Housing and Dwelling

Housing and Dwelling collects the best in recent scholarly and philosophical writings that bear upon the history of domestic architecture in the nineteenth and twentieth centuries. Lane combines exemplary readings that focus on and examine the issues involved in the study of domestic architecture. The extracts are taken from an innovative and informed combination of philosophy, history, social science, art, literature and architectural writings. The readings address, among other issues, the relation between the public and the private sphere, the gendering of space, notions of domesticity, the relation between domesticity and social class, the role of builders and prefabrication, and the relationship between architects and the inhabitants of dwellings.

Uniquely, the readings in *Housing and Dwelling* underline the point of view of the user of a dwelling and assess the impact of varying uses on the evolution of domestic architecture.

Housing and Dwelling is a valuable asset for students, scholars and designers alike. The book explores the extraordinary variety of methods, interpretations and source materials now available in this important field. For students, it opens windows on the many aspects of domestic architecture. For scholars, it introduces new, interdisciplinary points of view and suggests directions for further research. It acquaints practising architects in the field of housing design with history and methods and offers directions for future design possibilities.

Barbara Miller Lane is Professor Emeritus in the Humanities, Professor Emeritus of History, and Mellon Emeritus Fellow at Bryn Mawr College. She founded the College's Growth and Structure of Cities Program and served as its director from 1971 to 1989, and again in 1996 to 1997. She has published numerous books and articles on architectural and urban history.

Housing and Dwelling

Perspectives on Modern
Domestic Architecture

**Edited by
Barbara Miller Lane**

Routledge
Taylor & Francis Group

LONDON AND NEW YORK

First published 2007 by Routledge
2 Park Square, Milton Park, Abingdon, Oxon OX14 4RN

Simultaneously published in the USA and Canada
by Routledge
270 Madison Avenue, New York, NY 10016

Routledge is an imprint of the Taylor & Francis Group, an informa business

Typeset in Galliard by Bookcraft Ltd, Stroud, Glos.
Printed and bound in Great Britain by
The Cromwell Press, Trowbridge, Wilts.

British Library Cataloguing in Publication Data
A catalogue record for this book is available from the British Library

Library of Congress Cataloging in Publication Data
Housing and dwelling: perspectives on modern domestic architecture / edited by
Barbara Miller Lane.
    p. cm.
Includes bibliographical references and index.
1. Architecture, domestic. 2. Architecture—19th century. 3. Architecture—20th
century. I. Lane, Barbara Miller.
NA7110.H69
2006 728–dc22   2006012527

ISBN10: 0-415-34655-x (hbk)
ISBN10: 0-415-34656-8 (pbk)
ISBN10: 0-203-79967-4 (ebk)

ISBN13: 978-0-415-34655-9 (hbk)
ISBN13: 978-0-415-34656-6 (pbk)
ISBN13: 978-0-203-79967-3 (ebk)

For Jon, who made my houses, and taught me about them

Contents

Illustrations

Acknowledgements

This book owes a great deal to my Bryn Mawr, Haverford, University of Delaware and University of Pennsylvania students who took the course on "Housing and Dwelling" that I taught three times after retirement. Their passion for the subject, their enthusiasm for writing family history and oral history, went a long way toward convincing me to put together this anthology. I wish I could have included more excerpts from their papers, because I learned so much from each of them. Many of these students also provided me with useful suggestions about the character and length of the selections; these suggestions have influenced my choices and editing.

Bryn Mawr College contributed generously to this volume. It provided me with funding for research assistants, and supported the visual component of the anthology by scanning, editing, and helping to collect the images. I am especially indebted to Joan Beaudoin, Del Ramers, Laura Blankenship, Nancy Halli, Scott Silverman – and to Elliott Shore who put the resources of the Bryn Mawr College Information Services at my disposal at crucial moments.

I am extremely grateful to the Architectural History Foundation for its timely support of the project.

Special thanks go to my research assistants and student helpers (graduate and undergraduate): Deborah Barkun, Jennifer Bopp, Claire Mahler, Jordan Teel. And especially to Helen Vong and Tienfong Ho, who nailed it all down in the last year and a half. Each of these people has been deeply engaged with the content and argument of the project, and has offered important criticisms.

Without the encouragement of Despina Stratigakos, I would never have begun this enterprise, and she has prompted me throughout the process. Other friends and colleagues have also given me vitally important critical readings at various points: Gary McDonogh, Jeffrey A. Cohen, Daniela Voith, Carola Hein, Andy Shanken, Leslie Topp, and Sandy Isenstadt.

Caroline Mallinder's faith in the project kept me going, and Matthew Brown made it all happen. My heartfelt thanks to them too.

As always in the past, the support of my family, Jonathan Lane, Steven Lane and K. Signe Hansen, Ellie Lane and Richard Webber, and their children Erlend, Rowena, and Simon, has been decisive for my writing and thinking. The ways that the generations of my family dwell have also influenced my interpretations.

1
Introduction

This collection of scholarly writings and source materials attempts to lay the basis for new kinds of discussion and research in the history of domestic architecture. For a long time, historians of architecture paid attention only to a few of the buildings where people lived. These were the great palaces and villas of the wealthy, together with the houses designed in the modern period by a few recognized "great architects". Most writers were convinced by Nikolaus Pevsner's famous dictum that while cathedrals (and other major public buildings) are "architecture", the "bicycle shed" (and all other utilitarian structures) is merely "building".[1] In other words, to merit the attention of architectural historians, a structure had to be large, expensive, and beautiful.

Any glance at an aerial view of city, town, or countryside shows that such buildings are few and far between. The vast majority of built structures are (and have been at all periods) dwellings: detached houses, row houses, apartment blocks of various heights (Figs. 1–4). Today, new generations of scholars have begun to look at the history of these "ordinary" dwellings of the modern period. Stimulated by the pioneering work of Gwendolyn Wright, Alan Gowans, Anthony King, Dell Upton, and other writers of the 1980s,[2] new histories of builders' houses, apartment dwellings, working-class housing, mass housing of all types, and the housing of marginal populations and slaves, now diverge from Pevsner's restrictive formula. Not only the major turning points of "high-style" architectural design – the large houses of the Victorian era, the modernist villas of the 1920s and 1930s – are being analyzed, but also buildings previously thought to be particularly unbeautiful: farmhouses, builders' houses of the later nineteenth century, "tract houses" of the 1950s, mobile and manufactured homes, high-rise housing towers of the later twentieth century. These latter kinds of buildings are now often described as "vernacular architecture".[3]

The terms of analysis have also changed: scholars are now looking not only at the façade composition and the geometry of the plan, but also at issues such as the organization within and around the dwelling of public and private space, the importance of work and household structure, the gendered character of interior and exterior spaces, the influence of consumption patterns on spaces and decoration, the ways that lines of sight organize perceptions of space, and many other aspects of the inhabitants' experiences. The part played by politics in shaping building form and location is often discussed, as are the effects of population pressure and technological development on the creation of mass housing.

Scholars now pay considerable attention to the users of buildings, whose creative impulses are reflected in their dwellings. To a degree that has seldom been recognized in the past, the users, whether we mean the owner of the dwelling or the family group that resides there, shape their dwellings. Sometimes they design them themselves, and build with their own hands. Sometimes they design them, and hire a carpenter or builder or architect. Sometimes they influence the design by choosing from among a series of patterns, as in the case of the builders' houses and "tract" houses of the last two centuries. But always the users make and remake their spaces – by rebuilding, remodeling, decorating, furnishing, landscaping, or simply by dwelling within the forms and spaces of domestic architecture. Thus the places where people dwell are now understood to demonstrate their ideas of individuality, privacy, family, politics and society; to create, in other words, the general cultural patterns of an era. But there is little agreement as to how ideals and aspirations are formed – do the ideals of those who select and remodel their dwellings come from the "great minds" of the era, or is the reverse true? Do the great minds (or leading architects) simply reflect the taste of their times? And is "taste" a set of preferences created by advertising, or do the mass media simply respond to the wishes and demands of the public? Some historians have turned fruitfully to the study of popular media – to domestic advice writings, advertisements, plan books – and for recent periods, to film and television, to answer these questions.[4] Such materials, though, entail their own problems – how does one decide who decides the content of films, television programs, advertisements? In any case, the growing fields of media studies, and the history of consumption patterns have much to offer the historian of modern domestic architecture.

A number of these issues and questions have a long history in the traditional humanistic and social science disciplines. But their appearance in the study of domestic architecture is relatively new. To a considerable extent the emergence of new perspectives and emphases in this field is a consequence of the writings of feminist scholars, who have themselves drawn upon a variety of disciplines. This is surely not surprising: the role of women within the so-called domestic sphere in the modern period is an important subject within the history of women more generally. As the selections included here demonstrate, feminist scholarship has been decisive in bringing to bear new viewpoints upon the development of domestic architecture. Not only have feminist writers helped to overturn traditional approaches, but they have also mobilized insights from archaeology, sociology, anthropology, psychoanalysis, film studies, economic and social history, politics and government, oral history, social psychology, literary theory, art-historical theory, landscape history, and the history of technology, in the study of the history of domestic architecture.

Of course, many of these perspectives themselves are relatively new, and have influenced a variety of scholars, not just feminist scholars. A number of new "disciplines" have formed out of older ones in the last fifteen to twenty years: anthropological archaeology, landscape history (sometimes called history of the built environment, sometimes environmental history, depending on its emphasis), literary theory and studies, film studies, and the various fields normally grouped together as "cultural studies": popular culture, material culture, visual culture. Behind these new scholarly clusters are often new philosophical positions: structuralism and post-structuralism, neo-Marxism, and what we tend now to call the philosophy of "the Everyday".[5]

Feminist scholarship itself has changed significantly over the last twenty-five years. In the field of domestic architecture, early feminist writers focused on the exploitation of women within the "separate" domestic sphere, by a male "patriarchal" structure. Hence, feminist writers initially wrote extensively about the plan of the upper-middle-class Victorian house, with its segregated and specialized spaces, which were seen as the result of male domination, and about the separation of male "work" and female "home". Within the separate domestic sphere, the wife and mother was said to preside over a "cult of domesticity" (or "cult of true womanhood"), caring for her nuclear family and decorating the interior of her home. Starting from the same point of view, feminist writers identified the utterly different tract houses of the 1950s suburbs, with their small lots, open plans, high-tech appliances, mass-media-inspired decoration, as yet another patriarchal creation – one that isolated women from community and work.[6]

Despite the importance of these insights, such evaluations of the domestic architecture of the Victorian and modern periods have now been extensively amended. Our definitions of "private" and "public", for decades inappropriately derived from the writings of Jürgen Habermas, are now undergoing careful redefinition by sophisticated political philosophers like Jeff Weintraub and Krishan Kumar.[7] Thus current writers, including feminist scholars, have begun to see an interpenetration of public and private "spheres" even in the Victorian dwelling and have modified the view of the suburban "tract house" to include an understanding of its appeal to rural, individualistic, and populist strains within modern thought.

Our older definitions of what is meant by "domesticity", along with what has been meant by "home" in recent centuries, are also under review. For a while, historians equated these notions with the "rise" of the nuclear family, and sought the origins of this type of family structure in a specific turning point in the past.[8] Others saw modern ideas of home and domesticity as resulting from the institutions of "patriarchy" and attempted to trace these institutions back through western history at least as far as antiquity.[9] Philippe Ariès and his followers argued that modern attitudes to childhood arose in the seventeenth and eighteenth centuries among the upper classes and then spread gradually to all classes in the nineteenth and twentieth centuries.[10] Simon Schama and Witold Rybczynski located the origins of a modern sense of "family, intimacy, and a devotion to the home" in the Netherlands of the seventeenth century.[11]

But now, with the writings of Steven Ozment, both on the family and on the history of the notion of privacy, together with the massive new Yale *History of the European Family* (2001–4),[12] we can be relatively sure of the following: the nuclear family is not new, but it is better studied as a part of the household; middle-class family and household size increased rather than decreased in the nineteenth century, decreasing only in the twentieth; our views of children have not changed very much over time; the legal situation of middle-class women was worse in the latter half of the nineteenth century than ever before or after; the separation between work and home has varied dramatically among countries in the modern era; middle-class and working-class families have been thoroughly different in their attitudes to work and privacy throughout history.

Writers such as Elizabeth Cromley and Elizabeth Blackmar now argue that the emotional attachment to "home" usually equated with domesticity was a modern invention, a by-product of the experiences of transience and uprooting that characterized the industrial revolution.[13] As art historian Heidi De Mare has written, "Not till the nineteenth century did the inner emotional world become extended, taking over the space within the four walls of the house and dominating concepts of the 'home' until far into the twentieth century".[14] Still other authors are questioning the domestic roles of both women and men during the modern period by looking at gender relations in domestic settings, while economic historians like M. J. Daunton point to the importance of class in influencing ideas of home and domesticity.[15]

Other factors that have contributed to new perspectives in the history of domestic

architecture include recent developments in urban and city planning history; the population explosion of the last three decades throughout the world; the development of
modern communication systems and the concomitant growth of rootlessness and transience among large populations; and the urgent issues created by "homelessness" almost
everywhere. The British "Planning History Group", founded in 1974 by Gordon Cherry
and others at the University of Birmingham, originally focused to a considerable extent
on British town planning issues, including housing history. That organization has transformed itself over the last ten years into the International Planning History Society, holds
international conferences, and publishes its own journal.[16] One result of this evolution is
that almost every new planning history text includes a consideration of housing history,
often drawn from a background of politics and economics. Works with important implications for the history of domestic architecture have resulted, including the writings and
compilations by Anthony Sutcliffe on urbanization, and the comprehensive *Cambridge
Urban History of Britain*, a model for national histories elsewhere.[17]

   Experiences of extraordinary population growth and of homelessness (a result of political
laissez-faire in the United States, of geopolitical upheavals elsewhere, and of hyper-
urbanization in non-Western countries) have deeply affected the recent history of
domestic architecture. An emphasis on the importance of participation in housing
design, especially for the poor, has been apparent in the lives and writings of architects
and planners since the 1960s and 1970s.[18] The technological challenges of housing large
numbers of people, a focus of early modern architecture, have come to the fore again in
widespread discussions of high-rise housing, prefabrication, and the features necessary to
the "minimal dwelling".[19] Issues of privacy and individual preference inevitably arise in
discussions of mass housing, giving further stimulus to the study of participatory design.

   It can be argued that the issue of individual preference, and the desire by some for a
demonstrative form of self-expression, has been a continuing thread in European and
American domestic architecture. The practice of building a dwelling for purposes of
self-display (or, more often, display of the importance of one's household) has been
obvious among the rich and powerful in western history at least since the early Middle
Ages. But the desire to represent one's own eccentricity and subjectivity through the
creation of a new kind of dwelling, like modern ideas of home and domesticity, probably
begins with the industrial revolution and with Romanticism.[20] As Amos Rapoport
remarks in *House Form and Culture*, "our culture puts a premium on originality, often
striving for it for its own sake".[21] On the other hand, most people throughout history
have chosen (as a result of personal preference, religion, or politics), or been compelled
(by available building materials and housing stock), to live in dwellings that appear quite
similar to one another on the outside. Gwendolyn Wright was one of the first to consider
this issue,[22] but new studies of apartment dwellings and row housing touch upon it as
well. Recent work in social psychology, anthropology, vernacular architecture, and visual
culture shows that the desire for individual expression in such contexts has often found an
outlet in interior decoration, renovation, and interior and exterior remodeling.[23]

   With the help of these perspectives, it should soon be possible to integrate our understanding of all the formal aspects of dwellings with their cultural, social, political, and
individual underpinnings, at least for the modern period. The newest work by architectural historians (especially those who practice the study of "vernacular" architecture)
begins to take into account these points of view. But there are as yet no overarching
works that have been able to accomplish this goal. Norbert Schoenauer's large history of
house forms (like that of Ettore Camesasca before him) is useful but narrow in focus.[24]

Julienne Hanson's *Decoding Homes and Houses*, an interesting attempt to map zones of use ("space syntax") in examples drawn from all periods and places, never proceeds beyond the issue of the uses of space, and is in fact too encyclopedic as to time and place to shed light on particular periods.[25] Paul Oliver's *Dwellings: The House Across the World* (University of Texas, 1987) is broader in focus but says little about Europe or the United States, and was written too early to take advantage of the recent outpouring of scholarship.[26] There are important national histories, such as Ingeborg Flagge's large compilation for Germany, or the books by Gwendolyn Wright, Alan Gowans, and Dolores Hayden, but these are, of course, limited in scope, and in the case of the American authors, somewhat dated.[27]

One problem is that few people command all the disciplines from which these different viewpoints derive. Another is that those who write about domestic architecture from different points of view do not agree as to the raw materials for their work. When I began to teach a course on the subject five years ago, I was not able to find any general readings that took into account all or even the majority of the new developments in scholarship. Thus I set out to gather together a selection of texts and source materials that touch on a large number of them, and that seem to me to illustrate the major themes and materials in the modern history of housing and dwelling in Europe and the United States.

One of the most difficult kinds of source material to find is precisely that which supports the study of the architecture of "the Everyday". The photographs, façade illustrations, and measured drawings of the plan that architectural historians have traditionally used are themselves representations and as such need to be carefully interpreted. But once they are interpreted, how does one penetrate beyond them, in order to learn about the ways houses have been used, modified, and valued? Personal letters and diaries have often been the recourse of historians looking at such questions, but they are few, winnowed out by the passage of time. Literary works and works of art have provided recent historians with ways of answering these questions. Histories of rooms such as the parlor, the boudoir, or the kitchen, and of interior decoration draw heavily on these materials.[28] But literary works, and all works of art, present formidable interpretative problems because they depict, not reality, but the ideas of the author. The selections on literature and art that are included here are therefore drawn from writers that make plain these interpretative difficulties (see especially Sharon Marcus in Chapter 5, Susan Sidlauskas in Chapter 6). In a few cases I have included fiction selections too (by Tony Earley, Émile Zola and Anthony Burgess), selections that seemed to me to be close enough to reality to be stimulating and helpful or that powerfully symbolized and stimulated public opinion.[29]

An important but neglected source for understanding the desires and actions of the inhabitant of the dwelling is oral or family history, as it has been practiced in the United States and other countries for at least four decades. In the course that I taught at Bryn Mawr College, students interviewed family members of several generations about such questions as the style and plan of the dwelling, the manner of its construction or choice, its uses by family or household members, the nature of public and private roles in the dwelling, the relations between inside and outside, the gendering of spaces. Not only did such studies reveal the nature of housing choices and dwelling usages; they also provided an unusual look at the varieties of "ordinary" dwellings. I have included brief extracts from two of these papers among the selections.

Illustrations follow and amplify each section. In choosing these images, I have been mindful of the need to illustrate the individual selections with the usual architectural views – exteriors, interiors, plans – but I have also added a variety of other materials. Cartoons, movie and television stills, advertisements, images from advice books, sales brochures, help to indicate the range of visual sources that are useful to the student of domestic architecture.

This anthology focuses on Europe and America in the nineteenth and twentieth centuries. Here modern industrialization began, bringing with it for the first time rapid urbanization, massive technological change, incredible population growth requiring extraordinary numbers of new dwellings, the rise of new classes with new attitudes to social status, unprecedented mobility and instability in relationship to class structures, new communications, and novel and frightening forms of warfare. The experience of industrialization co-existed with the birth of Romanticism, Marxism, nationalism (and later internationalism), and was welded on to very particular ideas of class, rural life, ethical values, creativity, and homeland. These developments, however, took place at different times in different places, and the whole process, rapid as it was, was nevertheless drawn out over a period of two centuries, unlike the experience of "modernization" in twentieth-century non-European countries. This unique and indissoluble blend of experiences necessarily found its expression in domestic architecture. In contrast to the centuries before industrialization, these experiences led to new, more subjective, more intimate and expressive relationships between users and dwellings. Thus, the development of housing and dwelling in Europe and America in the nineteenth and twentieth centuries had its own specific dynamic, never repeated, and never quite replicated elsewhere.

The practice of studying history must be guided by intelligent questions that are themselves the result of a reasoned theoretical framework, but it is obvious from what has been said so far that it is currently extremely difficult to formulate a single approach to the history of domestic architecture. Thus this collection begins with an extended group of selections (Part I) exemplifying as many as possible of the major theoretical and methodological perspectives that have inspired recent scholarship. Part I begins with selections characteristic of the principal viewpoints in interpretation (Chapter 2) and continues in Chapter 3 with a series of approaches, philosophical and methodological, to the question "What is home?". Chapter 4 then offers a series of writings, from varied methodological perspectives, of issues of perception, memory, and performance in domestic settings.

In Part II, nine themes in the history of modern domestic architecture are delineated and serve to organize the groups of primary and secondary source materials. In choosing the selections, I have attempted to include varied methodologies and conflicting points of view. The themes themselves are organized roughly chronologically, beginning with Chapter 5, "Living downtown: nineteenth-century urban dwelling". While people have always lived in cities, the rapid increases in urban populations during the early industrial revolution led to new dwelling types and unique dwelling experiences. New relationships between public and private life emerged, as did defensive reactions to the experience of "living with strangers", so that "living downtown" was a catalyst for profound social and cultural change. Not only did this experience give rise to new ideas about domesticity among the new urban middle classes, but the ideals of older urban residents were transformed in response. In the process, a variety of older architectural models ("French flats", aristocratic palaces, monasteries and other institutional structures) helped to give form to large numbers of new urban dwellings.

Some of the writers in Chapter 5 deal with Victorian domestic ideals, but an intensive discussion of the subject is reserved for Chapter 6, "Victorian domesticity: ideals and realities". The large, single-family "Victorian house" has been a focus of scholarly attention, both from architectural historians, because of its size and architecturally inno-vative character, and from feminist writers because of its apparent embodiment of upper-middle-class patriarchal society. Such houses, usually located outside the central areas of major cities (frequently in new suburbs), and often modeled distantly on English manor houses, have long been thought to display a strong separation between home and work, public and private life, male and female, parents and children, masters and servants. Here, the selections begin with the evolution of Victorian house plans and interiors, and then provide conflicting points of view on Victorian ideals of home and domesticity.

Chapter 7 introduces the theme of "Rural memories and desires" in the context of rapid urbanization. To a greater extent than in any other country, the American farm building has had a formative influence upon domestic architecture. Here the best bedroom was usually at the first floor front, the kitchen was the principal living space, and the front porch was the second principal living space. The users were not only the extended family, but also, during parts of the day, neighbors and farm workers as well. The rural ideal in Britain and continental Europe has been rather different, focusing in the former on the manor houses of the gentry and in the latter (as we see in the Heidegger and Bachelard selections in Chapters 3 and 4) on the dwellings of well-to-do peasants. The idea of the wilderness retreat, influenced in part by the experience of the frontier, and in part by early nineteenth-century Romantic ideals, also had a powerful influence in the United States, but it was paralleled by the phenomenon of National Romanticism in the Scandinavian countries. The selections here trace the rural ideal from Andrew Jackson Downing through Thoreau (as radically reinterpreted by William Barksdale Maynard), to wilderness ideals in late nineteenth-century America and Europe. Two writers demon-strate the actualities of farm life and the role of farmers in shaping their environment, while another suggests the relationship of rural and rustic ideals to the formation of suburban dwellings and their gardens.

Chapter 8, "Modernism, technology, and utopian hopes for mass housing", takes up the theme of technological innovation already raised by writers in other sections, and focuses on the Germany of the Weimar Republic. Here many of the principal founders of international modernism espoused new technologies in an effort to create housing for the masses that would be consistent with a new architecture and a new society. With the encouragement of public officials and working within a new legal framework, radical architects succeeded in building large numbers of housing developments in the 1920s. Among the features of public housing during the Weimar Republic were the search for the ideal "minimal dwelling", new attitudes to the role of the "new woman" in domestic affairs, and utopian hopes that technology could transform society. The aesthetic of the new architecture, bare and extremely simplified, derived partly from working-class dwell-ings, partly from the architects' conception of machine production, and partly from the kind of non-objective painting and innovative interior design that was taught at the Bauhaus. Scholars have long disagreed about the centrality of technology to this new architecture, and about the relative importance in Weimar housing of social concerns and new artistic conceptions. The selections included here illustrate the importance of ideas of prefabrication in German dwelling design of the period, but at the same time underline the utopian social concerns displayed by Weimar housing.[30]

Chapter 9, "Mass housing as single-family dwelling", is devoted to the American suburb of the 1950s and 1960s, which developed a far more widespread and successful form of mass housing than that introduced in Germany in the 1920s. Suburbs go back at least to the early nineteenth century in America and Britain, where they were formed by members of the well-to-do middle classes fleeing the new city and proximity to workers, or simply seeking a rustic ideal (see Chapters 5, 6, and 7). But it was only after the Second World War, with the help of the FHA and GI Bill financing and with the spread of the automobile, that the mushrooming suburbs of the United States became the location of choice for great numbers of the lower middle classes and the better-off working classes. Such suburbs, laid out by developers and mass produced, responded to the desires of tens of thousands of Americans for a "rural-looking" single-family house in its own yard with its own front lawn that was nevertheless "modern". Yet the suburban developments of this period were regarded with contempt by architects and social critics. Partly as a result, they have been ignored by scholars until quite recently.[31] The selections here include some of the best new evaluations by younger architectural historians.

Chapter 10, "Participatory planning and design: initiatives in self-help housing, renovation, and interior decoration", treats the participation of the individual and household in the creation of dwelling spaces. This participation is not a new phenomenon, but it has emerged as a focus of debate since the 1960s. Not only leading intellectuals but also architects and planners were drawn to this subject by the experience of hyper-urbanization in non-Western countries and by the new social consciousness of the 1960s. Sociologists, ethnographers, and housing specialists have begun to discuss these issues, but, so far, architectural historians have neglected them.[32] Selections range from considerations of the ways in which squatters create their own dwellings, challenging traditional forms of architecture and community, to issues of self-expression through interior and exterior renovation.

Chapter 11, "Twentieth-century apartment dwelling: ideals and realities", attempts to present a few of the dimensions of the bitter and as yet unresolved debate over high-rise apartment buildings that took place after the Second World War. The need to provide mass housing in a period of ever-increasing population, together with the development of new technologies and the inspiration of architects such as Le Corbusier and Alison and Peter Smithson, led postwar governments to create "tower blocks" for subsidized housing, usually for housing the poor. The multiple failures of such high-rise structures, which included both construction inadequacies and severe social dislocations, led to a storm of criticism, especially in Britain and the United States. Many such projects were demolished, and, especially in the United States, few were built after the 1970s. Yet both Alison Ravetz (excerpted here) and Sam Davis agree that the failure of these projects resulted more from a lack of planning and foresight than from deficiencies in the form itself.[33] Where high-rise apartment buildings have been erected that are responsive to the needs of inhabitants, with good construction and amenities, and integrated into the surrounding community (as in European new towns), they have proved very successful. Selections here trace the controversy, offer explanations, and include analyses of two successful solutions. The high density of such buildings continues to offer a badly needed solution to the housing shortages of the future.[34]

Chapter 12, "Some possible futures", offers speculations about the future, when needs for large numbers of dwellings can only increase. The twenty-first century, with its population pressures and the extreme mobility of various segments of the population may well witness the end of the ingrained dwelling patterns and affections of the nineteenth and twentieth centuries. Longstanding desires for personal expression in the dwelling are hard to reconcile with the almost invariably large-scale housing construction of the present day. Similarly, participatory planning and individual intervention in design through renovations, remodeling, and decorating, become ever more difficult. Modern housing density will almost certainly preclude a return to the rustic tradition of the "studio in the wilds". Will the need for new dwellings be met by cooperative arrangements which recall the older village, by the individualism of the mobile home (prefabricated and uniform in appearance even when truly mobile), by new forms of minimal dwelling in high-rise structures, by the proliferation of tract housing which now attracts even the wealthy to gated communities of repetitive-looking "McMansions", or by new forms of "living downtown" in which older housing is "gentrified" and older commercial and industrial structures are remodeled? The future, of course, is unpredictable. At the time of writing this, some young architects are experimenting with factory-produced low-cost housing in the form of modular units that can be stacked up and turned into high-rise mass housing. Others are combining the notion of the minimal dwelling with custom design for rural settings.[35] But these efforts are highly experimental. The responses in this section, from political scientists, architects, and landscape historians, discuss models that appear to be currently feasible.

Chapter 13 raises the question, "Where is home?". The world population explosion since the Second World War, the spread of modern communications technology (high-speed rail, more and more automobiles, airplanes), and economic globalization have made this a more acute question than at any time in the past, except perhaps at the very beginning of the modern period. Already in 1961, the Twentieth Century Fund, studying dwelling and commutation patterns on the eastern seaboard of the United States, hypothesized the existence of "Megalopolis", a giant form of conurbation in which people live at great distances from their work, and move their dwellings frequently from place to place (Fig. 5). This notion now clearly applies to other areas of the United States (Fig. 6), and links such areas to similar places in other countries. Leisure activities too, have come to produce patterns of unprecedented mobility. When seen in combination with the urban sprawl and high-density building of the last fifty years, Robert Day's cartoon of 1954 – "I'm Mrs. Edward M. Barnes. Where do I live?" (Fig. 7) – seems to offer an almost universal truth.[36]

At the same time, the mass economic and political dislocations of the postwar period have produced new generations of people who are not just disoriented, like Mrs Barnes, but genuinely without adequate shelter. Some are the desperately poor of modern society, others are the dispossessed refugees of modern catastophes – war, ethnic cleansing. For such writers as Martin Heidegger and Yi-Fu Tuan, the notion of home or dwelling is inextricably linked to the notion of homeland or home place. Without these, people are "homeless". But what, after all, is homelessness? Is it simply the lack of adequate shelter, or the result of dense and repetitive development, or the consequence of new kinds of mobility in pursuit of work and leisure? Or is it also the loss of connection to a familiar past? Selections in this section address the issue of attachment to home and place, question the future viability of this attachment and also refer to contemporary movements to create "housing for the dispossessed". At the end of the section, the German television series *Heimat* is summarized and illustrated: *Heimat* sums up the dilemmas of homelessness in the later twentieth century.[37]

These nine chronologically organized sections do not, of course, exhaust the subject matter of the history of modern housing and dwelling. Notably lacking in this anthology is a consistent discussion of either the history of "style" or the work of "great architects". Only a few of the major façade and plan types and only a few well-known architects are represented, in brief selections. Frank Lloyd Wright's passage in Chapter 2 expresses the view, typical among modern architects, that only the architect can interpret the dwelling. Walter Gropius's 1910 proposal for prefabrication (Chapter 8) signals the adoption of mass production techniques by international modernism. The two pieces by Le Corbusier and Alison and Peter Smithson in Chapter 11 are included because of the extraordinary influence of these architects on the building of high-rise dwellings. Much of the best new scholarship on the canonical "masters of modern architecture", also not included here, deals with patrons, and the important ways in which the patrons' views and wishes affected the buildings of the "master".[38] Absent too is any systematic history of community or urban planning, even though this subject is closely relevant to the history of housing types. Other important issues not specifically dealt with, either because they would produce too long a volume or because they are as yet ill-supplied with scholarship, include the contribution of Romanticism to modern ideas of the home (see above, note 20), the history of utopian housing, the role of village models as a source of modern design (touched upon by Spencer-Wood in Chapter 6 and McCamant in Chapter 12), and the special contributions of industrial design since the mid-nineteenth century.[39] A larger volume, or a two-volume collection (as one of my readers kindly suggested) ought to include sections on earlier periods in the history of housing and dwelling, and on dwelling design in non-American and non-European areas. This last is of course an enormous subject, but of the greatest importance even for the materials included here, for it has been precisely the work of anthropologists, ethnographers, and sociologists working outside European and American subject matters, that has provided strikingly important stimuli for new perspectives on our own domestic spaces and designs.[40]

But I think that this anthology will serve as a good starting point. These missing pieces are suggested here, if not amplified upon. And the materials in this volume have the virtue of belonging to a tightly-knit historical dynamic. I am assuming that when the collection is used in relatively traditional architectural or planning history courses, additional information will be provided in lectures or in supplemental readings from the readily available existing histories. And I hope that the anthology will be more broadly useful too; that it will serve not only as a tool for teachers and students on a variety of courses, but also as a stimulus for future scholars and practitioners among all the disciplines related to the history of domestic architecture.

The footnotes and bibliography included here should assist wider reading on the subjects raised in the different sections. But there is a caveat. This is a collection of excerpts, short pieces drawn from much longer and richer texts. Those who find a selection particularly interesting will be rewarded by first giving careful attention to the original work before beginning a more extended study of the subject.

Notes

1   Pevsner, *An Outline of European Architecture*, Harmondsworth and Baltimore: Penguin, 1968 (first pub. 1943), p. 15: see Ch. 2 of selections. Sir Nikolaus Pevsner (1902–83) was in many respects the founder of modern architectural history. He was not constrained in his other works by a single-minded focus on "great" buildings. In these writings he urged attention to the history of the crafts, to the evolution of building types, and to the exploration of "vernacular" architecture (*Pioneers of Modern Design from William Morris to Walter Gropius*, New Haven, Conn.: Yale University Press, 2005, first pub. 1936; *A History of Building Types*, Princeton, N.J.: Princeton University Press, 1976; *The Buildings of England* series, Harmondsworth: Penguin, 1952–83 ff.). But his invidious comparison of the bicycle shed to the cathedral dominated the practice of architectural historians for a long time.

2 Gwendolyn Wright, *Moralism and the Model Home: Domestic Architecture and Cultural Conflict in Chicago 1873–1913*, Chicago, Ill.: University of Chicago Press, 1985; Alan Gowans, *The Comfortable House: North American Suburban Architecture 1890–1930*, Cambridge, Mass.: MIT Press, 1986; Anthony D. King, *Buildings and Society: Essays on the Social Development of the Built Environment*, London: Routledge, 1980; *The Bungalow: the Production of a Global Culture*, London: Routledge & Kegan Paul, 1984; Dell Upton and John Michael Vlach (eds), *Common Places: Readings in American Vernacular Architecture*, Athens, Ga.: University of Georgia Press, 1986. See also the pathbreaking work on American vernacular housing by Henry H. Glassie, *Folk Housing in Middle Virginia*, Knoxville, Tenn.: University of Tennessee Press, 1975. Glassie has recently published a distinguished volume that sums up three decades of his work: *Vernacular Architecture*, Bloomington, Ind.: Indiana University Press, 2000.

3 There is not, however, broad agreement among scholars as to what "vernacular architecture" is. Amos Rapoport distinguishes among primitive building, pre-industrial vernacular, and modern vernacular (see below), and expresses doubt as to whether there is such a thing as a modern version, since he believes vernacular architecture involves a lack of self-consciousness and a neglect of common building traditions and common symbolisms. The seminal work of Dell Upton and Henry H. Glassie for the United States does in fact focus on traditional, largely pre-industrial patterns, while Paul Oliver's *Encyclopedia of the Vernacular Architecture of the World* (3 vols., New York and London: Cambridge University Press, 1997) deals primarily with non-Western "traditional" building types. But the publications of Robert Venturi and Denise Scott Brown (Venturi, Scott Brown, and Steven Izenour, *Learning from Las Vegas*, Cambridge, Mass.: MIT Press, 1972; Venturi, *Complexity and Contradiction in Architecture*, New York: MOMA, 1966; Venturi *et al.*, *Signs of Life: Symbols in the American City*, Washington: Renwick Gallery, 1976) on the importance of "ordinary buildings" of all types, together with the growing fields of landscape and environmental history, have produced a more inclusive understanding of vernacular architecture. The excellent journal *Perspectives in Vernacular Architecture* (Columbia, Mo., and London: University of Missouri Press, 1982–) deals with all periods and all building types. The selections by Sandy Isenstadt, David Smiley, Thomas Hubka, Sue Bridwell Beckham, and John Brinckerhoff Jackson included here represent a few of these more recent approaches. The new book by Isenstadt addresses many of these issues: *The Modern American House: Spaciousness and Middle-Class Identity, 1850–1950,* New York and London: Cambridge University Press, 2006.

4 See, for example, Karal Ann Marling, *As Seen on TV: The Visual Culture of Everyday Life in the 1950s*, Cambridge, Mass.: Harvard University Press, 1994; Thomas Elsaesser, "Tales of Sound and Fury: Observations on the Family Melodrama", in Bill Nichols (ed.), *Movies and Methods*, Berkeley, Calif.: University of California Press, 1976; Christine Gledhill, (ed.), *Home is Where the Heart Is*, London: BFI Pub., 1987; Lynn Spigel, *Welcome to the Dreamhouse: Popular Media and Postwar Suburbs*, Durham, N.C.: Duke University Press, 2001; A. Appadurai (ed.), *The Social Life of Things: Commodities in Cultural Perspective*, New York and London: Cambridge University Press, 1986; Grant McCracken, *Culture and Consumption: New Approaches to the Symbolic Character of Consumer Goods and Activities*, Bloomington, Ind.: Indiana University Press, 1988; and Victoria De Grazia with E. Furlough, *The Sex of Things: Gender and Consumption in Historical Perspectives*. Berkeley, Calif.: University of California Press, 1996.

5 After Henri Lefebvre, *Everyday Life in the Modern World*, New Brunswick, N.J.: Transaction Books, 1984 (originally Paris, 1968) and Michel De Certeau, *The Practice of Everyday Life*, Berkeley, Calif.: University of California Press, 1984 (originally Paris, 1980). For recent writings that call for the study of "the everyday" within architectural history, see Mary McLeod, "Everyday and 'Other' Spaces", in Debra Coleman *et al.*, *Architecture and Feminism*, New York: Princeton Architectural Press, 1996, 1–37.

6 On the successive stages in feminist writing, see Linda K. Kerber, *Toward an Intellectual History of Women: Essays*, Chapel Hill and London: University of North Carolina Press, 1997, especially "Separate Spheres, Female Worlds, Woman's Place: The Rhetoric of Women's History", pp. 159–99.

7 Craig Calhoun (ed.), *Habermas and the Public Sphere*, Cambridge Mass.: MIT Press, 1992, especially Seyla Benhabib, "Models of Public Space: Hannah Arendt, the Liberal Tradition, and Jürgen Habermas", pp. 73–97, and Mary P. Ryan, "Gender and Public Access: Women's Politics in Nineteenth-Century America", pp. 259–88; Jeff Weintraub, "The Theory and

Politics of the Public/Private Distinction", in Weintraub and Krishan Kumar (eds), *Public and Private in Thought and Practice: Perspectives on a Grand Dichotomy*, Chicago: University of Chicago Press, 1997, pp. 1–42, and Krishan Kumar, "Home: The Promise and Predicament of Private Life at the End of the Twentieth Century", ibid., pp. 204–36.

8   See especially Richard Goldthwaite, "The Florentine Palace as Domestic Architecture", *American Historical Review* 77 (1972): 977–1012.

9   The view that there is any lasting or well-defined social system that can be described as "patriarchy" has long fallen out of favor among anthropologists and ethnographers. For reasons why such a system should not be sought in antiquity, see Spencer-Wood, this volume and, among others, Mary R. Lefkowitz and Joyce E. Salisbury (eds), *Encyclopedia of Women in the Ancient World*, Santa Barbara, Calif.: ABC-CLIO, 2001. Nevertheless, some architectural historians still make this argument.

10 Philippe Ariès, *Centuries of Childhood: A Social History of Family Life*, New York: Knopf, 1962.

11 Simon Schama, *The Embarrassment of Riches*, New York: Knopf, 1987; Witold Rybczynski, *Home: A Short History of an Idea*, New York: Penguin, 1986.

12 Steven Ozment, *Ancestors: The Loving Family in Old Europe*, Cambridge, Mass.: Harvard University Press, 2001; Ozment, *Flesh and Spirit: Private Life in Early Modern Germany*, New York: Viking, 1999; David I. Kertzer and Marzio Barbagli (eds), *The History of the European Family*, New Haven, Conn.: Yale University Press, 3 vols., 2001–4.

13 Blackmar and Cromley, this volume.

14 Heidi De Mare, "Domesticity in Dispute: A Reconsideration of Sources", in Irene Cieraad, *At Home: An Anthropology of Domestic Space*, Syracuse, N.Y.: Syracuse University Press, 1999, pp. 13–30, p. 30.

15 Hilde Heynen and Gülsüm Baydar (eds), *Negotiating Domesticity: Spatial Productions of Gender in Modern Architecture*, London and New York: Routledge, 2005. Daunton's work is excerpted in Ch. 5.

16 *Planning Perspectives*, London: Spon/Routledge, 1986–.

17 Anthony Sutcliffe (ed.), *Multi-storey Living: The British Working Class Experience*, London: Croom Helm, 1974; Sutcliffe, *Towards the Planned City: Germany, Britain, the United States, and France, 1780–1914*, New York: St Martin's Press, 1981; Sutcliffe (ed.), *British Town Planning: the Formative Years*, New York: St Martin's Press, 1981; Sutcliffe and Derek Fraser (eds), *The Pursuit of Urban History*, London: E. Arnold, 1983; Sutcliffe (ed.), *Metropolis, 1890–1940*, Chicago and London: University of Chicago Press and Mansell, 1984; Sutcliffe and Theo Barker (eds), *Megalopolis: The Giant City in History*, New York: St Martin's Press, 1993. Peter Clark and M. J. Daunton (eds), *The Cambridge Urban History of Britain*, New York and London: Cambridge University Press, 2000. The discussions of building orientation and siting, of the evolution of notions of "front" and "back" presented by Daunton, Hubka, and Cromley in this volume, owe a good deal to this kind of planning history.

18 See the selections by Turner, Davey, Egelius and Ravetz in Ch. 10. See also Sam Davis: *The Architecture of Affordable Housing*, Berkeley, Calif.: University of California Press, 1995.

19 See the selections by Gropius, Herbert, and Henderson in Ch. 8 and by Ravetz in Ch. 11. The impact of modern technology, on building construction and prefabrication, heating and lighting, household appliances, and access to communications, is central to understanding the forms and uses of modern domestic architecture. Many selections included here touch on these issues, but there are few systematic efforts to address the relationships between technology and domestic architecture. Susan Strasser (*Never Done: A History of American Housework*, New York: Pantheon Books, 1982) and Ruth Schwartz Cowan (*More Work for Mother: The Ironies of Household Technology from the Open Hearth to the Microwave*, New York: Basic Books, 1983) offer useful surveys of the evolution of appliances, and discuss at some length the influence of new forms of heating and lighting. Among general histories of technology, those by Thomas P. Hughes are notable for referring to influences upon architecture; see especially his *Networks of Power: Electrification in Western Society, 1880–1930*, Baltimore: Johns Hopkins University Press, 1983; and *Human-built World: How to Think about Technology and Culture*, Chicago: University of Chicago Press, 2004. Also useful is Knut H. Sørensen and Merete Lie, *Making Technology our Own: Domesticating Technology into Everyday Life*, Oslo and Boston: Scandinavian University Press, 1996.

20 For the contribution of Romanticism to the idea of the home, see Barbara Miller Lane, "The Home as a Work of Art", in *National Romanticism and Modern Architecture in Germany and the*

Scandinavian Countries, New York and London: Cambridge University Press, pp. 79–162, excerpted briefly in this volume, Ch. 7. W. Barksdale Maynard's essay on Thoreau, also in Ch. 7, stresses the connections between the Picturesque (foreshadowed by Romanticism) and wilderness ideals. Andrew Jackson Downing, in Ch. 7, and elsewhere in his *The Architecture of Country Houses*, New York and Philadelphia: Appleton, 1850, speaks of the necessity for a house to express the character of its owner. To my knowledge, however, there is as yet no comprehensive study of the contributions of Romanticism to the desire for personal expression and originality in domestic architecture.

21 Rapoport, this volume, pp. 26–31.

22 See the chapters on Puritan dwellings and on slave housing in Gwendolyn Wright, *Building the Dream: A Social History of Housing in America*, Cambridge, Mass.: MIT Press, 1981.

23 See the selections in Chs 10 and 12. See also M. Csikszentmihalyi and E. Rochberg-Halton, *The Meaning of Things: Domestic Symbols and the Self*, New York and London: Cambridge University Press, 1981; Adrian Forty, *Objects of Desire: Design and Society 1750–1980*, New York: Pantheon Books, 1986; Terry Smith, *Making the Modern: Industry, Art, and Design in America*, Chicago: University of Chicago Press, 1993; Kristina Wilson, *Livable Modernism: Interior Decorating and Design during the Great Depression*, New Haven, Conn.: Yale University Press, 2004.

24 Norbert Schoenauer, *6000 Years of Housing*, New York: Norton, 2000 (1981). Ettore Camesasca, *History of the House*, London: Collins, 1971 (originally Milan, 1968).

25 Julienne Hanson, *Decoding Homes and Houses*, New York and London: Cambridge University Press, 1998.

26 Paul Oliver, *Dwellings: The House Across the World*, Austin: University of Texas Press, 1987.

27 Ingeborg Flagge (ed.), *Geschichte des Wohnens*, 5 vols., Stuttgart: Deutsche Verlags-Anstalt, 1996–9. Wright, *Building the Dream*; Gowans, *Comfortable House*; Dolores Hayden, *Redesigning the American Dream: The Future of Housing, Work, and Family Life*, New York: W. W. Norton, 1984 (new edn, 2002).

28 See, for example, Ed Lilley, "The Name of the Boudoir", *Journal of the Society of Architectural Historians*, 53 (June 1994), 193–8; Thad Logan, *The Victorian Parlour: A Cultural Study*, New York and London: Cambridge University Press, 2001; Kristin Hoganson, "Cosmopolitan Domesticity: Importing the American Dream, 1865–1920", *American Historical Review* 107 (2002), 55–83; Ellen Lupton and J. Abbott Miller, *The Bathroom, the Kitchen, and the Aesthetics of Waste: a Process of Elimination*, Cambridge, Mass.: MIT Press, 1992; and Elizabeth Collins Cromley, "A History of American Beds and Bedrooms", in Thomas Carter and Bernard L. Herman (eds), *Perspectives in Vernacular Architecture IV*, Columbia and London: University of Missouri Press, 1991, pp. 177–86.

29 Anthony Burgess's *A Clockwork Orange* (excerpted in Ch. 11) helped to influence public rejection of high-rise dwellings. On Burgess's novel and its influence, see especially Stuart Y. McDougal (ed.), *Stanley Kubrick's A Clockwork Orange*, New York and London: Cambridge University Press, 2003. The selection by Tony Earley in Ch. 2 and that by Émile Zola in Ch. 5 get quite close to reality. Émile Zola wrote what he called "the naturalist" novel, based on huge quantities of what would now be called "field work". For his Rougon-Macquart series of novels, he closely observed Parisian working-class life, and attempted to render its patterns and dialects with care and accuracy. Nevertheless, he had his own agenda – to arouse sympathy for the worker and to demonstrate the relative roles of heredity and environment in human affairs – and he had his own biases. Gervaise, the heroine of the novel excerpted here, probably reflects some of Zola's own middle-class attitudes. On Zola's belief in the importance of the family to the moral health of children, see Sylvia Schafer, *Children in Moral Danger and the Problem of Government in Third Republic France*, Princeton, N.J.: Princeton University Press, 1997; on Zola more generally see Sharon Marcus, "Zola's Restless House", in *Apartment Stories: City and Home in Nineteenth-Century Paris and London*, Berkeley, Calif.: University of California Press: 1999, pp. 166–98.

30 The affirmation of modern technology by Bruno Taut, Walter Gropius, and other architects of the Weimar Republic has led certain scholars to see connections between international modernism and Nazi architecture. Closely linked to this view is the issue of the "modernity" of Nazism itself – were the Nazis and their architecture "rational" and favorable to modernity or not? See for example Jeffrey Herf, *Reactionary Modernism: Technology, Culture, and Politics in Weimar and the Third Reich*, New York and London: Cambridge University Press, 1984;

Hilde Heynen, *Architecture and Modernity, A Critique,* Cambridge, Mass.: MIT Press, 1999; and Mark Antliff, "Fascism, Modernism, and Modernity", *Art Bulletin* 84, 1, March 2002, 148–69. I myself have always denied any ideological link between modernism and Nazism: see Barbara Miller Lane, *Architecture and Politics in Germany 1919–1945*, Cambridge, Mass.: Harvard University Press, 1968, new edn, 1985; Lane, "Interpreting Nazi Architecture: the case of Albert Speer", in Börje Magnusson *et al.* (eds), *Ultra terminum vagari: Scritti in onore di Carl Nylander*, Rome: Edizioni Quasar, 1998, 155–169; and Lane, "Die Moderne und die Politik in Deutschland zwischen 1919 und 1945", in Vittorio Magnago Lampugnani and Romana Schneider (eds), *Moderne Architektur in Deutschland, 1900 bis 1950*, vol. 2., *Expressionismus und neue Sachlichkeit*, Frankfurt am Main, 1994: Deutsches Architekturmuseum, pp. 224–49 (from which the selection included in Ch. 8 is drawn).

31   J. W. R. Whitehand and C. M. H. Carr, *Twentieth-century Suburbs: A Morphological Approach*, London: Routledge, 2001, trace a similar pattern of contempt and neglect in Britain.

32   Exceptions are Peter Davey and Mats Egelius (excerpted here); the selections included in Russell Ellis and Dana Cuff (eds), *Architects' People*, Oxford and New York: Oxford University Press, 1989; Peter G. Rowe, *Modernity and Housing*, Cambridge, Mass.: MIT Press; and the works of Sam Davis: *Affordable Housing*, cited above, and *Designing for the Homeless: Architecture that Works*, Berkeley, Calif.: University of California Press, 2004.

33   But see Ravetz on high-rise housing in Ch. 11, and Davis, *Affordable Housing*, passim.

34   The debate over high-rise housing is extremely complex, and involves, especially in the United States, longstanding fears of "living downtown" and "living with strangers". Jane Jacobs, *The Death and Life of Great American Cities*, New York: Random House, 1961, gave a powerful impetus to renewed appreciation of city life, provided it involved low-rise apartment buildings with a strong relationship to the street. Oscar Newman, in *Defensible Space: Crime Prevention through Urban Design*, New York: Macmillan, 1972, reinforced Jacobs's arguments and persuaded much of the American public that high-rise structures for the poor will inevitably lead to crime and social upheaval. British writers Miles Glendinning and Stefan Muthesius, on the other hand, hold out more hope for high-rise structures, even for the poor (*Tower Block: Modern Public Housing in England, Scotland, Wales, and Northern Ireland*, New Haven, Conn.: Yale University Press, 1994). A very useful analysis of high-rise housing in terms of the relations of public and private space is provided by Roderick J. Lawrence, "Public Collective and Private Space: A Study of Urban Housing in Switzerland", in Susan Kent (ed.), *Domestic Architecture and the Use of Space: An Interdisciplinary Study*, New York and London: Cambridge University Press, 1990, pp. 73–91.

35   The idea of factory-produced modules has been prominent among visionary architects outside of America since the 1960s, in the thought of Archigram, for example, or that of the Metabolists. Moshe Safdie's Habitats have also followed this model. But the only successful factory-produced house in the USA has been the mobile or 'manufactured" home, and since these are lightly constructed and usually one story, it is hard to find a way to stack them. See Davis, *Designing for the Homeless*, pp.62–6, who discusses several experiments and reviews the impediments to factory-construction of low-cost dwellings in the USA. Charlie Lazor, recent founder of the furniture design studio Blu Dot, has designed a panelized FlatPak House that can be shipped long distances. Jay Shafer, of the "Tumbleweed Tiny House Company", proposes tiny minimal dwellings (one of which is named after Thoreau's hut at Walden) which can be shipped on trucks and installed by crane. He envisages most of them in wilderness settings, though "clusters" are also possible (see www.tumbleweedhouses.com). The firm called *Resolution: 4 Architecture* utilizes existing techniques of producing modular homes to produce custom designs. Rocío Romero has created the "L.V. House", a sleek-looking modernist box that is shipped in large components. Yet, so far at least, none of these recent experiments is suited to low-cost mass housing. Relevant current websites include www.housingprototypes.org and www.thedwellhome.com. See also Robert Kronenburg, *Portable Architecture,* Oxford and Boston: Architectural Press, 2000; Alejandro Bahamón (ed.), *Prefab: Adaptable, Modular, Dismountable, Light, Mobile Architecture*, London: Hi Marketing, 2002; and Paul Goldberger, "Some Assembly Required: A Modern Way to Make a Modern House", *The New Yorker*, 17 October 2005, 180–2.

36   See for example the reports, by critics of high-rise housing, of lost children in high-rise apartment buildings discussed by Ravetz in Ch. 11. On "Megalopolis", see Jean Gottmann, *Megalopolis: the Urbanized Northeastern Seaboard of the United States*, New York: Twentieth Century

Fund, 1961 and Wolf Von Eckardt, *The Challenge of Megalopolis: a Graphic Presentation of the Urbanized Northeastern Seaboard of the United States*, New York: Macmillan, 1964.

37 Writing in the mid-1950s, Heidegger observed a kind of "homelessness" that resulted from lack of roots, and from the absence of older kinds of group identity. Deborah Tall reaffirms this kind of concern half a century later in Ch. 13. Other writers believe that homelessness is first and foremost the absence of adequate shelter. In addition to the "Mad Houser" dwellings described here by journalist Bo Emerson, see also Davis, *Designing for the Homeless*, on the homeless condition, and especially on Habitat for Humanity and analogous organizations. See also the current work of Cameron Sinclair and the Architecture for Humanity group in providing crisis housing for those dispossessed by war and disaster (briefly described in Alastair Gordon, "Designing for the Dispossessed", *New York Times*, 28 August 2003, and much more fully in the recent volume: Cameron Sinclair, Kate Stohr and Architecture for Humanity (eds), *Design Like You Give a Damn: Architectural Responses to Humanitarian Crises*, London: Thames & Hudson, 2006). Habitat for Humanity has been active in hurricane and Tsunami relief. Useful current websites are www.madhousers.org, www.architectureforhumanity.org, and www. habitat.org/disaster.

On Edgar Reitz's *Heimat*, see especially Kenneth Barkin, "Heimat: Eine deutsche Chronik", *American Historical Review* 96, 4 (October 1991), 1123–6; Christopher J. Wickham, "Representation and Mediation in Edgar Reitz's *Heimat*", *The German Quarterly* 64, 1, (Winter 1991): 35–45; and Richard Kilborn, "Retrieving and Remembering the Past: Edgar Reitz's *Heimat* (1984)", *Forum for Modern Language Studies* 31, 1, (January 1995): 84–98. Readers are urged to view the film itself: *Heimat, eine deutsche Chronik*, television series 1984, fifteen and a half hours, directed by Edgar Reitz, written by Edgar Reitz and Peter Steinbach. With English subtitles: Facets Multimedia, Chicago: video 1987, 1996; DVD 20005.

38 See for example, Alice Friedman, *Women and the Making of the Modern House: A Social and Architectural History*, New York: Abrams, 1998; Daniela Hammer-Tugendhat and Wolf Tegethoff (eds), *Ludwig Mies van der Rohe: the Tugendhat House*, Vienna and New York: Springer, 2000; Kathryn Springer, *Frank Lloyd Wright, Hollyhock House and Olive Hill: Buildings and Projects for Aline Barnsdall*, New York: Rizzoli, 1992; Franklin Toker, *Fallingwater Rising: Frank Lloyd Wright, E. J. Kaufmann, and America's Most Extraordinary House*, New York: Knopf, 2004.

39 See, for example, Dolores Hayden, *Seven American Utopias: The Architecture of Communitarian Socialism, 1790–1975*, Cambridge, Mass.: MIT Press, 1976; Gillian Darley, *Villages of Vision*, St Albans: Granada, 1978; Terry Smith, *Making the Modern: Industry, Art, and Design in America*, Chicago: University of Chicago Press, 1993; and Lisa Taylor (ed.), *Housing: Structure, Symbol, Site*, New York, Cooper-Hewitt Museum, 1990.

40 As for example in the selections included here by Rapoport and Tuan. A superb and powerfully influential further example is Pierre Bourdieu's essay "The Kabyle House: or, The World Reversed", first pub. 1970 ("La Maison Kabyle ou le monde renversé", in Jean Pouillon and Pierre Maranda (eds), *Échanges et communications: Mélanges offerts à Claude Lévi Strauss à l'occasion de son 60e anniversaire*, The Hague: Mouton, 1970, pp. 739–58). Here Bourdieu examines the dense symbolisms of all aspects of the Kabyle house, including shape, orientation, siting, materials, interior furnishings and decorations, and patterns of use.

Figure 1
Sacré Coeur and Montmartre,
Paris, aerial view.

Figure 2
Edward L. Angell, row houses,
241–9 Central Park West, New
York City, 1887–8.

Figure 3
Single-family dwelling, suburban Philadelphia,
c. 1890.

Figure 4
Chamberlin, Powell and Bon, Barbican,
London, 1956–82.

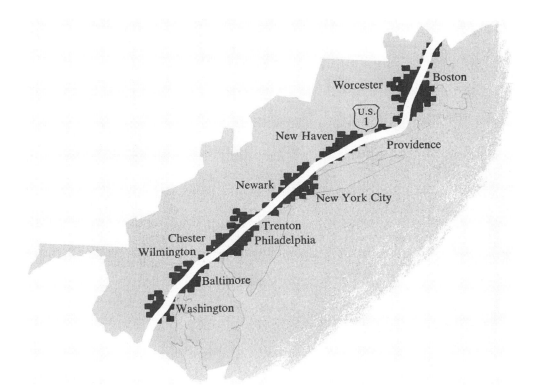

Figure 5   Jean Gottmann, Megalopolis, 1961.

Figure 6   Beverly Hills, Los Angeles, aerial view 1975.

"I'm Mrs. Edward M. Barnes. Where do I live?"

Figure 7   "I'm Mrs. Edward M. Barnes. Where do I live?", cartoon by Robert Day, *The New Yorker*, 1954.

PART I
Methods and interpretations

2

Who interprets?

The historian, the architect, the anthropologist, the archaeologist, the user?

These selections present some of the principal types of interpretation that have been or can be employed in thinking about domestic architecture. Nikolaus Pevsner states the old-fashioned definition of the subject matter of architectural history as pursued by the scholar. Frank Lloyd Wright expresses the olympian view of the modern architect who hopes to constrain patrons, forms and furnishings in the service of his own creations, and who as "form-giver" is the sole authority on the building. Amos Rapoport brings to bear on the subject the perspective of the cultural anthropologist who interprets the symbolism of domestic practices, and also raises important questions about the nature of "vernacular" architecture. Archaeologist Suzanne Spencer-Wood attacks the "andro-centric" conventions of all history writing as it has been practiced from the nineteenth century on, urging that we turn to non-patriarchal, non-art-historical, materials-based methods in the study of domestic architecture. Tony Earley's short story, depicting the maturing of a young man interacting with the spaces of a family dwelling, helps us think about the users of domestic spaces.

An outline of European architecture

Nikolaus Pevsner (1943)

A bicycle shed is a building; Lincoln Cathedral is a piece of architecture. Nearly every-thing that encloses space on a scale sufficient for a human being to move in is a building; the term architecture applies only to buildings designed with a view to aesthetic appeal. Now aesthetic sensations may be caused by a building in three different ways. First, they may be produced by the treatment of walls, proportions of windows, the relation of wall-space to window-space, of one story to another, of ornamentation such as the tracery of a fourteenth-century window, or the leaf and fruit garlands of a Wren porch. Secondly, the treatment of the exterior of a building as a whole is aesthetically significant, its contrasts of block against block, the effect of a pitched or flat roof or a dome, the rhythm of projections and recessions. Thirdly, there is the effect on our senses of the treatment of the interior, the sequence of rooms, the widening out of a nave at the crossing, the stately movement of a Baroque staircase. The first of these three ways is two-dimensional; it is the painter's way. The second is three-dimensional, and as it treats the building as volume, as a plastic unit, it is the sculptor's way. The third is three-dimensional too, but it concerns space; it is the architect's own way more than the others. What distinguishes architecture from painting and sculpture is its spatial quality. In this, and only in this, no other artist can emulate the architect. Thus the history of architecture is primarily a history of man shaping space, and the historian must keep spatial problems always in the foreground. This is why no book on architecture, however popular its presentation may be, can be successful without ground plans.

But architecture, though primarily spatial, is not exclusively spatial. In every building, besides enclosing space, the architect models volume and plans surface, i.e. designs an exterior and sets out individual walls. That means that the good architect requires the sculptor's and the painter's modes of vision in addition to his own spatial imagination. Thus architecture is the most comprehensive of all visual arts and has a right to claim superiority over the others.

This aesthetic superiority is, moreover, supplemented by a social superiority. Neither sculpture nor painting, although both are rooted in elementary creative and imitative instincts, surrounds us to the same extent as architecture, acts upon us so incessantly and so ubiquitously. We can avoid intercourse with what people call the Fine Arts, but we cannot escape buildings and the subtle but penetrating effects of their character, noble or mean, restrained or ostentatious, genuine or meretricious. An age without painting is conceivable, though no believer in the life-enhancing function of art would want it. An age without easel-pictures can be conceived without any difficulty, and, thinking of the predominance of easel-pictures in the nineteenth century, might be regarded as a consummation devoutly to be wished. An age without architecture is impossible as long as human beings populate this world.

The very fact that in the nineteenth century easel-painting flourished at the expense of wall-painting, and ultimately of architecture, proves into what a diseased state the arts (and Western civilization) had fallen. The very fact that the Fine Arts today seem to be recovering their architectural character makes one look into the future with some hope. For architecture did rule when Greek art and when medieval art grew and were at their best; Raphael still and Michelangelo conceived in terms of balance between architecture and painting. Titian did not, Rembrandt did not, nor did Velazquez. Very high aesthetic achievements are possible in easel-painting, but they are achievements torn out of the common ground of life. The nineteenth century and, even more forcibly, some of the most recent tendencies in the fine arts have shown up the dangers of the take-it-or-leave-it attitude of the independent, self-sufficient painter. Salvation can only come from architecture as the art most closely bound up with the necessities of life, with immediate use, and functional and structural fundamentals.

That does not, however, mean that architectural evolution is caused by function and construction. A style in art belongs to the world of mind, not the world of matter. New purposes may result in new types of building, but the architect's job is to make such new types both aesthetically and functionally satisfactory – and not all ages have considered, as ours does, functional soundness indispensable for aesthetic enjoyment. The position is similar with regard to materials. New materials may make new forms possible, and even call for new forms. Hence it is quite justifiable if so many works on architecture (especially in England) have emphasized their importance. If in this book they have deliberately been kept in the background, the reason is that materials can become architecturally effective only when the architect instils into them an aesthetic meaning. Architecture is not the product of materials and purposes – nor by the way of social conditions – but of the changing spirits of changing ages. It is the spirit of an age that pervades its social life, its religion, its scholarship, and its arts. The Gothic style was not created because some-body invented rib-vaulting; the Modern Movement did not come into being because steel frame and reinforced concrete construction had been worked out – they were worked out because a new spirit required them.

Thus the following chapters will treat the history of European architecture as a history of expression, and primarily of spatial expression.

Building the new house
Frank Lloyd Wright (1954)

First thing in building the new house, get rid of the attic, therefore the dormer. Get rid of the useless false heights below it. Next, get rid of the unwholesome basement, yes abso-lutely – in any house built on the prairie. Instead of lean, brick chimneys bristling up everywhere to hint at Judgment, I could see necessity for one chimney only. A broad generous one, or at most two. These kept low down on gently sloping roofs or perhaps flat roofs. The big fireplace in the house below became now a place for a real fire. A real fireplace at that time was extraordinary. There were mantels instead. A mantel was a marble frame for a few coals in a grate. Or it was a piece of wooden furniture with tile stuck in it around the grate, the whole set slam up against the plastered, papered wall. Insult to comfort. So the *integral* fireplace became an important part of the building itself in the houses I was allowed to build out there on the prairie.

It comforted me to see the fire burning deep in the solid masonry of the house itself. A feeling that came to stay.

Taking a human being for my scale, I brought the whole house down in height to fit a normal one – ergo, 5′ 8½″ tall, say. This is my own height. Believing in no other scale than the human being I broadened the mass out all I possibly could to bring it down into spaciousness. It has been said that were I three inches taller than 5′ 8½″ all my houses would have been quite different in proportion. Probably.

House walls were now started at the ground on a cement or stone water table that looked like a low platform under the building, and usually was. But the house walls were stopped at the second-story windowsill level to let the bedrooms come through above in a continuous window series below the broad eaves of a gently sloping, overhanging roof. In this new house the wall was beginning to go as an impediment to outside light and air and beauty. Walls had been the great fact about the box in which holes had to be punched. It was still this conception of a wall-building which was with me when I designed the Winslow house. But after that my conception began to change.

My sense of "wall" was no longer the side of a box. It was enclosure of space affording protection against storm or heat only when needed. But it was also to bring the outside world into the house and let the inside of the house go outside. In this sense I was working away at the wall as a wall and bringing it towards the function of a screen, a means of opening up space which, as control of building-materials improved, would finally permit the free use of the whole space without affecting the soundness of the structure.

The climate being what it was, violent in extremes of heat and cold, damp and dry, dark and bright, I gave broad protecting roof-shelter to the whole, getting back to the purpose for which the cornice was originally designed. The underside of roof-projections was flat and usually light in color to create a glow of reflected light that softly brightened the upper rooms; overhangs had double value: shelter and preservation for the walls of the house, as well as this diffusion of reflected light for the upper story through the "light screens" that took the place of the walls and were now often the windows in long series.

And at this time I saw a house, primarily, as livable interior space under ample shelter. I liked the *sense of shelter* in the look of the building. I still like it.

The house began to associate with the ground and become natural to its prairie site.

And would the young man in Architecture believe that this was all "new" then? Yes – not only new, but destructive heresy – ridiculous eccentricity. All somewhat so today. Stranger still, but then it was *all* so *new* that what prospect I had of ever earning a livelihood by making houses was nearly wrecked. At first, "they" called the houses "dress reform" houses because Society was just then excited about that particular reform. This simplification looked like some kind of reform to the provincials.

What I have just described was on the *outside* of the house. But it was all there, chiefly because of what had happened *inside*.

Dwellings of that period were cut up, advisedly and completely, with the grim determination that should go with any cutting process. The interiors consisted of boxes beside boxes or inside boxes, called *rooms*. All boxes were inside a complicated outside boxing. Each domestic function was properly box to box.

I could see little sense in this inhibition, this cellular sequestration that implied ancestors familiar with penal institutions, except for the privacy of bedrooms on the upper floor. They were perhaps all right as sleeping boxes. So I declared the whole lower floor as one room, cutting off the kitchen as a laboratory, putting the servants' sleeping and living quarters next to the kitchen but semidetached, on the ground floor. Then I screened various portions of the big room for certain domestic purposes like dining and reading.

There were no plans in existence like these at the time. But my clients were all pushed toward these ideas as helpful to a solution of the vexed servant problem. Scores of unnecessary doors disappeared and no end of partition. Both clients and servants liked the new freedom. The house became more free as space and more livable too. Interior spaciousness began to dawn.

Thus came an end to the cluttered house. Fewer doors; fewer window holes though much greater window area; windows and doors lowered to convenient human heights. These changes once made, the ceilings of the rooms could be brought down over on to the walls by way of the horizontal broad bands of plaster on the walls themselves above the windows and colored the same as the room-ceilings. This would bring ceiling-surface and color down to the very window tops. Ceilings thus expanded by way of the wall band above the windows gave generous overhead even to small rooms. The sense of the whole broadened, made plastic by this means.

Here entered the important new element of plasticity – as I saw it. And I saw it as indispensable element to the successful use of the machine. The windows would sometimes be wrapped around the building corners as inside emphasis of plasticity and to increase the sense of interior space. I fought for outswinging windows because the casement window associated house with the out-of-doors, gave free openings outward. In other words, the so-called casement was not only simple but more human in use and effect. So more natural. If it had not existed I should have invented it. But it was not used at that time in the United States so I lost many clients because I insisted upon it. […]

Here was an ideal of organic simplicity put to work, with historical consequences not only in this country but especially in the thought of the civilized world.

Simplicity

[…] In architecture, expressive changes of surface, emphasis of line and especially textures of material or imaginative pattern, may go to make facts more eloquent – forms more significant. Elimination, therefore, may be just as meaningless as elaboration, perhaps more often is so. To know what to leave out and what to put in; just where and just how, ah, *that* is to have been educated in knowledge of simplicity – toward ultimate freedom of expression.

As for objects of art in the house, even in that early day they were bêtes noires of the new simplicity. If well chosen, all right. But only if each were properly digested by the whole. […] Better in general to design all as integral features.

I tried to make my clients see that furniture and furnishings that were not built in as integral features of the building should be designed as attributes of whatever furniture *was* built in and should be seen as a minor part of the building itself even if detached or kept aside to be employed only on occasion.

But when the building itself was finished the old furniture they already possessed usually went in with the clients to await the time when the interior might be completed in this sense. Very few of the houses, therefore, were anything but painful to me after the clients brought in their belongings. […]

Human beings must group, sit or recline, confound them, and they must dine – but dining is much easier to manage and always a great artistic opportunity. Arrangements for the informality of sitting in comfort singly or in groups still belonging in disarray to the scheme as a whole: *that* is a matter difficult to accomplish. But it can be done now and should be done, because only those attributes of human comfort and convenience should be in order which belong to the whole in this modern integrated sense. […]

Plasticity

[…] Classic architecture was all fixation-of-the-fixture. Yes, entirely so. Now why not let walls, ceilings, floors become *seen* as component parts of each other, their surfaces flowing into each other. To get continuity in the whole, eliminating all constructed features … Here the promotion of an idea from the material to the spiritual plane began to have consequences. Conceive now that an entire building might grow up out of conditions as a plant grows up out of soil and yet be free to be itself, to "live its own life according to Man's Nature". Dignified as a tree in the midst of nature but a child of the spirit of man.

I now propose an ideal for the architecture of the machine age, for the ideal American building. Let it grow up in that image. The tree.

But I do not mean to suggest the imitation of the tree.

Proceeding, then, step by step from generals to particulars, plasticity as a large means in architecture began to grip me and to work its own will. Fascinated I would watch its sequences, seeing other sequences in those consequences already in evidence: as in the Heurtley, Martin, Heath, Thomas, Tomek, Coonley and dozens of other houses.

The old architecture, so far as its grammar went, for me began, literally, to disappear.

As if by magic new architectural effects came to life – effects genuinely new in the whole cycle of architecture owing simply to the working of this spiritual principle. Vistas of inevitable simplicity and ineffable harmonies would open, so beautiful to me that I was not only delighted, but often startled. Yes, sometimes amazed.

I have since concentrated on plasticity as physical continuity, using it as a practical working principle within the very nature of the building itself in the effort to accomplish this great thing called architecture.

The nature and definition of the field

Amos Rapoport (1969)

Architectural theory and history have traditionally been concerned with the study of monuments. They have emphasized the work of men of genius, the unusual, the rare. Although this is only right, it has meant that we have tended to forget that the work of the designer, let alone of the designer of genius, has represented a small, often insignificant, portion of the building activity at any given period. The physical environment of man, especially the built environment, has not been, and still is not, controlled by the designer. This environment is the result of vernacular (or folk, or popular) architecture, and it has been largely ignored in architectural history and theory. Yet it has been the environment of the Athens of the Acropolis, of the Maya cities and the towns next to Egyptian temples and tombs or around Gothic cathedrals – as it has been of remote villages and islands, whether of Greece or the South Seas. In addition, the high style buildings usually must be seen in relation to, and in the context of, the vernacular matrix, and are in fact incomprehensible outside that context, especially as it existed at the time they were designed and built.

In archeology, the interest shifted a while ago from temples, palaces, and tombs to the whole city as an expression of a culture and a way of life, although the house, the most typically vernacular building type, is still frequently ignored. Similar shifts have taken place in general history, in the history of art, and in that of music, to an extent. In architecture, however, such an interest is only now starting, and it has not yet gone very far nor beyond the purely visual. It is therefore a topic which has been rather neglected.

This neglect of the bulk of the built environment, the tendency to see mud hovels or insignificant grass shacks where there are, in fact, buildings of great quality with much to teach us, has given rise to two standards – one for "important" buildings, especially those of the past, and another for "unimportant" buildings and the environment which they compose. [...] Yet we must look at the whole environment in order to understand it, and it is in this sense that we must study the history of built form. If we look at only the smallest part of the work, that part tends to assume undue importance; if we look at it in isolation, we cannot grasp its complex and subtle relation to the vernacular matrix with which it forms a total spatial and hierarchic system. Neglect of the vernacular buildings which form the environment has had the effect of making the latter seem unimportant; it is consequently neglected physically and constantly deteriorates.

What then do we mean by folk architecture and by the terms *primitive* and *vernacular* as they apply to building forms? [...]

We may say that monuments – buildings of the grand design tradition – are built to impress either the populace with the power of the patron, or the peer group of designers and cognoscenti with the cleverness of the designer and good taste of the patron. The folk tradition, on the other hand, is the direct and unselfconscious translation into physical form of a culture, its needs and values – as well as the desires, dreams, and passions of a people. It is the world view writ small, the "ideal" environment of a people expressed in buildings and settlements, with no designer, artist, or architect with an axe to grind (although to what extent the designer is really a form *giver* is a moot point). The folk tradition is much more closely related to the culture of the majority and life as it is really lived than is the grand design tradition, which represents the culture of the élite. The folk tradition also represents the bulk of the built environment.[1]

Within this folk tradition we may distinguish between primitive and vernacular buildings, with the latter comprising preindustrial vernacular and modern vernacular. Present-day design, while part of the grand design tradition, is characterized by a greater degree of institutionalization and specialization. [...]

Since the average member of the group builds his own house, he understands his needs and requirements perfectly; any problems that arise will affect him personally and be dealt with. There are, of course, prescribed ways of doing and not doing things. Certain forms are taken for granted and strongly resist change, since societies like these tend to be very tradition oriented. This explains the close relation between the forms and the culture in which they are embedded, and also the fact that some of these forms persist for very long periods of time. With this persistence the model is finally adjusted until it satisfies most of the cultural, physical, and maintenance requirements. This model is fully uniform, and in a primitive society all the dwellings are basically identical.

As I have suggested, a satisfactory definition of *vernacular* is more difficult. At the moment, the most successful way of describing it seems to be in terms of process – how it is "designed" and built.

When building tradesmen are used for construction of most dwellings, we may arbitrarily say that primitive building gives way to *preindustrial vernacular.*[2] Even in this case, however, everyone in the society knows the building types and even how to build them, the expertise of the tradesman being a matter of degree. The peasant owner is still very much a *participant* in the design process, not merely a *consumer;* this applies to the townsman of a preindustrial culture to a greater extent than it does to the townsman of today, since participation tends to decrease with urbanization and greater specialization. This change to the use of tradesmen marks the beginning of the process of increasing specialization of trades, although at the outset of this process the tradesman is ... only part-time, and is still also a peasant. The two methods of building may, in fact, coexist as they do in the primitive context. In preindustrial vernacular the accepted *form* still exists, thus offering a way of arriving at a definition of vernacular by looking at the "design process".

The vernacular design process is one of models and adjustments or variations, and there is more individual variability and differentiation than in primitive buildings; it is the *individual specimens* that are modified, not the *type*. When a tradesman builds a farmhouse for a peasant, they both know the type in question, the form or model, and even the materials. What remains to be determined are the specifics – family requirements (although this is also less variable than is true today), size (depending on wealth), and relation to the site and micro-climate.[3] Since both tradesman and peasant agree on what is wanted, there is, in effect, a model which is adjusted and adapted as one proceeds; this is as true of the Danish farmer as of the French or Yugoslav peasant. [...]

The characteristics of vernacular building as I see them [are]: lack of theoretical or aesthetic pretensions; working *with* the site and micro-climate; respect for other people and *their* houses and hence for the total environment, man-made as well as natural; and working within an idiom with variations within a given order. There are many individual variations within a framework which can be adapted in various ways. Although a vernacular always has limitations in the range of expression possible, at the same time it can fit many different situations, and create a *place* at each. It is, of course, precisely this limitation of expression which makes any communication possible. To communicate, one must be prepared to learn as well as use the language – which implies the acceptance of authority, trust, and a shared vocabulary.

Another characteristic of vernacular is its additive quality, its unspecialized, open-ended nature, so different from the closed, final form typical of most high-style design. It is this quality which enables vernacular buildings to accept changes and additions which would visually and conceptually destroy a high-style design. Vernacular is also characterized by the greater importance and significance of relationships between elements, and the manner in which these relationships are achieved, rather than by the nature of the elements themselves. This, however, leads us into the realm of urban design, which is the topic for another book.

The model itself is the result of the collaboration of many people over many generations as well as the collaboration between makers and users of buildings and other artifacts, which is what is meant by the term *traditional*. Since knowledge of the model is shared by all, there is no need for drawings or designers. A house is meant to be like all the well-built houses in a given area. The construction is simple, clear, and easy to grasp, and since everyone knows the rules, the craftsman is called in only because he has a more *detailed* knowledge of these rules. Size, layout, relation to site, and other variables can be decided by discussion and, if necessary, set down in a written contract. The aesthetic quality is not specially created for each house – it is traditional and handed down through the generations. Tradition has the force of a law honored by everyone through collective assent. It is thus accepted and obeyed, since respect for tradition gives collective control, which acts as a discipline. This approach works because there is a shared image of life, an accepted model of buildings, a small number of building types, and, finally, an accepted *hierarchy* and hence an accepted settlement pattern. As long as the tradition is alive, this shared and accepted image operates; when tradition goes, the picture changes. Without tradition, there can no longer be reliance on the accepted norms, and there is a beginning of institutionalization. The introduction of pattern books is the first step in this process, as in the United States with barns and houses and in Japan with houses. Tradition as a regulator has disappeared – notably in our own culture – for a number of reasons.

The first reason is the greater number of building types, many of which are too complex to build in traditional fashion. This rise of specialization and differentiation is paralleled in the spaces within the buildings and the various trades and professions involved in their design and erection.

The second reason is loss of the common shared value system and image of the world, with a consequent loss of an accepted and shared hierarchy – and generally a loss of goals shared by designers and the public. This results in the disappearance of that spirit of cooperation which makes people respect the rights of adjoining people and their buildings, and ultimately the rights of the settlement as a whole. Lack of cooperation leads to the introduction of such controls (going beyond pattern books) as codes, regulations, and zoning rules concerning alignments and setbacks, which also existed in some preindustrial towns.

For example, in Latin America under the Spanish, the Laws of the Indies prescribed narrow streets for shade, uniformity of façades, and orientation for winds; while Peking had rules regulating the hierarchy of colors. These rules do not usually work as well as the voluntary controls of public opinion. The distinction between traditional and modern societies can be understood in terms of the contrast between informal controls, affectivity, and consensus in the former, and impersonality and interdependent specialization in the latter,[4] which would seem to correspond to Redfield's concept of substitution of the technical order for the moral order.[5] While these concepts have usually been applied to social mechanisms and cities, they are useful to an understanding of the processes of creating vernacular buildings and settlements.

The third reason for the disappearance of tradition as a regulator is the fact that our culture puts a premium on *originality*, often striving for it for its own sake. As a result, society becomes dissatisfied with traditional forms, and the vernacular process can no longer work. This dissatisfaction is often based on nonfunctional considerations and is linked to socio-cultural factors. In most traditional cultures, novelty is not only not sought after, but is regarded as undesirable.

This book is concerned only in passing with modern vernacular and the question as to whether, in fact, it exists at all. Neither is it really concerned with architect-designed buildings. However, some reference needs to be made to these in order to complete the definition of vernacular and to clarify the areas of our concern. Avoiding for the moment the problem of whether a vernacular architecture is possible with modern communications and self-consciousness, I would suggest that there *is* a modern folk idiom, and that this is primarily, although not exclusively, one of *type*. Most of the folk architecture in contemporary America has been in terms of new types – the motel, the diner, drive-ins of all types – all of which originated outside the design professions and have, as it were, come up from "below". The forms themselves have been those currently fashionable and commonly used; their wide dissemination by the various news media, films, and travel make it impossible to create forms in the traditional manner. I have already suggested that relationships between these buildings can no longer be achieved through the informal controls typical of traditional vernacular. Those forms which are still partly of that style – the Doggie Diners, concrete doughnuts, and so on – are designed *for* the popular taste, not *by* it, but they, as well as popular housing, continue to show some commonly held values more clearly than does the design subculture.

Finally we find that due to the causes already enumerated – greater complexity of problems and greater specialization – the design of buildings and settlements is increasingly the concern of professional designers. [...]

Let us turn to the Western world, and see whether the basic framework suggested helps us in any way to understand the form of the popular house.

The prevalent attitude toward planning and design in the United States makes the norm the white, middle-class family of parents and two children typified by advertising. This leaves out millions who have different values and do not fit this package, even though these subcultural differences are of great importance. Consider, for example, the way working-class people use part of the settlement – the neighborhood – in a manner much more closely related to the Mediterranean tradition than to the Anglo-American one.[6] This will have, or *should* have, profound effects on the image and form of the house and settlement ...

Definition of the image and meaning of the house is of great importance; it can help explain the difference between houses on the East Coast and California, and can be an important aspect in low-cost housing. For example, agricultural workers in the Central valley of California, in self-help housing, build "ranchhouses" based on the popular press image, a symbol of belonging through the middle-class house. These people are not confident enough to be different, to express their own traditions, or even to respond directly to the needs of the area. It may well be that the expression of subcultural traditions is more likely in areas such as Latin America, Africa, and Asia, where these cultures are stronger than among, say, Mexican-Americans.[7]

Within the middle-class culture itself, dwelling forms change to accommodate people outside the "standard family" through new types of popular housing. An example is the recent development of a new type of apartment for single people in cities.[8] I have already suggested ... that the vernacular today may be one of *type* rather than of form. This particular type came from the needs of a specific group, felt by an entrepreneur; the need was real, as shown by the great success of his efforts. The new social role this housing fills has strong form consequences in the stress placed on communal and recreational facilities, and the way in which spaces are used to fulfill this new role.

Turning to the single family house and its parts, there is still a link between behavioral patterns and form.

Consider the impact of attitudes toward eating, for example, on house form. It makes a major difference whether one has a formal family meal in a separate dining room or eats in the kitchen; whether everyone eats separately whenever he wishes or all eat together; or whether one eats indoors at all. The prevalence of the barbecue in Los Angeles affects more than just house form, since increasing use of the backyard, with its barbecue and swimming pool, makes it, and the house, more than ever the center of life. Patterns of formality or informality in dining still play an important role in molding childhood attitudes, and to that extent the house is still a mechanism for shaping character.

Attitudes toward the bathroom in the United States ... are largely cultural. A recent major study of the topic shows clearly that the form of the bathroom is the result of attitudes about the body, relaxation, privacy, and so on.[9] It has frequently been observed by visitors that American houses are advertised by the number of bathrooms they possess, which often exceeds the number of bedrooms. This brings us back to the problem of *basic needs*. The same fundamental problems of hygiene have always existed, but the importance attached to them, and the forms used, have been very different, depending on beliefs, fears, and values rather than utilitarian considerations. For example, the choice between tub and shower is largely a matter of attitudes and images.[10]

In the same way, attitudes toward privacy are still very much culturally shaped, and have great impact on house form. These attitudes not only differ between Germany and the United States, and even England and the United States,[11] but also among different subcultures in this country. [...]

It may be that the modern house orients itself to the view, beach, sun, and sky, and that this orientation, and the picture window, replace the religious, symbolic orientation of the past. Therefore, a new symbol takes over – health, sun, and sport *as an idea*. We could say that in the United States the ideal of health becomes a new religion.[12]

What then does "house" mean to Americans? They have a dream "home – the very word can reduce my compatriots to tears",[13] and builders and developers never build houses, they build homes. The dream home is surrounded by trees and grass in either country or suburb, and must be *owned* ... It is not a real need but a symbol.

This symbol means a freestanding, single family house, *not* a row house, and the ideal of home is aesthetic, not functional.[14] ... The symbol is not necessarily good or reasonable in terms of utility, and has, in fact, been criticized, but it is real and represents a world view and an ethos. This becomes particularly clear if the American attitude is compared with a study in Vienna, where 61 per cent of the people wanted apartments in the center of town, 51 per cent preferred multistory buildings, and other preferences were equally different from the prevailing American attitude.[15] [...]

As one example, consider the fence. Visitors from Australia and England are struck by the lack of fences in American suburbs, and find it difficult to understand. The front fence, in those other countries gives no real visual or acoustic privacy, but symbolizes a frontier and barrier. [...]

In the same way, "roof" is a symbol of home, as in the phrase "a roof over one's head", and its importance has been stressed in a number of studies. In one study, the importance of images – i.e., symbols – for house form is stressed, and the pitched roof is said to be symbolic of shelter while the flat roof is not, and is therefore unacceptable on symbolic grounds.[16]

Notes

1   Even today the figure for architect-designed buildings worldwide is reliably estimated at five percent. See Constantinos A. Doxiadis, *Architecture in Transition*, London: Hutchinson, 1964, pp. 71–5. The maximum, he estimates, is reached in England where architects may be responsible for 40 percent of the buildings. In most of the world their influence is "precisely nil" (p. 71), five percent of all buildings being designed by architects. Most buildings are built by the people or by tradesmen.

2   An alternative way of drawing a distinction between primitive and vernacular is suggested by an analogy with Robert Redfield's *Peasant Society and Culture*, Chicago: University of Chicago Press, 1956, pp. 68–9, 71, where primitive is defined as isolated and self-contained – if not in terms of other primitive cultures then in terms of some *high* culture – while peasant cultures (i.e., vernacular) must be seen in the context of the coexisting high cultures. They are replenished and influenced by the high culture because they are aware of it, and the high and low cultures are interdependent and affect each other. [...]

3   See J. A. Bundgaard, *Mnesicles*, Copenhagen: Gyldendal, 1957, in which he suggests that Greek temples are vernacular forms in this sense.

4   Gerald Breese, *Urbanization in Newly Developing Countries*, Englewood Cliffs, NJ: Prentice-Hall, 1966, p. 7. See also Eric Wolf, *Peasants*, Englewood Cliffs, NJ: Prentice-Hall, 1966, p. 11, in which he similarly distinguishes between primitive and "civilized" in terms of specialization and differentiation.

5   Robert Redfield, *The Primitive World and Its Transformations*, Ithaca, NY: Cornell University Press, 1953 and Robert Redfield, "The Cultural Role of Cities", *Economic Development and Cultural Change*, 3, October 1954, 56–7.

6   See Marc Fried, "Functions of Working Class Community in Modern Urban Society: Implications for Forced Relocation", *Journal of the AIP*, XXXIII, no. 2, March 1967, 90ff., especially 92, 100, and references on 102; see also Marc Fried, "Grieving for a Lost Home", in Leonard Duhl (ed.) *The Urban Condition*, New York: Basic Books, 1963.

7   Even in the United States one can find examples of the expression of cultural differences. A student of mine – Mr. Edward Long – found that Mexican and Japanese neighborhoods in Los Angeles, which began with identical houses, took on very different characteristics because of the symbolism of the landscaping. (This is my interpretation, not his; he was concerned with a different aspect of the problem.)

8   *Time* LXXXVIII, no. 9, August 26, 1966, 49.

9   Alexander Kira, *The Bathroom*, Ithaca, NY: Cornell University Center for Housing and Environmental Studies, Research Report no. 7, 1966. It is interesting that most reviewers stressed the physical, rather than the cultural and psychological, aspects of the study.

10 Ibid., pp. 8–10.

11 E. T. Hall, *The Hidden Dimension*, Garden City, NY: Doubleday and Co., 1966, pp. 123–37.

12   See H. G. West, "The House is a Compass", *Landscape* I, no. 2, 1951, 24–7. This topic has been studied by J. B. Jackson. He suggested this view to me in personal conversation and also during a seminar at the Department of Landscape Architecture, University of California, Berkeley, Winter 1967; see also his "The Westward Moving House", *Landscape* II, no. 3, 1953, 8–21, on how three attitudes toward life in the United States produced three different types of house.

13   John Steinbeck, "Fact and Fancy", *San Francisco Examiner,* March 30, 1967.

14   See Richard D. Cramer, "Images of Home", *AIA Journal* XLVI, no. 3, 1960, 41, 44; also "The Builder's Architect", *Architectural Forum* XCV, no. 6, 1951, 118–25, which discusses public house preferences in the tract house field. It is clear that these preferences are symbolic.

15   Cited in *Landscape* VII, no. 2, 1957–58, 2.

16   Richard D. Cramer, "Images of Home", *AIA Journal* XLVI, no. 3 (Sept. 1960), 42.

The world their household
Changing meanings of the domestic sphere in the nineteenth century

Suzanne M. Spencer-Wood (1999)

This chapter shows how our understanding of household activities in other cultures has been shaped by archaeological projections of an élite Victorian gender ideology as the universal gender system from early prehistory through Classical cultures to the nine-teenth century. Archaeologists have created distorted constructions of past cultures by selecting and interpreting evidence to validate an assumed gender dichotomy. Feminist theory and research has questioned assumed stereotypes, revealing previously overlooked evidence of multiple diverse gender ideologies and practices from prehistory to the present. This chapter demonstrates that the élite Victorian gender ideology was not even universal in the nineteenth century.

The first section of this chapter discusses how feminist theoretical critiques have revealed androcentric biases produced by projecting Victorian-derived modern gender stereotypes as universal. Partial understandings of the past have been created by dichotomizing cultural activities into dominant-public-male versus subordinate-domestic-female roles. Feminist theorizing has revealed that belief in the reality of dualistic gender ideology is supported at deeper levels by language and an epist-emological belief in the universality of structuralist binary thinking.[1] The next section discusses how nineteenth-century classicists legitimated their élite Victorian gender ideology by claiming it originated in Classical Greece. Feminist research is presented showing that a gender dichotomy was not universally espoused or practiced in Classical Greece. [...]

Feminist critiques of male-biased frameworks

Starting in the 1970s third-wave feminist analyses have revealed how a self-reinforcing structure of Victorian-derived androcentrism deeply permeates all aspects of western culture, including anthropology, archaeology, scientific epistemology, language, and values. Multiple levels of male bias support and reinforce each other in a comprehensive androcentric system of thought that is represented as objective in ungendered text and discourse. As a result most of us have at some point unconsciously used widely accepted but androcentric paradigms, methodology, models, assumptions or taxonomies. Androcentrism can be most simply defined as an ideology of sexist prejudice resulting from a male-centered point of view. Androcentrism constructs gender in a universal structural dichotomy between opposed gender stereotypes. In androcentric ideology men are identified as public, cultural, rational, active, powerful, superior and naturally dominant over women, who are devalued as subordinate, domestic, natural, emotional, powerless, passive and inferior. Women and households have been devalued to the point that they have often been excluded entirely from large-scale constructions of the past in apparently objective ungendered text. Androcentric archaeology and anthropology are fundamentally political in supporting the oppression of women in the present by creating partial distorted constructions of cultures that represent male dominance and female subordination as universal, natural, and inevitable.[2] This section discusses feminist critiques of androcentric biases at a number of levels, from supposedly ungendered text and discourse, through constructions of cultures in gender dichotomies, to the underlying epistemology of structuralism.

The disappearance of women and households in androcentric ungendered discourse

The political standpoint of an individual or group is revealed by the questions that are not asked as much as the questions that are asked. Traditionally most archaeological research has not explicitly considered gender, although it is a foundational cultural construct that structures all social life. Supposedly objective ungendered text, discourse, constructions of cultures and evolution reveal unquestioned sexist assumptions about gender. Prior to feminist archaeology gender was not researched as a cultural construct because it was unproblematically reduced to biologically determined models of sex in which weak domestic women were dependent on strong public men.[3] According to this ideology, because men are dominant their viewpoints and behavior are of primary importance, while domestic women are subordinate and unimportant. Therefore, supposedly ungendered constructions of other cultures usually represent men's behaviors and viewpoints as those of the whole society, often masked as cultural norms.[4] The primacy and dominance of men over women is reinforced at the deepest cultural level by the linguistic convention of always putting men before women. Further, women disappear and are excluded from the past by the linguistic convention of using male nouns and pronouns to represent androcentric text and discourse as ungendered and universal.[5] Women and children often disappear from the past in ungendered text that purports to represent them but is actually exclusively about men.

The tradition of subsuming women and children within male-biased language extends as well to male-defined categories. For instance, in historical archaeology households usually have been identified only by the male head.[6] This continues the historic western cultural practice in which each man legally controlled and represented "his" household of women and children in the public community of men.[7] Women and children have disappeared, not only in male-defined households but also in classes defined according to men's occupations by economists, historians and archaeologists.[8] At the larger scale cultures are often defined according to male-controlled social, political and economic structures. Households and women disappear as they are subsumed in classes. For instance, Henretta's[9] androcentric research on the social structure of colonial Boston only discussed men, their sons, and their occupations, as if households, women and girls didn't exist. Henretta ignored female-domestic households and families as unimportant to men's public history. Yet colonial women in households produced significant quantities of goods for public sale, including textiles, butter, eggs and chickens. Further, many houses included rooms where public sales occurred, whether stores, craft shops, or print shops such as Ben Franklin's in Philadelphia. Often women worked in household stores, in craft shops, and in the industrial system of "putting out" to households the production of goods such as shoes and straw hats. Widows usually became proprietors of household businesses after their husbands died.[10] Androcentric bias in ungendered text and discourse is often apparent from the fact that only men are mentioned, excluding women's contributions to history.

Henretta exemplifies the fundamental assumption among androcentric historians and anthropologists: what men did was always more important and powerful than what women did. Some early feminist anthropologists analyzed how androcentric anthropologists produced male-biased ethnographies by accepting the viewpoints of male informants as the monolithic truth for a culture.[11] Men have been viewed by many anthropologists and historians as the only important social agents, the makers of male-defined large-scale political history. This definition of what is important in the past limits research questions to men's public actions and excludes women and households from the past because they are assumed to be only domestic and therefore irrelevant to history by definition. Thus women and households have disappeared in androcentric constructions of the past as sequences of men's public events, including wars, conquests, and kings.

In processual archaeology those questions considered most important and accorded the highest status have been male-defined and limited to the identification of ungendered large-scale public external variables considered to determine small-scale internal socio-cultural variables such as ethnicity, class, and gender.[12] Many large-scale external causal variables are androcentrically assumed to be controlled by men, such as exploration, wars, trade, and governmental or religious cultural contacts. The systems theory model of culture has focused research on large-scale processes in functional perspective, making small-group actions, roles and choices invisible as sources of cultural change.[13] Large-scale public constructions of the past subsume and therefore exclude from consideration the essential contributions of households to economies, social and political systems. Prior to feminist critique and research household archaeology was considered a less important … topic due to its association with women. Households were not often explicitly related to larger scale descriptions of cultural systems. […] The large-scale focus is on men's public activities, whether hunting, agriculture, production of goods for trade or political leadership. The household is subsumed under these ungendered but male-represented categories and is seldom mentioned at the large scale.

Projecting the ideology of dichotomies as the universal reality

Large-scale cultural processes, cross-cultural generalizations, theories, methods and questions are considered most important in the search for scientific laws of culture change. At a deeper epistemological level the positivistic paradigm of science used in the "new" archaeology is based on a historically situated gender ideology. In the eighteenth century Descartes drew from the gender ideology opposing rational man versus emotional woman to create the ideology that objectivity is opposed to subjectivity.[14] Yet the subjective elements in the objective scientific method include the selection of research question[s], data, and methods of analysis that together determine research results.[15] Claims that the scientific method is absolutely objective have been bolstered by the use of omniscient language that removes the subjective observer, making it difficult to reveal assumptions masked in passive voice statements that "The data show this to be true".[16] However, the interpretation of meanings of data is shaped by theory and method. Androcentric frameworks, assumptions and methods that classify data as either domestic or public can create the finding of a sexual division of labor as the result of circular reasoning.[17]

Starting in the 1970s some feminist anthropologists and archaeologists began to critique androcentric biases involved in the explicit construction of gender as a universal structural dichotomy, in which public active men dominated women who were devalued as domestic, passive, and subordinate.[18] This practice of reproducing androcentric models and assumptions by explicitly constructing gender in sexist dichotomies has been called the "add women and stir" approach.[19] [...]

The construction of cultures, evolution, and science in simplistic dichotomies is supported at an epistemological level by structuralism, which considers dualistic either/ or thinking to be the universally natural pattern of thought. The widespread acceptance of structuralism has resulted in monolithic constructions of cultures as sets of dichotomies,[20] even in post-processualism, although it was strongly influenced at the theoretical level by feminist critiques of dichotomies and concerns for individual social agency.[21] Structuralist thinking classifies the diversity of human cultural behavior into either one or the other of only two categories that are constructed as polar opposites. Unfortunately, some early attempts to engender other cultures used a structuralist methodology that resulted in monolithic categorizations of women as domestic and subordinate to dominant public men. In Rosaldo and Lamphere's 1974 edited volume they and other authors such as Ortner uncritically used an over-generalizing cross-cultural methodology to find universal dominance by public men and subordination and devaluation of domestic women.[22] This exemplifies how some early feminists reinforced gender stereotypes by uncritically accepting male-biased frameworks, methods, ethnographies and data. The ranking inherent in the creation of dualistic oppositions in binary structuralist thinking results in the high status accorded large-scale male-public constructions of the past and the low status accorded small-scale female-domestic pasts.

Dichotomized constructions of household roles and spaces

Gender dichotomies, structuralist thinking and methods can produce distorted constructions of households in a number of ways. First, the dichotomizing of gender into male-public and female-domestic spheres results in the *a priori* categorization of all household tasks as domestic, although many public tasks and events can occur in households, such as production of goods for public sale, public waged labor (as in taking in laundry and the putting-out system), production of public labor, and public entertainments from political receptions to parties, dinners and teas.[23] Second, dualistic gender ideology is often simplistically projected as actual practice so that household tasks and roles are unproblematically assigned to women. Even when it is acknowledged that both genders had household roles, they are commonly constructed as structurally opposed in a static normative sexual division of labor. Documented dualistic gender ideology is uncritically accepted as historic reality and is projected onto archaeological data.[24] Within the structuralist framework of gender dichotomy household spaces, features and artifacts are assigned fixed mutually exclusive identities as either male or female.[25] The subjectivity of structuralist constructions of gender and households is usually masked in apparently objective text using the passive voice of omniscient authority to claim that artifacts, features and spaces associated with men were, by definition, public, while those associated with women were domestic. In sum, concepts of gender and the household are not problematized except by feminists.[26]

In historical archaeology Yentsch[27] similarly projected this idealistic gender dichotomy onto American colonial households, monolithically categorizing the front parlor, dining room, white ceramics and other tableware as male, public and cultural versus women's domestic kitchen space ... This could have been a useful critique of the categorization of households as solely domestic, but instead the mutual exclusivity of the male-public versus female-domestic dichotomy was just imposed on household material culture. The problem with this framework is that women as well as men displayed their status to "public" outsiders in the parlor and hosted "public" dinners in the dining room. Household spaces were used for public activities at least as much by women as by men. Women often hosted "public" teas where they displayed their social status to women and sometimes men from other households. Women's and men's public activities in the home often overlapped in the same spaces. In addition, by the nineteenth-century upper- and middle-class homes often included separate men's parlors and women's parlors where each gender could publicly display their social status and wealth to people outside the household. Yet in the distorted double standard of dualistic gender ideology men's parlors are labeled public while women's parlors are labeled domestic. Finally, men were also not always excluded from household kitchens and pantries, since high status was expressed by having male black servants to serve public meals (e.g. the [male] butler's pantry).

Inclusive feminist frameworks

Many feminists have thrown off the bonds of structuralist thinking that dichotomizes cultures into mutually exclusive *either* male-public *or* female-domestic activities, roles, artifacts, and spaces. The actual complexity and diversity in real gender systems can seldom be accurately represented by simplistic dichotomies. Instead, I have suggested a more open-minded inclusive *both/and* contextually situated epistemology that more objectively analyzes all the evidence to determine whether it supports a whole range of gender behaviors. I've proposed modeling diversity in any dimension as a continuum that includes all the shades of gray between the two ends of the range of variation, whether two supposed opposites or the beginning and end of a historical developmental continuum.[28] For instance, the social dimension of degree of gender segregation in household behaviors, spaces or artifacts can each be modeled as a continuum from complete spatial separation of women's and men's activities, artifacts or spaces at one end, to complete flexibility in gender roles and multiple uses of artifacts and spaces at the other end. Between these two poles the continuum includes the whole range of variation possible in combining gender-segregated and shared household spaces and artifacts. Tasks and artifacts that were not gender segregated can overlap in household spaces that also include gender-segregated tasks and artifacts. [...]

Feminists have critiqued gender stereotypes basically in two ways: evidence has been found that women as well as men were important powerful cultural agents both (1) in the domestic sphere and (2) in the public sphere, even in male-dominated cultures. Most feminists, while not denying evidence of male domination and oppression of women in many situations, have also sought and found evidence of women's many sources of social and cultural power. Feminists have argued that women's public positions cannot be dismissed as exceptions, but instead invalidate the identification of women as only domestic. However, fewer feminists have challenged the solely male-public definition of importance by showing that women's domestic roles were important by themselves and not just for what they contributed to public history.[29]

Differentiating gender ideologies from practices

The universality of gender stereotypes can be further critiqued by differentiating gender ideology from reality. Gender ideals constructed in stereotypes and dichotomies do not represent the full diversity, complexity and flexibility in actually practiced gender roles and behaviors.[30] The linguistic root of the confusion of ideals with practice is the definition of a role as "the characteristic and expected social behavior of an individual" which represents ideals and normative practice as monolithic synonyms, ignoring variation in individual behavior that is the basis for processes of culture change. Since the culturally constructed categories of women and men both included important domestic as well as public actors, the idealistic gender dichotomy did not exist as a monolithic reality.[31]

The gender dichotomy between public men versus domestic women can also be critiqued as only one gender ideology, albeit a dominant one, among many gender ideologies. Many people today have other gender ideologies that support women in working outside the home and support male contributions to housework. Not only are there many alternative ideologies today, there were also a number of alternative ideologies in the past. Feminists have shown that the meaning of the female-domestic versus male-public dichotomy changed through time and was only one among a variety of gender ideologies.

The legitimation of élite Victorian ideology by classical archaeology

This section discusses feminist critiques of the use of Classical scholarship to materially legitimate modern and Victorian gender stereotypes as universal. In 1980 Rosaldo critiqued the universalization of modern gender stereotypes by revealing their roots in the élite Victorian gender ideology of separate spheres for dominant public men versus subordinate domestic women. Subsequently feminist historians have shown that this dominant gender ideology was only one of many nineteenth-century gender ideologies… The Victorian separate spheres gender ideology was dominant because it was espoused by most people in the upper and middle classes.[32] Most nineteenth-century scholars were élite men who believed in the superiority of western culture and projected their Victorian separate spheres gender ideology to dichotomize classical cultures into mutually exclusive male-public versus female-domestic spheres, spaces and artifacts.[33]

This ideology was supported by the structuralist school in anthropology founded in the 1950s by Lévi-Strauss, and by earlier Enlightenment philosophers from Descartes to Locke and Rousseau.[34] Nineteenth-century male scholars materially legitimated their élite Victorian gender ideology by tracing its descent from the misogynist Classical Greek gender ideology exemplified in Aristotle's writings, which had been recorded and passed down to Victorians through a long line of male scholars in exclusively male academic institutions. Further, Victorian classicists uncritically accepted male-dominated Classical gender ideology as historic reality and proceeded with structuralist interpretations of Classical artifacts and spaces at sites, including house sites, as either male-public or female-domestic.[35] [...]

Summary

This section has shown how nineteenth-century classicists inaccurately projected their élite Victorian gender ideology as actual practice throughout Classical Greece. In addition, scholars legitimated their élite Victorian gender ideology that devalued women as domestic, irrational and subordinate, by tracing it to Aristotle. Further, the similar dominant Classical Greek gender ideology was considered universal, overlooking the diversity of alternative gender ideologies by both men and women. Men have needed to legitimate their dominance because some women and men have contested male dominance from Classical Greece,[36] through medieval times and the seventeenth century through the twentieth century.[37]

This section has shown that a richer understanding of Classical Greek cultural complexities is generated by feminist critiques and research on the diversity in gender ideologies and actual practices. In this volume [Allison (ed.), *The Archaeology of Household Activities*] both Allison and Goldberg reject the projection of élite Victorian gender ideology to universally segregate Classical households into mutually exclusive *either* male-public *or* female-domestic spaces and artifacts. Instead they each found that most household spaces included both female and male activities, supporting a feminist both/and inclusive approach. [...]

The rest of this chapter argues that the élite Victorian ideology of nineteenth-century classicists cannot be considered a universal gender structure because it wasn't even universally espoused or practiced by nineteenth-century Americans or Europeans [*See below, Chapter 6, Ed.*]. [...]

In this chapter feminist questions revealing the diversity of Victorian and Classical Greek ideologies and behavior have challenged monolithic definitions of *the* gender roles, *the* gender ideology, or *the* typical household in a culture. Further, feminist critiques of binary thinking have revealed how sexist gender ideology has been selectively reproduced and represented as *the* universal ideology and practice from ancient Greece to the twentieth century. Androcentric constructions of the unitary gender ideology and norms of a culture, region, or time period, can be corrected with feminist theory, methods and research on the diversity in cultural ideologies, practices and material culture.

Notes

1   Suzanne M. Spencer-Wood, "Toward the Further Development of Feminist Historical Archaeology", *World Archaeological Bulletin* 7, 1993, 118–36.
2   Spencer-Wood, "A Feminist Agenda for Non-Sexist Archaeology", in L. A. Wandsnider (ed.) *Quandaries and Quests: Visions of Archaeology's Future*, Carbondale: South Illinois University Press, 1992.
3   Sandra Harding, "The Instability of the Analytical Categories of Feminist Theory", in Sandra Harding and Jean O'Barr (eds) *Sex and Scientific Inquiry*, Chicago: University of Chicago Press, 1987, p. 299.

4 Margaret Conkey and Janet Spector, "Archaeology and the Study of Gender", *Advances in Archaeological Method and Theory*, vol. 1, 1984, 4.

5 Spencer-Wood, "Towards a Feminist Historical Archaeology of the Construction of Gender", in Dale Walde and Noreen Willows (eds) *The Archaeology of Gender: Proceedings of the 22nd [1989] Chacmool Conference*, Calgary: University of Calgary Archaeological Association, 1991.

6 Ibid.

7 Sheila Rowbotham, *Hidden From History: Rediscovering Women in History from the 17th Century to the Present*, London: Pluto Press, 1973, pp. 4, 43, 48–50, 55–6.

8 Spencer-Wood, "Towards a Feminist Historical Archaeology", p. 236.

9 James Henretta, "Economic Development and Social Structure in Colonial Boston", in Robert Fogel and Stanley Engerman (eds) *The Reinterpretation of American Economic History*, New York: Harper and Row, 1971.

10 Barbara Wertheimer, *We Were There: The Story of Working Women in America*, New York: Pantheon Books, 1977, pp. 12–20, 51.

11 Ruby Rohrlich-Leavitt, Barbara Sykes, and Elizabeth Weatherford, "Aboriginal Woman: Male and Female Anthropological Perspectives", in Rayna Reiter (ed.) *Toward an Anthropology of Women*, London: Monthly Review Press, 1975.

12 Alison Wylie, "Gender Theory and the Archaeological Record: Why Is there no Archaeology of Gender?", in Joan Gero and Margaret Conkey (eds), *Engendering Archaeology: Women and Prehistory*, Oxford: Basil Blackwell, 1991, p. 221, critiquing Lewis Binford, *Working at Archaeology*, New York: Academic Press, 1983.

13 Conkey and Spector, "Archaeology and the Study of Gender", 22–3.

14 Susan Bordo, "The Cartesian Masculinization of Thought", *Signs* 11, no. 3, 1986, 439–56.

15 Helen Longino and Ruth Doell, "Body, Bias and Behavior: A Comparative Analysis of Reasoning in Two Areas of Biological Science", *Signs* 9, no. 2, 1983, 206–27.

16 Spencer-Wood, "Toward the Further Development of Feminist Historical Archaeology", 130.

17 See Mary Kennedy and Patty Jo Watson, "The Development of Horticulture in the Eastern Woodlands of North America: Women's Role", in Gero and Conkey, *Engendering Archaeology*.

18 E.g. Rayna Reiter, "Introduction", in Reiter (ed.) *Toward an Anthropology of Women*.

19 Charlotte Bunch, *Passionate Politics: Essays 1968–1986 – Feminist Theory in Action*, New York: St. Martin's Press, 1987, p. 140.

20 E.g. James Deetz, "Material Culture and Worldview in Colonial Anglo-America", in Mark Leone and Parker Potter, Jr (eds) *The Recovery of Meaning: Historical Archaeology in the Eastern United States*, Washington, D.C.: Smithsonian Institution Press, 1988.

21 Ian Hodder, "The Contextual Analysis of Symbolic Meanings", in Ian Hodder (ed.) *The Archaeology of Contextual Meanings*, Cambridge: Cambridge University Press, 1987, pp. 6–9; Hodder, *Theory and Practice in Archaeology*, London: Routledge, 1992, pp. 84–5.

22 Sherry Ortner, "Is Female to Male as Nature Is to Culture?", in Michelle Rosaldo and Louise Lamphere (eds) *Woman, Culture, and Society*, Stanford: Stanford University Press, 1974; Rosaldo, "Woman, Culture and Society: A Theoretical Overview", in ibid., pp. 23, 29, 35, 41; Rosaldo and Lamphere, "Introduction", in ibid., pp. 4, 8, 13–4.

23 Spencer-Wood, "Feminist Historical Archaeology and the Transformation of American Culture by Domestic Reform Movements, 1840–1925", in Lu Ann De Cunzo and Bernard Herman (eds) *Historical Archaeology and the Study of American Culture*, Winterthur, Del.: Winterthur Museum; Knoxville: University of Tennessee Press, 1996, p. 399; Spencer-Wood, "A Feminist Agenda for Non-Sexist Archaeology", p. 237.

24 E.g. R. Jameson, "Purity and Power at the Victorian Dinner Party", in Hodder, *The Archaeology of Contextual Meanings*.

25 Critiqued by both Penelope Allison and Marilyn Y. Goldberg, in Penelope M. Allison (ed.), *The Archaeology of Household Activities*, London and New York: Routledge, pp. 57–77, 142–61.

26 E.g. Sarah Nelson, *Gender in Archaeology: Analyzing Power and Prestige*, Walnut Creek: Altamira Press, 1997; Reiter, "Introduction", pp. 12–16; Linda Stine, "Early Twentieth Century Gender Roles: Perceptions from the Farm", in Walde and Willow, *The Archaeology of Gender*, pp. 496–501.

27   Anne Yentsch, "The Symbolic Divisions of Pottery: Sex-Related Attributes of English and Anglo-American Household Pots", in Randall McGuire and Robert Paynter (eds) *The Archaeology of Inequality*, Oxford: Basil Blackwell, 1991.

28   Spencer-Wood, "Introduction to Critiques of Historical Archaeology", Paper presented at the 1992 Annual Society for Historical Archaeology Conference, Kingston, January 6, 1992.

29   Spencer-Wood, "Toward the Further Development of Feminist Historical Archaeology".

30   Spencer-Wood, "Towards an Historical Archaeology"; Spencer-Wood, "Diversity in Nineteenth Century Domestic Reform: Relationships among Classes and Ethnic Groups", in Elizabeth Scott (ed.) *Those "Of Little Note": Gender, Race and Class in Historical Archaeology*, Tucson: University of Arizona Press, 1994.

31   Spencer-Wood, "Toward the Further Development of Feminist Historical Archaeology", 128.

32   Spencer-Wood, "Towards an Historical Archaeology", p. 223.

33   Critiqued by Lucia Nixon, "Gender Bias in Archaeology", in Léonie J. Archer, Susan Fischler and Maria Wyke (eds) *Women in Ancient Societies: An Illusion of the Night*, London: Macmillan, 1994, pp. 8–13.

34   Andrea Nye, *Feminist Theory and the Philosophies of Man*, New York: Routledge, 1988, p. 6.

35   Critiqued for Greece by Goldberg and for Romans by Allison in Penelope M. Allison (ed.), *The Archaeology of Household Activities*, London and New York: Routledge, pp. 57–77, 142–61.

36   Eva Cantarella, *Pandora's Daughters: The Role and Status of Women in Greek and Roman Antiquity*, Baltimore: Johns Hopkins University Press, 1987, p. 56.

37   Gerda Lerner, *The Creation of Feminist Consciousness: From the Middle Ages to Eighteen-Seventy*, Oxford and New York: Oxford University Press, 1993.

The hallway

Tony Earley (2001)

The story goes like this: my sister was born angry. She had colic as a newborn and cried for six weeks. After that, she just cried. We lived then with my maternal grandparents in North Carolina. My father was away on temporary duty in the air force and traveled the western part of the country, installing radar systems. Mama did not want to be alone in a bad neighborhood in Texas with two babies in diapers. She and Granny Ledbetter stayed up in shifts. Shelly wore them both out. Paw-paw could not stand to hear a baby cry. He was softhearted and nervous. He paced and smoked and sat and rocked on the porch. Shelly cried and cried. I was the only person in the house who slept much. I was fifteen months old, and had spent my life until then in small houses beneath the runway approaches of air force bases. Shelly had dark skin and black hair and eyes when she was born, but fair skin and blond hair and blue eyes by the time Daddy came back from TDY. He did not recognize her. She cried when he picked her up. Everyone agreed that Shelly cried because she was mad, but they could not figure out what she was mad about. It is said that the only thing that would make her stop crying in the morning was the sound of my grandfather's footsteps in the hallway.

Or this: my great-grandmother kicked my great-grandfather out of their bed after my grandfather was born. My great-grandfather, Bill Ledbetter, slept in the hallway, near the front door, beside the steps leading upstairs. The hallway was unheated, and in the winter he slept under a great pile of quilts. In the summer he slept with the front and back doors open and lay comfortably in the breeze that traveled between the doors late at night. […]

Bill Ledbetter hired the carpenter Guilford Nanney to build the house for him in 1917, in the fork of a road, down the hill from Rock Springs Baptist Church. The site is on an upland farm, on the spine of a ridge ringed in the distance by mountains. The house is white, surrounded on three sides by a porch. The steep roof is covered with red tin, through which the upstairs dormer windows peer out. The hallway is forty-one feet long and just over six feet wide. It bisects the middle of the house. Its ceiling is nine feet, two inches high. Its walls and ceiling are unfinished heart pine tongue and groove, red and dark now with age. The walls are marked with hundreds of faint, yellow streaks where for years Paw-paw struck stick matches to light his cigarettes. The streaks are curved upwards at the ends, like fish hooks, where the match sparked and Paw-paw lifted it away from the wall. The floor is made of four-inch pine boards, which were covered with carpet in 1978.

If you stand at the front door and look down the hallway to the back of the house, you will see on your left the doors to the living room, dining room, and kitchen. On your right you will see two windows, the halltree, the stairway curving up, the doors to the canning closet beneath the stairs, and two bedrooms. My family knows the bedrooms as the front room and the back room. The doors, stair steps, banister, and railing are also unfinished pine. The doors have brass knobs; the railing is bright, and smooth enough to slide on. Three rooms are upstairs: the big room, the junk room, and Uncle Tom's room. My grandmother is displeased by the junk room. Early in their marriages her children asked her if they could store a few things upstairs that they did not have room for in their small, rented houses, and then never came back to get them.

Before she married Bill Ledbetter, my great-grandmother was Sallie Ursula Egerton. The Egertons, it is said, were granted a significant chunk of western North Carolina by an English king. Nobody remembers anymore exactly how much land, or even which king. It is doubtful that even the Egertons at the time ever fully realized the extent of their holdings. They were rich as only people in a new world can be rich. They owned everything they could see. They owned the mountains in the distance. But generations passed. The Egertons married local. There was no one else to marry. They gradually began to forget where they were from. They came to think of themselves as Carolinians, and then Americans, and then Confederates. They divided their land among themselves and among the mountain boys who married their daughters, and then divided it again. Over the course of two hundred years, North Carolina changed them from English aristocracy to country people with straight backs. Their dignity survived intact, but the family itself did not take a good hold. Their numbers did not improve over time, and their lot diminished. They began to die out.

While we lived with Granny and Paw-paw, Mama put my playpen in the hallway, in the spot where Bill Ledbetter's bed used to be, so I could see out the front door. Paw-paw's beagles occasionally stopped at the screen and looked in. This made me laugh. Mama and Granny were busy with Shelly, or napping for the next shift. They were not able to pay me much attention. I sat in the playpen, so the story goes, and looked at a *Reader's Digest*. I did not chew on it. I did not rip the pages out. Once I fell asleep with it covering my face. I would not touch a *Progressive Farmer* or look at a *Life*. Do not ask me why. Paw-paw drove an old, green Lincoln. Mama and Granny say that every afternoon I announced his impending arrival by making a noise like a car.

The last Egerton to live on the Egerton homeplace on Walnut Creek was my great-grandmother's uncle, Tom Egerton. People said that Tom Egerton wasn't right. He never married and lived alone in a dignified, bewildered squalor. His dogs and chickens wandered in and out of the house. Some people believed he had a fortune squirreled away; his father had been known as Squire, and the Egerton slaves were buried on the hill above the house. The way Tom Egerton lived made the people who believed in the fortune angry. They tried to cheat him out of money. It felt to them like a right, a settling up. Tom Egerton gave away what little money he had, and offered the people who came to cheat him sweet potatoes. He cooked the potatoes in the coals in his fireplace. His obliviousness and eccentricity embarrassed the few Egertons who were left. By the end of his life, Tom Egerton had to sleep in the crib to keep people from stealing his corn. After he died, people broke into his house and ripped down the wallboards and pried up the hearth stones. My great-grandmother inherited his farm. It became known as Bill Ledbetter's. My family refers to it as "down on the creek". […]

Bill Ledbetter married up. Sallie Egerton married well. Bill Ledbetter was a huge, strong man. In pictures his face is biblical and sharp, like Lincoln's. As a young man he watched the sun rise and set with the reins from his team of plow horses draped around his neck. The fields turned green and lush behind him. He started with nothing save prodigious strength and an unreasonable ambition, but was prosperous by the time he married Sallie Egerton. He opened a general store. He bought a second farm, black bottomland on the Broad River. When his wife inherited Tom Egerton's place, he made the days long enough to work three farms at once. He hired field hands to help him, many of them black men named Egerton. Lazy men could not work for Bill Ledbetter. He ran them off if they didn't quit first. When he hoed or picked cotton, he lapped everyone else in the field. He had water hauled to the hands in the rows so they would not waste time walking to the bucket. […]

My cousins and I loved running up and down the hallway, but Paw-paw and Granny did not like for us to run inside the house. He was afraid we would fall and get hurt; she was afraid one of Paw-paw's guns would fall to the floor and discharge and kill us. Paw-paw kept shotguns and rifles hanging from the hat hooks on the halltree, and from the hat hooks on the wall. All of his guns stayed loaded. Paw-paw said there was no reason to keep a gun in the house if it wasn't loaded. Granny said there was no reason to keep a gun in the house if it was. This was one of the few points on which I ever heard them disagree.

Running up and down the hallway was one of the few ways we even considered disobeying Paw-paw and Granny. They were loath to spank us and rarely had to. We found the thought that one of them might be angry at us deterrent enough. But the hallway was our temptation, a fine line along the edge of their good graces. It was long enough to race in full speed. It demanded we run. Our feet pounding on the wooden floor thundered inside the tall, enclosed space. We became a herd, a posse. The brass doorknobs rattled as we passed. We made more noise than we absolutely had to. We made an altogether satisfactory racket.

Even under direct orders, a sideways look as we came into the front door was enough to propel the whole lot of us down the hallway. What happened then was always the same. Paw-paw rapped his knuckles against the living-room wall and said, "I'm gonna jerk a knot in somebody's tail", but by then we were pulling up at the opposite end of the house, where we met Granny coming out of the kitchen.

She said, "You jaybirds stop all that running before one of those guns falls".

Guilford Nanney traveled the countryside building the tall houses he saw in his head. He was not a carpenter to whom you could present a plan drawn by someone else. You told him how many rooms you wanted, and he built you a house. That was the transaction. He would not suffer interference and meddling. The inordinate length of the hallway, the extravagant line and steep pitch of the roof were his idea alone. He lived in a small shack on the property, and started work mornings as soon as he could see. He sawed all of the framing for Bill Ledbetter's house and piled it in the front yard before he ever drove a nail. He did not use a blueprint, but when he put the house together, all the pieces fit. There were no studs or rafters or joists left over. He did not find this remarkable. The roof, seen from any angle, comprises a series of triangles, offset so that your eye is drawn upward as it is when you look at mountains and find yourself seeking the tallest peak. From the front door, the back door at the other end of the house seems as far away as the altar of a cathedral. The landing at the top of the stairs is cantilevered, and floats out over the hallway without betraying the intricacy of the structure that supports it, or the complexity of thought behind it.

My cousins and sister ran barefoot up and down the hallway in the summer, and someone always pulled up lame and crying, with a long, jagged splinter impaled in the heel or toe. Granny rounded up the injured cousin and sat him or her down in a straight chair in the kitchen. She dug at the splinter with a needle sterilized in alcohol. The cousin screamed and flailed; Granny threatened and scolded and cajoled. She swore that in just a minute she was going to pop somebody if the racket didn't stop; she said she would get a switch after the whole lot of us if we didn't get out of her light so she could see.

When the splinter came loose she presented it to the sobbing cousin for inspection. She applied red Mercurochrome, which didn't burn, or orange Methylate, which did, to the wound. We all sucked in our breath and watched the cousin's face when it was Methylate. The cousin limped down the hallway with the needle to show the splinter to Paw-paw. The rest of us followed along behind, grumbling by then at the cousin's hysteria. Paw-paw took the cousin up into his lap and patted him or her on the leg and pretended not to be able to see the splinter, it was so small. He looked carefully at the red or orange stain on the bottom of the cousin's foot and said that he thought it was going to be all right. The rest of us gathered around Paw-paw's chair and leaned toward him. He smelled like aftershave and Vitalis. Each of us secretly wished we had been fortunate enough to have been injured so grievously.

It is said that as Bill Ledbetter watched the tall, skeletal peaks of his new roof rising, he was sickened by the amount of lumber Guilford Nanney used. Bill Ledbetter was not by nature an extravagant man. He wanted a big house, but could not sanction waste. While it is unknown whether he said anything to Guilford Nanney about what he considered gratuitous use of material, it is known that Guilford Nanney left the job suddenly while there was still trim work to be done around the doors and windows upstairs. He took a job building the first set of steps to the top of Chimney Rock, a mountain visible from Bill Ledbetter's front yard. Rich men were making the mountain

into a park. No one knows if Bill Ledbetter complained about Guilford Nanney's deser-
tion. He simply finished the house himself. While Bill Ledbetter's carpentry work is
level and adequate and square, it is not hard to spot. The only hammer marks in the
whole house belong to Bill Ledbetter. It is easy to tell at the top of the stairs where one
man left a job, and another man took it up.

Sallie Ledbetter was never a robust woman and did not bear children easily. The first child
she had with Bill Ledbetter was a girl, Clydie Belle. Clydie was frail from the time of her
birth and did not live to see a healthy day. She died of colitis when she was seven months
old. Their second child, a son, was born prematurely and lived only an hour. They did not
name him. My grandfather, William Dan, was their third and last child. As a baby he was
small and sickly and Sallie Ledbetter feared for his health. She kept him in her bed to keep
him warm. She was afraid Bill Ledbetter would turn over on the baby in his sleep and
banished him to another bed.
    When Bill Ledbetter moved his family into the new house Guilford Nanney built, he
put his bed in the hallway and slept there for the next thirty years. My grandfather slept in
the front room, in the bed with his mother, until he was a tall and gangly boy. When Bill
Ledbetter finally made Paw-paw move to another room, Sallie Ledbetter did not ask him
to return to her bed, or perhaps by then he did not want to go. My family is unsure how
this part of the story goes. Bill Ledbetter did not sleep again in the same room with his
wife until 1947, when he was an old man sick with lung cancer. He had his bed moved to
the front room from the hallway because in his illness he could no longer keep warm.

My story goes like this: I jerked the front screen door open and ran as hard as I could. The
house was Fenway Park in Boston, the hallway the first-base path. The door swinging
shut behind me a throw whizzing in from first. If I hit the back door before the front
door slammed, I was safe. If the front door slammed first, I was out. I hit the back screen
running and crossed the porch in a step and jumped off into the yard and kept going. I
went for extra bases. The game then became problematic, a matter of judgment and
honesty. The spring on the back door was pulling it closed. The clothesline pole was too
close, too easy to reach in time, to be an acceptable base; the woodshed was too far away.
There was no quantitative way to make the call of safe or out. I had to decide when the
door slammed where I was on the field. Sometimes I slowed up with a single, disappointed skip and slapped my hands on my thighs and turned toward the dugout. I was
out. Sometimes I clapped my hands once and reached out to accept the congratulatory
handshake of an imaginary teammate. *Earley scores! He has good speed! He's having a heck of
a year!* In my mind's eye, I was always on television. I interviewed myself in the woodshed, where no one could see me from the house. I took off my cap and wiped my brow
with the back of my arm. I spoke into a piece of kindling. I said, *"Thanks. I felt good today.
I'm just glad I could help the team"*.

A corner cupboard from the Egerton homeplace used to sit in the dining room. It was
built by Egerton slaves out of wide oak boards. It was big and dark and solid as a vault.
When I was a little kid I had to stand on a chair to see what was inside it. Paw-paw stored
his tools on the top three shelves. Behind the wide doors he kept dark, heavy wrenches
and hammers and screwdrivers and files, and old coffee cans filled with nuts and bolts and
screws and the occasional, odd shotgun shell. There were leftover balls of baling twine,
and twisted leather gloves fragrant with grease, and inscrutable pieces of machinery, parts

of tractors and balers and combines and trucks; there were chains and spare tines from cultivators and planters and plows. Granny kept tablecloths and towels and napkins and washcloths on the bottom two shelves. The cupboard smelled like washing powder and clean cotton stiffened by the sun – like rust and leather and creosote. It smelled simultaneously like a warm barn and fresh sheets.

Paw-paw showed the cupboard once to an antiques dealer. The man wanted immediately to buy it. He tried to buy it for years. Paw-paw did not sell it until 1978, after he was sick, when the house had begun to seem big and cold. The antiques dealer gave five hundred dollars for the cupboard. Paw-paw and Granny used the money to carpet the hallway. Granny says today that she does not wish the cupboard back, even though it would be worth thousands of dollars. She says the only furniture she's ever known was dark and ponderous and ugly to look at. Much of it came from the Egertons' and was old already when she married Dan Ledbetter in 1933 and moved into the house. She does not understand the modern Southern passion for antiques. She would not walk to the mailbox for a truckload. She has wanted her whole life to get rid of old things and replace them with new. She especially does not miss sweeping the hallway. Forty-five years was long enough. She memorized the grain in the flooring. She wore out more brooms than she cares to remember. She still considers the cupboard for the carpet a good trade.

And this: Granny and Paw-paw slept in the front room. Paw-paw kept a loaded .38 revolver in a cigar box in the nightstand by the bed. On Sundays after church I used to sneak down the hallway and into their room to look at it. It was a black, antique Smith & Wesson. I was strictly forbidden to touch it. One Sunday I pulled the hammer back and cocked it. At that moment I felt the gun become a living thing in my hand. It felt dangerous as a coiled snake. I was afraid to breathe. I was nine or ten years old. I didn't know what to do. I couldn't call for help because I would get into trouble; I couldn't put it back into the cigar box because it was cocked.

I was afraid to uncock the gun because it might fire. I had seen people uncock guns on television hundreds of times. They held the hammer back with a thumb and pulled the trigger, but they were Marshall Dillon and Mannix and McGarrett and Gil Favor. If the hammer slipped from beneath my thumb the gun would go off. It would kill me or shoot through one of the walls. I became conscious of where my family was in the house. Mama and Granny were in the kitchen cooking dinner. Daddy was in the living room reading and Paw-paw was sitting on the front porch with his feet on the railing. I didn't know where Shelly was. There seemed to be no safe place to point the gun. I was sure I was going to kill someone, and the fear I felt turned also into a kind of sadness, and anticipation of loss. I moaned out loud, although I did not want or mean to. I prayed for God to help me. I gasped and closed my eyes and pulled the trigger. The gun did not fire. The hammer came loose between my thumbs and I held it poised for a moment above the firing pin. Then I lowered it slowly into place. The gun returned to sleep in my hand. I placed it back in the cigar box. I put the cigar box back in the nightstand. I wiped my hands on my pants and backed into the hallway. I ran down the hallway hard as I could and through the back door and across the porch and jumped off into the yard. I was almost to the woodshed before the back door slammed.

It is a credit to my grandmother that to this day she will not speak ill of Sallie Ledbetter. Granny's maiden name was Clara Mae Womack. She grew up on a small farm where Walnut Creek empties into the Green River, several miles below Tom Egerton's place. She married Dan Ledbetter in 1933, when she was nineteen years old. He was twenty-eight. She did not kiss him until they were engaged, and then she put a chair between them so he couldn't get his arms around her. They had planned to live in the small house the Ledbetters had lived in before the big house was built, but Sallie Ledbetter forbade her son to move out. Later she had the older house torn down.

While the big house with the red roof was known as Bill Ledbetter's place, it was Sallie Ledbetter who decreed what was what inside it. When Clara Mae Ledbetter moved in, Sallie Ledbetter stopped cooking altogether. Granny cooked breakfast before dawn, a big dinner for the field hands at noon, and supper for the family in the evening. She did most of the cleaning and washing. Her life was not easy. If she and Paw-paw went upstairs together during the day, Sallie Ledbetter called her daughter-in-law back downstairs because it did not look proper. She scolded the two of them if they went for a walk alone.

When my uncle Tom was born, Sallie Ledbetter insisted the baby sleep with her. The room Paw-paw and Granny slept in did not have a stove, and Sallie Ledbetter said the baby would get sick in the cold. She did not express the same concern later for my mother and my aunt Barbara, who slept in unheated rooms from the time they were born until they married and moved away. Uncle Tom slept with Sallie Ledbetter until he was a tall and gangly boy. She would not let him eat watermelon because she thought watermelon had given Clydie the colitis that killed her. Granny could not put her foot down because it was not her house, and Paw-paw would not stand up to his mother. Bill Ledbetter had no interest in the affairs of women. Inside the house Sallie Ledbetter's every wish hardened into stone as soon as she uttered it. Granny had nowhere to turn. She could not run the house the way she saw fit until Sallie Egerton Ledbetter died in 1953. Sallie Ledbetter also died of lung cancer, although neither she nor Bill Ledbetter ever smoked.

I chased my cousin Janet up the front steps. She squealed and opened the front door and ran into the house. We started down the hallway at a dead run. The screen door slammed behind us. A double-barreled twenty-gauge shotgun slipped from the top row of hat hooks on the halltree and fell and clattered onto the floor. Janet and I stopped in our tracks. We tiptoed back down the hallway and stared at the shotgun. It hadn't fired.

Paw-paw ran from the living room. Granny came down the hallway at a gallop from the kitchen. The falling gun had split the halltree seat half in two. Janet and I were terrified. We said that we hadn't done it, that we were just running down the hallway and the gun fell. Paw-paw's face flushed red. He began to shake. His fists were clenched at his sides. We could tell he didn't know what to do next. Janet and I held our breath. We had never seen him that angry.

"Damn", Paw-paw said.

"Dan!" Granny said. Paw-paw didn't believe in cursing.

"Damn, damn, damn, damn, damn", Paw-paw said. He seemed to like it, though, once he got started. He unbuckled his belt. He had never whipped any of us before. Granny did all the spanking, and she popped us so lightly that sometimes it was hard not to laugh. Paw-paw jerked his belt out through the loops. Janet and I began to cry. Paw-paw was tall as a giant. "How many times have I told you not to run in this house?" he said.

"Please don't whip us, Paw-paw", we said.

"Dan Ledbetter", Granny said, "you're not going to whip anybody. You're lucky that gun didn't go off. I've told you and told you not to keep those guns loaded".

Paw-paw and Granny stared at each other and went out the front door and down the steps and around the side of the house. Janet and I tiptoed into the living room and peeked out the window. We could see them arguing through the gap between the two heating oil tanks at the side of the house, but the window was closed and we couldn't hear what they said. We had never seen them argue before and it scared us to watch. Paw-paw still held his belt in his hand. Janet said later she thought they were going to get a divorce.

Paw-paw pointed at the house and said something angry to Granny. We could tell he was talking about us. Granny pointed at the house and said something angry back. She was talking about him. Paw-paw spun away from her and walked away. We ran to the window on the other side of the room to see where he went. He walked quickly across the front yard and got in his car and drove away. Granny came back inside and ordered me into the back room and Janet into the front room. She told us that if she heard one sound out of either of us she would get a switch after us, and we could tell she meant what she said. I don't know about Janet, but I cried into the pillow on the bed in the back room. I was sure Paw-paw hated me.

While Dan Ledbetter grew to be as tall as Bill Ledbetter, he did not inherit his father's strength or stamina. He was 6'4", but so skinny that he seemed to have been constructed from spare parts. In photographs his legs seem much too long and delicate, the rest of his body ill-supported, dangerously high above the ground. Only near the end of his life, when he grew a small, incongruous potbelly, did he ever weigh more than one hundred and fifty pounds. He wore only long-sleeved shirts, whose cuffs he kept tightly buttoned at the wrist. And if he suffered in physical comparison with Bill Ledbetter, Paw-paw fared no better in comparison of accomplishment. Even on a tractor, he could never do in a day the work his father did in the same amount of time with a team of horses. The sun never stood still above the fields in which he worked. [...]

That people looked to Dan Ledbetter to match his father in word and deed, when he was incapable of doing so, was perhaps my grandfather's heaviest burden. While Bill Ledbetter delighted in firing both barrels of his massive 10-gauge shotgun at once, Paw-paw found shooting the gun one barrel at a time as unpleasant as any other ordinary man. The one time Paw-paw fired both barrels simultaneously, the recoil turned him around in his tracks. He never planted a cash crop for which there was a demand a year before there was a supply. He never considered his opinions worthy of a journey to Raleigh. He never bought land or led the singing in church. He spent his life presiding over the slow dissipation of Bill Ledbetter's immaculate farms. Through no fault of his own he became the measuring stick people used to construct Bill Ledbetter's legend. That stick was in turn used to measure him.

After a while Paw-paw blew the horn in the front yard. Janet and I opened the doors and looked tentatively out into the hallway. Every day Paw-paw rode down on the creek to feed the cows. It was a favorite expedition among the cousins. Granny came out of the kitchen with Paw-paw's cap and a plastic margarine dish filled with food scraps from dinner. Paw-paw always took food scraps for the cats who lived in the barn. The cats rubbed against his legs, but ran away when we tried to touch them. Granny motioned for us to follow her and walked down the hallway and held the screen door open. She handed me the scraps for the cats and Paw-paw's cap. Paw-paw didn't like to go anywhere without his cap. He had left the house without it earlier. "Go on out there", Granny said. "He's not mad at you".

Janet and I went slowly down the front steps and walked across the yard toward the car. The motor was running. Paw-paw watched us through the windshield. We walked up close to the car and stopped. I couldn't tell if he was mad or not. I was afraid to say anything. I handed him his cap through the window. He said, "You knotheads going with me?"

We ran around the car and opened the door and climbed in. Janet slid up close beside Paw-paw. I rolled down the window. On the way to the creek Paw-paw stopped at Ed Bailey's store and bought each of us a Mountain Dew and a pack of M&M's. He did not mention the halltree, then or ever. He had a carpenter glue the two halves of the seat back together. If you examine the seat today, you cannot tell it was ever broken.

Bill Ledbetter made no provision for his family after his passing, other than leaving them the land he had accumulated over the years. He did not believe in insurance. When his general store burned down years before, he had not been able to replace it. He died in 1947 after a long stay at Baptist Hospital in Winston-Salem, leaving behind a sheaf of bills thick enough to be the story of his life. My family found itself land rich, but cash poor. Paw-paw had to sell the farm on the river to pay the medical bills. That first spring, he had to hire someone to lay out the corn rows in the remaining Ledbetter bottoms because he didn't know how. He was forty-two years old and had farmed his entire life, but his father had never trusted him with anything important. Bill Ledbetter had reserved for himself the labors that required thought or skill. The fields Paw-paw planted in sweet potatoes that year came up in Johnson grass and did not make a crop.

For years I tried to jump high enough to touch the ceiling in the hallway. In the slow movement of time as it is measured by children, I had been trying to touch the ceiling forever. I never came close until the Sunday my middle finger brushed the wood. I was fourteen years old and could not believe I had finally done it. I jumped again to verify what had happened, and again my middle finger brushed the dark pine. I had crossed some threshold I couldn't name, but felt a profound, if equally nameless, pleasure at finding myself on the other side. One Sunday I couldn't jump high enough to touch a ceiling nine feet, two inches above the floor, but the next Sunday I could. This simple fact came to stand during my adolescence as a constant, quantifiable measurement of *something*. I checked it every Sunday the way a meteorologist might check gauges. That I could always touch the ceiling when I jumped provided a small, welcome comfort, a slight marking of joy.

Soon I could touch the ceiling with increasingly larger portions of my hand: two fingers, then three fingers, then four. By the time Shelly died in December 1979 I could jump high enough to place both palms flat against the ceiling. I checked this measurement immediately after her funeral, still wearing my suit and dress shoes. Paw-paw died the following June, shortly before my nineteenth birthday, of heart disease and emphysema. If my family thought I was being disrespectful by jumping in the hallway after his funeral, while the house was still full of visitors, I don't remember them telling me so.

After Shelly died I continued jumping in the hallway, but came to view the fact that I could still slap my hands on the ceiling as verification of nothing so much as God's unfairness. I wanted to know why Shelly had died and I had lived; I became so adamant in the face of the unanswerable that my life unraveled around the question. Shelly's lifelong anger not only filled me with regret at the times I had deserved to be its object, but with certainty that it had been a premonition she had been unable to voice. I hadn't understood what she was trying to say until it was too late to make amends. Although we no doubt loved each other, we never really got along. It seemed to me then, and – in the secret part of my heart where I hold unreasonable truths – seems to me still, that Shelly came into this world knowing she would not be here long. She spent her short life in a howl of protest untranslatable by the people she loved most.

I also came to believe that I was somehow a beneficiary of Shelly's death, that an account had been settled in my favor. I began to think I was invincible. I thought I would live forever. My jumping took on a desperate, daredevil quality. In the woods behind Granny's house I vaulted over the chest-high barbed-wire fence that separated her property from her neighbor's. I took running starts and leaped over picnic tables and shrubs, and once over a parked MG Midget. I stood flat-footed and jumped over chairs, trash cans, lengthwise over coffee tables, up four, five, six steps of my dormitory stairwell. What I did not take into account when jumping was the accumulated violence of landing. I jumped as if my immortality had been bought and paid for, without realizing that each time my feet hit the ground I paid a corresponding physical price. Eventually, my knees and feet began to give out. By the time I was twenty-five, I was hesitant to jump over the net on a tennis court, a leap I would have taken without thinking a few years before. I was afraid of how much it would hurt when I landed.

As I write this, I no longer jump particularly well. On a good day I can touch the hallway ceiling with my three longest fingers. Although I didn't realize it at the time, the thing I began measuring with that first jump was the inevitable arc of my own mortality. The day is approaching when I won't be able to touch the ceiling at all. And while I realize the vanity and uselessness and ingratitude inherent in any evaluation of self-worth based solely on accomplishment of the body, it is still a day I dread. I am sensitive to the power of metaphor to the point of superstition. It was metaphor that frightened Bill Ledbetter the first morning the cancer sprouting in his lungs prevented him from going to the fields and doing a day's work. Metaphor was the stranger outside in the dark from whom my grandfather sought to protect himself and his family with the shotguns and rifles that lined the hallway, and it was metaphor that rode as a friend in his left breast pocket until it finally killed him. It was metaphor that left sulfurous tracks on the walls of the hallway you can still see today. The last five years of his life Paw-paw had to sleep sitting up in order to catch his breath. While I cannot recall the sound of his voice, I can still hear him cough. It was metaphor that kept us all awake and listening during those nights. We were afraid with each cough that Paw-paw was going to die, until eventually he did. The metaphors of his life hardened into facts. That I remember almost nothing of what my sister said to me is a fact. That Granny is eighty-six years old is a fact. I wish that with these words I could turn the hallway into perfect metaphor, an incantation that would restore everyone who ever walked its length to the person they wanted most in their best heart to be, but the fact is that the hallway is simply a space forty-one feet long, nine feet, two inches high, and just over six feet wide, through which my family has traveled for eighty-four years. Of all the facts we have gathered and stored in the hallway, this one troubles me most: stories in real life rarely end the way we want them to. They simply end.

3

What is home?

Before one can explore the history of domestic architecture, it is necessary to arrive at a definition of the home, house, or dwelling. Historians, philosophers, architects, social scientists and social critics have differed extravagantly in their approaches to this issue. Philosopher Martin Heidegger, mid-century definer of phenomenology and existentialism, has been influential in architectural thought since the 1960s. For Heidegger, "building" and "dwelling" are a single phenomenon, the creation by the individual consciousness out of its rootedness in culture, time, and place. Reyner Banham was closely affiliated with the visionary British Archigram group in the 1960s, and then took on the role of gadfly to modern architectural historians. Banham argues that the modern home is a set of modern appliances and services, not bound to any location and therefore essentially rootless. Sociologist and economist Mary Douglas suggests that home is a place where households organize themselves over time by practicing the planning of resources and by developing household rituals; for Douglas, home is thus an early form of social organization. English professor and social activist bell hooks reminds us that the home, for African-Americans, is a place of resistance to the norms of a hostile society.

Building, dwelling, thinking

Martin Heidegger (1954)

In what follows we shall try to think about dwelling and building. This thinking about building does not presume to discover architectural ideas, let alone to give rules for building. This venture in thought does not view building as an art or as a technique of construction; rather it traces building back into that domain to which everything that *is* belongs. We ask:

1.   What is it to dwell?
2.   How does building belong to dwelling?

Part one

We attain to dwelling, so it seems, only by means of building. The latter, building, has the former, dwelling, as its goal. Still, not every building is a dwelling. Bridges and hangars, stadiums and power stations are buildings but not dwellings; railway stations and high-ways, dams and market halls are built, but they are not dwelling places. Even so, these buildings are in the domain of our dwelling. That domain extends over these buildings and yet is not limited to the dwelling place. The truck driver is at home on the highway, but he does not have his shelter there; the working woman is at home in the spinning mill, but does not have her dwelling place there; the chief engineer is at home in the power station, but he does not dwell there. These buildings house man. He inhabits them and yet does not dwell in them, when to dwell means merely that we take shelter in them. In today's housing shortage even this much is reassuring and to the good; residential buildings do indeed provide shelter; today's houses may even be well planned, easy to keep, attractively cheap, open to air, light and sun, but – do the houses in themselves hold any guarantee that *dwelling* occurs in them? Yet those buildings that are not dwelling places remain in turn determined by dwelling insofar as they serve man's dwelling. Thus dwelling would in any case be the end that presides over all building. Dwelling and building are related as end and means. However, as long as this is all we have in mind, we take dwelling and building as two separate activities, an idea that has something correct in it. Yet at the same time by the means–end schema we block our view of the essential relations. For building is not merely a means and a way toward dwelling – to build is in itself already to dwell. […]

Part two

In what way does building belong to dwelling? The answer to this question will clarify for us what building, understood by way of the nature of dwelling, really is. We limit ourselves to building in the sense of constructing things and inquire: what is a built thing? A bridge may serve as an example for our reflections.

The bridge swings over the stream "with ease and power". It does not just connect banks that are already there. The banks emerge as banks only as the bridge crosses the stream. The bridge designedly causes them to lie across from each other. One side is set off against the other by the bridge. Nor do the banks stretch along the stream as indif-ferent border strips of the dry land. With the banks, the bridge brings to the stream the one and the other expanse of the landscape lying behind them. It brings stream and bank and land into each other's neighborhood. The bridge *gathers* the earth as landscape around the stream. Thus it guides and attends the stream through the meadows. Resting upright in the stream's bed, the bridge-piers bear the swing of the arches that leave the stream's waters to run their course. The waters may wander on quiet and gay, the sky's floods from storm or thaw may shoot past the piers in torrential waves – the bridge is ready for the sky's weather and its fickle nature. Even where the bridge covers the stream, it holds its flow up to the sky by taking it for a moment under the vaulted gateway and then setting it free once more.

The bridge lets the stream run its course and at the same time grants their way to mortals so that they may come and go from shore to shore. Bridges lead in many ways. The city bridge leads from the precincts of the castle to the cathedral square, the river bridge near the country town brings wagons and horse teams to the surrounding villages. The old stone bridge's humble brook crossing gives to the harvest wagon its passage from the fields into the village and carries the lumber cart from the field path to the road. The highway bridge is tied into the network of long-distance traffic, paced as calculated for maximum yield. Always and ever differently the bridge escorts the lingering and hastening ways of men to and fro, so that they may get to other banks and in the end, as mortals, to the other side. [...]

The bridge *gathers* to itself in *its own* way earth and sky, divinities and mortals. [...]

To be sure, the bridge is a thing of its *own* kind; for it gathers the fourfold [*i.e., earth and heaven, divinities and mortals, Ed.*] in *such* a way that it allows a *site* for it. But only something *that is itself a location* can make space for a site. The location is not already there before the bridge is. Before the bridge stands, there are of course many spots along the stream that can be occupied by something. One of them proves to be a location, and does so *because of the bridge*. Thus the bridge does not first come to a location to stand in it; rather, a location comes into existence only by virtue of the bridge. [...]

Only things that are locations in this manner allow for spaces. What the word for space, *Raum*, *Rum*, designates is said by its ancient meaning. *Raum* means a place cleared or freed for settlement and lodging. A space is something that has been made room for, something that is cleared and free, namely within a boundary, Greek *peras*. A boundary is not that at which something stops but, as the Greeks recognized, the boundary is that from which something *begins its presencing*. That is why the concept is that of *horismos,* that is, the horizon, the boundary. Space is in essence that for which room has been made, that which is let into its bounds. That for which room is made is always granted and hence is joined, that is, gathered, by virtue of a location, that is, by such a thing as the bridge. *Accordingly spaces receive their being from locations and not from* "*space*".

Things which, as locations, allow a site we now in anticipation call buildings. They are so called because they are made by a process of building construction. Of what sort this making – building – must be, however, we find out only after we have first given thought to the nature of those things which of themselves require building as the process by which they are made ... . The relation between location and space lies in the nature of these things *qua* locations, but so does the relation of the location to the man who lives at that location. Therefore we shall now try to clarify the nature of these things that we call buildings by the following brief consideration.

For one thing, what is the relation between location and space? For another, what is the relation between man and space?

The bridge is a location. As such a thing, it allows a space into which earth and heaven, divinities and mortals are admitted. The space allowed by the bridge contains many places variously near or far from the bridge. These places, however, may be treated as mere positions between which there lies a measurable distance; a distance, in Greek *stadion*, always has room made for it, and indeed by bare positions. The space that is thus made by positions is space of a peculiar sort. As distance or "stadion" it is what the same word, *stadion*, means in Latin, a *spatium*, an intervening space or interval. Thus nearness and remoteness between men and things can become mere distance, mere intervals of intervening space. In a space that is represented purely as *spatium*, the bridge now appears as a mere something at some position, which can be occupied at any time by something else or replaced by a mere marker. What is more, the mere dimensions of height, breadth and depth can be abstracted from space as intervals. What is so abstracted we represent as the pure manifold of the three dimensions. [...]

The spaces through which we go daily are provided for by locations; their nature is grounded in things of the type of buildings. If we pay heed to these relations between locations and spaces, between spaces and space, we get a clue to help us in thinking of the relation of man and space.

When we speak of man and space, it sounds as though man stood on one side, space on the other. Yet space is ... neither an external object nor an inner experience ... If all of us now think, from where we are right here, of the old bridge in Heidelberg, this thinking toward that location is not a mere experience inside the persons present here; rather, it belongs to the nature of our thinking *of* that bridge that *in itself* thinking gets through, persists through, the distance to that location. From this spot right here, we are there at the bridge – we are by no means at some representational content in our consciousness. From right here we may even be much nearer to that bridge and to what it makes room for than someone who uses it daily as an indifferent river crossing. Spaces, and with them space as such – "space" – are always provided for already within the stay of mortals. Spaces open up by the fact that they are let into the dwelling of man. To say that mortals *are* is to say that *in dwelling* they persist through spaces by virtue of their stay among things and locations. And only because mortals pervade, persist through, spaces by their very nature are they able to go through spaces. But in going through spaces we do not give up our standing in them. Rather, we always go through spaces in such a way that we already experience them by staying constantly with near and remote locations and things. When I go toward the door of the lecture hall, I am already there, and I could not go to it at all if I were not such that I am there. I am never here only, as this encapsulated body; rather, I am there, that is, I already pervade the room, and only thus can I go through it. [...]

Man's relation to locations, and through locations to spaces, inheres in his dwelling. The relationship between man and space is none other than dwelling, strictly thought and spoken.

When we think, in the manner just attempted, about the relation between location and space, but also about the relation of man and space, a light falls on the nature of the things that are locations and that we call buildings. [...]

This is why building, by virtue of constructing locations, is a founding and joining of spaces. Because building produces locations, the joining of the spaces of these locations necessarily brings with it space, as *spatium* and as *extensio*, into the thingly structure of buildings. But building never shapes pure "space" as a single entity. Neither directly nor indirectly. Nevertheless, because it produces things as locations, building is closer to the nature of spaces and to the origin of the nature of "space" than any geometry and mathematics. [...]

Building thus characterized is a distinctive letting-dwell. [...] For building brings ... *forth* the thing as a location, out into what is already there, room for which is only now made *by* this location. [...]

The nature of building is letting dwell. Building accomplishes its nature in the raising of locations by the joining of their spaces. *Only if we are capable of dwelling, only then can we build.* Let us think for a while of a farmhouse in the Black Forest, which was built some two hundred years ago by the dwelling of peasants [*Fig. 8*]. Here the self-sufficiency of the power to let earth and heaven, divinities and mortals enter *in simple oneness* into things, ordered the house. It placed the farm on the wind-sheltered mountain slope looking south, among the meadows close to the spring. It gave it the wide overhanging shingle roof whose proper slope bears up under the burden of snow, and which, reaching deep down, shields the chambers against the storms of the long winter nights. It did not forget the altar corner behind the community table; it made room in its chamber for the hallowed places of childbed and the "tree of the dead" – for that is what they call a coffin there: the *Totenbaum* – and in this way it designed for the different generations under one roof the character of their journey through time. A craft which, itself sprung from dwelling, still uses its tools and frames as things, built the farmhouse.

Only if we are capable of dwelling, only then can we build. Our reference to the Black Forest farm in no way means that we should or could go back to building such houses; rather, it illustrates by a dwelling that *has been* how *it* was able to build.

Dwelling, however, is *the basic character* of Being in keeping with which mortals exist. Perhaps this attempt to think about dwelling and building will bring out somewhat more clearly that building belongs to dwelling and how it receives its nature from dwelling. Enough will have been gained if dwelling and building have become *worthy of questioning* and thus have remained *worthy of thought*.

But that thinking itself belongs to dwelling in the same sense as building, although in a different way, may perhaps be attested to by the course of thought here attempted.

Building and thinking are, each in its own way, inescapable for dwelling. The two, however, are also insufficient for dwelling so long as each busies itself with its own affairs in separation instead of listening to one another. They are able to listen if both – building and thinking – belong to dwelling, if they remain within their limits and realize that the one as much as the other comes from the workshop of long experience and incessant practice.

We are attempting to trace in thought the nature of dwelling. The next step on this path would be the question: what is the state of dwelling in our precarious age? On all sides we hear talk about the housing shortage, and with good reason. Nor is there just talk; there is action too. We try to fill the need by providing houses, by promoting the building of houses, planning the whole architectural enterprise. However hard and bitter, however hampering and threatening the lack of houses remains, the *real plight of dwelling* does not lie merely in a lack of houses. The real plight of dwelling is indeed older than the world wars with their destruction, older also than the increase of the earth's population and the condition of the industrial workers. The real dwelling plight lies in this, that mortals ever search anew for the nature of dwelling, that they *must ever learn to dwell*. What if man's homelessness [*Heimatlosigkeit, Ed.*] consisted in this, that man still does not even think of the *real* plight of dwelling as *the* plight? Yet as soon as man *gives thought* to his homelessness, it is a misery no longer. Rightly considered and kept well in mind, it is the sole summons that *calls* mortals into their dwelling.

But how else can mortals answer this summons than by trying on *their* part, on their own, to bring dwelling to the fullness of its nature? This they accomplish when they build out of dwelling, and think for the sake of dwelling.

A home is not a house

Reyner Banham (1965)

When your house contains such a complex of piping, flues, ducts, wires, lights, inlets, outlets, ovens, sinks, refuse disposers, hi-fi reverberators, antennae, conduits, freezers, heaters – when it contains so many services that the hardware could stand up by itself without any assistance from the house, why have a house to hold it up? When the cost of all this tackle is half of the total outlay (or more, as it often is) what is the house doing except concealing your mechanical pudenda from the stares of folks on the sidewalk? Once or twice recently there have been buildings where the public was genuinely confused about what was mechanical services, what was structure – many visitors to Philadelphia take quite a time to work out that the floors of Louis Kahn's laboratory towers are not supported by the flanking brick duct boxes, and when they have worked it out, they are inclined to wonder if it was worth all the trouble of giving them an independent supporting structure.

No doubt about it, a great deal of the attention captured by those labs derives from Kahn's attempt to put the drama of mechanical services on show – and if, in the end, it fails to do that convincingly, the psychological importance of the gesture remains, at least in the eyes of his fellow architects. Services are a topic on which architectural practice has alternated capriciously between the brazen and the coy – there was the grand old let-it-dangle period, when every ceiling was a mess of gaily painted entrails, as in the council chambers of the U.N. building, and there have been fits of pudicity when even the most innocent anatomical details have been hurriedly veiled with a suspended ceiling.

Basically, there are two reasons for all this blowing hot and cold (if you will excuse the air conditioning industry's oldest-working pun). The first is that mechanical services are too new to have been absorbed into the proverbial wisdom of the profession; none of the great slogans – form follows function, *accusez la structure*, firmness commodity and delight, truth to materials, *wenig ist mehr* – is much use in coping with the mechanical invasion. The nearest thing, in a significantly negative way, is Le Corbusier's *pour Ledoux, c'était facile – pas de tubes*, which seems to be gaining proverbial-type currency as the expression of profound nostalgia for the golden age before piping set in.

The second reason is that the mechanical invasion is a fact, and architects – especially American architects – sense that it is a cultural threat to their position in the world. American architects are certainly right to feel this, because their professional specialty, the art of creating monumental spaces, has never been securely established on this continent. It remains a transplant from an older culture and architects in America are constantly harking back to that culture. The generation of Stanford White and Louis Sullivan were prone to behave like *émigrés* from France, Frank Lloyd Wright was apt to take cover behind sentimental Teutonicisms like *lieber Meister*, the big boys of the thirties and forties came from Aachen and Berlin anyhow, the pacemakers of the fifties and sixties are men of international culture like Charles Eames and Philip Johnson, and so too, in many ways, are the coming men of today, like Myron Goldsmith.

Left to their own devices, Americans do not monumentalize or make architecture. From the Cape Cod cottage through the balloon frame to the perfection of permanently pleated aluminum siding with embossed wood-graining, they have tended to build a brick chimney and lean a collection of shacks against it. When Groff Conklin wrote (in "The Weather-Conditioned House") that "a house is nothing but a hollow shell … a shell is all a house or any structure in which human beings live and work really is. And most shells in nature are extraordinarily inefficient barriers to cold and heat…", he was expressing an extremely American view, backed by a long-established grass-roots tradition.

And since that tradition agrees with him that the American hollow shell is such an inefficient heat barrier, Americans have always been prepared to pump more heat, light, and power into their shelters than have other peoples. America's monumental space is, I suppose, the great outdoors – the porch, the terrace, Whitman's rail-traced plains, Kerouac's infinite road, and now, the Great Up There. Even within the house, Americans rapidly learned to dispense with the partitions that Europeans need to keep space architectural and within bounds, and long before Wright began blundering through the walls that subdivided polite architecture into living room, games room, card room, gun room, etc., humbler Americans had been slipping into a way of life adapted to informally planned interiors that were, effectively, large single spaces.

Now, large single volumes wrapped in flimsy shells have to be lighted and heated in a manner quite different and more generous than the cubicular interiors of the European tradition around which the concept of domestic architecture first crystallized. Right from the start, from the Franklin stove and the kerosene lamp, the American interior has had to be better serviced if it was to support a civilized culture, and this is one of the reasons that the U.S. has been the forcing ground of mechanical services in buildings – so if services are to be felt anywhere as a threat to architecture, it should be in America.

"The plumber is the quartermaster of American culture", wrote Adolf Loos, father of all European platitudes about the superiority of U.S. plumbing. He knew what he was talking about; his brief visit to the States in the nineties convinced him that the outstanding virtues of the American way of life were its informality (no need to wear a top hat to call on local officials) and its cleanliness – which was bound to be noticed by a Viennese with as highly developed a set of Freudian compulsions as he had. That obsession with clean (which can become one of the higher absurdities of America's lysol-breathing Kleenex-culture) was another psychological motive that drove the nation toward mechanical services. The early justification of air-conditioning was not just that people had to breathe: Konrad Meier ("Reflections on Heating and Ventilating", 1904) wrote fastidiously of "…excessive amounts of water vapor, sickly odors from respiratory organs, unclean teeth, perspiration, untidy clothing, the presence of microbes due to various conditions, stuffy air from dusty carpets and draperies … cause greater discomfort and greater ill health".

(Have a wash, and come back for the next paragraph.)

Most pioneer air-conditioning men seem to have been nose-obsessed in this way; best friends could just about force themselves to tell America of her national B.O. – then, compulsive salesmen to a man, promptly prescribed their own patent improved panacea for ventilating the hell out of her. Somewhere among these clustering concepts – cleanliness, the lightweight shell, the mechanical services, the informality and indifference to monumental architectural values, the passion for the outdoors – there always seemed to me to lurk some elusive master concept that would never quite come into focus. It finally became clear and legible to me in June 1964, in the most highly appropriate and symptomatic circumstances.

I was standing up to my chest hair in water, making home movies (I get that NASA kick from taking expensive hardware into hostile environments) at the campus beach at Southern Illinois. This beach combines the outdoor and the clean in a highly American manner – scenicly it is the old swimmin' hole of Huckleberry Finn tradition, but it is properly policed (by sophomore lifeguards sitting on Eames chairs on poles in the water) and it's *chlorinated* too. From where I stood, I could see not only immensely elaborate family barbecues and picnics in progress on the sterilized sand, but also, through and above the trees, the basketry interlaces of one of Buckminster Fuller's experimental domes. And it hit me then, that if dirty old Nature could be kept under the proper degree of control (sex left in, streptococci taken out) by other means, the United States would be happy to dispense with architecture and buildings altogether.

Bucky Fuller, of course, is very big on this proposition: his famous nonrhetorical question, "Madam, do you know what your house weighs?" articulates a subversive suspicion of the monumental. This suspicion is inarticulately shared by the untold thousands of Americans who have already shed the deadweight of domestic architecture and live in mobile homes which, though they may never actually be moved, still deliver rather better performance as shelter than do ground-anchored structures costing at least three times as much and weighing ten times more. If someone could devise a package that would effectively disconnect the mobile home from the dangling wires of the town electricity supply, the bottled gas containers insecurely perched on a packing case, and the semi-unspeakable sanitary arrangements that stem from not being connected to the main sewer – then we should really see some changes. It may not be so far away either; defense cutbacks may send aerospace spin-off spinning in some new directions quite soon, and that kind of miniaturization talent applied to a genuinely self-contained and regenerative standard-of-living package that could be towed behind a trailer home or clipped to it could produce a sort of U-haul unit that might be picked up or dropped off at depots across the face of the nation. Avis might still become the first in U-Tility, even if they have to go on being a trying second in car hire.

Out of this might come a domestic revolution beside which modern architecture would look like Kiddibrix, because you might be able to dispense with the trailer home as well. A standard-of-living package (the phrase and the concept are both Bucky Fuller's) that really worked might, like so many sophisticated inventions, return Man nearer to a natural state in spite of his complex culture (much as the supersession of the Morse telegraph by the Bell Telephone restored his power of speech nationwide). Man started with two basic ways of controlling environment: one by avoiding the issue and hiding under a rock, tree, tent, or roof (this led ultimately to architecture as we know it) and the other by actually interfering with the local meteorology, usually by means of a campfire, which, in a more polished form, might lead to the kind of situation now under discussion. Unlike the living space trapped with our forebears under a rock or roof, the space around a campfire has many unique qualities which architecture cannot hope to equal, above all, its freedom and variability.

The direction and strength of the wind will decide the main shape and dimensions of that space, stretching the area of tolerable warmth into a long oval, but the output of light will now be affected by the wind, and the area of tolerable illumination will be a circle overlapping the oval of warmth. There will thus be a variety of environmental choices balancing light against warmth according to need and interest. If you want to do close work, like shrinking a human head, you sit in one place, but if you want to sleep you curl up somewhere different; the floating knucklebones game would come to rest somewhere quite different from the environment that suited the meeting of the initiation rites steering committee … and all this would be jim dandy if campfires were not so perishing inefficient, unreliable, smoky, and the rest of it.

But a properly set-up standard-of-living package, breathing out warm air along the ground (instead of sucking in cold along the ground like a campfire), radiating soft light and Dionne Warwick in heartwarming stereo, with well-aged protein turning in an infrared glow in the rotisserie, and the icemaker discreetly coughing cubes into glasses on the swing-out bar – this could do something for a woodland glade or creekside rock that *Playboy* could never do for its penthouse. But how are you going to manhandle this hunk of technology down to the creek? It doesn't have to be that massive; aerospace needs, for instance, have done wild things to solid-state technology, producing even tiny refrigerating transistors. They don't as yet mop up any great quantity of heat, but what are you going to do in this glade anyhow; put a whole steer in deep freeze? Nor do you have to manhandle it – it could ride on a cushion of air (its own air-conditioning output, for instance) like a hovercraft or domestic vacuum cleaner.

All this will eat up quite a lot of power, transistors notwithstanding. But one should remember that few Americans are ever far from a source of between 100 and 400 horse-power – the automobile. Beefed-up car batteries and a self-reeling cable drum could probably get this package breathing warm bourbon fumes o'er Eden long before micro-wave power transmission or miniaturized atomic power plants come in. The car is already one of the strongest arms in America's environmental weaponry, and an essential component in one nonarchitectural antibuilding that is already familiar to most of the nation – the drive-in movie house. Only, the word *house* is a manifest misnomer – just a flat piece of ground where the operating company provides visual images and piped sound, and the rest of the situation comes on wheels. You bring your own seat, heat, and shelter as part of the car. You also bring Coke, cookies, Kleenex, Chesterfields, spare clothes, shoes, the Pill, and god-wot else they don't provide at Radio City.

The car, in short, is already doing quite a lot of the standard-of-living package's job – the smoochy couple dancing to the music of the radio in their parked convertible have created a ballroom in the wilderness (dance floor by courtesy of the Highway Dept., of course) and all this is paradisal till it starts to rain. Even then, you're not licked – it takes very little boosting, and the dome itself, folded into a parachute pack, might be part of the package. From within your thirty-foot hemisphere of warm dry *Lebensraum* you could have spectacular ringside views of the wind felling trees, snow swirling through the glade, the forest fire coming over the hill, or Constance Chatterley running swiftly to you know who through the downpour.

But … surely, this is not a home, you can't bring up a family in a polythene bag? This can never replace the time-honored ranch-style trilevel with four small boys and a private dust bowl. If the countless Americans who are successfully raising nice children in trailers will excuse me for a moment, I have a few suggestions to make to the even more countless Americans who are so insecure that they have to hide inside fake monuments of Permastone and instant roofing. There are, admittedly, very sound day-to-day advan-tages to having warm broadloom on a firm floor underfoot, rather than pine needles and poison ivy. America's pioneer house builders recognized this by commonly building their brick chimneys on a brick floor slab. A transparent airdome could be anchored to such a slab just as easily as could a balloon frame, and the standard-of-living package could hover busily in a sort of glorified barbecue pit in the middle of the slab. But an airdome is not the sort of thing that the kids, or a distracted Pumpkin Eater, could run in and out of when the fit took them – believe me, fighting your way out of an airdome can be worse than trying to get out of a collapsed rain-soaked tent if you make the wrong first move.

But the relationship of the services kit to the floor slab could be rearranged to get over this difficulty; all the standard-of-living tackle (or most of it) could be redeployed on the upper side of a sheltering membrane floating above the floor, radiating heat, light, and whatnot downward and leaving the whole perimeter wide open for random egress – and equally casual ingress, too, I guess. That crazy modern movement dream of the inter-penetration of indoors and outdoors could become real at last by abolishing the doors. Technically, of course, it would be just about possible to make the power membrane liter-ally float, hovercraft style. Anyone who has had to stand in the ground-effect of a heli-copter will know that this solution has little to recommend it apart from the instant disposal of waste paper. The noise, power consumption, and physical discomfort would be really something wild. But if the power membrane could be carried on a column or two, here and there, or even on a brick-built bathroom unit, then we are almost in sight of what might be technically possible before the Great Society is much older.

The basic proposition is simply that the power membrane should blow down a curtain of warmed/cooled/conditioned air around the perimeter of the windward side of the un-house, and leave the surrounding weather to waft it through the living space, whose relationship in plan to the membrane above need not be a one-to-one relationship. The membrane would probably have to go beyond the limits of the floor slab, anyhow, in order to prevent rain blow-in, though the air curtain will be active on precisely the side on which the rain is blowing and, being conditioned, will tend to mop up the moisture as it falls. The distribution of the air curtain will be governed by various electronic light and weather sensors, and by that radical new invention, the weathervane. For really foul weather automatic storm shutters would be required, but in all but the most wildly inconstant climates, it should be possible to design the conditioning kit to deal with most of the weather most of the time, without the power consumption becoming ridiculously greater than for an ordinary inefficient monumental type house.

Obviously, it would still be appreciably greater, but this whole argument hinges on the observation that it is the American Way to spend money on services and upkeep rather than on permanent structure as do the peasant cultures of the Old World. In any case, we don't know where we shall be with things like solar power in the next decade, and to anyone who wants to entertain an almost-possible version of air-conditioning for absolutely free, let me recommend "Shortstack" (another smart trick with a polythene tube) in the December 1964 issue of *Analog*. In fact, quite a number of the obvious common-sense objections to the un-house may prove to be self-evaporating: for instance, noise may be no problem because there would be no surrounding wall to reflect it back into the living space, and, in any case, the constant whisper of the air-curtain would provide a fair threshold of loudness that sounds would have to beat before they began to be comprehensible and therefore disturbing. Bugs? Wild life? In summer they should be no worse than with the doors and windows of an ordinary house open; in winter all right-thinking creatures either migrate or hibernate; but, in any case, why not encourage the normal process of Darwinian competition to tidy up the situation for you? All that is needed is to trigger the process by means of a general purpose lure; this would radiate mating calls and sexy scents and thus attract all sorts of mutually incompatible predators and prey into a compact pool of unspeakable carnage. A closed-circuit television camera could relay the state of play to a screen inside the dwelling and provide a twenty-four-hour program that would make the ratings for *Bonanza* look like chicken feed.

And privacy? This seems to be such a nominal concept in American life as factually lived that it is difficult to believe that anyone is seriously worried. The answer, under the suburban conditions that this whole argument implies, is the same as for the glass houses architects were designing so busily a decade ago – more sophisticated landscaping. This, after all, is the homeland of the bulldozer and the transplantation of grown trees – why let the Parks Commissioner have all the fun?

As was said above, this argument implies suburbia which, for better or worse, is where America wants to live. It has nothing to say about the city, which, like architecture, is an insecure foreign growth on the continent. What is under discussion here is an extension of the Jeffersonian dream beyond the agrarian sentimentality of Frank Lloyd Wright's Usonian Broadacre version – the dream of the good life in the clean countryside, power-point homesteading in a paradise garden of appliances. This dream of the un-house may sound very antiarchitectural but it is so only in degree, and architecture deprived of its European roots but trying to strike new ones in an alien soil has come close to the anti-house once or twice already. Wright was not joking when he talked of the "destruction of the box", even though the spatial promise of the phrase is rarely realized to the full in the all-too-solid fact. Grass-roots architects of the Plains like Bruce Goff and Herb Greene have produced houses whose supposed monumental form is clearly of little consequence to the functional business of living in and around them.

But it is in one building that seems at first sight nothing but monumental form that the threat or promise of the un-house has been most clearly demonstrated – the Johnson House at New Canaan [*Fig. 9*]. So much has been misleadingly said (by Philip Johnson himself, as well as others) to prove this a work of architecture in the European tradition, that its many intensely American aspects are usually missed. Yet when you have dug through all the erudition about Ledoux and Malevich and Palladio and stuff that has been published, one very suggestive source or prototype remains less easily explained away – the admitted persistence in Johnson's mind of the visual image of a burned-out New England township, the insubstantial shells of the houses consumed by the fire, leaving the brick floor slabs and standing chimneys. The New Canaan glass house consists essentially of just these two elements, a heated brick floor slab, and a standing unit which is a chimney/fireplace on one side and a bathroom on the other.

Around this has been draped precisely the kind of insubstantial shell that Conklin was discussing, only even less substantial than that. The roof, certainly, is solid, but psychologically it is dominated by the absence of visual enclosure all around. As many pilgrims on this site have noticed, the house does not stop at the glass, and the terrace, and even the trees beyond, are visually part of the living space in winter, physically and operationally so in summer when the four doors are open. The "house" is little more than a service core set in infinite space, or alternatively, a detached porch looking out in all directions at the Great Out There. In summer, indeed, the glass would be a bit of a nonsense if the trees did not shade it, and in the recent scorching fall, the sun reaching in through the bare trees created such a greenhouse effect that parts of the interior were acutely uncomfortable – the house would have been better off without its glass walls.

When Philip Johnson says that the place is not a controlled environment, however, it is not these aspects of undisciplined glazing he has in mind, but that "when it gets cold I have to move toward the fire, and when it gets too hot I just move away". In fact, he is simply exploiting the campfire phenomenon (he is also pretending that the floor heating does not make the whole area habitable, which it does) and in any case, what does he mean by controlled environment? It is not the same thing as a uniform environment, it is simply an environment suited to what you are going to do next, and whether you guild a stone monument, move away from the fire, or turn on the air conditioning, it is the same basic human gesture you are making.

Only, the monument is such a ponderous solution that it astounds me that Americans are still prepared to employ it, except out of some profound sense of insecurity, a persistent inability to rid themselves of those habits of mind they left Europe to escape. In the open-fronted society, with its social and personal mobility, its interchangeability of components and personnel, its gadgetry and almost universal expendability, the persistence of architecture-as-monumental-space must appear as evidence of the sentimentality of the tough.

The idea of a home
A kind of space

Mary Douglas (1993)

The more we reflect on the tyranny of the home, the less surprising it is that the young wish to be free of its scrutiny and control. The evident nostalgia in much writing about the idea of home is more surprising. The mixture of nostalgia and resistance explains why the topic is so often treated as humorous. Dylan Thomas left home at an early age. His *Portrait of the Artist as a Young Dog* has a story about two men, outcasts from seaside suburbia, standing under the pier and wistfully speculating on what would be happening at home. Given that it is five o'clock in the evening, they know quite precisely that curtains are being drawn, the children being called in to tea, and even what tea will comprise. In *Less than Angels* Barbara Pym, that coolly detached recorder of homes, has an ironic passage about the suburban home of two sisters. After supper the dishes are cleared and the house made ready for night; every day before retiring one sister sets the table for tomorrow's breakfast, then both go up to bed; every night, before extinguishing the light, the other sister creeps down again to have one last look at the breakfast table in case something has been forgotten, and is very relieved if she manages to avert catastrophe by straightening a fork or adding a plate that should be there. These are affectionate images of home as a pattern of regular doings. Other images are frankly hostile. The very regularity of home's processes is both inexorable and absurd. It is this regularity that needs focus and explaining. How does it go on being what it is? And what is it?

Home certainly cannot be defined by any of its functions. Try the idea that home provides the primary care of bodies: if that is what it does best, it is not very efficient; a health farm or hotel could do as well. To say that it provides for the education of the infants hardly covers what it does, and raises the same question about whether specialized school or orphanages would not do it better. We will dismiss the cynical saying that the function of the home in modern industrial society is to produce the input into the labor market. As to those who claim that the home does something stabilizing or deepening or enriching for the personality, there are as many who will claim that it cripples and stifles. This essay makes a fresh start by approaching the home as an embryonic community. If it sounds platitudinous it is because many sociologists think of the embryonic community as modeled on the idea of a home. This relic of nine-teenth-century romantic enthusiasm has been a stumbling block in sociology, where it is assumed too easily that the survival of a community over many vicissitudes does not need explaining. On this line of thought both home and community are supposed to be able to draw upon the same mysterious supply of loyal support, and further, their inner sources of strength are unanalyzable: thanks to a kind of mystic solidarity home and small local community are supposed to be able to overcome the forces of fission that tear larger groups apart.[1] This essay will approach solidarity from a more pragmatic point of view. It will try to answer the question, What makes solidarity possible? not by theorizing but by empirical observations on what strategies people adopt when they want to create solidarity.

What kind of space?

We start very positivistically by thinking of home as a kind of space. Home is "here", or it is "not here". The question is not "How?" nor "Who?" nor "When?" but "Where is your home?" It is always a localizable idea. Home is located in space, but it is not necessarily a fixed space. It does not need bricks and mortar, it can be a wagon, a caravan, a boat, or a tent. It need not be a large space, but space there must be, for home starts by bringing some space under control. Having shelter is not having a home, nor is having a house, nor is home the same as household.[2] For a home neither the space nor its appurtenances have to be fixed, but there has to be something regular about the appearance and reappearance of its furnishings. The bedding in a Japanese home may be rolled away, and rolled back, morning and night. The same with the populations; people flow through a home too, but there are some regularities. Happiness is not guaranteed in a home. It is possible to be happy in a hotel or a transit camp, but they are nonhomes. Here is an instance of a happy, serviceable space that fails the test.

> His Knightsbridge home was expensive, but it looked as if he were in the process of either moving in or moving out, and it had looked like that for the past sixteen years … Vince was surrounded by packing cases, half laid carpets and paintings waiting to be hung. He was sitting in the middle of the floor, eating fish fingers, drinking whiskey and listening to a Linguaphone course.[3]

This nonhome was a fixed and solid building, full of domestic things, but it was all beginnings and incomplete projects, with no sign of coming out of the state of confusion that would lead one day to the regular cycles of home life. So a home is not only a space, it also has some structure in time; and because it is for people who are living in that time and space, it has aesthetic and moral dimensions. Compare the Knightsbridge nonhome with the African homes described by anthropologists.[4] The minimum home has orientation even if it lacks any inside–outside boundary; usually it has both, so that the cardinal points are not mere coordinates for plotting position but "directions of existence".[5] Most of the homes we know are not organized on lateral principles, right and left, but on a front–back axis. Sometimes the orientation of a home marks all four axes, back–front, up–down, two sides, and inside–outside. Why some homes should have more complex orienting and bounding than others depends on the ideas that persons are carrying inside their heads about their lives in space and time. For the home is the realization of ideas.

A memory machine

[…] The home makes its time rhythms in response to outside pressures; it is in real time. Response to the memory of severe winters is translated into a capacity for storage, storm windows, and extra blankets; holding the memory of summer droughts, the home responds by shade-giving roofs and water tanks. Those are annual rhythms, but there are longer cycles, as testified by the standard pair of coffin stools always ready for the funeral wake in East Anglian houses. And shorter ones: to the onset of evening, the home responds with lighting; to strong light, with blinds. Children reading *Robinson Crusoe* are transfixed by his work of anticipation: candles, firewood, containers to catch and hold the rain, planks and other provisions from the wreck. The squirrel's autumn shopping cache, the storage arrangements of *Swiss Family Robinson* , the annual autumn shopping expedition in *The Little House in the Big Wood*, have the same essential appeal as the weekly shopping of the Yeoman's family before World War I:

> Tuesday had a special magic for me, when at four o'clock Mother and Father arrived home from market and unloaded the groceries from the high trap. Into the kitchen came a smell spicy as an Indian market. No sterile pre-packed food in plastic bags, but provisions selected by Mother like a connoisseur: cheese she had "tasted", tea to her own blending, dates in large lumps carved from an even bigger block on the grocer's counter. I sniffed and guessed at the contents of the dark blue bags of rice, sago, spices, sultanas and other wonders. Out came biscuits in seven-pound tins, custard powder, candles, lampwicks, and elastic for garters and bloomers: packet after packet! Surely we should never want for anything again.[6]

Storage implies a capacity to plan, to allocate materials between now and the future, to anticipate needs. A stocking-up anticipates a running-down of supplies, which implies continual reallocation, repair, renewal, in short an intelligent plan. For the sake of the plan, space is differentiated, parceled out, allotted to different intentions. This happens, obviously, in a railway station or a hotel. What makes storage different in a home is the scope of the intentions. A home has a much more comprehensive expectation of service. People do not normally expect to give birth or to die in hotels or railway stations, and the management gets upset when they do. Even the one-occupant home is a general service utility, an institution whose uses cannot be defined except as a presentation of a general plan for meeting future needs.

The commons dilemma

[…] The home's capability to allocate space and time and resources over the long term is a legitimate matter for wonder. We are not surprised that the cupboard is often bare; what should amaze us is that it often contains an extraordinary variety of things that are going to be used through the year, mentally ticketed for different kinds of expected events. Even more amazingly, they have been stacked so that they can be found at the right times. The most precious, to be used on the grandest occasion, are safely on the highest shelves, out of reach because they are least frequently wanted, while the most everyday stuff, hardier and cheaper to replace, stands near at hand. The spacing of provisions provides another aide-memoire for the totality of life within the home. In a much longer essay it would be possible to compare homes on the basis of how strongly the members are committed to the production of a collective good, or how much of it they succeed in producing, and to say more about the other kind of homes which aim to produce spaces for individuals. For introducing the idea of the home as a collective good it will be enough to concentrate only on one kind of home, an extreme type in which the members have been working successfully for a long time on the common objective. […]

A home is a model for kinds of distributive justice. The reference to morality points a major difference between a home and a hotel. Both plan for the future, but the planning of the hotel follows criteria of cost efficiency. The reason why the home cannot use market reasoning is, to extend Suzanne Langer's term, that it is a virtual community. It is not a monetary economy, though a household could be. Suppose a group of people sharing the rent of a house, each with his or her own timed access to the cooker and corner of the larder, each coming and going independently of the others, each autonomously making plans and keeping careful check of requital for services rendered by the others – that would be a household. They would settle conflicts over scarce resources by bargaining on semimarket principles. They would argue about their claims in terms of functional priorities or in terms of relative contributions. Inputs would be measured against outputs. This is the kind of institution which the "human capital" theorists can analyze with ease. At the other end of the scale from market to nonmarket is the home, with its laughably complex, tyrannical rules, unpredictably waived and unpredictably honored, and never quite amenable to rational justification. The question for the theory of collective choice is how a home manages to demand and to get sacrifices from its members, how it creates the collectivity which is more than the sum of parts. […]

Coordination

[…] Coordination might seem to pose a problem of its own: it is not so obviously easy to arrange. But the home has an easy solution: its characteristic method of coordinating is to maintain open, constant communication about fair access to resources. Like fairness, coordination is regarded as a public good. How can the home be run if no one knows who is coming and who is going? It is not a hotel, goes the complaining refrain. Coordination is achieved in three ways: coordinated work is on a functional basis, coordinated access to the fixed resources is governed by rotation, and distributions of movables by synchrony, which ensures visibility. As in other institutions, work tends to get allocated in lumps, according to space used and periodicity of tasks.[7] Someone doing one task, say in the kitchen, might as well save on transaction costs by doing others in the same place, say the kitchen, if they occur at the same time. So the home has a tendency to develop a simple division of labor, by age and sex.

However, the functional basis only goes a short way to provide coordination. Rotation is the principle used to control access to fixed space, the bathroom for example, if there is one, the outside privy if there is not. Whoever tries to monopolize that specialized space gets fiercely criticized. The criticism is in the name of the collective good: what sort of home is it where one person can hog the bathroom? Who do they think they are? Have they bought it up? The same attack is made on other offenses against the collectivity: "Dropping your sweet papers on the floor … who do you think is going to clean up after you?" "Marching in and out, without so much as by your leave; do they think this is a hotel?" The idea of the hotel is the standard "Other", where every comfort has to be paid for, the mercenary, cold, luxurious counterpart against which the home is being measured.

The home's technique is to use synchrony and order to protect fair access to other goods, movables and perishables. Synchrony and order effectively combine to show up delinquency. Round the table each knows where to sit, the order of seating corresponds to other orderings, such as the order of chores, the order of privileges and birth, the order of bedtime. Rankings are scored in space. The positions indicate the fairness of the distribution of food. Anyone who tries to get in first to take the best food or larger amounts will hear about fairness. The problems of fair access and distribution are anticipated by synchronicity, and there is always post hoc criticism as a last resort. No one can get in first, or secretly, before the others, because everyone has to be physically present. Charity has to be discreet, even secret, but in a home gifts have to be delivered and opened publicly, so that everyone can enjoy the display of finely cadenced distinctions. Although all distributions are visible and publicly monitored, everyone will tell you that monitoring for fairness is not an intention. Indeed, when intentions are closely integrated none are primary. Everything that is done together in the home has multiple purposes. That is why it is of little use to ask members of a home why they do anything the way they do it.

Much of the burden of organization is carried by conspicuous fixed times. The order of day is the infrastructure of the community. In a home there is no need to look for someone: it should be possible to work out where everyone is at any given time, that is, if it is functioning well. But home is a fragile system, easy to subvert. It is generally well recognized that the main contribution of members to the collective good is to be physically present at its assemblies. An act of presence is a public service.[8] Absence is to be deplored. Perhaps the most subversive attack on the home is to be present physically without joining in its multiple coordinations. To leave erratically, without saying where or for how long, to come back and go upstairs without greeting, these lapses are recognized as spoliation of the commons. In one of her autobiographical essays Colette describes her mother coming into the garden and calling: Where are the children? No answer. They are up in the trees, stretched out in the boughs, or curled up in the grass, in the stable, hiding, sleeping, reading. She gets no answer, and her disregarded call bespeaks the weakness of that home shortly to be disbanded.

The time devoted to the common meal is a conclave, used for coordinating other arrangements, negotiating exemptions, canvassing for privileges, diffusing information about the outside world, agreeing on strategies for dealing with it and making shared evaluations. The conclave invents exceptions to its rules: permissions to be late, to skip a meal. A home is a tangle of conventions and totally incommensurable rights and duties. Not a money economy, the home is the typical gift economy described by Marcel Mauss.[9] Every service and transfer is part of an ongoing comprehensive system of exchanges, within and between the generations. The transactions never look like exchanges because the gesture of reciprocity is delayed and disguised. No one can know the worth of their own contribution to the home. It is not just that calculation is too difficult, but more that it suits no one to insist on a precise offsetting of one service against another. Debts are remembered well enough, but by keeping them vague there is the hope that repayment may be more than equivalent. Direct reciprocity is avoided. In the most extreme, perfectly abstract, complete instances of a home, there would be no free gifts, no loose ends, and nothing meaningless at all. Every smallest gesture would be laden with information, every greeting and every meal a celebration of the system itself. A virtual community is in place, from which vantage point clans, tribes, and phratries [*tribal subdivisions, Ed.*] can be surveyed – and hotels.

From set times for meals flow further rules about timing. Not just mealtimes, but throughout the meal even, the synchronized attack with knives and forks on the plates is finely tuned. Members of a home eat level, drink level, get reproached for eating too fast or too slow. Synchrony guarantees fair distribution: no second helpings can be given until the last slow eater has cleared his plate. The home requires apology or explanation from one caught raiding the larder ahead of the mealtime or after it or between meals. Why was he hungry? Where was he last mealtime? The expectation of synchrony gives a right to a vast amount of information about members' doings.

Tyrannies of the home

This is how the home works. Even its most altruistic and successful versions exert a tyrannous control over mind and body. We need hardly say more to explain why children want to leave it and do not mean to reproduce it when they set up house. When we add the possibilities of subversion, the case for rejecting the idea of the home is even stronger. The free-rider on the collectivity may be the authoritarian father, or it may be the youngest child, or the mother herself. There is no space here today to talk about the model subverted to an individual's private self-interest. Nor is it necessary to say much about the inadvertent interruptions of the proper flow of claims and counterclaims which block the perception of the collective good. For a thousand reasons, the home becomes inefficient in its own terms. It is rigid: mealtimes cannot be suddenly changed to accommodate a visitor lest cascading disorder overthrow its subsystems. Warmth and friendship may take second place in its priorities.

Apart from its tyranny over times, the home tyrannizes over tastes. In the name of friendly uniformity, the menus tend to be designed not to satisfy food preferences but to avoid food hates. One person's rooted dislike or medical prohibition results in certain foods being totally eliminated even if they are everyone else's favorite food, so in the regular menu everyone gets what they are indifferent to, and no one ever gets their favorite dish.[10]

The home also censors speech. It has slots for different tones of voice, conversational topics, and even language. In the name of the community, referred to as "we" or "everyone", neither shouting (because it dominates) nor whispering (because it is secret and exclusive) is allowed, and no private conversations at meals. The rank order which shows in the order of seating and the order of serving imposes restrictions on topics – "Not in front of the children" – or on language – "Not in front of your mother-in-law".[11] "Don't sing at the table", says the mother in *The Little House on the Prairie*, and then, realizing they are sitting by the wagon with no table, she amends it to a rule against singing at mealtimes.[12] Obscenities and talk about money problems at mealtimes are ruled out for different reasons. We have already said that though the family may depend on money coming in, in its internal dealings it is essentially a nonmonetary arrangement. A truce on money talk at table is a truce in the name of the home on all the private struggles that are going on to negotiate a share of the budget for particular projects. Finding the right time to talk about something can be quite a problem in a highly coordinated home.

The idea of the hotel is a perfect opposite of the home, not only because it uses market principles for its transactions, but because it allows its clients to buy privacy as a right of exclusion. This offends doubly the principle of the home whose rules and separations provide some limited privacy for each member. Even when the space is at a premium, by conventions of eyes averted and speech controlled, privacy is cherished in the home. The home protects a person's body from voyeurism and intrusive scatology. Whatever the distinctions that govern the home's procedures, and for whatever reasons they are instituted, one of their effects is to honor a person's incumbency of space. To some extent the old, whose bodily infirmities belie their dignity, are protected from ridicule by the practice of ranked space and time. The child owes its safety from parental incest to rules separating bodies and times. To infringe these boundaries is to threaten the collectivity itself. This explains why the home generally makes a ban on obscenity. What forms are banned depends where the thresholds of privacy are drawn. Spoken or graphic obscenity invades the privacy which the community affords to its members, and will be put under control.

A self-organizing system

On this account, home as a virtual community is often absurd, and often cruel. We have tried to interrogate its life to understand community sources of solidarity. The result of the inquest is to show that those committed to the idea of home exert continual vigilance in its behalf. The vigilance focuses upon common presence at fixed points in the day, the week, the year, on elaborate coordination of movements and far-reaching surveillance of members' claims and counterclaims. If we were to follow further Suzanne Langer's ideas about virtual time and virtual space in artistic creation, we would try to draw a clear series of pictures of the assemblies and dispersals which pattern different virtual ethnic domains. If we had to choose an index of solidarity from the time–space structure of homes, the strongest indicator would not be stoutness of the enclosing walls but the complexity of coordination.[13] Complexity is more surprising than simplicity or confusion. From an information-theoretic point of view its presence needs to be explained. The persons who devote vigilance to the maintenance of the home apparently believe that they personally have a lot to lose if it were to collapse. This is the point at which biological pressures to provide for the care of the young have to be invoked. Other embryonic communities have more trouble about mustering solidarity and demanding sacrifice. To this extent the sociologists are right who attribute to primordial passions the survival of families and small communities.

We have been contrasting the home explicitly with a hotel, and contrasting a virtual community with a virtual market. The type of home that has been taken as exemplary has a lot of authority at its disposal, but it is not authoritarian or centralized. Everything happens by mutual consultation. Mutual adjustment of interlocking rules combines to meet functional requirements, personal claims on scarce amounts of time, space, and other resources. That is what makes this home so complicated, difficult to enter and difficult to change. This home emerges as the result of individual strategies of control defended respectively in the name of the home as a public good. Ideally the mother operates the system, so does the father, and so, undoubtedly, do the children. It is extremely coercive, but the coercion is anonymous, the control is generalized. The pattern of rules continually reforms itself, becomes more comprehensive and restrictive, and continually suffers breaches, fission, loss at the fringes.

It is not authoritarian, but it has authority. It is hierarchical, but it is not centralized. The best name for this type of organization is a protohierarchy. It is recognizable because it springs up, spontaneously, to meet certain recurring conditions of organization. It is a multipeaked, rationally integrated system which we find in villages, districts, kingdoms, and empires. Highly efficient for maintaining itself in being, it is easily subverted and survives only so long as it attends to the needs of its members.

Notes

1 Mary Douglas, *How Institutions Think*, Syracuse: Syracuse University Press, 1986, pp. 21–43.
2 This may come as a surprise to the judges in divorce courts who try to allot the custody of children to the spouse who has a home.
3 Francis Durbridge, *The Geneva Mystery*, 1982.
4 Mary Douglas, "The Body of the World", *International Social Science Journal* 42, August 1990, 395–9.
5 J. Littlejohn, "The Temne House", *Sierra Leone Studies* (New Series) 14, December 1960, 63–7.
6 H. St. George Cramp, *A Yeoman Farmer's Son: A Leicestershire Childhood*, Oxford: Oxford University Press, 1986, p. 67.
7 Mary Douglas and Baron Isherwood, *The World of Goods*, New York: Basic Books, 1979, ch. 6.
8 See the account of "consumption services" in ibid.
9 Marcel Mauss, *The Gift: The Form and Reason for Exchange in Archaic Societies*, W. D. Halls (trans.) London: Routledge, 1990.

10 G. Mars and V. Mars, unpublished manuscript on cultural theory applied to London families.
11 An American sociologist commented that this description of the home as a system of rules and rankings was distinctly elitist. Particularly the control on speech recalls the family in the American south in which children had to wash their mouths with soap if they used foul language. It is necessary to say that the details of the rules vary slightly, but the general concern to make an equitable, structured space for living is reported for many civilizations. The examples from English autobiographies and children's stories quoted here are not upper class. In Africa the control on speech takes the form of prescribing categories of kin who are allowed to joke with one another, thus defining others before whom obscenity is ruled out.
12 Laura Ingalls Wilder, *Little House on the Prairie*, New York: Harper and Row, 1953.
13 Jonathan Gross, "Measuring Cultural Complexity", in Mary Douglas (ed.) *Food in the Social Order*, New York: Russell Sage Foundation, 1984.

homeplace
a site of resistance

bell hooks (1990)

When I was a young girl the journey across town to my grandmother's house was one of the most intriguing experiences. Mama did not like to stay there long. She did not care for all that loud talk, the talk that was usually about the old days, the way life happened then – who married whom, how and when somebody died, but also how we lived and survived as black people, how the white folks treated us. I remember this journey not just because of the stories I would hear. It was a movement away from the segregated blackness of our community into a poor white neighborhood. I remember the fear, being scared to walk to Baba's (our grandmother's house) because we would have to pass that terrifying whiteness – those white faces on the porches staring us down with hate. Even when empty or vacant, those porches seemed to say "danger", "you do not belong here", "you are not safe".

Oh! that feeling of safety, of arrival, of homecoming when we finally reached the edges of her yard, when we could see the soot black face of our grandfather, Daddy Gus, sitting in his chair on the porch, smell his cigar, and rest on his lap. Such a contrast, that feeling of arrival, of homecoming, this sweetness and the bitterness of that journey, that constant reminder of white power and control.

I speak of this journey as leading to my grandmother's house, even though our grandfather lived there too. In our young minds houses belonged to women, were their special domain, not as property, but as places where all that truly mattered in life took place – the warmth and comfort of shelter, the feeding of our bodies, the nurturing of our souls. There we learned dignity, integrity of being; there we learned to have faith. The folks who made this life possible, who were our primary guides and teachers, were black women.

Their lives were not easy. Their lives were hard. They were black women who for the most part worked outside the home serving white folks, cleaning their houses, washing their clothes, tending their children – black women who worked in the fields or in the streets, whatever they could do to make ends meet, whatever was necessary. Then they returned to their homes to make life happen there. This tension between service outside one's home, family, and kin network, service provided to white folks which took time and energy, and the effort of black women to conserve enough of themselves to provide service (care and nurturance) within their own families and communities is one of the many factors that has historically distinguished the lot of black women in patriarchal white supremacist society from that of black men. Contemporary black struggle must honor this history of service just as it must critique the sexist definition of service as women's "natural" role.

Since sexism delegates to females the task of creating and sustaining a home environment, it has been primarily the responsibility of black women to construct domestic households as spaces of care and nurturance in the face of the brutal harsh reality of racist oppression, of sexist domination. Historically, African-American people believed that the construction of a homeplace, however fragile and tenuous (the slave hut, the wooden shack), had a radical political dimension. Despite the brutal reality of racial apartheid, of domination, one's homeplace was the one site where one could freely confront the issue of humanization, where one could resist. Black women resisted by making homes where all black people could strive to be subjects, not objects, where we could be affirmed in our minds and hearts despite poverty, hardship, and deprivation, where we could restore to ourselves the dignity denied us on the outside in the public world.

This task of making homeplace was not simply a matter of black women providing service; it was about the construction of a safe place where black people could affirm one another and by so doing heal many of the wounds inflicted by racist domination. We could not learn to love or respect ourselves in the culture of white supremacy, on the outside; it was there on the inside, in that "homeplace", most often created and kept by black women, that we had the opportunity to grow and develop, to nurture our spirits. This task of making a homeplace, of making home a community of resistance, has been shared by black women globally, especially black women in white supremacist societies.

I shall never forget the sense of shared history, of common anguish, I felt when first reading about the plight of black women domestic servants in South Africa, black women laboring in white homes. Their stories evoked vivid memories of our African-American past. I remember that one of the black women giving testimony complained that after traveling in the wee hours of the morning to the white folks' house, after working there all day, giving her time and energy, she had "none left for her own". I knew this story. I had read it in the slave narratives of African-American women who, like Sojourner Truth, could say, "When I cried out with a mother's grief none but Jesus heard". I knew this story. I had grown to womanhood hearing about black women who nurtured and cared for white families when they longed to have time and energy to give to their own.

I want to remember these black women today. The act of remembrance is a conscious gesture honoring their struggle, their effort to keep something for their own. I want us to respect and understand that this effort has been and continues to be a radically subversive political gesture. For those who dominate and oppress us benefit most when we have nothing to give our own, when they have so taken from us our dignity, our humanness that we have nothing left, no "homeplace" where we can recover ourselves. I want us to remember these black women today, both past and present. Even as I speak there are black women in the midst of racial apartheid in South Africa, struggling to provide something for their own. "We ... know how our sisters suffer" (Quoted in the petition for the repeal of the pass laws, August 9, 1956). I want us to honor them, not because they suffer but because they continue to struggle in the midst of suffering, because they continue to resist. I want to speak about the importance of homeplace in the midst of oppression and domination, of homeplace as a site of resistance and liberation struggle. Writing about "resistance", particularly resistance to the Vietnam war, Vietnamese Buddhist monk Thich Nhat Hanh says:

> … resistance, at root, must mean more than resistance against war. It is a resistance against all kinds of things that are like war … So perhaps, resistance means opposition to being invaded, occupied, assaulted and destroyed by the system. The purpose of resistance, here, is to seek the healing of yourself in order to be able to see clearly … I think that communities of resistance should be places where people can return to themselves more easily, where the conditions are such that they can heal themselves and recover their wholeness.[1]

Historically, black women have resisted white supremacist domination by working to establish homeplace. It does not matter that sexism assigned them this role. It is more important that they took this conventional role and expanded it to include caring for one another, for children, for black men, in ways that elevated our spirits, that kept us from despair, that taught some of us to be revolutionaries able to struggle for freedom. [...]

Though black women did not self-consciously articulate in written discourse the theoretical principles of decolonization, this does not detract from the importance of their actions. They understood intellectually and intuitively the meaning of homeplace in the midst of an oppressive and dominating social reality, of homeplace as site of resistance and liberation struggle. I know of what I speak. I would not be writing this essay if my mother, Rosa Bell, daughter to Sarah Oldham, granddaughter to Bell Hooks, had not created homeplace in just this liberatory way, despite the contradictions of poverty and sexism.

In our family, I remember the immense anxiety we felt as children when mama would leave our house, our segregated community, to work as a maid in the homes of white folks. I believe that she sensed our fear, our concern that she might not return to us safe, that we could not find her (even though she always left phone numbers, they did not ease our worry). When she returned home after working long hours, she did not complain. She made an effort to rejoice with us that her work was done, that she was home, making it seem as though there was nothing about the experience of working as a maid in a white household, in that space of Otherness, which stripped her of dignity and personal power.

Looking back as an adult woman, I think of the effort it must have taken for her to transcend her own tiredness (and who knows what assaults or wounds to her spirit had to be put aside so that she could give something to her own). Given the contemporary notions of "good parenting" this may seem like a small gesture, yet in many post-slavery black families, it was a gesture parents were often too weary, too beaten down to make. Those of us who were fortunate enough to receive such care understood its value. Politically, our young mother, Rosa Bell, did not allow the white supremacist culture of domination to completely shape and control her psyche and her familial relationships. Working to create a homeplace that affirmed our beings, our blackness, our love for one another was necessary resistance. We learned degrees of critical consciousness from her. Our lives were not without contradictions, so it is not my intent to create a romanticized portrait. Yet any attempts to critically assess the role of black women in liberation struggle must examine the way political concern about the impact of racism shaped black women's thinking, their sense of home, and their modes of parenting.

An effective means of white subjugation of black people globally has been the perpetual construction of economic and social structures that deprive many folks of the means to make homeplace. Remembering this should enable us to understand the political value of black women's resistance in the home. It should provide a framework where we can discuss the development of black female political consciousness, acknowledging the political importance of resistance effort that took place in homes. It is no accident that the South African apartheid regime systematically attacks and destroys black efforts to construct homeplace, however tenuous, that small private reality where black women and men can renew their spirits and recover themselves. It is no accident that this homeplace, as fragile and as transitional as it may be, a makeshift shed, a small bit of earth where one rests, is always subject to violation and destruction. For when a people no longer have the space to construct homeplace, we cannot build a meaningful community of resistance.

Throughout our history, African-Americans have recognized the subversive value of homeplace, of having access to private space where we do not directly encounter white racist aggression. Whatever the shape and direction of black liberation struggle (civil rights reform or black power movement), domestic space has been a crucial site for organizing, for forming political solidarity. Homeplace has been a site of resistance. Its structure was defined less by whether or not black women and men were conforming to sexist behavior norms and more by our struggle to uplift ourselves as a people, our struggle to resist racist domination and oppression.

That liberatory struggle has been seriously undermined by contemporary efforts to change that subversive homeplace into a site of patriarchal domination of black women by black men, where we abuse one another for not conforming to sexist norms. This shift in perspective, where homeplace is not viewed as a political site, has had negative impact on the construction of black female identity and political consciousness. Masses of black women, many of whom were not formally educated, had in the past been able to play a vital role in black liberation struggle. In the contemporary situation, as the paradigms for domesticity in black life mirrored white bourgeois norms (where home is conceptualized as politically neutral space), black people began to overlook and devalue the importance of black female labor in teaching critical consciousness in domestic space. Many black women, irrespective of class status, have responded to this crisis of meaning by imitating leisure-class sexist notions of women's role, focusing their lives on meaningless compulsive consumerism. […]

This contemporary crisis of black womanhood might have been avoided had black women collectively sustained attempts to develop the latent feminism expressed by their willingness to work equally alongside black men in black liberation struggle. Contemporary equation of black liberation struggle with the subordination of black women has damaged collective black solidarity. It has served the interests of white supremacy to promote the assumption that the wounds of racist domination would be less severe were black women conforming to sexist role patterns.

We are daily witnessing the disintegration of African-American family life that is grounded in a recognition of the political value of constructing homeplace as a site of resistance; black people daily perpetuate sexist norms that threaten our survival as a people. We can no longer act as though sexism in black communities does not threaten our solidarity; any force which estranges and alienates us from one another serves the interests of racist domination.

Black women and men must create a revolutionary vision of black liberation that has a feminist dimension, one which is formed in consideration of our specific needs and concerns. Drawing on past legacies, contemporary black women can begin to reconceptualize ideas of homeplace, once again considering the primacy of domesticity as a site for subversion and resistance. When we renew our concern with homeplace, we can address political issues that most affect our daily lives. Calling attention to the skills and resources of black women who may have begun to feel that they have no meaningful contribution to make, women who may or may not be formally educated but who have essential wisdom to share, who have practical experience that is the breeding ground for all useful theory, we may begin to bond with one another in ways that renew our solidarity.

When black women renew our political commitment to homeplace, we can address the needs and concerns of young black women who are groping for structures of meaning that will further their growth, young women who are struggling for self-definition. Together, black women can renew our commitment to black liberation struggle, sharing insights and awareness, sharing feminist thinking and feminist vision, building solidarity.

With this foundation, we can regain lost perspective, give life new meaning. We can make homeplace that space where we return for renewal and self-recovery, where we can heal our wounds and become whole.

Notes

1   Thich Nhat Hanh, *The Raft Is Not the Shore*, Boston: Beacon Press, 1975.

Figure 8
Seventeenth-century farm-
house in the Black Forest,
Germany.

Figure 9   Philip Johnson, Johnson House, New Canaan, Connecticut, 1945–9.

4

Domestic spaces as perceptual, commemorative, and performative

This chapter offers examples of important psychological and perceptual interpretations of domestic spaces. For psychologist and philosopher Gaston Bachelard, the "oneiric" house (*oneiric*: of dreams) is a metaphor of the psyche, and memories of its spaces, colors, and odors help to structure the personality of the adult individual. Anthropological geographer Yi-Fu Tuan draws on theories of spatial perception to show that buildings are understood through movement, and by the various senses – touch, smell, vision, awareness of light and dark. For Tuan, these perceptions are made conscious by the experience of architecture itself. Architectural historian and critic Beatriz Colomina uses the ideas of Freud, Lacan, and recent film theory to analyze the role of lines of sight in buildings by Adolf Loos; she also discusses interior spaces as related to theatrical practices. Historian of vernacular architecture Sue Bridwell Beckham employs the ideas of sociologist Erving Goffman and anthopologist Victor Witter Turner about performance and ritual in order to analyze the American front porch as a performative space. Art historian Adina Loeb develops further the ideas of Beckham and Colomina in her oral history of a tiny Yorktown apartment of the 1940s and 1950s.

The oneiric house

Gaston Bachelard (1948)

[…] The child is there by his mother, living in the middle part. Will he go with the same courage to the cellar and to the attic? The worlds are so different from each other. In one darkness, in the other light; in one muted sounds, in the other clear ones. The phantoms above and the phantoms below have neither the same voices nor the same shadows. The time spent in each does not have the same tonality of anguish. And it is quite rare to find a child who has courage enough for both. Cellar and attic can be detectors of imagined miseries, of those miseries which often, for all of life, leave their mark on the unconscious.

But let's not live only the images of a tranquillized life, in a house carefully exorcised by good parents.

Let's descend to the cellar, as in older times, candle in hand. The trap-door is a black hole in the floor; the night and its freshness are under the house. How many times in dreams will one make again this descent into a sort of walled night? The walls too are black under the gray hangings of the spider. Oh, why are they *slippery*? Why is there a stain on the dress? A woman must not descend into the cellar. It is the business of the man to go fetch the new wine. As Maupassant said: "For only males go to the cellar".[1] How steep and worn the staircase is, how the steps shine! All those generations when the stone steps were not washed. Above, the house is so clean, so bright, so well ventilated!

And then here is the earth, the black and humid earth, the earth under the house, the *earth of the house*. Some stones to wedge the wine barrels. And under the stone, a dirty creature, the wood louse, who finds a way – like so many parasites – to be fat at the same time as he is flat! How many dreams, how many thoughts come in the time it takes to fill a liter from the barrel!

Once one has understood the oneiric necessity to have lived in a house that comes forth from the earth, that lives rooted in its black earth, one reads with infinite dreams that curious page where Pierre Guéguen describes the "Treading of the New House": "Once the new house was finished, one forced the earth to become a solid and flat base under one's boots. For this one mixed sand and slag together, plus a magical binder made of sawdust and sap, and one invited the young people of the town to come stamp on this mud".[2] And an entire page tells us of the unanimous will of the dancers who, under the pretext of making the soil solid and firm, set themselves to bury the evil spirits.[3] Do they not in this way fight against the repressed fears, against the fears that will transmit themselves from generation to generation, in this refuge constructed upon trampled earth? Kafka too lived for an entire winter in a dwelling on the ground. It was a little house in Prague on Alchymistengasse. He writes (as Max Brod cites): "It is a very particular feeling to have one's own house, to be able to close the door – not of one's room, not of one's apartment, but that of one's whole house – on the world; to tread on the snow that covers the silent street directly upon leaving one's lodging …".[4]

In the attic are lived the hours of long solitude, hours that range from sullenness to contemplation. It is in the attic that one sulks in absolute abandon, sulks unwitnessed.

The child hidden in the attic basks in his mother's anguish: where is he, that sulker?

It is also in the attic that one does interminable reading, far from those who pick up books because they have already read too much. In the attic one dresses up in the costumes of one's grandparents, with shawl and ribbons.[5] What better museum for reveries than a crowded attic! There old things attach themselves for life to the soul of a child. A reverie brings back to life a family's past, the youth of one's ancestors. In four lines a poet sets into movement the shades of the attic: *In some corners / of the attic I found / living ghosts / stirring*.[6]

Then too the attic is the domain of the dry life, of a life that is preserved through drying.[7] Here is the withering linden flower, crumbling in one's hand, and here are the raisins hanging in the hoop of a wine barrel, marvelously lustrous like the clusters of grapes with their clear lights … For all fruits the attic is a world of autumn, a world of October, the most suspended of all the months …

If one has the chance to ascend to the family attic by a narrow stair, or by a stair without bannister, squeezed a little between the walls, one can be certain that a beautiful diagram will inscribe itself for life in the dreamer's soul. Through the attic the house takes on a singular height; it participates in the aerial life of nests. In the attic the house is in the wind.[8] The attic is truly "the lightweight house", like that in the dream of d'Annunzio, living in a chalet in Landes: "The house on the branch, light, sonorous, quick".[9]

Moreover, the attic is a changing universe. The attic in evening has great terrors. Alain-Fournier's sister has noted its dread: "But all that is the garret by day. That of the night – how will Henri be able to stand it? How will he be able to put up with it? How will he stand to be alone in this other universe into which one enters above, without forms or limits, open under the dead nocturnal clarities to a thousand presences, a thousand rustlings, a thousand whispering transactions?"[10] And by the half-open door Alain-Fournier in *Le Grand Meaulnes* sees again the attic: "And all night we feel around us, penetrating into our bedroom, the silence of the three attics".[11]

Thus there is no true oneiric house that is not organized vertically. With its cellar well in the earth, its ground floor for daily life, the floor where one sleeps, and the attic next to the roof, such a house has all that is necessary for symbolizing deep fears, the platitudes of daily life almost touching the ground, and sublimations. Clearly a complete oneiric topology would demand detailed studies; it would also require one to consider refuges that are sometimes very particular: a cupboard, the undercroft of a stairway, an old fireplace can offer suggestive outlines for the psychology of the enclosed life. This life must, moreover, be studied in the two opposite senses of prison and refuge. But in totally adhering to the intimate life of the house that we are characterizing in these pages, we leave to one side the rages and fears nourished in a child's prison. We speak only of positive dreams, of dreams that will return all through life, impelling innumerable images. Thus one can state as a general law the fact that every child who is enclosed desires an imaginary life; and dreams, it seems, are the grander the smaller the refuge in which the dreamer feels himself to be. As Yanette Delétang-Tardif says: "The most enclosed being is a *generator of waves*".[12] Loti renders to perfection this dialectic of the dreamer huddled in his solitude and these waves of reveries in quest of immensity. "When I was a small child I had here some little nooks which represented Brazil to me, where I truly succeeded in giving myself the impressions and fears of the virgin forest".[13] One gives the child a profound life by according him a place of solitude, a corner. A Ruskin, in the great dining room of his parents, passed long hours confined in his "corner".[14] He speaks of it at length in his memories of childhood. At base, the closed-in and the extroverted life are both psychic necessities. But so as not to become abstract formulas, it is necessary that they be psychological realities with a setting, a decor. For these two lives, the house and the fields are both necessary.

Can one sense now the difference in oneiric richness between the country house constructed truly on the earth, in an enclosure, in its own universe, and the edifice in which a few compartments serve for our lodging and which is constructed only on the asphalt of cities? Is this paved room where more trunks than wine barrels are piled up a cellar?

Thus a philosopher of the imaginary encounters – he too – the problem of the "return to earth". One must excuse his incompetence, given that he is treating this social problem only at the level of a study of the dreaming psyche; he would be satisfied if only he could engage the poets to construct for us, with their dreams, "oneiric houses" with cellar and attic. They would help us to shelter our memories, to shelter them in the unconscious of the house, in accord with the symbols of intimacy to which real life has not always the possibility of giving root.

Notes

1　Guy de Maupassant, *Mont-Oriol*, vol. 3.
2　Pierre Guéguen, *Bretagne*, p. 44.
3　In an article in *Journal Asiatique* ("La Maison védique"), October 1939, Louis Renou indicates a rite, prior to the building of the Vedic house, of "appeasement of the ground".
4　Cited by Max Brod, from *Franz Kafka*, p. 184.

5   See Rainer Maria Rilke, *The Notebooks of Malte Laurids Brigge*, New York: W. W. Norton, 1949, pp. 92–3.
6   Pierre Reverdy, *Plupart du temps*, p. 88.
7   Anyone who would like to live, with Mary Webb, in the attic of Sarn, will know these impressions of the *economized life*.
8   See Giono, *Que ma joie demeure*, p. 31.
9   *Contemplation de la mort*, p. 62.
10   *Images d''Alain-Fournier*, p. 21.
11   Alain-Fournier in *Le Grand Meaulnes*, ch. 7.
12   Yanette Delétang-Tardif, *Edmond Jaloux*, p. 34.
13   Loti, *Fleurs d'ennui. Suleima*, p. 355.
14   See J.-K. Huysmans, *Against the Grain*, Harmondsworth: Penguin Books, 1971, p. 26. Des Esseintes installs in his living room "a series of niches".

Architectural space and awareness

Yi-Fu Tuan (1977)

Many animals, like human beings, live in environments of their own construction rather than simply in nature. And evolutionarily advanced animals such as birds and mammals are not the only species that can build. Even single-celled organisms construct shells for themselves out of things like sand grains. We say, however, that animals build instinctively, that each species of weaverbird has an inherited instinct to make a nest of a particular shape, some round, others pear-shaped. Yet we know that some weaverbirds build better nests in their second year than they did in the first. Weaverbirds are capable of learning from experience, which means that not all the details of their performance are controlled by heredity. As another illustration of architectural prowess, consider the termites. They live in a built environment that is vast in proportion to their own size. They make nests that soar like skyscrapers. Termites' nests contain not only elaborate ventilated living quarters for themselves but also fungus gardens for their form of food production. Moreover there appear to be local traditions in architecture that determine how, for instance, the ventilation should be arranged; termites of the same species adopt different systems in Uganda and on the west coast of Africa.[1]

Compared with the termite's skyscraper, the lean-tos and thatched mud shelters of the human being look crude. If humans nonetheless claim certain superiority, the claim must rest on grounds other than architectural achievement. It must rest on awareness. The assumption is that the Bushman, when he makes his lean-to shelter, is more aware of what he does than the weaverbird and the termite as they make their fancier homes.

What is the quality of this awareness? What is the human builder conscious of as he first creates a space and then lives in it? The answer is complex because several kinds of experience and awareness are involved. At the start, the builder needs to know where to build, with what materials, and in what form. Next comes physical effort. Muscles and the senses of sight and touch are activated in the process of raising structures against the pull of gravity. A worker modifies his own body as well as external nature when he creates a world. Completed, the building or architectural complex now stands as an environment capable of affecting the people who live in it. Man-made space can refine human feeling and perception. It is true that even without architectural form, people are able to sense the difference between interior and exterior, closed and open, darkness and light, private and public. But this kind of knowing is inchoate. Architectural space – even a simple hut surrounded by cleared ground – can define such sensations and render them vivid. Another influence is this: the built environment clarifies social roles and relations. People know better who they are and how they ought to behave when the arena is humanly designed rather than nature's raw stage. Finally, architecture "teaches". A planned city, a monument, or even a simple dwelling can be a symbol of the cosmos. In the absence of books and formal instruction, architecture is a key to comprehending reality. Let us look at these kinds of experience and awareness in greater detail.

Where shall one build, with what materials, and in what form? Such questions, it has been said, do not worry builders in preliterate and traditional societies. They work from ingrained habit, following the procedure of unchanging tradition. They have, in any case, little choice since both the skill and the materials at hand are limited. Some types of dwelling, such as the beehive houses of Apulia, the black houses of the Outer Hebrides, and the Navajo hogans, have not changed since prehistoric times. Habit dulls the mind so that a man builds with little more awareness of choice than does an animal that constructs instinctively. At the opposite pole from the primitive builder is the modern master architect. He feels the call to be original. He can, if he likes, select and combine from the numerous styles offered by the world's cultures, past and present. He has almost unlimited technical means at his disposal to achieve his final vision. Given a project, the master architect is obligated to conceive in his mind and on paper a range of architectural forms, all of which serve the project's purpose but only one of which will be selected because it is deemed the best, for reasons that may not be clear to the architect himself.[2] In the preliminary steps of design the architect's consciousness is almost painfully stretched to accommodate all the possible forms that occur to him.

This contrast between primitive builder and modern architect is, of course, an exaggeration: the one is not wholly chained to custom and the other does not have unlimited choice. What sorts of decisions does the primitive builder make? What are his options? These are pertinent questions because a person is most aware when he has to pause and decide. Unfortunately we lack the evidence for clear answers. Few ethnographic surveys report on building activity as a process of making up minds, of communication and learning. Rather huts and villages are described as though they simply appeared, like natural growths, without the aid of cogitating mind. Such portraitures are, to say the least, misleading. In any human life choices arise and decisions must be made, even if they are not especially demanding. Nomads, for example, need to decide where to stop for the night, where to establish their camps. Shifting agriculturalists must know where to make a clearing and build a village. These are locational choices. Material and form also require selection. The natural environment is never static or uniform. Materials available to the human builder vary, however slightly, in time and place, forcing him to think, adjust, innovate. [...]

[Another] cause of heightened awareness is the fact that with many primitive and traditional peoples the act of construction is a serious business that calls for ceremonial rites and perhaps sacrifice.[3] To build is a religious act, the establishment of a world in the midst of primeval disorder. Religion, since it is concerned with stable truths, contributes to the conservatism of architectural form. The same shaped house and city are made again and again as though they come out of the mold of some unthinking process of mass production; yet each is probably built with a sense of solemnity. The builder, far from feeling that he is doing routine work, is obliged by the ceremony to see himself as participating in a momentous and primordial act. The occasion elevates feeling and sharpens awareness, even though the actual steps to be followed in construction fall into a more or less prescribed pattern.

A type of spatial consciousness that people of a simple economy do not experience is systematic and formal design, the envisagement of the final result by drawing up plans. Any large enterprise calls for conscious organization. This can be done verbally and by example on the work site. However, an order of complexity develops, at which point instruction has to be more formally presented if it is to be effective. A technique in formal learning and teaching is the plan or diagram. By making sketches the architect clarifies his own ideas and eventually arrives at a detailed plan. With the same means he helps others to understand what is to be done. The plan is necessary to any architectural enterprise that is sustained over a period of time and executed by a large team of more or less specialized workers. Conceptualizing architectural space with the help of plans is not, of course, a modern device. According to John Harvey, from Egypt in the middle of the second millennium B.C. there is a continuous chain of evidence for architectural scale drawing, throughout all the higher cultures of the Near and Middle East and in classical and medieval Europe.[4] [...]

Building is a complex activity. It makes people aware and take heed at different levels: at the level of having to make pragmatic decisions; of envisioning architectural spaces in the mind and on paper; and of committing one's whole being, mind and body, to the creation of a material form that captures an ideal. Once achieved, architectural form is an environment for man. How does it then influence human feeling and consciousness? The analogy of language throws light on the question. Words contain and intensify feeling. Without words feeling reaches a momentary peak and quickly dissipates. Perhaps one reason why animal emotions do not reach the intensity and duration of human ones is that animals have no language to hold emotions so that they can either grow or fester. The built environment, like language, has the power to define and refine sensibility. It can sharpen and enlarge consciousness. Without architecture feelings about space must remain diffuse and fleeting.

Consider the sense of an "inside" and an "outside", of intimacy and exposure, of private life and public space. People everywhere recognize these distinctions, but the awareness may be quite vague. Constructed form has the power to heighten the awareness and accentuate, as it were, the difference in emotional temperature between "inside" and "outside". In Neolithic times the basic shelter was a round semisubterranean hut, a womblike enclosure that contrasted vividly with the space beyond. Later the hut emerged above ground, moving away from the earth matrix but retaining and even accentuating the contrast between interior and outside by the aggressive rectilinearity of its walls. At a still later stage, corresponding to the beginning of urban life, the rectangular courtyard domicile appeared. It is noteworthy that these steps in the evolution of the house were followed in all the areas where Neolithic culture made the transition to urban life.[5]

The courtyard house is, of course, still with us – it has not become obsolete. Its basic feature is that the rooms open out to the privacy of interior space and present their blank backs to the outside world. Within and without are clearly defined; people can be certain of where they are. Inside the enclosure, undisturbed by distractions from the outside, human relations and feelings can rise to a high and even uncomfortable level of warmth. The notion of inside and outside is familiar to all, but imagine how sensibly real these categories become when a guest – after a convivial party – leaves the lantern-lit courtyard and steps through the moon gate to the dark wind-swept lane outside. Experiences of this kind were commonplace in traditional Chinese society, but they are surely known to all people who use architectural means to demarcate and intensify forms of social life. Even contemporary America, with its ideal of openness symbolized by large windows and glass walls, has created the enclosed suburban shopping center. How will the shopper experience such a place? As he approaches it in his car across the vast expanse of the parking lot, he can see only the center's unperforated outer sheath which, except for a large trade sign, makes no attempt to lure people in. The image is bleak. He parks the car, steps inside the center's portal, and at once enters a charmed world of light and color, potted plants, bubbling fountains, soft music, and leisurely shoppers.[6]

Spatial dimensions such as vertical and horizontal, mass and volume are experiences known intimately to the body; they are also felt whenever one sticks a pole in the ground, builds a hut, smoothes a surface for threshing grain, or watches a mound of dirt pile up as one digs a deep well. But the meaning of these spatial dimensions gains immeasurably in power and clarity when they can be seen in monumental architecture and when people live in its shadow. Ancient Egypt and Mesopotamia have enlarged mankind's consciousness of space, heightened people's awareness of the vertical and the horizontal, of mass and volume, by constructing their exemplars in the towering shapes of pyramids, ziggurats, and temples.[7] We have inherited this knowledge. Modern architects design with these dimensions in mind. The layman, sensitized to the dramatic play of thrust and repose, learns to appreciate it wherever it appears, in nature as well as in man-made objects that have no aesthetic pretension. We see drama and meaning in the volcanic neck standing above the flat plateau and in the silos of Nebraska. [...]

[Another] example of how architecture can educate people's awareness and conception of reality is from the domain of the illuminated interior. Interior space as such is a commonplace experience. We have already noted the enduring and universal antithesis between "inside" and "outside". Historically, interior space was dark and narrow. This was true not only of humble dwellings but also of monumental edifices. Egyptian and Greek temples commanded external space with their polish and imposing proportions; their interiors, however, were gloomy, cluttered, and crudely finished. European architectural history has seen many changes of style but... among ambitious builders the development of an illuminated and spacious interior was a common ideal from the Roman to the Baroque period. An early success was Hadrian's Pantheon. [...]

How does modern architectural space affect awareness? In important respects, the principal ways by which it influences people and society have not changed. Architectural space continues to articulate the social order, though perhaps with less blatancy and rigidity than it did in the past. The modern built environment even maintains a teaching function: its signs and posters inform and expostulate. Architecture continues to exert a direct impact on the senses and feeling. The body responds, as it has always done, to such basic features of design as enclosure and exposure, verticality and horizontality, mass, volume, interior spaciousness, and light. Architects, with the help of technology, continue to enlarge the range of human spatial consciousness by creating new forms or by remaking old ones at a scale hitherto untried.

These are the continuities. What are some of the changes? Active participation is much reduced. In the modern world people do not, as in nonliterate and peasant societies, build their own houses, nor do they participate even in a token manner in the construction of public monuments. [...] Modern society is also increasingly literate, which means that it depends less and less on material objects and the physical environment to embody the value and meaning of a culture: verbal symbols have progressively displaced material symbols, and books rather than buildings instruct.

Symbols themselves have lost much of their power to reverberate in the mind and feeling since this power depends on the existence of a coherent world. Without such a world symbols tend to become indistinguishable from signs. Gas stations, motels, and eateries along the highway have their special signs which are intended to suggest that these are not only convenient but good places for the motorists to pause. [...] Consider the modern skyscraper. People who take note of it are likely to offer a broad range of opinions concerning its worth and meaning. To some it is aggressive, arrogant, and monolithic; to others, on the contrary, it is daring, elegant, and lithe. Such divergent – even opposing – views exist despite the fact that the high-rise is the product of an age to which we all belong ...

Notes

1 Karl von Frisch, *Animal Architecture*, New York: Harcourt Brace Jovanovich, 1974.
2 See Christopher Alexander, *Notes on the Synthesis of Form*, Cambridge: Harvard University Press, 1964. On the stability of certain folk architectural forms, Alexander gives the following references: L. G. Bark, "Beehive Dwellings of Apulia", *Antiquity* 6, 1932, 410; Werner Kissling, "House Tradition in the Outer Hebrides", *Man* 44, 1944, 137; and H. A. and B. H. Huscher, "The Hogan Builders of Colorado", *Southwestern Lore* 9, 1943, 1–92.
3 Pierre Deffontaines, *Géographie et religions*, Paris: Librairie Gallimard, 1948; Mircea Eliade, *The Sacred and the Profane*, New York: Harper and Row, 1961; Lord Raglan, *The Temple and the House*, London: Routledge and Paul, 1964. On the animal and human sacrifices in the building of a Royal City, see T. K. Chêng, *Shang China*, Toronto: University of Toronto Press, 1960, p. 21.
4 John Harvey, *The Medieval Architect*, London: Wayland Publishers, 1972, p. 97.
5 For the courtyard house in Mesopotamia see C. L. Woolley, "The Excavations at Ur 1926–27", *The Antiquaries Journal* 7, 1927, 387–95. For a summary of changes in the style of the house in the ancient Near East see Sigfried Giedion, *The Eternal Present*, New York: Pantheon Books, 1964, pp. 182–9. For the evolution of house shape from oval to rectangular in ancient Egypt see Alexander Badawy, *Architecture in Ancient Egypt and the Near East*, Cambridge: MIT Press, 1966, pp. 10–14. For changes in house type from the round semi-subterranean dwelling to the courtyard pattern in Boeotia see Bertha Carr Rider, *Ancient Greek Houses*, Chicago: Argonaut, 1964, pp. 42–68. On Crete, however, Neolithic houses were predominantly rectangular. See D. S. Robertson, *Greek and Roman Architecture*, Cambridge: Cambridge University Press, 1969, p. 7. For the development of the Chinese house since Neolithic times see Kwang-Chih Chang, *The Archaeology of Ancient China*, New Haven, Conn.: Yale University Press, 1968, and Andrew Boyd, *Chinese Architecture and Town Planning, 1500 B.C.-A.D. 1911*, Chicago: University of Chicago Press, 1962. For prehistoric Mexico see Marcus C. Winter, "Residential Patterns at Monte Alban, Oaxaca, Mexico", *Science* 186, no. 4168, 1974, pp. 981–6.
6 Neil Harris, "American Space: Spaced out at the Shopping Center", *The New Republic* 173, no. 24, 1975, 23–6.
7 Giedion, *The Eternal Present*, particularly "Supremacy of the Vertical", pp. 435–92.

The split wall
Domestic voyeurism

Beatriz Colomina (1992)

"To live is to leave traces", writes Walter Benjamin, in discussing the birth of the interior. "In the interior these are emphasized. An abundance of covers and protectors, liners and cases is devised, on which the traces of objects of everyday use are imprinted. The traces of the occupant also leave their impression on the interior. The detective story that follows these traces comes into being … The criminals of the first detective novels are neither gentlemen nor apaches, but private members of the bourgeoisie".[1]

There is an interior in the detective novel. But can there be a detective story of the interior itself, of the hidden mechanisms by which space is constructed as interior? Which may be to say, a detective story of detection itself, of the controlling look, the look of control, the controlled look. But where would the traces of the look be imprinted? What do we have to go on? What clues?

There is an unknown passage of a well-known book, Le Corbusier's *Urbanisme* (1925), which reads: "Loos told me one day: 'A cultivated man does not look out of the window; his window is a ground glass; it is there only to let the light in, not to let the gaze pass through.'"[2] It points to a conspicuous yet conspicuously ignored feature of Loos's houses: not only are the windows either opaque or covered with sheer curtains, but the organization of the spaces and the disposition of the built-in furniture (the *immeuble)* seems to hinder access to them. A sofa is often placed at the foot of a window so as to position the occupants with their back to it, facing the room. This even happens with the windows that look into other interior space – as in the sitting area of the ladies' lounge of the Müller house (Prague, 1930). Moreover, upon entering a Loos interior one's body is continually turned around to face the space one just moved through, rather than the upcoming space or the space outside. With each turn, each return look, the body is arrested. Looking at the photographs, it is easy to imagine oneself in these precise, static positions, usually indicated by the unoccupied furniture. The photographs suggest that it is intended that these spaces be comprehended by occupation, by using this furniture, by "entering" the photograph, by inhabiting it.[3]

In the Moller house (Vienna, 1928, Figs 10, 11) there is a raised sitting area off the living room with a sofa set against the window. Although one cannot see out the window, its presence is strongly felt. The bookshelves surrounding the sofa and the light coming from behind it suggest a comfortable nook for reading. But comfort in this space is more than just sensual, for there is also a psychological dimension. A sense of security is produced by the position of the couch, the placement of its occupants, against the light. Anyone who, ascending the stairs from the entrance (itself a rather dark passage), enters the living room, would take a few moments to recognize a person sitting in the couch. Conversely, any intrusion would soon be detected by a person occupying this area, just as an actor entering the stage is immediately seen by a spectator in a theater box.

Loos refers to the idea of the theater box in noting that "the smallness of a theater box would be unbearable if one could not look out into the large space beyond".[4] While Kulka, and later Münz, read this comment in terms of the economy of space provided by the *Raumplan*, they overlook its psychological dimension. For Loos, the theater box exists at the intersection between claustrophobia and agoraphobia.[5] This spatial-psychological device could also be read in terms of power, regimes of control inside the house. The raised sitting area of the Moller house provides the occupant with a vantage point overlooking the interior. Comfort in this space is related to both intimacy and control.

This area is the most intimate of the sequence of living spaces, yet, paradoxically, rather than being at the heart of the house, it is placed at the periphery, pushing a volume out of the street façade, just above the front entrance. Moreover, it corresponds with the largest window on this elevation (almost a horizontal window). The occupant of this space can both detect anyone crossing-trespassing the threshold of the house (while screened by the curtain) and monitor any movement in the interior (while "screened" by the backlighting).

In this space, the window is only a source of light (not a frame for a view). The eye is turned towards the interior. The only exterior view that would be possible from this position requires that the gaze travel the whole depth of the house, from the alcove to the living room to the music room, which opens onto the back garden. Thus, the exterior view depends upon a view of the interior.

The look folded inward upon itself can be traced in other Loos interiors. In the Müller house, for instance, the sequence of spaces, articulated around the staircase, follows an increasing sense of privacy from the drawing room, to the dining room and study, to the "lady's room" (*Zimmer der Dame*) with its raised sitting area, which occupies the center, or "heart", of the house.[6] But the window of this space looks onto the living space. Here, too, the most intimate room is like a theater box, placed just over the entrance to the social spaces in this house, so that any intruder could easily be seen. Likewise, the view of the exterior, towards the city, from this "theater box", is contained within a view of the interior. Suspended in the middle of the house, this space assumes both the character of a "sacred" space and of a point of control. Comfort is paradoxically produced by two seemingly opposing conditions, intimacy and control.

This is hardly the idea of comfort which is associated with the nineteenth-century interior as described by Walter Benjamin in "Louis-Philippe, or the Interior".[7] In Loos's interiors the sense of security is not achieved by simply turning one's back on the exterior and immersing oneself in a private universe – "a box in the world theater", to use Benjamin's metaphor. It is no longer the house that is a theater box; there is a theater box inside the house, overlooking the internal social spaces. The inhabitants of Loos's houses are both actors in and spectators of the family scene – involved in, yet detached from, their own space.[8] The classical distinction between inside and outside, private and public, object and subject, becomes convoluted.

The theater boxes in the Moller and Müller houses are spaces marked as "female", the domestic character of the furniture contrasting with that of the adjacent "male" space, the libraries. In these, the leather sofas, the desks, the chimney, the mirrors, represent a "public space" within the house – the office and the club invading the interior. But it is an invasion which is confined to an enclosed room – a space which belongs to the sequence of social spaces within the house, yet does not engage with them. As Münz notes, the library is a "reservoir of quietness", "set apart from the household traffic". The raised alcove of the Moller house and the *Zimmer der Dame* of the Müller house, on the other hand, not only overlook the social spaces but are exactly positioned at the end of the sequence, on the threshold of the private, the secret, the upper rooms where sexuality is hidden away. At the intersection of the visible and the invisible, women are placed as the guardians of the unspeakable.[9]

But the theater box is a device which both provides protection and draws attention to itself. Thus, when Münz describes the entrance to the social spaces of the Moller house, he writes: "Within, entering from one side, one's gaze travels in the opposite direction till it rests in the light, pleasant alcove, raised above the living room floor. Now we are really inside the house".[10] That is, the intruder is "inside", has penetrated the house, only when his/her gaze strikes this most intimate space, turning the occupant into a silhouette against the light.[11] The "voyeur" in the "theater box" has become the object of another's gaze; she is caught in the act of seeing, entrapped in the very moment of control.[12] In framing a view, the theater box also frames the viewer. It is impossible to abandon the space, let alone leave the house, without being seen by those over whom control is being exerted. Object and subject exchange places. Whether there is actually a person behind either gaze is irrelevant:

> I can feel myself under the gaze of someone whose eyes I do not even see, not even discern. All that is necessary is for something to signify to me that there may be others there. The window if it gets a bit dark and if I have reasons for thinking that there is someone behind it, is straightway a gaze. From the moment this gaze exists, I am already something other, in that I feel myself becoming an object for the gaze of others. But in this position, which is a reciprocal one, others also know that I am an object who knows himself to be seen.[13]

Architecture is not simply a platform that accommodates the viewing subject. It is a viewing mechanism that produces the subject. It precedes and frames its occupant.

The theatricality of Loos's interiors is constructed by many forms of representation (of which built space is not necessarily the most important). Many of the photographs, for instance, tend to give the impression that someone is just about to enter the room, that a piece of domestic drama is about to be enacted. The characters absent from the stage, from the scenery and from its props – the conspicuously placed pieces of furniture – are conjured up.[14] The only published photograph of a Loos interior which includes a human figure is a view of the entrance to the drawing room of the Rufer house (Vienna, 1922). A male figure, barely visible, is about to cross the threshold through a peculiar opening in the wall.[15] But it is precisely at this threshold, slightly off stage, that the actor/intruder is most vulnerable, for a small window in the reading room looks down onto the back of his neck. This house, traditionally considered to be the prototype of the *Raumplan*, also contains the prototype of the theater box.

In his writings on the question of the house, Loos describes a number of domestic melodramas. In *Das Andere*, for example, he writes:

> Try to describe how birth and death, the screams of pain for an aborted son, the death rattle of a dying mother, the last thoughts of a young woman who wishes to die… unfold and unravel in a room by Olbrich! Just an image: the young woman who has put herself to death. She is lying on the wooden floor. One of her hands still holds the smoking revolver. On the table a letter, the farewell letter. Is the room in which this is happening of good taste? Who will ask that? It is just a room![16]

One could as well ask why it is only the women who die and cry and commit suicide. But leaving aside this question for the moment, Loos is saying that the house must not be conceived of as a work of art, that there is a difference between a house and a "series of decorated rooms". The house is the stage for the theater of the family, a place where people are born and live and die. Whereas a work of art, a painting, presents itself to critical attention as an object, the house is received as an environment, as a stage.

To set the scene, Loos breaks down the condition of the house as an object by radically convoluting the relation between inside and outside. One of the devices he uses is mirrors which, as Kenneth Frampton has pointed out, appear to be openings, and openings which can be mistaken for mirrors.[17] Even more enigmatic is the placement, in the dining room of the Steiner house (Vienna, 1910), of a mirror just beneath an opaque window.[18] Here, again, the window is only a source of light. The mirror, placed at eye level, returns the gaze to the interior, to the lamp above the dining table and the objects on the sideboard, recalling Freud's studio in Berggasse 19, where a small framed mirror hanging against the window reflects the lamp on his work table. In Freudian theory the mirror represents the psyche. The reflection in the mirror is also a self-portrait projected onto the outside world. The placement of Freud's mirror on the boundary between interior and exterior undermines the status of the boundary as a fixed limit. Inside and outside cannot simply be separated. Similarly, Loos's mirrors promote the interplay between reality and illusion, between the actual and virtual, undermining the status of the boundary between inside and outside.

This ambiguity between inside and outside is intensified by the separation of sight from the other senses. Physical and visual connections between the spaces in Loos's houses are often separated. In the Rufer house, a wide opening establishes between the raised dining room and the music room a visual connection which does not correspond to the physical connection. Similarly, in the Moller house there appears to be no way of entering the dining room from the music room, which is 70 centimeters below; the only means of access is by unfolding steps which are hidden in the timber base of the dining room.[19] This strategy of physical separation and visual connection, of "framing", is repeated in many other Loos interiors. Openings are often screened by curtains, enhancing the stagelike effect. It should also be noted that it is usually the dining room which acts as the stage, and the music room as the space for the spectators. What is being framed is the traditional scene of everyday domestic life.

Notes

1   Walter Benjamin, "Paris, Capital of the Nineteenth Century", in *Reflections*, Edmund Jephcott (trans.) New York: Schocken Books, 1986, pp. 155–6.
2   "Loos m'affirmait un jour: 'Un homme cultivé ne regarde pas par la fenêtre; sa fenêtre est en verre dépoli; elle n'est là que pour donner de la lumière, non pour laisser passer le regard.'" Le Corbusier, *Urbanisme*, Paris, 1925, p. 174. [...]
3   The perception of space is not what space *is* but one of its representations; in this sense built space has no more authority than drawings, photographs, or descriptions.
4   Ludwig Münz and Gustav Künstler, *Der Architekt Adolf Loos*, Vienna and Munich, 1964, pp. 130–1. English translation: *Adolf Loos, Pioneer of Modern Architecture*, London, 1966, p. 148.
5   Georges Teyssot has noted that "The Bergsonian ideas of the room as a refuge from the world are meant to be conceived as the 'juxtaposition' between claustrophobia and agoraphobia. This dialectic is already found in Rilke". Teyssot, "The Disease of the Domicile", *Assemblage* 6, 1988, 95.
6   There is also a more direct and more private route to the sitting area, a staircase rising from the entrance of the drawing room.
7   [...] Benjamin, "Paris, Capital of the Nineteenth Century", p. 154.
8   This calls to mind Freud's paper "A Child Is Being Beaten" (1919) where, as Victor Burgin has written, "the subject is positioned both in the audience *and* on stage – where it is both aggressor *and* aggressed". Burgin, "Geometry and Abjection", *AA Files* 15, Summer 1987, 38. The *mise-en-scène* of Loos's interiors appears to coincide with that of Freud's unconscious. [...] In relation to Freud's paper, see also: Jacqueline Rose, *Sexuality in the Field of Vision*, London: Verso, 1986, pp. 209–10.
9   In a criticism of Benjamin's account of the bourgeois interior, Laura Mulvey writes: "Benjamin does not mention the fact that the private sphere, the domestic, is an essential adjunct to the bourgeois marriage and is thus associated with woman, not simply as female, but as wife and mother. It is the mother who guarantees the privacy of the home by maintaining its respectability, as essential a defense against incursion or curiosity as the encompassing walls of the home itself". Mulvey, "Melodrama Inside and Outside the Home", *Visual and Other Pleasures*, London, 1989.
10   Münz and Künstler, *Adolf Loos*, p. 149.

11   Upon reading an earlier version of this manuscript, Jane Weinstock pointed out that this silhouette against the light can be understood as a screened woman, a veiled woman, and therefore as the traditional object of desire.

12   In her response to an earlier version of this paper, Silvia Kolbowski pointed out that the woman in the raised sitting area of the Moller house could also be seen from behind, through the window to the street, and that therefore she is also vulnerable in her moment of control.

13   Jacques Lacan, *The Seminar of Jacques Lacan: Book I, Freud's Papers on Technique 1953–1954*, Jacques-Alain Miller (ed.), John Forrester (trans.), New York and London: W. W. Norton, 1988, p. 215. [...]

14   There is an instance of such personification of furniture in one of Loos's most autobiographical texts, where he writes: "Every piece of furniture, every thing, every object had a story to tell, a family story". See Adolf Loos, "Interiors in the Rotunda", in J. O. Newman and J. H. Smith (eds), *Spoken into the Void: Collected Essays 1897–1900*, Cambridge, Mass.: MIT Press, 1982, p. 24.

15   This photograph has only been published recently. Kulka's monograph (a work in which Loos was involved) presents exactly the same view, the same photograph, but without a human figure. The strange opening in the wall pulls the viewer toward the void, toward the missing actor (a tension which the photographer no doubt felt the need to cover). This tension constructs the subject, as it does in the built-in couch of the raised area of the Moller house, or the window of the *Zimmer der Dame* overlooking the drawing room of the Müller house.

16   Adolf Loos, *Das Andere*, no. 1, 1903, p. 9.

17   Kenneth Frampton, unpublished lecture, Columbia University, Fall 1986.

18   It should also be noted that this window is an exterior window, as opposed to the other window, which opens into a threshold space.

19   The reflective surface in the rear of the dining room of the Moller house (halfway between an opaque window and a mirror) and the window on the rear of the music room "mirror" each other, not only in their locations and their proportions, but even in the way the plants are disposed in two tiers. All of this produces the illusion, in the photograph, that the threshold between these two spaces is virtual – impassable, impenetrable.

The American front porch
Women's liminal space

Sue Bridwell Beckham (1988)

Sitting on the Porch
An event, in those days
for which one freshened up.
The houses were close to the street
and to sit on the porch
meant to be accessible
to visit, to chat and receive,
to be public and on display.
My grandmother did not
sit on the porch
before four o'clock
but sometimes stayed there
through sweet summer evenings.
And when I was with her

I thought of it as
an occasion.[1]

Every evening of a summer, after supper dishes were done, my mother-in-law insisted that the whole household gather on the front porch to "cool off". The ritual made good sense before her husband persuaded her to let him install air conditioners in their Mississippi home, but long after the house was kept at a comfortable 70 degrees, Ms. Beckham continued to insist that we all troop out on the porch after supper to cool off. Whenever I tried to beg off because I wished to read a book or watch a television show, the lady was convinced that nothing less than a rift with some family member would keep anybody indoors. And she was equally certain that whatever pique there was would disappear once I occupied a rocker on the front porch and communed with the group. Clearly, her faith in the ministry of the porch went deeper than relief from the heat. The porch for my mother-in-law was, as it was for Mary Easter, author of the poem above, and her grandmother, a ritual space. For those women, it was a space which met certain largely female needs, a space which, like a church, required compliance with certain forms for maximum benefit – and also, like a church, permitted the casting off of other social forms in order to realize a largely hidden self.

While virtually all American porches owe their architectural being to forms developed in other cultures, the American front porch is a peculiarly American institution. The earliest porches in recorded history were ceremonial. Porticoes on Greek temples and on the ceremonial buildings of America's Mississippian Indians alike blurred boundaries between the populace outside and the high priests performing their rituals in the inner sanctum. They were bridges between the sacred and the profane from which the highly revered could speak with the lowly and on which they could perform public rites for untutored – or unsanctified – audiences on the outside. It is far in space and time from Greek temples and pre-Columbian Indians to the porches on American houses and yet, unless the function were somewhat similar, my mother-in-law would not have placed so much faith in her porch and its restorative power. Nor would Mary Easter have recalled the ritual of freshening up at the appropriate time of day for the "occasion" of sitting on the porch.

Those authors, particularly women, who write of the American experience have long been aware that a ritual significance attaches to the front porch; the absence of direct allusion to that significance, however, suggests the realization to have been subconscious. In *The Ballad of the Sad Café*, for example, Carson McCullers recounts the peculiar use her protagonist, Miss Amelia Evans, made of her porch. Having lost her mother in early childhood and her father at the vulnerable age of nineteen, Miss Amelia, six feet tall and utterly masculine in build, had not learned – or chosen to acknowledge – the womanly virtues, but implicitly she understood the proprieties of a woman living alone. In the daytime, she admitted men to the store on the ground floor of her house where they bought necessities such as feed, fertilizer and snuff. In the evening, when male visitors inside would have been improper, she sold men her moonshine through the kitchen door – liquor she would never permit to be consumed in her house or her store.

Miss Amelia did, however, permit the men to drink her liquor on her front porch. The porch was Miss Amelia's property, readers are told, but this intensely possessive woman "did not regard [it] as her premises; the premises began at the front door and took in the entire inside of the building".[2] Clearly Miss Amelia understood the porch to be neither her home nor public property. She allowed the men to consume her liquor on the porch and to enjoy a certain amount of social interchange, but all the time she remained standing in the doorway guarding the inner sanctum and presiding over the proceedings. For this woman and for the town in which she lived, the porch was a space "betwixt and between" private and public, and once we consider the special properties attributed to the liquor consumed there, it becomes a place for ritual communion as well:

> For the liquor of Miss Amelia has a special quality of its own. It is clean and sharp on the tongue, but once it is down a man it glows inside him for a long time afterward. And that is not all. It is known that if a message is written with lemon juice on a clean sheet of paper there will be no sign of it. But if the paper is held for a moment to the fire then the letters turn brown and the meaning becomes clear. Imagine that the whisky is the fire and that the message is that which is known only in the soul of a man – then the worth of Miss Amelia's liquor can be understood.[3]

[…] The porch for Miss Amelia … – and for millions of women from the mid-nineteenth century to the mid-twentieth – was a sort of "liminal space". Anthropologist Victor Turner speaks of a "liminal state" which occurs in those more primitive cultures studied by anthropologists – a time when the participants in a ritual are "betwixt and between" two cultural states – neither completely inside the culture nor yet outside it since their position is a transitional one.[4] Among those Turner describes as liminal are stone age peoples undergoing puberty rituals and medieval squires practicing the rites preparatory to knighthood. Two comparatively modern female liminal states are experienced by women who have declared their availability for marriage but who have not yet been claimed (debutantes, for example) and engaged women – both betwixt and between the protection of their parents and that of their husbands.

During their liminal period, such people are neither children nor adults, neither aspiring nor fully achieving. Using Turner's model, the front porch becomes a liminal space – neither sanctified as the hearth nor public as the road. One must be *invited* to sit on the porch, but, on the other hand, one has the right to *expect* that invitation because a person sitting on the porch has declared herself "to be accessible/to visit, to chat and receive/to be public and on display". Occupants of a porch are betwixt and between because they are neither fully sheltered from the elements nor fully exposed to them – neither fully a part of the workings of the public sphere nor fully excluded from them.

Although every structural feature of the porch is borrowed from another culture, the domestic front porch is an American institution – owing its origin to the Southeastern climate and gradually spreading into the fabric of American life in all geographic regions. While it was English settlers and African slaves who conceived of and built the first American front porches early in the seventeenth century, they borrowed concepts from the Indian bungalow, the Haitian "shotgun" house, and the French side and back "galleries".[5] Later, wealthier English stock tempered the practical porch with majestic columns and ornate porticoes borrowed from the ancient Greeks. While those formal porches testify to the architectural genius of such men as George Washington and Thomas Jefferson, and even the more humble porches of the common people were usually conceived and built by men, one suspects that women had something to do with their proliferation and their pervasiveness by the mid-nineteenth century.

The widespread use of the domestic front porch in the United States came at a time when the functions of male heads of households and of their female counterparts were being redefined. Late in the eighteenth century and early in the nineteenth, the Industrial

Revolution for the first time made working away from home the order of the day for great numbers of people. Before that, soldiers and adventurers left home for months on end, hunters for shorter periods. Wealthy Europeans, perhaps, maintained multiple dwellings and moved freely among them as they do today. But the masses of the earth's people lived and worked together in exceedingly small geographic areas. While their chores were often delineated by sex, both men and women were involved in work in or near the dwelling – even when, as with nomads, home itself moved seasonally. Families and groups of families could count on social intercourse and highly valued work. In the western world of the nineteenth century, however, all that would change. Particularly in the United States, the industrial revolution and unbridled capitalism brought about for all classes a departure from traditional ways of life. And it brought about corresponding changes in domestic architecture. One historian of American domestic architecture characterizes the new culture of the American mid-nineteenth century this way:

> The dynamic of this entire era was nothing less than the industrialization of America … Life itself was harder and more cynical. The old Jeffersonian vision of an agrarian democracy, of independent men, rooted in the security of their own land or their own handicraft skills, had become more dream than actuality. The ruptures, dislocations, and insecurities of wage work and absentee ownership were increasingly the realities of American life.
>
> But with these miseries came also the optimism that was part of a period of phenomenal growth. It was the opening of an age of untrammeled *laissez-faire* capitalism, of rugged individualism, of unparalleled opportunity … America felt herself to be the inheritor of all the riches of the historic past and scientific present, claiming furthermore an inalienable right to do with her inheritance exactly as she wished. This was true no less in architecture than in the mining, lumbering, and marketing conquest of a continent.[6]

American men may certainly have enjoyed that sense of unparalleled opportunity and the inalienable right to do with their political inheritance exactly as they wished. Women, however, are notably absent from that female writer's concept – and with good reason. With the industrial revolution and the rise of the middle class in European and American societies, it became possible for large numbers of families to "enjoy the luxury" of sending their men out to earn a living while the women stayed home and "enjoyed" the pleasures of domestic life. Wealthy women, of course, still could employ servants to handle domestic chores and carriages to move about in society. At the other end of the spectrum, every able bodied member of less fortunate families was required to work for wages just to keep food on the table.

But increasingly, the class which could neither afford servants nor needed the proceeds of every member's work to survive became the dominant class. What developed was a caste of women whose roles kept them largely indoors and solitary during the day. These women were to engineer domestic bliss, "influence" the children in Christian virtue, and act as moral guides to their men. Much has been written about the stress and frustration women suffered in this period because of their isolation and the gradual devaluation of their work. And much has already been written about ways they devised to deal with it. But one strategy women used to maintain contact with the community remains unconsidered.

The author of the quote above who celebrated the unparalleled opportunity for

American men and the accompanying effervescence in domestic architecture of the period includes in her book dozens of drawings of representative American houses built between 1860 and 1941. And virtually every one of those examples has a front porch of some sort. And yet, like the women of the period she celebrates, the porches seem to be invisible. As in most other histories of American architecture, porches are virtually unmentioned in this book and, while architecture is seen as indicative of the consciousness which spawned it, no quarter is given to implications of ubiquitous porches.

It is probably impossible to prove that women had any direct influence on the porch mania that swept America from this period through the early 1940s. But it is a notable coincidence that, in the era in which the house became woman's domain and man exited to the market place, porches blossomed with an unprecedented abandon and pervasiveness. Before that time, American porches were confined to the Southeast where climate demanded the indoor-outdoor space. Beginning in the 1850s, however, virtually every domestic structure was built with a porch. And to those whose builders failed to catch on to the trend soon enough, porches were sure to be added. A careful look at older residential sections of almost any American community reveals a healthy sprinkling of appended porches among the more common houses on which the porches are integral.

Whether or not women were responsible for the explosion of porches spanning three generations, there can be no doubt that indoor/outdoor living space became for them a way of countering domestic isolation, at least during the warm months. For women, kept at home by children in need of care and the labor necessary to keep a household going, the porch functioned as a social place – their own space – at home yet not inside – a space simultaneously work place and salon – where they could visit, keep track of neighborhood activities and exchange news flashes with passers by while they watched their children and performed their more portable and sedentary chores. Middle class women could – and did – sit on the porch swing to prepare vegetables and fruits for cooking, even for preservation. Shelling peas, peeling apples and peaches, snapping beans, shucking corn – all were acceptable porch activities. So were hand sewing, endless mending, knitting in preparation for the colder indoor months and the more leisurely "fancy work". And while women performed those chores, they could keep an eye on the children – those middle aged people who today remember the porch as partially sheltered playground.

The more fortunate women who had a back porch as well could do their more strenuous and less presentable chores in the back. Their poorer sisters, however, often actually canned those peeled apples and shelled peas on the front porch. The cramped kitchen would have been just too hot. The porch also served as summer laundry room. Today, adults from the South especially recall playing the familiar automobile game of "counting washing machines on the front porch" in the late thirties, the forties and into the fifties. Those washing machines had replaced earlier boilers and washtubs.

Porches did make heavy chores more pleasant in hot weather, and they did offer the opportunity to take quieter tasks into the semi-public, but the most liberating use women found for the porch, one imagines, was social. On the porch, the casual visitor, the maid separated from the family by class and caste, the family itself experienced "communitas". One characteristic Turner ascribes to people in a liminal state is "Communitas" – the temporary but vital attachment that only people caught between cultural states can establish. Communitas, according to Turner, is "undirected, equalitarian, direct, nonrational, existential". Thus behavior in the liminal space is "spontaneous, immediate, concrete". The rules that apply to relationships and behavior in the structured environment on either side of the liminal space do not apply within it. So it is with the porch. There, betwixt and between absolute private and absolute public, relationships that would be impossible elsewhere can flourish for however brief a time – and they can be spontaneous. Thus, bashful and protected youth in the first flush of intimacy are free to experiment with new relationships; thus, caste and class can be suspended and commonality explored; thus the boundary between friend and stranger breaks down; thus, the powerless are empowered; and thus, established relationships are freed from the constraints and tensions of business on the outside and busy-ness indoors to commune and, if my mother-in-law is to be taken seriously, to heal.

The communitas established on the porch has contributed to the transmission of culture from generation to generation. In the evening, when whole families gathered on porches, family lore was passed in the guise of stories of old times. On my grandfather's porch, in the long televisionless summer evenings, I learned family history – and family legend. But in the day, with my grandmother, I learned my proper place. The turn of the century girl child … learns from a female family retainer how to sweep a porch – and the importance of keeping it swept. At the turn of the century, at the height of Jim Crow, she also learned that it was sometimes socially acceptable for blacks to sit with whites – at least with white children – on porches, but never in living rooms. On some porches white female employers could indulge the friendships they formed with black employees without public censorship. It was my mother-in-law's custom to invite her maid for a mid morning Coke on the screened part of the front porch – and again in the mid afternoon. Ida Rebecca Baker's realm was more strict. Her black maid and lifelong friend Annie was permitted the sanctity of a porch rocker only in times of sickness or death and then only … in the company of children.[7] It was a reward for service rendered.

The porch also provided a setting within which blacks could maintain social relationships with whites. A white woman who would never have entered her black friend's living room unless it was to impart some matriarchal service could sit on the black woman's porch with impunity. When he filmed *The Color Purple*, Steven Spielberg retained Alice Walker to advise him on cultural mores with which he was unfamiliar. In the film he illustrated proper decorum for whites visiting blacks. When Sophia's white employer brought Sophia to spend the day with her relatives, she could not start the car to return home. One of Sophia's sisters, eager not to have her celebratory dinner interrupted while her menfolks ministered to the white woman's car, offered to fix her a plate of food and serve it on the porch. While the white woman refused the proffered gift, it is clear that eating "colored" food on the porch was permissible. The liminal porch was clearly a place where the color barrier could be weakened if not destroyed.

The sex barrier was also weakened on the front porch. In literature and the popular arts, as in life, the porch was the place for innocent courting. Young men have always been more or less able to come and go as they please. Not so young women. Traditionally, they must wait for men to come along, men to make the first move toward courtship, men to suggest marriage.

Most of us know that while women did often initiate acceleration of a relationship, the myth of the male initiator was a charade that had to be maintained, and it was maintained with the help of the porch. Since it was inappropriate for women to go into the public arena in search of potential mates, they needed a way to shop and to sample before making a selection – while all the time seeming to acquiesce in a male decision. Thus the porch, betwixt indoors and out, between public and private, became a sexual market place where the woman seemed to be on display but where she actually sampled wares presented before her.

The nineteenth century was a time, it must be remembered, when peddlers sold house to house, when dressmakers brought their bolts and patterns to the consumer, when fruits and vegetables were delivered to the back door. So it was with men. While Amanda Wingfield in Tennessee Williams' semi-autobiographical *The Glass Menagerie* does not mention her front porch, we are rather certain her living room would not have contained the seventeen gentlemen callers who visited her one fateful Sunday afternoon. And both Margaret Mitchell and David O. Selznik opened *Gone With the Wind* with Scarlet surveying masculine wares on the front veranda. Incidentally, Selznik was at least subconsciously aware of the ritual significance of a porch. While Scarlet is at her feminine best, the veranda is intact. When she returns to Tara to take over the man's job of running the place and even working in the fields, the porch is gone. We are led to believe that Yankees destroyed it, but the subtext is that a gritty female farmer has no use for the accoutrements of a girl whose only responsibility was to snare a husband.

It was for good reason that the porch was the place to entertain gentlemen callers. Inside the rules of propriety and chaperonage were restrictive. On the porch, neither in the parents' parlor nor in the forbidden public arena, certain rules could be broken. A girl on her mother's porch was properly chaperoned, but so long as her mother was inside, she could steal a touch or even a kiss and, in the cover of night, she could talk of subjects inappropriate indoors. […]

In *The Awakening*, when Kate Chopin's protagonist, Edna Pontellier begins to awaken to the limiting nature of her role as a Creole wife, much of the action takes place on the porch of her summer cabin. Vacations are suggested by Turner to be liminal periods when the vacationers temporarily move outside the expectations of their culture. Resorts then, must be themselves liminal spaces. Thus Edna, summering at a vacation spot where many of her daily routines are suspended, is outside her culture enough to examine her lifestyle. And she doesn't like what she sees.

Edna's culture, however, has not taught her fulfilling alternatives. Even so, timidly at first, she begins to experiment. One experiment she tries is flirtation. At the resort, that is entirely acceptable. When she entertains her chosen gentleman friend on her own porch, her husband remarks how pleased he is that she has the young man to keep her amused while he is away during the week attending to business. It is only when, back in the city in colder weather, Edna invites her guests *indoors* in her husband's absence that family and friends perceive something untoward in her search for self. […]

Edna, of course, becomes acutely aware that her life thus far has been a series of command performances. In *The Presentation of Self in Everyday Life*, Erving Goffman outlined his now classic contention that in their everyday lives virtually all people present themselves to others in full fledged performances that include costume, setting and, most of all, acting. Thus, the place where people act becomes a stage and the witnesses an audience. Preparation for such a performance, of course, demands a backstage. In his chapter on "Regions and Regional Behavior", Goffman discusses "front places" and "back places".[8] A front place is where performances are staged. A back place, on the other hand, is not only where the actor prepares for performance, but where she can be herself. For women and their porches, a strange reversal of back and front sometimes occurs. We have already seen that for Edna Pontellier, the front porch in full view of friends and neighbors – the audience – is where she feels most free to try being herself. Indoors, in the bedroom, one of the most back places for Goffman, with only her husband for audience, Edna must act the role of perfect wife and mother. […]

Nineteenth and early twentieth century women seem to have been more free to be themselves on porches than any place else. They could enjoy the communion of passers by and chance visitors on the porch while they watched children and did some of their more portable chores. And they could keep up with community news via casual exchanges with people on the street. As a matter of fact those people on the street were very important in building a porch culture. The porch served a dual role as stage and orchestra for Goffmanesque performances. As Mary Easter indicates, sitting on the porch at certain times of day, was "an occasion". People planned it; people freshened up for it. Women retired to their porches after demands of the protestant work ethic had been met to see and be seen. From their perch above the street, they could look down on passers by, wave, greet, and, after the passer had gone, comment. Each new event on the street was occasion for new stories or for dragging out old ones. And at the same time, those who walked by were audience for the performance on the porch.

Except at resorts and vacation cottages, the stage function of the porch seems to have been the only part of women's porch culture to survive into the 1980s. True, people do still sit on porches – when they have them – in the spring and fall, but it seems usually to be a sentimental harkening to days gone by. When it gets really hot, they huddle indoors with their air conditioning. Women, equipped with cars and telephones, no longer need to sit outdoors to maintain social contact. Television supplies continuous undemanding entertainment for those who are bored. And most women of the eighties are too busy performing the superwoman roles today's society has assigned them to have time to sit outdoors to greet and be greeted. In our frenetic society, a new need for "privacy" demands that what serious outdoor activity remains be relegated to decks at the rear of newer homes. And houses are seldom built with porches any more. […]

Last summer I visited my home town in Kentucky to show my children where I grew up and, incidentally, to photograph porches. As we strolled by one of the grandest houses from my day – the house of the federal judge – I was telling my children how excited I had been when the judge's granddaughter invited me to play with paper dolls on that very porch when we noticed in the corner of that great front porch, a tiny, shriveled up woman. Her live-in companion confirmed that the woman on the porch was the judge's wife and grandmother of my childhood friend and invited me to speak with her, warning me she wouldn't know me. True, she did not recognize me, but she would never forget the ritual of the porch. Strapped in her chair so that she wouldn't fall, bereft of most of the knowledge she had accumulated in ninety odd years, she greeted me as she had hundreds of other visitors to her porch over all those years – as if it were once again 1951, and she had yet to have a car of her own, the only air conditioning was to be found in movie houses, televiewing was relegated to those who had a stomach for professional wrestling, and the ritual of the porch had never ended. She had freshened up to sit on the porch, she was "assessable, receiving", and I was a neighbor who passed on the street and stopped to chat.

Women of her era, often foggy about the present, have no difficulty recalling the porch's meaning for women for over a century of American history. For her, for me, and for countless other women the front porch will remain an artifactual testimony to the isolation women once experienced and the resourcefulness with which they overcame it.

Notes

1   Mary Easter, "Sitting on the Porch", in Beverly Voldseth and Karen Herseth Wee (eds) *Absorb the Colors: Poems by Northfield Women Poets*, Northfield, Minn.: privately published, 1986, p. 15.

2   Carson McCullers, *The Ballad of the Sad Café*, in Charles Clerc and Louis Leiter (eds) *The Ballad of the Sad Café: Seven Contemporary Short Novels*, 3rd edn, Glenview, IL: Scott, Foresman and Company, 1982, p. 118.

3   Ibid., p. 107.

4   All information on Turner's liminality and communitas is drawn from Victor Turner, *Dramas, Fields and Metaphors: Symbolic Action in Human Society*, Ithaca: Cornell University Press, 1974, Chapters 1 and 7, although he has written of the concepts in many of his writings.

5   Material on the actual history of porches is difficult to find, and most of what is available is impressionistic – as is this article. The most serious scholarship on the front porch as significant domestic architecture to date is a mere two pages by John Michael Vlach, in *The Afro-American Tradition in Decorative Arts*, Cleveland, Ohio: The Cleveland Museum of Art, 1978, pp. 136–8, Vlach has carefully documented the African and Caribbean origins of the traditional American front porch. Ruth Little-Stokes reported the same origins in "The North Carolina Porch: A Climactic and Cultural Buffer" [in Douglas Swaim (ed.) *Carolina Dwelling*, Raleigh: North Carolina State University, 1978], but her essay is primarily interpretive. Davida Rochlin's essay, "The Front Porch" [in Charles W. Moore, Katheryn Smith, and Peter Becker (eds) *Home Sweet Home: American Domestic Vernacular Architecture*, New York: Rizzoli, 1983] reports the social significance of American porches but eschews history. In his classic history of architecture, Sir Bannister Fletcher [*A History of Architecture*, 17th edn, New York: Charles Scribner's Sons, 1983] acknowledges the ancient European origins of the "grand porticoes" and galleries of the early American Southeast, but porches *per se* are beneath his concern. Other sources have undoubtedly mentioned perfunctorily the appendages on American houses, but the architectural history of porches is most significant for its invisibility.

6   Mary Mix Foley, *The American House*, New York: Harper and Row, 1980, p. 163.

7   Russell Baker, *Growing Up*, New York: Congdon and Weed, 1982, p. 42.

8   Erving Goffman, *The Presentation of Self in Everyday Life*, Garden City, NY: Doubleday, 1959, pp. 106–40.

Excavation and reconstruction
An oral archaeology of the deLemos home

Adina Loeb (2003)

The deLemos apartment remembered

Few remnants remain of the home [of] my great-grandparents. As newlyweds in 1897, Adolph deLemos (b. 1872) and Hannah Morris deLemos (b. 1876) moved into a brand new "railroad flat" on New York's Upper East Side, in an area known as Yorkville. They lived there for the entire duration of their more than 55-year marriage. When Adolph died in 1953, his youngest daughter Norma deLemos Loeb, my paternal grandmother, and her family moved into the Yorkville apartment with Hannah.

The Loebs lived in the deLemos apartment with Hannah for the better part of a decade; it thus became known as "home", perhaps more than any other place for Norma's children, my aunt [Judy] and my father.[1] After more than [sixty-four] years, my great-grandmother finally moved with my grandparents to another apartment in 1961 – less than a year before her death and only a few years before the Yorkville building was demolished in the mid–1960s. Today, a luxury high-rise apartment building stands in its place.

Having spent most of her adulthood in the Yorkville apartment, my great-grandmother's story is inextricably woven into the history of the apartment itself. In this paper,

I will attempt to reconstruct and analyze the physical space of the deLemos apartment, based on interviews [with] my aunt and my father. In my analysis of the deLemos apartment, I will attempt to piece together a plan and provide a sketch of space utilization, while at the same time giving a sense of the actual family life lived within that space. My project will pay particular attention to the use of space over time, with a special focus on my great-grandmother, who lived there longer than any of the other apartment inhabitants. This focus will lead to a close study of Hannah's favorite space in the house, a chair at the living room window [...]

[My thinking has been] colored by my father's and aunt's stories as well as by family photo albums. [For me], the indelible image of that vanished existence is that of my aging great-grandmother sitting in a straight-backed wooden chair, before the over-exposed white of an uncovered window. In more than one photograph, she sits facing the camera, her chair angled perpendicularly towards the window, so she could clearly view the bustle of Second Avenue below ...

Located at 1677 Second Avenue between 86th and 87th Street, the deLemos home was a third-floor walk-up, three-bedroom apartment that stood in the heart of Yorkville. This area of the Upper East Side, between 72nd and 100th Street to the east of Lexington Avenue, was particularly known for the large number of German immigrants who moved there from the mid-nineteenth century until the 1930s.[2] My great-grandparents were both German Jewish immigrants, who came to the United States during the 1880s as children, settling with their families in New York City. Though not specifically a Jewish neighborhood, many German Jews who came to America before the Nazi regime moved to German neighborhoods, such as Yorkville, where they could comfortably communicate in their native language and live within a culture familiar to them.[3]

The deLemos apartment building was one section of a block-long set of four-story buildings on the west side of Second Avenue, with six entrances and a continuous façade, giving it the appearance of a single building. Standing between street-level storefronts, each entrance led to a separate three-story apartment building starting one floor above the street level, with two apartments per floor, one on each side of a central stone-floored staircase. Airshafts on either side of the six buildings divided them from behind the street-facing façade.

[...] My Aunt Judy's ... first memory of her grandparents' apartment is of "schlepping groceries up and down stairs", to and from the third floor.[4] Although the kitchen was equipped with a dumbwaiter, it was used only for garbage by the time the Loebs lived there and is said to have had a terrible smell. Judy's descriptions often deal with sensory impressions of remembered odors, the darkness of the rooms, the summer heat, and sounds within the apartment and outside. To Judy, the already compact apartment felt smaller because there were simply "too many people" living within its confines. [...]

The division and use of space

To deal with the crowdedness of the apartment and accommodate a multiplicity of needs, the members of the family used its spaces in different ways. The division of space according to function was based primarily on temporal considerations. Rooms served different purposes at different times of day and night. The bedrooms, bathroom, and kitchen were more singular in purpose than the living room and dining room – notably the two largest rooms in the apartment. Moreover, the utilization of space depended on the generation. While my great-grandparents, who spent most of their time in the apartment, had established territorial spaces in the living room and divided the use of space by gender when entertaining guests, my grandparents did not make such designations [*Fig. 12*].

When asked where adults went for privacy, my father responds that there was no real privacy in the house. Yet certain times and spaces did allow for private moments. Somehow, personal issues were resolved either in front of the family or in the quiet of night, the only time when the family members were in separate spaces.

[…] My father remembers that the living room had no door and [therefore] did not physically delimit a private space for his parents even during sleeping hours. However, Judy recalls that she and my father did not go into the living room at night, thus respecting the temporal privacy the space assumed.

Within the apartment, play, work, entertainment, and eating all took place in the shared spaces of the living room, dining room, and kitchen. The living room was the primary gathering space for the family, but much time was also spent at the dining room table, where they ate meals together … Phone conversations took place in the dining room, as the apartment's only phone was located there. My father describes doing his homework at the dining room table and sometimes taking friends there to play board games. […]

For more active playing, my father would go to the urban outdoor playground of the street. Played on the three concrete steps of the building's six-foot wide stoop, stoopball became a favorite, albeit dangerous, pastime alongside the busy traffic on Second Avenue. In the winter, my father and his friends used to chase trucks down the street and throw snowballs at them. He also frequently joined a larger group of boys on 87th Street for games of stickball.

[…] Most of my aunt and father's memories take place in the multi-purpose space of living room, which, not coincidently, happened to be the largest room in the apartment. This space is also of greatest interest to me because it served more functions than any other room. It was not only the main familial gathering space by day, for playing, reading, interacting, listening to the radio, and, later, watching the television, but the living room also served as my grandparent's bedroom for a decade. […]

The living room and Hannah's window

The living room was also the space where my great-grandmother spent her days. White-haired and with wrinkled hands in the photographs we have of her in the apartment, Hannah sat at the living room window for as far back as my father and aunt can remember. From her space by the window, Hannah read the newspaper and met with friends, but mostly watched the goings-on of the people along Second Avenue and told stories about them.

Approximately three feet wide and six feet high, Hannah's favorite window was the southernmost of two, cut into the east wall of the living room. Coming down nearly to lap level, the two unbarred living room windows, when opened, were the cause of considerable anxiety for Norma who worried about her children and elderly mother falling out. A [BB bullet], shot from the elevated train that once ran up and down Second Avenue, punctured a neat hole nearly at the center of each window. Long after the Second Avenue rail line was taken out in the 1930s, the small holes remained in the windows, never to be repaired.

Directly opposite the entrance to the room, Hannah's chair stood near a stand-alone wooden radio and a floor lamp, facing the sofa along the south wall, which doubled as my grandparent's bed at night. Adolph sat in a chair immediately adjacent to Hannah's, against the portion of wall between the two windows and facing west. When my father initially described the position of the chairs, I was surprised by their orientation: Hannah, in fact, sat with her back to Adolph's armchair. Though close in proximity, the chairs hardly encouraged direct conversation. My father remembers that his grandparents did sometimes interact while sitting in their respective chairs, yet he does not recall much conversation between them nor either of them ever turning their chairs or bodies in order to face one another. Quiet by nature, my great-grandmother was also hard of hearing, which necessarily would have made extensive spoken conversation difficult.

While Adolph met with his friends or played cards in the living room, often "smoking cigars like a chimney", my father explains that Hannah would often sit in her chair, sometimes participating in their conversation but usually looking out the window. According to my father, she spent so much time at the window, Hannah "probably knew everybody in the street by sight", whether she knew anything of them personally or not. Unsure if any of her stories were true, he recalls that Hannah's tales were a creative and lasting source of entertainment … Not only did Hannah craft stories about the people she saw, but Judy recalls that her stories were ongoing, like the unfolding narrative of a novel. Of the various sequences, Judy remembers a tragic story of a sailor whose wife had died and who was raising his motherless children alone.

Women at windows: pastime, liminality, and power

Having lived there for more than a half century, my great-grandmother did in fact know many of the people who frequented her block of Second Avenue. For Hannah, the window was her portal to the outside world. As a young woman, she participated in that outside world, walking with friends, running errands, going to visit people in their homes. In her older age, however, as she became more feeble and her ability to walk more limited, Hannah spent increasingly more time by the window [*Fig. 13*].

Adolph, who remained active outside of the apartment, had relatively little interest in looking out the window. When at home, he was oriented towards home, as his chair and attention faced inward. Inside the apartment most of the time, Hannah, on the other hand, seemingly longed for greater contact with what existed outside. From her chair at the window, she interacted with the city below, mostly by watching the world of the street and creating a semi-fictional model of that world by crafting stories about what she saw.

Sue Bridwell Beckham, in her 1988 essay, "The American Front Porch: Woman's Liminal Space" [*this volume*], examines the implications of the front porch for women in nineteenth and early twentieth century American culture. Beckham utilizes Victor Turner's model of the "liminal state", during which participants in a ritual are in a transitional space that is "betwixt and between" two cultural states. […] While the interaction between a woman three floors above street-level and the world outside certainly had limitations, it was a space from which my great-grandmother remained connected to the life of the street. Even at the age when she could no longer frequent the city below, she often opened the window and called down greetings to friends or requests to relatives passing by.

My great-grandmother's construction of this liminal space took place over time, the window ultimately serving as her enclosed urban front porch, a viewing space onto the lives of those outside. Though indoors and therefore not in the semi-exposed position of an actual front porch, Hannah's window functionally served as a front porch not only for viewing but also for participating in the life of the street.

Sometimes, my father, playing stoop-ball on the stairs of the front stoop or on his way home from school, would yell up to Hannah to check in and see if she needed anything. Though hard of hearing, she would often see his approach, open the window and call to him, asking him to pick up bread or cakes from a nearby bakery or the like. Occasionally, Hannah threw keys down to friends or relatives, so they could let themselves into the apartment. My aunt also recalls that Hannah would often remind her from the window, as she left the building, to wear her scarf because of cold weather or to come back up to take an umbrella for a forthcoming rainstorm.

This use of the window as a front porch, overlooking and communicating with the street, was not unique to my great-grandmother. As my aunt explains, she and my father interacted from the street with cousins Willy and Hansie through their living room window as well. According to Judy, Willy worked for what became "*Time-Life* magazines or something", and used to give them comic books. Judy remembers calling up to Willy and Hansie's front window, and yelling, "Throw us something!" or "Throw us a joke book!" Their request was commonly met by a comic book flying out from the living room window down to my father and aunt below.

This kind of interaction was probably even more frequent in the early years of the apartment, when there were no buzzers to let people into the building electrically. My father recalls stories of Hannah using buckets to lower money down to street peddlers, who were selling goods from a carriage or pushcart. The peddlers would then take the payment and place the sold fruit or vegetables in the bucket for the family to pull back up to the apartment.

Hannah's … framed vision of Second Avenue functioned as a source of unending entertainment. While there was eventually a television in the apartment, aside from a soap opera or two, Hannah hardly watched it during the day. Nor did she seem to listen to the radio. Perhaps as a result of her poor hearing or simply a greater interest in seeing and participating in the actual life unfolding on Second Avenue, Hannah found what seemed to be her greatest fascination through the somewhat removed view from the living room window. At night, when the excitement on Second Avenue diminished, Hannah would more frequently watch the television, always from her chair by the window.

Hannah's window became a locus of controlled and empowered looking. From her chair, my great-grandmother not only commanded the view of the street and entryway to the building from the window on her left but also of the threshold to the apartment itself with a direct line of sight to the front door on her right. In her essay, "The Split Wall: Domestic Voyeurism" [*this volume*] Beatriz Colomina examines a comparable viewing space in the raised sitting alcove of Adolf Loos's Moller house. Colomina explains that the occupant of the couch placed against the window in this interior space is empowered to act as a sentinel of sorts, able to guard the space, [as] Hannah could, by detecting movement both at the threshold of the house outside and in the interior itself. However, Colomina argues that the covered window in the case of the Moller house is only a source of light, rather than a frame for a view outside, thus turning the eye of the occupant of the space towards the interior. I would suggest the opposite case for my great-grandmother, whose position would certainly allow for watching and participating in the interior space of the house, but whose gaze was nonetheless directed to the exterior.

[…] Hannah's privileged position, with access to a view within the apartment and to the outside, also recalls the empowered liminality of the *portière* in nineteenth century Paris, as examined by Sharon Marcus in *Apartment Stories: City and Home in Nine-teenth-Century Paris and London* [*this volume*]. Marcus explains that the porter's lodge was a space at the seam of the Parisian apartment building, with visual access to both the public and private realms. From there the female porter possessed [a] certain power in her ability to act in that space as a mediator between the public street and private home(s) of her building.

Marcus, Colomina, and Beckham each deal with the female occupant of a designated space: at a window, on a porch, or in the porter's lodge. From these spaces, the female occupant engaged in the activity of viewing others and being viewed. Male viewing from these spaces is not the focus of their analyses. This emphasis on looking and being looked at from constructed spaces introduces a theme of performance in each example. The three authors touch on the staged realm of domestic and urban life, whether citing Walter Benjamin's observations of Paris, whose houses he considered to be part of the urban theater, or Erving Goffman's sociological analysis of life as a theater, with the requisite costume, setting, and acting, in *The Presentation of Self in Everyday Life*.[5] [...]

For my great-grandmother, whose apartment became very much an extension of herself, the [living room] window served not only as an important light source for seeing within the house but also occupied a central role for her as a front porch of interaction with the outside, a framed view for entertainment, a fantastical realm of the imagination, and a stage from which she performed much of her domestic life. [...]

Notes

1 I will use the terms "apartment" and "home" interchangeably, since these ostensibly had the same meaning for the occupants of the dwelling space in question.

2 Avraham Barkai, *Branching Out: German-Jewish Immigration to the United States, 1820–1914*, New York: Holmes and Meier, 1994, p. 137.

3 In his examination of the German Jewish community of Washington Heights, Steven M. Lowenstein argues that German Jewish immigrants no longer moved to German neighbor-hoods like Yorkville after the 1930s, but avoided them as such neighborhoods often harbored members of the pro-Nazi German-American Bund. Instead the mid-twentieth century immigrants tended to move to Jewish rather than German neighborhoods. See Steven M. Lowenstein, *Frankfurt on the Hudson*, Detroit: Wayne State University Press, 1989, pp. 45–6. Antisemitism was not a major concern for my great-grandparents, who immigrated to the U.S. in the 1880s.

4 All accounts by Judy Loeb Ellis are based on interviews that took place on April 14 and April 30, 2003.

5 Marcus and Colomina both use Benjamin's model of Paris as the world theater ..., while Beckham refers to Goffman's sociological analysis of the stage and backstage performances in everyday life... See Walter Benjamin, in Rolf Tiedemann (ed.) *Paris, capitale du XIXe siècle: le livre des passages*, trans. Jean Lacoste, Paris: Editions du cerf, 1989, and Erving Goffman, *The Presentation of Self in Everyday Life*, Garden City, NY: Doubleday Anchor Books, 1959.

Figure 10
Adolf Loos, Moller House,
Vienna, 1928, exterior.

Figure 11   Loos, Moller House, interior.

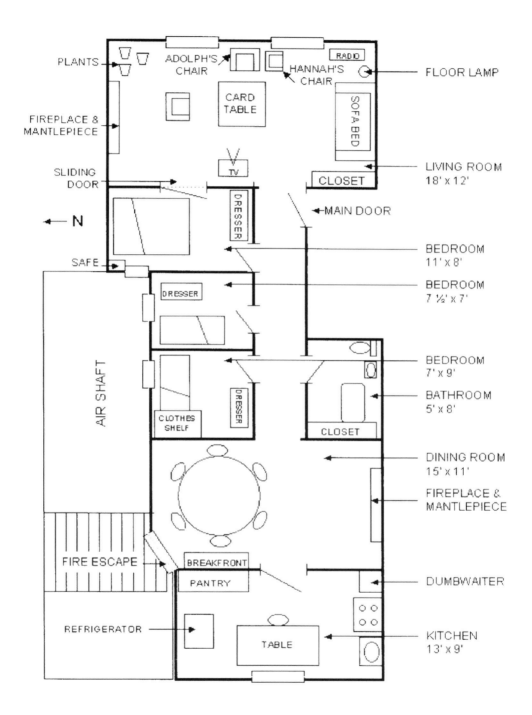

Figure 12 DeLemos apartment, Yorkville, New York City, floor plan 1897–1961, drawn by Adina Loeb.

Figure 13
Hannah Morris deLemos
at her living room
window, 1950s.

PART II
Themes in modern domestic architecture

5

Living downtown

Nineteenth-century urban dwelling

Historians Elizabeth Collins Cromley, Elizabeth Blackmar and Paul Groth discuss the attractions and repulsions of the new living situations in New York and San Francisco (apartment buildings, hotels, rooming houses): the freedom of individuals to move easily and frequently, both in location and in social status; the anxieties of families to assert their social status in shockingly new circumstances. These three, together with historian Donald Olsen, demonstrate that in these new circumstances, architects and builders often turned to pre-existing models: in America, the so-called French flat; in Vienna, the palaces of the aristocracy; everywhere, the larger institutional structures of the past such as monasteries. In a close analysis of Parisian apartment buildings (which were also modeled on aristocratic prototypes) as seen through the novels of Balzac, literary historian Sharon Marcus shows that these most desirable dwellings of the French middle classes exhibited transparency toward their urban surroundings. These buildings, unlike their British and American counterparts, housed several different social classes and often included commercial enterprises. Economic historian M. J. Daunton, writing about the British working class, argues that a gradual reorientation toward the street, away from more communal types of spatial configuration, was a by-product of early-nineteenth-century middle-class efforts in planning reform, developing household technologies, and the changing aspirations of working-class people themselves. Selections from the greatest of Émile Zola's urban novels, *L'Assommoir* (1876), suggest in a vivid and concrete way the housing experiences of the Parisian working classes during the period of Baron von Haussmann's replanning of Paris. Paris is viewed through the eyes of Gervaise, a laundress.

Alone together
A history of New York's early apartments

Elizabeth Collins Cromley (1990)

Reports from Paris

It was not unusual for New Yorkers in the 1850s and 1860s, faced with a shortage of affordable middle-class houses and disappointed with ad hoc solutions such as living in hotels and boardinghouses, to turn to Europe for ideas about urban housing. Urban

Europeans had been living in apartment buildings of various kinds for generations, and the mid-nineteenth century had seen a tremendous growth in newly constructed apartments. Calvert Vaux's apartment proposal of the 1850s was called Parisian Buildings; the New York City Buildings Department recorded the new multiple dwellings of the early 1870s under names like "Parisian dwellings" and "French flats". These names acknowledged that the new housing type was linked to foreign models. [...]

[But] for American observers, the ... traditional apartment building in Paris with its mixture of classes stirred fears of strangers. Middle-class New Yorkers, uncertain of their social status, needed to assure themselves that they were, in fact, rising on the social ladder and could not afford to risk their new sense of social worth by mixing with people less prosperous than themselves.[1] The old Parisian neighborhoods with their mixture of all kinds of residents and services were a parallel to the conditions in antebellum New York that had represented threats to emerging middle-class sensibilities. [...]

Buildings Department inspectors adopted the name "French flat" in the early 1870s as a way to make social class distinctions between kinds of multifamily dwellings. [...] In various locations – on Fifty-eighth Street between Second and Third avenues, on Fiftieth Street between First and Second, on West Forty-seventh and Forty-eighth streets – third-class buildings were going up which inspectors called French flats. An average size for a French-flat building in 1874 was 20 to 30 feet wide and 60 to 75 feet deep. Most of these flat buildings were intended to house three or four families in four stories, and some included a shop on the ground floor. They often had brownstone fronts instead of cheaper brick, though that is not a determining factor for a French-flat designation. [...]

Richard Morris Hunt's 1869–70 Stuyvesant Apartments on East Eighteenth Street, ... and the Albany, designed in 1874 by John C. Babcock, on Broadway between Fifty-first and Fifty-second streets ... illustrate the norms and variations within the size range of typical walk-up French flats of the first generation.[2] [...] Hunt's Stuyvesant buildings occupied four contiguous lots with a frontage of 112 feet, preserving something of the scale of a set of row houses; Babcock's Albany occupied ten contiguous house-sized lots, or the full end of a block (approximately 200 feet of frontage on Broadway).[3]

The Stuyvesant Apartments [*Figs. 14, 15*], described by a contemporary as "somewhat grotesque but highly picturesque", was a seventy-foot-high building of five stories – four floors of family units and the mansarded fifth floor of artists' studios.[4] Although the building was as long as four row houses, and therefore massive in context, in height the Stuyvesant conformed to familiar private house sizes. Its materials of brick and stone were not unusual for residential architecture in New York, but its ornament and wrought-iron balconies, combined with its somewhat over-scaled mansard roof, probably suggested Parisian style to contemporary viewers. Through its incomplete match with ordinary private houses and other familiar dwelling forms, the building's style hinted at unusual uses within. [...]

The [roof] of the Stuyvesant ... unifies the whole, through its imposing size, and reiterates the four-part division of the interior seen in plan, four parts representing four family units per floor. Hunt does indicate, by means of window changes and ornamental details, that there are breaks between individual family units on each floor, but the first-time viewer might easily find the image ambiguous. There are no clear clues by which residents could identify the extent of their individual domains from the exterior. It is very difficult to think of this building's features as representing any one family's status — only a generic social status for all the tenants at once. [...]

The four-story Albany begun in 1874 filled a whole block along Broadway. Initially the architect had filed plans for a set of ten individual French-flat buildings on the same site, but plans were changed to make a single, large apartment block instead. The Albany's identity at first glance seems equivocal. Because the entire site's ten building lots were occupied by a single mass, viewers might have read it as a commercial block, or perhaps have seen in it kinship to a hotel. Along the Broadway façade a series of eight shop-fronts at ground level made the building fit into neighboring blocks of commercial development. Its brick façade with sandstone trim had simple ornamental details to give it character, and over the raised center of the Broadway façade its own name was presented in relief. This name was probably chosen to preserve the name of a unique early nineteenth-century apartment house in Piccadilly, London.[5] [...]

Social rank and strangers

[...] Imagine tenants who were attempting apartment life for the first time moving into the Bella Flats, a small French-flat building that opened in the 1870s on the corner of Twenty-sixth Street at 358 Fourth Avenue.[6] The people who found themselves living together in this building comprised fourteen household units and included married couples with and without children, a widower, single men sharing a "bachelor flat", a janitor, and servants. Among the male heads of households living at the Bella, three were lawyers, two were in banking, and one was a physician, one a clergyman, one a stock-broker, one a bookkeeper, and one a gentleman at leisure. In addition there were several businessmen engaged in wine importing, silks, and produce. Of the married women tenants, all but one listed their occupations as "housekeeping"; the remaining one was an artist. The children living in the Bella Flats ranged in age from infancy to twenty-two years. Most of the families with children had one, two, or three children, but one family, headed by a widower, had six.

Every Bella household but one had at least one live-in servant, several had two, and one family had three; all the servants at the Bella were Irish. Four of the households also had lodgers living with them; a single lodger in two cases, and three lodgers in two other cases. The last family in residence was the janitor with his wife, son, and daughter. They lodged two servants who worked at the general upkeep of the Bella Flats.[7]

This cross section of genteel occupations and a fairly homogeneous tenancy of mostly small families would have characterized "the neighbors" for anyone moving into the Bella Flats. Living among clergymen, physicians, stockbrokers, and lawyers could be socially comfortable for these tenants; yet nonetheless every other family was still made up of "strangers". Did the married people find their bachelor neighbors a problem? Was it comfortable for families of related individuals to live with "families" of couples with lodgers? Did the clergyman have doubts about the morals of the wine importer? How did all those "housekeeping" wives treat the one woman pursuing her own career? Confronting unknown neighbors was only one of the several novelties that tenants encountered when they chose to try apartment life.

Notes

1   See Catharine Beecher, *Treatise on Domestic Economy*, New York: J. B. Ford, 1869, for ante-bellum fears of social risk in encounters with strangers. Karen Halttunen, *Confidence Men and Painted Women*, New Haven, Conn.: Yale University Press, 1982, explores the continuing history of Americans' suspicions of strangers through the 1870s.

2   These buildings also signify the social acceptability of apartments, evidenced by the fact that many of their occupants were listed in *Phillips' Elite Directory* in the 1870s and 1880s. Phillips listed twenty-six "visitable" Albany tenants in the 1879 directory, including one woman with her own flat, a "Mrs."; in 1880–81 the directory listed two "Drs." at 21 East Twenty-first St., and the following year, four; Mr. and Mrs. Calvert Vaux were included among the residents of the Stuyvesant in 1886–87.

3   [...] Plans were published for Hunt's Stuyvesant Apartments in Montgomery Schuyler, *American Architecture and Other Writings*, 2 vols., Willian Jordy and Ralph Coe (eds), Cambridge, Mass.: Harvard University Press, Belknap Press, 1961, p. 519 (showing a parlor and a library as the front rooms), and in Andrew Alpern, *Apartments for the Affluent: A Historical Survey of Buildings in New York*, New York: Martin Brown, 1877, p. 12 (showing a parlor and a chamber as the front rooms). Plans for the Albany were published in *AABN* 1, December 23, 1876, following p. 412. Rental units were advertised in the *New York Times*, April 20, 1879, 11–12, where it was described as an elevator building (meaning dumbwaiter?). Babcock filed plans for the Albany's site originally as NBD, 1874, Plan no. 99, for ten third-class French-flat buildings estimated at $35,000, each with a store on the ground floor.

4   [Lewis Leeds], "Parisian Flats", *Appleton's Journal*, vol. 6, 1871, 562.

5   The Albany in London, where Lord Byron had rented rooms after the building was converted to flats in 1804, was described by Sydney Perks, *Residential Flats of All Classes, Including Artisans' Dwellings*, London: B. T. Batsford, 1905, pp. 18–20; illus. p. 19; New York's Albany building was described in *AABN* 1, December 23, 1876, 413.

6   The owner was Oswald Ottendorfer; the architect, William Schickel; the site was 50 by 150 feet. See "The Bella Apartment House", *Real Estate Record and Builders' Guide*, 21, March 23, 1878, 243.

7   Family data from federal census, 1880.

The social meanings of housing, 1800–1840

Elizabeth Blackmar (1989)

The "public" home

No institution in nineteenth-century America received more literary attention than the home. So many sermons, speeches, toasts, songs, novels, and articles extolled its virtues and satisfactions that the cultural value of home life seems self-evident. The home was the site of a loving family circle, of simple pleasures and intimacies, of cooperation and mutual trust. As in literary constructions of other ideal places – the wilderness, the country – the concrete referent, a physical site, its people, labors, and conflicts, often disappeared into abstract qualities. Housing's literary and ideological removal from the market and the "public sphere" underscored male privilege and denied class privilege by naturalizing gender prescriptions into a psychological landscape: men who braved the wilds of the marketplace could return to the safety and comforts of a hearth tended by women, be it in a hut, a log cabin, or a palace. For rich and poor, women and men, the home that sheltered the heart represented the possibility of human relations unqualified by a price.[1]

We in the twentieth century have inherited this elusive concept of the home as an emotional refuge that transcends specific conditions and relations of housing. And because the home is a place that exists primarily in imagination or in memory, because it represents such a depth of emotional attachment or longing, we tend to accept its inherently personal or private nature. But real homes have always had to exist in physical spaces, those spaces have been socially constructed, and they have changed their forms, uses, and meanings over time. Whatever the depth of psychological needs individuals brought to the construction of home life in antebellum New York City, they organized their housing to serve a wide range of social activities that differed from those of earlier generations and varied according to material means. In order to consider how particular cultural values and expectations shaped housing as a new social institution, we must move beyond its characterization as a "private sphere" and explore the publicity of new housing practices.

Dwellings and tenant houses evolved out of an earlier housing institution that, though private property, had not assumed the ideological attributes of a separate private sphere. Eighteenth-century integrated houses did not operate on a principle of exclusivity; sheltering trades or business alongside housework, they accommodated the traffic of customers and business associates as well as neighbors and kin. New Yorkers had ritually affirmed their "open houses" through the custom of New Year's visits. On January first, men and younger family members visited the houses of relatives and neighbors to wish the residents a prosperous new year; women stayed home to serve buffets of traditional liquors and sweets to members of the "community" who called to pay their respects. Nor were "private economical relations" opposed to public obligations: household heads' accountability for their dependents and the duties of public service attached housing to the civic order. And though family – and specifically conjugal – relations suggest personal privacy within houses, even domestic intimacy was not entirely free from exposure or publicity in a culture that sought to enforce a particular code of sexual morality and proscribed, for example, miscegenation and "unnatural" sexual acts as transgressions of social order.[2]

The only thing clearly private about eighteenth-century housing was proprietors' exclusive rights to the value of household resources and dependents' labor. The Bill of Rights, by protecting citizens' houses along with their persons, papers, and effects from unreasonable searches and seizures and by proscribing the quartering of soldiers, linked these property rights with political rights. But boundaries drawn between public and private with respect to state power and personal political rights did not construct spatial boundaries of social use or obligation. Rather, new boundaries were culturally constructed through custom, ritual, and prescription.

Even with the demise of trade uses, housing remained an intensely social, highly visible institution. Their rhetorical opposition notwithstanding, public and private "spheres" did not operate as either spatial or social polarities. In the eyes of propertied New Yorkers, respectable public and private spaces constructed one another through *continuities* of social traffic, activity, and conduct which established and maintained circles of obligation and trust beyond the family. The cultural definition of respectable housing opposed itself less to a "public sphere" than to perceptions of disreputable public and private continuities within tenant housing and neighborhoods.

Through its use for entertainment, meetings, religious life, and the marriage market, the dwelling stood at the center of circles of selective socializing that shaped public and private associational life into a class culture. A respectable home life suggested a person's capacity to enter into and to meet obligations within the community. In an era when New Yorkers were only beginning to establish financial institutions, they used kin networks, business associates, and acquaintances to certify reputation, and through reputation to gain access to property and credit. Propertied New Yorkers established their social standing and claims through rituals that affirmed their reciprocal obligations.

Unlike the fixed contractual relations of a cash bargain or a dated loan, the reciprocity enacted through home hospitality laid the ground for ongoing social exchanges and cooperation. In this respect, bourgeois New Yorkers did seek to distinguish the social world that moved through their homes from the anonymous "public" market and to store up social credit that could withstand sudden turns of fortune.

The dwelling's value as a social institution that organized acquaintanceship and certified public character emerged in contradistinction to the perceived limitations and dangers of alternative housing forms. In contrast to the carefully regulated social traffic of home hospitality, boarding and tenant houses appeared socially promiscuous, nonselective, and immediately vulnerable to market determinations of personal worth. [...] Tenant housing relations, in contrast, [were] perceived as imposing no social accountability for moral transgressions.

In the eyes of genteel New Yorkers, the "liberty" of boarding especially represented a condition of social immaturity that rejected the principles of family duty and selective obligation. The cultural characteristics attributed to unmarried boarders – youth, transience, freedom from family ties and long-term commitments – became all the more problematic in multifamily tenant housing. Viewed from a distance, the sharing of domestic space seemed to break down any one household's powers to define and order its relations with other households. What respectable New Yorkers overlooked, of course, were wage-earning tenants' own rituals and networks of obligation and sociability, often established through the very neighborhood institutions that most threatened the emerging bourgeois cultural definition of "proper" home life. [...]

In embracing "modern style" dwellings that differentiated formal "front" and family "back" parlors and featured dining rooms, prosperous New Yorkers expressed their perceptions of the necessity of public entertainment as much as a new impulse toward family privacy. If the level of investment in furniture and decoration is any indication of cultural priorities, a family's comfort in the "private" space of its back parlor mattered less than the accommodation of visitors. The city's social élite established the importance of dwellings as social institutions most clearly through the exchange of dinners, teas, receptions, and formal visits that rendered the new domestic standards of an emergent bourgeois class visible to itself. [...]

Propertied men used home hospitality to affirm among themselves the continuities of public and private responsibilities, values, and manners. Members of benevolent and political organizations generally assembled at such public sites as Tammany Hall, the New York Institution (the converted almshouse on Chambers Street), hotels, and taverns, but the formal and informal committees that managed these associations were as likely to meet in one another's parlors. [...]

If socializing within dwellings permitted propertied men to affirm a sense of mutual obligation and display qualities of magnanimity and character that redounded to their business and civic credit, women had a greater stake in constructing interlocking codes of public and private respectability. Only as the modern dwelling was understood to be a cultural necessity could women secure their claims on men for the improvement of housing as their workplace. As men used dwellings to form and confirm their business and civic networks, women defined the value of home life in relation to another social institution, the church. [...]

Beyond élite circles, much of the home's emerging cultural authority derived from perceptions that new codes of respectability revived, enacted, and recast precepts of family duty, Protestant piety, and republican virtue. But ... New Yorkers of different classes negotiated the meanings of "private" home life in relation to different arenas and forms of public interaction.

The conditions of housekeeping, for example, structured different kinds of public and private continuities for bourgeois and working-class women's activities. On the city's wealthiest clearly bounded residential blocks, town houses pulled back from the street and servants frequently acted as household agents to mediate relations with the neighborhood by performing errands and screening people who came to the door. The conceptual categories that defined the home as a private sphere (while incorporating church, charity, visiting, shopping, entertainment, *and* supervision of waged labor) drew a veil around bourgeois women's housework. The ability to assume that veil "in public" through particular styles of street dress and manners implicitly testified to "private" conditions of home life.

For most New Yorkers in tenant neighborhoods, there was a growing disjuncture between such codes and the conditions of housing, the physical environment in which wives, mothers, landladies, and servants secured household maintenance. The grounds of domestic work space in trade and tenant neighborhoods extended from the house and yard to the street and markets. Tenant women's domestic skills at bargaining for both goods and credit required personal familiarity with the neighborhood's social and economic resources and the "character" of particular shopkeepers and peddlers. Tenant women's housekeeping and socializing activities were thus more readily interchangeable.[3] [...]

In other contexts, the cultural concept of the private home assumed a different meaning. In the city's mixed-trade neighborhoods, the households of small masters and shopkeepers and wage-earning boarders and tenants (situated amid taverns, workshops, and groceries) maintained a sometimes uneasy coexistence as they negotiated the continuities and boundaries of private and public conduct. The "comfortable subsistence" that was replacing trade proprietorship as a marker of male maturity introduced new points of reference in establishing social accountability. The home's "private", "moral" character contrasted with more "public" housing arrangements, particularly boardinghouses, which in their alliance with commercial institutions threatened the traditional authority of household (and trade) hierarchies in maintaining social order.

Although households that took boarders were arrayed along the city's economic ladder, boarding houses had customarily been identified with transience and youth. Already suffering censure from their association with sailors and wharf-district epidemics, boardinghouses became a dominant housing form within the city's mechanic neighborhoods in the early decades of the nineteenth century. Boarding solved the problems of domestic maintenance for many young single men (and, to a far lesser extent, women) by liberating them from its labor. Boardinghouses frequently accommodated workers of the same trade or nationality, and meals served as an occasion for socializing; but the boardinghouse was less a center of social obligation to many residents than the place for meals and sleep within a daily circuit that included workshop and corner tavern. [...]

Rapidly expanding numbers of young boarding wage earners were not accountable to employers or parents – or to their boardinghouse landlords – for their public conduct. Their popular amusements – gambling, drinking, cockfights, boxing, bear baiting, fire fighting, and the boisterousness that accompanied these activities – were not new. What was distinctively new was the concentration of young men between the ages of fourteen and twenty-five who had the personal "liberty" to engage in these recreational pursuits.[4]

Through the early decades of the century evangelical artisan householders in the city's mechanic wards (Wards 5, 6, 7, 10, and 14) joined more influential citizens in repeatedly appealing to the Common Council to control young men's rowdiness and disrespect, particularly on Sundays, when churchgoing, the promenade, and labor's day of rest brought New Yorkers together onto the streets ...

Artisan householders who may not have identified with bourgeois codes of respectability nonetheless sought to preserve their own moral standards (and particularly their religious values) within their neighborhoods. [...]

The tensions between those shopkeepers and artisans who upheld the new codes of public propriety and those who ignored them reveal competing economic interests as well as moral values. Proprietors who sold "home" services as well as shelter to thousands of boarders and tenants depended on young wage earners' spending for their own livelihoods. By 1827, for example, more than three thousand licensed grocers and tavernkeepers provided the city's journeymen and laborers not merely with drink and food but also with heat and amusements lacking in their domestic accommodations.

Notes

1   For the shifting literary construction of ideal places, see Raymond Williams, *The Country and the City*, Oxford, Engl. and New York: Oxford University Press, 1973. I find Nina Baym, *Woman's Fiction: A Guide to Novels by and about Women in America, 1820–1870*, Ithaca: Cornell University Press, 1978, a particularly useful reading of the literature of domesticity. See also Ann Douglas, *The Feminization of American Culture*, New York: Knopf, 1977, and Karen Halttunen, *Confidence Men and Painted Ladies: A Study of Middle-Class Culture in America, 1830–1870*, New Haven, Conn.: Yale University Press, 1982.

2   Pintard recalled New York City's "boisterous" New Year's visiting in the 1760s, with a "dram at every house". To "keep up acquaintance with kindred branches", children "were universally sent to visit the family relations". *Letters of John Pintard*, 2: 382 (Dec. 27, 1827). Paul Gilje describes colonial New Yorkers' tolerance of plebeian "frolics" on New Year's in *The Road to Mobocracy: Popular Disorder in New York City, 1763–1834*, Chapel Hill: University of North Carolina Press, 1987, pp. 21–2, 252. For regulation of sexual mores, see John D'Emilio and Estelle Freeman, *Intimate Matters: A History of Sexuality in America*, New York: Harper and Row, 1988, pp. 30–2, 34–8.

3   Christine Stansell, *City of Women: Sex and Class in New York, 1789–1860*, New York: Knopf, 1986, pp. 41–62, gives a vivid portrait of antebellum tenant neighborhood life. See also Jeanne Boydston, "To Earn Her Daily Bread: Antebellum Housework and Working-class Subsistence", *Radical History Review* 35, 1985; and Carol Groneman, "'She Earns as a Child; She Pays as a Man': Women Workers in a Mid-nineteenth-century New York Community", in Milton Cantor and Bruce Laurie (eds) *Class, Sex, and the Woman Worker*, Westport, Conn.: Greenwood, 1977, pp. 83–100.

4   See, for example, *MCC, 1784–1831*, 3:101, August 5, 1802, 4:71, August 26, 1805. On the male youth in the city, see Diane Lindstrom, "The Economy of Antebellum New York City", paper presented to the Social Science Research Council, New York, November 1983, table 7, p. 24. On journeymen's popular culture, see Sean Wilentz, *Chants Democratic: New York City and the Rise of the American Working Class*, Oxford, Engl. and New York: Oxford University Press, 1984, pp. 52–6; on hours, Howard Rock, *Artisans of the New Republic*, New York: New York University Press, 1979, pp. 250–2.

YMCAs and other organization boarding houses

Paul Groth (1994)

As rooming houses and their residents proliferated downtown, religious and other phil-anthropic leaders worked to bring back old-fashioned boarding houses at a larger scale and with more centralized administration. Providing vigilant supervision of the tenants and offering some sort of group parlor life (while at the same time prohibiting card playing and drinking) were seen by reformers – overwhelmingly Protestants – as minimal replacements for the safeguards and respectability of a private family house. Thousands of downtown residents seemingly agreed with these social and architectural guarantees of respectability (at least for short periods) as organization boarding houses were built in great numbers and were almost always full.

The Young Men's Christian Association and the Young Women's Christian Associa-tion, transplanted from England to the United States in 1851 and 1866, respectively, pioneered in providing inexpensive, morally conservative homes for city residents who otherwise might have lived in a rooming house [*Fig. 16*].[1] Historically, because of their sharp disadvantage in salaries, women relied more on institutionally subsidized rooms than did men. Although the founders of women's boarding institutions stereotyped women living apart from families as helpless and incapable of managing their own lives, both men and women knew the advantages of Ys and other subsidized rooming houses: they were generally clean, dependable, respectable, and cheap. The combined room and food costs were often less than just the price of a room at a commercial rooming house.[2]

Especially between 1890 and 1915, other charitable boarding house organizations joined the movement. These homes were often sponsored according to ethnicity, race, or religion, since not all Ys accepted everyone. In 1915, New York City had fifty-four orga-nized, nonprofit lodgings for women; Chicago had thirty-four, not counting homes run for special groups such as immigrants or unmarried mothers. From 11 to 320 women lived in each home; managers wrote that 90 to 125 tenants constituted the optimal client group.[3] The YMCA opened its doors more widely in 1925, offering membership to Jews, Catholics, and people with no religious affiliation. Each city made its own rules regarding integration of black and white members; through World War II, the YMCA typically built separate facilities for blacks and Asians. More fully integrated chapters became more common in the 1940s and particularly after the beginning of national desegregation in 1954. In some chapters, blacks could stay as transient guests but not as permanent resi-dents.[4]

Ys and other organization boarding houses often occupied America's most specialized boarding house buildings. The eight-story, 211-room Evangeline Residence built by the Salvation Army in San Francisco opened in 1923 on a site just a block from the new Civic Center. The T-shaped plan imitated the best middle-income apartment buildings and hotels. The Evangeline, however, had very small rooms, no private baths, and very plain and economical interior construction. Its managers compensated for these with a sun deck on the roof and several social spaces in addition to the lobby, dining room, and reading room. […]

For many people, rooming houses were acceptable because of their similarities with college dormitories, fraternities and sororities, retirement homes of fraternal, ethnic, and benevolent societies (such as the Oddfellows' retirement homes), and orphanages, together with the monasteries and convents of religious orders. Institutions like these have been and still are providers of thousands of subsidized housing units in every large American city.[5] [...]

The vast majority of single-room residents in turn-of-the-century rooming houses were young men and women recently arrived in the city. In 1906, the sociologist Albert Wolfe characterized the rooming house residents of Boston's South End as a "great army of clerks, salesmen, bookkeepers, shop girls, stenographers, dressmakers, milliners, barbers, restaurant-keepers, black railroad porters and stewards, policemen, nurses, ... journeymen carpenters, painters, machinists, and electricians".[6] In more clinical terms, Wolfe had found an army of low-paid but skilled white-collar and blue-collar workers, rarely immigrants but usually American-born of northern European and most often Protestant stock.

These city recruits struggled with their uncertain standing: they often held strong family values but were living outside a family; they were capable of being well dressed but only in one or two outfits; they aspired to material comfort but had access to very little of it; they aimed for economic security but lived with uncertain incomes. Typically, work had lured rooming house residents to the city, and it was the realities of their work that kept them in an economic and residential limbo. Rooming house women and men shared similar employments but had sharply differing incomes. The women's situation was the more acute. Women represented a third to a half of the people in American rooming houses.[7] In Wolfe's 1906 study, about one-sixth of the women were wives with no employment outside their homes. Single elderly women, or as Wolfe put it, "old ladies, most of them living on modest incomes, or supported by some relative or by charity", made up 8 percent of the women in his study. Stenographers, waitresses, dressmakers, saleswomen, and clerks roughly tied as the most common occupations among the working women, with 6 to 8 percent apiece.[8] ... In San Francisco, women's average pay in similar jobs in 1920 was still typically too low for women to live alone in a rooming house as men did ... Thirty to 60 percent of San Francisco's working women could not afford a room alone, especially before 1920, and they doubled up with another woman to share the rent. The only lower pay rates in San Francisco were those of Chinese laborers and children.[9]

After 1920, new industrial and commercial jobs and the sudden rise of entry-level white-collar work helped more women migrate to the city and live outside a family. [...]

In many cities skilled workers were common in rooming houses. In San Francisco, for instance, a fourth of the city's carpenters in 1900 were boarders or lodgers, most of them living downtown. [...]

For both men and women in rooming houses, frequent moves were common. Half the roomers in a city moved within a typical year, usually from one rooming house to another. Frequent moves were also part of the work life for machinists, cigar workers, and people in construction trades. Layoffs were another major factor in this rooming house mobility. [...]

Nineteenth-century rooming house residents also sorted themselves by ethnic, racial, and occupational considerations. Some housekeepers preferred Catholic or Protestant tenants, or mechanics over clerks. These distinctions became less common after 1900. When blacks moved into Chicago rooming house areas, the population pyramids and age-sex formations did not change, although racial discrimination meant that crowding was far worse inside black rooming houses.[10]

Not everyone in rooming houses was single or living alone. Couples, either married or unmarried, ranged from 7 to 38 percent of the roomers. White couples often rented two-room suites. Crowded conditions in black rooming houses largely precluded more than one room. After World War II, some rooming house districts had a higher proportion of couples (again, both married and unmarried) than those neighborhoods had seen in the 1920s. The life-style remained similar to the earlier period. [...]

The low prices in rooming houses kept an independent low-paid work force available to downtown industries and also helped young single Americans forge personal independence and a subculture separate from the city's family zones. The rooming house district became notable for both of these roles ...

In addition to many rooms at low prices, rooming house residents needed at least two other features: easy access to work places, and a surrounding neighborhood with mixed land use including stores, bars, restaurants, and clubs for association with friends and commercial recreation. Few outsiders questioned the first of these two needs. However, the retail mixtures of rooming house neighborhoods caused concern within the dominant culture. They also reinforced the liminal status of rooming house residents ...

Work places and rooming houses were inextricably linked. Especially during boom times, employers needed a ready supply of help on short notice, and workers could afford only so much time and money for their journey to work. Given the erratic availability of employment, they also needed to be within easy reach of many different companies. Roomers rarely owned cars. Thus, rooming house areas were usually within half a mile of varied jobs. For the greatest number of rooming house residents, work was downtown in the retail shopping district in the office core, or in a warehouse, shipping, or manufacturing zone very close to the center of the city. Higher-paid white-collar workers could afford to commute on streetcars to an outlying rooming house area. Streetcar transfer locations like these were exceptions to the dominant pattern, but made up between 5 and 10 percent of San Francisco's rooming house supply by 1930.[11]

Rooming houses might have seemed unnecessary to downtown, but they were just as essential for urban economic growth as the family tenements that stretched next to factories and just as basic as the new downtown skyscrapers and loft buildings. At the turn of the century, urban Americans knew at least two different types of rooming house areas: districts of old-house rooming houses, and newer purpose-built rooming house districts.

Notes

1 See Mary S. Sims, *The Natural History of a Social Institution: The Young Women's Christian Association*, New York: Woman's Press, 1936; and Sherwood Eddy, *A Century with Youth: A History of the YMCA from 1844–1944*, New York: Association Press, 1944.

2 On independence sought by women, see Joanne J. Meyerowitz, "Holding Their Own: Working Women Apart from Family in Chicago", Dissertation, Stanford University, 1983, pp. 77, 84–90, 120. In the 1920s in New York, the cheapest women's residence clubs charged from $3 to $8 a week without board. Other institutional residence clubs typically charged from $7 to $12 for combined board and room. In contrast, the YWCAs charged 50 cents a day for meals with a dormitory bed or cubicle, up to $1.50 a day for rooms (with meals); James Ford, *Slums and Housing: History, Conditions, Policy with Special Reference to New York City*, Cambridge: Harvard University Press, 1936, p. 755. Girls Housing Council in San Francisco, "Where Is Home? A Study of the Conditions for Non-family Girls in San Francisco", Mimeographed report [in the San Francisco State University library], 1927, pp. 14, 18–20, reports similar prices in San Francisco. See also Essie Davidson, "Organized Boarding Homes for Self-Supporting Women in Chicago", Dissertation, University of Chicago, 1914.

3 U.S. Bureau of Labor, "Boarding Homes, Aids for Working Women", 31–57; Fergusson, "Boarding Houses and Clubs for Working Women", in *Working Women in Large Cities*,

Report of the Commissioner of Labor, Washington, D.C.: U.S. Government Printing Office, 1888, pp. 141–95; Arnold M. Rose, "Interest in the Living Arrangements of the Urban Unattached", *American Journal of Sociological Review* 12, 1947, 488–9; Girls Housing Council, "Where Is Home?", p. 14; Meyerowitz, "Holding Their Own", pp. 78–82, 121–2.

4   Clifford Drury, *San Francisco's YMCA: 100 Years by the Golden Gate, 1853–1953*, Glendale, Calif.: Arthur Clark, 1963, p. 233; on integration of blacks, J. Howell Atwood, *The Racial Factor in YMCAs*, New York: Association Press, 1946, pp. 48–51, and National Council of YMCAs, *Negro Youth in City YMCAs*, New York: Association Press, 1944, pp. 5–9, 59.

5   In the 1920s, ethnic homes for the elderly charged a monthly fee of about $40 or a lifetime entrance fee of about $2,000; University of California, the Heller Committee for Research in Social Economics, *The Dependent Aged in San Francisco*, University of California Publications in Economics, vol. 5, no. 1, Berkeley: University of California Press, 1928, pp. 26–9, 83–6. Hospitals, institutional residences for the handicapped, tuberculosis sanatoriums, prisons, and army bases add other urban dwellings that the census counts as "institutional group quarters"; few of these met rooming house standards and typically substituted for lodging house quarters.

6   Albert Benedict Wolfe, *The Lodging House Problem in Boston*, Boston: Houghton Mifflin, 1906, pp. 1, 5–6; Wolfe reported that the roomers made up 14 percent of the population of Boston's inner wards. See also Mark Peel, "On the Margins: Lodgers and Boarders in Boston, 1860–1900", *Journal of American History* 72, no. 4, 1986, 817; and Harvey Warren Zorbaugh, "The Dweller in Furnished Rooms", *Papers and Proceedings of the American Sociological Society* 20, 1925, 84–5.

7   Boston in 1906 had a 1:1 ratio of men to women; Wolfe, *The Lodging House Problem*, p. 82. Data from Chicago in 1929 reported 52 percent men, 10 percent single women, and 38 percent couples; Harvey Warren Zorbaugh, *Gold Coast and Slum: A Sociological Study of Chicago's Near North Side*, Chicago: University of Chicago Press, 1929, p. 71. Philadelphia in 1912 had similar ratios; Franklin K. Fretz, "The Furnished Room Problem in Philadelphia", Dissertation, University of Pennsylvania, 1912, p. 50. A Los Angeles study in 1949 reported about one-third of the 600 interviewees were women; Lillian Cohen, "Los Angeles Rooming-house Kaleidoscope", *American Sociological Review* 16, no. 3, 1951.

8   Wolfe, *The Lodging House Problem*, p. 94. Wives with no outside employment made up 16.5 percent of the sample of 200 women. Stenographers and waitresses made up 8 percent each; dressmakers, 7.5; saleswomen and nurses, 6.0 each; and clerks, 5.0.

9   Employment figures from U.S. Census, *Fourteenth Census of the U.S. Vol. 4, Population 1920*, 222–38; wages from California State Bureau of Labor Statistics, *20th Biennial Report, 1919–1920*, Sacramento, State Printing Office, 1920, p. 228; on vying with Chinese, see Jules Everett Tygiel, "Workingmen in San Francisco: 1880–1901", Dissertation, University of California, Los Angeles, 1977, p. 23; on few living in commercial housing, Girls Housing Council, "Where Is Home?", pp. 5–6, 37. In the Housing Council's sample, a third of the single women lived away from their families, but only one out of twelve girls lived in a commercial rooming house or hotel. The rest were boarders or lodgers.

10 On ethnic and religious distinctions, see Peel, "On the Margins", 816; Robert F. Harney, "Boarding and Belonging: Thoughts on Sojourner Institutions", *Urban History Review* 78, 1978, 8–37. On blacks, see Charles Hoch and Robert A. Slayton, *New Homeless and Old: Community and the Skid Row Hotel*, Philadelphia: Temple University Press, 1989, pp. 24–5; Norman S. Hayner, *Hotel Life*, Chapel Hill: University of North Carolina Press, 1936, p. 86; and R. D. McKenzie, *The Metropolitan Community*, New York: McGraw-Hill, 1933, pp. 243–7.

11 On the half-mile figure for San Francisco, see Neil Shumsky, "Tar Flat and Nob Hill: A Social History of San Francisco in the 1870s", Dissertation, University of California, Berkeley, 1972, p. 138. On journey to work issues for women, see Meyerowitz, "Holding Their Own", pp. 111–13. For descriptions of pedestrian job searches, see Dorothy Richardson, *The Long Day: The Story of a New York Working Girl* (first published in 1905), in William O'Neill (ed.) *Women at Work*, Chicago: Quadrangle Books, 1972, and Bessie and Marie Van Vorst, *The Woman Who Toils; Being the Experiences of Two Ladies as Factory Girls*, New York: Doubleday, Page and Company, 1903.

Inside the dwelling
The Viennese *Wohnung*

Donald J. Olsen (1986)

"We Viennese very seldom feel truly at home in our rented flats", admitted the *Allgemeine Bauzeitung* in 1860. "The *chez soi* of the French, the *at home* of the English express a comfort unknown to us".[1] Describing the splendid buildings of the Ringstrasse to the Congress of French Architects in 1884, Paul Sédille commented that "behind their rich decoration, there is very little. Plan hardly exists. There are none of those niceties of distribution which render life so easy and comfortable in our Parisian interiors". Jacob von Falke found Viennese flats, "in which kitchen, sitting room, and bedroom all lie in a row and one cannot reach the last room without passing through all the others: an unheard-of situation in England!" a matter for general reproach [*Figs. 17, 18*].[2]

The Viennese middle classes, Thomas Blashill told the Royal Institute of British Architects (RIBA) in 1888, "pay nearly twice as much in rent and other outgoings for very scanty accommodation on the upper floors of these grand houses, as would be paid here for a separate house and garden". Victor Tissot gave a French audience a similarly bleak picture. In the suburbs family accommodation was badly furnished and congested, with rents a third higher than in Paris. Subletting was commonly practiced, and in working-class areas houses generally resembled *hôtels garnis*.[3]

According to the census of 1910, 75 percent of the dwellings in Vienna consisted of *Kleinstwohnungen*, comprising a single living room (*Zimmer*) with in most cases a tiny kitchen annex, and in some a smaller sleeping chamber (*Kabinett*) attached.[4] Overcrowding affected a large proportion of the middle as well as the lower classes. Under such circumstances analyses of the room arrangements of most Viennese flats tell us much about what they had to endure, but little about what they would have wished for themselves. If we can say with some confidence that Notting Hill and St. John's Wood and Highgate reflected the chosen styles of living and scale of values of their residents, we cannot do the same even for the relatively prosperous Mariahilf or Josefstadt. Here, all too often, the domestic environment imposed rather than reflected a life-style.

More revealing are the *Grosswohnungen* of the Ringstrasse and the substantial villas of Türkenschanz and Hohe Warte. Tissot believed that the well-off bourgeoisie lived at least as well as in Paris.[5] But their definition of comfort, the qualities they particularly prized in a flat, were different. A French critic, writing in 1873, thought the Viennese building owner cared more than his Parisian equivalent about an impressive façade, less about internal arrangements. "If he finds the rooms dark, the *dégagements* inconvenient, the smaller rooms badly ventilated, he is convinced that things couldn't have been otherwise and puts up with them, especially if his façade does him honor".[6] Actually the Viennese paid great attention to the details of internal distribution but approached them as they did the details of external decoration, seeking representation rather than comfort.

At one extreme petit bourgeois families sacrificed domestic comforts in order to maintain an appearance of gentility. Tissot described one such family in which the mother, the three daughters, and the two sons slept in the same room, with the beds pressed tightly one against the other. By such an expedient they were able to make one of their rooms a *salon*, containing a small set of shelves displaying busts of Schiller and Goethe and volumes of their poetry, and where they could receive guests.[7] In Vienna bourgeois families made the kind of sacrifice of space that working-class families in England made to have a Sunday-best parlor, "not to be used for relaxation", but "as a more controlled and formal social environment".[8]

At the other extreme were the *Herrschaftswohnungen*, occupying the entire first floor of buildings in the Ringstrasse and City. Here, too, space was devoted to public rooms at the expense of private family quarters. *Sacrifice* may not be quite the word, but the largest Ringstrasse flats were better suited for giving smashing evening parties than for a life of personal withdrawal or domestic intimacy.

The London suburban villa was trying to be a miniature country house, while the Parisian luxury flat aspired toward the condition of an *hôtel privé*. By contrast the Ringstrasse *Mietpalast* was just that: an imitation palace in which bourgeois householders could pretend to be old aristocracy. Among aristocracy and bourgeoisie alike, vestiges of an older way of living persisted well into the nineteenth century. As for the working classes, severe economic constraints kept them, until well into the twentieth century, from participating even in the moderate degree of separation and withdrawal possible for the English working classes.

Yet to Ferdinand Fellner in 1860 the contrast with eighteenth-century domestic habits was already great. Viennese burghers and manufacturers no longer ate in the kitchen at the same table with their workers, but withdrew to a private dining room. Their children would no longer share a bed under the roof with the apprentices.[9] Social distance was reshaping domestic life…

It was only gradually and hesitantly that even the grandest apartments in the City and Ringstrasse acquired corridors. Although Ludwig von Förster boasted that the principal rooms in the Renngasse flat he designed in 1847 for Adolph Freiherr von Pereira-Arnstein had facilities for "the greatest possible *dégagement*", many of its principal reception rooms were accessible only by passing through other rooms.[10] The banker and wholesale merchant Ludwig Ladenberg specified in 1863 that in the owner's flat in his building at Opernring 17 "one be able to go from the anteroom into the breakfast room and the bedroom, as well as from the kitchen, without having to go through the dining room in order to reach the living rooms".[11] Heinrich von Ferstel was careful to provide in his buildings a corridor paralleling the *enfilade* (or *Zimmerflucht*) of reception rooms.[12]

Corridors, however, were conspicuously absent from the plans of the house of the Count von Hoyos-Sprinzenstein in the Kärntner Ring, later part of the Hotel Bristol, and also designed by Förster. That this was not unusual is suggested by the comment of the *Allgemeine Bauzeitung* that "the inner arrangement of the building … is appropriate to the requirements and wishes of the noble family and the flats are set up according to the ordinary practice in Vienna".[13]

In the *Herrschaftswohnungen* of the 1870s there was a tendency to expand the anteroom by means of a corridor along the central wall, in contrast to the sixties when thoroughfare rooms were still the rule. Yet an extensive development of middle-class housing by Prince Schwarzenberg in Wieden in the 1880s was "based on the older system of Viennese planning, the rooms being without distinct corridor communication". It was noteworthy that in the *Sühnhaus*, in the Schottenring, "there are only two principal rooms on the whole floor which are not entered directly from the vestibule or corridor".[14]

With or without corridors, all the flats of any social pretension strove to maximize the size, number, and splendor of reception rooms, arranged in a row along the main façade. Vast apartments, lavishly supplied with suites of public rooms, often offered no more than two bedrooms, one each for husband and wife. Where, one can only ask, were the children expected to sleep?[15] In smaller establishments, temporary beds might be set up in corridors, or revealed in curtained alcoves, but the seeming disregard for such practical needs as sleeping accommodation in flats of imposing size and splendor stands in striking contrast to the English obsession with separate bedrooms. [...]

Middle- and upper-class flats became less splendid and more comfortable as 1914 approached. The formal antechamber became the convenient corridor, space that would once have been devoted to seldom used reception rooms was now given up to daily family purposes, bathrooms became standard fixtures in middle-sized as well as large flats.[16] Yet although running water, gas lighting, central heating, and fixed baths were introduced into favored buildings about as early as in Paris, they reached a small proportion of the residential buildings. As late as 1910, no more than seven percent of all dwellings had bathrooms, and only twenty-two percent private water closets. Kitchens in all but luxury flats rarely had their own water supply, but depended on a *Basena* in the public corridor. Of a sample survey of twenty thousand dwellings made in 1919, sixty one percent lacked both gas and electricity.[17]

Even so, F. Leonhard, after an extended examination of the blocks of flats erected, mostly in the City and Ringstrasse zone, over the previous forty years, concluded in 1905 that their tenants had every reason to be satisfied. Room dimensions were larger than in London, Paris, and Berlin, and the dark and narrow corridors of flats in other cities were absent in the best Viennese buildings. He praised the superior standards of building construction in Vienna, where thicker walls provided better protection against both sudden changes in temperature and outside noise. There was, admittedly, frequent incongruity between exterior display and interior reality: "The Viennese loves ... to adorn his house, often indeed more than is its due".[18] It is hard in retrospect to reproach the Viennese of past generations for such harmless vanity, considering the pleasure the exuberant domestic façades have given generations of pedestrians.

Notes

1   *Literatur- und Anzeigeblatt für das Baufach. Beilage zur allgemeinen Bauzeitung* 6, 1860, 288–93; quoted in Klaus Eggert, *Der Wohnbau der Wiener Ringstrasse im Historismus: 1855–1896*, vol. 7, in Renate Wagner-Rieger (ed.) *Die Wiener Ringstrasse: Bild einer Epoche*, Wiesbaden: Franz Steiner, 1976, pp. 8–9.
2   *Builder* 46, 1884, 940; Jacob von Falke, "Das englische Haus", *Zur Cultur und Kunst*, Vienna, 1878, p. 53.
3   Thomas Blashill, "The Recent Development of Vienna", Royal Institute of British Architects, *Transactions*, vol. 4, 1888, 38. Victor Tissot, *Vienne et la vie viennoise*, 19th edn, Paris: E. Dentu, 1878, pp. 453–4.
4   Charles O. Hardy, *The Housing Program of the City of Vienna*, Washington, D.C.: Brookings Institution, 1934, p. 15.
5   Tissot, *Vienne et la vie viennoise*, p. 455.
6   J.-L. Pascal, in *Revue générale de l'architecture* 30, 1873, col. 208.
7   Tissot, *Vienne et la vie viennoise*, p. 455.
8   M. J. Daunton, *House and Home in the Victorian City*, London: Edward Arnold, 1983, p. 280.
9   Ferdinand Fellner, *Wie soll Wien bauen*, Vienna, 1860, pp. 1–18; quoted in Eggert, *Der Wohnbau der Wiener Ringstrasse in Historismus*, pp. 7–8.
10 *Allgemeine Bauzeitung* 12, 1847, 242.
11 *Allgemeine Bauzeitung* 31, 1866, 341; quoted by Hannes Stekl in Franz Baltzarek et al., *Wirtschaft und Gesellschaft der Wiener Stadterweiterung*, vol. 5 of Renate Wagner-Rieger (ed.) *Die Wiener Ringstrasse: Bild einer Epoche*, Wiesbaden: Franz Steiner, 1975, pp. 328–9.
12 Norbert Wibiral and Renata Mikula, *Heinrich von Ferstel*, vol. 8 (3) of Renate Wagner-Rieger (ed.) *Die Wiener Ringstrasse: Bild einer Epoche*, Weisbaden: Franz Steiner, 1974, p. 154.

13 *Allgemeine Bauzeitung* 29, 1864, 3.
14 Elizabeth Lichtenberger, *Wirtschaftsfunktion und Sozialstruktur der Wiener Ringstrasse*, vol. 6 of Renate Wagner-Rieger (ed.) *Die Wiener Ringstrasse: Bild einer Epoche*, Vienna: Hermann Böhlaus Nachf., 1970, p. 43; Frederick R. Farrow, "The Recent Development of Vienna", Royal Institute of British Architects, *Transactions*, n.s. 4, 1888, 34–5.
15 Lichtenberger, *Wirtschaftsfunktion und Sozialstruktur der Wiener Ringstrasse*, pp. 43–4.
16 Hans Bobek and Elizabeth Lichtenberger, *Wien: Bauliche Gestalt und Entwicklung seit der Mitte des 19. Jahrhunderts*, Graz: Hermann Böhlaus Nachf., 1966, p. 106.
17 Hardy, *The Housing Program of the City of Vienna*, pp. 15–16.
18 F. Leonhard, "Städtische Miethäuser", in Paul Kortz (ed.) *Wien am Anfang des XX. Jahrhunderts*, Vienna: Gerlach & Wiedling, 1905, 2: 425.

Seeing through Paris, 1820–1848

Sharon Marcus (1999)

Why did apartment houses become the dominant architectural elements in the Parisian landscape during the last decades of the Restoration (1814–30) and throughout the July Monarchy (1830–48)? Their popularity owed much to two factors: they provided spatially compact housing in a city with a rapidly increasing population and offered an expanding middle class opportunities for investing in relatively inexpensive and profitable properties. Demography and economics, however, do not sufficiently account for Parisians' adoption of the apartment building as their chief residential form … although London's population also expanded dramatically throughout the nineteenth century, Londoners did not build apartment houses. In order to understand the Parisian enthusiasm for apartment buildings, we need to excavate the cultural beliefs about domestic and urban space embedded in the discourses of Parisian architecture and everyday life. Apartment buildings appealed to Parisians as a material figure of broad social conceptions of private and public life: the containment of social heterogeneity in a unifying framework; the imbrication of the domestic and the urban; and the transparency and fluidity of every component of urban space.

Paris in the first half of the nineteenth century reflected, in intensified form, the extreme social mobility that characterized France in the years following the fall of the old regime. Many of the aspects of urban modernity that marked Second Empire and fin-de-siècle Paris were already in place by the 1820s, including a culture based on commodification, spectacle, and speculation, and a legible urban space easily mapped and navigated by the upwardly mobile.[1] The premium on legible urban space was matched by a desire to decipher the exact social position and moral character of any Parisian in a glance, as a series of urban "physiognomists" claimed the power to do. Within the July Monarchy's capitalist democracy, the desire for transparent space and citizens, whose exteriors would be windows onto their interiors, emphasized reading people in terms of commodities and wealth; by the cut of a man's suit, you could assess his income.[2] Specific as it was to that new regime, however, transparency also had deep roots in French political culture, which from Rousseau through the Revolution had decried obscurity, duplicity, and theatricality as antithetical to democracy.[3]

The historiography of an urban culture and space as open as the society that generated them coexists uneasily, however, with the historiography of nineteenth-century domesticity, which describes a segregated private realm that emerged in the wake of the French Revolution, a realm strictly separated from public spaces and functions. That separation was most evident in political and medical discourses that aligned women with the private space of the home and excluded them from a public sphere of abstract masculine political activity as well as from a set of collective exterior urban spaces (the street, the café, the theater).[4]

Scholarly assumptions about domestic space as a separate sphere have occluded more representative discourses about Paris, discourses so invested in the notion of a legible, transparent urban space conducive to easy circulation and observation that they actively incorporated domestic space into the city and even extended urban mobility to the emblematic figures of the private sphere – women of all classes, and especially the women who lived in the middle-class apartment building. The first section of this chapter studies both apartment-house designs and architectural pattern books to demonstrate how the apartment house embodied the cultural amalgamation of private and public spaces. The next section turns to the vast descriptive literature produced about Paris, particularly during the July Monarchy, and shows how the discourse of urban observation described the apartment building as a typical and integral physical feature of the Parisian landscape and, strikingly, as a figure for the objects and activity of urban observation itself. The apartment building's ability to unify its disparate residents within a single frame mirrored the efforts of urban observers to contain Parisian heterogeneity within a single text; its transparency illustrated the fluid relationship between apartments and the city's exterior spaces, as well as the accessibility of every space in Paris, even domestic space, to urban observers. The strength of the urban observers' commitment to mobility, transparency, and visibility can be measured by their insistence that even married women circulate within the city, and by their deployment of a female figure, the *portière*, to personify the apartment building and the activity of urban observation ...

Architectural discourse and the continuum of street and home

[...] During the Restoration and the July Monarchy, from the 1820s through the 1840s, the characteristic Parisian house took on a new form, that of the modern six- to eight-story apartment building with shops on the ground floor and an imposing entrance supervised by a porter [*Figs. 19, 20*]. In terms of both their form and the ways that their form was perceived, apartments embodied an urban domesticity that aligned them simultaneously with private homes and with public structures such as monuments, cafés, and streets.

The new apartment house represented a shift from earlier architectural articulations of private and public space. On the one hand, nineteenth-century apartment units were more self-contained and hence provided more spatial privacy than eighteenth-century housing for the middle and working classes; on the other hand, the increased size of nineteenth-century buildings, and their incorporation of vestibules, lobbies, and elaborate stairways, meant that these edifices brought more strangers into contact, in more places, than earlier ones had.[5] The apartment house partly owed its unique synthesis of publicity and privacy to its dual architectural sources, the *maisons à allée* and the *hôtels privés*. Most eighteenth-century apartment houses were *maisons à allée*, which lacked vestibules and were entered either through alleys off the street or through ground-floor shops. Internal apartments were formed by blocking off varying sets of rooms according to the needs of individual tenants and often consisted of suites of rooms distributed over several floors;

this arrangement tended to multiply contact with other occupants, since one tenant might have to cross another's room to reach her own.[6]

Nineteenth-century apartment *units* were spatially self-contained and thus offered tenants greater seclusion within an individual apartment, but nineteenth-century apartment *buildings* maintained and even extended the public nature of the *maisons à allée*, since their larger scale (five to six stories) gathered greater numbers of residents together under one roof, while their inclusion of clearly articulated common spaces for entrance and egress formalized interaction among tenants. Like the *maisons à allée*, the new buildings had shops on the ground floor and thus continued to mix commerce and private life, though tradespeople and merchants were more common than artisans and manufacturers in more costly buildings.

The nineteenth-century apartment house did not evolve exclusively from earlier models of communal housing. Apartment house architects also drew on the aristocratic private townhouse, the *hôtel privé*, in their designs for the imposing double doors (*portes cochères*), elaborate vestibules, and porter's lodges that stood between the apartment building and the street ... But significant differences existed between the two building types.[7] The apartment brought public and private rooms into greater proximity with one another than the *hôtel* had. The *hôtel* separated reception rooms such as salons, which were open to strangers and designed for social occasions and display, from the bedrooms, studies, and cabinets intended for retirement and solitude. The apartment not only placed both types of rooms on a single floor but often placed them in direct communication with one another, so that one might enter an apartment's salon by passing through its main bedroom ...

Apartment buildings and *hôtels privés* also differed in their orientation toward their urban surroundings ... The *hôtel* turned its back to the street, since its primary, highly decorated front and its most important rooms (dining room, salon, bedrooms) faced a private garden ... Apartment buildings, by contrast, were situated directly on the street, entered from the street, made to be viewed from and to provide views of the street. Builders constructed apartment buildings with strong front/back axes, aligned façades with the sidewalk, and emphasized the importance of the street front by lavishing better materials and more intricate designs on it. The most sought-after apartments were those closest to the street, and the most prized rooms of an apartment – living room, dining room, and main bedroom – faced the street, while the kitchen, servant's room, and storage rooms faced the courtyard.[8]

Apartment-house design also bore a conceptual similarity to urban street systems. The ordered grid of the apartment-house façade, like that of city streets, worked to abstract individual details into an aggregate public form. Their unity and symmetry gave façades a decorative power of generalization over the particularities of the rooms behind them in a process related to the urban consolidation of heterogeneous individuals into a public. The windows in a building's street façade often matched one another in size, shape, and design, even when the rooms behind them were different sizes or belonged to apartments separated from one another by vertical or horizontal partitions.[9] [...]

Apartment buildings displayed and oriented a collective domesticity that communicated fully with the public street. [...] The space of early nineteenth-century Parisian buildings mingled with the space of streets in concrete, quotidian ways. As prefect of Paris after 1833, Claude Rambuteau installed benches on all the major boulevards, a practice that made the comfort and stillness conventionally associated with the home available on the street; he also increased the number of public urinals on the sidewalks.[10]

Apartment buildings began literally to enter the street when an 1823 ordinance of Louis XVIII allowed façades to project into the street, albeit in very restricted ways, for the first time since 1607. That ordinance also decreed that street widths would determine the height of a building and whether it could have balconies, thus deriving the façade's dimensions and design from those of the street.[11] Houses, like streets, became more rationalized, more subject to surveillance, better lit, and better marked …

By the end of the July Monarchy, the apartment house was the most frequent and consistent element of the urban landscape … Pattern books combined a canonical emphasis on architectural composition and the presentation of every building from three perspectives – cross-section, floor plan, and elevation – with a modern interest in construction techniques and the design of elements such as doors, cornices, and balconies.[12]

Architectural pattern books rarely used terms like "private" or "public" to describe the new residences; indeed, they barely distinguished the apartment building as a unique type at all, suggesting that its relative lack of privacy did not pose a problem for architects or their clients, and that urban homes were not defined in terms of privacy, nor in contradistinction to streets and other exterior spaces. Most architects simply called apartment buildings *maisons*, a general term meaning both "house" and "home", whose use emphasized the apartment building's similarity to other housing types, even more private ones, making the apartment house representative of the house in general … Indeed, the apartment house was so typical of Parisian domestic architecture, and its congruence with the term *maison* so established, that some Parisians perceived the single-family house as lexically indescribable …

Architectural texts linked the public spaces of the street and the private spaces of the residence by consistently associating apartment houses with the urban progress and modernity that twentieth-century historians have attributed only to public spaces such as boulevards and cafés. […] Others similarly associated apartment buildings with the modern qualities of contemporaneity and progress. […]

English observers often criticized Parisian home life for its lack of privacy, not only because they took the single-family house as an architectural standard, but also because they defined domesticity in opposition to the marketplace, and the *maison de rapport* brought economics close to home. French architects, however, did not consider the apartment house's associations either with the street or with urban speculation to disqualify it from a domestic function; they continued to call apartment buildings and units *maisons* or private houses (*maisons particulières*) even after the late 1840s, when financial speculators had begun to build apartments on an almost industrial scale and landlords were commonly depicted as impersonal administrators who rarely lived in the buildings they owned.[13] […]

Architects also placed apartment houses on a continuum with the imperial, royal city of imposing monuments and the modern, bourgeois city of boulevards, boutiques, and cafés.[14] Pattern books praised the ways that apartment houses combined public scale and private character. The apartment loomed larger than any residential building ever had, horizontally as well as vertically, and practices such as making the balconies of separate buildings continuous promoted the monumentality of apartments by emphasizing the mass block formed by their contiguity. The increased use of stone façades, often signed by stonecutters as artists would sign works of art, also contributed to the sense that the apartment building's exterior was, as one architectural historian puts it, "an enormous monumental sculpture facing the street".[15] …

Just as architects saw similarities between the monumental and the residential, between public and private building types, they also promoted designs that emphasized the similarity between a building's exterior, potentially more public face, and its interior, the space conventionally associated with privacy; indeed, architectural historians define Restoration architecture in terms of its "transposition of a building's indoor ornament onto its façade".[16] Authors of pattern books frequently compared apartment buildings to stores, cafés, and theaters and recommended incorporating elements from commercial and civic buildings into apartment-house decor. The stores, cafés, and restaurants that occupied the ground floor of most apartment buildings lent residences a commercial note, while the large sheets of plate glass that began to be incorporated into shops from the 1820s on made the apartment buildings that housed trade more physically open and transparent to the street.

Conversely, because café, restaurant, and shop interiors used the same decorating principles and materials as domestic ones, commercial spaces often resembled apartments, but apartments open to public view and entry. The mirrors commonly placed behind plate-glass store windows reflected pedestrians just as looking glasses on salon walls mirrored people at home. The Café de Paris "retained the appearance of an apartment in the grand style: high ceilings, antique mirrors, magnificent carpets",[17] and Thiollet's 1837 *Nouveau recueil de menuiserie et de décorations intérieures et extérieures* used the same criteria to evaluate stores, arcades, and apartments. Thiollet wrote that a "shop interior" possessed "the true character of a drawing room whose fireplace faces the entryway and whose principal ornaments are mirrors", and he praised the contemporary rapprochement of interiors and exteriors as a modern advance in decorating. [...]

The *tableaux de Paris* and the apartment-house view

Beginning in the 1830s, an unprecedented number of books about Paris not only posited a continuum between the apartment house and the street but also presented the apartment house as an ideal framework for visual observations of the city. The texts that critic Margaret Cohen has identified as "a characteristic nineteenth-century genre for representing the everyday" were known as *tableaux de Paris* and were accompanied in the early 1840s by an important subgenre, the *physiologies*.[18] Authored mostly by professional writers who worked for the popular press and wrote criticism, prose, and plays, the *tableaux* and *physiologies* mapped the new types, places, and trends of contemporary Paris for a reading and viewing public eager to consume images of the city. [...]

Because the *tableaux* and the *physiologies* understood the city as a site in which events unfurled and as a decor within which character emerged, they frequently treated apartments as settings for the various episodes and types they recounted. Unlike architectural pattern books, which by convention eliminated all representations of people from their illustrations, the *tableaux* defined Paris as much by its population of *parisiens* and *parisiennes* as by its physical environment.[19] Apartment houses were seen as privileged settings for Parisians and their plots, as figures for "this big city where misfortune, good fortune, pain and pleasure frequently live under the same roof", and as sites of a narrative available only to the urban initiate, who with the aid of the urban observer would become aware of "entire novels hidden in the walls of ... [a] house".[20] [...]

The writers who represented the city to itself thus not only emphasized apartment houses as elements of the Parisian landscape but also *saw through* the apartment house, treating it as a lens or as a point of view and not simply as an opaque visual object. In the process, they imagined apartment houses to be as transparent as they wanted the city to be. And by depicting the apartment house as though its façades and walls were transparent, Parisian chroniclers demonstrated that even the city's most private spaces posed no impediment to their vision. In a sketch called "Les Drames invisibles", which exemplified the *tableaux*'s representation of the apartment building, Frédéric Soulié, a frequent contributor to the genre, deployed the common device of describing Parisian society through a single apartment building. Even the most private events within the apartment house – what should be the "invisible dramas" of the title – become visible, with the narrator exposing blackmail and suicide on one floor and a concealed pregnancy on another. […]

[In his] preface to the fifteen-volume *Paris, ou le livre des cent-et-un* (1831), … Jules Janin consolidated [this] representational process into an allusion to a single figure, Asmodeus, the devilish hero of Lesage's *Le Diable boiteux* (1707), who removed roofs and peered inside houses. His reference suggested that Paris itself was reducible to a series of domestic interiors, and that those interiors were the primary objects of an ambulatory urban gaze.[…]

A decade later, in the 1840s, Asmodeus began to peel away apartment-house façades, and even when he approached apartments from the sky, he aligned his viewpoint with a building's vertical front. […] As a result, both streets and apartment buildings were equally described as areas of display and contact, open to effortless visual penetration …

Urban discourses also represented women as mobile urban observers, because to do otherwise would have been to acknowledge a limit to the transparency and accessibility of urban space. Indeed, even the most blatant examples of male voyeurism in the *tableaux* worked not only to constitute women as sexualized objects of a male gaze but also to liquidate the barrier potentially posed by the private space of the home. As a result, the objectification of women viewed either in the street or in their apartments had the unintended effect of bringing women into the city or bringing the city to women. […]

The *portière* and the personification of urban observation

The *tableaux* and *physiologies* directed their most concentrated animus against a female type whom they themselves associated with the power to see into apartment buildings – the *portière*.[21] By the 1840s the *portière* had become a standard presence even in buildings that lacked a formal entrance or porter's lodge. She often selected tenants for the landlord and collected rents; within the building, she distributed mail, cleaned landings and entrances, and did light housekeeping for some tenants (especially unmarried men); and she responded when tenants (who did not have keys to the main door) and visitors rang the bell.[22] The *portière* personified the passage between the street and the apartment because she let tenants into the building; because, as the historian Jean-Louis Deaucourt puts it, she "appeared everywhere, in the building's semiprivate spaces, in the open space of the street"; and because her *loge*, located off the building's vestibule or courtyard, was a "space both closed and open at the same time, eminently theatrical … propitious for exchanges, for comings and goings".[23] …

Urban literature characterized the *portière* as an adept observer: her duties as mail distributor, rent collector, and maid gave her an intimate and composite overview of the building's individual parts that perfected the totalizing yet local vision of the Parisian microcosm sought after by the authors of the *tableaux*. […]

Physiologists represented the porter as a personification of their own project of rendering the city "legible" by describing her as an Asmodeus figure, a knowing urban observer and an expert reader of physiognomies.

Notes

1   For a history of Paris during the July Monarchy, see Philippe Vigier, *Nouvelle histoire de Paris: Paris pendant la monarchie de juillet (1830–1848)*, Paris: Hachette, 1991. On the modernity of July Monarchy Paris, see Nicholas Green, *The Spectacle of Nature: Landscape and Bourgeois Culture in Nineteenth-Century France*, Manchester: Manchester University Press, 1990.

2   On the encoding and decoding of personal appearance during the earlier years of the Directory, see Margaret Waller, "Disembodiment as Masquerade: Fashion Journalists and Other 'Realist' Observers in Directory Paris", *L'Esprit créateur*, Spring 1997, 44–54.

3   On transparency in Rousseau, see especially Jean-Jacques Rousseau, *Lettre à Monsieur d'Alembert sur les spectacles* (1758) and Jean Starobinski, *Rousseau: la transparence et l'obstacle*, Paris: Gallimard, 1971; on transparency in the French Revolution, see Lynn Hunt, *Politics, Culture, and Class in the French Revolution*, Berkeley: University of California Press, 1984; and Susan Maslan, "Representation and Theatricality in French Revolutionary Theater and Politics", Dissertation, Johns Hopkins University, 1997.

4   One of the most explicit articulations of this view is Erna Olafson Hellerstein, "Women, Social Order, and the City: Rules for French Ladies, 1830–1870", Dissertation, University of California, Berkeley, 1980. Hellerstein focuses on medical literature, which along with educational tracts and political writings was the most emphatic discourse of separate spheres in France. See also Janet Wolff, "The Invisible *Flaneuse*: Women and the Literature of Modernity", in *Feminine Sentences: Essays on Women and Culture*, Berkeley: University of California Press, 1990, pp. 34–50. [...] My claim is not that a gendered distinction between public and private simply did not exist, but that it did not structure Parisian everyday life and its representations in the ways that previous scholarship would lead us to assume. [...] However, pressure has also been applied to several other assumptions implicit in histories of everyday life that argue for the separation of public and private during the nineteenth century, in particular the assumption that an abstract public sphere can be mapped onto actual public spaces. For example, while many people defend the equation of a political public sphere with urban, collective spaces by citing Jürgen Habermas's discussion of the role of coffeehouses in the development of public opinion, Susan Maslan has shown that Habermas in fact separates a virtual public sphere, constituted by writing, from the materialized public spaces peopled by crowds. See Susan Maslan, "Resisting Representation: Theater and Democracy in Revolutionary France", *Representations* 52, Fall 1995, esp. 29–30. For an incisive analysis of the contradictions endemic to any attempt to separate public and private spheres, see Joan Wallach Scott, *Only Paradoxes to Offer: French Feminists and the Rights of Man*, Cambridge, Mass.: Harvard University Press, 1996.

   Separating the abstract political realm from concrete public spaces also allows us to see that while women may have been excluded from political participation, they were actively present in many public spaces. Recent work on Paris cafés shows not only that women from all classes often frequented them, but also that cafés were both urban hubs open to a general public and places where patrons conducted domestic business. See W. Scott Haine, *The World of the Paris Café: Sociability Among the French Working Class, 1759–1914*, Baltimore: Johns Hopkins University Press, 1996, esp. pp. 33–58.

5   I draw here on the two major works on Parisian domestic architecture in the nineteenth century: Monique Eleb-Vidal and Anne Debarre-Blanchard, *Architectures de la vie privée: maisons et mentalités XVIIe–XIXe siècles*, Brussels: Archives d'Architecture moderne, 1989; and François Loyer, *Paris: Nineteenth-Century Architecture and Urbanism*, trans. Charles Lynn Clark, New York: Abbeville Press, 1988. [...]

6   This arrangement seems less startling when we take into account that sixteenth- and seventeenth-century society barely distinguished between rooms in which one sat and rooms through which one passed. See Monique Eleb-Vidal, "Dispositifs et moeurs: du privé à l'intime", *In Extenso* 9, November 1985, 217, 223. This vertical organization persisted well into the eighteenth century; see Annik Pardailhé-Galabrun, *The Birth of Intimacy: Privacy and Domestic Life in Early Modern France*, trans. Jocelyn Phelps, Cambridge: Polity Press, 1991,

pp. 52–3; and Jean-Pierre Babelon, *Demeures parisiennes sous Henri IV et Louis XIII*, Paris: Le Temps, 1965, p. 94.

7   The *hôtel privé* was also interchangeably called the *hôtel particulier*. On the *hôtel* as the origin of the bourgeois apartment building in Paris, see Patrick Céleste, "L'immeuble et son intérieur", *In Extenso* 9, November 1985, 75–6; and Eleb-Vidal and Debarre-Blanchard, *Architectures de la vie privée*, which argues that architects transposed the *hôtel*'s design onto the apartment, leading to an opposition between the two types when the *hôtel*'s several stories were compressed into the apartment unit's one. This argument is convincing, but incomplete … A fuller account of the development of the apartment house would include (1) its partial origins in the *maison à allée*, a building type rarely erected by trained architects; (2) economic factors that helped make rental property built to the maximum allowable height an increasingly attractive investment; and (3) the interaction of building type with urban form and culture, which I explore in detail here …

8   See Loyer, *Paris*, pp. 22–4. In buildings with several units per floor the cheapest, smallest apartments faced the courtyard. Loyer specifies that units close to the street were prized not only because their tenants had to climb fewer stairs, but because Parisians valued proximity to the density and exchanges of the street.

9   Building styles varied: sometimes window size was constant over the entire façade, sometimes only within sets of two or three stories, but in both cases the need for symmetry in the façade predominated over the varied proportions of the rooms behind the windows. […]

10 See *Les Grands boulevards*, Paris: Musées de la ville de Paris, 1985, p. 209.

11 A 1607 edict of Henri IV had forbidden all *saillies* and *encorbellements* in order to create a city of flat façades; Louis XVIII's legislation allowed pilasters up to 10 cm deep and enabled people to apply for permission to build balconies that could not extend more than 80 cm and would be at least 6 m above street level. See Paul Léon, "Maisons et rues de Paris", *Revue de Paris*, August 1910, 848–9. The law specified that only nonpublic buildings were to be regulated by street size … See M. Toussaint, *Nouveau manuel complet d'architecture ou traité de l'art de bâtir*, Paris: Roret, 1837, p. 42. The interpenetration of the spaces of the apartment building and the street is also evident in Balzac's suggestion that balconies serve as awnings for pedestrians in the rain (Honoré de Balzac, "Histoire et physiologie des boulevards de Paris, de la Madeleine à la Bastille", *Le Diable à Paris*, Paris: Hetzel, 1846, vol. 2, p. 94) and in the structure of arcades (*passages*), in which mezzanine apartments overlooked the enclosed commercial thoroughfares.

12 On the technological developments that shaped architectural pattern books and their methods of representing buildings, see Antoine Picon, "Du traité à la revue: l'image d'architecture au siècle de l'industrie", in Stéphane Michaud, Jean-Yves Mullier, and Nicole Savy (eds) *Usages de l'image au XIXe siècle*, Paris: Créaphis, 1992, pp. 153–64. On architectural training in the first half of the nineteenth century, see David Van Zanten, *Developing Paris: The Architecture of Duban, Labrouste, Due, and Vaudoyer*, Cambridge, Mass.: MIT Press, 1987; and Annie Jacques, *La Carrière de l'architecte au XIXe siècle*, Paris: Editions de la réunion des musées nationaux, 1986.

13 For a late July Monarchy take on the hostile relations between landlords and tenants, see the Daumier series *Locataires et propriétaires*, reprinted in Loys Delteil, *Le Peintre-graveur illustré (XIXe et XXe siècles): Honoré Daumier (V)*, vol. 24, Paris: Chez l'auteur, 1926, pp. 1594–628. […]

14 For discussions of the evolution of the modern city from the imperial city, see Van Zanten, *Developing Paris*; Richard Becherer, *Science Plus Sentiment: César Daly's Formula for Modern Architecture*, Ann Arbor: UMI Research Press, 1984; and Anthony Vidler, "The scenes of the street: transformations in ideal and reality, 1750–1871", in Stanford Anderson (ed.) *On Streets*, Cambridge, Mass.: MIT Press, 1978, pp. 29–112.

15 Loyer, *Paris*, pp. 99, 144.

16 Ibid., p. 98.

17 *Les Grands boulevards*, p. 171.

18 Margaret Cohen, "Panoramic Literature and the Invention of Everyday Genres", in Leo Charney and Vanessa R. Schwartz (eds) *Cinema and the Invention of Modern Life*, Berkeley: University of California Press, 1995, pp. 227–52. […]

19 Viollet-le-Duc was an exception to this rule of depopulated architecture: he included people in his architectural drawings, both to convey a sense of building scale and to insist on the imbrication of architectural and social structures. See Picon, "Du traité à la revue", p. 162.

20   Paul de Kock et al., *La Grande ville: nouveau tableau de Paris,* Paris: Maulde et Renou, 1843–44, 1:139, and Frédéric Soulié, "La Maîtresse de maison de santé", *Les Français peints par eux-mêmes*, Paris: Curmer, 1841, 4:350.
21   Some writers associated female types other than the *portière* with a combination of urban and domestic knowledge; see, for example, L. Roux, "La Sage-femme", *Les Français peints par eux-mêmes*, 1:177–184; and Madame de Bawr, "La Garde", in ibid., 1:129–137.
22   For a social history of male and female porters in the nineteenth century, see Jean-Louis Deaucourt, *Premières loges: Paris et ses concierges au XIXe siècle*, Paris: Aubier, 1992; Deaucourt's thorough work is compromised by his insistence on reading descriptive and even literary texts as transparent sources of empirical data about the daily lives and duties of his subjects.
23   Deaucourt, "Paris et ses concierges au 19e siècle", Dissertation, University of Paris, 1989, pp. 488, 742.

Public place and private space
The Victorian city and the working-class household[1]

M. J. Daunton (1983)

It is time … that the development of the city was viewed from below through the eyes of the slum dweller or the cottage tenant.

The task will not be an easy one, for the residents were not consulted at the time about their feelings on their accommodation. Nevertheless, it is important to move beyond a mere description of the physical structure of cities … Much of the work of housing reform may be interpreted as an attempt to change social behavior via physical change; an attempt which was often frustrated or deflected by a conflict between the donor's and recipient's expectation of how the environment should be made effective.[2] […] The effective environment was the creation of an interplay between managers and users, in which working-class attitudes formed in the past and aspirations for the future had their role to fulfill …

The form of working-class districts … did indeed change in the early and mid-Victorian years from a *cellular* and *promiscuous* to an *open* and *encapsulated* residential style. Most working-class housing had been located in self-contained little worlds of enclosed courts and alleys; but within each cell, the residents shared space and facilities in a communal way. Each group of houses formed its own private world within the larger city, and within that private world, space was a shared asset. […]

There were two trends away from such a pattern. The first was to break down the self-contained worlds, to open up the cells. Dead-ends were anathema [to reformers and planners] in the late Victorian city. The cellular pattern gave way to an open layout where everything connected with everything else. The second trend was to turn each house upon itself as its own private world. Its facilities were not to be shared with its neighbors, the space assigned to it was not to be part of the common property of a group of houses; instead each house was to be rigidly encapsulated. This all amounts to a realignment of the relationship between what was private and what was public: a change from inward-looking dead-ends turning their backs on the public thoroughfares to outward-looking streets; and from a pooling of space between houses to a definite allocation of space to each house. The threshold between the private and public spheres had been redrawn and made much less ambiguous. What was not now encapsulated, within the private sphere of the individual unit, was now totally public rather than communal to a group of neighbors, and hence open to view and to regulation. [...]

The trend towards an open and encapsulated layout was not confined to working-class housing; it was apparent also in the housing of other classes and in non-residential features within the Victorian city. The middle class was also retreating into a more private residential style which was most obvious in London but was soon followed in the provinces. The transition was from the town house to the villa, the detached or semi-detached house which became for a century and a half the preferred form of middle-class residence. The town house typified Bloomsbury which was developed from the 1820s; the communal space was the square.[3] The transitional stage was the Ladbroke estate which was developed in the 1840s, with houses backing onto private gardens which then led into a communal garden.[4] The suburban house with its private garden was the middle-class equivalent of the backyard; in each case, outdoor life was ceasing to be a social life and disappearing from view behind the garden hedge or the yard walls. The first villas dated from the 1820s on the Eyre estate in St. John's Wood, though the swing in balance in London might be as late as the 1850s.[5] And many other social functions became contained within specific spaces where they could be regulated. Partly this was a private assertion of responsibility for commercial reasons, partly a governmental assertion of public order. The space in the city between buildings, the interstices of the urban form, tended to become socially neutral, rather than social arenas in their own right.

Recreation is one example of the process. The street life and fairs of an earlier age were undermined in a number of directions.[6] One was the municipal park, with the careful delineation of recreation ground from flower beds, with keepers, bye-laws, specific hours of admission, booking procedures for pitches, and the pervasive iron railings.[7] Another was the building of separate stadia under private management for football or cricket, with turnstiles for admission and regulation not only of the players on the pitch but of the crowds on the terraces.[8] [...] The same applies to retailing. Where street traders continued, they were licensed and controlled; on the whole market trading retreated from the streets to covered market halls owned by the municipality and subject to the regulation of a code of bye-laws and a municipal officer.[9] The commercial expression of the same phenomenon would be the shopping arcade and the department store, with their doorkeepers and codes of behavior.[10] The factory similarly entailed a retreat from the scattered and unregulated workshops and outwork towards centralization within a specialist space which was regulated not only by the owner with his rules and work discipline, but also by government inspectors and act of parliament.[11]

Urban social life was increasingly carried on within specialist space controlled and regulated by its owner, whether commercial or municipal. The pattern of the late Victorian city was that people could assemble, but in a passive rather than participatory role, always under the control of a definite regulatory agency.[12] The communal, ad hoc and participatory life of the early Victorian city had been severely curtailed, and this links with the changed style of working-class housing. The trend in housing and in these other aspects of the urban form was two-fold. First, what remained in the public sphere was to be as open and regulated as possible; it was to be sterilized, made anonymous. Secondly, social functions were to be encapsulated within managed, contained environments, whether under the authority of a governmental agency, a private business, or the family itself. When people met, it was to assemble for a particular function, rather than to participate in a communal activity; space which remained in the public sphere rather than assigned to a particular function was declared neutral and anonymous. Working-class housing accords with these trends. Each house was to lie between the anonymous and public space of the street and the individual and private space of the yard, whereas previously it had lain within space lacking total privacy but also lacking the anonymity of public and impersonal control.[13]

Such, at least, was the intention. The explanation of the change is a subject in its own right; the concern at present is how this potential environment was made effective. Of course, the switch to an open and encapsulated form dictated the bounds of what was possible, but the working-class residents were not entirely passive recipients. Tensions did develop in the use of the public and anonymous street, and the utilization of the encapsulated house did accord with particular working-class aspirations. The process of change was not entirely one way. [...]

"Privatization" and "encapsulation" involved a wide range of social and economic factors. One was the spur of profit in response to increased incomes. Specialization is limited by the extent of the market: increased purchasing power generated change in shopping habits and leisure pursuits;[14] it also led to the wider adoption of factory production with its attendant work discipline.[15] Of course, this links with the development of housing, for the home was where the goods were consumed.[16] On the most general level, there was a reorientation of working-class culture from being work-centered to home-centered. Of course, this was not a uniform trend; it applied less to mining towns, for example, than to large industrial towns where work-place and residence were distant. But generally, shorter working hours and increased real wages eroded work-centered culture and increased the role of the home as a center of life.[17] G. J. Crossick has indicated how artisans in Kentish London were absorbing "privatized and family-centered values".[18] This was not merely the filtering down of ideas from above, for he suggests a specifically working-class justification, the residential form being part of the artisan's claim to respectability. This was impossible if he were forced to live cheek by jowl with those lacking respectability, and there was an often articulated desire to escape from promiscuous mixing and sharing.[19] The working-class acceptance of privatized and family-centered values had both a negative and positive dimension. In a negative sense, the stress upon the home as the crucial element in life was in part a defensive retreat from the loss of control over work, a compensation in the home for an increased sense of dependence in the work place. In a positive sense, many working-class families in the last quarter of the nineteenth century had increased real wages, and could direct the budgets toward improved standards of accommodation and home-based consumption ...

How, then, did the inside of the house change as its threshold became more defined? [...]

The trend in working-class housing in the second half of the nineteenth century was towards encapsulation from its neighbors, and towards separation of function within the house. Houses in their internal arrangement came to have separate rooms for distinct purposes as the city came to have precise locations for various functions. As this occurred, the facilities available within the house improved. If the front parlor for "best" occasions became a shrine of respectability, its idol was the piano ... The piano was a potent symbol. It links with the desire of temperance reformers to woo men from the public houses. [...] Perhaps more important than a demand for pianos ... was a growing demand for basic furnishings. For example, the interiors of working-class houses were transformed by the availability of cheap wall and floor coverings. [...] Such home-based consumption concentrated on the parlor. "There is", remarked Fred Willis in his memoirs, "something almost sacred about this choice apartment", with its rare and costly contents.[20] […]

In the 1890s there was a major change in the availability of energy for working-class households. Until then, most working-class houses had relied upon the paraffin lamp and the triple-purpose coal-fired range. The range heated the room, provided hot water from a back boiler, and supplied cooking facilities in an oven. Of course, this was an improvement on what went before, but there were many disadvantages, for the range was dirty; it necessitated the use of the kitchen as a living room to obtain heat; cooking and heating water in summer meant over-heating the room.[21] So far as lighting is concerned, between the 1860s and 1890s it was mainly supplied by paraffin lamps. Paraffin, it was said in 1898, "is, on account of its low price, the 'poor man's light'".[22]

Gas provided a more sensitive source of heat and light. […] The crucial breakthrough was the development of the slot meter [*a meter that provides a fixed amount of gas when a coin is inserted, Ed.*]. "Prior to the invention of the Slot Meter so few weekly tenants in London used gas that it may be taken as correct to say that gas was practically unknown in the dwellings of the working classes. They would not incur the expense of putting in the gas fittings and pipes, and the payment of a quarterly gas bill was also a difficulty".[23] The slot meter was pioneered by Liverpool in the early 1890s.[24] The South Metropolitan Company started installation in London in 1892, the number of slot meters rising from 439 at the end of 1892 to 80,115 at the end of 1898, of which 62,845 were also supplied with stoves.[25] … The working-class demand for gas increased rapidly, and at an average consumption of 16,000 cubic feet per meter accounted for an eighth of the gas consumed in the South Metropolitan district.[26] Even "the very, very poor people go in for it".[27] […] Gas contributed to a changed use of space, for the cooker could be relegated to the scullery along with the sink, so removing cooking from the kitchen, which now became a general dining and living room.[28] […]

The general argument of this paper is that the historians of housing should turn their attention in two directions. One is to what Chadwick called the external economy of housing, the environment in which the house was located. It is suggested that a realignment took place in the early and mid-Victorian city in the manner in which the house was located in urban space, which entailed a redefinition of the relationship between public and private space, an increased emphasis upon the threshold between the two. The second area of concern has been the late Victorian transformation of the internal economy of housing, a process which entailed cooperation between the property owner on the one hand, and on the other the municipality and gas undertaking, both of whom were willing to make an investment in the house whether to raise the standard of sanitation or to extend the market for gas. These developments entailed a trend towards domestic-based consumption within a more private, internal life which was very different from the experience of the early Victorian city. Daily life became less public and less communal, more private and more introverted.

The agencies for change were many. These included imposition from above, out of concern for hygiene and public order; commercial motivations as in the extension of gas supply; as well as the working-class dynamic of respectability. Underlying everything else were the permissive factors of land availability and capital flows. Attention should be given to the way in which the residents utilized their accommodation and how this related to changes in other parts of the urban environment and to the social history of the working class. Furthermore, the physical superstructure of the city in itself created social relationships between its owners, managers and users. It might be asked how the development of the law relating to eviction determined the power balance between tenants and landlords; whether the landlords formed pressure groups to influence municipal financial policy; if the social composition of ownership changed; what power landlords gave to house agents. Houses were not merely built in greater or lesser numbers, of rising or falling standards, but generated complex social relations.

All these points are obvious, but are not very apparent in the writings of urban historians. The history of housing should involve far more than a Whig interpretation of the coming of council initiative, or a concern for the building cycle; the history of the urban form should entail more than an analysis of segregation and the development of town planning. The approach suggested here involves crossing what Richard Cobb has called "the tempting threshold between what is public and visible and what is private, yet suggestible",[29] but only if it is realized that the threshold itself was shifting and being redefined.

Notes

1   This paper is a preliminary and condensed version of a wider analysis in my forthcoming book on *House and Home: Working-Class Housing in the City, 1850–1914*. I would like to thank Duncan Bythell, Neil Evans and Ranald Michie for their comments.

2   Donald J. Olsen, *The Growth of Victorian London,* New Haven, Conn. and London: Yale University Press, 1976, pp. 279–81.

3   Hermione Hobhouse, *Thomas Cubitt, Master Builder*, London: Macmillan, 1971, chapter IV, and Olsen, *Town Planning in London: the Eighteenth and Nineteenth Centuries*, New Haven, Conn.: Yale University Press, 1964.

4   *Survey of London, vol. XXXVII, Northern Kensington*, London, 1973, pp. 196, 204.

5   Ibid., pp. 21–2; John Summerson, *Georgian London*, London: Pleiades Books, 1945, pp. 158–9.

6   For the earlier pattern, see Robert W. Malcomson, *Popular Recreations in English Society 1700–1850*, Cambridge: Cambridge University Press, 1973.

7   There is no good history of public parks. On ideas about layout, see George F. Chadwick, *The Park and the Town. Public Landscape in the Nineteenth and Twentieth Centuries*, London, 1966; the best survey of a particular town is the unpublished study in Cardiff; A. A. Pettigrew, *The Public Parks and Recreation Grounds of Cardiff*, Central Library, volumes I-VI, 1926, rev. 1933–4. See also Helen E. Meller, *Leisure and the Changing City 1870–1914*, London: Routledge, 1976, for some remarks on Bristol.

8   For example, C. P. Korr, "West Ham United Football Club and the Beginnings of Professional Football in East London, 1895–1914", *Journal of Contemporary History* 13, 1978, 224–6.

9   On the building of public markets, see J. Blackman, "The Food Supply of an Industrial Town: A Study of Sheffield's Public Markets, 1780–1900", *Business History* V, 1963. For the building of the Grainger covered market in Newcastle, see L. Wilkes and G. Dodds, *Tyneside Classica. The Newcastle of Grainger, Dobson and Clayton*, London: J. Murray, 1964, pp. 75–7.

10 See Alison Adburgham, *Shops and Shopping 1800–1914: Where, and in What Manner the Well-dressed Englishwoman Bought Her Clothes*, London: Allen and Unwin, 1964.

11 E. P. Thompson, "Time, Work Discipline and Industrial Capitalism", *Past and Present* 38, 1967; B. L. Hutchins and Amy Harrison, *A History of Factory Legislation*, London: P. S. King and Son, 1911.

12 Stephen Yeo, *Religion and Voluntary Organizations in Crisis*, London, 1976, p. 310.

13 A. Errazurez, "Some Types of Housing in Liverpool, 1785–1900", *Town Planning Review* XIX, 1943–7, 68; on this process see Sam Bass Warner, "The Public Invasion of Private Space and the Private Engrossment of Public Space", in Swedish Council for Building Research, *Growth and Transformation of the Modern City*, Stockholm, 1979.

14 For changes in leisure, see Yeo, *Religion and Voluntary Organizations*; on shopping, see, for example, P. Mathias, *Retailing Revolution*, London, 1967.

15 D. Bythell, *The Sweated Trades. Outwork in Nineteenth-Century Britain*, London, 1978, chapter 4.

16 Yeo, *Religion and Voluntary Organizations*, pp. 305–6.

17 G. Stedman Jones, "Working-Class Culture and Working-Class Politics in London, 1870–1900", *Journal of Social History* VII, 1973–4, 485–7.

18 G. J. Crossick, *An Artisan Elite in Victorian Society. Kentish London 1840–80*, London, 1978, p. 146.

19 Ibid., pp. 135–6; R. Gray, *The Labor Aristocracy in Victorian Edinburgh*, Oxford, 1976, chapter 7; G. Stedman Jones, *Outcast London. A Study in the Relationship between Classes in Victorian Society*, Oxford, 1971, pp. 226–7.

20 F. Willis, *101 Jubilee Road. A Book of London Yesterdays*, London, 1948, p. 102.

21 Political and Economic Planning, *Report on the Gas Industry in Great Britain*, London, 1939, p. 85. See Alison Ravetz, "The Victorian Coal Kitchen and its Reformers", *Victorian Studies* XI, 1967, on the development of coal and gas ranges.

22 PP 1898 XI, Report from the Select Committee on Petroleum, p. ix.

23 PP 1899 X, Report from the Select Committee on Metropolitan Gas Companies, p. 315.

24 Ibid., Q. 1472.

25 Ibid., 297–8, 315. In addition to the 62,845 stoves supplied to slot meter consumers, 40,601 were let on hire [*i.e. rented, Ed.]* in 1898.

26 Ibid., Qq. 235, 1477–8, 315.

27 Ibid., Q. 2085.

28 PP 1908 CVII, *Report on an Enquiry by the Board of Trade into Working-Class Rents, Housing and Retail Prices*, 359, for change in Blackburn; *An Enquiry into People's Homes. A Report Prepared by Mass-Observation for the Advertising Service Guild*, London, 1943, pp. 99–101.

29 Richard Cobb, "The Tempting Threshold", *The Listener*, April 6, 1978, 438.

L'Assommoir

(The Dram Shop)

Émile Zola (1876)

[*The novel, which traces the life of Gervaise Macquart, takes place during the Second Empire, from about 1850 to about 1870. Gervaise, a young laundress from the provincial southern town of Plassans (Aix-en-Provence), comes to Paris with her lover Lantier and two of their children. He neglects and then leaves her, and she eventually marries the roofer Coupeau, bearing him another child, Nana. Things go well for the Coupeaus until the roofer falls, injuring himself, and takes to drink. Gervaise establishes a successful laundry business with the help of the black-smith Goujet, but gradually, the weight of debts and Coupeau's mistreatment drag her down, the laundry fails, she is reduced to prostitution and dies, starving and alone, in a closet of the same tenement building that had housed the laundry. The following selections, from chapters 1, 2, 4, and 10, trace her life and exemplify Zola's masterly evocation of the Parisian working-class environment. The novel was often performed in theatrical adaptations, and inspired René Clément's motion picture "Gervaise" of 1956 (Figs. 21, 22). Ed.*]

The boarding-house [*where Gervaise and Lantier first stay*] stood on the Boulevard de la Chapelle, to the left of the Barrière Poissonnière.[1] It was a dump, three stories high, painted reddish purple as far as the second floor, with wooden shutters rotted by the rain. Above a lantern with cracked panes, one could just make out the words: HÔTEL BONCOEUR, OWNER MARSOULLIER, between the two windows, in large yellow letters, though bits of this inscription had fallen away with the decaying plaster. The lantern got in Gervaise's way and she stood on tiptoe with her handkerchief to her lips, looking to the right, towards the Boulevard de Rochechouart, where the butchers stood in groups, in their blood-stained aprons, in front of the slaughterhouses, and, from time to time, the cold wind brought a foul odor, the crude smell of slaughtered animals. Then she looked to the left, her eyes threading along the ribbon of the avenue that came to a halt almost exactly in front of her in the white mass of the Lariboisière Hospital, at that time still being built. Slowly, her eyes traced the boundary wall as far as it could be seen in both directions; sometimes, at night, she could hear the screams of people being murdered behind it; and now she searched its far recesses and dark corners, stained with damp and filth, afraid that she might come across Lantier's body, his belly punctured with knife wounds. When she looked up beyond the endless gray wall that circled the city with its strip of wasteland, she saw a great glow, a sprinkling of sunlight, already humming with the early-morning sounds of Paris. [...]

[*Ch. 2. Sitting with Coupeau, the roofer.*] Gervaise had picked up her basket. However, she did not stand up, keeping it on her knees instead and staring into the distance, dreaming, as though the young workman's words had stirred in her some distant memories of a different life. Then she went on slowly, without any apparent link to what had been said before:

"Heavens! I'm not ambitious, I don't ask for much ... My dream would be to work quietly, eat bread every day and have a fairly decent place to sleep: you know, a bed, a table and two chairs, nothing more ... Oh, I'd also like to bring up my children and make good citizens of them, if I could ... If there was anything else I'd like, it's not to be hit, if ever I did settle down again with someone ... That's all, you know, nothing more ...". [ellipses the author's]

She looked around, analyzing her desires and not finding anything much apart from this that appealed to her. However, with a little hesitation, she continued:

"Yes, perhaps in the end one would like to die in one's bed. After slaving away all my life, it would be nice to die in my bed, at home". [...]

She was about to set off down the boulevard, but he took her hand and would not let go, saying:

"Why not come along with me, then? Go down the Rue de la Goutte-d'Or, it's no further, really ... I have to go to my sister's before returning to work ... We can keep one another company".

In the end, she accepted, and they went slowly up the Rue des Poissonniers, side by side, but not arm in arm. He told her about his family. [...] One of his sisters ... had married Lorilleux, a chain-maker with a deadpan sense of humor. This was the one they were going to see in the Rue de la Goutte-d'Or, where she lived in the large house on the left. In the evenings, he went to eat with the Lorilleux: it was cheaper for all of them. In fact, the reason he was going now was to tell them not to expect him today, because he had an invitation from a friend. [...]

While they were talking, they had already gone a hundred yards down the Rue de la Goutte-d'Or, where he stopped, looked up and said:

"This is the house. I'm not far away myself, at No. 22. But I must say this place is a fine old pile! It's like a barracks, it's so large inside there".

Gervaise looked up and examined the front of the house. On the street side, it had five stories, each with a row of fifteen windows, their black shutters with broken slats lending an air of desolation to the huge expanse of wall. Below, on the ground floor, there were four shops: to the right of the door: a huge greasy chop house, at the left: a coal merchant's, a draper's and an umbrella shop. The house seemed all the more vast since it stood between two low, puny little buildings that huddled against it; and, square-set, like a crudely cast block of cement, decaying and flaking in the rain, its huge cube stood out against the clear sky above the neighboring roofs, the mud-colored sides unrendered and having the endless nakedness of prison walls, with rows of join stones[2] resembling empty jaw-bones gaping in the void. But Gervaise was chiefly looking at the door, a huge arched doorway rising to the second floor and making a deep porch, at the far end of which one could see the dim light from a large courtyard. Through the middle of the entrance, which was paved in the same way as the street, ran a gutter along which some water, colored soft pink, was flowing.

"Come on in", Coupeau said. "No one's going to eat you".

Gervaise wanted to wait for him in the street, but she could not resist stepping through the doorway as far as the concierge's lodge, which was on the right. Here, on the threshold, she looked upwards once again. On the inside, the four regular façades surrounding the huge square courtyard rose to six stories. They consisted of gray walls, with leprous yellow patches, rising featureless from the paving-stones to the roofing slates without any moulding, and streaked with stains that had trickled off the roof; the only irregularity was where the downpipes bent at each floor where the cast-iron of the gaping cisterns left rusty stains. The windows had no shutters, but exhibited their bare panes, which had the blue-green tint of murky water. Some were open, to allow blue check mattresses to hang out and air, while others had cords stretched across them with clothes on, a whole family's washing: the man's shirts, the woman's camisoles, the children's pants. From one, on the third floor, hung a child's nappy, smeared with filth. From top to bottom, cramped dwellings spilled outside, letting scraps of their poverty escape through every opening. Below, on each side, a high, narrow doorway, without any wooden frame, cut directly out of the plasterwork, led into a cracked hallway, at the far end of which was a staircase with muddy steps and an iron railing; so there were four such stairways, designated by the first four letters of the alphabet, which were painted on the wall. Huge workshops had been fitted out on the ground floor, behind windows that were black with grime: a locksmith's forge blazed away, while farther off one could hear the sound of a carpenter's plane, and near the concierge's lodge a dye-works was gushing out the pale pink flood that ran beneath the porch. Puddles of dye-water, wood shavings and coal-dust dirtied the courtyard, grass grew round its edges, between the uneven flag-stones, and it was lit by a harsh light that seemed to cut it in half at the point where the sun stopped. On the shaded side, beside a standpipe with a dripping tap, which ensured that the area was permanently damp, three small hens with muddy claws were pecking the ground in search of worms. And Gervaise slowly took it all in, her eyes descending from the sixth floor downwards to the pavement, then back again, surprised at the vastness of it, with the sensation of being inside a living organism, at the very heart of a city, regarding the house with the same interest as she would had she been confronted by a giant being. […]

She did not find it ugly. Among the rags hanging from the windows, there were splashes of jollity: a wallflower in a pot, a cage of canaries twittering, shaving-mirrors shining like bright stars in the shadowy depths. Downstairs, a cabinet-maker was singing to the accompaniment of the regular whistling noise of his trying-plane, while in the locksmith's workshop, the hammers beat rhythmically in a great silvery din. Meanwhile, at almost every open window, against the glimpses of the poverty behind, children showed their grubby, laughing faces or women sat sewing, their calm profiles bent over their work. Men had gone back to their work outside after the midday break and the rooms were empty, the house returning to a great tranquility, unbroken except for the noises of craftsmen and the lulling sound of a refrain, always the same, repeated hour after hour. But the courtyard was a little damp; if Gervaise had lived there, she would have wanted an apartment at the back, on the side that got the sun. She had taken five or six steps and could smell the musty aroma of poor dwellings, a smell of old dust and rancid grime; but since it was covered by the acrid smell of water from the dyeworks, she decided that it was far preferable to that of the HÔTEL BONCOEUR. She was already choosing her window, in the left-hand corner where there was a little window-box with some runner beans, their slender stems beginning to wind around a cat's-cradle of strings.

"I kept you waiting, didn't I?" said Coupeau, whom she suddenly heard close to her. "They make a fuss when I don't have dinner with them, especially today, because my sister had bought some veal".

And, since she had started a little with surprise, he continued, examining the surroundings in his turn:

"You were looking at the house. It's always let, from top to bottom. There are three hundred tenants, I think … Now, if I'd had any furniture, I'd have kept an eye open for a room here myself. It would be nice, don't you think?"

"Yes, it would", Gervaise murmured. "In Plassans, there were fewer people in our street … Oh, look, that's pretty, the window on the fifth floor, with the runner beans". […]

"They're waiting for you", Coupeau said, as they were walking round [a few weeks later], through the Rue des Poissonniers. "Oh, they're starting to get used to the idea of my getting married. They seem very pleasant this evening. And, if you've never seen someone making gold chains, it will be amusing for you to watch. As it happens they have an urgent order for Monday". […]

Meanwhile, they had gone through the arched door and across the courtyard. The Lorilleux lived on the sixth floor, Staircase B. Coupeau laughed and called to her to take a firm hold on the banister and not to let it go. She looked up and blinked, seeing the high empty tower of the stairwell, lit by three gaslights, one every second floor. The last, right at the top, looked like a twinkling star in a black sky, while the other two cast long beams of light, oddly broken up where they fell across the endless spiral of stairs. […]

Staircase B, gray, dirty, with its greasy steps and banisters, and plaster showing through the scratched paint on its walls, still reeked of an overpowering smell of cooking. From every landing, corridors led off echoing with noise, and yellow doors opened, blackened around the locks with marks from dirty hands; and the cistern, level with the window, gave off a fetid dampness, its stench mingling with the sharp odor of cooked onions. From the ground floor to the sixth, one could hear the sounds of washing-up, the rinsing of pots, the scraping of pans with spoons to clean them. On the first floor, Gervaise glanced through an open door, with the word Draughtsman on it in large letters, and saw two men sitting in front of an oiled tablecloth after the dishes had been cleared away, having a heated discussion amid the smoke from their pipes. The second and third floors were quieter: one could hear only the rocking of a cradle through the gaps in the woodwork, the stifled cries of a child's or a woman's thick accent pouring out like the dull murmur of running water, without any distinguishable words; and Gervaise could read placards nailed to the doors, giving the inhabitants' names: Madame

Gaudron, carder;[3] and, further on, Monsieur Madinier, packing shop. There was a fight in progress on the fourth floor: such a stamping that the floor trembled, furniture overturned, and a dreadful racket of blows and curses – though it didn't stop the neighbors opposite from playing cards with the door open to let in the air. But when she reached the fifth floor, Gervaise had to pause for breath. She was not used to climbing; the constantly winding wall and the apartments, half glimpsed as they went by, made her head spin. In any case, there was a family blocking the way on the landing: the man was washing dishes on a little clay stove near the cistern while the mother, leaning back against the ramp, was cleaning the child before putting him to bed. All the time, Coupeau was urging her on: they were nearly there; and when at last they reached the sixth floor, he turned round to help her with a smile. She had her head lifted, trying to decide where a particular voice was coming from, shrill and clear, which she had been hearing above the other sounds right from the first step. It was a little old woman who lived under the roof and sang as she dressed dolls costing thirteen *sous*. Also, as a tall girl was returning with a pail to one of the neighboring rooms, Gervaise caught sight of an unmade bed, where a man was waiting in shirtsleeves, sprawling and looking towards the ceiling; when the door shut, a handwritten visiting card announced: MADEMOISELLE CLÉMENCE, IRONING. At that, reaching the very top, breathless, her legs aching, curiosity made her lean over the banisters: now, it was the ground-floor gaslight that looked like a star, at the bottom of the narrow well, six stories deep; and the smell and vast rumbling life of the house was wafted up to her in a single breath, a hot blast breaking over her anxious face, making her feel as though she were perched on the edge of an abyss.

"We're not there yet!" Coupeau said. "It's quite a journey!"

He had turned left, down a long corridor. He took two further turnings, the first again to the left, the next to the right. The corridor continued, branched, narrowed, cracked and crumbling, lit at long intervals by a slender tongue of gas; and the doors, each one like the next, lined up like the doors of a prison or a convent, but almost all wide open, continued to reveal scenes of poverty or labor, interiors that the warm June evening filled with a reddish mist. At last, they reached the end of a completely dark passage.

"This is it", the roofer said. "Look out! Keep to the wall: there are three steps to go down".

Gervaise took a further ten paces, cautiously, in the dark. She stumbled, then counted the three steps; but Coupeau, at the end of the passage, had just pushed open a door, without knocking. A harsh light shone across the floor. They went in.

The room was constricted, a sort of funnel looking like nothing more than an extension of the corridor. A faded woolen curtain, held up for the time being by a piece of string, divided the funnel in two. The first compartment contained a bed, wedged under the sloping mansard roof, a cast-iron stove still warm from dinner, two chairs, a table and a cupboard with part of the beading sawn off so that it could fit between the bed and the door. The second compartment served as the workshop: at the far end, a small forge and bellows; on the right, a vise fixed to the wall, beneath a shelf covered in scraps of metal; and on the left, by the window, a tiny workbench, littered with pliers, shears and minute saws, all greasy and very dirty. […]

[*Ch. 4. After Gervaise and Coupeau marry*], there followed four years' hard work.[4] In their neighborhood, Gervaise and Coupeau were a good couple, who kept themselves to themselves, didn't fight and took a regular Sunday walk over to Saint-Ouen. […]

However, especially in the early days, they had to scrimp and save to make ends meet.

The wedding had left them with a debt of two hundred francs. Then, they hated living at the HÔTEL BONCOEUR. They found it disgusting and full of undesirable types. They dreamed of having their own home, with their own furniture, which they could take care of. Twenty times, they worked out how much they would need: in round figures, it came to three hundred and fifty francs, if they wanted to start off without having a hard time to keep their heads above water and have a saucepan or casserole dish when they needed it. They could see no chance of saving such a large sum within two years; but then they had a stroke of luck: an old gentleman from Plassans asked them to send him Claude, the elder of the two boys, so he could put him in boarding-school – a generous notion on the part of an eccentric art-lover who had been very impressed by some sketches of people that the kid had done. Claude had been costing them the shirts off their backs, and now that they had only the younger boy, Etienne,[5] to support, they put aside the three hundred and fifty francs in seven and a half months. On the day when they bought their furniture, at a second-hand shop in the Rue Belhomme, they went for a walk before going home along the outer boulevards, their hearts bursting with great joy. They had a bed, a bedside table, a chest of drawers with a marble top, a cupboard, a round table with a waxed cloth and six chairs, everything in old walnut – not to mention the bedclothes, linen and almost-new kitchen utensils. To them, this seemed to mark the moment when they finally and seriously took their place in life – an event that, by making them owners of property, gave them some standing among the well-set-up people of the neighborhood.

For the past two months, they had been concerned with the choice of somewhere to live. What they wanted most of all was to rent a flat in the big house in the Rue de la Goutte-d'Or, but there was not a single room to let, so they had to give up this long-cherished dream ... They looked elsewhere ... And finally they did find somewhere, a big room, with a small room off it and a kitchen, in the Rue Neuve de la Goutte-d'Or, almost opposite the laundry [where Gervaise was working]. It was a little, one-story house, with a steep staircase at the top of which were just two apartments, one on the right, the other on the left; the lower floor being occupied by a man who gave carriages out for hire and kept them in sheds round a huge courtyard opening into the street. The young woman was delighted: it was like living in a small town again: no busybodies next door, no gossip to worry about, just a tranquil spot that reminded her of a backstreet in Plassans, behind the ramparts; and, to cap it all, she could see her own window from the laundry, if she craned her neck, without putting down her iron.

They moved on the April quarter-day.[6] Gervaise was now eight months pregnant; but she showed a fine spirit, laughing and saying that the child would help her while she was working; she could feel its little fists pushing inside her and giving her strength. What! She took not the least notice of Coupeau when he said she should have a lie down and take it easy! She'd lie down when the contractions started. That would be quite soon enough, because now, with another mouth to feed, they would really have to put their backs into it. She was the one who cleaned the apartment, before helping her husband to put back the furniture. She worshipped that furniture, wiping it down lovingly and breaking her heart at the slightest scratch. She would stop dead, as though she had hit herself, when she knocked any piece of it with the broom. The chest of drawers was especially dear to her: she thought how beautiful and solid it was, with that air of seriousness about it. One of her dreams, which she did not dare mention to anyone, was to have a clock to put on it, right in the middle of the marble top – the effect would be quite splendid. Had it not been for the baby that was on the way, she might have risked buying her clock, but as it was she put it off until later, with a sigh.

The family were enchanted with their new abode. Etienne's bed was in the small room, which was large enough for another child's cot. The kitchen was no bigger than the back of your hand and very dark; but if you left the door open you could see quite well. After all, Gervaise did not have to cook for thirty people; all she needed was room to make a stew. As for the main room, it was their pride and joy. As soon as they got up, they drew the curtains across the recess – curtains in white calico – and at once the bedroom was transformed into a dining-room, with the table in the middle and the wardrobe and chest of drawers facing one another. As the open fire could consume as much as fifteen *sous'* worth of coal a day, they blocked it off. Instead a little iron stove, standing on the marble slab, gave them heat even in the depth of winter for seven *sous.* Coupeau had done his best to decorate the walls, while promising further embellishments later on. A tall engraving showing a Marshal of France,[7] prancing about with his baton in his hand, between a cannon and a heap of cannon-balls, took the place of a mirror. Above the chest of drawers were the family photographs, in two rows, to the right and left of an old china stoup for holy water, with gilt decoration, where they kept the matches. On a corner of the wardrobe stood a bust of Pascal, and on the other side, one of Béranger,[8] the first grave, the other smiling, close to the cuckoo clock, so that they seemed to be listening to its ticking. It really was a lovely room. [...]

The Rue Neuve de la Goutte-d'Or itself played a large part in their feeling of satisfaction. Gervaise lived in the street, constantly going back and forth from her own house to Mme. Fauconnier's. Coupeau, nowadays, would go downstairs in the evening to smoke his pipe on the doorstep. The street, which had no pavement and was full of pot-holes, went uphill. [...] The most cheerful part of the street was in the middle, where the buildings were lower and more widely-spaced, letting in air and light ... Patches of wasteland and narrow alleyways, running between the black walls, turned this part of the street into a village. Coupeau, amused by the sight of the occasional passer-by hopping over the constant streams of soapy water, said that it reminded him of a little place in the country where one of his uncles had taken him when he was five. Gervaise's great joy, to the left of her window, was a tree in a courtyard, an acacia with one of its branches reaching out, its meager greenery enough to lend charm to the whole street. [...]

Gervaise had managed to bring up the girl [Nana] while never losing more than two days of work in a week. She had become a skilled worker for fine linen and earned up to three francs a day ... When their savings reached the sum of six hundred francs, the young woman started to lose sleep over it, obsessed by her daydream of setting up her own business, renting a little shop and employing her own workers. She had it all figured out. After twenty years, if the enterprise prospered, they might be able to purchase an annuity, which could keep them for the rest of their lives, somewhere in the country. But she was afraid to take the risk. She said that she was still looking for a shop, so that she could have time to consider it. The money was quite safe in the savings bank; in fact, it was multiplying. In those three years, she had satisfied only one of her desires: she had bought herself a clock; and even then this timepiece, a rosewood clock with twisted columns and a copper gilt pendulum, had to be paid off over a year, at the rate of five francs every Monday. She got cross when Coupeau said he would wind it up, because only she was allowed to take off the glass globe and religiously wipe the columns, as though the marble top of her chest of drawers had been transformed into a chapel. Under the glass cover, behind the clock, she hid the savings book. And often, when she was dreaming about her shop, she would sit there, miles away, in front of the dial, staring at the turning hands, for all the world as if she was waiting for some particular, solemn moment before she made up her mind. […]

The very day when Nana reached three, Coupeau came back from work to find Gervaise in a dreadful state …

"Well, if you must know", she confessed at last, "the little draper's shop in the Rue de la Goutte-d'Or is up to rent. I saw it an hour ago, when I went to buy some thread. It gave me a real turn".

It was a very clean shop, which happened to be in the large house where they had once dreamed of finding somewhere to live [the tenement where the Lorilleux live]. There was the shop and the living quarters behind, with two other rooms, to right and left. In short, just what they wanted, rather small rooms, but well-arranged. The only trouble was, she thought it a little over-priced: the owner was talking about five hundred francs. […]

The next day, when she was alone, she could not resist the urge to lift the glass dome off the clock and consult the savings book. Just imagine: her shop was in there, in those pages blackened with nasty scribbles! […]

[*Ch. 5*] On the day of the actual letting [*of the new laundry in the big tenement house*], when the Coupeaus went to sign the lease, Gervaise had a lump in her throat as she passed under the high door on to the street. She was really going to live in this house, as large as a small town, the endless thoroughfares of its stairs and corridors crossing and stretching into the distance. The gray frontage with the clothing drying out of the windows in the sun, the dingy courtyard with its uneven stones like a public square, and the murmur of sounds from those working behind the walls, all caused her great emotion, joy at last in being able to fulfill her ambition, and fear that she might not succeed, but be crushed in this huge struggle against hunger, the faint sounds of which she could hear around her. She felt that she was doing something very daring, throwing herself in to the very middle of an active piece of machinery, while the locksmith's hammers and the cabinet-maker's planes banged and whistled inside the ground-floor workshops. That day, the water from the dyeworks that flowed under the front porch was a very gentle apple-green. She stepped over it with a smile: the color seemed to her a good omen. […]

The following Monday, the decorators arrived. The buying of the paper was a tremendous affair. Gervaise wanted some gray paper with blue flowers, to make the walls light and merrier. Boche [the concierge] offered to take her: she would choose. But he had strict orders from the owner: they were not to go above fifteen *sous* a roll. They spent an hour at the paper shop. The laundress kept coming back to a very sweet chintz at eighteen *sous* a roll, and was desperate to have it, finding all the other papers horrible. Finally, the concierge gave in: he would fix it, charging for an extra roll if he had to. […]

The shop was to be ready in four days. The work lasted three weeks. Originally, there was talk only of washing down the paintwork; but the painting, which had once been maroon in color, was so dirty and so dingy that Gervaise let herself be persuaded to have all the front done in light blue, with yellow lettering. Then, the redecoration went on and on. […] Gervaise was going out of her mind. Suddenly, in two days, it was all finished, the painting done, the paper hung, the rubbish thrown into a truck. The workmen had dashed it off as though it were a game, whistling on their ladders or singing loud enough to deafen the whole neighborhood.

The move took place immediately afterward. For the first few days, Gervaise was as happy as a child with a new toy, when she crossed over the street after going on some errand or other. She dawdled there, so that she could enjoy her home. From a distance, in the midst of the black row of other shop-fronts, hers seemed to her so light, so new and so merry, with its soft-blue sign, on which the words High Quality Laundry were painted in large yellow letters. In the window, which was closed in at the back with little muslin curtains and lined with blue paper to show off the whiteness of the clothing, some men's shirts were on show, with women's hats hanging above them, their ribbons tied to lengths of brass wire. And she thought her shop very pretty, with its sky-blue color. Inside, you walked into more blue: the paper, an imitation of Pompadour chintz, represented a trellis with bindweed growing up it. The work-table, a huge piece of furniture that filled two thirds of the room, had a thick blanket over it, and, over that, to hide the trestles, a piece of cretonne with a design of large blueish leaves. Gervaise would sit on a stool, sighing with contentment, pleased with her fine property and gloating over her new tools. But the first thing she always looked at was her "machinery", a cast-iron stove on which ten irons could heat up at a time, placed round the fire on sloping stands. She would go and kneel in front of it, examining it with the constant fear that that flibberti-gibbet of an apprentice of hers might have cracked it by stoking it up with too much coke.

The living quarters, behind the shop, were very satisfactory. The Coupeaus slept in the first bedroom, where they also ate and did the cooking; a door, at the back, opened into the courtyard. Nana's bed was in the right-hand room, a large box-room lit by a round fanlight, near the ceiling. As for Etienne, he shared the left-hand room with the dirty washing: there were always huge piles of that lying around on the floor. There was just one disadvantage, which the Coupeaus did not want to admit at first: the damp positively pissed out of the walls and you could not see clearly after three in the afternoon.

The new shop caused a great stir around and about. The Coupeaus were accused of going too fast and asking for trouble. It was true that they had spent the Goujets' five hundred francs [a loan from Gervaise's friends] just moving in, and not even kept enough to live on for a fortnight, as they had promised each other they would. On the day when Gervaise took down the shutters for the first time, she had just six francs in her purse. But she wasn't worried: customers had started to come and business looked good. A week later, on the Saturday before she went to bed, she spent two hours doing her sums on a piece of paper; and she woke Coupeau up, her face shining, to tell him that, if they were careful, they would make pots of money. [...]

In the midst of this tittle-tattle, Gervaise, calm, smiling, on the front porch of her shop, greeted her friends with an affectionate little nod. She liked to come out there for a minute or two, taking a break from her ironing, to smile at the street with the swelling pride of a shopkeeper who has a piece of pavement to herself. The Rue de la Goutte-d'Or belonged to her; so did the streets around it and, indeed, the whole neighborhood. When she put her head out of the door, in her white bodice, her arms bare and her blonde hair disheveled by the work, she looked right and left, to both ends of the street, taking in the passers-by, the houses, the pavement and the sky in a single glance. To the left, the Rue de la Goutte-d'Or led off, peaceful and empty, towards a small town where the women held murmured conversations at their doorsteps; to the right, a few yards away, the Rue des Poissonniers brought a din of traffic and the continual march of the crowd backwards and forwards, which made this end a whirlpool of milling people. Gervaise loved the street, the jolting of wagons over the pot-holes between the rough humped cobbles and the jostling of people along the narrow pavements, interrupted by steep piles of gravel. The three meters of gutter in front of her own shop took on immense importance: a broad river, which she thought of as very clear, a strange, living river, its waters colored by the dyeworks in the most fantastic hues amid the black mud. Then she was interested in the other shops: a huge grocer's with a display of dried fruit held together by finely meshed nets; a workers' draper and outfitter, displaying smocks and blue overalls with legs and arms spread wide, swaying at the slightest breeze. In the fruiterer's and the tripe shop, she glimpsed the ends of counters where splendid cats were calmly snoring. Her neighbor, Mme. Vigouroux, the coal merchant, returned her greeting: a small, plump woman, with a black face and shining eyes, who lazed around, laughing with the men, slouching against the front of the shop, which was adorned with logs in a complicated design painted against a maroon background, to give it the appearance of a rustic chalet. The Cudorges, mother and daughter, her other neighbors who kept the umbrella shop, never showed themselves, but left their window dark and their door shut, decorated with two little metal parasols thickly painted with bright vermilion. But, before going inside, Gervaise always glanced across at the big white wall on the opposite side, with no windows in it, only a vast doorway through which you could see the blazing furnace, in a yard littered with carts and carriages with their shafts in the air. On the wall was written the word FARRIER in large letters, surrounded by a semi-circle of horseshoes. All day long, the hammers rang on the anvil and showers of sparks lit up the dismal gloom of the yard. And, beneath this wall, at the bottom of a hole no larger than a cupboard, between a scrap-iron merchant and a chip shop, there was a watchmaker, a decent-looking gentleman in a frock-coat, who was continually probing watches with tiny tools at a bench where delicate things slept under glass covers while, behind him, the pendulums of two or three dozen tiny cuckoo clocks were swinging at once, in the dark squalor of the street, in time to the rhythmical hammering from the farrier's yard.

The neighborhood considered Gervaise very sweet … She was coming up to twenty-eight and had filled out a bit. Her fine features had become fleshier and her movements had a contented slowness. Nowadays, she would sometimes let her mind wander, sitting on the edge of a chair while her iron was heating, with a vague smile, her face suffused with joyful repletion. She was getting fond of her food, everyone said that; but it was no great sin, on the contrary. When one earns enough to pay for delicacies, it would be stupid to eat potato peelings, wouldn't it? Apart from which, she always worked hard, taking endless trouble for her customers and even working through the night, herself, with the shutters up, when there was an urgent job to do. […]

[But] Nana upset the whole house. She was now six. […] The whole building teemed with kids, to an extraordinary extent, swarms of them pouring down the four stairways at all hours of the day and streaming out across the yard, like flocks of noisy, ravaging sparrows … Hordes emerged from every room. And, in the midst of this milling throng of pink-nosed parasites, washed clean every time it rained, there were some tall, stringy ones, others fat, already pot-bellied like grown men, and some tiny little ones, straight from the cradle, still uneasy on their feet, who went back to traveling on all fours when they needed to run. Nana reigned over this heap of brats … Under her leadership, they were always getting into trouble. The gang would paddle in the colored waters from the dyeworks, emerging with their legs dyed blue or red up to the knees. Then she would dash off to the locksmith's to pinch nails and iron filings, before setting off again to plunge into the shavings from the carpenter's shop, great piles of shavings, good fun in themselves, where you could roll around and show your bottom. The yard was her kingdom, echoing with the clatter of little shoes frantically tumbling around and the high screech of voices that rang out whenever the swarm resumed its flight. Some days, even the courtyard was not large enough, so the gang would pour down into the cellars, then run back up, climb the whole length of a staircase, set off along a corridor, then come down a stairway again, follow another corridor, and so on, for hours on end without tiring, constantly screaming, shaking the massive building like a stampede of dangerous wild animals let loose from every side. [...]

[*Ch. 10. After Gervaise loses the shop, she and the disabled Coupeau move to a room in the tenement building where the laundry had been.*] One room and a box-room, nothing more. This is where the Coupeaus lived now. And the room was only as big as the palm of your hand. They had to do everything there: sleep, eat and all the rest. Nana's bed just fitted into the box-room; she had to get undressed in her parents' bedroom and they left the door open at night so that she would not suffocate. The place was so small that Gervaise had handed over some of her things to the Poissons when she left the shop, since she couldn't fit it all in. With the bed, table and four chairs, the apartment was full ... One of the casements was broken and blocked off, which reduced the amount of light and added to the gloom. When she wanted to look out into the yard, since she was getting very fat, she had to squeeze into a space narrower than her own width, leaning sideways and craning her neck before she could see anything.

Notes

1 *Barrière Poissonnière*: the action of the novel takes place on the northern outskirts of Paris in what is now the area behind the Gare du Nord. The Barrière Poissonnière was one of the historic gateways into the city.
2 *join stones*: *pierres d'attente*: the bricks or stones on the end walls of a house, ready to link it to the next building alongside it. References in the novel to building, including Coupeau's profession as a roofer, help to fix it at a time (the 1860s) when Paris was being extensively rebuilt.
3 *carder*: a woman who cards wool.
4 *four years' hard work*: this chapter covers the period from 1850 to 1854.
5 *Claude ... Etienne*: Claude and Etienne reappear in the Rougon-Macquart cycle, the first as the painter in *L'Oeuvre* (1886) and the second as the miner in *Germinal* (1885). Another son of Gervaise and Lantier makes a belated appearance in *La Bête Humaine*; this is Jacques, who was apparently born to the couple before their departure for Paris and left behind in the South. Zola needed a third child to show the effects of a hereditary weakness for alcohol. [...]
6 *quarter-day*: the day when rents were due.
7 *Marshal of France*: no doubt, one of Napoleon's marshals from the days of the (first) Empire.
8 *Pascal ... Béranger*: the mathematician and philosopher Blaise Pascal (1623–62) was famous for his meditations on religious topics; Pierre-Jean de Béranger (1780–1857) was a writer of songs, enormously popular under the Bourbon Restoration, when he represented the voice of patriotic opposition to the regime.

Figure 14
Richard Morris Hunt,
the Stuyvesant
Apartments, 142 East
Eighteenth Street,
New York City, 1870.

Figure 15
The Stuyvesant
Apartments, half of
one floor plan.

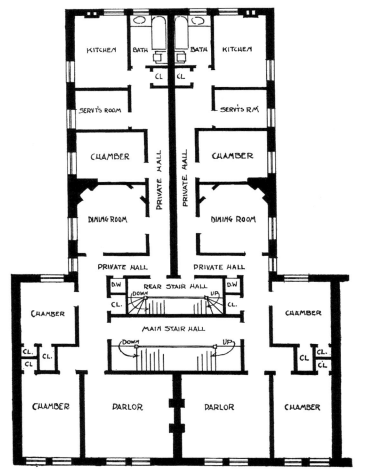

Figure 16
A 68-year-old
railroad employee in
his YMCA room in
Gibson, Indiana,
1943.

Figure 17
Theophil Hansen, Vienna
apartment building
"Heinrichshof", 1861–3,
exterior.

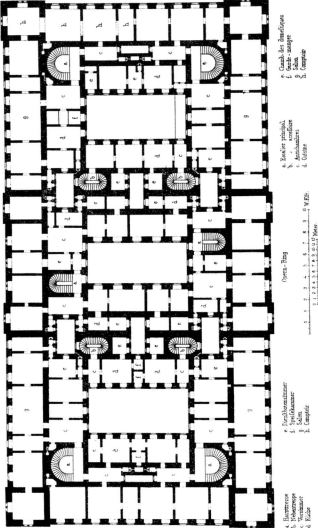

Figure 18
"Heinrichshof", plan.

Figure 19
Paris street: Giuseppe
Canella, *La rue de
Castiglione*, 1829.

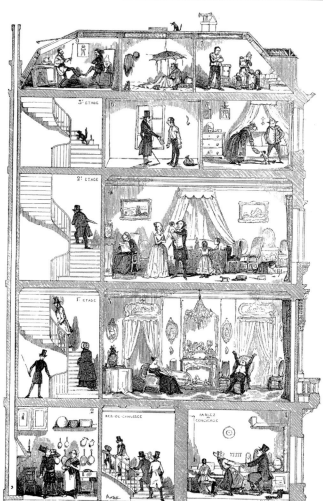

Figure 20
Edmund Texier,
cross-section of a Parisian
apartment building, 1852.

Figure 21 Gervaise Macquart and two of her children, from *Gervaise*, 1956, directed by Réné Clément and starring Maria Schell.

Figure 22 Gervaise setting up her laundry.

6

Victorian domesticity

Ideals and realities

It has long been believed that a particular ideal of domesticity inspired the middle-class Victorian house. With men at work away from the home, it has been argued, women were left behind to provide a safe haven for husband and children within the very private "domestic sphere". Here women and their families worshiped the "Cult of True Womanhood", the belief in a morally pure and sequestered motherhood. Sociologist Mike Hepworth outlines this version of the Victorian ideal, with its religious overtones, using evidence from Victorian literature and painting (see Fig. 23). As a result of this ideal, the dwelling is thought to have evolved in distinctive ways, with great emphasis on "front" and "back", on "public" and "private" spaces, and on a proliferation of rooms with special purposes. Attention has focused particularly on the parlor, full of knick-knacks, where the central life of the family was supposed to take place, and which also served as the main reception room (Fig. 24). As Elizabeth Blackmar shows in Chapter 5, the inclusion of a parlor in middle-class dwellings was already taking place in the early nineteenth century. But a principal inspiration for the parlor, and for Victorian ideas of spaces and privacy more generally, was provided by the writings and designs of British architect Robert Kerr. Included here are excerpts from his *The Gentleman's House* of 1864, and architectural designs that show his emphasis on the multiplication of spaces for specific purposes (Figs. 25, 26). Many of these spaces, but especially the parlor (or "Drawing-room" in Kerr's terminology), reappeared in the later nineteenth century in a wide range of American dwellings, from architect- through builder- to factory-designed houses (Figs. 27, 28, 29 and 30; see also Fig. 24). Yet Suzanne Spencer-Wood challenges traditional views of Victorian domesticity and Victorian housing design, showing far more interpenetration of "public" and "private" activities than has usually been observed. Spencer-Wood argues that "the Cult of True Womanhood", rather than confining women to the home, actually provided a springboard for women's leadership in political, social and architectural reform movements. And art historian Susan Sidlauskas, analyzing a single painting by Edgar Degas, reminds us of the darker side of Victorian domestic life – of the sexual conflicts and gender uncertainties that took place in the private spaces of Victorian dwellings.

Privacy, security and respectability
The ideal Victorian home

Mike Hepworth (1999)

It is difficult to exaggerate the influence of Victorian images on present-day beliefs about the "ideal home". Rapid social and economic changes since the close of the nineteenth century have done little to change the Victorian belief in the home as a private retreat within which a personal life can be enjoyed in peace and security. The term "Victorian" is, of course, derived from the name of Queen Victoria, who ruled from 1837 to 1902 over what was once an extensive British Empire. But, like the empire she once ruled, "Victorian" has come to refer to a series of attitudes and values whose influence goes well beyond the shores of Britain and the boundaries of the nineteenth century. As Grier has noted in her study of culture and comfort in the middle-class North American drawing room or "parlor", the concept of Victorian can be defined in more global terms as the "Anglo-American, transatlantic, bourgeois culture of industrialising western civilisation".[1]

Grier's definition suggests that, seen as a global feature of industrializing western civilization, Victorian culture is dauntingly complex. The aim of this chapter, therefore, is to draw attention to only a single yet nevertheless highly significant strand in Victorian thought, namely the contribution that images of the ideal Victorian home have made to the distinctive features of the idea of home in western society. Images, both visual (photographs, paintings, book illustrations etc.) and verbal (novels, poems, biographies, autobiographies, histories etc.), are closely connected with expressions of the ideal because they often give shape to the hopes and fears of people living during a specific historical period. Mundane everyday life can be seen as a constant struggle to give meaning to life in terms of contemporary cultural ideals. As an image, the "ideal home" is an expression of value: the kind of private life that individuals hope to achieve. As conceived by the Victorians, the image of the ideal home is an essential link between the public and the private domestic world, at once a coveted symbol of success in both these spheres, and of the effort to achieve normality and respectability by its residents.

It is not stretching the argument too far to say that the image of home dominated the Victorian collective vision of a stable and harmonious social environment in the private and public spheres and also in this world and the next. In his study of the roles of hymns and hymn singing in Victorian everyday life, I. Bradley noted that a constantly recurring image in "the depiction of heaven in Victorian hymns is that of the happy home, with work over for the day, the table spread and the family gathered together".[2] If the home in its ideal expression was analogous to heaven, it was also, as Jalland observed, the place where many people hoped to die.[3] Certainly for the middle and upper classes, the family home was the appropriate place to confront and come to terms with the harsh realities of painful terminal illness and death; an essential link between the secular and the sacred. In these social circles "death bed scenes were private affairs which were usually limited to a relatively small number of members of the immediate family, together with a nurse or a servant, and occasionally a doctor".[4] The home, then, was described not only as a retreat from the not infrequently harsh realities of the Victorian world but also as a secluded place to struggle with those realities such as illness and death which succeeded in breaching the walls.

Two important features of the ideal home as a retreat were particularly significant. The first was the constructed façade – the physical structure of stone, bricks and mortar which helped to conceal the residents from public view – and the second has been neatly described by Marshall and Willox as the "home within".[5] The home within was the social organization of private life inside the private spaces such as bedrooms, studies and the various forms of specific social interaction that were possible in these rooms. Because the external structure of the houses built during the building booms of the Victorian period were often uniform in external appearance, as is the case today, it was the home within which gave these homes their individual character and which encouraged an increasing fascination of outsiders (newspaper reporters, novelists, gossips) with the lives of those inside.

While the hedges, fences and walls surrounding residents guaranteed some kind of protection against the world outside, it is important to remember that private spaces of the home were not always sacrosanct and were often open to the scrutiny of other members of the family, especially the "head of the household" and servants. For this reason, as Bailin has indicated, the sickroom was often especially valued as "a haven of comfort", order and "natural affection".[6] Because behavior and expressions of emotions normally repressed in polite society were permissible when someone became ill, the sickroom was the one place within the home where an individual could retreat from the demands of family life and be himself/herself. One of the consolations of illness, as Florence Nightingale discovered during the later part of her life, was that the conventions surrounding the sickroom made it possible for the ill person to abandon the highly disciplined rigors and rituals of respectable conduct and to "express feelings and essential truths about the undisfigured self".[7]

It is important to recognize that the Victorian home was not simply a place for a relaxed presentation of a "real" self away from the prying eyes of the world but a complex arrangement of spaces for the presentation of a miniaturized array of variable domestic selves. There is therefore an evident tension here between the idealized image of the home as a private haven for the self and the practical everyday activities of family life and relationships. For those who lived in polite society, the home was as much a display cabinet of social virtues as it was a haven for an army of would-be social reclusives. Standards had to be maintained both within and without its confines and the ideal Victorian home is therefore more accurately defined as a kind of battleground: a place of constant struggle to maintain privacy, security and respectability in a dangerous world.

It was also, of course, a gendered place. While historians such as Tosh[8] have shown how men became increasingly drawn to the rewards of a domesticated life during the Victorian period, the key role for respectably active women was, as George Elgar Hicks's series of three paintings entitled *Woman's Mission* (1863) graphically asserted, the domestic caregiver. Casteras has recorded that *The Times* newspaper described the trilogy as depicting:

> "woman in three phases of her duties as ministering angel", … Hicks himself believed that woman fulfilled a sacrosanct function as wife and mother and wrote, "I presume no woman will make up her mind to remain single, it is contrary to nature".[9] […]

Respectability and social deviance: the ideal home as fortress

[…] During the early nineteenth century the gradual separation of paid employment from the domestic sphere helped create a new concept of a realm ruled over by women, bringing with it what some social analysts controversially regard as a form of empower-ment in the private sphere.[10] The central contrast between the home and the outside world placed the onus on women to carry out the emotional and moral labor necessary to create and maintain the ideal home: in other words to transform the image into reality. According to Halttunen it was the main responsibility of women to create a world free from the dissimulations, manipulations and heartlessness of the outside world.[11] "By defi-nition", she writes, "the domestic sphere was closed off, hermetically sealed from the poisonous air of the world outside".[12]

According to this analysis of middle-class domestic culture in America, 1830–1870, the location of a staged meeting point between the external potentially threatening world of strangers and the internal domestic sphere of intimates was the parlor. "Geographically", Halttunen observes, the parlor

> lay between the urban street where strangers freely mingled and the back regions of the house where only family members were permitted to enter uninvited. According to the cult of domesticity, the parlor provided the woman of the house with a "cultural podium" from which she was to exert her moral influence.[13]

Within this private sphere clear distinctions were made between deviance and respect-ability. The parlor was the acme of the latter: a purified social arena subject to constant surveillance dictated by the proliferating rules of etiquette. The private world was estab-lished as a respectable social space in constant contrast to the dangers and deviations located in the competitive battlefield of the male-dominated public world where the money was made to furnish the "soft furnishings" of the home.

As the stage on which respectable domestic social performances took place, the parlor was suitably dressed and embellished. Furnishings and decorations were designed and marketed according to complex rules of moral consumption which it was essential for the successful housewife to command as she moved through her prescribed life course from newly married woman to matron:

> The right furniture was thought to ease social intercourse by helping visitors to look their best, and, when correctly arranged, by encouraging circulation. Similarly, the hostess who tastefully arranged potted shrubs, plants, and flowers throughout the room helped "brighten" and "enliven" the company by placing them in "almost a fairy-like scene". In addition she selected and displayed the "curiosities, handsome books, photographs, engravings, stereoscopes, medallions, any works of art you may own", which were the stage properties of polite social intercourse. Such conversation pieces, according to one etiquette manual, were the good hostess's "armor against stupidity". The polite Victorian hostess was not simply an actress in the genteel performance; she was also the stage manager, who exercised great responsibility for the performances of everyone who entered her parlor.[14]

A key feature of these genteel performances was the careful maintenance of the privacy of the back regions of the house. Household manuals advised that the "internal machinery of a household" should be carefully concealed from public view.[15] In these segregated areas could be found members of the family who had not yet been civilized (infants in the nursery) or whose social status was changed in respect of debilitating illnesses, mental or physical (the sickroom) or the decrements of old age (seated before the kitchen fire).

The housewife was entrusted with the discipline of maintaining the decoration of the home and the smooth running of the material mechanisms of family life and also with the maintenance of the healthy physical bodies of members of her family and the support staff. Above all, the Victorian middle-class home was a privatized arena where comfort and etiquette softened the deviant "angles" and "defects" of human character.[16] As we noted above, the Victorian home was not only a haven from deviance but also a place where it was possible for deviance to occur and which must therefore be an arena for constant vigilance. In her study of the culture of comfort, Grier, like Halttunen, focuses on the parlor as one of the places "intended to serve as the setting for important social events and to present the civilized façades of its occupants".[17] The intention was to convey domesticity through "comfort" and cosmopolitanism through "culture". The term "comfort" "designates the presence of the more family-centered, even religious values associated with 'home,' values emphasizing perfect sincerity and moderation in all things. Social commentators claimed comfort to be a distinctively middle-class state of mind".[18]

Hearth and home

As an example of the processes which Grier and Halttunen regard as central to the construction of the middle-class home, it is useful to refer to McNair Wright's *The Complete Home: An Encyclopaedia of Domestic Life and Affairs* (1881): "Between the Home set up in Eden, and the Home before us in Eternity, stand the Homes of Earth in a long succession … Every home has its influence, for good or evil, upon humanity at large".[19] The home of Earth thus takes on a mediating function between the secular and the sacred function. The home and home making were dignified as institutions endowed by God as his ideal of human life and (as noted previously) heaven was conceptualized as an ideal home.

Because of its traditional sacred associations, the fireplace played a special role in the symbolic representation of the ideal home. During the nineteenth century the fireplace, writes Litman,[20] was "an all-pervasive symbol". "Homes lacking fireplaces literally and figuratively lack warmth".[21] In this sense the hearth, as the place where heat is generated before the invention of central heating, is closely associated with the heart as the organ which gives life and is traditionally regarded as the source of human emotion. To be welcomed at the hearth is to anticipate a closer and more intimate form of human relationship. Images of hearths filled with burning logs at Christmas are only one idealized set of images of hearth and home. The sacred symbolism of the hearth was not confined to the bourgeois drawing room or parlor but was part of the wider Victorian concern with the moral implications of architecture. Litman shows how the Victorian reading of architectural forms corresponded with the physiognomic or close scrutiny of external appearances of human beings for evidence of their inner moral character which exercised such an influence on Victorian painters.[22] Mary Cowling has shown how the interpretation of character types by painters of modern Victorian life was influenced by the physiognomic tradition dating principally from the dominant influence in the latter half of the eighteenth century of the Zwinglian minister, Lavater. Victorian audiences were well versed in physiognomic codes deriving from his work and Victorian artists were skilled in drawing on these symbols to comply with the demands of popular taste. Painters and public subscribed to what Cowling describes as a "shared system of beliefs about human character, and its physiognomic expression" and we should not therefore be surprised that the paintings were "read so easily".[23]

The widespread belief in the idea that the moral quality of a person, a place or a building could be determined through a close scrutiny of external appearance and structure inevitably included the home. The pervasive influence of the so-called science of physiognomy was such that significant connections were made between architecture and the visual and literary arts.[24] Thus, as Litman notes, "The great mid-century American architectural theorist, Andrew Jackson Downing, put it succinctly: 'We believe much of the character of every man may be read in his house.'"[25] [...]

In this expanding and symbolically complex arena of ideal homes and gardens the role of the woman as the quintessential housewife remained crucial. Modern developments in consumer culture, particularly the department store, reinforced the Victorian ideal of woman as home maker by playing an important part in educating women as modern housewives.[26] In the department store the housewife learnt both to indulge what were regarded as typical "feminine" whims and fancies, expressed in an "impulsive" fascination with shopping, yet at the same time to temper her desires with a rational eye to the exigencies of "good housekeeping". As Laermans has observed, the department store reinforced the traditional distinction between the home as woman's realm and work as the male sphere of influence. These developments perpetuated the powerful series of symbolic associations established between mundane objects and broader social and spiritual values which were essential to the Victorian images of the ideal home. Grier observes that "Sentimental poetry and fiction not only helped to demonstrate the way in which such chains of association worked in connection to objects such as furniture, but they probably also served to perpetuate conventional associations".[27] She quotes the example of the poem "The Old Arm-Chair" by Eliza Cook published in *Godey's Lady's Book* in March 1855. "The Old Arm-Chair" was hallowed because it had belonged to the owner's deceased mother and reminded her of childhood teachings at her mother's knee. She cannot bear to be parted from it because it represents in material form the union between their two souls – a union made, it need scarcely be added – within the sanctity of the home.

Conclusion

This chapter has surveyed what are considered by historians and sociologists to be some of the key characteristics of the ideal Victorian home. It has for the most part been concerned with images, or representations in visual and verbal form, of hopes (and fears) concerning the role of the home in the wider society, a society which was undergoing rapid upheaval and change. The Victorians were, therefore, extremely conscious of the instability of society and the need to establish a basic series of ground-rules for moral conduct – a clear set of boundaries between deviance and respectability. The Victorian home can be seen, in its ideal version, as a controlled private realm within whose walls even more controls had to be established to maintain a desired congruence between appearance and reality. The moral home life not only had to be lived on a daily basis but also had to be seen to be lived. Hence the need to continue to reproduce these images in art, literature and consumer culture. Inevitably these pressures produced conflict and the symbolic richness of the Victorian home, as displayed for example in the increasingly popular collections of Victorian domestic design, must be examined in the context of a continuous struggle to reconcile the demands of the ideal with the exigencies and contingencies of everyday living. All the signs are that just as present-day conceptions of family life have been heavily influenced by Victorian ideas so we can continue to learn from their success, and failures, in making the ideal a practical reality.

Notes

1 Katherine Grier, *Culture and Comfort: People, Parlors and Upholstery: 1850–1930*, Rochester, NY: The Strong Museum, 1988, p. 2.
2 Ian Bradley, *Abide with Me: The World of Victorian Hymns*, London: SCM Press, 1997, p. 118.
3 Patricia Jalland, *Death in the Victorian Family*, Oxford: Oxford University Press, 1996.
4 Ibid., p. 26.
5 John Marshall and Ian Willox, *The Victorian House*, London: Sidgwick and Jackson, 1986, p. 57.
6 Miriam Bailin, *The Sickroom in Victorian Fiction: The Art of Being Ill*, Cambridge: Cambridge University Press, 1994, p. 6.
7 Ibid., p. 24.
8 John Tosh, "New Men'? The Bourgeois Cult of Home", *History Today* 46, no. 12, 1996, 9–15.
9 Susan Casteras, *Images of Victorian Womanhood in English Art*, Rutherford, NJ: Fairleigh Dickinson University Press, 1987, pp. 51–2.
10 See Dennis Chapman, *The Home and Social Status*, London: Routledge and Kegan Paul, 1955, chapter 13.
11 Karen Halttunen, *Confidence Men and Painted Women: A Study of Middle Class Culture in America, 1830–1870*, New Haven, Conn.: Yale University Press, 1982.
12 Ibid., p. 59.
13 Ibid.
14 Ibid., p. 105.
15 Ibid.
16 Grier, *Culture and Comfort*, p. 1.
17 Ibid.
18 Ibid.
19 Quoted in Asa Briggs, *Victorian Things*, Harmondsworth: Penguin, 1990, p. 213.
20 Vicki Litman, "The Cottage and the Temple: Melville's Symbolic Use of Architecture", *American Quarterly* 21, no. 3, Autumn 1969, 630–8.
21 Ibid., 632.
22 Mary Cowling, *The Artist as Anthropologist: The Representation of Type and Character in Victorian Art*, Cambridge: Cambridge University Press, 1989; Mike Hepworth, "Wrinkles of Vice and Wrinkles of Virtue': The Moral Interpretation of Aging", in Cornelia Hummel and Christian Lalive d'Epinay (eds) *Images of Aging in Western Societies*, University of Geneva: Center for Interdisciplinary Gerontology, 1995.
23 Cowling, *The Artist as Anthropologist*, p. 5.
24 Graeme Tytler, *Physiognomy in the European Novel: Faces and Fortunes*, Princeton, NJ: Princeton University Press, 1982.
25 Litman, "The Cottage and the Temple", 630.
26 R. Laermans, "Learning to Consume: Early Department Stores and the Shaping of the Modern Consumer Culture", *Theory, Culture and Society* 10, no. 4, 1993, 79–102.
27 Grier, *Culture and Comfort*, pp. 8–9.

The gentleman's house
(or, how to plan English residences)

Robert Kerr (1864)

"A Gentleman's House" – the common phrase which we have taken leave to employ as a technical term (simply because it really is so in ordinary conversation, signifying an idea not otherwise easily expressed) – implies of course that we do not propose to deal in any way with inferior dwellings, such as Cottages, Farmhouses, and Houses of Business. But at the same time it is not necessary, or even desirable, to apply the term in any more restricted sense. No question of mere magnitude is involved; no degree of embellishment; no local or personal peculiarity: but there is indicated an entire class of dwellings, in which it will be found, notwithstanding infinite variety of scale, that the elements of accommodation and arrangement are always the same; being based, in fact, upon what is in a certain sense unvarying throughout the British Islands, namely, the domestic habits of refined persons. To put the case familiarly, there are houses in which the accommodation is of the smallest, and the expenditure the most restricted, whose plan nevertheless is such that persons who have been accustomed to the best society find themselves at ease; and there are others upon which ample dimensions, liberal outlay, and elaborate decoration have entirely failed to confer the character of a Gentleman's House.

A scheme of classification which shall be applicable alike to houses of all degrees of importance is not perhaps easily contrived; but the following is offered as being at least practical and simple.

Primarily the House of an English gentleman is divisible into two departments; namely, that of THE FAMILY, and that of THE SERVANTS. In dwellings of inferior class, such as Farmhouses and the houses of tradesmen, this separation is not so distinct; but in the smallest establishment of the kind with which we have here to deal this element of character must be considered essential; and as the importance of the family increases the distinction is widened, – each department becoming more and more amplified and elaborated in a direction contrary to that of the other. […]

The qualities which an English gentleman of the present day values in his house are comprehensively these:

> Quiet comfort for his family and guests, —
> Thorough convenience for his domestics, —
> Elegance and importance without ostentation. […]

Privacy

The idea here implied has already been suggested; being, indeed, the basis of our primary classification. It is a first principle with the better classes of English people that the Family Rooms shall be essentially private, and as much as possible the Family Thoroughfares. It becomes the foremost of all maxims, therefore, however small the establishment, that the Servants' Department shall be separated from the Main House, so that what passes on either side of the boundary shall be both invisible and inaudible on the other. The best illustrations of the want of proper attention to this rule must necessarily be obtained from houses of the smaller sort; and here cases more or less striking are unfortunately by no means rare. Not to mention that most unrefined arrangement whereby at one sole entrance-door the visitors rub shoulders with the trades people, how objectionable it is we need scarcely say when a thin partition transmits the sounds of the Scullery or Coal-cellar to the Dining-room or Study; or when a Kitchen window forms in summer weather a trap to catch the conversation at the casement of the Drawing-room; or when a Kitchen doorway in the Vestibule or Staircase exposes to view the dresser or the cooking-range, and fills the house with unwelcome odors …

On the same principle of privacy, as we advance in scale and style of living, a separate Staircase becomes necessary for the servants' use; then the privacy of Corridors and

Passages becomes a problem, and the lines of traffic of the servants and family respectively have to be kept clear of each other by recognized precautions; again, in the Mansions of the nobility and wealthy gentry, where personal attendants must be continually passing to and fro, it becomes desirable once more to dispose the routes of even this traffic so that privacy may be maintained under difficulties. In short, whether in a small house or a large one, let the family have free passage-way without encountering the servants unexpectedly; and let the servants have access to all their duties without coming unexpectedly upon the family or visitors. On both sides this privacy is highly valued.

It is matter also for the architect's care that the outdoor work of the domestics shall not be visible from the house or grounds, or the windows of their Offices overlooked. At the same time it is equally important that the walks of the family shall not be open to view from the Servants' Department. The Sleeping-rooms of the domestics, also, have to be separated both internally and externally from those of the family, and indeed separately approached.

The idea which underlies all is simply this. The family constitute one community: the servants another. Whatever may be their mutual regard and confidence as dwellers under the same roof, each class is entitled to shut its door upon the other and be alone.

When the question of the privacy of Rooms comes into notice more properly, in our examination of the apartments in detail, the development of the principle at large will further appear. We may, however, here refer to one point at least of general application, namely, the comparative merits of Italian and Elizabethan plan in respect of the privacy of Thoroughfares. In the Classic model, privacy is certainly less. The Principal Staircase especially is almost invariably an instance of this; so also are the various forms of Cortile, Central Hall, and Saloon; all are in a manner public places. But in the Medieval model, privacy is never difficult of accomplishment. The Staircase, for example, is generally secluded; and even a Gallery, if properly planned, becomes almost a Family-room. In other words, it may be said that the open central lines of thoroughfare in Italian plan must necessarily favor publicity, whilst the indirect routes of the Medieval arrangement must equally favor privacy. Or it may be put thus: the Italian model, legitimately descended from the Roman, still suggests its origin in the open-air habits of a Southern climate; whilst the old English model, the growth of Northern soil, displays a character of domestic seclusion which seems to be more natural to the indoor habits of a Northern home …

Comfort

What we call in England *a comfortable house* is a thing so intimately identified with English customs as to make us apt to say that in no other country but our own is this element of comfort fully understood; or at all events that the comfort of any other nation is not the comfort of this. The peculiarities of our climate, the domesticated habits of almost all classes, our family reserve, and our large share of the means and appliances of easy living, all combine to make what is called a comfortable home perhaps the most cherished possession of an Englishman. […]

In its more ordinary sense the comfortableness of a house indicates exemption from all such evils as draughts, smoky chimneys, kitchen smells, damp, vermin, noise, and dust; summer sultriness and winter cold; dark corners, blind passages and musty rooms.[1] But in its larger sense comfort includes the idea that every room in the house, according to its purpose, shall be for that purpose satisfactorily contrived, so as to be free from perversities of its own, – so planned, in short, considered by itself, as to be in every respect a comfortable room of its kind. [...]

Drawing-room

This is the Lady's Apartment essentially, being the modern form of the *Lady's With-drawing-room*, otherwise the *Parlor*, or perfected *Chamber* of Medieval Plan. If a Morning-room be not provided, it is properly the only Sitting-room of the family. In it also in any case the ladies receive calls throughout the day, and the family and their guests assemble before dinner. After dinner the ladies withdraw to it, and are joined by the gentlemen for the evening. It is also the Reception-room for evening parties. There is only one kind of Drawing-room as regards purpose: there is little difference, except in size and evidence of opulence, between that of the duchess and that of the simplest gentlewoman in the neighborhood. Consequently, although in most respects the chief room of the house, it is, perhaps, the most easily reduced to system of any.

The *character* to be always aimed at in a Drawing-room is especial cheerfulness, refinement of elegance, and what is called lightness as opposed to massiveness. Decoration and furniture ought therefore to be comparatively delicate; in short, the rule in everything is this – if the expression may be used – to be entirely *ladylike*. The comparison of Dining-room and Drawing-room, therefore, is in almost every way one of contrast.

The proper *Aspect* for a Drawing-room must, of course, be such as to meet sunshine and mild weather, so that the ladies may enjoy the most free and direct communication with the open air. Southward will consequently be the general tendency; and the precise point of the compass which is most eligible will be determined by an avoidance on the one hand of the bitter and unhealthy East winds, and on the other of the quarter of wet winds and sultry sunshine. [...]

Prospect is generally held to be the most important of all considerations in the disposition of a Drawing-room; and certainly it must always be matter for regret if this room cannot be made to look out upon the very best view that the house commands. But let it never be forgotten that here especially aspect also is of the greatest moment; and if, when all the resources of end-windows and bay-windows are exhausted, the desired prospect is not obtained, the effort, in all but very exceptional cases, ought scarcely to go further. The prospect may probably be turned to account in some other way; but the discomfort of a Drawing-room which presents itself unfavorably to the weather or the sun will never cease to make itself felt.

In their general scheme the *internal arrangements* of a Drawing-room have several times been alluded to as those of the sitting-room or *Parlor*. This scheme starts with the principles (speaking of a very common room), first, that the door should be far from both the fire and the window, on account of the draught; secondly, that the window should be near the fire, for the sake of light at the fireside and warmth at the window; thirdly, that the door should not come between the fire and the window; fourthly, that the window should light both sides of the fire; and fifthly, that the fire should have a central position in the room. Accordingly the fireplace, in ordinary cases, is best situated in the middle of one side ..., and opposite the windows. [...]

The *Furniture* of a Drawing-room is not such as to require any special arrangements of the architect's plan; provided the desire to render the room graceful and light has not induced him to give window-space in such excess as to occasion an embarrassing deficiency of wall space. In a small room there will be probably a center table, perhaps with chandelier over, the usual chairs and couch, occasional table, sofa-table, or writing-table, occasional chairs, a chiffonier generally, or one or more fancy cabinets, perhaps one or more pier-tables, a whatnot or the like, one or more mirrors, and a cabinet pianoforte. If there be sufficient space there may be an ottoman settee; perhaps a pair of wall settees also. In a large room the principle of furnishing is still the same; everything becomes doubled in number or more; varieties of chairs, lounges, tables, cabinets, and so on, are multiplied; the pianoforte becomes a grand; sculptures are perhaps introduced; instead of a single chandelier there are two (although one is still preferable generally), and accessory lights are added at the walls; but nevertheless the comparatively simple idea of a Parlor or Sitting-room is always preserved.

The architect ought never to allow himself, unless in extraordinary cases, and with a very clear understanding of the case, to make unusual provisions for furniture. Even as regards mirrors, for example, although there are instances when an architectural effect may be aimed at, the architect must not venture to reckon without in the first place his client, and in the second his client's upholsterer. At the same time it must be admitted that if architect and upholsterer can be made to work together intelligently and artistically, very charming effects can be realized; the architect's decorations bearing to the hangings, mirrors, and the rest, the relations of a framework whose own integrity is left untouched, and the work of the tradesman serving to fill up all gaps of design, and give richness to the architectural arrangements.

A door of *intercommunication* is admissible in a Drawing-room when opening to the Boudoir, if any, the Library, or the Morning-room. For a small room such a door is never to be too readily accepted; but that the ladies find it to be occasionally of service, especially in large establishments, cannot be disputed. Its general purpose, however, being less for mere intercommunication than for private exit or *escape,* the connection in this way of the Drawing-room with the Morning-room or its equivalent is perhaps all that is necessary in the house. To correct the disturbance of privacy which a door of intercommunication appears to involve, a small intervening lobby and two doors, or even a set of double doors, may often be judiciously employed. By this means at least the chance of one's conversation being overheard is done away with ...

In respect of *external position* the Drawing-room must face upon open Lawn or Flower-garden, or, what is perhaps best, a combination of both. In superior houses a *Terrace* is frequently formed along the Drawing-room front, an admirable feature in landscape-gardening, as well as in architectural design; but in massive Classic compositions it sometimes interposes a barrier to that communication between the Drawing-room and the Lawn, which is so much valued as matter of domestic enjoyment; and this must always be taken into account. [...]

The *internal position* of the Drawing-room ought to be such as to afford an easy, but nevertheless sufficiently stately, access from the Entrance door. The route from Drawing-room to Dining-room must also be similarly contrived ...

It is plain that we have been considering the Drawing-room all this time as a Ground-floor apartment; and so it ought always, if possible, to be. In town, however, the *First-floor Drawing-room* must be accepted, simply for want of area. All that can then be done is to carry out the spirit of the foregoing rules as circumstances best permit. [...]

A closing observation under the head of the Drawing-room may refer to the fact that it is generally the Music-room of the house, and that it is well therefore to construct it accordingly; but this question we leave to be treated of under the head of *Music-room* in the sequel ...

Boudoir

The proper character of a Boudoir is that of a Private Parlor for the mistress of the house. It is the *Lady's Bower* of the olden time. In this light it does not serve in any way to relieve the Drawing-room; nor is it even supplementary or accessory to that apartment; but as the personal retreat of the lady, it leaves the Drawing-room – and the Morning-room if any – still occupied by the family and guests.

In some cases, however, what is called the Boudoir is simply a secondary and smaller Drawing-room. It is then generally turned to account in the way of ordinary use, especially in a small family, so as to preserve the Drawing-room for occasions of more importance. When the Drawing-room itself is very large, this arrangement may have its advantages; but it is manifest that such a Boudoir is really a Morning-room.

The Boudoir in any case follows, in respect of *situation*, *aspect*, *plan*, *furniture*, etc., the ordinary regulations for a small Drawing-room; that is to say, it is to be a Sitting-room, and to open if possible from the principal Corridor of the house. It may, however, be somewhat retired in situation; although such retirement ought not to prejudice free access, it being in many respects the lady's business-room. […]

If circumstances cause the Boudoir to be placed *on the Bedroom story*, this is no objection, provided the access be well contrived. It may then be attached to the Mistress's Bedroom as in the case of the Private Suite. […]

Library

The degree of importance to be assigned to the Library in any particular house would appear, theoretically, to depend altogether upon the literary tastes of the family, and to be, indeed, so far, a criterion of those tastes. But there is a certain standard room, irrespective of such considerations, which constitutes the Library of an average Gentleman's House; and the various gradations by which this may be either diminished or augmented in importance are easily understood. It is not a Library in the sole sense of a depository for books. There is of course the family collection; and the bookcases in which this is accommodated form the chief furniture of the apartment. But it would be an error, except in very special circumstances, to design the Library for mere study. It is primarily a sort of Morning-room for gentlemen rather than anything else. Their correspondence is done here, their reading, and, in some measure, their lounging; – and the Billiard-room, for instance, is not infrequently attached to it. At the same time the ladies are not exactly excluded. […]

The *Fireplace* ought to be placed so as to make a good winter fireside, because this is in great measure a sitting-room. The *door* ought to stand in relation to the fire according to the principles already explained for such a room … A sash door to the open air is not desirable, except in some special case. […]

It is to be observed that we have been hitherto dealing with the ordinary Library of an average house, and no more; but when the owner is a man of learning, we must either add a *Study* or constitute the Library itself one. In the latter case, in order to prevent disturbance, the door will be more conveniently placed, not in the main Corridor, but indirectly connected therewith; no door of intercommunication ought to connect it with any other room (except possibly the Gentleman's-room); and the position externally ought to be more than ordinarily secluded. Double-doors also may be required. In short, the Library, which has hitherto been a public room, and somewhat of a lounge, becomes now essentially a private retreat. […]

An ordinary bedroom

[...] The *primary features* of plan in a Bedroom are, first, the door or doors, the fireplace, and the windows; and secondly, the bedstead, the dressing-table, and the wardrobe; and it has to be remembered that every Bedroom must be considered not merely as a sleeping-room, but as occasionally a sick-room.

Take the most usual kind of Bedroom, namely, one for a married couple with a Dressing-room attached for the gentleman. This may be considered as a room of good size, about square in form, with the window in the middle of one side, the fireplace in the middle of another side, and the door in one angle. Now we shall suppose the position of the *window* alone to be determined. We may generally make it a rule to place the *bedstead* (its head being to the wall after the English manner) with its *side* to the window, rather than its foot. By this means the light is favorably placed, whether for a sleeper or for a sick person: experiment must prove this. The next rule is that the side next the window ought to be the *left* side. [...]

Whilst, however, all this may be theoretically correct, it is certainly very often made the rule, especially in large rooms, to place a four-post-bedstead with its foot to the light. The principle chiefly in view is that a draught from the window is thus rendered impossible. Besides, the fireside, if the doors be well placed, may be more snug. In the case of an oblong room, with two or more windows along one side, this arrangement is frequently rendered inevitable.

If the bedstead be placed after the *French* manner, with one side to the wall, the head ought to be in the direction of the light rather than the foot, and the fireplace if possible, rather than the window, in front.

The best French arrangement (Italian also) places the bedstead in an *Alcove*, as is well known; but it is to be noted that this is done more on Sitting-room considerations than otherwise, the characteristic French Bedroom of the present day being so far very much like the old English "Parlor". At the same time, as a merely pleasant feature, the alcove in question is certainly worth copying in English plan, provided, of course, it is not to be occupied by a four-post-bedstead. This kind of room appears particularly suitable for the occupation of young ladies. [...]

The *Furniture* in a good ordinary Bedroom is as follows. There will be a small writing-table to be accommodated, which may stand almost anywhere near the fire; a washstand in the light; a pier-glass with its back to the light; a wardrobe facing the light, and in a central position; a couch, chairs, easy chairs; a chest of drawers, perhaps a chiffonier or cabinet, and so on, according to the size of the room. [...]

A very convenient form of Bedroom is that which has an *Alcove dressing-place*. When the room is to be used by a bachelor, for instance, who makes it his private retreat during the day, or "own room", this arrangement answers well; in case of sickness also it is sometimes to be appreciated. [...]

Family bedchamber-suite

Although the mistress of a hospitable English house will desire to give her guests every preference, yet this need not deprive her own rooms of their right to conditions in every way favorable. The situation in all external and internal relations ought to be so selected and contrived as to combine the best that can be had of cheerfulness, aspect and prospect, convenience of access in various directions, and special retirement.

In superior houses privacy will require to be now carried so far that probably these rooms may form a department by themselves, entirely separated. Here there are two models chiefly in use. In the one the Suite is placed on the principal Chamber-story, as a *Bedchamber Suite*, and connected with the Gentleman's-room and Boudoir below by means of a Private Staircase … ; in the other it is placed on the Ground-floor, and in direct combination with the Gentleman's-room and Boudoir, thus constituting the *Private Family Suite* …

A complete Bedchamber Suite on the former of these models consists of the Bedroom, either one Dressing-room or two, a Bath-room, a Water-closet (or one to each Dressing-room), very often a special Wardrobe-room, always a private Passage or Lobby or its equivalent, and, when the suite is upstairs, sometimes a private Staircase. If a Lady's-maid's-room be provided in conjunction, it ought not to be so placed as to be actually within the Suite. The outer door of the private Passage or Lobby, when there is no private Stair, will open from the principal Chamber Corridor or its equivalent; and in the case of there being a private Stair, a door of connection between this and the principal Chamber Corridor will follow the same rule.

The best position for the *Private Staircase* for such a Suite is one that shall allow it to ascend from a point beside the doors of the Gentleman's-room and the Boudoir below; and obviously it must on no account be liable to be mistaken for any other Stair. It may perhaps serve also for the Nurseries, as in the case before described in the *Private Family Suite*.

The *Gentleman's Dressing-room* need not be of any more importance than the best of its kind. The *Lady's Dressing-room*, however, may be required to be a very elegant apartment, as a second or even sole Boudoir. In this case let its door be opposite the entrance from the Corridor, so that it may be of direct and somewhat stately access. The *Bathroom* ought to communicate with the Bedroom, having also, if possible, a second entrance from the private Passage. It ought certainly to have a fireplace. The *Wardrobe* may be either a small room, a closet, or a lobby, containing large presses; sometimes a fireplace may be serviceable. Care will especially be required that all these and other smaller apartments, including the private Passage or Staircase, shall be well lighted and ventilated. This problem, if to be solved with due regard to compactness of arrangement, is not always easy. [...]

Other special bedchambers

Bachelors'-Bedrooms, so called, are generally provided in a large establishment, as a number of smaller single rooms, placed together in a secondary position, with some sort of separate access, such as to enable the occupants to pass to and fro without ascending the Principal Staircase, or otherwise using the chief lines of Bedroom thoroughfare. The object is chiefly to provide for the sons of the family, and other young men, unceremonious apartments, and an unceremonious access thereto. The arrangement described a few pages back …, which gives the Bedroom an attached alcove for dressing, is very useful here; as a single gentleman more than any one else is glad to make his bedroom a "sanctum". [...]

Notes

1   It appears to have been matter of disappointment to some readers of our first edition that we do not deal with this class of questions in detail, by way of pointing out the means of prevention and

cure; but a moment's reflection will show that, our subject being *Plan* only, these considerations as a class cannot come formally into our program. Several of them, however, are frequently spoken of incidentally throughout the work.

The world their household
Changing meanings of the domestic sphere in the nineteenth century

Suzanne M. Spencer-Wood (1999)

Alternative Victorian gender ideologies and practices

The rest of this chapter argues that the élite Victorian ideology of nineteenth-century classicists cannot be considered a universal gender structure because it wasn't even universally espoused or practiced by nineteenth-century Americans or Europeans. Ideals of women's exclusive domesticity were practiced neither by working women nor by middle- and upper-class women who delegated child rearing to servants. Further, large numbers of people rejected the dominant Victorian gender ideology that devalued women as inferior and subordinate and made them economically dependent on men while exploiting their domestic labor. For instance, many working women and middle-class reformers rejected the élite Victorian ideal of idle domestic womanhood as sinful and instead extolled the virtues and godliness of labor.

Overview of domestic reform

This section discusses a wide variety of social movements that I call "domestic reform" because they sought through diverse gender ideologies and practices to transform western culture by raising the status of women and domestic labor to be equal to the status of men and public labor. Traditional histories that focus on the male public sphere largely overlook women's domestic reform movements as private organizations insignificant to history. Domestic reform was researched by feminist historians starting in the late 1970s, and in 1981 Hayden categorized a number of women's reform movements as "material feminists". I have coined the term "domestic reformers" for these movements because many reformers opposed female suffrage at least initially and their reforms were directed at re-forming the household or domestic sphere.[1] Because women's domestic sphere was defined in relation to men's public sphere, redefining the domestic sphere also meant redefining the public sphere, resulting in the transformation of western culture and gender ideology from the nineteenth century into the twentieth century.

Domestic reformers were mostly middle-class women and some men who changed dominant Victorian ideology by redefining women's domestic sphere in relation to men's public sphere. The reformers resisted male dominance by arguing that women should control an expanded household that included both the domestic sphere and parts of the public sphere. In a number of different ways the reformers conflated the meanings of domestic and public by making the domestic sphere public and the public sphere domestic. The boundary between the supposedly separate gender spheres blurred as they were combined fundamentally in two ways.[2]

First, domestic reformers made parts of the domestic sphere public by transforming many of women's household tasks into public female professions which were acceptable for women within the dominant gender ideology because they were arguably "domestic" professions. Domestic reformers argued that just as women were innately best suited to take care of the private family and household, women were also best suited to be the caretakers or mothers of the community-as-household.[3] By extending women's private household roles into the public community, domestic reformers created a powerful positive solution to the fundamental nineteenth-century social problem of "whether the existence of the marital family is compatible with that of the universal family which the term 'Community' signifies".[4] Cooperative housekeeping expanded the meaning of "family" and "household" from private homes to the public community. Second, domestic reformers applied men's public sphere rational thinking, scientific methods and technology to both private and public households in order to transform housework into a profession equivalent to men's public professions. The professionalization of housework was symbolized and implemented with special scientific equipment and classes and schools in domestic science, scientific cooking, housekeeping and home economics. In sum, the reformers sought to raise women's status by transforming domestic work into women's professions both in the private household and in the public sphere.[5]

Reformers socialized many household tasks to create women's public housekeeping cooperatives, in which individual women cooperated for the rational efficient production of household tasks and products. Cooperatives resisted male-dominated individual households in which the same tasks were repeated by each woman in isolation. The idea of public housekeeping cooperatives spread from Europe to the United States in the late eighteenth century and in the nineteenth, often as a result of American women's experiences and observations when studying or visiting in Europe. Cooperatives included day nurseries, kindergartens, playgrounds, cooking, dining, and laundry cooperatives, working women's cooperative homes, public kitchens, and social settlements. The reformers symbolized and implemented the professionalization of domestic tasks by founding industrial schools for girls and adult schools and classes that created higher levels of female teaching professions, such as college professors in home economics and early childhood education (e.g. kindergartens, Montessori, etc.). By socializing aspects of housework in the public sphere the reformers created many women's public professions that are still major female-dominated professions today such as kindergarten and nursery school teaching, home economics, nursing, nutrition, social work and public health. Domestic reformers also successfully argued that some male-dominated professions should become female-dominated because women's supposedly innate domestic abilities made them better suited than men to be grade-school teachers, sales clerks, typists, secretaries, bank tellers and telephone operators.[6]

Documentary and material evidence shows that domestic reform movements taken together transformed western culture by redefining the dominant gender ideology to make it acceptable for women to work in what was considered men's public sphere. Further, domestic reform movements were instrumental in creating a majority for female suffrage in Britain and in the United States. The effectiveness and importance of a wide variety of domestic reform organizations and programs is amply demonstrated by their rapid growth in numbers and membership, their spread across the western world, and the long-term utility of many of these social service organizations up to the present day.[7]

Domestic reform ideologies

Domestic reform was supported by a great diversity of ideologies, but was united by some shared beliefs. The belief that every aspect of social life had "domestic meaning"[8] redefined the household and domestic reform activities as virtually unlimited. Most domestic reformers believed in the Cult of True Womanhood[9] or Domesticity that defined women as domestic, but combined it with Enlightenment egalitarian beliefs and the democratic ideology of the American and French republics (ideologically drawing on men's Classical education stressing the socio-politics of the Greek and Roman worlds), to create an ideology of equality between women's domestic sphere and men's public sphere. Domestic reformers combined Enlightenment beliefs in the perfectibility of society with the development of science to advocate perfecting housework tasks by rationalizing them with efficient scientific methods and equipment. Applying rational, scientific principles to housework was also supported by the popular "religion of science" that viewed scientific laws of nature and principles of order as manifestations of the symmetry and harmony of God's creation.[10]

In cooperative housekeeping movements, women applied their domestic values and superior morality to reform what they saw as the corruption and sin resulting from capitalism and usury in men's public sphere.[11] Their goal, as president of the Women's Christian Temperance Union Frances Willard put it, was to "make the whole world homelike".[12] Evangelical Christian reformers sought to reform and perfect society for the second coming of Christ in the Millennium.[13] Evangelical Christians rejected Puritanical beliefs in original sin and predestination to transform American culture with beliefs in original purity and the possibility of redemption and salvation through good deeds and benevolence, including many domestic reform institutions. The socialization of household tasks into public housekeeping cooperatives in communes and in urban areas was supported by Utopian religious ideology about community families and households, Enlightenment perfectionist and egalitarian beliefs, Communitarian Socialist beliefs in the scientific efficiency of collective labor, and Plato's philosophy of an élite egalitarian cooperative, proposed in *The Republic*.[14]

American historians, in most cases feminists, have identified a number of cults that ideologically supported domestic reform in both America and Europe. The status of women and their household roles was raised by the Cult of True Womanhood, or Domesticity, the Cult of Home Religion, and the Cult of Republican Motherhood. Women's public professions were legitimated and supported by Republicanism, the Cult of Single Blessedness and the Cult of Real Womanhood. The Cult of Domesticity argued that women's domesticity made them superior to men both in domestic ability and morally. Reformers resisted male dominance in the household by arguing that women's supposedly innately superior domestic abilities made them better suited to control their domestic sphere. Women's superior morality was established because their domestic sphere was separated from the supposedly sinful capitalism and usury in men's public sphere.[15] This logically led to the Cult of Home Religion which advocated household worship in the more moral domestic sphere.[16] The reformers created the Cult of Republican Motherhood to argue for women's equal rights to education as the mothers of the next generation of male democratic leaders, extending American and French egalitarian democratic ideals from men to women.[17] These cults raised the status of women and their domestic roles in the household.

Women's public professions were legitimated and supported by Republicanism, the Cult of Single Blessedness and the Cult of Real Womanhood. From Republicanism some women argued that they were public independent republics deserving suffrage, in resistance to the *femme coverte* tradition of married men representing their wives.[18] Both republican ideology and religious ideology about the high status of nuns as the brides of Christ were the background to the development of the Cult of Single Blessedness in 1780, which advocated that women not marry but instead become economically independent through public professions, to redress the economic dependence on men that made women subordinate. And in fact the proportion of unmarried women in America increased from approximately 7 percent in the 1830s to approximately 11 percent in 1870.[19] As late as the 1910s a newspaper article asked whether most employed women ascribed to the "Cult of Single Blessedness" and pointed out that most women journalists were married.[20] In the second half of the nineteenth century the Cult of Real Womanhood advocated that women should be educated, marry carefully, maintain health and physical fitness, and be trained for a profession in case they should need to support their families.[21]

These ideologies supported educational, economic, and physical sources of power for women and the development of women's public professions by domestic reformers. My research has revealed how women reformers created and drew on such alternative ideologies of equality to change the meaning of the domestic/public dichotomy in élite Victorian gender ideology. Using an inclusive feminist approach, I seek not simply to validate materially any single historic gender ideology, but ask instead what the evidence indicates about the extent to which the variety of alternative gender ideologies affected material culture used in actual historic behaviors.

Historical archaeology of domestic reform

A historical archaeology of domestic reform is particularly useful because reform ideologies were symbolized and implemented with material culture. Further, both documentary data and archaeological data need to be analyzed conjunctively in order to develop an understanding of how ideologies were realized in actual practices of domestic reform. The documents of domestic reform are largely prescriptive, detailing ideal religious or scientific material culture to be used to symbolize and implement different ideologies of domestic reform. Ideologies and prescriptions of ideal material culture are important contributions to ideological and intellectual histories, but must not be mistaken for actual practices. Archaeological research on the material culture and built environments actually used for domestic reform can provide insights into the relationships between ideals and practices. Material culture and architecture used to implement domestic reform may be found above or below ground, or in the few documents and depictions concerning the actual operation of domestic reform institutions, enterprises, and programs. More domestic reform material culture may be excavated in site yards in poor or rural neighborhoods that lacked municipal trash collection, and in site yards used by children who were more likely to lose artifacts than were adults.

In many cases it may be difficult or impossible to distinguish architecture or material culture used in domestic reform from ordinary domestic architecture or equipment. However, by using documents to identify and locate domestic reform sites archaeological excavation can be used to determine the extent to which ordinary material culture or ideal domestic reform artifacts and architecture were used at these sites. Both innovative and ordinary material culture were consciously given new meanings to symbolize and implement domestic reform. This corresponds well with a material feminist approach that views material culture not simply as a product or reflection of cultural behavior or ideology but as an active social agent shaping behavior. Domestic reform also demonstrates how cultural materials, buildings, and spaces have no fixed meaning or gender identity, but rather change meanings in different subcultural contexts. These meanings may only be ascertained through the synergistic contextual interpretation of documents and material culture which is the essence of historical archaeology.

The rest of this chapter will reveal that domestic reform was not monolithic, but included a wide variety of social movements and reformers who espoused many different gender ideologies and operated a great diversity of institutions, organizations, and programs. Examples of the diversity of domestic reform ideologies, practices, architecture and distinctive material culture will be discussed in sequence for public housekeeping cooperatives in communal societies, followed by urban public housekeeping cooperatives with or without kitchenless houses or apartments, and finally domestic reform of the household.

Public communal households

The earliest domestic reform movements were European communal societies of the seventeenth century that combined heretical religious ideologies with socialism and communalism. Many communes were heretical sects that emigrated to America to avoid persecution by state churches. Socialist communes were often founded first in Europe and then replicated in America. The most renowned heretical sect with cooperative housekeeping that fled to America were the Shakers, who founded nineteen Societies from Maine to Kentucky (1774–1826) under the leadership of Ann Lee, who in 1759 had become a leader of the Shakers in England (which was founded by a married couple).[22] Other heretical sects that fled Europe to found communes with cooperative housekeeping in the United States included three Harmony Society towns (founded by George Rapp 1805–24), and seven Amana Inspirationist communes (founded by women and men, starting 1855) that still thrive today. An American heretic, John H. Noyes, founded the three towns of the Oneida Perfectionists (1847–78). The most renowned socialist communal experiments included a few Fourierist Phalanxes and Owenite communities in Europe and in the United States: fifteen Owenite communes (1820s–1830), Brook Farm (1841–6), and thirty Fourierist Associations (1840–60), which combined science and religion.[23] Communes often influenced each other, as exemplified by the inspiration the Oneida Perfectionists gained from Brook Farm, Shaker communalism, and socialism, while rejecting Fourierism. People in communal societies felt that they could not reform the whole society and therefore withdrew to form a perfect cooperative society in miniature – a heaven on earth.[24]

Commune ideologies

The egalitarian ideologies of communes were drawn from a great historical depth and diversity of sources. The diverse egalitarian ideologies of religious communes developed from different interpretations of the Bible, especially Christ's Sermon on the Mount, the Apostolic communal church, Gnosticism brought back from the Crusades, Deism, and books such as St. Thomas More's *Utopia*, which derived almost entirely from the élite commune proposed in Plato's *Republic*. Socialist communes combined the "religion of science", Enlightenment egalitarian ideology, and Communitarian Socialism that also drew on the ideology in Plato's *Republic*. Thus most communes believed in gender, racial and ethnic equality as well as communal property, but differed from Plato by abolishing slavery in any form. The great diversity in egalitarian communal ideologies can be illustrated by a few examples. The Shakers believed that God was bisexual and created female and male "in our image". Biblical authority for the absence of marriage in Heaven was interpreted by the Shakers and most other heretical sects to justify celibacy, while the Oneidans interpreted the same text to justify promiscuity. Fourier's "religion of science" belief that God created a harmonious universe was combined with a fanciful scheme of cosmological evolution, including seas turning into lemonade, polyandry with concubinage, and "attractive industry" on a cooperative basis.[25] While both Owen and Fourier believed that character was shaped by environment rather than heredity, Fourier went beyond Owenite arguments for gender equality through collective housekeeping by claiming that "The degree of emancipation of women is the natural measure of general emancipation" and "the extension of the privileges of women is the fundamental cause of all social progress".[26]

Commune gender practices

The egalitarian ideologies of communal societies were practiced by women who transformed domestic production into public cooperative housekeeping that was equal in status to men's cooperative agricultural and craft production. Some communes permitted or practiced some form of marriage, but most religious communes practiced celibacy and asceticism that with egalitarian cooperative living had a long tradition in Christian monasteries, nunneries, abbeys and heretical sects.[27] Men and women often worked in gender-segregated groups. Despite egalitarian ideologies, women were usually paid less than men.[28] Women cooperatively performed most household tasks and produced goods such as clothing, milk, butter, cheese, vegetables, fruit and eggs, while men worked cooperatively in fields, craft shops and mills to produce goods such as meat, grain, flour, lumber, buildings, and furniture. In a few communes, such as the Social Palace in Guise, France, and at Oneida, both genders worked in communal factories that provided strong economic bases for these communes.[29]

Most communes were founded and led by men, although a few were founded and led by women or leaders of both genders. My feminist both/and approach can be used to model the diversity in gendered leadership practices as a continuum from exclusively male leadership at one extreme to female leadership at the other extreme, with the shared leadership of the Shakers in between. The diversity of communal governments can be modeled on a continuum from completely autocratic at one end to entirely democratic at the other end, with many communes falling somewhere in between. These two leadership practices intersect at different points along these continuums to model the autocratic male leadership of George Rapp, the mixed gender autocratic leadership of the Shakers, the partial democracy (for men and unmarried women) of the Amana Inspirationists, and the consensus government of the Oneidans.[30]

Archaeology of communal households

Archaeologists can gain information about the degree of cooperation, centralization and segmentation of tasks in communes from the size and configuration of buildings.

Applying my inclusive both/and feminist paradigm, degree of cooperative architecture can be modeled on a continuum from private households at one end to public community cooperative households at the other end, with combinations in between. The social dimension of degree of centralization can also be modeled on a continuum measuring the number of cooperative tasks performed in single large buildings versus the number of cooperative tasks in separate buildings. The kinds of cooperative tasks in different buildings may be indicated by types of artifacts lost or discarded near buildings. Most communes segregated cooperative tasks into different buildings to some extent. Many communes, especially religious sects, were organized as one community household in a large structure. In the United States, Shaker "families", the Oneida Perfectionists, and Fourierists lived in large buildings with cooperative facilities including at least a kitchen, dining room and meeting room, plus separate buildings for other cooperatives. In the early 1860s the Oneida Perfectionists constructed a single building that housed mixed gender living quarters as well as the cooperative kitchen, dining hall, workshops and a nursery. The cooperative laundry and older childcare were in separate buildings, as well as the carpentry shop, barns, and factories. A Fourierist Phalanstery building for cooperative living often included a laundry and bakery, while the Shakers used separate buildings.

Excavations at American Shaker villages have uncovered the foundations of buildings used for cooperative housekeeping by a Shaker "family" that had gender-segregated living quarters. Excavation uncovered the huge stone base of a large fireplace/stove for cooperative cooking, large pots and serving dishes for cooperative eating, as well as artifacts in other structures indicating cooperative weaving and education.[31] The Amana Inspirationists built separate small kitchenless houses of four apartments each that would leave clusters of small foundations around a larger cooperative house for every fifty residents with a large kitchen and chimney base, dining room, and laundry that might be identifiable if large soapstone sinks remained. Nearby were communal kindergartens, schools and workshops. The Rappites built family row houses with private kitchens that would leave a long subdivided foundation with a small chimney base in each unit, plus a large cooperative building foundation with a large chimney base for cooperatively cooking of feasts. The Fourierist Social Palace built in 1859 at Guise, France, housed 350 ironworkers and their families in large buildings containing separate family apartments with private kitchens, plus separate buildings for a public community cooperative bakery, café, schools, theater, restaurant and butcher shop. The largest central apartment house included a cooperative nursery and kindergarten specially designed for children.[32] [...]

Public cooperative households

The idea of cooperative housekeeping spread from communitarian socialist ideology and communes to cooperative hotels and apartments. Fourier's early call for shared facilities in Parisian apartment buildings was followed by designs for cooperative apartments by American reformer Melusina Fay Pierce in 1869 and subsequent designs by a number of mostly male architects that were constructed in cities from Boston and New York to London, Paris and Moscow. Starting in the 1870s middle- and upper-class cooperative apartment hotels offered collective dining, and cooking, laundry, housework, and childcare by servants, transforming the stigmatized occupation of domestic service into higher status hourly waged occupations with regular hours. Some hotels also offered private dining rooms and kitchens in the apartments. Apartment hotels offered economies through cooperative domestic services and women were freed from organizing servants so they could organize social movements such as domestic reform. Some commercial cooperative hotels were also constructed for single working women who were willing to pay for cooperative parlors, dining rooms, cooking, and laundry. Socialist and communist workers' organizations hired architects to design a number of cooperative apartment houses, starting in the United States in the 1910s and in Paris and Moscow by the 1920s. Workers cooperatively built and owned these apartment houses and paid for cooperative domestic services such as dining clubs, tearooms, cafeterias or restaurants, bakeries, day nurseries, kindergartens, playgrounds, and laundries. Some included libraries, auditoriums, schools, and health centers, as well as tailors, butchers, and grocery stores.[33]

Non-commercial cooperative homes for the increasing numbers of single working women in the 1890s were either organized by working women or by domestic reformers. Working women sometimes arranged to live together, cooperatively sharing housework and rent and supporting each other in times of unemployment and strikes, as at the Jane Club in Chicago. Women reformers and religious orders created non-profit cooperative homes for working women in order to prevent the financial and sexual exploitation of women by unscrupulous commercial boarding-house keepers. Cooperative homes for working women were the most widespread type of cooperative housekeeping institution, including both religious and non-sectarian homes. The most widespread and numerous type of cooperative home for working women which also offered educational classes and employment services were the YWCA homes. Modeled after the YMCA, the first YWCA was created in London in 1855 thence spreading to America and Australia. The YWCA offered not only cooperative dining rooms, kitchens, parlors and laundries, but also lecture halls, class rooms, reading rooms, gymnasiums, cafés and club rooms.[34]

College-educated women and men reformers cooperatively lived in social settlement houses in poor neighborhoods in order to offer poor families a wide variety of programs. Settlement houses run by male reformers in London inspired Jane Addams to found the first American settlement house in 1889 in Chicago, which started a large movement in the United States. Women reformers sought to alleviate working women's double burden of work and housework by offering childcare and education in cooperative day nurseries and kindergartens. To prepare the unskilled, mostly immigrant, poor to become employed citizens, settlements and industrial schools operated by women and/or men offered classes in subjects ranging from mathematics and English, to printing, typing, dressmaking, cooking, housekeeping and domestic science. Classes were included both for children and for adults, sometimes segregated by gender. Programs to keep latchkey children from the immoral temptations of the streets after school included playgrounds, gardens and clubs in subjects such as history, biology, music, dancing and reading.[35] [...]

Public cooperative housekeeping enterprises

Domestic reformers also founded cooperative housekeeping enterprises outside of cooperative households. In most cases public cooperative housekeeping enterprises did not completely replace private housekeeping in homes. Rather, household tasks were separately socialized in cooperative institutions, including neighborhood cooperative kitchens, dining cooperatives, cooked food delivery services, public kitchens, day nurseries, and kindergartens.

Childcare cooperatives

The idea of day nurseries that provided physical care for infants spread from French crèches run by nuns to nurseries in communes and day nurseries as separate institutions. Later in the nineteenth-century day nurseries often included kindergarten classes for older children.[36] Following Robert Owen's innovations in developmental childhood education for working mothers at his Institute for the Formation of Character (1800–24) in Scotland, the kindergarten was invented in 1837 in Germany by Friedrich Froebel.[37] He developed the kindergarten ideology of discovery learning through which children harmoniously developed their God-given mental and physical capacities by playing with specially designed educational toys, called Froebelian gifts. Starting in 1838 German immigrants founded German-language kindergartens in the United States. The American kindergarten movement was led by Elizabeth Peabody, who founded the first English-speaking kindergarten in Boston in 1860. Around the turn of the century Italian Maria Montessori created Montessori schools that stressed more structured individualized learning of skills and scientific principles. Although some American women educators translated and advocated Montessori's methods in the 1910s, and a 1913 American lecture tour by Montessori was sponsored by notables including Thomas Edison, Alexander Graham Bell and Margaret Wilson (the President's daughter), Froebel's more playful and socially oriented kindergartens continued to predominate.[38] Montessori developed her own special equipment for teaching shape distinctions, mathematics and principles of physics. […]

Public cooperative kitchens

Public cooperative kitchens were charitable institutions established to feed the poor, nutritiously and scientifically at low or no cost. The first public kitchens were in European almshouses such as the Munich House of Industry founded in 1790 by Count Rumford in order to make experiments in feeding the poor "scientifically" with his innovative efficient stove design. Public kitchens were also founded as separate cooperative institutions in Vienna, Leipzig and Berlin, where a soup kitchen for the poor was founded in 1866 by Lina Morgenstern. A similar philanthropic kitchen, or *cucini populari*, was founded in Modena, Italy. In the United States Ellen Swallow Richards and Mary Hinman Abel drew on these earlier public cooperative kitchens to found the New England Kitchen in 1890 in Boston, followed by the Rumford Kitchen exhibited at the World's Columbian Exposition in 1893. The resulting publicity led to the spread of public cooperative kitchens to many other cities in the United States. Public kitchens used scientific weights and measures and Aladdin Ovens that slowly cooked food with the heat of gas lamps funneled into metal-lined insulated boxes with shelves on which dishes of food were stacked. […]

In neighborhood cooperative kitchens, including dining clubs and cooked food delivery services, meals were cooperatively prepared for a number of families who either ate together in dining cooperatives or received delivery of their meals at their individual houses. Communes such as the Rappites that had individual family houses with kitchens as well as a cooperative community kitchen and dining room were precedents for neighborhood cooperative kitchens and dining rooms, usually set up in an ordinary house. Usually a middle-class member of a dining cooperative would oversee servants who cooperatively produced meals for the other middle-class households who were members of the dining cooperative. Cooperative kitchens and cooked food delivery services both transformed an aspect of low-status domestic service into a higher waged occupation with regular, though still long, hours. The precedents for cooked food delivery services included cook shops that sold hot food in Europe and the United States and the urban English custom of taking family roasts or cakes to be baked in bakers' ovens. Cooked food delivery services first developed in Europe and then spread to the United States, where in 1868 Harriet Beecher Stowe published an article about her cooked-food-delivery experience from living in Europe. Community cooperative kitchens were given added impetus by World War I kitchens in Europe, especially the 1,000 National Kitchens in English cities, and mobile kitchens established in trams in Halifax, England and in devastated areas of France. […]

Community cooperatives and kitchenless households

As the urban middle class moved from city apartments, sometimes with cooperative housekeeping services, into more private individual suburban houses, domestic reformers built on the idea of dining clubs to create suburban neighborhood cooperatives, sometimes in conjunction with kitchenless houses. American reformers such as Marie Howland, Edward Bellamy and Charlotte Perkins Gilman inspired both American and European architects to design and build a number of experimental neighborhoods of kitchenless houses with central cooperatives. English architect Ebenezer Howard became renowned for his Garden City town plan, for which he and his associates designed the Cooperative Quadrangle – a square of attached kitchenless row houses with a central dining room, kitchen and laundry in one corner. Between 1909 and 1924 Howard's architectural firm designed four Cooperative Quadrangles that were built in London suburbs. Some were reminiscent of university quadrangles, and Tudor revival architectural style was frequently used to evoke the coherence of pre-industrial villages. Domestic services were supplied by paid employees, who in some cases were supervised by lady tenants who took turns as unpaid managers. Howard, as well as Fourier, influenced French cooperative housing designs. In the United States, kitchenless houses with central cooperatives were built in a few summer communities for affluent New Yorkers. For instance, in 1922 Ruth M. Adams designed Yelping Hill Connecticut's seven kitchenless houses, some Tudor style, and remodeled an old barn as a community center with a cooperative kitchen, dining room, living room, childcare, and guest quarters. Inspired by Howard's Garden City, two architects in California, the Heineman brothers, in 1910 designed the bungalow court – moderately priced single and double bungalows bordering a center garden with a central building housing a sewing room and laundry over a covered play area.[39] …

Archaeological survey of domestic reform sites in Boston

My survey of over 120 Boston domestic reform sites founded from 1860 to 1925 shows how the rapid growth of women's cooperative housekeeping enterprises physically contested male dominance on the public landscape and moved the built environment toward gender equality. Further, women's public professions and institutions grew to dominate parts of many public urban landscapes, in contrast to the ideal of an exclusively male public-sphere landscape.[40] Public and private were physically conflated as reformers built prominent public institutions in residential neighborhoods, while housing other public cooperative housekeeping enterprises in typical domestic structures.

The survey further revealed geographical relationships between the reformers and participants in reform. Some reformers lived in settlement houses in poor immigrant neighborhoods where they offered cooperative childcare and numerous educational programs. Other reformers lived in private homes or cooperative hotels in posh neighborhoods and volunteered or worked in schools for cooking and housekeeping, or in cooperatives in nearby poor neighborhoods. With a feminist approach I sought and found evidence that participants in reform were not passive, but negotiated with reformers for programs and material culture that would meet their needs.[41] For instance, working-class families protested the bland north eastern United States "Yankee" menu offered them at public kitchens, saying "You can't make a Yankee out of me by making me eat that", and "I'd ruther eat what I'd ruther".[42] The reformers responded by offering more ethnic dishes that were not slow-cooked in the scientific Aladdin oven until they lost flavor. Archaeological evidence may indicate the extent to which this oven and its scientific cooking methods were actually used in enterprises such as public kitchens and cooking cooperatives.[43]

Domestic reform of the private household

My research on American domestic reform of the household, conducted within this larger context, shows how reformers conflated women's domestic roles with men's public roles. Rational principles, scientific methods and equipment used by men in their public businesses were adapted by women reformers and applied to organize and mechanize housework for increased efficiency. In contrast to histories that have portrayed women only as consumers of men's household inventions,[44] feminist research has revealed that some women earned income as early as the 1860s by inventing, patenting and sometimes undertaking factory production of their scientific designs for household equipment such as a stove, a washing machine, irons and sewing devices.[45]

Women's domestic reform ideology was instrumental in applying rational scientific methods and equipment to housework. In domestic advice manuals reformers presented pictures and drawings of innovative equipment arranged to increase the efficiency and healthiness of housework in both middle-class and working-class homes. The evidence that women's domestic manuals both verbally and materially transformed gender ideology and relationships corrects male-centered histories that did not consider women's domestic advice literature important.

The American Woman's Home, by Beecher and Stowe

The earliest domestic reform ideology appeared in the most popular mid-nineteenth-century domestic manuals by Catherine Beecher and her famous sister, Harriet Beecher Stowe. Drawing on the ideology of Republican Motherhood, which pointed out the importance of the profession of motherhood in raising tomorrow's male political leaders, their aim was to "elevate both the honor and remuneration" of women's household tasks to professions "as much desired and respected as are the most honored professions of men". This goal was materially symbolized and implemented by raising the kitchen from its frequent location in the basement to a central position on the more public ground floor. Kitchen doors for shutting in cooking smells could be opened at other times, expressing the interconnectedness of the domestic sphere. The rational arrangement of furniture and equipment supposedly expressed the order and harmony in "divine nature". Innovative shelf boxes stored materials beneath working surfaces while hooks and shelves above held cooking utensils and dining tableware.

Beecher and Stowe used the popular Cult of Home Religion to raise women's domestic role to the exclusively male status of a minister, and elevated food preparation and service as analogous to communion. They justified their and other women's house designs by quoting the Bible: "The wise woman buildeth her house". Reformers drew on evangelical Protestantism to contend that women were naturally more pious and moral due to their closeness to God and nature in a domestic sphere separated from a men's capitalistic public sphere which was corrupted by the sin of usury. Women's supposedly innately superior domestic morality was symbolized with a cruciform house, gothic furnishings, gothic doorways, gothic corner niches with religious statues, and romantic religious and bucolic pictures. A Gothic arched central recess in the entrance hall held the small round table that with a Bible was the normative symbol for family communion in the church of the home. The Beecher sisters designed a public entry space filled with symbols of the preeminence of woman's role as minister of the home church. They also designed a bow-windowed conservatory in each of the two ground-floor rooms, where they recommended that women and children grow houseplants, bringing God's nature into the home. The simple house design did not include a large men's parlor separate from the usually smaller women's parlor which in wealthy Victorian houses physically expressed the relative status of the separate female domestic and male public spheres. Instead Beecher and Stowe contended that woman should control the entire domestic sphere and cooperatively organize her children's labor as the "sovereign of her empire".[46]

The archaeology of household domestic reform

Archaeologists excavating house sites often find flowerpots without realizing that they could symbolize the Cult of Home Religion. Gothic and floral designs popular on mid-nineteenth-century household tableware also symbolized women's supposedly naturally superior piety. Of course household ceramic choices could also be driven by cost, availability, aesthetics, or some combination of factors.[47]

Archaeologists may be able to contribute to the important question of to what extent documented ideal domestic reform equipment and designs for the home were actually used, and by whom. This may be indicated in historic documents, photos, or above ground material culture. The preserved historic house of Harriet Beecher Stowe in Hartford, Connecticut, includes some kitchen furniture similar to what she and her sister recommended. Archaeologists may find material evidence of the undocumented extent to which other people implemented distinctive foundation features and artifacts in the basement design, including the ice closet, the washtub drains, water pipes, laundry stove and the drying rack.

Further developments in efficient arrangements of furniture and equipment in Christine Frederick's early twentieth-century domestic manual include photographs of designs she and some friends implemented in their houses. Frederick's basement laundry materially organized the process from a laundry shute to sorting table to large metal tubs, a washing machine, and a metal drying rack heated by a stove, followed by an ironing board, mangle and table for folding clean clothes. Archaeologists could find many parts of large metal laundry equipment in rural or town dumps. Frederick's kitchen was arranged on one side for food preparation, from a refrigerator raised by a dumbwaiter from the basement to kitchen, to a cabinet which Frederick invented and which integrated cupboards with a work surface, to a metal oil stove, and a serving table over a fireless cooker chest in which food was slowly cooked by heated soapstones beneath insulated buckets. The other side of the kitchen included a cable for stacking dishes next to a sink with drain boards, and shelves and closets for storing clean dishes. Frederick and her friends, the Noyes at Oneida, also hung utensils on the walls, and had dishwashers and vacuum cleaners.[48]

The question of to what extent domestic reformers' designs were adopted in other households is seldom documented. Cohen's research found that the simple wood furniture suggested by reformers was not adopted by most of the working class, which sought plush furniture and carpets as high status furnishings.[49] Frederick showed photos of her kitchen designs implemented both in a large kitchen and in a small apartment.[50] Ellen Swallow Richards in her manual on the cost of housing illustrated a remodeled apartment kitchen that included some of her suggestions to facilitate sanitation, such as [floor covering] laid up the wall a few inches, glass shelves, and a glass table. However, aside from hanging pots under the glass table and a cooking range with overhead shelves and boiler, this kitchen did not implement reformers' designs for efficiently arranging domestic equipment.[51]

Archaeologists might find evidence of the degree of adoption of innovative domestic equipment advocated by reformers by excavating community dumps or house sites in rural or poor neighborhoods that lacked municipal garbage collection. However, the degree to which ordinary domestic utensils and equipment were used to implement reform could not be identified without documenting reform sites, as I have in my surveys of Boston and Cambridge.[52]

Conclusion

[...] This chapter has shown how nineteenth-century western culture, gender ideology and practice were materially transformed by alternative domestic reform ideologies and practices. The diversity of domestic reform gender ideologies had roots in Classical Greek philosophies, as well as fundamentalist Christian beliefs. Victorian women's domestic reform ideologies redefined and conflated the meanings of domestic and public to successfully contest the exclusion of women from the public sphere, creating a large number of female public professions that were acceptable within the dominant ideology because they could be labeled "domestic". Further, women and men reformers combined the supposedly separate female/domestic and male/public spheres to argue that women's housework should be a paid profession equivalent to men's professions.

Public cooperative housekeeping enterprises that socialized private household tasks challenged any unitary definition of the household as exclusively familial and private. Cooperative housekeeping institutions materially blurred the distinction between community and family household. Communes created economically cohesive community-scale households. Kitchenless houses and apartments also materially changed the traditional definition of a household. [...]

Notes

1   Dolores Hayden, *The Grand Domestic Revolution: A History of Feminist Designs for American Homes, Neighborhoods, and Cities*, Cambridge: MIT Press, 1981; Suzanne M. Spencer-Wood, "A Survey of Domestic Reform Movement Sites in Boston and Cambridge, ca. 1865–1905", *Historical Archaeology* 21, no. 2, 1987, 7–36; Spencer-Wood, "Towards an Historical

Archaeology of Domestic Reform", in Randall H. McGuire and Robert Paynter (eds) *The Archaeology of Inequality*, Oxford: Basil Blackwell, 1991.

2   Ibid.; Spencer-Wood, "Diversity in Nineteenth Century Domestic Reform: Relationships among Classes and Ethnic Groups", in Elizabeth M. Scott (ed.) *Those "Of Little Note": Gender, Race and Class in Historical Archaeology*, Tucson: University of Arizona Press, 1994.

3   Priscilla Robertson, *An Experience of Women: Pattern and Change in Nineteenth-Century Europe*, Philadelphia: Temple University Press, 1982, p. 166; Spencer-Wood, "Towards an Historical Archaeology".

4   D. S. Smith, "Family Limitation, Sexual Control, and Domestic Feminism in Victorian America", in Nancy F. Cott and Elizabeth H. Pleck (eds) *A Heritage of Her Own*, New York: Simon and Schuster, 1979, p. 238.

5   Spencer-Wood, "Towards an Historical Archaeology".

6   Bonnie S. Anderson and Judith P. Zinsser, *A History of Their Own: Women in Europe from Prehistory to the Present II*, New York: Harper and Row, 1988, pp. 177, 193–6, 246, 389, 393–4; Hayden, *The Grand Domestic Revolution*; Robertson, *An Experience of Women*, pp. 395–6, 398, 423–4, 444–6, 452–3.

7   Spencer-Wood, "Towards an Historical Archaeology".

8   William Leach, *True Love and Perfect Union: The Feminist Reform of Sex and Society*, New York: Basic Books, 1980, p. 209.

9   Barbara Welter, "The Cult of True Womanhood: 1820–1860", *American Quarterly* 18, no. 2, part 1, 1966, 151–74.

10   Leach, *True Love and Perfect Union*, p. 136; James Turner, *Without God, Without Creed: The Origins of Unbelief in America*, Baltimore: Johns Hopkins University Press, 1985, pp. 181–3.

11   Nancy F. Cott, *The Bonds of Womanhood: Woman's Sphere in New England, 1780–1835*, New Haven, Conn.: Yale University Press, 1977, pp. 66–8; Robertson, *An Experience of Women*, pp. 13–9, 31–2; Barbara Welter, "The Feminization of American Religion: 1800–1860", in Mary Hartman and Lois Banner (eds) *Clio's Consciousness Raised: New Perspectives on the History of Women*, New York: Harper Colophon Books, 1974, pp. 145–6.

12   Hayden, *The Grand Domestic Revolution*, p. 153.

13   Amanda Porterfield, *Feminine Spirituality in America: From Sarah Edwards to Martha Graham*, Philadelphia: Temple University Press, 1980, pp. 99–120, 155–88.

14   Hayden, *The Grand Domestic Revolution*; Mark Holloway, *Heavens on Earth: Utopian Communities in America 1680–1880*, 2nd edn, New York: Dover, 1966, p. 24.

15   Robertson, *An Experience of Women*, pp. 13–9; Welter, "The Cult of True Womanhood".

16   David P. Handlin, *The American Home: Architecture and Society, 1815–1915*, Boston: Little Brown and Co., 1979, pp. 4–19.

17   Catherine E. Beecher and Harriet Beecher Stowe, *The American Woman's Home, or Principles of Domestic Science*, New York: J. B. Ford and Co., 1869–1985; Robertson, *An Experience of Women*, pp. 15–7.

18   Carol Hymowitz and Michaele Weissman, *A History of Women in America*, New York: Bantam, 1978, pp. 22–5.

19   Lee Virginia Chambers-Schiller, *Liberty a Better Husband. Single Women in America: The Generations of 1780–1840*, New Haven, Conn.: Yale University Press, 1984, pp. 3–5, 21–3.

20   *Chronicle Telegraph, Literary Learns Mr. Bolt Proves that Love and Literature are Not at War: Matrons and Spinsters*, January 18, Pittsburgh, in Andrews Scrap Album of Laura C. Holloway Langford, in the Shaker Collection, Joseph Downs Collection of Manuscripts and Printed Ephemera, The Winterthur Library, Henry Francis Du Pont Winterthur Museum, Winterthur, Delaware, 1891.

21   Frances B. Cogan, *All-American Girl: The Ideal of Real Womanhood in Mid-Nineteenth-Century America*, Athens: University of Georgia Press, 1989.

22   Holloway, *Heavens on Earth*, pp. 55–9.

23   Hayden, *The Grand Domestic Revolution*, pp. 33–9.

24   Ibid., p. 96; Holloway, *Heavens on Earth*, pp. 34–5, 184–5.

25   Ibid., pp. 18, 24, 64, 104, 134–42, 182–3.

26   Hayden, *The Grand Domestic Revolution*, pp. 33–5.

27   Holloway, *Heavens on Earth*.

28   Hayden, *The Grand Domestic Revolution*, p. 39.

29   Ibid., p. 37; Holloway, *Heavens on Earth*, pp. 188–9.

30 Ibid., pp. 59, 67–8, 95, 172, 192.
31 D. R. Vaillancourt, "Archeological Excavations at the North Family Dwelling House Site, Hancock Shaker Village, Town of Hancock, Berkshire County, Massachusetts", Unpublished manuscript, Project, Rensselaer Polytechnic Institute, Troy, New York, 1983.
32 Hayden, *The Grand Domestic Revolution*, pp. 37–45, 96.
33 V. A. Buchli, *The Battle Against Microbes and Counter-Revolutionaries: The Soviet Domestic Front (1920–1931)*, unpublished Harriman Institute Certificate Essay, Columbia University, 1996, p. 10; Hayden, *Seven American Utopias*, pp. 69–86, 254–9.
34 Moses King, *King's Handbook of Boston, 1885*, Cambridge, Mass.: Moses King, 1885, p. 205; M. G. Wilson, *The American Woman in Transition: The Urban Influence, 1870–1920*, Westport, Conn.: Greenwood Press, 1979, p. 99.
35 Jane Addams, *Twenty Years at Hull-House*, New York: New American Library, 1910–1981; Robert A. Woods and Albert J. Kennedy (eds), *Handbook of Settlements*, New York: Charities Publications Committee, 1911.
36 Agnes Snyder, *Dauntless Women in Childhood Education 1856–1931*, Washington, DC: Association for Childhood Education International, 1972, pp. 9–12, 19–21, 41, 58; Margaret Steinfels, *Who's Minding the Children?*, New York: Simon and Schuster, 1973, pp. 34–9, 42–55; E. S. Beer, *The Day Nursery*, New York: E. P. Outran, 1942, pp. 33–41, 48–51, 144–51.
37 Hayden, *The Grand Domestic Revolution*, pp. 33, 97–9.
38 D. Howes, M. L. Braun, and R. Garvey (eds), *American Women: The Standard Biographical Dictionary of Notable Women III 1939–40*, Los Angeles: American Publications, 1939, p. 290.
39 Hayden, *The Grand Domestic Revolution*, pp. 230–9, 260–3.
40 Spencer-Wood, "Diversity in Nineteenth Century Domestic Reform".
41 Spencer-Wood, "A Survey of Domestic Reform Movement Sites"; Spencer-Wood, "Diversity in Nineteenth Century Domestic Reform".
42 Addams, *Twenty Years at Hull-House*, p. 102.
43 Spencer-Wood, "Towards an Historical Archaeology".
44 E.g. Earl Lifshey, *The Housewares Story: A History of the American Housewares Industry*, Chicago: National Housewares Manufacturers, 1973; L. Wright, *Home Fires Burning: The History of Domestic Heating and Cooking*, London: Routledge and Kegan Paul, 1964.
45 Anne L. Macdonald, *Feminine Ingenuity: Women and Invention in America*, New York: Ballantine Books, 1992, pp. 38–47, 60–3, 196, 385–6, 393.
46 Beecher and Stowe, *The American Woman's Home*, pp. 17–36, 222, 442–5; Handlin, *The American Home*, pp. 4–19.
47 Spencer-Wood, "Feminist Historical Archaeology and the Transformation of American Culture by Domestic Reform Movements, 1840–1925", in L. A. De Cunzo and B. L. Herman (eds) *Historical Archaeology and the Study of American Culture*, Knoxville: Winterthur Museum and University of Tennessee, 1996, pp. 419–20.
48 Christine Frederick, *Household Engineering: Scientific Management in the Home*, 5th edn, Chicago: American School of Home Economics, 1923, pp. 32, 64, 98, 110, 114.
49 L. Cohen, "Embellishing a Life of Labor: An Interpretation of the Material Culture of American Working-class Homes, 1885–1915", *Journal of American Culture* 4, 1980, 752–5.
50 Frederick, *Household Engineering*, pp. 40, 178.
51 Ellen H. Richards, *The Cost of Shelter*, New York: John Wiley and Sons, 1905, pp. 70–2.
52 Spencer-Wood, "A Survey of Domestic Reform Movement Sites"; Spencer-Wood, "Towards an Historical Archaeology"; Spencer-Wood, "Diversity in Nineteeth Century Domestic Reform"; Spencer-Wood, "Feminist Historical Archaeology".

Degas and the sexuality of the *Interior*

Susan Sidlauskas (2000)

Introduction

For the generation that came of age during the 1850s and 1860s, subjectivity was thought to be most authentically imagined and experienced in relation to one's intimates – intimacy being "a nineteenth-century invention".[1] The visual, literary, and theatrical cultures of these years attest that the relation of body to place – still the measure of private identity – was negotiated through sometimes complementary, sometimes competing, interactions with yet *another* body, or bodies – often, but not necessarily, of the opposite sex. Not surprisingly, that interaction most often took place within the private interior, which by 1860 had become a stage for the enactment of an entire range of affective, intimate dramas. Subjectivity was not simply pictured within the domestic interior; it was here that it *came into being*. With the painting *Interior* [*Fig. 31*], Degas fashioned a new kind of content by marrying the two-dimensional fusion of space and subject advocated by Lecoq de Boisbaudran to an anxiety about how the lived, sexual body was both exposed and constrained within its intimate world.[2]

Degas's *Interior* dramatizes the fraught, wordless aftermath of some kind of sexual encounter between a man and woman who have retreated to opposite sides of a sparsely furnished room. The apocryphal, but nonetheless persistent, informal title of the work, *The Rape*, is sensational rather than explanatory: there is no visual or narrative evidence that a rape has occurred.[3] Nonetheless, the designation captures something of the painting's initial effect, which might best be described as a potent sensation of sexual menace.

The man stands nearly erect, while the woman is huddled in a self-protective curve, suspended somewhere between sitting and crouching. In contrast to her companion's impeccable *haut bourgeois* costume, she is clothed only in a chemise, which has fallen – or been made to fall – to expose her left shoulder and the curve of her back. The mass of purplish drapery lying limply in her lap may be her discarded dress. Her facial expression is indecipherable, lost in the shadows around her. The combination of bared shoulder and shadowed face makes the woman seem simultaneously more exposed and more remote than her companion. The man's physiognomy, on the other hand, is starkly apparent and eerily irradiated by a dull yellow glow. Early critics focused on the so-called bestiality of his features, for this fueled the story of violation they saw in the painting – most often, in their telling, the story of a virginal servant girl who has been brutally assaulted by her upper-class employer.[4] Degas kept this painting largely hidden in his studio until 1905, when he decided to end thirty-five years of solitary possession and offer it for sale at the Galérie Durand-Ruel.[5] [...]

There is no conventional "solution" to *Interior* (though viewers will doubtless continue to look for one), but I believe that the painting possesses a dominant theme: the strains and failures of bourgeois sexuality. Moreover, this theme is wrought in explicitly spatial terms. Degas visualized sexual desire *confounded*, and he did so by embedding the uneasiness of the encounter within the very structure of the composition. Any prior volatility between the man and woman is thereby suppressed and remains unresolved. Degas's own sexual anxieties may have played a role in shaping at least the outlines of this enigmatic scenario. But if so, his preoccupations resonated with those of his generation, as did the means he used to explore them. Georges Bataille has suggested that spatial transformation possesses a fundamental eroticism of its own. Degas's painting implies that eroticism suppressed or frustrated *also* generates a particular spatial transmutation, one that, in turn, shapes the bodily constitution of those who experience it.[6] [...]

Degas's *Interior* is a space whose structure, figural arrangements, proportions, scale, and atmospheric effects have all been calculated to disallow or preempt any acts of seduction. Its distorted perspective, asymmetric arrangements, and irrational lighting effects shape a pictorial field of sexual despair, in which the pleasure in looking and touching is prohibited. As surrogates for the viewer, these stranded, withdrawn figures elicit a bodily empathy that is intensified by their spatial isolation from one another, an isolation that is effectively cemented by their heightened visual interdependence with the room in which they are confined. This conflict between affective and spatial isolation, on the one hand, and visual fusion, on the other, generates a sensation of acute strain, a tense equipoise felt – by extension – in the spectator's own body, a tension that resists dissipation. Sexual tension does not simply run beneath the surfaces of *Interior*, as it arguably did in the daily life of the French bourgeoisie; it is embedded in its very constitution.

The intimate life of the bourgeoisie

The sexualized fusion of body and place on which *Interior* depends reflects a widespread contemporary preoccupation with how the bourgeoisie lived in their domestic spaces. The discussion about domesticity was carried on within many venues, from the loftiest of architectural volumes to the illustrated pages of the daily press. In the first category, César Daly led the way. Beginning around 1860, he directed his long-standing interest in people's response to space and structure toward life in the private "habitat", as he called it. In his opus, *Architecture privée* (1864), he defined the house as "the clothing of the family. It is in effect destined to serve as an envelope for them, to shelter them and to yield to all their movements".[7] Daly was one of the first to insist that the "aesthetic geometry" of domestic architecture did not simply reflect the tenor of family life; its structures and spaces could actually *determine* its psychological quality – for good or ill: "According to the appearance of the house, its lines, its exterior and interior decoration flatter or offend the taste of anyone who inhabits it, it is for him a pleasure or a pain each day; for certain dispositions, it is an occasion of triumph or of permanent humiliation".[8] When properly housed, the aesthetically balanced family could relate appropriately and constructively to the world outside. The usual habits and chores of domestic life could be carried out either "easily or with pain", depending upon the congeniality of the environment. Internal rapport was necessary before a family could function well outside the walls of the domestic sanctum.[9] Daly's writing was prescriptive as well; he had definite ideas about what constituted the proper encasement for family life. He believed that the ideal house's decor consisted of "delicate and harmonious details, and well-balanced lines". Everything should "caress the eye and satisfy the affections".[10]

Degas's *Interior* adamantly defies the architectural and decorative conventions for ensuring family harmony. Few harmonious elements grace the room's architecture. The man and woman are both placed at a distance from the table – that anchor for family togetherness. The flowered wallpaper (which Degas may have touched up around 1895) seems almost a mockery of the despairing scene. Surely, Daly would not have approved of such a space for *any* family, for there is little to caress the gaze or satisfy the spirit. The softening surface coverings so commonplace in nineteenth-century bourgeois decor – and so prominent in Walter Benjamin's analysis of the interior – are nearly absent, except for the skimpy rug that emphasizes the bareness of the floor. There are no draperies, as called for by Daly, because there are no windows (although one may be discernible in the unrevealing mirror reflection) and the only egress – the door on the right – is securely closed.

Degas may not have known Daly's publications directly, but he was certainly aware of the popular prints that promulgated a cruder visualization of the same belief: that there was an inextricable tie between the decor and structure of the habitat and the quality of private life. By the 1860s, Parisians were accustomed to categorizing images of domestic interiors by signs of class so conventional that they amounted to a visual code. Even the casual observer became adept at assessing class affiliation according to the relative height of ceilings, the lavishness or spareness of decor, and the comparative scale of windows and doors.[11] Some new multifamily dwellings consisted of a variety of *appartements-à-loyer*: adjacent, discontinuous rooms let to boarders, often with a commercial enterprise on the street level. For these city-dwellers, class was inversely proportionate to height from the street. Spacious bourgeois dwellings were situated just above the shop, and middle-class quarters were on the level just above that. In both classes of apartments, the family's most private rooms (the bedrooms) were farthest away from the street, and thus most remote from light and air. At the top of the building were the grim garrets that housed the Second Empire's marginal citizens: the starving actor, the struggling artist and writer, the seamstress, and the prostitute.[12]

Could Degas's room represent such a garret? While the room as painted is certainly modest, with its low ceiling, bare floor, and thin rug, it is not unequivocally lower-class. Consider the refinements in the decor: the gold-framed mirror and the glass-shaded lamp – elements more at home in a bourgeois parlor or sitting room. The small framed images distinguish the room from the grim topmost quarters of Texier's 1852 *Tableau de Paris* *[Fig. 20]*, for instance, although it shares its drab decor with the rooms just below. In addition, the lace collar and thread on Degas's pedestal table, along with the embroidery hoop visible inside the box, suggest the sewing activities of a gentle needlewoman rather than a seamstress-for-hire. And if Degas intended the woman to be a prostitute, why has her "client" lingered, in the aftermath of what was obviously an unsatisfactory encounter? Perhaps *Interior* depicts a more *public* private space – a room in a hotel, for instance. Otherwise, why have the bonnet and cloak been tossed on the bed, apparently in haste, rather than hung on a coatrack in the foyer or downstairs at the entrance? The question remains to a large degree unanswerable, for while the reductive setting and scattered clothing imply that this is a transient place, the sewing box is planted on the table like a domestic fixture. Presumably, such an object would be an unwieldy accompaniment to a quick assignation.

It is impossible to establish with certainty *Interior*'s class or location, and even the identity, and thus the gender, of its primary inhabitant. This is a room that was "built" for expressive effect. Indeed, the room itself is clearly an *agent* of effect, as Daly contended was the case with any domestic setting. Daly's belief that a house should envelop, should virtually *clothe*, the family within, was a metaphorical turn of phrase, to be sure. But his musings confirm, nonetheless, the nineteenth-century obsession with the material sensuality of the surfaces and objects that constituted the private interior. Benjamin believed that the need to "leave traces", as he put it, was a defining feature of the bourgeois's living habits.[13] All those antimacassars, runners, and upholstered surfaces doubled the sensation of touch and served as material evidence of the multiple acts of physical possession by which middle-class identity was constructed and represented. These tactile surfaces served as repositories for the inhabitants' visceral connection to their intimate surround-ings, a liminal space where body actually verged into place.

The impact of Degas's *Interior* depends in part on a thematics of touch or, more precisely, on the consequences of the refusal or suppression of touch. Not only are surface coverings scarce, but the fire is remote and the bedstead is metal. The space is chilly and barren – overdetermined, it would seem, for domestic *dis*harmony. Paradoxically, this sensation of touch withheld or rejected was constructed through a delicately modulated fusion of figure to ground. Sexual aversion is conjured through the pressure of a succes-sively greater pictorial integration. As Degas adjusted the woman's proportions to recede more seamlessly into the room's distorted perspective; as he distanced her farther from the table and the sewing box upon it; as he stiffened her companion's body and submerged his legs into murky shadow, he dramatized the sexual and psychological abyss between them. Pictorial integration exacted a psychological price … As the animacy of the shifting surfaces, enlivened objects, and expressive furniture became subtly height-ened in the course of Degas's studies for the picture, the figures became more fixed, locked into space in a way that gives visual form to the sensations of futility and defeat. In the visual and psychological interdependence of these phenomena is embedded the insep-arability of sexual and spatial identity in nineteenth-century culture.

The engendering of space

[…] Recently, feminist scholars have begun to urge that women's public lives must be considered in tandem with their intimate experiences; that men were not the only ones who navigated the public world of the Second Empire.[14] I would add that *men's* interior lives must be considered as well – especially those of men whose most searching reflec-tions appear to have occurred either at home (in the case of Vuillard), or within the private interiors of friends (as in Sargent's work and life), or inside the extended home of their studios (as with Degas). In Degas's *Interior*, neither protagonist enjoys a privileged position – despite initial impressions to the contrary. The anxieties and preoccupations of a man *and* a woman (which are presented as being very different) collide and intermingle. Degas painted this work at a critical juncture in his career and, I would venture, at a pivotal moment in the evolution of his own masculine identity. The waning years of the Second Empire saw much confusion about men's and women's public and private roles, and, in particular, about the fortunes of their intimate relations. Many wondered how an authentic intimacy might be identified, how it should be acted out and preserved. What were its psychological and social costs?[15]

Degas's *Interior* is neither entirely feminine nor masculine, although it contains signs of both. There is, on the one hand, the flowered wallpaper, the sewing box, the lace collar, and the corset collapsed on the floor. On the other hand, there is the man's top hat and the map just above it. The right corner of the room might be construed as "feminine", with its small framed images, single pillow, and delicate tones in the towels beside the bed. Yet this is precisely the side of the room in which the man stands – the realm he seems, at first, to command. Likewise, the male "attributes", the map and top hat, pene-trate what might be understood initially as the woman's territory.[16] This room is neither a woman's space nor a man's. It is rather a place where the social and sexual signs of *both* femininity and masculinity are constrained and imperiled.

A family portrait

I have said earlier that *Interior* visualizes the strains and failures of bourgeois sexuality. This suggests a familial tie, that this man and woman are already intimately known to each other; they could be a couple – perhaps even a married couple – in extremis. The characterization may seem far-fetched at first, for sexual alienation hardly seems the conventional subject for a "family portrait", as we usually understand it. But a variety of evidence supports such a claim, beginning with Degas's own name for *Interior*: "my genre painting". The title indicates that the artist imagined a broader framework for his painting, a more general interpretation of this seemingly private and obsessive theme. His designation does raise the question, however, of how such a theme ever came to constitute a plausible scene from "everyday life". Whose everyday life do we see represented here? And why *this* particular moment from that life?[17]

Degas did seem to harbor a personal skepticism about the possibilities for domestic happiness, but the theme of alienation between men and women, within and without marriage, was very common during these years, inspiring countless novels, plays, illustrations, and paintings.[18] Conjugal violence, the specter of divorce, marriages of convenience, and victimized working girls flooded mid-century domestic dramas such as Alexandre Dumas *fils*'s *La Femme de Claude*, *La Question d'Argent*, and *Le Fils Naturel*.[19] Characteristic of such plays is the following vision of marriage; in one scene of the first play, the protagonist Claude says to his wife: "I don't know who you are. There is only a bondage between us. There is nothing more than the chain which the law imposes on us".[20] In the literature of Degas's own generation, examples of sexual misalliances are legion. Duranty's *Combats de Françoise Du Quesnoy* (1873) was actually the first suggested literary source for the *Interior*. In Emile Zola's *Thérèse Raquin* (1867), the most often mentioned "source" for the painting, the grim fate of the protagonists, Thérèse and Laurent, is prefigured by their murder of her husband, Camille. In *Madéleine Férat* (1868), Zola's heroine's destructive affair with Jacques leads ultimately to her suicide. The Goncourts charted the violence between the painter Coriolis and his model Manette Salomon in their novel of that name (1867), a novel that we know deeply preoccupied Degas around this time.[21] At the center of Flaubert's *L'Education Sentimentale* (1869) is the doomed affair between Frédéric and Madame Arnoux. Not surprisingly, most of these relationships' culminating intimate scenes were staged in *interiors*, decorated either sparingly or lavishly to enhance the effect. [...]

Interior melodramas

When Degas staged a more contemporary sexual conflict within an interior, he drew upon that space's identification with family privacy. In so doing, he unmasked the fragility of the interior as a sanctum. Writing about cinematic melodrama, Laura Mulvey has argued that "the family is the socially accepted road to respective normality, an icon of conformity, and at one and the same time, the source of deviance, psychosis and despair. In addition to these elements of dramatic material, the family provides a physical setting, the home, that can hold a drama in claustrophobic intensity and represent, with its highly connotative architectural organization, the passions and antagonisms that lie behind it".[22]

Discussing the same cinematic devices, Thomas Elsaesser contrasts the intense psychological conflict on which melodrama depends to the more "theatrical" gestures of an epic form such as the Western. In melodrama, Elsaesser writes, the social pressures are such, the frame of respectability so sharply defined, that the range of "strong" actions is limited. The tellingly impotent gesture, the social gaffe, the hysterical outburst replaces any more directly liberating or self-annihilating action and the cathartic violence of a shoot-out or chase becomes an inner violence, often one which the characters turn against themselves ... The dramatic configuration, the pattern of the plot makes them, regardless of any attempt to break free, constantly look inwards, at each other and themselves.[23]

With certain adjustments, this could be a telling description of Degas's *Interior*, in which the viewer is drawn in, again and again, to speculate about a conflict that has no obvious resolution. *Interior* contains *some* signs of the world exterior to its limited space – the outer garments of both the man and the woman, the map, and the framed pictures. But nearly all architectural clues to the space external to the room have been studiously expunged. The room is turned back on itself. There is no light, except for the artificial glow of the glass oil lamp; there is no air; nor is there a window to relieve the room's claustrophobia. The spectator both projects and absorbs this sensation of entrapment, which is intensified with every look. [...]

There are other disturbing spatial anomalies that viscerally affect the spectator. *Interior*'s foreground recedes too rapidly toward the distant wall and the ceiling that descends to meet it. With its combination of widened floor and lowered ceiling, the space seems at once claustrophobic and unprotected: the man and woman seem both too near and too far away. The painted floorboards, which act as schematic orthogonals, underscore the impression that the figures are stranded on either side of an abyss. Objects and figures are crowded into the left side of the composition, while the space on the right seems to yawn, an effect that intensifies the general sense of destabilization, as does the figures' uncertain attachment to the tilting floor. The glow of the hearth appears at the perspectival vanishing point, but its orange light seems futile and remote; Degas subtly exaggerated the distance between the foreground and the far wall by compressing the rear plane disproportionately to make it seem even farther away.

The spectator is almost unconsciously implicated in this spatial distension and perspectival retreat. [...] The active pressure that Degas applies to his interior is evident in the "reasoned distortions" he employed, distortions that actualize Lecoq's recipe for the envisioning of subjectivity through the charged relations of body to place, figure to ground. Like the room's skewed perspective and telescoped rear plane, *Interior*'s dramatic projections into light and recessions into shadow are greatly exaggerated.[24] Light seems to emanate *from* the opened sewing box – for reasons I will explore later – and the shadow cast on the door behind the man displays the silhouette and force of an independent entity. Neither effect can be accounted for entirely by the only source of strong illumination, the glass oil lamp, whose light spills directly, and impossibly, onto the mirror reflection behind.[25] [...]

Animism

[...] The nineteenth-century bourgeoisie carried on ambivalent relationships with their ever-present "bibelots". Their drawing rooms were notorious for the proliferation of surface coverings, upholstered chairs, and "knickknacks". Edmond de Goncourt dubbed the taste for crammed rooms and cosseted furniture "bricàbracomania". Although such objects and coverings were presumably selected and arranged by their owners, their sheer profusion called the primacy of human inhabitants into doubt. Duranty's short story *Bric-à-Brac* (1876) is a humorous account of a family of collectors whose limbs are indistinguishable from the legs of their oversized furniture. According to both Charles Baudelaire and Edgar Allan Poe, the wrong furniture, or an unpleasing arrangement of it, could positively ruin a room.[26] And in the writings of Guy de Maupassant, furniture could even come alive – to the susceptible imagination, at least.[27]

Sexual attraction was believed to heighten the imagined animacy of objects even further. In 1858, this commentary about the vitality of matter appeared in the periodical *L'Artiste*: "The sister-molecules, separated by the arbitrary force of man, yield spontaneously only to the sweet law of attraction ... Living a life of their own, animated by an individual spirit, they obey only one law: the law of love".[28] These comments anticipate by over a century Elaine Scarry's emphasis on the importance of animism as a practice for orienting the self in the world. She writes, "it is the work of the imagination (rather than the object) to make the inanimate world animate-like, to make the world outside the body as responsible as if it were not oblivious to sentience".[29]

Degas achieves something very close to this: he fosters the *expectation* of animacy by staging a series of dynamic oppositions between objects and bodily configurations that are gendered as masculine or feminine, rather than by using an accumulation of anecdotal clues. In *Interior*, certain obvious emblems of gender, such as the sewing box and the top hat, are contrasted through the associations they inspire; the openness of the sewing box might stand for a certain feminine vulnerability, for instance, while the map suggests a world of masculine adventure. Yet postures, gestures, physiognomies, and costume are directly opposed within the structure of the painting itself ... In other words, Degas painted not just a sewing box, but a sewing box that serves as a pivotal point from which the body of a woman turns away; a corset cast down between the couple; and a top hat that rests at the opposite side of a room from its putative owner. [...]

Despite its apparent spareness, *Interior* is dense with visualizations of desire confounded and of touch denied: the sewing box opened but abandoned, the tools of handiwork set aside, the garments cast off and strewn carelessly over the bed frame. The exposed flesh of the woman's shoulder embodies touch as an act of violation, as does her corset, that most intimate of bodily encasements, now collapsed unceremoniously at midpoint between the couple.

The corset's condition and its distance from the woman's body testify to the volatility of the earlier encounter.[30] Like the rug, the corset is thinly painted, almost ghostly in its immateriality, with its laces spilling toward the viewer. The ephemerality of its form contradicts its loaded meaning, for no corset can be dismissed, no matter how reductively it is painted. One early critic, Georges Grappe, called it "a symbol of powerful restraint", evidence that the woman was forcibly undressed.[31] But as we have seen, the painting is far more ambiguous than this. The corset's equidistance from both man and woman raises the unanswerable question of how it fell to the floor in the first place. Did the woman cast it away of her own volition, all the while knowing its abandonment would be a sure prelude to female dishonor?[32] Or was it included as an assurance of the realism of the image? [...]

Pandora's box

For early critics of *Interior*, the sewing box confirmed the asymmetry of the protagonists' respective class status and reinforced the bestiality of the man. The woman, according to

Georges Grappe, was "the little worker", whose employer has "lost his head … his composure returning as he contemplates his grief".[33] Cainille Mauclair, a well-known Symbolist critic, concurred in 1924, bemoaning the agony of the "little victim", with her "embroiderer's work basket", sobbing in the aftermath of the "brutal struggle". The man, who has "satisfied his lust, is once more composed, but mournfully so".[34]

Some authors have argued that the box on the table is a valise, pointing to its commodious proportions and conspicuous presence.[35] Indeed, a box of approximately this size *could* function as a general index for femininity, for it resembles a milliner's case, as well as a traveling seamstress's workbox. But Degas seems relatively indifferent to the actual details of sewing and embroidery as activities, as he was to their customary moralizing associations. The scissors, ball of thread, lace collar, and embroidery hoop do not collectively serve as implements for a project. Instead, they act as a cumulative inventory of references to the significance of the *act* of sewing.

Historically, sewing had been represented as a virtuous activity. Practitioners ranged from the Virgin Mary to the beneficent matron pictured in Jacques-Louis David's *The Marquise de Pastoret and her Son* (ca. 1792; Chicago, The Art Institute). Nineteenth-century popular illustrations are full of seamstresses working alone in their damp, ill-lit garrets. Working-class seamstresses were vulnerable to the predatory bourgeois, who is represented in some illustrations as a menacing, top-hatted silhouette lurking just outside the seamstress's shop.[36] […]

The sewing box serves not only as the visualization of virtue longed for but lost, but also as the materialization of sensual, female flesh. This was precisely the claim made in the catalogue of the Degas retrospective organized by the Musée d'Orsay and the Metropolitan Museum of Art in 1988, where the author of the entry on *Interior* asserted that "there had not been a more expressive symbol of lost virginity than that gaping box, with its pink lining glaringly exposed in the lamplight".[37] […]

For the *Interior*, Degas opened the box, and therein lies the crucial difference. Luminous rose tones seem to pulse from the box's interior. A constellation of pink and red hues – the woman's rosy cheek, the red stripes of the rug, the red- and pink-flowered sprigs on the glass chimney – coalesce around the box to cement its unambiguous association with the woman. In *The Poetics of Space*, Gaston Bachelard described the small chest as an "interior within an interior". Its relation to the larger space it inhabits is equivocal, depending entirely on whether it is open or closed. "Chests, especially small caskets, over which we have more complete mastery, are objects *that may be opened*. When a casket is closed, it is returned to the general community of objects; it takes its place in exterior space. But it opens! … a new dimension – the dimension of intimacy – has just opened up".[38]

Ludmilla Jordanova links the closed object containing a hidden interior with female sexuality and thus with the danger of the secrets that might be revealed. And secrecy is seductive. She writes: "Women and their secrets have a decidedly ambiguous status, being both desired and feared … Men desire to possess both women and knowledge, and they pay a cost for both".[39] That Degas felt acutely the perilous nature of this dual possession is suggested in his pronouncement about the difficulties of making art: "Art is vice. You don't marry it, you rape it. Whoever says art says artifice".[40] For Degas, the metaphorical possession of the female body that was a necessary prelude to transmuting it into art was fraught with anxiety, and perhaps even with shame.

The best-known box in the modern history of sexuality belonged to Freud's patient "Dora". As Janet Malcolm has put it: "The case rattles with boxes; you practically trip over one wherever you turn. There is a jewelry box in the first dream ... there are two boxes in the second dream ... and there is the ... reticule, which Dora pokes her finger in and out of".[41] Freud himself recorded his comments to Dora after she recounted for him a dream in which she was offered a jewel case. "Perhaps you do not know that jewel-case [*Schmuckkästchen*] is a favorite expression for the same thing that you alluded to not long ago by means of the reticule you were wearing – for the female genitals, I mean".[42]

Freud's analysis of Dora was a notorious failure, largely because he was unable to cope with the countertransference inspired by this intelligent, challenging, young woman.[43] Malcolm asks, "Who could Dora be but Pandora? ... the authoress of all our ills", a combination of "great beauty and a bad character".[44] As for the Pandora myth itself, according to Elaine Showalter, it is "a parable of defloration".[45] Less literally, the myth is also about the dangers of satisfying one's curiosity, "a reification and displaced representation of female sexuality as mystery and threat".[46] If Pandora's box distills the fear of women's secrets, of their hidden anatomy, and their potential treacheries, then Degas's open sewing box evokes both the seductions and the dangers of an erotic encounter. Indeed, the idea that female sexuality presented a distinct threat to masculine autonomy was a commonplace in Degas's day, one acutely felt within his own circle. Roy McMullen has pointed out that many of Degas's friends and colleagues remained unmarried, while others delayed the "march to the altar". McMullen also notes that Degas was deeply absorbed in Edmond and Jules de Goncourt's volatile tale of sexual obsession, *Manette Salomon*, at the end of 1867, just when he began the sketches for *Interior*. The novel tells of a wealthy and talented painter, Coriolis, who succumbs to the erotic charms of Manette, an illiterate Jewish model. Coriolis's obsession with Manette dissipates his drive to create and destroys his career. Degas identified *Manette Salomon* as a "direct source" for his "new perception" of painting.[47] If *Interior* exemplifies this new approach to his work, then Degas himself, at the age of thirty-four, seems to have possessed a deeply conflicted understanding of the role of masculine authority, as well as a significant confusion about the proper response to those who might challenge it.

When Freud's analysis of Dora came to its unexpected end, the psychoanalyst nonetheless boasted to his friend Wilhelm Fliess that "the case has opened smoothly to my collection of picklocks", a comment that depends quite obviously on metaphors of penetration. Such penetration could be simply psychoanalytic – the obdurate dreams and fantasies yielding to the insightful powers of Freud's technique. But we know that Freud himself associated the key, or picklock, with male sexuality.[48] The word that Dora used for box, *Schachtel*, was also a deprecatory word for woman. As Freud mused, "'Where is the *key*?' seems to me to be the masculine counterpart to the question 'Where is the *box*?'"[49]

Honor

Degas may not have represented the key itself in *Interior*, but he did represent the lock plate. In an early oil sketch – the same study that shows the fully dressed woman about to enter the room – the man leans heavily against the opened door. Below his elbow is a conspicuous rectangular lock plate with a keyhole at its center – a striking detail given the provisional nature of the study. In the final painting, the man's body occludes the keyhole, but the connotation of privileged entry is preserved in the bold red color and clear rectangular contour of the lock plate. Both lock and keyhole are now absorbed directly into the masculine body that presses against the (now) closed door; the visible portion of the lock plate acts less as an accessory or attribute than as a partially hidden body part. Degas certainly understood the sexual significance attached to the lock plate or latch, as seen in paintings such as Fragonard's *The Bolt* (ca. 1778; Paris, Musée du Louvre), in which a man overcomes the objections of his lover (or rather, his victim) by sliding the bolt across the doorjamb. Degas's own collection of prints by Gavarni included an image of a man conspicuously sliding back the bolt of a lock to secure his privacy.[50] The partial obscuring of the lock in *Interior* is but one aspect of Degas's envisioning of a contemporary man fixed in a position that is both compromising and compromised. Degas pictured a masculine subjectivity that seems without authority, without freedom and, above all, without honor.

Degas's male protagonist is in many ways more enigmatic than his female counterpart. His class identity seems at first to echo the artist's own, for he is garbed much as Degas himself dressed during these years … [But] Degas did not reveal himself directly in his works. He proceeded by indirection, painstaking reformulation, and charged juxtapositions. If his own sexual preoccupations were implicated – perhaps unwittingly – in *Interior*, the painting's power stems in great part not from its personal revelations, but from the fact that Degas gave figural and spatial form to a far more general uncertainty about the nature and appearance of masculine authority. There is a strategic difference between "solving" a complex painting and striving to understand the more general significance of its complexities. It is true that the interior state of a man who lingers in the aftermath of a failed sexual encounter is something that a high-strung, unmarried man of thirty-four may well have speculated about.[51] We shall never know. Nor do we need to, for Degas's *Interior*, despite the persistence of our ignorance about its "origin" in the mind of the artist, demonstrates that, in the nineteenth century, spatial identity – how and where a man stood in relation to the milieu and the figures around him – *was* sexual identity. […]

In mid-century France, two characteristics were essential to the preservation of masculine honor: the mastery of involuntary or indecorous emotion, and sexual potency. Propagating the species was a solemn duty of the exemplary French citizen, and "only a man who was sexually potent could live in and through the heirs who received both his good name and the imprint of his person". He who departed from the standard "dishonored himself and brought shame to his family – a judgement applied with equal severity to both the bachelor and the homosexual".[52] […]

In Degas's day, much bourgeois effort was directed toward mastering emotion or involuntary urges within the interior. The male's "unshakeable sang-froid", according to Nye, "not only promoted social mobility, but conferred, it would appear, a selective advantage on the men who possessed it in the highest degree".[53] The male protagonist of *Interior* initially appears to be the very picture of self-possession. He is contained and aloof; moreover, Degas exaggerates his bodily presence. He extends the length of his legs by fusing them with the shadows they cast on the floor, and he amplifies the force of his body with a nearly independent shadow on the door behind him. But this effect of dominance is subtly undermined, not only by the hands encased in pockets, but by his physiognomy and the startling manner in which it is lit. His face is distinctly unappealing. He is not grotesque or bestial – as early critics insisted – but his features are aberrant enough to warrant attention.[54] His physiognomy was carefully shaped in a series of studies, in which Degas discarded the handsome face and engaged demeanor of the earlier version for a man whose forehead is too narrow, nose too large, eyes too small, and eyebrows too close together. A sizable fleck of white paint fills the man's left eye and, most unsettling of all, the man's ear seems ever-so-slightly pointed. […]

Degas's protagonist is … a man whose masculine honor has been compromised. His sang-froid has been shaken – perhaps more by a recognition of his own lapse than by any actual harm he has inflicted on the woman who crouches before him. More than any other feature, the flash of white paint in the man's eye aroused the animosity of early critics. (As Grappe put it: "A lewd fire burns in his gaze – oh, that white point on his pupil!")[55] It is unsettling but ambiguous, because even as it rivets the spectator's attention to the male gaze, it conceals both its direction and expression. Armstrong has argued that the man's gaze, and its deflection by the woman's back, is the central theme of the painting, a supposition reinforced to some degree by the conventional understanding of male sexuality in these years. Nye writes: "Males alone were believed capable of a subjective orientation toward sexuality; women, though they were regarded as eminently capable of subjectivity, were simply the objects of this gaze".[56] But Degas's man gazes without pleasure or authority. His face supplies little evidence of the "bestial" creature critics saw; instead, it is a site of emotion masked, emptied, or restrained.

The man's gaze and his constrained posture suggest what may be another theme within the *Interior*: the mutual endurance of sexual shame. The picture's protagonists seem forever trapped in a space that at once suffocates and divides them. The relinquishing of self under the press of desire has consigned each character to an unending, and unbreachable, isolation. The signs of humiliation are more overt in Degas's female protagonist: the dishevelment of her dress, the dispersal of both her inner and her outer garments, the reflexive curve of her body, the dramatic exposure of the sewing box's interior. But she is not the only character to have lost honor. Her male companion is stranded too, fixed by perspective, proportion, and atmosphere – by *paint* – in a space riven by irreparable tensions.[57]

Interior envisions how sexual identity – for men and women – was imagined during a most unstable period in the history of private life … While much of the art I examine in this book preceded Freudian psychoanalysis by two decades, the kinds of sexual tensions it claimed to elucidate were first visualized in works such as Degas's painting. Because the artist's protagonists are visually fused to a space that acts out their sexual alienation, their conflict is reimagined – and *felt* in the body – by every viewer who stands before them. Perhaps this is why everyone who sees the painting tries to invent a convincing solution to its mystery. Irresolution may be the truest stance toward *Interior*, but it remains an uncomfortable one, even for the late-twentieth-century viewer.

Robert Nye has claimed that "we cannot easily penetrate the veil that cloaks private sexual experience and identity in the past, but the representations in the surrounding culture to which they are dialectically bound have left abundant traces in the public record".[58] Degas's *Interior* provides just such a trace, a trace which, moreover, invites the responsive spectator to experience viscerally an exceptionally strained and intimate encounter, the kind of encounter that, in life, would have no witnesses. While we are not admitted, exactly, into the metaphorical interior of Degas's own sexual anxieties, we are given a glimpse of the larger stage on which those anxieties may have been imagined, masked, or, in the language of the post-Freudian age, repressed. Traces of renunciation and paralysis are embedded in *Interior*'s very form, but can be pried out, can be *seen* and *felt*, through a process of immersion that preserves the enigma of Degas's sexuality but delivers the viewer to the very brink of a revelation about the unvoiced but abiding bonds that, at one and the same moment, connected *and* isolated bourgeois men and women of the nineteenth century.

Notes

1   René König, *Sociologie de la mode*, Paris: Payat, 1969, p. 136, quoted in Rémy Saisselin, *The Bourgeois and the Bibelot*, New Brunswick, N.J.: Rutgers University Press, 1984, p. 40.

2   Degas knew of Lecoq's ideas through his friendships with Legros, Cazin, Fantin-Latour, and Whistler. In addition, Edmond Duranty referred to the drawing master fairly often in his own essays for *Réalisme* and, later, in his art reviews and in *The New Painting*.

3   For the use of *Le Viol* as an alternate title, see Marcia Pointon, *Naked Authority*, New York and Cambridge: Cambridge University Press, 1990, p. 119; and Carol Armstrong, "Edgar Degas and the Representation of the Human Body", in Susan Suleiman (ed.) *The Female Body in Western Culture*, Cambridge, Mass.: Harvard University Press, 1985, pp. 223–42, 225 …

4   Early comments to this effect came from Georges Grappe, *Degas. L'art et beau* 3 (1), Paris: Librairie artistique Internationale, 1908, p. 7; and Camille Mauclair, *Degas*, Paris: Editions Hypérions, 1924, p. 31 … The most substantial writings on the painting to date have been by: Theodore Reff, whose original interpretation appeared as "Degas's 'Tableau de Genre,'" *Art Bulletin* 54, no. 3, September 1972, 316–37, and was later collected in his *Degas: The Artist's Mind*, New York: Metropolitan Museum of Art with Harper and Row, 1976; Carol Armstrong, *Odd Man Out: Readings of the Work and Reputation of Edgar Degas*, Chicago: University of Chicago Press, 1991, pp. 93–100; and, more recently, by John House, "Degas's 'Tableau de Genre,'" in Richard Kendall and Griselda Pollock (eds) *Dealing with Degas: Representations of Women and the Politics of Vision*, New York: Universe, 1992, pp. 80–94.

5   See Jean Sutherland Boggs, with Douglas Druick, Henri Loyrette, Michael Pantazzi, and Gary Tinterow (eds), *Degas*, exhibition catalog, New York: Metropolitan Museum of Art, 1988, pp. 143–46, for the painting's provenance and exhibition and critical histories. […]

6   Jean François de Bastide, *The Little House: An Architectural Seduction*, trans. Rodolphe El-Khoury, New York: Princeton Architectural Press, 1996, pp. 16–17 …

7   César Daly, *L'Architecture privée aux XIXe siècle urbaine et suburbaine*, Paris: A. Morel et cie., 1864, p. 10. The home should be "le vêtement de la famille. Elle est en effet destinée à lui servir d'enveloppe, à l'abriter et à se prêter à tous ses mouvements" (p. 22).

8   Ibid., p. 12. On Daly's ideas about "aesthetic geometry", see Ann Lorenz Van Zanten, "Form and Society: César Daly and the *Revue Générale de l'Architecture*", *Oppositions* 8, Spring 1977, 137–45, esp. 140. For an analysis of *Architecture privée*, see Hélène Lipstadt, "Housing the Bourgeoisie: César Daly and the Ideal Home", ibid., 34–47 …

9   Daly, *L'Architecture privée*, p. 12. […]

10 Daly, "Villa", *Revue Générale de l'Architecture*, 32, 1875, 272–3. […]

11 For publications on nineteenth-century decoration, see J. Feray, *Architecture intérieure et décoration en France: Des origines à 1875*, Paris: Berger-Levrault: Caisse Nationale des Monuments Historiques et des Sites, 1988, and T. Lambert, *Décorations et ameublements intérieurs*, Paris: C. Schmid, 1906.

12 For illustrations that document the relationship between class and urban accommodations, see Edmond Texier, *Tableau de Paris*, vol. 1, Paris: Paulin et Le Chevalier, 1852, in particular, p. 65.

13 Walter Benjamin, "Paris: Capital of the Nineteenth Century", in *Reflections*, trans. Edmund Jephcott, New York: Schocken Books, 1986 …

14 This point is addressed by Carolyn Steedman, *Strange Dislocations: Childhood and the Idea of Human Interiority, 1780–1930*, Cambridge, Mass.: Harvard University Press, 1995; also, see Part Three ("A Woman's Place") of Suzanne Nash (ed.) *Home and Its Dislocations in Nineteenth-Century France*, Albany: State University of Albany Press, 1993; and Carroll Smith-Rosenberg, *Disorderly Conduct: Visions of Gender in Victorian America*, New York and Oxford: Oxford University Press, 1985; and Rachel Bowlby, *Shopping with Freud*, London: Routledge, 1993.

15 The most comprehensive study of intimate life in the nineteenth century is Peter Gay's three-volume series, *The Bourgeois Experience: Victoria to Freud*, esp. vol. 1, *The Education of the Senses*, New York: W. W. Norton, 1984. See Debora Silverman, *Art Nouveau in Fin-de-Siècle France: Politics, Psychology and Style*, Berkeley and Los Angeles: University of California Press, 1989, pp. 186–206, for an analysis of the feminization of the decorative arts.

16 The most influential argument about the feminization of the spatial strategies employed by artists such as Cassatt and Morisot remains Griselda Pollock, "Modernity and the Spaces of

Femininity", in *Vision and Difference: Femininity, Feminism, and the Histories of Art*, London and New York: Routledge, 1988, pp. 50–90. I believe that Degas both exploits and subverts the usual gendered associations of the domestic interior, and thus serves as a counterexample to Pollock's thesis.

17   For an analysis of the respective status of history and genre painting around 1867, particularly the fluctuating stature of history painting as an "official art", see Patricia Mainardi, *Art and Politics of the Second Empire: The Universal Expositions of 1855 and 1867*, New Haven and London: Yale University Press, 1987 ... See Armstrong, "Edgar Degas and the Representation of the Female Body", pp. 73–100, for the relation of Degas's work to earlier painting, both history and genre.

18   For popular imagery on the subject, see Beatrice Farwell, *The Cult of Images: Baudelaire in the Nineteenth Century*, Santa Barbara: Santa Barbara Art Museum, University of California, 1977. A valuable overview of the theme in drama is found in Charles Edward Young, "The Marriage Question in Modern French Drama", *University of Wisconsin Bulletin* 5, no. 4, 1912. See also Linda Nochlin, "A House Is Not a Home: Degas and the Subversion of the Family", in Kendall and Pollock, *Dealing with Degas*, pp. 43–65. The course of the fallen working girl was charted in many *feuilletons*, which are surveyed in Farwell, as above.

19   See Young, "The Marriage Question", for an overview of the genre of the domestic drama during the nineteenth century.

20   Quoted in ibid., p. 410.

21   See Roy McMullen, *Degas: His Life and Time*, Boston: Houghton Mifflin Company, 1984, pp. 151–82, for discussions of the books and ideas Degas was interested in at this time.

22   Laura Mulvey, "Melodrama Inside and Outside the Home", in *Visual and Other Pleasures*, Bloomington: Indiana University Press, 1989, pp. 63–80, 74 ...

23   Thomas Elsaesser, "Tales of Sound and Fury", in Bill Nichols (ed.) *Movies and Methods*, vol. 2, New York: Columbia University Press, 1985, p. 177.

24   J. J. Gibson, *The Senses Considered as a Perceptual System*, Boston: Houghton Mifflin Company, 1955, p. 202.

25   Degas made a number of remarks in his notebooks of this period about the effects of artificial light. The relevant studies and comments are in Degas's Notebook 23, p. 45. See Theodore Reff, *The Notebooks of Degas*, 2 vols., Oxford and London: Oxford University Press, 1976.

26   Georges Teyssot, "The Disease of the Domicile", *Assemblage* 6, June 1988, 73–97, 92.

27   Guy de Maupassant's fanciful "observations" are quoted by Teyssot, ibid., 91.

28   Anonymous, "La Vie de la Forme", *L'Artiste* 2, 1858, 156–57. […]

29   Elaine Scarry, *The Body in Pain: The Making and Unmaking of the World*, Oxford, Engl. and New York: Oxford University Press, 1985, p. 306.

30   Corsets were not generally worn by working-class women in the mid-nineteenth century ...

31   Grappe, *Degas*, p. 27.

32   Hollis Clayson has noted that "the abandonment of stays had long been a symbol of female dishonor, of taking leave of social decencies"; see Clayson, "Avant-Garde and Pompier Images of Nineteenth-Century French Prostitutes: The Matter of Modernism, Modernity and Social Ideology", in Benjamin Buchloh, Serge Guilbaut, and David Solkin (eds) *Modernism and Modernity: The Vancouver Papers*, Halifax: The Press of the Nova Scotia College of Art and Design, 1983, pp. 43–64, 56.

33   For imagery of the seamstress in contemporary prints, see Farwell, *The Cult of Images*, and Farwell, *French Popular Lithographic Imagery 1815–1870*, Chicago: University of Chicago Press, 1981. See Grappe, *Degas*, p. 7, on the man's "bestiality".

34   Mauclair, *Degas*, p. 31. Other like-minded interpretations include Arsène Alexandre's in "Degas", *L'art et les artistes* 29, no. 154, February 1935; and Meier-Graefe, *Degas*.

35   Armstrong calls the box a valise. See Armstrong, "Edgar Degas and the Representation of the Female Body", p. 228.

36   See Farwell, *The Cult of Images*, for related illustrations.

37   See Boggs et al., *Degas*, p. 146.

38   Gaston Bachelard, *The Poetics of Space*, trans. Maria Jolas, Boston: Beacon Press, 1958, p. 85.

39   Ludmilla Jordanova, *Sexual Visions: Images of Gender in Science and Medicine between the Eighteenth and Twentieth Centuries*, Madison: University of Wisconsin Press, 1985, quoted by Laura Mulvey in "Pandora: Topographies of the Mask and Curiosity", in Colomina, *Sexuality and Space*, pp. 53–72, 61, and 96–7.

40 "L'Art, c'est le vice. On ne l'épouse pas légitimement, on le viole. Que dit Art dit Artifice. L'Art est malhonnête et cruel"; quoted in, among other places, F. Sevin, "Degas à travers ses mots", *Gazette des Beaux Arts* 86, no. 1, 1975, 36.

41 Janet Malcolm, "Reflections; j'appelle un chat un chat", *The New Yorker*, April 20, 1987, 84–102, 98.

42 Sigmund Freud, quoted in Peter Gay (ed.) *The Freud Reader*, New York and London: W. W. Norton, 1989, from the "Fragment of an Analysis of a Case of Hysteria ('Dora')", pp. 172–239, 210. [...]

43 See Charles Bernheimer and Claire Kahane (eds) *In Dora's Case: Freud-Hysteria-Feminism*, New York: Columbia University Press, 1985.

44 "If Freud's countertransference invested Dora with all the seductiveness and dangerousness of Eve, if he saw her not as the messed-up little Viennese teenager she was but as Original Woman, in all her beauty and evil mystery, it is no wonder that he treated her as he did", Malcolm, "Reflections", p. 98.

45 Elaine Showalter, *Sexual Anarchy: Gender and Culture at the Fin de Siècle*, New York: Penguin Books, 1990, p. 137.

46 Mulvey, "Pandora", p. 57.

47 On Degas's unmarried state, see McMullen, *Degas*, pp. 261–83. On Degas and the Goncourts' novel, see ibid., pp. 130–1.

48 As Showalter has put it: "There's more than a hint in this language of sexual assault, but also of rational penetration. If Dora's 'case,' like Pandora's box, held the secrets of female sexuality, Freud's key – the new science of psychoanalysis – could unlock it". She quotes Freud: "No one who disdains the key will ever be able to unlock the door". See Showalter, *Sexual Anarchy*, p. 137.

49 Freud's note to Fliess is reprinted in Gay, *A Freud Reader*, p. 22. [...]

50 The Gavarni print was in Degas's own collection and was part of the *Lorette* series, but is not illustrated in the catalog by Ann Dumas, Colta Ives, Susan A. Stein, and Gary Tinterow, *The Private Collection of Edgar Degas*, exhibition catalog, New York: Metropolitan Museum of Art, 1997.

51 On Degas's social interactions during the 1860s, see McMullen, *Degas*, pp. 165–82.

52 Robert Nye, *Masculinity and Male Codes of Honor in Modern France*, New York and Oxford: Oxford University Press, 1993, p. 67: "As we have seen, male sexual potency was a qualifying feature for full citizenship in the modern state".

53 Ibid., p. 129. [...]

54 See Reff, *Degas*, pp. 217–20, for a discussion of physiognomic theories relevant to the *Interior*, and p. 329, n. 76, and 82, for references to Caspar Lavater. [...]

55 On the "lewd white speck" see Grappe, *Degas*, p. 52, and Reff, *Degas*, pp. 217–8. [...]

56 On the gaze of the male protagonist, see Armstrong, "Edgar Degas and the Female Body", pp. 228–9. Also see Nye, *Masculinity*, p. 114.

57 It may be relevant that the only recorded note we have of Degas's own apparently limited sexual experience revolves around the sensation of shame: "I cannot say how much I love this girl since she turned me down on Monday, 7 April. I cannot refuse to ... say it is shameful ... [illegible] a defenceless girl". This remark is recorded in Reff, *Notebooks of Degas*, Notebook 6, BN, Carnet II, p. 21. It is also quoted in Boggs et al., *Degas*, p. 146.

58 Nye, *Masculinity*, p. 10.

Figure 23
Charles West Cope, *A Life Well Spent*, 1862.

Figure 24
Victorian parlor: "Glen Roy" interior, Wake Green Road, Mosley, 1891.

Figure 25
Robert Kerr, Bear Wood,
near Wokingham, Berk-
shire (1865–74), exterior.

Figure 26
Bear Wood, plans

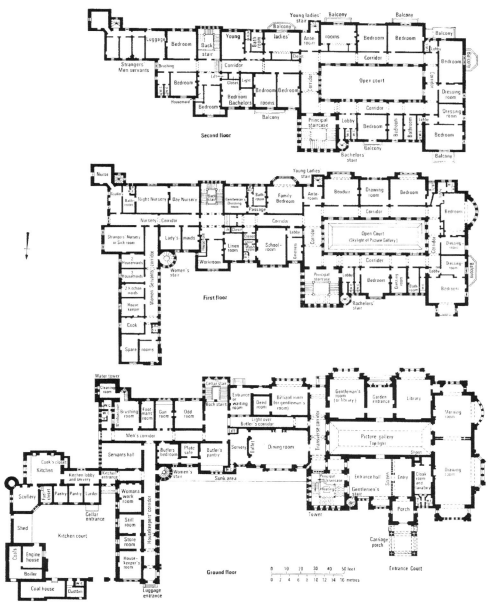

Figure 27
American shingle-style
house, 1882, exterior
and plan.

Figure 28
George and J. P.
Kingston House,
Worcester, Mass.,
c. 1897, exterior.

Figure 29
Kingston House, plan.

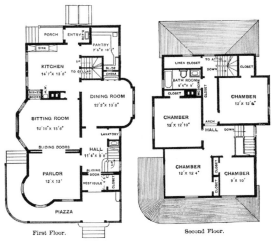

Figure 30
Sears, Roebuck and
Company Modern Home
#111 (The Chelsea),
1908, exterior and plan.

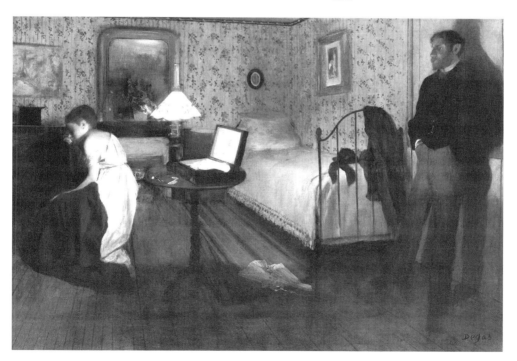

Figure 31   Edgar Degas, *Interior*, 1868–9.

7

Rural memories and desires

The farm, the suburb, the wilderness retreat

In this section, the influential mid-nineteenth-century architect and theorist Andrew Jackson Downing describes the proper appearance of a farmhouse (Fig. 32), and stresses its importance for American values. Art historian William Barksdale Maynard reinterprets the significance of Thoreau, seeing him as a proponent both of suburbanization and of the wilderness experience, and setting his work in the context of contemporary garden and villa ideals (Fig. 33). Historian Barbara Miller Lane describes the evolution of wilderness retreats in late nineteenth- and early twentieth-century Finland and Sweden, where revivals of folk traditions helped to bolster nationalist feeling while inspiring innovative kinds of ideal dwellings (Figs. 34, 35 and 36). Closely resembling the Finnish works discussed by Lane were the Great Camps of the American Adirondacks, here described by National Parks historian Harvey H. Kaiser (Figs. 37, 38 and 39). Historian of vernacular rural architecture Thomas K. Hubka points to the gradual reorientation of American farm buildings toward the street during the course of the nineteenth century, thus supporting M. J. Daunton's hypotheses about the effects of urbanization on housing design. Hubka also suggests that farm buildings offered their owners considerable scope for architectural self-expression (Fig. 40). Sociologist Mike Hepworth argues that Victorian garden designs, executed in the suburbs, represented an effort to recapture rural origins in an era of rapid urbanization (Fig. 41). In her oral history of the life of her great aunt and uncle, planning student Dawni Freeman describes the attractions of farm life in the later twentieth century.

What a farm-house should be

Andrew Jackson Downing (1850)

In every agricultural country, the most numerous habitations that meet the eye of the traveler are farm-houses.

In this country, where a large proportion of the whole population is devoted to agriculture, this is especially the case. For every twenty persons who live in villas, suburban cottages, or town houses, there are eighty persons who live in farm-houses. It requires no argument, therefore, to prove that the comfort or convenience of farmers is of more weight and importance, numerically considered, than that of any other class; or that whoever desires to see his country adorned with tasteful dwellings, must not overlook its most frequent and continual feature – the farm-house.

Granting the importance of this branch of Rural Architecture, it is not a little singular that we, in America, so rarely see a satisfactory farm-house.

Most thinking persons explain this to themselves by saying that only those who have money to spare, can afford to build tasteful houses, and that the farmer has no money to spare for ornamental decoration. If, however, we have been rightly understood in our remarks on cottages, we trust we have plainly shown that beauty does not depend solely upon ornament, and hence that a house may be tasteful, without any additional cost, merely by exhibiting good forms.

Setting aside, therefore, this reasoning as insufficient, we must attribute the commonplace and meager character of farm-houses to two other causes – one, that Architects usually consider them beneath their notice; and the other, that farmers seldom consider what the beauty of a farm-house consists in.

It is not, perhaps, remarkable that foreign architects consider the farm-house as so little worthy of their attention. In countries where the farmers are serfs, as in Russia, or even tenants from year to year, as in England, wherever, in short, the farmer has no property in the soil he cultivates, we might naturally expect that the comfort and beauty of his habitations would be a matter of trifling consequence to architects, whose profession is dependent upon the wealthier class of landlords and proprietors. But in this country, where almost every farmer is a proprietor, where a large portion of the farmers are intelligent men, and where farmers are not prevented by anything in their condition or in the institutions of the country, from being among the wisest, the best, and the most honored of our citizens, the wants of the farming class deserve, and should receive the attention to which their character and importance entitle them.

We have said that farmers, generally, misunderstand the true sources of truth and beauty in a farm-house. Our farmers are by no means all contented with a comfortable shelter for their heads. On the contrary, we see numberless attempts to give something of beauty to their homes. The designs continually published by agricultural journals, most of which emanate from the agricultural class, show the continual aiming after something better, which characterizes every class in this country. Some of these designs are appropriate and tasteful. But a large number of the better and more substantial farm-houses, especially those where some effort at taste is apparent, are decidedly failures, considered either in a tasteful or architectural point of view.

They are often failures, indeed, not because there are no evidences of comfort or beauty in their exteriors or interiors; but because they are not intrinsically farm-houses; because they are not truthful; because they do not express the life and character of the farmer; because they neglect their own true and legitimate sources of interest, and aim to attain beauty by imitating or borrowing the style or decorations of the ornamental cottage or villa.

Now, if we have clearly explained, in a previous part of this work, the great value and importance of truthfulness in domestic architecture, it cannot but be plain to our readers that a farm-house must, first of all, look like a farm-house, or it cannot give us any lasting satisfaction; and that as one of the highest sources of beauty in domestic architecture is derived from its embodying the best traits of character of the man or class of men for whom it is designed, it is equally plain that to raise the farm-house in the scale of truth and beauty, we must make it express that beauty, whatever it may be, which lies in a farmer's life.

How shall we make a farm-house truthful and significant, so that it shall look like a farm-house? Only by studying the characteristics of the farmer's life, and expressing, first of all, in the forms of his dwelling, the peculiar wants and comforts of that life.

Some of these we conceive to be the following; extended space on the ground, to afford room for all the in-door occupations of agricultural life, which will always give the farm-house breadth rather than height; a certain rustic plainness, which denotes a class more occupied with the practical and useful than the elegant arts of life; a substantial and solid construction, which denotes abundance of materials to build with, rather than money to expend in workmanship.

The genuine farmer is peculiarly the man of nature – more sincere, more earnest than men of any other class; because, dealing more with Providence than with men, he is less sophisticated either in manners or heart, and, if less cultivated, is more frank, and gives us more homely truths and less conventional insincerity than dwellers in cities.

The farm-house, to be significant, should therefore show an absence of all pretension. It should not borrow Grecian columns, or Italian balustrades, or Gothic carved work from the villa; or merely pretty ornaments from the cottage ornée. It should rely on its own honest, straightforward simplicity, and should rather aim to be frank, and genuine, and open-hearted like its owner, than to wear the borrowed ornaments of any class of different habits and tastes. The porch or the veranda of the farm-house should not only be larger, but also simpler, and ruder, and stronger than that of the cottage, because there is more manly strength in the agriculturist's life than in that of any other class; the roof should be higher and more capacious, for it is to overshadow larger families and larger stores of nature's gifts; and, above all, the chimneys should be larger and more generous-looking, to betoken the warm-hearted hospitality of the farmer's home. Their large and simple tops should rather suggest ample hearths and good kitchens than small grates and handsome parlors.

Now, the real elements of beauty in the farm-house must be found in giving expression to the best and most beautiful traits in the farmer's life. And since the farmer's life is neither devoted to the elegant nor the ornamental arts, he should no more be expected to display a variety of architectural ornaments in the construction of his house than he would be to wear garments made by the most fashionable tailor in Broadway, or to drive to his market town in one of Lawrence and Collis's most modish carriages.

Expecting, as we do, to find every species of domestic architecture typifying the character of the man or class of men inhabiting it, we do not desire any elaborate artistic effect or anything like carefully studied attempts at architectural style in the farm-house. The farmer's life is not one devoted to aesthetics, and we do not look chiefly, for the evidences of carefully elaborated taste and culture in his house, as in the dwelling of the scholar and the man of letters.

But we ought to find, in every farm-house, indications of those virtues which adorn the farmer's character, and which, if expressed at all in his dwelling, must give the latter something of the same beauty as the former. His dwelling ought to suggest simplicity, honesty of purpose, frankness, a hearty, genuine spirit of good will, and a homely and modest, though manly and independent, bearing in his outward deportment. For the true farmer despises affectation; he loves a blunt and honest expression of the truth; and he shows you that he knows the value of a friend by shaking hands with you, as if his heart acted like a magnetic machine on the chords of his fingers.

It would be false and foolish to embellish highly the dwelling of such a man with the elaborate details of the different schools of architecture. We must leave this more scientific display of art and learning to villas and public edifices, and endeavor to make the farm-house agreeable, chiefly by expressing in its leading forms the strength, simplicity, honesty, frankness, and sterling goodness of the farmer's character. Although we must recognize, first of all, the constant industry which gives so much dignity and independence to his life, in the arrangement of the interior of his house mainly for useful ends, yet we would also introduce every comfort and convenience denoting the intelligence and ease of the successful farmer's life in a country where that life is so truly intelligent and reputable as our own. But in additing the veranda, the bay-window, and other architectural features significant of social cultivation and enjoyment, we should still bear in mind that these features are to be stamped with the strength, simplicity, and downrightness of character which denote that they belong to the dwelling of a man who cannot wear fine ornaments, even upon his house, because they are foreign to his nature – however significant the same ornaments may be of the life of another man or another class of men.

The principles which we would lay down for designing farm-houses may be stated as follows – so far as the production of *beauty* is concerned.

That the form of the building should express a local fitness, and an intimate relation with the soil it stands upon – by showing breadth, and extension upon the ground, rather than height.

That its proportions should aim at ampleness, solidity, comfort, and a simple domestic feeling, rather than elegance, grace, and polished symmetry.

That its details should be simple and bold, and its ornaments, so far as they are used, should rather be rustic, strong, or picturesque, than delicate or highly finished.

That in raising the character of the farm-house, the first step above the really useful, is to add the porch, the veranda, and the bay-window, since they are not only significant of real but of refined utility.

So far as the *useful* is concerned in the farm-house, its principles are better understood, but we shall do no harm in recapitulating the most important:–

The farm-house should be built of strong and enduring materials, whether of timber or stone, so that it may need repairs very seldom.

The pitch of the roof should always be high, not only to keep the chamber-floor cooler, and to shed the snows in a northern climate, but to give sufficient garret room for storing and drying many of the smaller products of the farm.

The *living-room* of the family should be a large, and usually the largest and most comfortable apartment; it should be so placed as to be convenient to the other apartments used in the every-day occupations of the family, and its size should never be sacrificed to that of the parlor. [...]

Thoreau's house at Walden

William Barksdale Maynard (1999)

The literary and historical stature of Henry David Thoreau grows with every passing year, it seems, and no episode in his career is more celebrated than his construction in 1845 of a little frame house for himself at Walden Pond, a mile and a half outside his native Concord, Massachusetts. For all its fame, however, this house has seldom been examined in the full context of contemporary architectural thought. This is not altogether surprising, as broadly contextual studies of Thoreau – long mythologized as a uniquely brilliant and self-sufficient figure – have been somewhat slow to appear. In particular, his decision to move to Walden, seemingly a bold rejection of society, has usually been ascribed to narrowly personal motivations – notwithstanding the fact that a number of British and American contemporaries made similar moves in the 1840s. Thoreau's Walden sojourn needs to be reevaluated in light of ideas current in his day, especially those concerning rural and suburban retirement put forth in dozens of "villa books" published in England and America between 1780 and 1850, including those by James Malton (d. 1803), William Fuller Pocock (1779–1849), John Claudius Loudon (1783–1843), and, in America, Andrew Jackson Downing (1815–1852). Building on pastoral conventions popularized by eighteenth-century poetry, these men advocated the habit of retirement and the reform of domestic architecture along the lines of the humble English cottage, a model of integrity, fitness, and the rustic Picturesque. Their ideas were enormously influential, being taken up as themes in general literature and ultimately becoming broadly assimilated into popular thought, providing the philosophical underpinnings for the early suburbanization of the landscape in England and America, a phenomenon in full swing outside Boston during Thoreau's young adulthood.

Viewed in the context of contemporary architectural thought, Thoreau's lakeshore experiment at Walden appears in a new light. Far from abandoning societal conventions, Thoreau in moving to the pond instead participated enthusiastically in the general cultural conversation regarding retirement and the villa. He relocated not to the wilderness but to a recently logged clearing in an intensively used landscape just minutes' walk from town. Here he erected a dwelling he described in terms of economy, sturdiness, and rusticity. The way he sited the structure and his descriptions of its arrangements suggest an awareness of specific dictates derived from villa books, as if he meant to offer a small-scale exemplar for the "villas which will one day be built here" (180).[1] His country house recalled several rustic types then popular – summerhouses, hermitages, and wilderness retreats – and seems to have been initially suggested by a Catskills "mountain house" he had recently admired. His Catskills trip (1844) has been virtually overlooked as an essential source of inspiration for Walden. In its wake, Thoreau creatively translated wilderness values to a suburban location as part of his desire "to live a primitive and frontier life, though in the midst of an outward civilization" (11). Following, in part, the lead of the villa books, he published his house design in *Walden; or, Life in the Woods* (1854), urging it as a model both intellectual and practical, stressing its complete opposition to all that was false and pretentious in the architecture of the day and highlighting its affinities to the so-called primitive hut, thereby joining the many contemporaries concerned with the origins of architecture and the promise, by return to "first principles", of true architectural reform. Viewed in context, the Walden experiment no longer seems, as it is so often portrayed, anomalous, antisocial, and escapist; instead, it may be understood as an intelligent and ambitious attempt to engage in current dialogues on the villa, the rustic, and the reform of domestic architecture, as Thoreau sought to participate in a popular new kind of lifestyle, suburban retirement …

The villa books comprised a diverse body of work, touching on many themes, but their basic purpose was to showcase models for progress in domestic architecture, and so they offer illustrated examples ranging from the humble summerhouse to sprawling neoclassical mansions. A frequent focus, however, is the suburban home of the gentleman of moderate means, which might more or less interchangeably bear the names "cottage", "villa", "country house", or "country seat". These books were texts addressed to members of an emerging middle class, economically tied to the burgeoning cities, who sought a return to traditional ways of living through retirement. The design of the dwellings they illustrate is highly varied, but the authors – usually practicing architects – tended to favor recognized historical styles of architecture for elaborate mansions and, more radically, astylar or rustic approaches for modest homes.

The books are more sophisticated intellectually than is sometimes warranted; far from being mere grab bags of eclectic ornament, the best of them offer in their prefaces serious-minded advice on domestic economy and architectural fitness, subjects inherited from eighteenth-century thought. As models of fitness, authors pointed to the vernacular architecture of the English countryside and specifically to the lowly cottage, stressing its intimacy with nature, its employment of locally available materials, and its lack of pretension. Thoreau frequently shows his understanding of such virtues, writing, for example, in *A Week on the Concord and Merrimack Rivers* (1849) that "humble dwellings, homely and sincere" are "more pleasing to our eyes than palaces or castles". In the villa books, a specifically "rustic" mode, Picturesque in its irregularity and resonating with theories of the primitive hut, was put forward as an alternative to the more pretentious architectural styles, and it was this mode that particularly appealed to Thoreau. The villa movement these books promoted was far more than a literary exercise; it was a cultural phenomenon of wide scope, fostered by the print explosion of the day. By Thoreau's time, the essential tenets of suburban thought as promulgated by the villa books – architectural fitness and humility, sensitivity to the landscape, the cult of the rustic – had been widely disseminated in journals and newspapers, poems and novels, letters and conversation, and would have been readily available to the young Concord writer.[2]

Thoreau's architecture

From July 4, 1845, until September 6, 1847, Thoreau (1817–1862) emulated the simple life of a classical philosopher in a house of his own fashioning on the shores of Walden … He was boarding with his mentor, Ralph Waldo Emerson, when Emerson bought thirteen and a half acres at Walden on September 21, 1844, with the intent to build "a cabin or a turret there".[3] Nothing came of these plans, but it was on Emerson's tract that Thoreau would erect his own house the following year – tiny, inexpensive, but achieving for its impecunious builder his long-standing dream of inhabiting a country house. Thoreau's decision to move to the pond likely owed in part to his growing awareness of the retirement idea, through exposure to the villa books or other sources. Crucial, too, was a conjunction of events in 1844 that together convinced Thoreau of the practicability of his dreams: his experience of helping build a house for his parents in the newly opened western (or "Texas") district of Concord; Emerson's enviable purchase of land; and the Catskills trip. That trip (see below) offered a vivid, experiential revelation of rustic ideas …

Thoreau lived at Walden for two years, two months, and two days, his return to town life being tied to the completion of the manuscript he had been writing at the pond (*A Week*) and to an invitation to manage Emerson's household while the older writer toured Europe. It is not surprising that Thoreau chose to return to "civilized life again" (3), for rustic retirement, as contemporaries conceived of it, was frequently short-term. William Wordsworth, for example, in escaping "the busy world" had allowed himself but "an allotted interval of ease, / Under my cottage-roof", and in this spirit Malton in 1802 had devoted a section of his *Collection of Designs for Rural Retreats* to "Reflections on the Necessity and Advantage of Temporary Retirement". To see Thoreau's sojourn in the context of the retirement phenomenon helps resolve a number of problems that have long troubled readers of *Walden*, including the apparent hypocrisy of the "solitary" author's frequent visits to town. In the course of retirement – always a genteel habit – one was expected to maintain close ties with friends and relatives. Downing recommended that persons planning to retire should by no means forsake the "charms of good society" and "should, in settling in the country, never let go the cord that binds them to their fellows".[4]

Popular misconceptions notwithstanding, Thoreau did not live in a "hut" or a "cabin" but in a tidy, one-room "house" – so he nearly always called it, with pride in its design and significance as a miniature country house. Nor was it a log house; he had not yet explored the Maine wilderness, where he would discover that logs provided "a very rich and picturesque look, far removed from the meanness of weatherboards".[5] As described in *Walden* (40–9, 240–6), his dwelling measured 10 by 15 feet, with two windows and a door. With his own hands he fashioned the frame of main timbers, floor timbers, studs, rafters, and king and queen posts. Certain parts he frugally recycled: boards from an Irishman's shanty (42–4), bricks from a 1790s chimney (240–1) …

The Walden house existed in two distinct phases: the breezy shelter of the summer of 1845, which Thoreau glowingly described in the language of the rustic, and the well-built, winterized home completed late that fall, with a chimney, plastered interior walls, and siding of shingles. That financial distress may have contributed to his departure from Walden is suggested by the fact that he sold the house to Emerson in 1847; eventually it was moved to a farm where it served as a grain storehouse until being dismantled in 1868. No photograph was taken of it, nor is there a fully reliable sketch; Thoreau complained of slight inaccuracies in its depiction on the frontispiece of *Walden*: "I would suggest a little alteration, chiefly in the door, in the wide projection of the roof at the front; and that the bank more immediately about the house be brought out more distinctly".[6] The remains of its foundations at the pond were discovered in the course of a 1945–46 archaeological investigation by Roland Wells Robbins (1908–1987). Several replicas of the house stand in the Concord area today, and the actual site, on a gentle hillside in the wooded Walden Pond State Reservation, is marked by granite posts.[7]

Thoreau's extensive accounts of his house in *Walden* demonstrate a lively appreciation of issues in current architectural thought. Pinning down his intellectual sources, however, often proves difficult, and it is uncertain whether or not he knew the villa books firsthand. There is some evidence that he was familiar with Downing, albeit at a later date than the Walden experiment. He mentions Downing's *A Treatise on the Theory and Practice of Landscape Gardening* (1841) and *The Fruits and Fruit Trees of North America* (1845) in a brief enumeration of books on a friend's shelf in 1857, and in a journal entry of 1852, he critiques the notion that one should "take up a handful of the earth at your feet & paint your house that color", a conceit that had appeared in Downing's writings in 1846 and 1850. Joseph J. Moldenhauer argues, however, that Thoreau's source was instead William Wordsworth's *Guide to the Lakes* (1810), a copy of which Thoreau owned (the fifth edition, of 1835, is an American compilation), in which the "handful of the earth" conceit is attributed to Joshua Reynolds (1723–1792) in conversation. Moldenhauer stresses that Thoreau's knowledge of Downing "is circumstantial rather than documentary"; nonetheless, the circumstantial evidence seems strong, given that Downing was at the height of his popularity and influence at the very moment of Thoreau's 1852 remarks.[8]

In any case, the substance of Thoreau's writings as early as the 1840s demonstrates his familiarity with Downingesque thought, from whatever sources he may have had it. In fact, a complex of ideas singled out by Moldenhauer as being notions that Thoreau held independently of Wordsworth – "the organic union of indweller and dwelling place", "concern with expense", and an "understanding of the dwelling as a point of mediation between the freedom and wildness of nature and the refinements and confinements of the social world"[9] – are all themes from the villa books. So, too, is Thoreau's call for the rejection of "luxury and heedless expense" in favor of "a rigid economy" (92), his famous cry of "simplicity, simplicity, simplicity!" (91), and his observation that "when the farmer has got his house, he may not be the richer but the poorer for it, and it be the house that has got him"; "we are often imprisoned" in our dwellings (33–4). Although Thoreau's sources for these ideas are unknown, Downing had derived similar notions from the English villa books. For example, he deplored in 1849 "the extravagance of Americans! … [author's ellipsis] Large estates, large houses, large establishments, only make slaves of their possessors … It is so hard to be content with simplicity!"[10] […]

[Thoreau] did not pioneer fitness, truth, or the "organic"; all these ideas he borrowed, shaping them to his own purposes and expressing them in bold, sharp words that Downing, bound by polite conventions, necessarily avoided. Rather than seeing Thoreau as an anomalous visionary, we should appreciate his shrewd grasp and effective rephrasing of the radical architectural ideas current in his day – ideas that would continue to shape architecture into the twentieth century. […]

Walden house and villa ideal

Construction of the Walden house in 1845 coincided with the height of the early villa craze in America. That cultural episode is sometimes attributed entirely to the influence of Downing, but in fact it was well under way before the horticulturist first put pen to paper, especially in suburban Boston. Downing repeatedly acknowledged that "the environs of Boston" were "more highly cultivated than those of any other city in North America. There are here, whole rural neighborhoods of pretty cottages and villas" (1841); "For that species of suburban cottage or villa residence which is most frequently within the reach of persons of moderate fortunes, the environs of Boston afford the finest examples in the Union" (1848); "In the suburbs of Boston, rural cottages are springing up on all sides" (1851).[11] Such Boston-area cottages and villas (again, the terms were often synonymous) were epitomized by William Bailey Lang's "Highland Cottages" at Roxbury, the designs for which were published just as Thoreau mortised his house frame in the Walden woods. Lang intended his villa book as a means "to assist in creating a taste for Rural Architecture", and he noted that "every year [is] bringing with it evidences of an increased taste for country life, and a better appreciation of natural scenery". His designs, derived from examples in the English villa books, featured wide eaves, Gothic gables with ornamented verge-boards, and the "rustic lean-to".[12] […]

In the months before he built his own lakeside house, Thoreau could hardly have been unaware of the villa mania sweeping the Boston suburbs. Indeed, he became caught up in it and yearned for a dwelling of his own, a desire perhaps stimulated by his experience of helping build his parents' "Texas" house. In *Walden*, he describes his attempts in 1841 to obtain the Hollowell farm for himself, which was just one episode in a larger personal obsession: "At a certain season of our life we are accustomed to consider every spot as the possible site of a house. I have thus surveyed the country on every side within a dozen miles of where I live … [author's ellipsis] Wherever I sat, there I might live, and the landscape radiated from me accordingly. What is a house but a *sedes*, a seat? – better if a country seat" (81). So Thoreau, mindful of Horace and Pliny, dreamed of a rural retreat years before he attained one, on a shoestring income, at Walden. [...]

"The future inhabitants of this region, wherever they may place their houses, may be sure that they have been anticipated", Thoreau wrote of his country-seat explorations, which culminated at Walden (81). In site as much as in architectural fitness, he intended his house to serve as a suitable example; after all, he imagined himself "a first settler" in the Walden region, "my house to be the oldest in the settlement".[13] In his accounts of the location of his dwelling he stresses exactly those aspects that loom large in contemporary recommendations on places of retirement. For example, architect Richard Elsam had suggested in 1803 that a cottage retreat be "situated near the city or town … [author's ellipsis] elevated upon rising ground, near to a public road, well sheltered by trees, and on a pleasant spot"; and in *Domestic Architecture* (1841), Richard Brown wrote that a country house should stand "in the vicinity of a town" with companionship "within reach", but not too near. Specifically, "the distance of a house from a town I should have at least two miles, and to be approached by a public road at no great distance".[14] To the reader of *Walden* Thoreau seems to emphasize his awareness of such dictates: his house is "seated … about a mile and a half south of the village of Concord" (86), "a mile from any neighbor" (3), with "the highway sixty rods off" (130).[15] [...]

In *Guide to the Lakes*, Wordsworth promoted the use of native flora around the cottage and warned that any "exotic plants" should be "confined almost to the doors of the house", and in 1823, Robert Lugar (ca. 1773–1855) cautioned that there should be "no dress trees" near a cottage, "but oak, elm, birch, and chestnut, with holly and broom" – native plants only.[16] Adapting such maxims for his own wild garden, Thoreau writes, "I have watered the red huckleberry, the sand cherry and the nettle tree" (18); "In my front yard grew the strawberry, blackberry, and life-everlasting, johnswort and golden-rod" (113). He several times mentions the sumac, as if to underscore his appreciation of a plant usually considered obnoxious: "The sumach, *Rhus glabra*, grew luxuriantly about the house … Its broad pinnate tropical leaf was pleasant though strange to look on" (114). Willis at his rural estate had written similarly, "I have propagated the despised sumach and the persecuted hemlock and 'pizen laurel.'"[17] These comments suggest the extent to which Willis and Thoreau – both enthusiastic participants in the dialogue on villas – were likewise kindred spirits of the contemporary Picturesque, a radically affirmative approach to landscape that contained many of the seeds of Thoreau's now-famous ecological consciousness. [...]

Rustic parallels

… In his accounts of the Walden house, Thoreau repeatedly employs the specific language of the rustic – appropriately enough, for his dwelling corresponded closely to a variety of rustic types popular at the time, including summerhouses, hermitages, and literary retreats.

The Walden dwelling in its first phase – as Thoreau described it, a "frame, so slightly clad", "not finished for winter, but … [author's ellipsis] merely a defence against the rain, without plastering or chimney" (84–5) – resembled that regular feature of the villa books, the rustic summerhouse. These abounded in England and America in Thoreau's day; in the former country, the landscape had come to be dotted with tiny "suburban retreats" resembling "the little cabins of the fly-boats on the junction canal".[18] Downing illustrated a "rustic seat" in New Bedford, Mass., as well as the "rustic covered seat" on an English estate – the latter a sheltered viewing place 150 feet from a lakeshore, akin in scale and purpose to Thoreau's "little house, which was all entry" (132).

Summerhouses, though small, loomed large in the world of architectural thought, as they were seen to embody cherished ideals; they were places affording poetic solitude and opportunities for nature worship, which were built of locally available materials and blended architecture with nature [*Fig. 33*]. The language Thoreau uses to describe his dwelling is exactly that of contemporary accounts of suburban summerhouses – that is, with the stress on the rustic: "the walls ... of rough weather-stained boards" (84); "I passed some cheerful evenings in that cool and airy apartment, surrounded by the rough brown boards full of knots, and rafters with the bark on high overhead" (242). He understands the rustic as described, for example, in T. J. Ricauti's 1842 *Rustic Architecture*: "The ceiling joist, collars, wall plates, &c. in the interior should not be concealed" and ought to be rough-textured.[19] Thoreau further asserts his fondness for the rustic when he decisively declares, "My house never pleased my eye so much after it was plastered" (242). [...]

Thoreau ... emphasized the cleanliness and freshness of his half-finished Walden summerhouse: it had "a clean and airy look, especially in the morning, when its timbers were saturated with dew, so that I fancied that by noon some sweet gum would exude from them" (84–5) – a reference to the famed medicinal qualities of a southern species, the sweetgum tree, *Liquidambar styraciflua*.[20] The healthfulness of his house stands in contrast to most homes, places of sickness and death that he compares to "an almshouse, a prison, or a splendid mausoleum" (28) and even to a "coffin, – the architecture of the grave" (48). In 1856 he observed that "staying in the house breeds a sort of insanity always. Every house is in this sense a hospital. A night and a forenoon is as much confinement to those wards as I can stand".[21] And at Walden he had written,

> from our village houses to this lodge on the shore of a beautiful lake in the midst of a green forest, where hardly any traces of man were visible, was a transition as from a dungeon to an open cage at least in a pleasant grove, where I could glimpse the light & the flowers through the bars ... [author's ellipsis] It was invigorating only to sit there and drink and be bathed in this unco[nta]minated current. The atmosphere of our houses has usually lost some of its life giving principle and it is necessary to our health and spirits frequently to go out, as we say, to take the air.[22]

In his affection for summerhouse architecture, which ought to be as open, breezy, and natural as possible – "a comfortable house for a rude and hardy race, that lived mostly out of doors" (29) – Thoreau again complements a contemporary dialogue, that of the healthfulness of the primitive hut and the rustic. Following Jean Jacques Rousseau, Chambers had celebrated the original state of humankind, when

> The first men, living in a warm climate, wanted no habitations: every grove afforded shade from the rays of the sun, and shelter from the dews of the night; rain fell but seldom, nor was it ever sufficiently cold, to render closer dwellings than groves, either desirable or necessary, even in the hours of repose: they fed upon the spontaneous productions of the soil, and lived without care, as without labor.[23]

Voicing a similar sentiment, Thoreau praises "the very simplicity and nakedness of man's life in the primitive ages" when he was "still but a sojourner in nature" and "stood under a tree for shelter" (37). For many contemporaries, this blissful picture constituted an ideal, and the imposition of architecture could only connote the loss of primeval vigor and freedom. Only the rustic remained as a truly healthy mode. [...]

A final parallel to the Walden house is the wilderness retreat. Some have supposed that Thoreau meant to play at log-cabin pioneer beside Walden, but his sojourn in fact bears closer affinities to the urbane custom of rustic retirement, which could, on the sliding scale of rural life, occasionally involve removal to places of considerable wildness. Thoreau was steeped in a culture in which, as Downing wrote in 1848, "country life is a leading object of nearly all men's desires" and "all sensible men gladly escape, earlier or later, and partially or wholly, from the turmoil of the cities". Downing recognized that most persons would prefer ample company in their retirement, but that a few "will, for the sake of the picturesque, settle on the banks of the Winipissiogee. These latter spots are for poets, artists, naturalists; men, between whom and nature there is an intimacy of a wholly different kind, and who find in the structure of a moss or the flight of a water fowl the text to a whole volume of inspiration".[24] These types, rather than rough pioneers or lumberjacks, were truly analogous to Thoreau – his frequent references to the rusticity of his Walden-area neighbors notwithstanding.

In a retirement adventure similar to Thoreau's, Joel Tyler Headley (1813–1897) escaped for two summers (1847–48) to the Adirondacks, as detailed in a book with a title identical to *Walden*'s subtitle: *Life in the Woods*. "How the soul awakes in this new existence", he rejoiced; "I love the freedom of the wilderness and the absence of conventional forms there". He found forest lakeshores peopled with city men ruined in the Panic of 1836, modern-day "Robinson Crusoes" who included at least one "wealthy manufacturer" ... In a similar spirit, Thoreau's colleague [Margaret] Fuller, on the Illinois frontier in 1843, commended a certain "double log cabin" as "the model of a Western villa", a place of "beauty", perfect for "the poet, the sportsman, the naturalist". Here "all kinds of wild sports, experiments, and the studies of natural history" could transpire ...

Thus, the contemporary habit of wilderness rustication, popularized by printed accounts, afforded precedent for Thoreau's lake-in-the-woods life at Walden – although his wilderness was mostly one of the imagination, given his location on a recently cleared suburban site just a mile and a half from Concord.

Revelation in the Catskills

An immediate and decisive stimulus for Thoreau's Walden experiment – one little noticed by scholars – came in the form of his 1844 trip to the Berkshires, in Massachusetts, and (joined by Channing) to the Catskills, in New York. This journey provided inspirational firsthand encounters with the rustic architecture of the wilderness, as well as with a memorable lake that awakened Thoreau to the possibilities latent in his familiar Walden Pond.[25]

Thoreau's first journal entry at Walden reads, "Walden Sat. July 5th – 45 Yesterday I came here to live. My house makes me think of some mountain houses I have seen, which seemed to have a fresher auroral atmosphere about them as I fancy of the halls of Olympus". There had been two "mountain houses", the first that of "a rude and inhospitable man" named Rice, high in the hills near Mount Greylock, Mass., "where the shaggy woods almost joined their tops over the torrent". "I was very much pleased with my host's residence", Thoreau wrote.[26] Apparently of greater significance was the second house, in the Catskills near Kaaterskill Falls, that mecca for the Picturesque tourist. In the first journal passage written at Walden, Thoreau described this dwelling, home to sawmiller Ira Scribner:

> I lodged at the house of a saw-miller last summer, on the Caatskills mountains, high up as Pine orchard in the blue-berry & raspberry region, where the quiet and cleanliness & coolness seemed to be all one, which had this ambrosial character. He was the miller of the Kaaterskill Falls[.] They were a clean & wholesome family inside and out – like their house. The latter was not plastered – only lathed and the inner doors were not hung. The house seemed high placed, airy, and perfumed, fit to entertain a travelling God. It was so high indeed that all the music, the broken strains, the waifs & accompaniments of tunes, that swept over the ridge of the Caatskills, passed through its aisles. Could not man be man in such an abode? And would he ever find out this grovelling life?[27]

For Thoreau, Scribner's house offered the instant revelation of a rustic architectural ideal: rough, unplastered, open to nature, clean, and healthful. It even resonated with the extraordinary virtues of the Parthenon, as he hints by calling it "high placed, airy, and perfumed, fit to entertain a traveling God" and by referring to its "aisles". For the classically inspired young writer with an enthusiasm for the primitive hut, Scribner's evidently seemed a latter-day Doric cabin.

Equally exciting and portentous for Thoreau was South Lake, less than half a mile to the east. Along with neighboring, smaller North Lake (with which it is today conjoined), its situation is unusual – it sits tarnlike on the mountainous Pine Orchard plateau that soars, with the abruptness of the Acropolis, 1,600 feet above the Hudson River valley. Distinctive were the numerous dead trees around its shoreline, the irregularity of which held irresistible charm for countless Picturesque-minded tourists, including Thomas Cole (1801–1848), who had inaugurated his career as a painter with *Lake with Dead Trees (Catskill)* in 1825, and Willis, who with artist William H. Bartlett (1809–1854) had featured those same trees in a chapter on "The Two Lakes and the Mountain House on the Catskills" in his 1840 *American Scenery*. Thoreau was doubtless struck by South Lake's similarity in size to Walden Pond – both are just over half a mile long – and conceivably it was while standing on its shores that he first appreciated the poetic possibilities that might unfold if he settled beside Walden. It is known for certain that within a few months, his traveling companion Channing was encouraging him to do so, as if they had discussed the matter previously.[28]

It seems that this dual encounter with rustic Scribner's and the nearby South Lake was crucial for Thoreau in formulating the Walden experiment of the following summer, when he would attempt to bring the Catskills' potent spirit of wildness home to Concord. As we have seen, his first, revealing thoughts on opening his journal at Walden were of the 1844 trip and its mountain houses. "The pond was like a mountain lake I had seen", he later observed, and he would recall in 1851 that when he came to live at Walden, "I had in my mind's eye a silent gray tarn which I had seen the summer before? High up on the side of a mt Bald Mt where the half dead spruce trees stood far in the water draped with wreathy mist ... Whose bottom was high above the surface of other lakes".[29] "Bald Mt", perhaps a recollection of the ledges above North Lake, has been interpreted as a reference to his trip to Mount Katahdin, in Maine (1846), but this possibility is obviated by "the summer before" and "the half dead spruce trees", which point to South Lake. [...]

The origin of Thoreau's Walden idea, it seems, was to join Scribner's "airy and unplastered cabin" (85) and the South Lake "tarn" into the conception of a rustic, lakeshore retreat of his own, one that would allow him to live the vigorous Catskills life not only in summer but all year long. By an effort of Transcendentalist imagination, a pond in a gradually suburbanizing landscape just fifteen miles from downtown Boston could become "a tarn high up on the side of a mountain, and the whole region where I lived" could seem to be "more elevated than it actually was" – a transformation of scene central to Thoreau's larger goal, "to live a primitive and frontier life, though in the midst of an outward civilization" (11).[30] And if South Lake of 1844 were translated into Walden Pond of 1845, then "high placed", "clean & wholesome" Scribner's, as an exemplar of the rustic, served as philosophical model for the Walden house. In the first version of *Walden*, written at the pond, Thoreau explicitly links his "clean and airy" house and the "ambrosial character" of Scribner's (see also *Walden*, 84–5), and of the latter dwelling he writes trenchantly, "such it seemed to me all our houses should be" – in other words, that all should derive from the rustic ideal.[31] By the time he wrote these words, he had already turned this bold conviction into tangible reality, having erected a rustic mountain house of his own beside a Concord pond, in fulfillment of a revelation he had experienced in the Catskills.

"More lives to live"

Thoreau's house at Walden, for all the deeply personal, Transcendentalist significance he gives it in his famous book, needs to be understood in a contemporary architectural context and in light of the current interest in returning to nature via suburban living. At the time of the Walden sojourn, Thoreau was apparently touched by the villa movement flourishing around him in the Boston suburbs, and retirement became his goal. He wrote in his journal during the winter of 1846–47, "I should not care if our village life were greatly modified or totally changed[.] It would be agreeable to me if men dwelt more in the country – a more rural life a life in the fields".[32] His Walden experiment made this dream a reality, giving him the opportunity to experience firsthand the possibilities of a country seat. In his passion for building, he was far from alone; in 1841, Downing had observed, "To have a 'local habitation,' – a permanent dwelling, that we can give the impress of our own mind, and identify with our own existence, – appears to be the ardent wish, sooner or later felt, of every man".[33] Thoreau's house – akin in scale and purpose to the portable "Substitute for a Country Residence" advertised in Loudon's villa book – was meant for temporary, not permanent, retirement, and was adapted to his limited income, but it nonetheless fully achieved for him this "ardent wish" for home ownership. He stressed that he had created a miniature version of a real country house, with, he insisted, all the amenities, and modest as it was, he proudly advertised it in print to his contemporaries. Viewed in context, the Walden house seems significant for its participation in a variety of architectural traditions: the summerhouse, the literary hermitage, and the wilderness retreat. All were rustic, an approach that Thoreau repeatedly endorsed. In its rustic flavor and its lakeshore setting, it reminded the wilderness-loving Thoreau of Scribner's and South Lake in the Catskills, his immediate sources of inspiration for the Walden adventure. As for his abandonment of the house after two years, several factors can be cited – the frequently short-term nature of retirement; his completion of the draft of *A Week*; the poverty that threw him back into Emerson's household; and his self-proclaimed intellectual restlessness: "Perhaps it seemed to me that I had several more lives to live, and could not spare any more time for that one" (323).

The house lived on, however, in the pages of *Walden*, where it proudly stood as a theoretical exemplar for future design. As a participant in the cultural conversation of the day, Thoreau celebrated in print his architectural achievements, namely, his having contrived a dwelling at one with its surroundings, expressive of the character of the indweller, and altogether clean, sturdy, and truthful. A primitive hut for modern times, it was ambitiously offered to the public, in the spirit of the villa books, as a paradigm of fitness and a model for future efforts at reform, a rustic shanty pointing to the day "when every country-seat will *be one*". Despite its apparent simplicity, this little suburban house was of profound significance as the embodiment of current architectural ideals, appropriated by Thoreau for his own intellectual and didactic purposes and thoughtfully translated into "boards & shingles lime & brick" on the shores of Walden Pond.

Notes

1   In the present article, page references to *Walden*, 1971, are given parenthetically in the text. Useful works on Thoreau include Joel Myerson (ed.), *The Cambridge Companion to Henry David Thoreau*, Cambridge: Cambridge University Press, 1995; Walter Harding (ed.) *Walden: An Annotated Edition*, New York: Houghton Mifflin, 1995; Harding, *The Days of Henry Thoreau: A Biography*, New York: Dover, 1982; Harding, "A New Checklist of the Books in Henry David Thoreau's Library", in Joel Myerson (ed.) *Studies in the American Renaissance*, Charlottesville: University Press of Virginia, 1983, pp. 151–86; Robert Sattelmeyer, *Thoreau's Reading*, Princeton: Princeton University Press, 1988; William Howarth, *The Book of Concord: Thoreau's Life as a Writer*, New York: Viking Press, 1982; and Raymond R. Borst, *The Thoreau Log: A Documentary Life of Henry David Thoreau, 1817–1862*, New York: G. K. Hall, 1992. Thoreau's house is discussed specifically in Dieter Schulz, "Thoreau's House", in Tibor Frank (ed.) *Values in American Society*, Budapest: Eötvös Loránd University, 1995, pp. 29–39; and in Marilyn R. Chandler, *Dwelling in the Text: Houses in American Fiction*, Berkeley: University of California Press, 1991, chapter 1.

2   Thoreau, *A Week on the Concord and Merrimack Rivers* (1849), Carl F. Hovde, William L. Howarth, and Elizabeth Hall Witherell (eds), Princeton: Princeton University Press, 1980, p. 241. [...]

3   "I want to go soon" in Henry David Thoreau, *Journal*, John C. Broderick and Robert Sattelmeyer (eds), 5 vols, Princeton: Princeton University Press, 1981–97 (hereafter "PJ",), vol. 1, p. 347 (Dec. 24, 1841); "Cabin or a turret" in Emerson to Thomas Carlyle, Sept. 30, 1844, in Joseph Slater (ed.) *The Correspondence of Emerson and Carlyle*, New York: Columbia University Press, 1964, p. 369. [...] For the history of the land around Walden, see Thomas Blanding, "Historic Walden Woods", *Concord Saunterer* 20, nos. 1–2, Dec. 1988, 2–86.

4   William Wordsworth, "When, to the Attractions of a Busy World" (1800–1802), lines 1, 53–4, in Jack Stillinger (ed.) *Selected Poems and Prefaces*, Boston: Houghton Mifflin, 1965, pp. 160–1; James Malton, *A Collection of Designs for Rural Retreats, as Villas: Principally in the Gothic and Castle Styles of Architecture*, London: J. and T. Carpenter, 1802, i; Andrew Jackson Downing, "On the Mistakes of Citizens in Country Life", *Horticulturist* 3, January 1849, 306.

5   Thoreau, "Chesuncook" (1858), in Joseph J. Moldenhauer (ed) *The Maine Woods*, Princeton: Princeton University Press, 1972, p. 124. Descriptions of log buildings are also to be found in "Ktaadn" (1848), in ibid., for example, pp. 25–6 ...

6   The drawing used as the basis of the wood-engraved frontispiece was by Thoreau's sister Sophia (1819–1876). Thoreau jotted his comments in the corrected proofs of *Walden*; see F. B. Sanborn, *The Life of Henry David Thoreau*, Boston: Houghton Mifflin, 1917, p. 338. Thoreau's friend Channing (whose remarks, it should be noted, are frequently suspect) later wrote in his own copy of *Walden*, "The picture (drawn by Sophia T[horeau]) is a feeble caricature of the true house"; Sanborn, *Recollections of Seventy Years*, vol. 2, Boston: Richard G. Badger, 1909, p. 390.

7 Robbins describes the archaeological dig he undertook at the Walden house site. See also Donald W. Linebaugh, "'The Road to Ruins and Restoration': Roland W. Robbins, Henry D. Thoreau, and the *Discovery at Walden*", *Concord Saunterer* n.s., 2, no. 1, Fall 1994, 33–62; see also Linebaugh's Ph.D. dissertation of a similar title, College of William and Mary, 1996. On Thoreau's house after 1847, see Jeanne M. Zimmer, "A History of Thoreau's Hut and Hut Site", *ESQ: A Journal of the American Renaissance* 18, no. 3, 1972, 134–40; Harding, *Walden*, 1982, pp. 222–4; and Stephen F. Ells, "Henry Thoreau and the Estabrook Country: A Historic and Personal Landscape", *Concord Saunterer* n.s., 4, Fall 1996, 145–8. There are at least four replicas of the Thoreau house in the Concord area today: two at the Roland Robbins estate, one at the Concord Museum, and one at the Walden Pond State Reservation.

8 Thoreau mentions two of Downing's books in his journal, Apr. 10, 1857, in Bradford Torrey (ed.) *The Writings of Henry David Thoreau: Journal*, vol. 9, Boston: Houghton Mifflin, 1906, p. 324. He critiques the "handful of the earth" conceit in PJ, vol. 4, p. 245 (Jan. 11, 1852); see also *Walden*, p. 48. The conceit appears in William Wordsworth, *Wordsworth's Guide to the Lakes* (1835), 5th edn; reprint, Oxford: Oxford University Press, 1970, p. 77. It also appears in Downing, "On the Color of Country Houses", *Horticulturist* 1, no. 11, May 1847, 491; and in Downing, *The Architecture of Country Houses*, 1850, reprint, New York: Dover, 1969, p. 201; and in Gervase Wheeler, *Rural Homes; or, Sketches of Houses Suited to American Country Life*, New York: Charles Scribner, 1851, p. 42. [...]

9 Moldenhauer, "*Walden* and Wordsworth's Guide to the English Lake District", p. 269. He lists Wordsworth, William Gilpin, and Horatio Greenough as "the three authorities" Thoreau rejects (271).

10 Downing, "On the Mistakes of Citizens in Country Life", pp. 307–9.

11 Ibid., 39; Downing, "Hints to Rural Improvers", *Horticulturist* 3, July 1848, 11–2; Downing, "A Few Words on Our Progress in Building", *Horticulturist* 6, June 1851, 249.

12 William Bailey Lang, *Views, with Ground Plans, of the Highland Cottages at Roxbury*, Boston: L. H. Bridgham and H. E. Felch, 1845, n.p.

13 PJ, vol. 2, p. 215 (winter 1845–46); see also *Walden*, p. 264.

14 Richard Elsam, *An Essay on Rural Architecture*, London: E. Lawrence, 1803; reprint, Westmead, Eng.: Gregg, 1972, p. 8; Theodore M. Brown, "Thoreau's Prophetic Architectural Program", *New England Quarterly* 38, no. 1, March 1965, 92–5.

15 Sixty rods is about a thousand feet. The path Thoreau took to the highway covered more than twice this distance, however, being "about half a mile long" (265). Walking to his parents' "Texas House", he generally avoided the highway altogether, preferring the shortcut provided by the railroad tracks.

16 Wordsworth, *Wordsworth's Guide to the Lakes*, p. 83; R. Lugar, *Architectural Sketches for Cottages, Rural Dwellings, and Villas, in the Grecian, Gothic, and Fancy Styles* (1805), London: J. Taylor, 1823, p. 13.

17 Willis, "Letter to the Unknown Purchaser and Next Occupant of Glenmary", in Nathaniel Parker Willis (ed.) *Rural Letters and Other Records of Thought at Leisure*, New Orleans: Burnett and Bostwick, 1854, p. 209 ...

18 Shirley Hibberd, *Rustic Adornments for Homes of Taste* (1856), 2nd edn, London: Groombridge and Sons, 1857, p. 496.

19 T. J. Ricauti, *Rustic Architecture: Picturesque Decorations of Rural Buildings in the Use of Rough Wood, Thatch, Etc.*, London: James Carpenter, 1842, n.p.

20 The inner bark and gum of the sweetgum tree were "traditionally chewed for sore throats, coughs, colds, diarrhea, dysentery, ringworm; used externally for sores, skin ailments, wounds, piles ... Considered expectorant, antiseptic, antimicrobial, anti-inflammatory"; Steven Foster and James A. Duke, *The Peterson Field Guide Series, Field Guide to Medicinal Plants: Eastern and Central North America*, Boston: Houghton Mifflin, 1990, p. 280.

21 Thoreau, Dec. 29, 1856, in Bradford Torrey (ed.) *The Writings of Henry David Thoreau: Journal*, vol. 9, p. 200 ...

22 Thoreau, *Walden*, first version, 1846–47 [hereafter WFV], in J. Lyndon Shanley, *The Making of "Walden", with the Text of the First Version*, Chicago: University of Chicago Press, 1957, pp. 137–8.

23 William Chambers, "Of the Origin, and Progress of BUILDING", in *A Treatise on the Decorative Part of Civil Architecture* (1791), reprint, New York: Benjamin Blom, 1968, p. 15.

24 Downing, "Hints to Rural Improvers", p. 9; "Winipissiogee" in Downing, "On the Mistakes of Citizens in Country Life", p. 306.

25 This outing "has not received the attention it deserves"; Thomas Woodson, "Thoreau's Excursion to the Berkshires and Catskills", *ESQ: A Journal of the American Renaissance* 21, no. 2, 1975, 82. Almost alone among scholars, he argues that there was an important link between this trip and Thoreau's Walden sojourn.

26 First Walden entry in PJ, vol. 2, p. 155 (July 5, 1845); Greylock house in PJ, vol. 2, pp. 96–9 (after Aug. 1, 1844). On the latter, see Thoreau, *A Week on the Concord and Merrimack*, pp. 203–9; William Howarth, *Thoreau in the Mountains*, New York: Farrar, Straus, Giroux, 1982, p. 59; and Donald M. Murray, "Thoreau's Uncivil Man Rice", *New England Quarterly* 56, no. 1, Mar. 1983, 103–9.

27 PJ, vol. 2, p. 155 (July 5, 1845). [...]

28 South Lake appeared in Nathaniel Parker Willis, *American Scenery*, 2 vols., London: George Virtue, 1840, and in Cole's *Lake with Dead Trees (Catskill)*, now at the Allen Memorial Art Museum, Oberlin College, Ohio ...

29 WFV, p. 138; PJ, vol. 3, p. 213 (May 1, 1851).

30 WFV, p. 138.

31 Ibid.

32 PJ, vol. 2, p. 374 (winter 1846–47)

33 Andrew Jackson Downing, *A Treatise on the Theory and Practice of Landscape Gardening* (1841), 2nd edn, New York: Wiley and Putnam, 1844, pp. 339–40.

The home as a work of art
Finland and Sweden
Barbara Miller Lane (2000)

Introduction

In the new social and political circumstances of the eighteen nineties, it was housing design that first expressed new ideas about architecture and nationalism. This is not surprising, since the new era of state-formation in central Europe and Scandinavia brought great urgency to the question "what is home?" This question is a many-layered one, of course; the concept "home" or "homeland" (in German, *Heimat*, in Swedish, *hembygd*) refers to a sense of identity that may be national, regional, or local.[1] But, to an extent seldom recognized by historians, the identity of the dwelling place itself underlies all the issues of national, regional, and local loyalties. Thus a new domestic architecture was almost a necessary component of new ideas about the nation.

In both Germany and the Scandinavian countries, artists and architects created a new kind of ideal home. For the urban middle-class dwelling of the late nineteenth-century city, National Romantic artists and architects substituted as an ideal the dwelling embedded in nature, close to its earliest historic roots in the simple wooden structures of Northern antiquity.[2] Especially in Finland and Sweden, the ideal home was the "studio in the wilds",[3] the place where Anders Zorn, Carl Larsson, Akseli Gallen-Kallela, and their families created a new art and a new lifestyle far away from all modern conditions except those of the local peasantry and rural folk. The local environment was then depicted as the original home of the nation. This kind of regionalism was new. It stemmed from the ideas of the early nineteenth century about landscape and rural peoples, but it took on a different importance now as a context for speculations about the identity of the family, the folk, the individual, and their relationships to the nation. [...]

The new dwellings created first by artists and soon thereafter by architects were quite varied in their appearance. [...] Each evoked a different regional tradition. All were intensely idiosyncratic, vehicles for the self-expression of the designer and his family.

But despite the differences in appearance among them, these buildings represented a shared vision. Each was regarded by its creators as "a work of art". All were self-consciously humble in materials, furnishings, and the arrangement of spaces. They were embedded in nature, permitting new relationships between interiors and the exterior landscape. They were fashioned – inside and out – of local and natural materials and reflected some of the oldest traditions of the region or province in which they were built. The life-style that was imagined by their designers, closely related to contemporary "life-reform" movements, was one of great simplicity. Common spaces, often described as "great halls", provided the opportunity for new and more egalitarian relationships within the family or between the artist and his wife or partner. Women and children, and sometimes the artist/designer himself, were imagined as dressed in loose, peasant-inspired clothing. Great care was taken in arranging spaces for children. Interior furnishings, textiles and hangings were modeled on the traditions of folk art and often depicted mythological or "folk" themes in a flat, primitive, or even abstract manner. In housing design, the artist or architect found the opportunity to withdraw from the values of a society that he saw as too materialistic, too bourgeois, too bureaucratic, too academic, and neither "national" enough nor "free" enough.

These new kinds of dwelling were full of tensions and ambiguities. The artist or architect found in housing design an opportunity to create a total work of art, one in which the designer commanded the entire character of life, from household objects, clothing, the pattern of daily activities, to the relationship of the dwelling to its natural surroundings, local community, and province. These were large opportunities, providing a scope for self-expression that was not available within the academic or engineering professions. Perhaps as a result, it was housing design that launched the careers of the most innovative architects. At the same time, the image of the artist/architect as a solitary – almost godlike – creator, capable of standing above or apart from contemporary bourgeois society, was at odds with the egalitarian ideals and the social concerns of most National Romantics.

The relation of the male artist/architect to the woman who helped him create the ideal home was also a contradictory one. The wives and partners of artists played important roles as designers and as revivers of folk art, yet they did not share the creative stature of their husbands or lovers. The stress on the family contradicted the behavior of those intellectuals who tended to move from one lover to another and one family situation to another in rapid succession.

The rejection of the contemporary city, with its poverty and unwelcome structures of authority, that was implied in most of these dwelling designs was in conflict with the desire of innovative artists and architects to be close to the centers of intellectual life. The idealization of regional or national heroes, especially those who seemed to come from among the farmers, conflicted with artists' desire to depict the poor and humble circumstances of contemporary peasants. In general, the preoccupation with the peasant and with a rural way of life was hard to reconcile with the desire of many artists and architects, inspired by the teachings of Ellen Key, to provide a new ideal of beauty for the urban masses in an age of industrialization.[4]

Yet National Romantic housing designers managed to be nationalist, provincial, progressive, socially committed, elitist, feminist, misogynist, and modern, all at once. The child, both as inhabitant of the ideal home, and as a metaphorical presence, was particularly important to them: the innocence, simplicity, and primitive quality of the child seemed to them to be akin to the peasant, to one's earliest national forebears, to the worker, and to the revolutionary kind of "new humanity" they hoped to create. The next century, they said, would be "the century of the child". [...]

Karelia, the *Kalevala*, and Finnish art and architecture

The region known as Karelia came to play a role in Finnish National Romanticism similar to that of Telemark and Gudbrandsdal in Norway. Karelia was somewhat elastic in its definition, however. Karelians were one of the earliest prehistoric Finnish tribes. From the ninth to the twelfth century, Karelia was a populous area reaching from the eastern edge of the Gulf of Finland to Lake Onega, far into modern Russia. Conquered by Swedes and Russians in the later Middle Ages, the control of the area moved back and forth between these states. In the nineteenth century, a portion of southern and western Karelia lay within the Finnish province, but the eastern and northern parts were under Tsarist control. The old administrative districts lay on both sides of the Finnish/Russian border. In the twentieth century, eastern and western Karelia were joined and rejoined several times, forming in 1956 an autonomous Republic within the Union of Soviet Socialist Republics.

The landscape of Karelia was diverse, ranging from the flat and open lake districts of the south to the dense woods, sharply cut mountains, and roaring waterfalls of the north. Around the turn of the century, the northern parts were wild and sparsely populated; the southern dotted by farm villages along the lakes. In between, small farms were widely dispersed but recognizable in their traditional building techniques. Within the old administrative districts of Karelia, a variant of Finnish was spoken, and a distinctive culture still existed.

Karelia had been the site of the journeys made by Elias Lönnrot in the early nineteenth century to collect the songs of the *Kalevala*. As this national epic had grown in popularity, it was increasingly identified in the public mind with the border region that seemed to contain Finland's earliest history, its most powerful literature, and its most primitive landscape. As friction grew between Finns and Russians in the 1890s, Finnish nationalism came to focus on Karelian landscape and history.

The artists of the 1890s made frequent pilgrimages to Karelia, where they found a wilderness imagery that seemed to confirm their eagerness for independence from Russia. They brought back from Karelia an enthusiasm for folk art and a desire for wilderness studios organized around two-story central halls. At the same time, they entered into a mood of intense "*Kalevala* Romanticism": for Akseli Gallen-Kallela, Jean Sibelius, Pekka Halonen, Emil Wikström, Lars Sonck, and Eliel Saarinen, a few of the *Kalevala* stories seemed to be profoundly expressive of their national aspirations. Thus National Romanticism in Finland focused less upon a particular landscape or group of landscapes and more upon myth, a wilderness ideal, and a specific version of the home.

It was Akseli Gallen-Kallela (1865–1931), born Axel Gallén, who was most responsible for bringing the *Kalevala* before the public eye. He was the son of a minor official of the Russian government in southwest and then central Finland; his family were liberals, members of the group of Swedish-speaking middle-class people who were seeking a more representative legislature within the framework of Russian rule. Gallen-Kallela's family recognized his talent early and sent him to the Central School of Industrial Design in Helsinki. He also obtained private instruction from Albert Edelfeldt, one of the earliest artists of the nineteenth century to make the pilgrimage to Karelia. Gallen-Kallela studied in Paris from 1884 to 1889, and returned to Paris to exhibit for many years. From Paris he traveled to London and Berlin. He was close to the Norwegian artists of two generations and especially to Gerhard Munthe and Edvard Munch.

Well-regarded in Paris as the painter of realistic scenes of farm life in central Finland, Gallen-Kallela began in the early 1890s to dwell on wilderness landscapes and began to populate them with characters and stories from the *Kalevala*. Over the next decade, his depictions of the *Kalevala* stories became increasingly abstract, and very well-known in Finland. In his work, the shamans and heroes of Lönnrot's verses – Väinämöinen, Ilmarinen, Lemminkäinen, as they do battle with the forces of evil in order to protect the *sampo*, the precious talisman of the land of Kaleva – gained visual reality for Finland and Europe for the first time … Gallen-Kallela's elaboration of the *Kalevala* stories coincided with the building of his wilderness studio at Kalela, near Ruovesi, modeled on the farmhouses of Karelia.

Changing his name from Axel Gallén to Akseli Gallen-Kallela was an expression of his Finnish nationalism. The hopes that had been raised in the 1860s for more extensive representative institutions were disappointed in the 1890s by the vigorous Russification policies of Tsars Alexander III and Nicholas II. In 1891, Russia took over Finnish postal services, customs, and currency; in 1892 it began to abrogate Finnish religious freedoms. Under Governor General Bobrikow (1898–1904), Russian was to be the first language in the schools, Russians were to be the principal administrative officers throughout Finland; Finns were to be drafted into the Russian army. The rights of the Finnish Parliament were abrogated in a number of ways and the constitution itself was threatened. The independent kind of liberalism that had characterized Swedish-speaking Finns seemed no longer to be enough to resist the Russian onslaught; Finnish nationalism became widespread, sometimes violent, and overwhelmingly invested in the Finnish language. In May 1906, more than 16,000 Swedish-speaking families, especially artists and intellectuals, changed their names and the language of home and family to Finnish. Axel Gallén was one of these.

Kalela at Ruovesi

In 1890, Gallen-Kallela made the first of his trips to Finnish and Russian Karelia in search of the national origins. Accompanied by his bride Mary Slöör (1868–1947: herself a *Kalevala* specialist) and by his Swedish friend Louis Sparre, deeply moved by the unspoiled and primitive character of these rural areas, Gallen-Kallela came to believe that the farmhouses and crafts of Karelia represented the oldest Finnish culture …

Gallen-Kallela returned from Karelia to illustrate the *Kalevala*, design furniture and textiles for the new crafts workshops of Sparre (who had been similarly inspired in Karelia), and to design for himself a studio and home in the "wilderness" that would enable him to implement the lessons of Karelia. The log and plank country studio which he called Kalela was completed in 1895. The site was extraordinary: Gallen-Kallela's studio sat on a headland overlooking (to the south, east, and west) Lake Ruovesi, part of the complex and interconnected lake system that reaches from Tampere almost to Jyväskylä. Lake Ruovesi is part of the northern portion of this lake system (Kalela is about 120 miles northwest of Helsinki): it was at the time particularly remote, reachable only by steamboat from Tampere. When Kalela was built, the lake was surrounded by virgin pine forest.

Gallen-Kallela created winding paths around the headland that permitted distant views of the lake and close yet ever-changing views of native trees, ferns, stone, and lichen. The building, set upon a high cut stone base, is two stories high. With its steeply pitched roof, and square form, the building appears massive upon approach. Inside, a two-story hall, the studio, is surrounded on three sides by balconies and a stair leading to the second story loft rooms. The central hall is lit by a huge one-and-a-half story north-facing window, which bends back along the slope of the roof. Interior finishes were wood: the planks left unfinished, the balusters in some cases rough-hewn, elsewhere carved in geometric patterns or shaped into masklike forms. Gallen-Kallela designed the building according to what he thought were the principles of Karelian farmhouses; his designs for furniture, carvings, textiles, and "Rya" rugs (many of these were executed by Mary) were also inspired in part by Karelian motifs.[5] On the interiors, as on the exteriors, wood was idealized: doors and balusters were carved and patterned; door handles were twisted branches.[6] But Gallen-Kallela also opened up his studio to the light with the huge window cut through wall and ceiling. The interiors were self-consciously spare and light in ways that farmsteads never were. Gallen-Kallela and his family lived at Kalela almost continuously for four years, while he was planning the frescoes and furniture designs for the Finnish Pavilion at the Paris Exposition Universelle of 1900. Later on, they returned to Kalela at intervals, but also built a new studio and home nearer Helsinki (Tarvaspää, 1911–13). With a medieval-looking turret, Tarvaspää was the "castle" of Gallen-Kallela's early thoughts.[7]

Tuusula and Sonck

Gallen-Kallela was but one of a number of artists who were gripped by "Kalevala Romanticism" and Karelian enthusiasm. In the summer of 1894, Yrjö Blomstedt, Victor Sucksdorff, and Lars Sonck sought and obtained support from the Archaeological Society of Finland to travel to Russian Karelia and to publish the farm buildings they observed there. Other expeditions followed. Journal articles and books then made the design of the Karelian farmhouse well-known to the public between 1894 and 1901.[8] Throughout the 1890s other Finnish artists and architects built studios "in the wilderness" that derived from old Finnish and Karelian farmsteads. Karelian motifs also began to appear in furniture design from about the same date.[9]

The sculptor Emil Wikström (1864–1942), who had traveled to Karelia with Louis Sparre in 1892, built the studio villa "Visavuori" (1893–4) at Sääksmäki, modeling it partly on Karelian farmhouses and partly also on the Norwegian "dragon style" [*Fig. 34*].[10] Visavuori had the two-story hall with balcony above and alcoves below that Gallen-Kallela used at Ruovesi. The same plan – and a very similar design – reappeared at "Halosenniemi", built by the painter Pekka Halonen on a dramatic promontory at Lake Tuusula in 1899–1902 [*Fig. 35*]. Halonen, who also painted scenes from the *Kalevala* and often exhibited with Gallen-Kallela, was like his friend a zealous collector of folk art and peasant furniture, especially from Karelia. Some of this furniture was made of natural tree limbs, bent in contorted ways. Halonen's wife, Maija Mäkinen, was a Karelian farmer's daughter, and herself a textile designer. Halonen was also a central figure in founding at the lake an artists' colony which was shared by artists and musicians.[11] It was at Tuusula in 1904 that Lars Sonck erected a home and studio for Jean Sibelius, the great

Finnish composer who had drawn together themes from Finnish nationalism and the *Kalevala* in his Finlandia and other works.[12] "Ainola", Sibelius's home until his death, was considerably modified during the composer's lifetime: today it appears far less rustic than Kalela, Visavuori, or Halosenniemi. Originally, however, although the building massing was far more complex than these earlier buildings, the exterior was made of square-hewn unpainted logs. A two-story living hall with balcony still remains.[13] [...]

Zorn, Larsson, Dalecarlia, and the ideal home in Sweden

The most powerful and influential creation of a provincial identity as a setting for the ideal home was the work of the Swedish painters Anders Zorn (1860–1920) and Carl Larsson (1853–1919). Their love of Dalarna (Dalecarlia), a province in central Sweden, rivaled and paralleled the Finnish preoccupation with Karelia. But Dalarna was an existing province within modern Sweden. Zorn and Larsson helped to make it a symbol of true Swedishness for Swedes and of an idealized Northland for Germans. They both also became their own architects and made a major contribution to ideas about the ideal home in Sweden and outside of it.

Dalarna was (and still is) wild and exceptionally beautiful. Its craggy, densely wooded mountains were full of elk, boar, bear, and deer; its wide rivers, mountain streams, and crystalline mountain lakes offered a bountiful harvest of fish in the short summer season. Iron mining and a significant timber industry have existed there since the early Middle Ages; copper mining and production developed from the fourteenth century. Medieval patterns of life had undergone less change in the eighteenth and nineteenth centuries than elsewhere in Sweden. At the end of the nineteenth century, Dalarna's farmers still worked an open-field system; their large farmsteads, clustered around tiny villages and old churches, were much closer to their medieval prototypes than farm buildings in other Swedish provinces.

The district of Mora in Dalarna was of great political significance to the nation: here in the 1430s Engelbrekt Engelbrektsson had led farmers and miners in a successful revolt against Danish rule and here in 1521 Gustavus Vasa rallied the farmers, routed the Danes, and established an independent Swedish state. For its natural beauty, its simple rural customs, its links to the medieval past, and its importance to the nation, Dalarna had long been celebrated in song and story.[14] But it was only toward the end of the nineteenth century that Swedish artists and intellectuals came to regard Dalarna as the epitome of that which was truly "Swedish". Anders Zorn and Carl Larsson shaped this view through their art and through their architecture.

Anders Zorn, intimate of Auguste Rodin, Theodore Roosevelt, and Isabella Stewart Gardner, achieved world fame [as a painter]. [...] After their marriage in 1885, Zorn and his wife Emma Lamm spent their summers in Mora [his birthplace]. [...]

Zorn's Mora paintings strengthened the links between Dalarna and nationalist feeling among Swedish intellectuals at the turn of the century. But Zorn's Mora was to a great extent his own creation and this in a practical sense. He collected buildings from distant farms, as well as agricultural tools and furnishings, and assembled them on his own property and in an open-air museum that he created in Mora. He found and rebuilt old maypoles and gave them to surrounding hamlets. He collected and displayed folk art. He restored the church and bell-tower. He and Emma advised local residents on the details of traditional dress and organized the teaching of the Midsummer Night dance, which had fallen out of favor, owing to the opposition of church officials. Emma took up the study of

Swedish "home industries" (*hemslöjd*), the traditional handicrafts (furniture, textiles); she and Zorn founded a local Handicrafts Association to encourage the local farm people, who were very poor, to return to this old source of income and activity.[15] [...]

These ideals were embodied in Zorn's house. From 1887 to 1892, Anders and Emma added to his grandfather's cottage in "the Dalecarlian style", so that by 1892 the old house was encased in a new one. Like the old house, the new one combined logs and painted wood siding in traditional Dalecarlian colors.[16] Also in 1892, the Zorns brought a substantial log house from Vika and placed it next to the house as a studio; in 1894, they imported another small house for Zorn's mother. In 1897, they added a large two-story wing, a monumental timber construction that housed guest rooms and servants' quarters on the ground floor and on the upper floor a two-story "great hall" with a steeply sloping roof, gable windows, and small projecting balconies. The great hall, with exposed logs on interior and exterior, is reminiscent of ... Karelian farm buildings; it also has a resemblance to the "great camps" of the American Adirondacks.[17] [...]

Zorn's friend Carl Larsson also settled in Dalarna and did even more than Zorn to popularize the district as "the Swedish ideal". But unlike Zorn, who returned to his original home after achieving success in the outside world, Larsson came to rural Sweden from the city. Larsson's childhood was one of desperate urban poverty: he grew up in one of the worst slums of Stockholm's old city, the child of a poor woman (an occasional prostitute) and a disabled (and alcoholic) laborer. Rural Dalarna was the vehicle of Larsson's own success; he made it much more idyllic than Zorn had and far better known than Zorn ever could.

At an early age, Larsson taught himself to draw and paint; he managed to enter the Academy of Art in 1873. [...] [The academy] gave him a stipend to participate from 1882–85 in the Swedish artists' colony at Grèz-sur-Loing in France. Here and in Paris, Larsson began to paint *en plein air* and discovered his talent for watercolor. Here too he met and married Karin Bergöö, the daughter of a well-to-do Swedish merchant, herself an established artist. From Karin's aunts the Larssons inherited a log house on a small river in Sundborn, Dalarna, in 1888.[18] They began immediately to transform the "little mining cabin" ("Lilla Hyttnäs", "little smelting place") as a summer residence, adding a studio in 1890; they spent increasingly long periods of time there. In 1901, they made it their year-round home. A number of outbuildings were erected as Larsson's fortunes improved: in 1900, a new studio, enlarged by the addition of an old miner's cabin in 1912. In 1906, Karin and Carl added a working farm to their property. The development of "Larsson manor" was almost exactly contemporaneous with that of Zorn. And as at Zorn's, the original log building was encapsulated by the new home.

Lilla Hyttnäs provided the springboard for Carl Larsson's success and international reputation ... In 1893 or 1894 Larsson began a series of watercolors of the home and family (apparently at Karin's urging); twenty of these were exhibited at the Stockholm exhibition of 1897; then, together with an additional four, they were published as a book, *Ett hem* (*A Home*), in 1899.[19] The paintings and the book were immediate successes: the paintings were quickly exhibited in Berlin, St. Petersburg, and Chicago; the book was soon translated into German and went through a great number of German editions.[20] New editions of *Ett hem* and other watercolors and books containing them followed. All depicted a new kind of happy family life, plain and unpretentious, close to the soil, healthy, full of sunlight and outdoor living, focusing on children. A child (Kersti) invited the viewer to enter this life on the title page of *Ett hem*. Inside, children worked and played, family theatricals were held, light flooded in. Outdoors, "under the big birch" or along the river, the family ate, fished, worked and swam [*Fig. 36*]. This was, or appeared to be, an idyllic life. The child as an introduction to the house was repeated over and over by other artists and architects.[21] Translations of Larsson's books emphasized the role of light in the ideal home: "The House in the Sun", "Let the Light in!"[22] A long series of visitors, ranging from Serge Diaghilev, Strindberg, Ellen Key, and Zorn to Prince Eugen, reinforced these impressions by writing about Lilla Hyttnäs.

Although Lilla Hyttnäs was composed by joining and remodeling older buildings, it was to a great extent, like the life that was lived there, a new creation. Carl and Karin Larsson chose the wood siding for additions to the original building and the Dalarna ochre and red for the exterior. They added "dragon style" elements on the exterior. They landscaped and planted the grounds to create a particular set of views of the river and its islands. Inside, in the rather small rooms of the house, they juxtaposed furniture that they collected from local farmhouses and painted in bright, primary colors, with simple, heavy pieces of Carl's and Karin's design. At Lilla Hyttnäs, the Larssons created a new domestic atmosphere, one that was prefigured, or paralleled, in Zorn's house at Mora, but that was far more self-consciously humble and that focused (or appeared to focus) above all on the family – on Karin and the eight children.

Karin gave up her painting and devoted herself, together with Carl, to creating the home. She designed several pieces of furniture and designed and wove the textiles used in the house; her ideas are admired now for their combination of folk art traditions and innovative composition.[23] She helped to select the rest of the furniture and textiles; presumably, she also helped to create the overall character of the spaces. Influenced by the current feminist concern with dress reform, she also developed a new clothing style for herself and the children: their dresses were flowing and unconfined.[24] She and her husband worked on their home for years, changing, adding, painting over. Thus, the way of life that Carl Larsson depicted in his increasingly famous watercolors was to a considerable extent the creation of Karin Larsson and he often said that this was so.

On the other hand, Carl Larsson had a comprehensive view of the role of the artist. For him, it would be the painter who would lead the way for architects and all the other arts in achieving something necessary and new, by returning to the crafts and to the simplest forms and colors. He exhorted painters to:

> go out and preach to all the people the fair and joyful message of art … carve stoops and staves, make doors and cupboards, storm the china factories … learn to love the glorious material … climb up the walls and arouse the engineers, hypnotized by the Academy, who call themselves architects. Yes, painter, build the houses yourself, if your imagination has not been killed by all that tracing of monuments that the architects believe themselves at least capable of imitating.[25]

In spite of his frequent tributes to Karin's creative participation, there is considerable evidence that Larsson saw the role of this new kind of artistic leader as an exclusively male one.[26] And although he emphasized that Karin and the family were the center of life at home, sometimes he seemed to think of Lilla Hyttnäs as his alone. There is at least the implication in his art and his writings that he derived a strong, and perhaps his only, source of identity from his own family, his own wife, his own house, and his own grounds.

Lilla Hyttnäs always had two realities: the actual one, which changed greatly over time, and the published one of the watercolors and books. In the paintings, the house and grounds become a total universe. The family life that Larsson chose to represent in the paintings and books was idealized but also had within it elements of mystery. The outdoors rivals the indoors as a living space. The family eats, works, fishes, and swims outdoors, always in sunlight. Children dominate almost all the interiors and appear even in their father's studio. They seem to have a full share in the household tasks. Karin, when she appears, has aspects of a household goddess, one who watches over everyone. The family is presented as harmonious and egalitarian, a persuasive model for a loving and natural way of life. This life, however, is also quasi-religious: family ceremonies substitute to a considerable extent for those of the church; nature and Norse gods and goddesses are worshipped.[27] The truth, of course, was somewhat different: Larsson's attitudes to wife and children were ambivalent; he was subject to crippling depressions; and the sources of his success were not what he wanted them to be.[28] [...]

Did Zorn and Larsson take seriously their idealizations of Dalarna's peasant life, rural traditions, and Norse mythology? ... In his *Autobiography*, Larsson wrote that he liked to get back to Stockholm, "where I seek out people of my own kind".[29] Isabella Stewart Gardner remarked on Zorn's tendency to brag about his rural origins, to "act" like a homespun farmer, in order to please Americans.[30] At home, Zorn lived very richly indeed. Both men were peripatetic in the extreme: they were world citizens ... But although Zorn and Larsson did not really think of themselves as Dalarna rural folk, they did believe that simple peasant ways, traditional crafts and building types, the traditions of folklore and ancient myths offered new models for behavior, social relations, and a sense of national identity.

Notes

1   Best on this are Celia Applegate, *A Nation of Provincials: The German Idea of Heimat,* Berkeley and Los Angeles: University of California Press, 1990, and Benedict Anderson, *Imagined Communities: Reflections on the Origin and Spread of Nationalism*, London: Verso, 1983 ...

2   See Chapter 1 in Barbara Miller Lane, *National Romanticism and Modern Architecture in Germany and the Scandinavian Countries*, Cambridge: Cambridge University Press, 2000, for the teachings of mid-century scholarship as to the origins of Nordic or Germanic architecture in the earliest great hall structures.

3   This phrase is from Ritva Tuomi (Wäre), *Studios in the Wilds: Artists' Country Studios at the Turn of the Century*, Helsinki: Museum of Finnish Architecture, 1979 ...

4   Influential Swedish feminist, social philosopher and writer on aesthetics; well-known in English-language countries through the translations of Mamah Borthwick and Frank Lloyd Wright. See Lane, *National Romanticism*, pp. 122–6.

5   Ritva Wäre, "Kalela and Tarvaspää – the Wanderer's Homes", in Sinisalo, *Akseli Gallen-Kallela*, pp. 112–23, 113, explains that the main source for the studio was the *luhtiaitta*, a two-story "traditional Finnish storehouse with a narrow gallery". Gallen-Kallela, Sparre, and the other pilgrims to Karelia would have seen such storehouses there. [...]

6   Door handles at Kalela resemble those by Zorn and the furniture of bent and twisted wood that stemmed from Karelia and was collected by Pekka Halonen (see below, "Tuusula and Sonck"). [...]. There are also indications of influences upon German Expressionism [...]

7   ... Tarvaspää was poured concrete, with central heating. It is quite near Helsinki, on a promontory overlooking the sea.

8   Tuomi (Wäre), "On the Search for a National Style", p. 75 ...

9   On Karelian themes in Finnish furniture design, see Tuomi (Wäre), *Studios in the Wilds*, p. 76.

10   The villa was designed in 1893, built in 1894. It burned in 1896, was rebuilt in a similar fashion in 1899–1902, and extended from 1903–1912. [...]

11   See Tuomi (Wäre), *Studios in the Wilds,* Figs. 15–17; Roald Nasgaard, *The Mystic North: Symbolist Landscape Painting in Northern Europe and North America*, Toronto: University of Toronto Press, 1984, p. 54; Yrjö Hirn, "Kalevalaromantiken och Axel Gallen-Kallela", *L'ärt*

folk och landstrykare i det finska Finlands kulturliv, Stockholm and Helsinki: Wahlström & Widstrand, 1939, pp. 189–225, pp. 189–92, 204; Salme Sarajas-Korte, *Vid symbolismens källor: den tidiga symbolismen i Finland 1890–1895*, Jakobstad: Jakobstads Tryckeri och Tidning, 1981, p. 236. [...]

12   On Jean Sibelius (1865–1957), ... see Nils-Eric Ringbom, *Jean Sibelius: A Master and his Work*, trans. G. I. C. de Courcy, Norman: University of Oklahoma Press, 1954, and Erik Tawaststjerna, *Sibelius*, trans. Robert Layton, Berkeley: University of California Press, 1976. See also Nasgaard, *The Mystic North*, p. 57.

13   Construction of Ainola (named after Jean Sibelius's wife Aino) ... was begun in 1904. The roof, now tile, was originally shingled. The present vertical wood siding, painted white with green trim, was added in 1910. The top floor was finished only in 1911 ...

14   See Gustaf Näsström, *Dalarna som svenskt ideal*, Stockholm: Wahlström & Widstrand, 1937; Gerda Boëthius, *Dalarna: A Description of its Scenery, its People and its Culture*, Stockholm: Pettersons, 1930; Eva Eriksson, *Den moderna stadens födelse: Svensk arkitektur 1890–1920*, Stockholm: Ordfronts Förlag, 1990; and Elisabet Stavenow-Hidemark, *Villabebyggelse i Sverige 1900–1925. Inflytande från utlandet, idéer, förverkligande*, Lund: Nordiska museets Handlingar, 1971, p. 76. [...]

15   On the history of *hemslöjd* as an important economic activity in Sweden, see C. A. Montgomery, *The Rise of Modern Industry in Sweden*, London: King, 1939, and Elisabet Stavenow-Hidemark, "Sweden Goes English: A New Approach to the National Heritage", in Susanna Vihma (ed.) *Form and Vision*, Helsinki: The University of Industrial Arts, 1987, pp. 30–9. [...]

16   Ochre and red were most frequent in the farm buildings of Dalarna.

17   Did Zorn ever visit the "great camps"? It is tempting to think so, but the main features of Zorn's house antedate the more fully developed of the Adirondack camps. [...]

18   Sundborn, near the shores of Lake Toften, is at the eastern edge of Dalarna, near the town of Falun (a center of copper mining) ...

19   Carl Larsson, *Ett hem:24 målningar*, Stockholm: Bonnier, 1899. See also ... *Carl Larsson*, exhibition catalog, National Museum Stockholm, Stockholm: Bokförlaget Bra Böcker, 1992, p. 343; [and] Michael Snodin and Elisabet Stavenow-Hidemark (eds) *Carl and Karin Larsson: Creators of the Swedish Style*, exhibition catalog, London: Victoria and Albert Publications, 1997. [...]

20   Ulle Ehrensvärd, "De svenske i Chicago", in Erik Forssman et al. (eds) *Konsthistoriska studier tillägnade Sten Karling*, Stockholm: Universitet Konsthistoriska institutionen, 1966, pp. 341–60, 355–6; [...]Cecelia Lengefeld, *Der Maler des glücklichen Heims. Zur Rezeption Carl Larssons im wilhelminischen Deutschland*, Heidelberg: Universitätsverlag C. Winter, 1993 ...

21   [For example] in [Carl] Westman's drawing of Pressens Villa (1901 ...); by [Heinrich] Vogeler, in paintings of his daughter Mieke (especially *Im Frühling*, 1903) at Worpswede; and even in the photograph of Frank Lloyd Wright's Coonley House published in Frank Lloyd Wright, *Ausgeführte Bauten*, Berlin: Wasmuth, 1911, p. 119.

22   *Das Haus in der Sonne*, Düsseldorf and Leipzig: Langewiesche, 1909, contained selections of images and text from *Ett hem* and from the later publications *Larssons*, Stockholm: Bonniers, 1902, and *Spadarfvet, mitt lilla landtbruk*, Stockholm: Bonniers, 1906. [...]. *Lasst Licht hinein!*, Berlin: Bruno Cassirer, 1910, was the German title of *Åt Solsidan* ("On the Sunny Side"), Stockholm: Bonnier, 1910. See also Cecelia Lengefeld, "Translation and Transformation: Carl Larsson's Books in Europe", in Snodin and Stavenow-Hidemark, *Carl and Karin Larsson*, pp. 196–211.

23   Ulf Hård af Segerstad, "The Ideal Swedish Home", *Carl Larsson, 1853–1919*, exhibition catalog, Brooklyn: Brooklyn Museum, and New York: Rinehart and Winston, 1982, pp. 39–51; Madeleine von Heland, "Karin and Carl Larsson", in ibid., pp. 53–66; Ingrid Andersson, *Karin Larsson. Konstnär och konstnärshustru*, Stockholm: Gidlunds, 1986; Snodin and Stavenow-Hidemark, *Carl and Karin Larsson*.

24   Also influenced, certainly, by Kate Greenaway, who is quoted in the introduction to *Ett hem* ...

25   Quoted by Görel Cavalli-Björkman, Curator, National Museum, Stockholm, "Carl Larsson: A Brief Biography", in *Carl Larsson, 1853–1919*, p. 41.

26   Heland, "Karin and Carl Larsson", in ibid.; Georg Nordensvan, *Carl Larsson*, Stockholm: P.A. Norstedt, 1920–21, 2 vols.

27   The Larsson household paid tribute to Idun, the Norse goddess of nature and eternal life, whose name was the title of the leading Swedish women's magazine ... The birthday

celebrations (actually "name-day" celebrations) shown in the paintings are elaborate, theatrical, and ritualized. The family Christmas celebration is depicted as joining Christian and pagan traditions. Larsson rejected the church and refused to have his children baptized until the birth of the seventh in 1896.

28 On Larsson's ambivalence toward his wife and children, see Heland, "Karin and Carl Larsson", *Carl Larsson, 1853–1919*. On the depressions and the realities of his life in general, see his *Autobiography*, published posthumously; *Jag*, Stockholm: Bonnier, 1931, without subtitle. I have used the German and English editions primarily: *Ich: ein Buch über das Gute und das Böse*, Königstein im Taunus: Langewiesche, 1985, trans. from the Swedish edition of 1969; and *Carl Larsson: The Autobiography of Sweden's Most Beloved Artist*, John Z. Lofgren (ed.) trans. Ann B. Weissmann, Iowa City, Iowa: Penfield Press, 1992 …

29 *Autobiography*, p. 131.

30 Louise Hall Tharp, *Mrs. Jack. A Biography of Isabella Stewart Gardner*, New York: Peter Weed, 1965, p. 169.

Great Camps of the Adirondacks

Harvey Kaiser (1982)

When trying to define a "camp", one is reminded of Louis Armstrong's famous response to an often repeated question about jazz: "Man, if you gotta ask, you'll never know". To some who survived summers away from home under the watchful eyes of counselors, a camp was a refuge from city boredom, pains of adolescence, and shared homesickness. To some, it is a tar paper shack built by their grandfather near a trickle of a stream. And to others, it is a forty-room lodge with a servant and guide for every guest.

Alice M. Kellogg attested to the confusion, writing in *Broadway Magazine* in 1908: "A camp in the Adirondacks, then, may mean anything from a log fire in the woods to a hundred thousand dollar villa. The only places not called camps are the big hotels where guests dress formally for dinner". William Dix, gushing enthusiastically about a weekend at a luxurious camp, knew what a camp wasn't: "An Adirondack camp does not mean a canvas tent or a bark wigwam". But he also knew that it was distinctive: "a permanent summer home where the fortunate owners assemble for several weeks each year and live in perfect comfort and even luxury, tho in the heart of the woods, with no near neighbors, no roads and no danger of intrusion". The Great Camp, as it was termed in the more colorful periods of Adirondack history, meant usually the summer homes of the rich, the luxurious layouts where "roughing it" was a phrase without much meaning. The New York press and the popular magazines might describe an "Adirondack hunting lodge", but the owner always called it a camp.

The private log cabins and tents that grew up around Paul Smith's and other hotels were comfortable, but the most lavish camps were deeper in the woods. As the possession of an elaborate Adirondack hunting lodge became fashionable, the wealthy families looked for remote, isolated places surrounded by hundreds or thousands of private acres of land.

It is generally agreed that the first camps were more or less impromptu constructions. As with the development of other architectural styles, the Great Camps did not spring from any single source. Unspoiled nature, a hunger for greater privacy in the deep woods, ready availability of materials, and ample wealth to command absolute comfort mingled to produce the unique character of the Great Camps. A journalist in 1908 wrote: "The architectural perfection that is apparent in the Adirondack camps of the finer class is due, in great measure, to the artistic principle of suiting a design to its use and to its situation".

In the design of a Great Camp, most of the buildings demonstrated a special approach to their wilderness surroundings through deliberate esthetic choices. As one writer described the style: "Naturally no two are alike; some are elaborate, even to the point of questionable taste ... But the truest type is composed of a group of rustic buildings on the edge of a lake, with pathless forests in the rear" [*Fig. 37*].

Of the more prominent elements that can be considered standard features of the Great Camp, the use of log construction, whether true or simulated, is perhaps most striking. While ordinary balloon-frame construction composed the vast majority of country summer homes, logs, though construction was time-consuming and expensive, were laid up as walls, framed as trusses, used as supporting purlins for the roof, and peeled as beams and studs. Every detail possessed structural significance. Extensions of log ends, coping of intersecting logs, and crossbracing of poles became decorative elements.

While the Great Camps surpassed in size and structural complexity the simple log cabins of the early settlers, they conveyed the same sense of shelter from the severe climate, playing on romantic associations with the pioneering spirit and the simple life.

"Rustic work" is another distinctive camp characteristic. A contemporary definition from an architectural dictionary of the period defines the term as:

> decoration by means of rough woodwork, the bark being left in place, or by means of uncut stone, artificial rock-work or the like, or by such combination of these materials and devices as will cause the general appearance of what is thought rural in character. Where woodwork is used it is customary to provide a continuous sheathing as of boards, upon which is nailed the small logs and branches with their bark, moss, etc., carefully preserved.

Previously, rustic work was seldom used as architectural ornament, being confined primarily to nineteenth-century garden gazebos and summer houses and their furniture, or to country fences and estate entrance gateways. But in the Adirondacks, roughly dressed limbs and roots of the native trees were used to create imaginative, ornamental patterns, producing unique architectural embellishments. The same skills were applied by the guideboat builders as well, using native materials supplemented by craft, practicality, and some imposed materials. On building exteriors, rustic work included decorative application of peeled-bark sheathing, elaborate branch-work patterns on porch railings, and gable screens. Interiors incorporated it into fireplaces, decorative trim, and all types of imaginative woodland furniture produced on the site [*Figs. 38, 39*].

Another distinguishing feature of Adirondack camps is the tradition of individual buildings for separate functions as permanent buildings replaced tent platforms. Guests were generally lodged in cabins or perhaps on the second floor of the typical lakeside boathouse, separate from the camp owner's living unit. The dining room was often housed in an individual building, while the social gathering place, variously called "the casino", the game room, or the trophy lodge, was also a separate unit. Covered boardwalks or enclosed passageways connected the buildings, affording some shelter from the elements.

Separate buildings were particularly well-suited to expansions that continued through successive summers, the camp extending its size with each successive season. As camps grew, they took on the appearance of small settlements. The staff quarters – kitchens, icehouses, barns, workshops, carriage houses, and storerooms – became the service complex, a self-sufficient community in some cases several miles from the main camp.

Advice about building camps was published as early as 1888 by William S. Wicks in *Log Cabins: How to Build and Furnish Them*. Filled with valuable information on selecting a site, construction details and furnishings, plans and sketches, this popular book was published in many editions through the 1920s. Although the book may never have fallen into the hands of the Adirondack guides and local craftsmen, it provided a good primer in basic camp design for the owner or architect. The argument for log construction was set forth simply as a "civilized" choice: "The choice of material for a camp is, to a large extent, a matter of taste, expense or convenience … No material equals the log, and no cabin looks so well as the log cabin". Wick's designs were cabins of log construction, cut from timber on or near the site. Log notching was traditional; windows and doors were set by woodsman's methods; chimneys were of sound, functional design.

In 1931, almost a half century later, Augustus D. Shepard described the transition in camp design in *Camps in the Woods*. As an architect designing Great Camps for several decades at the same Adirondack League Club site as Wicks, Shepard had seen the basic log cabin translated into the elaborate hunting lodge. In Shepard's terms, although his camps were built of logs, they did not have the crude quality (Wicks called it charm), but were in reality "summer homes in the woods".

Desirability of a site was based on the available views, access, and a tree-protected waterfront, and, as Wicks said, "The structure should be the outgrowth of, and harmonize with the site". Shepard echoes this: "The buildings must be designed so that they actually appear to grow out of the ground. It should be hardly discernible to the eye where the building commences".

The most successful Great Camp designs followed the rule that building materials possess certain inherent qualities of the forest. This eliminated such materials as plaster, wallpaper, or paint – either inside or outside the building. The aesthetic point depended on the natural color, figure, and grain of the wood for decorative effects. Spruce, pine, hemlock, tamarack, and balsam were the best for structure; hardwoods were too heavy to handle. Spruce was best for roof boards; pine and spruce for ceilings; pine, spruce, cypress, and gumwood for wall and paneling; and birch, beech, maple, and fir for the floors and stairs.

Fall was the best time of the year to build, with the ground dry and hard, no heavy snows to obstruct the hauling of logs to camp, and bark clinging tightly to the trees. Logs for walls were fastidiously selected for straightness, shape, and taper, and had to be carefully placed to avoid contact with the ground, preventing dry rot. Foundations could take the form of piers or walls, preferably of local stone, although posts of cedar, hemlock, pine, or tamarack placed below frost level could be used instead. Camps like Santanoni, Kill Kare, or Uncas illustrate marvels of craftsmanship, all executed with the woodman's felling axe. In later years, when sawmills were more readily available, it became easier to flatten sides for a tight fit and to slot the length of a log for insertion of hemp weather barriers. But the intricate corner-notching and coping of logs to butt horizontally or at an angle could be done only by skilled workers. […]

Another highly skilled task was chimney construction. Just getting a fireplace to draw properly and not blow smoke and ash into the room was a difficult task; to make it decorative as well required art. One marvels at the massive hearths at Sagamore and Topridge, large enough to stand in and capped by stone mantles weighing tons. Cyclopean rocks were incorporated into fireplaces at Kill Kare and Nehasane with the apparent ease that ordinary bricklayers show with simpler materials.

The furniture and accessories of a Great Camp added to their character. Wicks urged that "as far as possible both log cabin and its furniture be made on the spot and with the material at hand". Beds, chairs, tables, cupboards, and decorative pieces of peeled poles, twigs, and birch bark were works of art, crafted by caretakers and guides over a long winter and presented to an owner upon arrival the following summer. William West Durant developed built-in bench seats, using bent poles polished with beeswax to reveal the natural grain, still fresh in appearance today after almost a century. Under the true craftsman, anonymous at Kamp Kill Kare or known like Ben Muncil, Jr., at Topridge, an interior of rustic furniture blended harmoniously with handrails, lighting fixtures, and the woods of interior surfaces. [...]

The history of tourism in the central Adirondacks during the last quarter of the nineteenth century is in large part the story of William West Durant. He was born in Brooklyn in 1850, scion of the railroad builder, Thomas C. Durant. When the famous steamship *Great Eastern* made her first Atlantic crossing in 1861, eleven-year-old William was a passenger, bound for a European education. Except for a few months' visit home in 1866, he remained abroad, studying in England and Germany and traveling extensively. In his early twenties, William became interested in exploring the Middle East. He was in Egypt in 1874 when called home by his father to help in developing the central Adirondacks. [...]

Upon his arrival at Raquette Lake in 1876, the son went to work on the father's plans for opening the central Adirondacks for tourism. The rigorous trip from the railhead at North Creek to Raquette Lake had to be improved to bring tourists to the central Adirondacks. A transportation system was planned linking the thirty miles from North Creek to Blue Mountain Lake by a stagecoach line. For the twelve-mile distance to Raquette Lake, he established a line of rowboats, later replacing them with several steamboats. At the same time, William's cousin Frederick, son of Charles W. Durant, came to build the Prospect House on Blue Mountain Lake. Setting aside his plans for hotels and clubs, William West Durant broke ground on his personal residence. In the summer of 1877 the elder Durant had built two or three simple one-story cabins on Long Point. During the building, one of the family had found a remarkable, three-foot-wide pine knot shaped like the hilt of a sword, which was quickly adopted as the camp totem. When William took over Camp Pine Knot in 1878, he gradually transformed the original, featureless buildings into "artistic" cabins of Swiss chalet lines. Pine Knot grew and evolved, ultimately becoming a cluster of buildings, large and small, connected and detached.

Durant built hunting camps on other holdings – south of Raquette Lake on Shedd and Sumner lakes and on Rich and Arbutus lakes in Essex County. His development schemes went forward, including camps, elegant hotels and golf courses, and modern transportation. Telegraph lines were strung into the region to bring the latest word from the outside. The line of rowboats along the Fulton Chain was replaced by a fleet of steamboats, the largest holding two hundred passengers. [...]

Although the undercurrents of an emerging, indigenous rustic style existed when Durant first came to the heart of the Adirondack wilderness in the 1870s, it was his creation of a harmonious woodland architecture that largely inspired and institutionalized the style as we know it today. Durant's simple design took the best features of the Adirondack early log cabin and combined them with the decorative features of the long, low Swiss chalet, making a building style that blended perfectly with a woodland or lakeshore setting.

The many buildings on the site were scattered in an informal manner, each separate from the next. Sites were selected for views, and within general proximity of each other for convenience of moving about in bad weather.

Durant's compound plan did not contain or define exterior space as did the functional structures of forested lands in northern Europe, Russia, or Japan. The scheme reflected the character of temporary woodsmen's or guides' camps, more or less random groupings of tent platforms. Rather than tack a new wing onto an existing structure to incorporate a new function, it was preferred to construct an entirely separate structure.

There were also practical reasons for the compound-plan tradition. A greater degree of privacy was afforded by the separated structures; at the same time, the sense of community, important in an isolated forest location, was provided by an extended complex. […]

Pattern in building and farming
Thomas C. Hubka (1984)

> No need to look around; all the farms around here are pretty much the same.
>
> Richard Chadbourne

From a passing car, connected farms sometimes appear to be strangely composed and haphazardly strung together. Present residents have also commented on the apparent whimsy of the farmers' planning decisions. But when Richard Chadbourne described the farms in the Ingalls Hill neighborhood of Bridgton, Maine, he knew that, despite some difference in appearance, most farms were organized and operated similarly. The visual variety among farmsteads was the result of a building tradition that allowed individual farmers a range of design choices within a uniform pattern of overall farmstead layout. This chapter outlines the major recurring patterns of spatial organization and activity usage that characterized most connected farmsteads in the nineteenth century.

The arrangement of buildings

Most connected farm buildings follow the organizational structure of the refrain, "Big house, little house, back house, barn". The distinguishing characteristic is that the big house and the barn are located at opposite ends of a string of connected buildings. Together they form either a straight or a staggered line of buildings in a flattened L- or U-shaped plan, usually aligned rectilinearly with the main road. The entire complex acted to shelter a south- or east-facing dooryard, protected from north and west winter winds by this line of connected buildings. More than 85 percent of the surveyed connected farms outside of town centers in Maine and eastern New Hampshire conform to the same organizational strategies of siting, linking, and connecting.

Siting the buildings

Three farm planning principles guided most farmers' decisions for the layout of a connected farmstead. The first, most consistent consideration was that all buildings, particularly the house, be aligned at right angles to the major road with the principal façade of the house facing the road. This may seem like an obvious consideration today, since nearly all buildings assume this orientation, but builders in rural New England have not always sited structures this way. Before 1800 rural builders usually aligned the front façades and doorways of most houses and barns southward, without particular regard for the orientation to the road. As late as 1830 an agricultural writer gave this advice to Maine farmers: "When the case will admit, the farm house, barn, etc., should front the south".[1] Today it is often possible to identify eighteenth-century houses and barns because of their now conspicuous nonalignment with the road. Where possible, buildings faced both south and the road, but southern orientation was the primary consideration. Between 1770 and 1830, most rural New England builders gradually came to favor an alignment in which the principal façades of new houses and barns, and particularly the formal front façade of the house, faced the major road without regard to southern exposure. This was a fundamental change in rural architectural planning and indicates that the rural population was relinquishing a nature-directed life-style in favor of a more road-directed, town-oriented way of life. It was almost as if the traditional building alignment of medieval origin was suddenly tugged out of its agrarian orientation by the increasing pull of economic and social influences of the town.[2] The swiftness and completeness of this conversion within a sixty-year period is one indication of the depth of this new town and commercial orientation for the rural population of New England. This change was to have important implications for the popularization of the connected building plan.

The second major siting consideration for connected farms was the provision for a southerly facing dooryard and kitchen ell. A southern or eastern exposure was important because farmers needed a dry, sunny work place for their many activities. A distinct benefit of the connected farm arrangement was that the line of attached buildings sheltered the dooryard, and to a lesser extent the barnyard, from northern and western winter winds and from excessive snow accumulation. The wisdom of this planning strategy is particularly evident in the early spring. Piles of melting snow and pools of muddy water make the shaded north side of a typical connected complex impassable, while the dooryard and the barnyard on the southern side are dry for early springtime chores. Because of the region's short growing season, an early spring start has always been critical to the success of agricultural activities. The environmental advantages of a south- or east-facing dooryard generally improved the quality of domestic and farm life, and it still has much to recommend it, even to those who no longer farm.

The orientation of the dooryard also affected many architectural features of the connected farm. A comparison of the front and back sides of a typical farm vividly demonstrates the response to climatic considerations that guided the planning of these structures. The south or east side facing the dooryard is usually perforated with doors, windows, porches, dormers, and building additions, while the north or west side usually lacks these amenities and is relatively blank and unadorned. Inside the buildings, the major rooms are also directed toward the south-facing dooryard, except for the parlor, which was usually oriented toward the front yard and road.

The third basic siting principle was to locate the barn's animal tie-up bay and barnyard in a southerly orientation and in close proximity to fields, pastures, roads, and wells. The consideration of a southern exposure for animal yards and their housing was echoed in all periods. [...] All [these] rules are perhaps so obvious to any New England farmer, past or present, that they may hardly seem worthy of comment. And that is precisely what these vernacular rules were: unarticulated, commonsense rules, ingrained in usage and habit, which became a standard part of the farming and building traditions of the region.[3]

Yet the layout and organization of many connected farms cannot be understood by simply following these general rules. Three other factors greatly complicate this tidy picture. First, the rules were not static but evolving in time. Much depended upon how strictly a guideline was followed and the degree to which it came into competition with previous rules or ideas. For example, the desire for a rectilinear alignment of the buildings, both to each other and to the road, gradually gained popularity in the late eighteenth and early nineteenth centuries and became accepted by most builders after the 1820s. But if a building was constructed between 1780 and 1820, the new consideration might only partially influence siting decisions; often only the house and not the barn would face the road, indicating a compromise between competing planning ideas ... Second, the planning rules that influenced connected farm layout and siting were frequently applied to existing, nonconnected farmsteads of various ages and configurations. These had usually been organized according to older vernacular rules. Consequently, the degree to which a new building idea could be implemented often depended upon the existing configuration of the farmstead ... A third, intangible factor was the effect of individual selection and choice by builders and owners in the planning decision-making process. Some farmers defied convention and made their building differently. [...]

Linking the buildings

A farmer had considerable choice about the way buildings were joined together ... The more common practice of offset building connection is a distinctive characteristic of many connected farmsteads (Fig. 40). Even to a sympathetic observer, the joining of individual buildings might sometimes appear to defy any organizational principles or rules, but the physical connection between most structures was not random.

From a practical standpoint, a staggered or offset building connection lessened the surface contact between two buildings joined together by allowing existing doors and windows to remain operable and thus minimizing the internal disruption to either building. This was an especially important consideration for New England farmers, who perfected a popular tradition of moving and realigning structures. A staggered building alignment also permitted the farmer to use each building independently and somewhat differently. This was an important overall consideration to the success of the connected farm plan because the presence of diverse, adjacent activities often required a degree of activity separation. [...]

An offset or nonsymmetrical connected building alignment for farm buildings was an ancient English tradition brought to America.[4] But there is, perhaps, another, more subtle reason for the persistence of this characteristic. The novelty of surface treatment in individual buildings suggests a certain amount of individuality, zealousness, even bravado, on the part of some farmers who might have enjoyed the juxtaposition and clash of different building forms. There may even have been a degree of anti-city formality or an individual pride in breaking formal rules – in this case, the genteel, aesthetic rules of uniformity and order that were frequently employed in fashionable connected town houses. Whatever the reason for this frequent juxtaposition of forms, it is important to emphasize the significant role of the builders and owners in designing these buildings. Within every connected building complex there were usually several different ways of aligning or offsetting, unifying or contrasting, and finishing or not finishing the buildings so as to achieve the same operational results (for example, the decision to rotate the English barn in the connected complex).[5] There was a significant degree of choice and individual expression, therefore, in the organization of connected farms, which many farmers chose to exploit for a variety of practical, aesthetic, and personal reasons.

Notes

1 *Maine Farmer*, January 6, 1830.
2 The transition from a medieval-agrarian to modern-industrial social and technological orientation has been treated by various New England historians, for example, Richard Bushman, *From Puritan to Yankee*, Cambridge, Mass.: Harvard University Press, 1967, pp. 73–6, 107–19; Robert Gross, *The Minutemen and Their World*, NY: Hill and Wang, 1976, pp. 75–9, 190–1; and Clive Day, "The Rise of Manufacturing in Connecticut 1820–1850", *Tercentenary Commission of the State of Connecticut*, Pamphlet no. XLIV, New Haven, Conn.: Yale University Press, 1935, pp. 28–30. Robert Gross has labeled this cultural reorientation an agricultural revolution ("Culture and Cultivation: Agriculture and Society in Thoreau's Concord", *Journal of American History* 69, no. 1, June 1982, 42), and his overall assessment of this profound reorientation experienced by nineteenth-century Massachusetts farmers is supported by the findings of this book.
3 The various methods by which building practices are maintained and transformed within folk tradition are analyzed by Henry H. Glassie, *Folk Housing in Middle Virginia*, Knoxville, Tenn.: University of Tennessee Press, 1975, pp. 19–21, 34, 66–8.
4 As shown in J. E. C. Peters, *The Development of Farm Buildings*, Manchester, England: Manchester University Press, 1969, pp. 48–59; and R. W. Brunskill, *Illustrated Handbook of Vernacular Architecture*, London: Faber and Faber, 1970, pp. 136–7.
5 The ability to manipulate independent portions of the architectural ensemble (the position of the barn) while maintaining the overall dependent arrangement (the connected building organization) is one of the primary methods by which folk designers achieve individuality within a traditional pattern of building. See also Glassie, *Folk Housing*, 1975, pp. 38–40.

Homes and gardens
The rural idyll

Mike Hepworth (1999)

Although the hearth has a strong claim on symbolic pride of place in all domestic architecture, the fireplace had a special virtue in another highly emotive symbol in Victorian domestic culture, the country cottage [*Fig. 41*]. Downing, whose principal work was published in 1851, believed that the countryside was the most appropriate location of the home, because in a rural environment domestic life was free to expand and "develop itself freely, as a tree expands which is not crowded by neighbors in a forest, but grows in the unrestrained liberty of the open meadow".[1] The most complete expression of the country home was the English cottage: "the domestic virtues, the love of home, rural beauty, and seclusion, cannot possibly be better expressed than in the English cottage, with its many upward pointing gables … and its walls covered with vines and flowering shrubs".[2]

It is the symbolic nature of the home, that "storehouse of signs"[3] where the home is "conceptualised both as a social symbol and an extension of the self",[4] which finds quintessential expression in the cottage in the country. As Clayton-Payne observes,

> The image of the cottage … was a potent one in the late nineteenth century. Its popularity can be seen in terms of a reaction against what was perceived as the ugliness of the Industrial Revolution … The simplicity and beauty of the past seemed still discoverable in rural villages and footpaths.[5]

Associations between the ideal home and the world of nature were expressed in their most contrived form in the Victorian garden, especially the flower garden. If access to a real cottage garden was not possible, a painting or reproduction of a painting could be purchased. The "development of flower garden painting began in the 1860s with the work of Frederick Walker and Birket Foster, still basically under the influence of picturesque values".[6] In paintings of flower gardens, human figures tend to derive their character from their physical surroundings. They are not present as identifiable individuals but as anonymous character types whose position in these floral surroundings reinforces the overall moral message of the tranquility of the garden. In, for example, Francis Wollaston Moody's *In Chelsea Gardens* (1858) an unnamed and unidentifiable Chelsea pensioner offers flowers to a child while the equally anonymous mother looks on fondly.[7]

Garden and cottage garden paintings reflected an increasing interest in the cultivation of flowers and gardens and a move away from the utilitarian idea of the garden as the provider of staple fare in a subsistence economy. Ironically, it is not the "useful" vegetable garden which comes to symbolize home in popular images but the "useless" flower. This in part reflects a greater interest in the cultivation of flowers alongside the staple vegetables which continued to play such an important part in the rural subsistence economy. It is also part-reflection of a longer tradition of floral symbolism as elaborated by the Victorians in paintings, poems and other works of art. By the mid-nineteenth century the better-off cottagers were cultivating bedding plants among their vegetables. For the socially advantaged the accent moved away from material subsistence towards colorful floral displays and the cottage garden was transformed into an aestheticized moral enterprise. In this floral enterprise there was a strong element of nostalgia and longing among an urbanized population, especially the affluent middle classes, for a rural idyll unspoiled by the forces of industrialization from which their wealth was derived.

The most ornamental and flowery cottage gardens were those created by landowners as a public display of their own taste. By the 1880s the cottage garden had been transformed into an indigenous gardening style. Painters played an important part in promoting what came to be known as the "cottage garden style"[8] and there was a slow effacement of the "distinction between the laborer's cottage and the middle class small house".[9] Alongside innovations in gardening and botany the Victorians elaborated a rich domesticated iconography of plant life. Grier cites a chapter in Richard Wells's *Manners, Culture and Dress*, frequently reprinted in the 1890s in the United States, as containing a list of the meanings of 318 flowers and plants: "A deep rose signaled 'bashful love'; an iris signaled 'melancholy.'"[10] The invention of photography and the concern of Pre-Raphaelite painters in Britain with the meticulous reproduction of the details of nature reinforced the symbolic appeal of plant life. Indeed, a preoccupation with accuracy of natural detail was bent to the service of symbolism. "With all their 'botanizing' associations", writes Bartram, "the plant images of the period have qualities transcending any scientific purpose", adding in a quotation from a review published in the *Athenaeum* in 1858:

> It is like reading Keats and Tennyson to look at the soft, white, velvet hair of the poisonous, veined nettle-leaves, green and rank, huddling up in a dark guilty mass to hide where the murdered child was buried, while the bee sings round the white diadems of their beguiling flowers as if nothing was wrong and earth was still a Paradise.[11]

The symbolic value of the home as rural haven and of the garden as a substitute for a full-blown rural life (homes and gardens) is thus reflected in the complex symbolism of plant life, especially flowers and gardens, evident in Victorian middle-class culture. As testified in the life of Charles Darwin, botany was regarded as one of the virtuous hobbies with close associations with gardening as both a science and an art. If the private Victorian home and garden represented a moral barrier erected against the enemy outside its walls, it also functioned to contain and discipline any enemies that may be found within. The cultivation of the garden as an aestheticized living space required the disciplining of deviant nature (weeding, pruning etc.) according to the tastes of the period reflected in images of ideal homes and gardens. Gardens were therefore part of what has been described as the "domestic scenery"[12] of the home. Alongside architectural design, furnishings and other choice domestic objects, they acted as a constant reminder to residents of the moral quality of their surroundings. [...]

Notes

1 Quoted in V. Litman, "The Cottage and the Temple: Melville's Symbolic Use of Architecture", *American Quarterly* 21, 1969, no. 3, 631.
2 Ibid.
3 Mihaly Csikszentmihalyi and Eugene Rochberg-Halton, *The Meaning of Things: Domestic Symbols and the Self*, London: Cambridge University Press, 1981, p. 139.
4 G. Barbey, "Spatial Analysis and the Experience of Time: Identifying the Dimensions of Home", in Ernesto G. Arias (ed.) *The Meaning and Use of Housing: International Perspectives, Approaches and their Applications*, Aldershot: Avebury, 1993, p. 103.
5 Andrew Clayton-Payne, *Victorian Flower Gardens*, London: Weidenfeld and Nicolson, 1988, p. 32.
6 Ibid., p. 9.
7 C. Wood, *Dictionary of Victorian Painting*, Woodbridge: Antique Collectors' Club, 1978, p. 670.
8 Clayton-Payne, *Victorian Flower Gardens*, p. 63.
9 Ibid., p. 68.
10 Katherine Grier, *Culture and Comfort: People, Parlors and Upholstery: 1850–1930*, Rochester, NY: The Strong Museum, 1988, p. 11.
11 Michael Bartram, *The Pre-Raphelite Camera*, London: Weidenfeld, 1985, p. 38.
12 Grier, *Culture and Comfort*, p. 6.

Home and work
The use of space in a Nebraska farmhouse

Dawni Freeman (2003)

[…] The house is white, with vinyl siding. It sits facing south on 1175 acres of Nebraska farmland in the Loup River valley, two miles southwest of Burwell, Nebraska. Behind the house is a ridge of hills that signal the beginning of Nebraska Sandhill country to the north and west. […]

The house has two stories and is spanned across its front by a screened-in front porch. There are six rooms on the main floor …, the mudroom, kitchen, bathroom, living room, back bedroom, … and [main] bedroom. In the upstairs there are three small bedrooms …

My Great-Aunt Lila and Great-Uncle Stan have lived in this house for forty-two years. They are cattle farmers. Originally they raised hogs and chickens, but as they expanded onto more and more land, they replaced the hogs and chickens with cows. Fifty-four of their acres are used to grow corn to feed their cattle, with two rows of sweet corn for summer eating and freezing for eating during the winter. The rest of the property is dry, rolling hills and cedar-choked canyons. […]

On the west side of the house there is a small garden [that] produces tomatoes, cucumbers, peppers, zucchini, rhubarb, onions, and melons. Next to the garden is a mid-sized elm tree, underneath which sits the picnic table for outdoor eating during the summer. Out in front of the house next to the cornfield are two machine sheds – one large enough for the tractors, the combine, and the feedwagon; and the other for my Uncle's trucks. Behind the house are the machine shop, three metal silos, and the barn …

[The farm] has gone through many changes [during] their … tenure there. The land and rooms have changed to better serve the needs of the family that inhabits them … When my Aunt and Uncle moved in, … [they eliminated] the wall that divided the living room and dining room. They did not need a formal dining room; they always ate in the kitchen. When the men came in from the fields at noon for dinner, the meal was taken outside or at the kitchen table. […]

My Aunt Lila was very involved in the running of the farm. She was my Uncle's partner in many necessary activities, including walking fence, cutting thistles, and feeding the cows. She rotated night watch with him during calving season when the newborn calves are most susceptible to the early spring cold. She spent the majority of the days out in the fields or pastures at my Uncle's side …

[But] my Aunt was [also] responsible for the cooking, canning, cleaning, laundry, and the general caretaking of the home. I doubt that my Uncle Stan ever cooked a meal for himself throughout the entirety of their fifty-seven year marriage … Other women would come over to "visit" while my Aunt was baking bread or canning tomatoes, … The women would sit around the kitchen table to gossip and drink coffee and smoke cigarettes. My Aunt would usually heat up a cinnamon roll …, or have fresh bread with homemade chokecherry jam … The kitchen [became] a public, social space … where women from the community would gather. […]

My Aunt and Uncle built an entirely new porch that extended across the front of the house. The porch served as another center of social activity in the house … I remember the porch as a place of lively conversation and also of quiet solitude for my Uncle. He had a comfortable chair there …, and his spittoon for the perpetual wad of tobacco he chewed always remained at his side. The porch faced the road and although the house sat several hundred yards from it, my Uncle could watch the cars and trucks and identify the people who were coming and going. [...]

The living room of my Aunt and Uncle's house acted as a multi-purpose space. It was the place for parties and event and so at times could be very social and public. [But when] there were smaller gatherings of people and family members, we either sat in the kitchen or on the porch. There was a T.V. in the living room, but I never remember it being on. Instead, there was a radio in the kitchen that played continuously at a low volume. The station it was set to rarely played music, except for hymns from the church service that was broadcast on Sunday. The majority of the time it was a fuzzy, scratchy rendition of the news announced by a man with a low, droning voice, [who] would publicize the latest price of pork bellies, the going rate for a bushel of corn, and the locations of the area's yard/farm sales. [...]

The influence of farming life on the home also had significant implications for my Aunt and Uncle's interaction with the wider community. Great distances separated individual farms and farmhouses and these gaps are expanding because of changes in farming technology ... [But] these great distances are surmounted by attachments to a common community.

My Aunt and Uncle have always been very familiar with all of their neighbors and describe them in relation to which edge of their property they border ... Some examples of neighborly interaction ... included rounding up escaped cattle and sharing expensive farming equipment. My Uncle also has a machine shop where he does welding and often trades favors with other farmers based on this service. [...]

I was particularly interested to learn about the number of strong women's organizations that my Aunt has been involved in over the years. These are not only limited to events such as the church bake sale and the Burwell flower show, but they also extend to purely social gatherings [such as] the women's bowling league ... I did not find similarly organized male groups that met solely for social purposes ... The prevalence of these organizations seems to me to be an elaborated form or outgrowth of the informal gatherings that take place in the women's kitchens. [...]

My Aunt and Uncle engage in a type of work that has the ability to shape their patterns of behavior and consequently this has affected the way they use the spaces within their home ... Their interactions with the community are based on the workings of their farm, but relationships are not only limited to work but also [involve] purely social activities as well.

Figure 32
Andrew Jackson Downing,
"Bracketed Farm-House",
1850, exterior and plan.

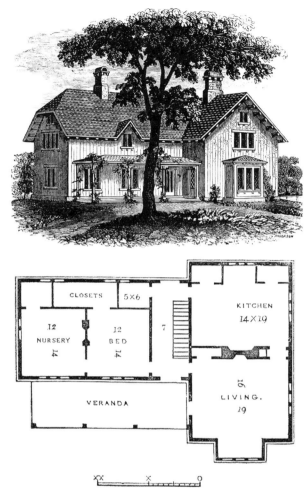

Figure 33
Bronson Alcott and Henry
David Thoreau, summerhouse
for Ralph Waldo Emerson in
Concord, Massachusetts, 1847.

Figure 34
Emil Wikström, Studio Villa
Visavuori, Finland, 1899–
1902, exterior.

Figure 35
Pekka Halonen,
Halosenniemi, Finland,
1899–1902, two-story living
room with bentwood chair.

Figure 36
Carl Larsson, *Breakfast under
the Big Birch*, 1899.

Figure 37
Aerial view, Wenonah Lodge,
Adirondack Mountains, archi-
tect unknown, *c*. 1915.

Figure 38
William West Durant, Camp
Pine Knot, *c*. 1876–80.

Figure 39 Rustic bedroom, Kamp Kill Kare, *c.* 1899–1902.

Figure 40 A connected farm complex in Fryeburg, Maine.

Figure 41 E. L. Lutyens, Munsted Wood, house and garden for Gertrude Jekyll, 1896.

8

Modernism, technology and utopian hopes for mass housing

The development of modern technology has been a central factor in shaping domestic architecture. M. J. Daunton in Chapter 5 shows the impact of gas heating and lighting on interior spaces; advances in prefabrication and factory forms of production are suggested by the Sears houses illustrated in Chapter 7, and discussed for Levittown by Curtis Miner in Chapter 9. It was in Germany just after the First World War, however, during a period of political revolution and severe housing shortages, that new technologies began to be the focus of widespread hopes for a new and modernist style. Walter Gropius's brief proposal of 1910 for new kinds of production methods for mass housing introduces that story; architect Gilbert Herbert then traces the progress of such hopes through the 1920s (Fig. 42). Architectural historian Susan Henderson focuses on the new housing in Frankfurt am Main, where the effort to evolve a "minimal dwelling" combined with factory modes of production and technological innovations such as the Frankfurt kitchen to produce huge new settlements in the modern style (Fig. 43). Henderson argues that despite the stated support of German modernists for gender equality, the Frankfurt kitchen involved the "redomestication" of women, so that the new household technology was at best an ambiguous benefit to women. Barbara Miller Lane, on the other hand, emphasizes the utopianism of German architects' attitudes to technology during the early Weimar Republic and the ways in which these attitudes permitted the embrace of revolutionary social and political ideals (Figs. 44, 45 and 46).

Program for the founding of a general housing-construction company following artistically uniform principles

Walter Gropius (1910)

The company to be established sees as its aim the industrialization of the building of houses, in order to provide the indisputable benefits of industrial production methods, best materials and workmanship, and low cost.

Abuses in the building industry of today

Due to extensive building speculation and poor management throughout the past decades, the state of building has deteriorated, both in taste and in durability, to such an extent that the public, consciously or unconsciously, suffers under these conditions. Anyone who has preserved his sensitivity for thoroughness must find unbearable the ostentatious, purely superficial appearance of comfort, which building contractors want in their buildings for the sake of publicity, but at the expense of good material, solid workmanship, distinction, and simplicity. Instead of good proportions and practical simplicity, pomposity and a false romanticism have become the trend of our time. The reason for this malaise is the fact that the public is always at a disadvantage, whether it builds with a building contractor or an architect. The contractor is understandably avoided, because he unscrupulously hurries projects through in order to save costs, but at the expense of quality. The architect, on the other hand, who only draws up the plans, is interested in increasing the building expenses, for his fee is determined by the total costs. In both cases it is the client who suffers. For him the ideal is the artist who sacrifices everything to his artistic aspirations and in the process suffers a financial loss.

The remedies

These points clearly evidence the unhealthy state of today's building industry. Enterprises whose production is based on craftsmanship (to a certain extent still including the building trade) can no longer bear the competition of industry. For, in the case of quantity production, the expenses for inventing and developing ideal prototypes are negligible in proportion to turnover, whereas in the production of single units they are prohibitive. The fundamental principle of all industry is the division of labor. The inventor concentrates all his mental energies on the viability of the idea, the invention; the manufacturer on cheap and durable production; and the merchant on organized marketing of the finished product. It is only with the aid of such specialists that it becomes possible to make the essential, i.e., the spiritual creation, economically feasible and at the same time provide the public with products of esthetically and technically good quality.

The very same conclusions may be drawn for the building of houses. To some extent, industrial production methods have already been introduced, but the prototypes built by the contractors in accord solely with economic considerations are immature and technically as well as esthetically bad and therefore inferior in quality to houses whose components are still produced by hand. However, the craftsman's work has proved to be too expensive and thus from the start has been eliminated wherever possible by those building contractors who seek lower production costs. Our organization now wants to draw the consequences from this situation and through the concept of industrialization unite the creative work of the architect with the economic talent of the contractor. This would improve on present conditions and produce striking advantages, particularly with respect to the quality of design. For whereas up to now the busy architect has had to rely more or less on trained assistants and was not able to attend personally to all the details of his designs, the projects of this company and the designs for their individual components can be painstakingly and thoroughly prepared down to the minutest detail by responsible designers before they are ready to be executed, for the expenses for this work would now be bearable. Thus, art and technology would be happily united and the public at large would be able to acquire truly mature, good art and solid, genuine goods.

Artistic uniformity – a prerequisite of "style"

Whereas the thorough development of all details benefits the individual residence, there is a deeper cultural implication underlying this principle. It is the concept of a "Zeitstil" [*style appropriate to its time, Ed.*] ...

A convention, in the best sense of the word, cannot be hoped for by emphasizing individuality. It results, rather, from the achievement of an integration that will develop from the rhythm of repetition and from the uniformity of proven and recurring forms. Our age, after a sad interregnum, is once again approaching a Zeitstil which honors tradition but fights false romanticism. Functionalism and solidity are once more gaining ground.

The necessity for a convention can also be demonstrated on practical grounds. An individual floor plan forfeits quality when it [deviates] from acknowledged [norms, which have resulted from the practical experience of countless predecessors]. But what applies to the floor plan applies to the entire house. Former cultural periods respected tradition. Even the Dutch brick house, the French block of flats of the 18th century, and the Biedermeier town house of about 1800 were repeated in series using the same forms. In England, this desire for conventional conformity, based on an urge to organize, led to the development of terrace housing, with each house looking exactly like the next and spreading in unbroken rows through whole districts. The result offered great economy and, even if unintentionally, produced artistic unity.

However, this company not only intends to supply its customers with low-cost, well-built, and practical houses in good taste, but it will also endeavor to comply with requests for individual variations, provided they do not intrude on the principle of uniformity based on industrial production.

The practical realization of the idea

I. *Use of the* same *building components and materials for all houses.* To implement the concept of the industrialization of house construction, the company will repeat individual components in all of its designs and hence facilitate mass production, promising low costs and easy rentability. Only through mass production can really good products be provided ... Industrial production methods can be applied to nearly all parts of a house ... The trend of our age to eliminate the craftsman promises far greater industrial rationalization, which for the time being still appears Utopian in our country. In America, Edison has already had entire houses including walls, ceilings, stairs, plumbing, etc., poured in concrete, using variable iron forms, and was even able to dispense with the bricklayer and the carpenter.

Standard sizes

For all essential building components the most advantageous dimensions were sought first of all, and these standard sizes form the actual basis for such designs and are to be retained in the new designs. Only with these methods can large-scale sales be guaranteed and special manufacturing in cases of additions and repairs be avoided.

Accommodation to individual needs

Each house maintains an individual personality through variations in form, material, and color …

II. *Multiple use of completed plans.* Out of the rich experience of many years and the study of traditional building methods of all civilized countries of the world, the best and most stimulating information was gathered and examined for its suitability to our time and our climatic conditions. Following this study of the proven traditions, old and living, there began an intensive task of planning, the result of which, after many experiments, was a series of designs for dwellings of various categories. These encompass the sum total of all practical, technical, and artistic experience and appear suitable for an exemplary standard on which multiple execution can be based, of course employing variable forms … The governing principle of the enterprise will be to make these houses comfortable, not in terms of overdone gilded pomp but rather in clear and open spatial arrangements and in the selection and application of proven materials and reliable techniques. What is to be offered here is excellence, to be guaranteed for many years …

The dream of the factory-made house
Walter Gropius and Konrad Wachsmann

Gilbert Herbert (1984)

The dream of the factory-made house

[…] The architectural profession has long been suffering from recurring bouts of the Henry Ford syndrome (Why can't we mass-produce houses – standard, well-designed, at low cost – in the same way Ford mass-produces cars?) encapsulated in a dream of a mechanically produced mass product which Siegfried Giedion once called the "Wohnford".[1] … From the Edinburgh iron founder C. D. Young's pronouncement in the 1850s that his three-story cast-iron houses "are susceptible of being carried out in ranges to any required extent, so as to form whole streets or squares",[2] to Buckminster Fuller's eulogy to technology in the Dymaxion house, designers have been seduced by the dream of the mass-produced house and entranced by its potentialities. […]

From the present-day view those engaged in the prefabrication of houses during the heroic period, the decades of the [nineteen] twenties and thirties, are usually regarded as being in the very vanguard of a new movement. Gropius and his colleagues are thus acclaimed as pioneers. In a sense they are – if the movement is defined in philosophical terms deriving from the principles of mass production enunciated by Henry Ford and is directed toward the expanding market of mass housing. But with slightly different perspectives we must acknowledge that there is a prehistory of prefabrication going back to the beginning of the nineteenth century or even earlier.

During the nineteenth century prefabrication (the manufacture of buildings in component form in workshops for transport to and ultimate assembly on a remote building site) developed from modest beginnings into an industry of quite substantial proportions.[3] From the joinery shops and iron foundries, the rolling mills and shipyards, from the specialized manufacturers of Britain, the continent of Europe, the United States of America, eventually even the countries of the colonial empires, there was a considerable outflow of buildings and structures in component form. These were destined for assembly and erection, occasionally in the home market, but predominantly in an astonishing variety of export markets embracing Europe, Africa, Asia, the Americas, and Australasia. There was an impressive range of products: hospitals and schools, warehouses and factories, market buildings and stores, churches and meeting halls, barracks and blockhouses, lighthouses and bridges, theaters and exhibition pavilions, offices and arcades, conservatories and farm buildings, gasworks and railway stations. They were produced in small workshops and large industrial plants employing a thousand men, businesses styling themselves variously as producers of iron churches, portable cottages, temporary buildings, which in sum constituted a new industry known today, but only since the 1930s, as the prefabrication industry. [...]

Then come the imperatives [of Le Corbusier]:

> *We must create the mass-production spirit. The spirit of living in mass-construction houses. The spirit of conceiving mass-production houses.*

If we examine Le Corbusier's proposals, we see that his main points are series or mass production; standardization in both the technical and aesthetic sense, with an ongoing search for standard types; modular and dimensional coordination; and the goal of "uniformity in detail and variety in the general effect". The call for industrialization that each point subsumes had already been clearly enunciated by Gropius in his memorandum of 1910. We cannot be sure if Le Corbusier had seen this document, although it must have been a subject of office discussion when he arrived at [the office of Peter] Behrens; certainly its spirit then reflected the Werkbund ethos that permeated the Behrens studio. Conceptually Le Corbusier adds nothing new to the basic formulations of Gropius. Yet ironically in the coming years it is Le Corbusier, not Gropius, who ignites the imagination of a generation of architects; it is not the reasoned arguments of Gropius but the stimulating force of Le Corbusier's visual images, and the evocative power of his prose, that leads the Modern Movement in its drive for industrialization and standardization.

The Bauhaus period

For more than a decade after the presentation of the abortive memorandum to Rathenau, Gropius did not return to the problem of the industrialized building process, nor did he again address the housing problem, until the 1920s. He was distracted from these earlier interests by momentous events on both a personal and national level. He entered into private practice,[4] whose main achievements, the Fagus Factory (1911) and the Werkbund model factory (1914), were buildings for industry rather than the exploitation of industry for building purposes. As the Werkbund exhibition opened in Cologne, World War I erupted, and Gropius, a serving officer in the German army, followed its cataclysmic course until the German surrender of 1918. Then, amid the economic and political chaos of the postwar era, Gropius became deeply involved in the politics of the emerging Modern Movement in architecture; he immediately plunged into what was to be his greatest challenge and his most enduring achievement, the establishment of the Bauhaus at Weimar in 1918.[5]

At Weimar, and subsequently at Dessau, the Bauhaus, while under Gropius's direction, did not deal substantially with the problems of prefabrication. Indeed it hardly dealt with any architectural problems, other than tangentially through the agency of Gropius's professional office … However, what the Bauhaus did concern itself with as basic were two issues central to the concept of industrialization generally. These issues were the relationship between art and industry and standardization of dimensional and typological norms. In other words, the Bauhaus continued to address itself to the two main themes of the Deutscher Werkbund.

Although Gropius's slogan, "Art and technology, a new unity",[6] was not uncontested, even within the Bauhaus,[7] the evolution in education and production from a handicrafts orientation to a fuller involvement in industry took place inexorably and reached its peak with the move from Weimar to Dessau. A marketing organization was established "in order to help establish contact between industry and the Bauhaus … [whose] function is to take care of the sale of prototypes to those branches of industry which can mass-produce from completed prototypes and market the product".[8] The designer's function, as Gropius came to see it, was as the designer of prototypes for industrial production. He had already spelled out his hopes in this direction in 1922.[9] Now, in a policy statement in 1926, he said: "The Bauhaus wants to serve in the development of present-day housing, from the simplest household appliances to the finished dwelling … The home and its furnishings are mass consumer goods, and their design is more a matter of reason than a matter of passion". The machine, Gropius went on, can provide the individual "with mass-produced products that are cheaper and better than those manufactured by hand".[10] It is evident that this policy statement is still informed by the spirit of the 1910 memorandum. The Bauhaus's theoretical and practical involvement in industrial mass production, although limited to domestic consumer products (textiles, furniture, light fittings, wall paper, heating stoves) was a significant preparation for a return to a concern with the wider issue of industrialized housing. It was an experiment in the sense of a limited learning experience of directing design to the specific tools and processes of industrial production. Out of this proving ground of trial and error there were lessons of a more universal nature to be learned.

In his statement on the principles of Bauhaus production, of 1926,[11] Gropius affirmed his belief that "the creation of standard types for all practical commodities of everyday use is a social necessity". Standardization was essential, he maintained, in order to exploit the effectiveness of the machine as a device for mass production of products "that are cheaper and better than those manufactured by hand". The drive toward standardization in the Bauhaus is expressed best by the attempt to crystallize a few, ideal, solutions to everyday problems. To this end the workshops of the Bauhaus were to be regarded, in Gropius's phrase, as "laboratories in which prototypes of products suitable for mass production and typical of our time are carefully developed and constantly improved".

There is no suggestion, at this stage, of regarding these industrially produced elements as part of a comprehensive system. Within one subsystem, as in the case of unit furniture designed by Marcel Breuer,[12] the interface between elements and the overall ordering principle of a modular grid governing standard sizes and variants might be seriously studied. This study of unit furniture followed on earlier experiments to standardize furniture notably by the Deutsche Werkstätten of Karl Schmidt, who had produced *Typenmöbel* [standardized furniture] as early as 1910.[13] In the Bauhaus, at this stage, this principle of integration and order was not extended in any systematic study to the overall system of dwelling and contents … Even Gropius and Meyer's proposal of the same year [1923] for Baukasten im Grossen, an adaptation of the concept of children's building blocks in terms of large-scale prefabricated elements, was an experiment that examined one partic-ular problem, that of variability within a standardized system[14] rather than the total problem of an overall system of prefabrication.

The architectural expression of this building system is, by the nature of things, cubic, boxlike, additive, austere … The Baukasten im Grossen project then may be considered not only important for its role in the history of prefabrication but also for its links – as an expression, if not a cause – with the subsequent evolution of a modern architectural style.

The first attempt to translate industrialized building from a theoretical postulate to a practical exercise came with Gropius's Reichsheimstättensiedlung, a housing scheme at Törten-Dessau built over the years 1926 to 1928 [*Fig. 42*].[15] The project was commis-sioned by the City of Dessau, and was based on extensive research both prior to and during the project, and sponsored after 1927 by the Reichsforschungsgesellschaft für Wirtschaftlichkeit in Bau- und Wohnungswesen, the national society for research into economic building and housing of which Gropius was an executive officer.[16] Planned for a population of 5,000, Törten-Dessau was carried out in stages over three years, 1926 to 1928, under Gropius's direction, and 316 of his two-story row-house units were constructed. These were of standard design, but with modifications from year to year, and were constructed of reinforced concrete and cinder blocks. Cross walls, beams, infill blocks, floors, and roofs were standardized and were manufactured on the site. Sand and gravel found on the site were suitable for concrete, and it was only necessary to transport cement and cinder. Materials were stored on site and moved by trolley along pre-laid tracks to casting areas between the houses, where the building elements were cast and cured, close to the point of use. When ready, they were hoisted by mechanical equipment and set in place by special teams. "The principle of work at the site was to reuse the same man for the same phase of the construction in each block of houses and thereby increase output", explained Gropius. "In order to insure the interlocking of the individual construction phases from the start of the rough construction and interior work, an accu-rate timetable was worked out, similar to the ones used by railroads".[17] The stages of construction were carefully articulated; the basic shell, for instance, was defined in four-teen constructional steps. A time chart was drawn out, and it provided both a visual survey of planned progress and a means of control. A photographic check on the progres-sive stages was maintained.

This project cannot be considered as prefabrication, nor did Gropius so consider it.[18] All work was carried out on the site, much of it by traditional means. Yet it is a form of industrialized building, with the organization of site operations as a whole work process analogous to the factory. We have here the concepts of standardization, mass production, specialization of labor, mechanization of operations, and rigorously planned organiza-tion of labor and materials, which are the characteristic features of the industrial system. Here these characteristics are transferred in a limited way, but with consistency, to the building process. Gropius is now exploring an alternative path to the industrialization of house construction to that adumbrated in his 1910 memorandum. In so doing, he is part of a wider movement; and Törten-Dessau must be seen as one of several significant experiments then being undertaken.

The first of these was Martin Wagner and Bruno Taut's Hufeisensiedlung, in Berlin-Britz, in 1925–27. As early as 1920 Taut had put forward, in *Die Auflösung der Städte*,[19] a system of house construction leading both to standardization and variability. In 1924 Taut wrote: "The problem of house-building today must be tackled along lines that are valid in industry for the production of machines, cars and similar objects".[20]

Now, in 1925, he approached this concept in practice, together with Wagner, tentatively and from a somewhat different point of view, as Gropius was soon to do at Dessau. Utilizing the cooperative building construction company organized by Martin Wagner, the two architects planned the comprehensive housing estate at Berlin-Britz in which they made use of large-scale mechanical equipment on the site such as traveling cranes, then an innovation, and set up a rigorous division of labor that involved specialization for specific repetitive tasks.[21]

A much more advanced scheme, built at about the same time as the first stage at Törten-Dessau, was initiated in Friedrichsfelde, Berlin, early in 1926.[22] Here a group of 31 three-story buildings was erected, using a pre-cast concrete system of construction based on the Bron patent, a Dutch method used for the first time in Germany. Pre-cast concrete construction was of course experimented with not only in Germany at this time but elsewhere in Europe. In addition to this Dutch system we also have notable examples in France, which, since [*François*]Hennebique and Perret Frères, had been a center of experiment and development.[23] The Bron system involved the casting of large story-height wall panels, complete with their windows and doors and all other components such as beams and slabs on the site, and then transporting them by a large overhead crane moving on tracks that straddled the line of buildings under construction.

This approach was developed even further in a large-scale housing scheme at Frankfurt, where at Praunheim in 1926–30 Ernst May built 1,400 dwellings.[24] Again rationalization and mass production were the key principles. Plans were limited to a few carefully thought-out types, and many details were standardized. *Frankfurter Normen* [Frankfurt guidelines], whose use was obligatory if a mortgage was desired, were laid down for doors, hardware, stoves, sanitary ware; the highly efficient "Frankfurt kitchen" [*Fig. 43*] was designed for standard use; and a construction system using prefabricated large-scale universal concrete panels, all 3.0 by 1.1 m, and pre-cast beams, was developed. This system was produced by the Frankfurter Montageverfahren, set up by May in a large empty machine hall, with the capacity to turn out a standard slab in three to five minutes, and was further promoted by the Reichsforschungsgesellschaft, the research organization in which, as we have seen, both May and Gropius were leading figures.

In all this activity we find the production emphasis in industrialization being shifted from the factory to the site, the technical solution becoming specific in relation to each project and no longer universal, and the conceptual solution to the housing problem moving inevitably from the private house (the main thrust of Gropius's memorandum to AEG in 1910) to mass housing, to the row houses and apartment blocks of the *Siedlungen* [*housing developments, ed.*]. The reasons for this expansion of scale may be found in the social and economic conditions of the times; in the magnitude of the housing shortage;[25] in the recovering economic situation of the post inflationary era and the considerable increase in housing investment; and in the highly volatile social and political situation, potentially threatening, for which housing was seen as an anodyne.

By the end of the decade, however, the pendulum had once more swung back. The promising economy of the late twenties became a casualty to world depression. Unemployment soared, and private investment in housing declined. Public spending on housing was cut drastically with the halving of the special rent tax, and new construction, as a consequence, was drastically curtailed.[26] The government, alarmed at the long-term prospects, began to encourage a return from town to country and the building of small cottages for workers. The back-to-the-land movement added an economic dimension to its inherent romantic appeal. After a few years of spectacular success the age of the

Großsiedlung was suddenly at an end and, with it, the brave program of experiment in the industrialization of mass housing, a program that, at Berlin, Frankfurt, and Dessau, was still in its infancy.

In the very heartland of the Modern Movement, with the most stalwart supporters of large-scale mass housing, interest in the one-family house revived, if indeed it had ever been abandoned. Perhaps it is nearer to the truth to say that work on the small house proceeded on a track parallel to that of the *Siedlung*. The design of the one-family house had always demanded a share of the architect's creative ability and interest disproportionate to its size but, psychologically speaking, commensurate with its significance as an environmental problem. The one-to-one relationship of family to house was close to the architect's heart, and even the advocates of apartment buildings often agreed with May's ideology that the ground-attached individual dwelling was the preferred solution to the problem of living. It was to be regretted therefore that it was not economically attainable, unless – and here the dream of the factory-made house reasserts itself – machine production could significantly reduce costs.

It is entirely understandable therefore that the problem of the prefabricated house continued to engage the inquiring spirit of Gropius and his colleagues at the Bauhaus, even at the time when they were involved in the large-scale Törten-Dessau housing scheme. The concept of the house as an industrial product was consistent with the Bauhaus philosophy; it epitomized at the most significant level, that of architecture itself, the Bauhaus vision of the unity of art and technology. It was fitting therefore that in December 1926, to coincide with the opening of the new Bauhaus building in Dessau, the Bauhaus was instrumental in erecting on a site at Törten an industrially produced house made of steel. […]

The next stage of [Gropius's] investigations was also limited to a case-study house, with no immediate practical consequences. This house was the widely publicized prefabricated house at the Weissenhofsiedlung, the Deutscher Werkbund model neighborhood of 1926–29, in Stuttgart.[27]

This house was one of two houses designed by Gropius for the exhibition, the other being only partially prefabricated. The fully fabricated house is a two-story structure, whose whole plan is reduced to a simple rectangle and whose form to an elementary prism. The term Gropius uses to describe its construction system is *Trockenmontage*, a dry assembly system. Upon an in-situ concrete foundation (the only exception to the "dry" rule, and a persistent problem in prefabrication), a steel frame is set up, consisting of Z-section uprights, channel section horizontals, and I-beams for floors. This frame is clad with asbestos sheeting on the outside, lignat sheeting (a cellulose fiber product) internally, and there are 80-mm-thick pressed cork slabs in between, as insulation, separated from each of the wall linings by an air space of 30 mm. The roof is of pre-cast cinder concrete blocks covered with metal. Floors are of wood, and ceilings of celotex sheets. Although the system resembles the Muche-Paulick system in some respects – the steel frame, the external sheet cladding, the insulation – it differs in its inner construction, which avoids such "wet" trades and in-situ work as plastering. The structural module is 1.06 m, to accommodate a standard doorframe. The planning module follows the structural grid, and all internal partitions are located on grid lines. It is apparent that Gropius has far greater understanding here of the design discipline that stems from the acceptance of a modular principle of structure.

The system remains elementary when broken down into its constituent components. Each steel section, wall lining, floorboard, and insulation slab is a separate industrially produced item. All have to be assembled on the site. There is no concept yet of subassemblies of entire building elements, such as wall panels or inner partitions, arriving ready-made from the factory. In other words, the system remains a primary one, with no clearly defined subsystems. It is essentially an open system, not dependent on the integrated output of a single production belt but incorporating a large variety of established industrial products of diverse origins. As a result the system is a flexible one, providing many alternatives, and responsive to change. The price paid is a considerable amount of site work, albeit of an assembly nature rather than construction in its traditional sense. But within these limitations we do have what was lacking in Gropius's memorandum of 1910, a coherent overall system. It is moreover the first system of prefabrication conceived and designed in all its technical details, if not by any architect, then certainly by an architect of Gropius's professional stature. The fact that this work was given great public and professional exposure, directly and in the press, because of its inclusion in the exhibition of the Weissenhofsiedlung, was of great importance to the movement for industrially built houses. Gropius therefore provided this movement with one if its first convincing practical demonstrations. He was to continue to be deeply involved in these empiric endeavors, as we shall see. But at this time his more important role was as the formulator and chief propagator of a coherent theory of industrialized building.

Notes

1 According to Werner Hebebrand, *Zur neuen Stadt*, Berlin, 1969, cited in Karin Wilhelm, "From the Fantastic to Fantasy", *Architectural Association Quarterly* 11, no. 1, 1979, p. 15, n. 22, Giedion had thus described Oud's housing at the Kiefhoek estate.

2 From the catalog of C. D. Young & Co., *Illustrations of Iron Structures*, c. 1856.

3 For an account of this development, in relation to Britain and its dependencies, see Gilbert Herbert, *Pioneers of Prefabrication: The British Contribution in the Nineteenth Century*, Baltimore: Johns Hopkins University Press, 1978; in the United States, see Charles E. Peterson, "Early American Prefabrication", *Gazette des Beaux-Arts* 6, no. 33, 1948; in general, Heinrich Wurm, "Vorgefertigte Bauwerke des 19. Jahrhunderts", *Technik-geschichte*, vol. 33, no. 3, 1966.

4 Gropius left Behrens's office in mid-June 1910 and entered into private practice in Berlin with his friend Adolf Meyer, also a former assistant of Behrens.

5 Gropius founded the Staatliche Bauhaus in Weimar in April 1919. He moved with the Bauhaus to Dessau in 1925 and remained the director until his resignation in February 1928.

6 The slogan: "Art and technology: a new unity", had first been put forward by Gropius in a lecture at the time of the Bauhaus exhibition in the summer of 1923. The next year, he included it in the draft of his "Breviary for Bauhaus Members". See Hans Maria Wingler, *Bauhaus*, Cambridge: MIT Press, 1969, pp. 69, 76.

7 It was not only opposed by the artist Feininger but also by the more technically oriented Muche. (Ibid., pp. 97, 113–4).

8 Ibid., p. 111.

9 In a circular to Bauhaus Masters on February 3, 1922, Gropius wrote: "It is possible that the work in the Bauhaus workshops will lead more and more to the production of single prototypes". (Ibid., p. 52).

10 Ibid., pp. 109–10.

11 Ibid., pp. 109–10.

12 Breuer, in 1925, designed unit furniture on the basis of a square modular grid of 33 cm. At no stage, however, was this module related to the architectural spaces containing the furniture.

13 According to Nikolaus Pevsner, *Pioneers of Modern Design: From William Morris to Walter Gropius*, rev. ed., Middlesex: Penguin Books, 1960, p. 35.

14 The drawings for the system had the following legend: "Lösung der gegensätzlichen Forderungen nach grösstmöglicher Typisierung (Wirtschaftlichkeit) und grösstmöglicher

Varibilität der Wohngebäude". Walter Gropius, *Apollo in the Democracy: The Cultural Obligation of the Architect*, New York: McGraw-Hill, 1968, p. 83.

15 The project was first reported by Gropius in "Der grosse Baukasten", *Das Neue Frankfurt* 1, no. 2, 1927–28, 25–30. The definitive account is Gropius, "Versuchsiedlung in Dessau", *Reichsforschungsgesellschaft für Wirtschaftlichkeit in Wohnungsbau*, vol. 7, 1929, pp. 1–136 (special number). Wingler gives a summary account in English in *Bauhaus*, 1969, pp. 126–7, 414–6, based in part on Gropius, *Bauhausbauten Dessau*, 1930.

16 This society was established in June 1927 in order to carry out research into sociological, economic, and technical aspects of housing. In addition to Gropius, architects such as Bartning and May were associated with it. For an account see Ronald Victor Wiedenhoft, *Workers' Housing in Berlin in the 1920s: A Contribution to the History of Modern Architecture*, London: Thames and Hudson, 1971, p. 111.

17 Wingler, *Bauhaus*, p. 414.

18 Gropius himself differentiated between the manufacture of building elements erected on site by mechanical equipment, such as pre-cast concrete panels, and pure factory-made systems ("Serienmässige, reinfabrikatorische Bau von Montagehäusern"). Gropius, "Der Architekt als Organisator der modernen Bauwirtschaft und seine Forderungen an die Industrie", in F. Block (ed.) *Probleme des Bauens*, vol. 1, Potsdam: Muller & Kiepenheuer, 1927.

19 See discussion in D. C. Anderson, "Architecture as a Means for Social Change in Germany, 1918–33", Dissertation, University of Minnesota, 1972, p. 56.

20 Cited in Wilhelm, "From the Fantastic to Fantasy", p. 7.

21 Discussed in Anderson, *Architecture*, p. 92.

22 For an account of this scheme see A. Lion, "Die ersten Wohnungsbauten aus Betonplatten in Deutschland", *Deutsche Bauzeitung*, August 15, 1926, 112–5.

23 See, for instance, Louis Perret's proposal, fully detailed and illustrated, for the design and erection of a prefabricated pre-cast concrete multistory block of flats, including pipe ducts, alternate allocation of floor spaces, stages of construction, and an explication of the advantages of prefabrication as a building system, which was published in Louis Perret, "L'Immeuble normalisé à montage rapide", *Arts et métiers* 94, July 1928, 241–6.

24 For an account of "Praunheim", see *Das Neue Frankfurt*, vols. 4–5, April-May 1930. See also Anderson, *Architecture*, p. 92; Wilhelm, "From the Fantastic to Fantasy", 7–8; Ferdinand Kramer, " Das Neue Frankfurt", *Architectural Association Quarterly* 11, no. 1, 1979, 44–9; Nicholas Bullock, "Housing in Frankfurt 1925 to 1931 and the New Wohnkultur", *Architectural Review* 163, no. 976, June 1978, 335–42.

25 According to Anderson, *Architecture*, p. 172, the housing shortage in Germany in 1920 was 1 million dwellings. The situation steadily deteriorated until 1924, when the major effort at rehousing commenced. By 1930 the cooperative housing movement alone had built 650,000 dwellings, housing 2,360,000 people.

26 This account is based on information in Mechtild Stratmann, "Housing Policies in the Weimar Republic", *Architectural Association Quarterly* 11, no. 1, 1979, 16–23; and Bullock, "Housing in Frankfurt", 335–42.

27 This house was exhaustively discussed by Gropius, "Siedlung in Stuttgart, Weissenhof", *Reichsforschungsgesellschaft für Wirtschaftlichkeit in Wohnungsbau*, vol. 7, 1929, 104–6, 133, 136, 144, 147, 148. In more accessible form it appears in H. and B. Rasch, *Wie Bauen?*, Stuttgart: Wedekind, c. 1927, pp. 142–3; and the Deutscher Werkbund publication, *Bau und Wohnung*, 1927, pp. 59–67.

A revolution in the woman's sphere
Grete Lihotzky and the Frankfurt Kitchen

Susan R. Henderson (1996)

The years between 1890 and 1918 were pivotal in the struggle for the rights of German women. The feminists of this radical period worked primarily within the political parties of the left, where they argued for total social and political equality for women. Women like Clara Zetkin, the leader of the women's branch of the Social Democratic Party, and communist Rosa Luxemburg were ultimately responsible for forcing the agenda of equality on their reluctant parties.[1] While the male majority of socialist opinion only recognized a "helpmeet" role for women, the leadership officially supported a limited progressive plank in the concept of separate-but-equal spheres. Thus, when the Social Democrats unexpectedly came to power in 1918, they fulfilled the political promises of the revolutionary days more from political embarrassment than conviction. The Weimar Constitution declared women to be the equals of men and granted them the vote.

Ironically, these legal victories were followed by a period of profound retrenchment within the feminist movement. The women who had achieved the great victories of the previous decade were entering their mature years, and young women, apparently feeling that political activism in the postrevolutionary period was passé, no longer joined the movement. As a result, the ranks of organized feminists fell precipitously in the Weimar years. Those stalwarts remaining faced overwhelming opposition, much of it from their own sex.

On the other hand, the introduction of new constitutional rights was paralleled by the advent of the New Woman, a complex and contradictory figure. Young women, it seemed, attempted to match the rising cult of modernity and their new freedoms with a model of contemporary woman of their own making. Their ideal was shaped by the images of women in advertisements and American films as sexually and socially liberated free spirits as much as by the growing numbers of young working mothers.

Even as an idealization, the New Woman was a phenomenon that seemed to portend a problematical fulfillment of constitutional promises. Though in her many incarnations she was not an overtly political being, in her style – the short hair and the "unfeminine" lines of her dress – and in her social behavior – working, often single, with no interest in a large family and little enthusiasm for homemaking – the New Woman embodied an independence and a modernity that was an anathema to the many self-appointed conservators of the home. [...]

This combination of factors – the veiled misogyny of the New Woman scare along with class and economic issues – resulted in a state policy called "female redomestication". With it, the effort to improve the lot of German women quickly narrowed its focus. Rather than striving to apportion women the same "basic duties and rights" as men, as the constitution promised, a loose coalition of interest groups sought to reassert the woman's sphere, at the same time bolstering it as the ideological equivalent to the male professions and distinguishing it from factory jobs, which were simply work.

As part of this program, state agencies and the liberal wing of the women's movement forged an ideal of the household as the "professional workplace" of women, one that needed the same studied research as the production line did for men. In one of the ironies of this history, they proposed that an aggrandized status for woman's sphere would be achieved by making it more like men's. The Weimar Republic became known not as an era when women joined the world of men, but as a time of modernization in the household sphere.

The strategic solution and promise of domestic reform was the elimination of drudgery. The "new housekeeping" took less time, was reputedly less tedious, and freed the housewife for more uplifting endeavors. […]

According to the experts, professionalization in the domestic sphere would be realized through simplified household design and the introduction of labor-saving appliances. Guided by the principles of scientific management that operated in modern industry, designers and reformers reshaped the household. Time and motion studies and the dogma of efficiency confirmed the efficacy of their work. The end product was quantifiable: an increase in productivity and less "wasted effort", resulting in a stable home life, a contented husband, and more and healthier children. Middle class women could now envision themselves pursuing housework with ease and grace, while working women could be expected to maintain two jobs with dexterity.

American women in the mid-nineteenth century had introduced the first reforms in household self-sufficiency and time-saving techniques. [*On the teachings of Catharine Beecher, Harriet Beecher Stowe, and Christine Frederick, see Spencer-Wood in Chapter 6, above, Ed.*] … Christine Frederick urged the same message in the twentieth century and became the torchbearer of scientific management in the home and the official founder of "domestic science". […]

Using time charts, meal plans, and inventories, women would become plant managers as Frederick rearmed the kitchen to become the woman's factory work station.

Frederick's works had a seminal influence in Europe. In Germany, the bourgeois women's movement embraced household reform in a campaign dubbed *Mütterliche Politik* (motherly politics). The ranks of the *Bund Deutscher Frauenvereine* (BDF) (Federation of German Women's Clubs), a coalition of bourgeois women's organizations, grew exponentially on the wave of patriotic sentiment and conservative reaction that followed the First World War. […]

In the modernist model, technology and the cult of rationalization were the methodological linchpins that ensured that progress was being made. And always in the back and forth between domestic scientists and architects was the presumption that the best social purpose of managerial and technical expertise was to bolster the existing model of the family and woman's role within it. These various currents effectively coalesced in 1927 at the Werkbund Exhibition in Stuttgart. Erna Meyer authored the household section, *Siedlung und Wohnungen* (*Settlement and Housing*), and displayed two demonstration kitchens of her own design, one in collaboration with architect J. J. P. Oud. Their kitchen became one of the best-known and frequently reproduced kitchens of the Weimar period. Though it is generally attributed to Oud with no mention of Meyer's contribution, at the time, its validity depended on the participation of an expert homemaker.

The New Frankfurt

Only twenty miles from Stuttgart, the city of Frankfurt am Main had gained international recognition for developing the social ideal of the *Neues Leben* (New Life) within a belt of modern settlements.[2] In 1927, the city architect Ernst May invited the thousands flocking to see the Weissenhof Settlement, the complex of modern housing built at the Werkbund Exhibition, to take tours of the new parks and housing estates of Frankfurt.

Ernst May viewed the woman's sphere primarily in terms of housekeeping. Its prominence in his program was largely due to the importance he accorded to *Wohnkultur* (domestic culture) in the program as a whole. The study of domestic life received unique emphasis in Frankfurt: May initiated research and published it in the journal *Das Neue Frankfurt* (*The New Frankfurt*), which extended from the household to the kitchen, from the consumer market in household products and appliances to the design of home economics classrooms. His design team studied psychology, material and product evaluations, and, of course, scientific management principles as applicable to the home. They scrutinized every aspect of household design to produce efficient and content housewives: color brightened the housewife's world, making housework more tolerable; enameled surfaces made for easy cleaning; and furniture with smooth lines eliminated dusting in hard-to-reach places.[3]

The modern Frankfurt household was to be based on this happy combination of a "scientifically" designed house and rationalized furnishings and equipment. While life in the new settlements offered the most complete array of conveniences, consumers living in older quarters could match some of its efficiency by purchasing items from *The Frankfurt Register*, a line of household furnishings by various manufacturers recommended by the municipal housing authority and published regularly in *Das Neue Frankfurt* and elsewhere.[4]

Modernizing efforts focused on the kitchen above all. The center of household labor, it became the professional "office" of the housewife and the subject of endless technological improvements. During the program's five years, several different designs were installed in the settlements, including Franz Schuster's all-purpose cupboard kitchen of 2.3 square meters and Anton Brenner's foldout model, both for use in small flats. Undoubtedly the best known project, however, was Margarete ("Grete") Schütte-Lihotzky's 1926 Frankfurt Kitchen [*Fig. 43*].

Margarete Schütte-Lihotzky

And, again, I was part of a group that stood up for certain principles and architectural ideas, and fought for them uncompromisingly.
Grete Schütte-Lihotzky on coming to Frankfurt in 1926[5]

Grete Lihotzky was the only woman architect on May's design team, but she gained international recognition for her design of the Frankfurt Kitchen.[6] Lihotzky was a socialist activist who dedicated her professional life to the embetterment of the working classes, beginning with her student days during the war.[7] After completing her studies at the *Wiener Kunstgewerbeschule am Stubenring* (Vienna School of Arts and Crafts), now the *Akademie für angewandte Kunst* (Academy of Applied Art), she began work in 1920 under Adolf Loos when he assumed the leadership of the Vienna Housing Authority. For the next five years, she worked for the city designing housing and new domestic facilities.[8]

With Loos, Lihotzky shared both a political outlook and an interest in the economizing strategies of rationalization – the reduction of living spaces to their smallest functional component. It was the same work that was being undertaken, more-or-less systematically, by professionals across Germany and Austria.

Ernst May and Lihotzky first met when May arrived in Vienna to visit Adolf Loos and to see his worker housing estates.[9] As Loos's assistant, Lihotzky acted as guide and emissary. She especially impressed May with her discussion of the work being done in household rationalization, an area May was concurrently exploring in the backwaters of Silesia, where he headed the *Schlesische Heimstätte* (Silesian Rural Housing Authority). In 1921, he asked her to become a contributor to the journal he was then publishing, *Schlesisches Heim* (*Silesian Home*). In the first article of her career, Lihotzky published a modular kitchen – a concrete, factory-assembled model, installed on site by crane, just as the Frankfurt Kitchen would be.[10] In 1925, May invited her to become part of his design team in Frankfurt, where he would direct one of the largest housing programs in the country.

Lihotzky's Frankfurt Kitchen became one of the most acclaimed creations of the Weimar housing programs.[11] In its gleaming metal surfaces, its high imagability, the specificity of its interlocking parts, its modular totality, and its largesse of technical fittings, it epitomized the transformation of everyday life in the modern age. Above all, Lihotzky's kitchen created an immediate photographic impact. Intricately coordinated and tightly configured, the Frankfurt Kitchen was the realization of the kitchen as machine.

Lihotzky's points of reference were far removed from the woman's sphere: ship galleys, the railroad dining car kitchen, and the lunch wagon.[12] As models, these commercial kitchens, developed to produce hundreds of food servings within short spaces of time, reduced domestic culture to a meals-per-minute equation. Thus, with Lihotzky, the kitchen came to full maturity as a piece of highly specialized equipment – a work station where all implements were a simple extension of the operator's hand. Its tiny plan of 1.9 by 3.44 meters was "scientifically" calculated as the optimal dimensions by which every movement was totally efficient and every operation coordinated.

Though several different versions were designed, including two larger ones for middle-class families with either one or two servants, the standard demonstration model was fully operable by one person. Continuous counter space encircled the worker/housewife; at the short end of the room was the cutting board fitted with its own small waste bin and directly lit by a window, and on one end a wooden plate holder, attached to the underside of the glass-faced cupboards, allowed wet dishes to drip in the drainage tray and sink below. Above, a row of hooks provided easy access to an array of special tools, and to the side eighteen labeled metal drawers stored flours and other staples. A square of open circulation space in the center of the kitchen was adjacent to the sliding door that led into the living room. Thus, as the housewife moved the meal to the table, her ambulatory movements were neatly confined to this small area. Light from the end window filled this cube of space, which Lihotzky freed from cabinets on the upper walls to create a feeling of spaciousness.[13]

Although in the rest of the house, plaster and enameled wood gave a homey quality to the scene, here (and in the bath) the machine age resonated in gleaming surfaces of tile, glass, and metal as Lihotzky experimented with new materials and simple, strong colors. The white of the plaster fabric on the walls and the ventilator hood reflected the light, while the aluminum sink, its splash tiles, and the aluminum storage bins were metal gray. The linoleum work surfaces, the stove top, and the tile floor were black, and the enameled cabinet fronts were a deep blue, a color that Lihotzky understood repelled flies.[14] [...]

There was yet another reason for the unique power of Lihotzky's design: among all the various proposals for kitchen modernization, hers was the only one that transformed the kitchen into a consumer product. The Frankfurt Kitchen was a factory-assembled module delivered to a building site and lifted into place by crane. Ten thousand were installed in the Frankfurt settlements alone, but individual units were also sold commercially as an item available from *The Frankfurt Register*. In contrast, Meyer and Oud's collaboration at the Weissenhof Settlement, or Georg Muche and Adolf Meyer's model kitchen at the *Haus am Horn* in Weimar seem fragmentary and unresolved.[15]

This conceptualization of the kitchen as a consumer product underscores the progressive commodification of household culture and the expansion of determinant market interests into the private domain. Lihotzky's design process depended on collaboration with industry – in this case Georg Grumbach, the manufacturer – and consultation with clients – women from middle-class *Hausfrauvereine* (housewives' clubs). May and Lihotzky regarded this collaboration as one of the singular successes of the Frankfurt Kitchen, a model of the ideal working relationship between the corporate structure and the welfare state:

> It is especially gratifying to see how closely in tune industry is with the practical concerns of the housewives.[16]

Thus the private patriarchy represented by the family was gradually given over to a public patriarchy dominated by industry and government. Increasingly, within the municipal housing programs like those headed by Ernst May in Frankfurt or Bruno Taut and Martin Wagner in Berlin, the lines between private and public were indistinct; indeed, the heroic nature of modernism depended on such comprehensivity, on a universal vision that overrode social and gender differences.

Lihotzky's kitchen was first demonstrated at Frankfurt's annual international trade fair of 1927, coincident with the Werkbund exhibition in Stuttgart. Like Meyer, Lihotzky set her kitchen within a larger context called *Die neue Wohnung und ihr Innenausbau* (*The New Housing and Its Interior*), an exhibit she designed that focused on Wohnkultur in the Frankfurt settlements.[17] Around a central display of Frankfurt housing and product samples, including a full-scale, concrete-plate model of a typical Frankfurt row house, photographs and models illustrated the work of Walter Gropius, Taut, Adolf Rading, Le Corbusier, P. Jeanneret, and Franz Schuster's work in Vienna and set the Frankfurt work in the larger context of the *Neues Bauen*.

Local housewives' clubs worked with Lihotzky to develop a subsection of the exhibit entitled *Der neuzeitliche Haushalt* (*The Modern Household*).[18] A didactic introduction to modern kitchen and household design, the display offered an array of technically sophisticated alternatives presented like museum period rooms. In conjunction with the exhibit, the housewives' clubs also sponsored a special lecture series addressing the practical arrangement of kitchen plans and living rooms; the labor-saving kitchen; the hygienic, problem-free bath; the latest in practical, inexpensive furniture; and the advantages of gas and electricity for a clean and efficient home.[19]

It was at this exhibit that the Frankfurt Kitchen first gained international recognition. In 1928, the French Labor Minister Loucheur proposed to purchase as many as 200,000 for his housing program, and it was such a critical success at the Stockholm exhibition of Weimar housing that within the year a Swedish version was put into production.[20] Subsequently, any professional critique of kitchen design in Germany was obliged to include it. Sociologist Ludwig Neundörfer discussed it in his professionally popular book *So wollen wir wohnen*, and in April 1929, the Department of Standards produced a special issue dedicated entirely to it, one that enlisted housewives' opinions. The reviews were generally admiring but mixed, even advocates of professionalization being somewhat alarmed by its absolute rigidity. Neundörfer, for example, criticized it as overdetermined, quipping "all you have to do is use it properly", and regretted that its small dimensions precluded two people working together.[21] Similarly, undazzled by its technical virtuosity, Erna Meyer complained that the Frankfurt Kitchen left too little to chance.[22] But even among critics, the Frankfurt Kitchen was widely acknowledged.

One of the chief innovations of the Frankfurt Kitchen and projects like it was the absolute embrace of modern technology. The postwar expansion of utility networks in Germany had already presupposed expanded private and commercial uses, and designers tended to view these opportunities as manifestations of progress. Largely as a result of the reciprocal relationship they developed with industry, new housing settlements became the proving ground for a commodity-oriented rethinking of the single-family home.

In Frankfurt, the expansion of utility networks began shortly before the war; the city enlarged existing power plants and built new ones. At the East Harbor, it added new electrical generating equipment to the gas plant and merged local servicing with the municipal heating network. By the war's end, the city had an energy production capacity far beyond the existing market, one readily filled by the introduction of new energy-consuming sources in the home.

Those who made the trip from the Weissenhof exhibition to visit Frankfurt were offered tours of the city's most famous settlement of Römerstadt (1927). Römerstadt offered not only a lush, modern version of the Garden City, it was the first completely electrified settlement in Germany. As its renown spread, appliance manufacturers used its image to advertise their products. Covering the opening of the settlement, the newspaper *Frankfurter General Anzeiger* saw the electricity as its most notable feature. It led with the headline: "America at the Gates: The electric stove. The permanently installed water heater. Everyone can hear the radio without an antenna".[23]

> The main thing is the electricity. Naturally, in the new current of 220 volts. In the new home it is "the servant girl who performs all tasks": it cooks the soup, grills the meat, bakes the cake, heats the bath and the cooking water – and, of course, lights the house.[24]

While the Frankfurt Kitchen was the locus for most of these innovations, the electrified communal laundry, complete with washers, dryers, mangles, and irons, was also hailed for its labor-saving potential. Lihotzky calculated that this facility, built in all the major new Frankfurt settlements, reduced a typical laundry day from fifteen to five hours.[25]

Frankfurt's public utility office was a major force behind these developments and actively pursued public education projects in modern housekeeping. Franz Tillmetz, the director of Frankfurt's utility division, sponsored a permanent exhibition space to display all the wonders of new kitchen technology. The scheme was implemented by architect Adolf Meyer, then one of the Frankfurt design team.[26] Meyer transformed the old shopping arcade "Kaiser-Wilhelm Passage" in the city center into the *Gaspassage*, a permanent forum for demonstrating the latest in gas appliances. Banking services located in the middle of the hall insured constant traffic through the space. Meanwhile, the passage itself was shorn of its nineteenth-century ornament in favor of Meyer's strong industrial forms, here concrete frames in a rectilinear grid. Heating equipment, including gas and electric ovens and stoves, hot water heaters, and various modern kitchen apparatus flanked the passage.[27]

Tillmetz's office also worked in cooperation with the local school authorities to create a model kitchen to occupy the front window. Designed by Lihotzky, it was used for daily demonstrations of the latest in cooking techniques. Courses in cooking and baking actively propagandized on the virtues of gas appliances.[28]

Schooling for the modern housewife

> The goal to rationalize housework will come to total fruition only in the next generation. The more we achieve widespread instruction within the Mädchenschulen on questions of labor-saving household operations, the more comprehensive this realization can become.
>
>   The most important teaching tool in domestic economy instruction is in the school kitchen. The transformation … of the kitchen … must be reflected in the arrangement of instruction rooms in which cooking is learned. Recently many labor-saving layouts and devices have been applied to the instructional kitchen. The entire planning of the space results from an analysis of the labor transaction.
>
> Grete Schütte-Lihotzky[29]

In the schools, redomestication began with the institution of required courses for young girls in domestic science and the allied household arts. In order to assert the new professional expertise over motherly example, classroom techniques, and indeed the classrooms themselves, replicated the aggrandized sphere of the domestic engineer, and the teacher gained a new authority in her command of a technology generally unavailable at home. The "laboratory" installed in new and remodeled schools around the country consisted of a complex of lecture, sewing, laundry, and dining rooms, with the kitchen as the centerpiece.

Initially, professionalization and hygiene were the two great themes in this pedagogical revolution, but as the German industrial economy slowly regeared toward peacetime production, training young women to be modern consumers gained equal importance. The kitchen classroom, like the *Gaspassage*, typically introduced the array of consumer choices; gas and electric appliances of German manufacture in a variety of models let the student appraise their particular advantages. In her design for the Professional Teachers' Institute in Frankfurt, for example, Lihotzky provided eight kitchen cubicles: five had gas stoves, two electric, and only one was of the old-fashioned coal-burning type. At the Varrentrapp School in Frankfurt, the electric cooker – a modern "miracle" – sat next to the teacher's demonstration table. Other more mundane designer features, like an overhead cupboard with its hanging utensils easy-to-hand, developed student awareness of the potentials of wise consumer choices in furnishing the home.

Lihotzky designed fourteen homemaking instructional facilities for the public schools of Frankfurt.[30] Her schoolroom kitchenette was a miniature version of the Frankfurt Kitchen, then being installed in new housing throughout the city. At Römerstadt, every unit had a Frankfurt Kitchen; at the same time, Martin Elsaesser and Wilhelm Schütte installed Lihotzky's kitchenettes in the domestic science "laboratory" at the local public school. A girl trained in the Frankfurt kitchenette could move into the new world of the Frankfurt settlements with full confidence in her modern homemaking skills.[31]

In comparing her kitchenette-equipped classroom with those in older schools, Lihotzky credited her analyses of "systematic labor" in generating the arrangement of utensils. The plan was a product of the path-diagram technique promoted by Frederick and Alexander Klein, intended to produce efficient circulation. Other contemporary examples like Otto Haesler's school at Celle, despite sharing the same consideration for light, cleanliness, and stylistic modernity, exhibited neither the precision of Lihotzky's kitchen designs nor the clear distinction between practice and study areas.[32]

At the Professional Teachers' Institute, designed by Max Cetto in 1928, Lihotzky was free to engender a more dynamic plan in the school kitchen and use the most deluxe equipment. In the rarefied air of this modern laboratory, the woman's sphere was characterized by sleek lines and sophisticated technology, and was peopled with uniformed girl-technicians in starched, white aprons. Reportedly, this rather complete embodiment of the domestic science ideal was greeted warmly by the school; it not only exemplified modern practice but lightened the work of the teachers as well. Above all, it was reported, the students engaged in their work more joyfully than before, since so little of their time was now given over to the drudgery of cleaning and maintenance.[33]

While the new housekeeping had important social objectives in better public health and hygiene, and fostered hopes for the rejuvenation of the German economy, the predominant message to students was imparted by the "scientific" atmosphere and a pedagogy dominated by rationalization concepts. The domestic science classroom represented a key moment in the challenge to women's authority over their traditional sphere.

Conclusion

> Recently, the subject of the house as workplace has again been taken up and researched, primarily by parts of the women's movement. On the one hand, one viewpoint advocates moving away from rigid house plans since they only strengthen stereotyped social roles. The champions of this position have thereby also viewed the Frankfurt Kitchen as a synonym for the oppression of the housewife, banished to the isolated kitchen, whereas (they believe) the new Wohnküche really can be liberating. Others, on the other hand, defend the opinion that the dissolution of the sex-specific practices of role behavior can in no way be expected from such an architectural/spatial transformation.
>
> Grete Schütte-Lihotzky, 1980[34]

Throughout her career, Lihotzky's belief in the importance of eliminating household drudgery through rationalization remained firm. In more recent times, she has proposed that with the reemergence of the "country kitchen", women have sacrificed efficiency and practicality to the whimsy of fashion and have left themselves with even a longer list of tedious chores.[35]

In the 1920s, however, the issue was much greater than a design fashion and concerned the technical and social transformation of an entire society. It is ironic that a politically engaged Lihotzky seemed to view the kitchen as the motor for change, rather than as a manifestation of larger redomestication issues.

Whether Lihotzky's Frankfurt Kitchen actually lessened the workload of the housewife is unclear – with women assuming jobs outside the home and becoming isolated in smaller family units, all indications are that their burden was growing rather than diminishing, and this in spite of labor-saving devices. At the same time, the professional dignity that the Frankfurt Kitchen was to confer on the role of housewife does not bear scrutiny.

The work station was not borrowed from the professional world, but from the factory, from labor characterized by single, repetitive, and mind-numbing operations. The notion of creativity was anathema to this model – it was for the manager/designer, the Taylorizer of the space, to blot out free action by delimiting an imperative "one best way". That this was not a situation compatible with household labor, with its myriad tasks and practices and varied member composition, was largely irrelevant to the overriding ideological notions of efficiency and scientism.

Indeed, household labor itself was revealed in the parallel made between the factory worker and the housewife to be a degraded process, as the persistent references to it as "drudgery" confirm. To all accounts, the "professional" housewife was admittedly committed to a life of grinding labor from which she could only be freed for brief moments through the application of techniques invented by authorities in the professional world. In the 1920s, there were few critics of this limited policy – few among the powerful women's groups, and fewer still within the ranks of the Social Democrats.

The backlash against the women's movement that followed World War I echoed this general erosion and devaluation of women's contribution to culture. At the same time, the positivist and male-defined architectural culture produced new artifacts of domesticity that fostered the development of the market in household goods. It also facilitated a new professional role for designers, one that might emerge only after the home had been newly consecrated as a professional realm and was largely shorn of its feminine attributes.

Lihotzky herself viewed this work primarily as part of a broader socialist enterprise, independent of any notion of feminist politics:

> My work was based on the idea of women who worked and not in cooking itself. I had never concerned myself with cooking in my life. Nowadays this is seen as feminist but it was not feminist at all.[36]

This last remark, that basing her research on women who worked was "not feminist at all", reflects the situation of would-be professional women in an era of limited options: either to embrace patriarchal culture as a New Woman, as Lihotzky did, or to support it from the vantage point of the helpmeet … Lihotzky's ideal, both personally and in her work on behalf of women, was clearly to reject the confines of home in favor of participation in the public world of men. Even backed by modernized domestic facilities, for most German housewives there was no such choice. The Frankfurt Kitchen may be taken as a kind of emblem of this cultural conundrum: a brief, if uncomfortable, resolution between women's culture and the ideal of a technological utopia.

Notes

1 On the history of the German women's movement see Barbara Aschoff-Greven, *Die bürgerliche Frauenbewegung in Deutschland, 1894–1933*, Göttingen: Vandenhoeck & Ruprecht, 1981, and Ute Frevert, *Women in German History. From Bourgeois Emancipation to Sexual Liberation*, trans. Stuart McKinnon-Evans, New York: St. Martin's Press, 1989.

2 Works on Ernst May and the Frankfurt housing program include Susan R. Henderson, "The Work of Ernst May, 1919–1930", Dissertation, Columbia University, 1990; and Christoph Mohr and Michael Müller, *Funktionalität und Moderne: Das Neue Frankfurt und seine Bauten, 1925–1933*, Cologne: Rudolf Müller Verlag, 1984.

3 The precepts of labor-saving house design came into currency in America before the war and were the subject of great interest among women's groups … [See] Dolores Hayden, *The*

Grand Domestic Revolution: A History of Feminist Designs for American Homes, Neighborhoods, and Cities, Cambridge: MIT Press, 1981, p. 200.

4 A supplement entitled "Das Frankfurter Register" appeared in each issue *of Das Neue Frankfurt* beginning with no. 1, 1928 through no. 4/5, 1931. There were seventeen entries to the register in all, including items such as the Kramer Oven, the Frankfurt Bed, Christian Dell lamps, Adolf Meyer lighting fixtures, and Bauhaus wall coverings and fabrics. May said the purpose of the register was to influence the public to purchase "good and price-worthy" household furnishings. Joseph Gantner, the editor of *Das Neue Frankfurt*, presented it as an overview of the best of mass-produced furnishings for the modern house.

5 Quoted from Burkhard Rukschcio and Roland Schachel, *Adolf Loos: Leben und Werk*, Vienna: Residenz Verlag, 1982, p. 575. Author's translation.

6 The only other major female contributor to the program was Grete Leistikow, who, with her brother Hans, designed many *Das Neue Frankfurt* covers. The photographer Grete contributed the images, and her brother designed the layouts. They produced nearly all the covers between no. 2 of 1929 and no. 9 of 1930. Though never directly employed by the Frankfurt Hochbauamt, Lilly Reich was also on the scene. [...]

7 Lihotzky is indeed an inspiring figure. She studied architecture against the best encouragement of her male teachers in Vienna and was the first woman graduate in her atelier. In 1930, she accompanied Ernst May in his voluntary exile to the Soviet Union, where she stayed to work for the state through 1937. In 1940, she left her work, then in Turkey, to join the Austrian resistance movement. She was arrested within weeks, narrowly missed a death sentence, and spent the subsequent four and a half years imprisoned. She continued an active career in Vienna through the 1970s and has since been working on various projects concerning her career and memoirs. Throughout her career Lihotzky remained a dedicated communist party member.

8 Lihotzky worked on *Winarskyhof* (today *Otto-Haas-Hof*) in Vienna in 1923. A collaborative effort, the coworkers included Peter Behrens, Josef Frank, Josef Hoffmann, Adolf Loos, Oskar Strnad, Oskar Wlach, and Franz Schuster ... Both Schuster and Lihotzky joined the Frankfurt team in 1925 and seem to have had a great influence on the evolution of May's modernist style. Rukschcio and Schachel, *Adolf Loos*, pp. 574–5.

9 Margarete Schütte-Lihotzky, *Erinnerungen aus dem Widerstand. 1938–1945*, Berlin: Verlag Volk und Welt, 1985, p. 13 ...

10 Grete Lihotzki [sic], "Einige über die Einrichtung österreichischer Häuser unter besonderer Berücksichtigung der Siedlungsbauten", *Schlesisches Heim* 8, August 1921, 217–22. Lihotzky's several articles for *Schlesisches Heim* were primarily concerned with kitchen design and garden huts. See her "Die Siedlungs-, Wohnungs- und Baugilde Österreichs auf der 4. Wiener Kleingartenausstellung", *Schlesisches Heim* 10, October 1922, 445–7; and "Wiener Kleingarten- und Siedlerhüttenaktion", *Schlesisches Heim* 4, April 1923, 83–7. Her resume, however, proves the bulk of her work to be concerned with other than explicitly women's design issues. Indeed, when she agreed to travel with May to the Soviet Union, one of her preconditions was that she not have to design any more kitchens.

11 For example, in the special RfG publication on kitchen design, Paul Mebes singled out Lihotzky's kitchen (for which he credited May) as the best solution to date for those without servants. Paul Mebes, "Gedanken zur Küchengestaltung", *Die Küche der Klein- und Mittelwohnung Reichsforschungs-gesellschaft für Wirtschaftlichkeit im Bau- und Wohnungswesen E. V. Sonderheft* 2, Group II 6, no. 2, June 1928, Year 1, 10. [...]

12 It was not a new idea. An earlier home efficiency expert, Catherine Beecher, was intrigued by the lunch wagon in the nineteenth century: ... [see] Catherine Beecher and Harriet Beecher Stowe, *The American Woman's Home*, Hartford, Conn.: Stowe-Day Foundation, 1975 [reprint of 1869 edition], p. 33. The parallels between the designs of Beecher and Lihotzky are also remarkable ...

13 Lore Kramer, "Biografie/Biography: Margarete Schütte-Lihotzky", in *Women in Design: Careers and Life Histories since 1900*, Stuttgart: Design Center Stuttgart, 1989, p. 165.

14 The best and most complete description of the Frankfurt Kitchen is in Grete Schütte-Lihotzky, "Arbeitsküche", *form + zweck* 4, 1981, 22–6.

15 Oud's Weissenhof kitchen appears in nearly all the major discussions of the kitchen after 1927. [...]

16 Lihotzky, "Die neuzeitliche Haushalt", 112. Author's translation.

17   "Vom neuen Bauen in Frankfurt am Main III: Ausstellung 'Die neue Wohnung und ihr Innenausbau' und 'Tagung der Baufachleute' am 28. und 29. März 1927", *Der Baumeister 25 Beilage*, 1927, 107.

18   Grete and Walter Dexel, *Das Wohnhaus von Heute*, Leipzig: Hesse & Becker, 1928, pp. 125–6. Descriptions of the exhibition can be found in Grete Lihotzky, "Rationalisierung im Haushalt", *Das Neue Frankfurt* 5, 1926/27, 120–2; and Werner Nosbisch, "Die neue Wohnung und ihr Innenausbau, der neuzeitliche Haushalt", *Das Neue Frankfurt* 6, 1926/27, 129–33.

19   Wilhelm Schütte, "Von neuen Bauen in Frankfurt am Main. II. Das Wohnungsprogram", *Der Baumeister*, 1927, 121.

20   "Das Programm Loucheur", *Das Neue Frankfurt* 9, 1928, 161; Lore Kramer, "Rationalisierung des Haushaltes und Frauenfrage – Die Frankfurter Küche und zeitgenössische Kritik", *Ernst May und Das Neue Frankfurt, 1925–1930*, exhibition catalog, Frankfurt am Main: Deutsches Architekturmuseum, 1986, p. 83. The French government suspended negotiations for the kitchen in 1929 when the intention to credit payment to a reparations account was called into question. "Frankfurter Normenbauteile für Frankreich", *Das Neue Frankfurt* 1, 1929.

21   Ludwig Neundörfer, *So wollen wir wohnen*, Stuttgart: Franckh'sche Verlagshandlung, 1931, pp. 55–6. Author's translation.

22   Erna Meyer, "Wohnungsbau und Hausführung", *Der Baumeister* 25, Supplement, 1927, 93.

23   "Die elektrische Römerstadt: Amerika vor den Toren", *Frankfurter General Anzeiger*, August 18, 1927. For more on the importance of electricity see Clara Mende, "Alte und neue Küchen", *Die Küche der Klein- und Mittelwohnung Reichsforschungsgesellschaft für Wirtschaftlichkeit im Bau- und Wohnungswesen E. V. Sonderheft* 2, Group II 6, no. 2, 8.

24   Ibid. Author's translation.

25   Grete Schütte-Lihotzky, "What is being done for the Women and Children in the new Residential Quarters and Colonies?", *Wohnen und Bauen*, July/August 1930, 158.

26   Adolf Meyer was an early partner of Walter Gropius's. They worked together on such projects as the Fagus Factory (1911) in Alfeld an der Leine and the Model Factory (1914) at the Werkbund Exhibition in Cologne. In 1926 he joined Ernst May's team in Frankfurt. His distinguished career was cut short by his premature death by drowning in 1929.

27   "Umbau der Frankfurter Gasgesellschaft in der Kaiser-passage. Frankfurt a. M.", *Das Neue Frankfurt* 5, 1928, 83–4; *Frankfurt am Main*, Frankfurt: Werner Rades, n.d., pp. 102–3.

28   Ibid., 84

29   Grete Schütte-Lihotzky, "Neue Frankfurter Schul- und Lehr-Küchen", *Das Neue Frankfurt* 1, January 1929, 18. Author's translation.

30   Lihotzky's kitchen cubicles were used at the Römerstadt *Volksschule*, at the *Eschersheim Ludwig-Richter-Schule* designed by Martin Elsaesser, and the *Niederursel Volksschule* designed by Franz Schuster. The semicircular plan of the *Berufspädagogischen Institut* was also repeated in the scheme for the unexecuted *Gewerbe- und Haushaltungsschule* designed by Elsaesser and Wilhelm Schütte (1930). On the three schools, see *Frankfurter Schulbauten 1929*; the *Gewerbe- und Haushaltungsschule* is published in *Martin Elsaesser. Bauten und Entwürfe aus den Jahren 1914–1932*, Berlin: Bauwelt Verlag, 1933, pp. 189–91.

31   She could also move back out into the work world: "One of the reasons for the stream-lining of the household was surely so that women could be moved into the factories on a moment's notice, just as the preoccupation with the health of the workers had military implications". Helene Röttiger, "Erfahrungen nach dem hauswirtschaftlichen Volljahr", *Die Frau* 32, 1925, 235. Author's translation.

32   Lihotzky, "Neue Frankfurter Schul- und Lehr-Küchen", 18. See Otto Haesler's school at Celle in N. L. Engelhardt, "Planning High School Buildings for Better Utilization", *Architectural Record* 66, 1929, 281.

33   Lihotzky, "Neue Frankfurter Schul- und Lehr-Küchen", 21.

34   Grete Schütte-Lihotzky, "Frauen, Räume, Architektur, Umwelt", *Beiträge*, vol. 4, Munich: Verlag Frauenoffensive, 1980, quoted in Günther Uhlig, "Margarete Schütte-Lihotzky: Textcollagen aus und zu ihrem Werk", *Um Bau* 5, December 1981, 31. Author's translation.

35   Kramer, "Biografie/Biography: Margarete Schütte-Lihotzky", 168.

36   Lihotzky, "Arbeitsküche", 26. Author's translation.

Modern architecture and politics in Germany, 1918–1945

Barbara Miller Lane (1994)

A view of society, and hence a view of politics, is always implicit in a building. When, however, buildings are paid for by political authorities, their political purposes become more obvious. There is, of course, no political position that is absolutely inherent in any particular architectural style: neoclassicism, for example, has been used by dictators and democrats, and the same is true for all varieties of modernism. Nevertheless, there have been many times in history when a particular style and particular kinds of buildings have been closely identified with a political regime and a political program. These connections between architecture and politics have then been imbedded in historical experience and in the collective memory: they have become part of the remembered content of architecture, and they affect our intentions about it and our responses to it.[1]

One of the most important of these moments took place in Germany from 1919 to 1945. Under the Weimar Republic, between 1919 and 1933, the artistic left set forth a vision of a new society, and a new, revolutionary political regime sponsored it. Unlike government sponsorship of architecture in other times and places, political patronage under Weimar focused mainly upon housing. After 1933, the Nazi Party overturned the government of the Weimar Republic, and persecuted or expelled most of the leaders of the modern movement, whose work had come to be seen as closely allied to the Republic. The Nazis then attempted to establish a new, ideologically appropriate, architecture of their own, without much room for modernism, and no room at all for those who had led the modern movement during the previous years. Above all, the Nazis stigmatized the kinds of housing that had been built in the previous era.

Modern architecture and the Weimar Republic

The origins of these events are many, but most important was Germany's experience during the first World War. In this war, Europe first encountered mass death on an immense scale. The characteristic, the most remembered, image of the war was the no-man's-land of the western front. Here, between the trenches, lay the dismembered corpses of Europe's young men, picked out at night by shell fire and searchlights. Though the theaters of war spread across Europe and the world, the experience of trench warfare took place almost entirely in Germany and France. And Germany lost the war. Young Germans, many architects among them, therefore discovered more painfully than anyone else the potentialities of early twentieth century technology. At the same time, they became convinced of the senselessness of the war, and the senselessness of the political values that had led to war. Trying to decide what realities he can hold on to, the front soldier of Remarque's novel *Im Westen Nichts Neues* (*All Quiet on the Western Front*) says "the world has become wobbly, like rubber".[2] Walter Gropius said something similar about the artists of his generation:

> Today's artist lives in an era of dissolution, without guidance. He stands alone. The old forms are in ruins, the benumbed world is shaken up, the old human spirit is

invalidated and in flux toward a new form. We float in space and cannot yet perceive the new order.[3]

The trauma of the war experience left expectations of, and desires for, a wholly new society – a "new order" – across the entire political spectrum, from right to left. The sense that a revolutionary change *must* come inspired the Spartacists and the USPD on the left, and the Frei Korps and the proto-Nazi völkisch movements on the right. Most earlier movements in politics and political thought were radicalized. This was true in the arts and architecture as well. For artists and architects, though, mere political change was not enough. "Not until the political revolution is perfected in the spiritual revolution can we become free", wrote Gropius in 1919; only then "will the people again join together in building the great art work of their time ... the freedom cathedral of the future".[4] I will return to this "freedom cathedral" shortly.

The actual political result of these expectations, the Weimar Republic, though revolutionary in the sense that it replaced an authoritarian with a republican form of government, was neither particularly radical nor very stable: it lasted only fourteen years. The Republic came into being as a result of revolutionary movements of the extreme left: workers' and soldiers' councils, the Spartacist movement, and the USPD. The Republic itself, however, was the creation of a middle-of-the-road coalition made up of the Social Democratic Party (SPD), the Democratic Party, and the Catholic Center: this was the "Weimar Coalition" that drew up the new constitution. The Republic was always vulnerable to anti-democratic political movements on both right and left, especially during the chaotic years of revolution and inflation (1919–23) and depression (1930–33). Gradually political leadership at the national level moved toward the right, although Social Democrats and Democrats continued in control in many municipalities and Länder.[5] But in the middle years of the Republic, from 1923, when the stabilization of the Reichsmark ended the inflation, until about 1930, with the onset of world depression, the Republic was quite stable, and during those years, the ideals of the Weimar Coalition set their stamp on many aspects of government, politics and policy.

The Weimar Coalition, and the Weimar Constitution itself, gave prominence to social legislation and especially to housing and urban needs. The principle that every citizen had the right to a sound dwelling within his means, enacted by the Prussian Landtag in 1918, was incorporated into the Weimar Constitution. Rent controls, state housing loans, the provision of public lands for new housing, state subventions for building societies, the creation of federally-supported housing research organizations such as the Reichsforschungsgesellschaft für Wirtschaftlichkeit im Bau- und Wohnungswesen, and the establishment of minimum standards for housing, combined to involve the government in the provision of housing to a degree never before experienced in Germany except in some municipalities.[6] The municipalities, too, enacted far-reaching housing reform measures, usually in collaboration with the gemeinnützige Baugenossenschaften and -gesellschaften. These reforms, at the federal, state and municipal levels, led to the construction of many new housing developments, usually at some distance from the city centers.

The patronage of the Weimar Coalition parties for public housing stemmed from various motivations. The Social Democrats wanted public housing above all for the workers, a policy inspired to a considerable extent by the trade union organizations. They [the Social Democrats and the trade union organizations] were particularly interested in buildings that would be quick and easy to build. The Catholic Center favored state-supported housing for large families. The Democratic Party, made up to a great extent of middle-class liberal intellectuals, the party of Theodor Heuss and Friedrich Meinecke, of "Vernunftrepublikaner", supported equal rights for all, often in the social as well as the political realm, and came to the support of public housing measures from this direction.

The Weimar Coalition, and especially the Social Democrats and Democrats, also supported new ideas in the arts, and freedom for individual artistic expression. It was often leading Democrats who were the principal patrons of modernism: Ludwig Landmann sponsored Ernst May's reforms in Frankfurt, Fritz Hesse nurtured the Bauhaus in Dessau, Adolf Hofacker advocated the dominance of modernists in the Weissenhof Siedlung in Stuttgart. The role of modernism in the arts was endorsed by state and federal cultural officials within the Social Democratic Party. And in many cases leading Social Democrats took public positions in support of modern art and architecture: they supported the Bauhaus in Thuringia, and the housing and planning programs of Bruno Taut and Martin Wagner in Berlin.

Nevertheless, the "fit" between the purposes of the Weimar governments (at the national, *Land* and municipal levels) and the ideas of avant-garde architects was never very complete. Government patrons wanted something new in architecture (something that appeared markedly different from architecture under the second Empire), that was obviously socially useful, but not too expensive, and quick to build. Above all they wanted a solution to the housing problem. The deferral of housing construction during the war, together with the hyper-urbanization necessitated by the organization of the economy for war, had created by 1919 an enormous housing deficit. When new housing construction began on a large scale, around 1924, a relatively small proportion of the new commissions was given to self-consciously "modern" architects.[7] But it was the work of the modernists that came to be most highly visible, associated in newspapers and journals and finally in the public mind with "the new Frankfurt", "the new Berlin", "the new Germany". The public fame of the "Neues Bauen" as representative of "the new Germany" probably reached its height in the 1927 Weissenhof Siedlung in Stuttgart, sponsored by the Deutsche Werkbund and the Reichsforschungsgesellschaft as a permanent exhibition of "the new dwelling". But for the architects who won these commissions, mass housing, and modernism itself, was part of a broader utopian program.

The vision of a new society among modern architects

The vision of a new society among the creators of the Neues Bauen was not stable either.[8] At its best it issued in the urbane environments created by May at Römerstadt, Praunheim, and Bruchfeldstrasse [*Figs. 44, 45, 46*], by Taut and Wagner at Britz and Zehlendorf, by Gropius and Meyer at Törten [*Fig. 42*], and by Mies and his international group of architects at Weissenhof. These Siedlungen represented a fusion of the utopian and often medievalizing ideas of expressionism, and the egalitarian and technological enthusiasm of "Neue Sachlichkeit" [New Objectivity]. These two movements were joined in the early and middle twenties; it is a mistake to see them as separate.[9] In the first years of the Weimar Republic, the future leaders of modernism participated in a series of "revolutionary" artists' organizations, such as the Arbeitsrat für Kunst [Work Council for Art] and the "Glass Chain". These same men, expressionists in the first years of the Republic, carried forward the ideas of the early Republic into the era of Neue Sachlichkeit, as members of the Ring [a pressure-group organized in 1924].

Gropius's exhortation in the first Bauhaus manifesto remains the best summary of the ideas of the Glass Chain architects at the beginning of the Weimar Republic:

> Architects, sculptors, painters, we must all return to craftsmanship … Let us all join together to desire, imagine, create the new building of the future which will be everything in one: architecture and sculpture and painting and which one day will rise up to heaven out of the hands of a million, the crystalline symbol of the new faith to come.[10]

Here and in other publications at the same time, Gropius also summoned contemporary artists to join in the "cooperative work" of "small fruitful communities, secret societies, brotherhoods … building guilds as in the golden age of the cathedrals!"[11]

The Bauhaus manifesto was accompanied by Lyonel Feininger's woodcut of a three-towered cathedral, lit by three stars, and, in the background, by searchlights [*Fig. 47*]. The cathedral, referred to in Bauhaus publications of the time as either "the cathedral of socialism", or "the cathedral of freedom", was described as crystalline. The faceted shapes of the building itself and the background, inspired perhaps by cubism, made a clear reference to current ideas of crystal, glass, and light. The image of the cathedral also referred to the idea of Gropius and others that the great "new building of the future" would be a total work of art, a Gesamtkunstwerk. And finally, the cathedral, like the manifesto which it illustrated, evoked the idea of the medieval building guild or masons' organization as a model for the society of the future.[12]

Gropius's and Feininger's reference to a crystalline architecture goes back … to Taut's Glashaus at the Werkbund Exhibition of 1914, to Scheerbart's *Glasarchitektur*, and, more immediately, to the publications of Taut right after the war. Already in 1914, Taut had called for the merging of the arts to form a great architecture,[13] and for a "glass architecture" that would banish hatred, war and aggression. In his *Alpine Architektur* of 1919, Taut proposed that modern technology, which had displayed its ability for sophisticated destruction during the war, should now take on constructive tasks, transforming the earth by beautiful faceted shapes of colored glass, lit at night by colored searchlights.[14] Soon thereafter, Taut wrote of new communities, shaped by glass, with new glass Volkshäuser [people's temples] at the center.[15] The idea of the "cathedral of the future" was linked with glass and crystal in the minds of Gropius and other Glass Chain architects. Feininger's cathedral was faceted, somewhat like a crystal. The visual implication of a faceted building can be one of breakdown, fragmentation. A crystal, on the other hand, is made up of many parts, or fragments, powerfully knit together by the forces of nature. Thus, the crystal, and crystalline forms, held the promise of reconstruction and regeneration too. And glass, especially colored glass, was for Taut and others like him an emblem of joy (in contrast to the pain of the war), but also a vehicle of quasi-religious mysticism, because of its reminiscences of stained glass in the medieval cathedrals.[16] […]

There is no reason to suppose that Taut, Gropius, Scharoun, Luckhardt, Mies or others expected in 1919 and 1920 to build cathedrals, or glass Volkshäuser, or glass monuments. Their manifestoes and projects were intended rather as exhortations – to other artists, to politicians, to "the people" in general, to turn away from the experience of war to the construction of peace. Taut moved quite quickly to the idea that "glass architecture" could be accomplished by color, in housing design.[17] After a brief experimentation with faceted shapes and stained glass in the Sommerfeld house, Gropius began to see the building blocks of the cathedral of the future in the housing modules exhibited at the Bauhaus in 1922.[18] Housing had always been an integral part of the architectural interests of both men, so the shift in their thinking was quite natural. In the housing designs that they and others executed during the middle years of the Weimar Republic, the mystical, communitarian, liberal, vaguely socialist, revolutionary, and utopian ideas of the first postwar years continued to be important. While none of these architects ever succeeded in reshaping a whole society – rather they designed and executed Siedlungen of limited size – they saw these Siedlungen as the microcosms from which the larger society would take its shape. In a few cases, they also began to develop a new view of the city.

The first large-scale housing developments executed by Taut in Berlin, together with Martin Wagner, show how the expressionist vision continued to be present during the era of Neue Sachlichkeit. The overall color schemes of the GEHAG Siedlungen at Britz and Zehlendorf (successfully restored in recent years), with their rust reds, brilliant yellows, strong greens and cobalt blues, give overall unity to each complex of dwellings. Each of these Siedlungen may thus be visualized as an abstract composition in color, as "glass architecture", and as a kind of a crystal, built up out of the individual housing units as modules. The housing units were often standardized in plan and located in apartment blocks. There was also a great deal of row housing. Widely spaced, separated by expanses of trees and grass, the rows of housing units at Britz framed or pointed to the central horseshoe, with its common green at the center. While the Horseshoe was not exactly a "Volkshaus", it served the purpose of focusing the entire organization of the housing development on a communal space.

The utopian ideas implied in modernist housing can be seen even more clearly in Ernst May's Siedlungen in Frankfurt am Main.[19] May's emphasis on the centrality of the community facility is clearly illustrated by the courtyard with Gemeinschaftshaus [community center] at Bruchfeldstrasse, where all the housing appears to focus on this central function [*Fig. 45*]. Within the Gemeinschaftshaus were meeting rooms, an office of the municipal welfare and health office, an electric-powered laundry, a kindergarten and an infant nursery. These facilities were especially useful to working women: it was assumed in Frankfurt that the new subsidized Siedlungen served both working men *and* women. The role of the "new woman" (working, participating in sport, voting, joining in the design of the new society) was made clearer in Frankfurt than in Berlin, although Taut had also heralded her importance in *Die Neue Wohnung, Die Frau als Schöpferin* (*The New Dwelling, the Woman as Creator*, Leipzig: Klinkhardt & Biermann, 1924). In Frankfurt publications, though, she is more often shown relaxing after work on an equal footing with her spouse [*Fig. 46*].[20]

Dwelling design at Frankfurt was thoroughly standardized and great effort was expended to achieve the minimal dwelling that would permit a good way of life, but would also hold costs down [*Fig. 44*]. To this end, Grete Schütte-Lihotzky and others on May's staff designed the famous "Frankfurter Küche" and "Frankfurter Bad" composed of prefabricated units that could be installed at the site.[21] Furniture was standardized and ingenious arrangements of slide-away or fold-up beds and tables made possible a maximal use of space. May also attempted to build some of the later units out of pre-cast panels, along the lines that Gropius was developing at Weissenhof and Törten.[22] Thus, the May Siedlungen were in one sense the most "rational" and technologically sophisticated of the Weimar Republic's new housing.

At Bruchfeldstrasse the "Volkshaus" held a laundry, kindergarten and infant nursery. There were community facilities in the other Frankfurt Siedlungen too – a communal laundry at Praunheim, for example. Another important aspect of communal life were the gardens and parks: public parks and walkways along the Nidda at Praunheim and Römerstadt, a sheepfold at Römerstadt, back gardens attached to all the row houses, and allotment gardens accompanying the apartment buildings and row houses. This land-scaping, together with some of the street layout, with its quasi-medieval, village-like feeling, was planned by Leberecht Migge from Worpswede. Migge had championed agricultural self-sufficiency in *Jedermann Selbstversorger* (Jena, 1916). Later he became a supporter of National Socialism.[23]

Beyond the village-like layout of each of the early Frankfurt Siedlungen, and linking them, were the great new boulevards, like Landmannstrasse, lined with balconied apart-ment buildings, connected to the center by municipally subsidized trolley systems. Although May had spent time working with Parker and Unwin in England, and although he had spent the early years of the Weimar Republic designing homestead buildings in rural Silesia,[24] he had grown up in Frankfurt, and his urban vision was influenced by Frankfurt's specific urban traditions: by the winding streets of the medieval quarters, by the great boulevards of the eighteenth and early nineteenth centuries, and by the sophisti-cated transportation systems of the late nineteenth and early twentieth centuries. The continuing presence of important medieval buildings in Frankfurt, such as the towers of the old walls, may also have served as an inspiration for the massing and spatial relation-ships in some of May's new Siedlungen.

Designed, like Britz and Zehlendorf, with overall patterns of strong color, the early Frankfurt Siedlungen demonstrate a complex vision of society and politics. They were full of inherent contradictions: Intended for the working classes (but not for the most part inhabited by them),[25] they were close to the soil, but mechanized in construction and offered a streamlined minimal design. They were arranged along broad boulevards but folded into a village-like street pattern, and were studded with parks and gardens designed to promote self-sufficiency. They were united by color and severe abstract pattern, yet they referred to a variety of medieval and early modern historical precedents, and focused (as at Bruchfeldstrasse) on a communal "Volkshaus". But it was perhaps just these contradictions – the sense that the best urban values of one of the oldest and proudest of German cities could be transformed under the rubric of the new aesthetic – that pleased the inhabitants so much.[26]

The Weissenhof Siedlung organized by Ludwig Mies van der Rohe and opened as a permanent exhibition of "Die neue Wohnung" in Stuttgart in 1927, displays many of the same features as the Siedlungen at Frankfurt and Berlin. Perhaps constrained by its curving, hilly site, its streets were winding and village-like, as at Frankfurt. The higher apartment buildings served as pivots to organize the arrangement of the whole. Color continued to be used, and for many participants, continued to reflect the ideal of a "glass architecture". But at Weissenhof color was no longer used as an organizing principle that would integrate the whole.[27] Gradually the modernist leaders were beginning to see white or off-white as purer and architecturally more forceful, as well as more practical and more rational. For Gropius at the Bauhaus, and increasingly for Mies and others as well, the use of large glass areas also came to substitute, in individual buildings, for color.

In all these buildings the home was seen as the microcosm of social change, as the source from which the "spiritual and cultural revolution" would come, and as the module from which the new society would be constructed – as the basic element in the crystal. It is no accident that along with the slogans the "new man", the "new woman", the "new Frankfurt", the "new Berlin", "the new Germany", it was "the new dwelling" – the leit-motif of the Weissenhof Siedlung – that was most often coupled with these other slogans.

Taut had written in *Die neue Wohnung* that the new dwelling must be full of sunlight, so that new, more honest, human relationships might take place within the home, establishing a model for a better society.[28] It is clear, even from the relatively few remaining interior photographs of Weimar housing, that the attention given by architects to large glass areas and to orientation to the sun was not just an issue of health. Interiors, such as that of Gropius's house at the Weissenhof, were flooded with light. Furnishings were spare and sparse, and rigorously geometric, inspired by the elements of interior design being taught at the Bauhaus.

These interiors have many implications for political and social views. Their light and spare quality was associated in Taut's thinking with honesty, and social equality. They had also shed the clutter of things associated with the interiors of bourgeois dwellings in the previous century, so they were seen as more spiritual, less materialistic, than the type of interior they had replaced, that was satirized in Taut's writings and other publications.[29] The design of their interior fittings was based on a simple geometry, on a minimalist aesthetic. The imagery of machine production was also very strong. The idea of good design for all, design that rejected bourgeois materialism, is related to both egalitarian and proletarian ideals. But Paul Tillich, writing about the interior design of these years, spoke of a religion of everyday life.[30] For many of the architects who had emerged from the utopian period after the war, simple geometric design, the new dwelling in all its parts, carried forward the search for transcendence, for the "new faith" that had been promised in the Bauhaus Manifesto. In a sense, then, the tables and chairs, the lamps and forks and spoons, designed at the Bauhaus and shown in contemporary pictures of bare, sunlit rooms – these were also seen as parts of the crystal, the building blocks and modules of the new society, the stuff of which the cathedral of the future would be made.

At their best, the new Siedlungen were a unique, humane accomplishment. They represented a pleasing but precarious balance, which might not, in any case, have lasted. Many writers have seen the later twenties and the early thirties as the time when modern architects decisively shifted away from their earlier ideas, in favor of "Zeilenbau" [*uniform-height slabs arranged in rows*], standardization, and rationalization.[31] Already at Georgsgarten in Celle, for example, and later at Westhausen in Frankfurt, in Hannes Meyer's projects and buildings, at Gropius's Siemensstadt, and in parts of the Haselhorst Siedlung in Berlin, row after row of stiff, same-looking buildings replaced the feeling of community that had been created by the varied massing, complex street layouts and coherent color patterns of the earlier Siedlungen. Some of this newer housing was higher, too: in the later twenties and early thirties, Gropius and others began to support the notion of relatively high-rise housing.[32]

Conceptually and formally, it was a short step from Zeilenbau to the monotonous and repellent urban architecture of Ludwig Hilberseimer, which Hilberseimer himself later described as "more a necropolis than a metropolis".[33] Mies too, in his designs for major urban complexes in the later twenties and early thirties – his project for the reconstruction of the Alexanderplatz in Berlin, 1928 and his Reichsbank competition entry of 1933 – produced grim and sterile slab-like buildings that offered no suggestion of any kind of community organization or unified urban vision. Some recent historians have seen these buildings as the result of the Weimar modern architects' excessive emphasis on technology, and have blamed them for all the ills of modern architecture in the late twentieth century.[34]

But it is by no means clear that either Zeilenbau, or the developing architecture of Hilberseimer and Mies, were the product of a sudden shift to ideas about standardization and rationalization, or to a new affection for technology. The interest of all the modernists in the use of technology for the purposes of social change, goes back at least to 1918.[35] Gropius was consistent in his belief that rationalization and technology were important only as means to the creation of the Neues Bauen and the new community.[36] The buildings of Taut and Scharoun, and the publications of Behne, May and Wagner, also continued the earlier synthesis.[37] But a shift in emphasis, in building and in writing, did occur toward the end of the decade, as the economic situation worsened. It seemed more and more important, especially during the depression, to present the Neues Bauen as both "scientific" and inexpensive.

Notes

1   See Barbara Miller Lane, "The Architecture of Nazi Germany", (review article), *Journal of the Society of Architectural Historians* 50 3, September, 1991, 325–8, and "Interpreting Nazi Architecture: The Case of Albert Speer", in Börje Magnusson et al. (eds) *Ultra terminum vagari: Scritti in onore di Carl Nylander* (Rome: Edizioni Quasar, 1998), pp. 155–69.
2   Erich Maria Remarque, *Im Westen Nichts Neues*, Berlin: Propyläen Verlag, 1928, p. 164.
3   *Ja! Stimmen des Arbeitsrates für Kunst in Berlin*, Berlin, 1919, p. 32.
4   "Baukunst im freien Volksstaat", in *Deutscher Revolutions-Almanach*, Hamburg, 1919, pp. 135–6.
5   The Social Democrats remained in control in Berlin and Prussia; Dessau and Anhalt. Elsewhere, as in Frankfurt, they continued to exercise great power through alliance with the Democrats.
6   Adelheid von Saldern, "Die Neubausiedlung der zwanziger Jahre", in Ulfert Herlyn et al. (eds) *Neubausiedlungen der 20er und 60er Jahre: Ein historisch-soziologischer Vergleich*, Frankfurt am Main: Campus Verlag, pp. 29–73, 32–3. See also Richard Pommer and Christian F. Otto, *Weissenhof 1927 and the Modern Movement in Architecture*, Chicago: University of Chicago Press, 1991, pp. 65–7; and Lane, *Architecture and Politics in Germany 1918–1945*, Cambridge, Mass.: Harvard University Press, 2nd ed., 1985, pp. 87–9, 117–23.
7   Perhaps five percent, according to von Saldern, "Die Neubausiedlung der zwanziger Jahre", 39. See also Albert Gut, *Der Wohnungsbau in Deutschland nach dem Weltkriege*, Munich, 1928; and discussion in Lane, *Architecture and Politics*, pp. 114–6.
8   I am focusing my discussion here mainly on Gropius, Taut, the Luckhardts, Häring, Scharoun, Mendelsohn, May, Wagner, and Mies. [...]
9   On the varying and even contradictory meanings of Neue Sachlichkeit as this term was used in the twenties, see Lane, *Architecture and Politics*, pp. 130–3.
10   "Programm des Staatlichen Bauhauses in Weimar", Weimar, 1919, in Hans Maria Wingler, *Das Bauhaus 1919–1933. Weimar, Dessau, Berlin und die Nachfolge in Chicago seit 1937*, Bramsche, 1962, p. 39.
11   Gropius in *Ja! Stimmen des Arbeitsrates*, pp. 32–3.
12   I am indebted for some of my interpretation of Feininger's woodcut to Karen Koehler, "'The Crystal Symbol of a New Faith' or the Shattered Symbol of an Old World?: the Bauhaus Manifesto and the Cathedral of the Future", paper presented at the Society of Architectural Historians Annual Meeting, Toronto, April, 1989.
13   "Eine Notwendigkeit", *Der Sturm* 196/197, February 1914, 174–5. See Vittorio Magnago Lampugnani, "From Fidus to the Early Bauhaus: a History of German Modern Architecture – part 2", *A + U* 260, May, 1992, 75.
14   Bruno Taut, *Alpine Architektur*, Hagen, 1919.
15   See *Die Stadtkrone*, Jena, 1919, and *Die Auflösung der Städte*, Hagen, 1920 ...
16   When the Glass Chain architects spoke of crystal, they always meant something that was glassy, but colorful; reflective *and* prismatic, in addition to being transparent ... On the history of the crystal as a symbol of regeneration, see Rosemarie Haag Bletter, "The Interpretation of the Glass Dream: Expressionist Architecture and the History of the Crystal Metaphor", *Journal of the Society of Architectural Historians* 40, 1981, 20–43.

17   Lane, *Architecture and Politics*, pp. 63–5; Pommer and Otto, *Weissenhof 1927 and the Modern Movement*, pp. 79–80.

18   Ibid., p. 76, and Winfried Nerdinger, *Walter Gropius*, Berlin and Cambridge, Mass.: A. Koch and Harvard University Art Museums, 1985, pp. 58–61.

19   On the Frankfurt Siedlungen in general, see Justus Buekschmitt, *Ernst May: Bauten und Planungen*, Stuttgart, 1963; Heicke Risse, *Frühe Moderne in Frankfurt am Main 1920–1933*, Frankfurt am Main: Societäts Verlag, 1984; Lane, "Architects in Power: Politics and Ideology in the Work of Ernst May and Albert Speer", in Robert I. Rotberg and Theodore Raab (eds) *Art and History*, Cambridge, Engl. and New York: Cambridge University Press, 1988, pp. 283–310; Ruth Diehl, "Die Tätigkeit Ernst Mays in Frankfurt am Main in den Jahren 1925–30 unter besonderer Berücksichtigung des Siedlungsbaus", Dissertation, Johann Wolfgang Goethe-Universität, Frankfurt am Main, 1976; and Susan R. Henderson, "The Work of Ernst May, 1919–1930", Dissertation, Columbia University, 1990.

20   The Weimar Constitution gave women the right to vote … Von Saldern, however (p. 72, n. ll), points out that a relatively small proportion of women in the new Siedlungen were actually employed full-time.

21   See Henderson, this volume. [...] See also Nicholas Bullock, "First the Kitchen – then the Façade", *AA Files* 6, 1984, 59–67.

22   *Das Wohnungswesen der Stadt Frankfurt am Main*, Frankfurt am Main: Das Neue Frankfurt, 1930.

23   Leberecht Migge, "Grünpolitik in Frankfurt am Main", *Der Städtebau* 24, 1929, 37–47 …

24   Henderson, "Ernst May and the Campaign to Resettle the Countryside: Rural Housing in Silesia, 1919–1925", *Journal of the Society of Architectural Historians* 61 2, 2002, 188–211. May also visited the United States in 1924, and, together with Martin Wagner, helped to publicize American building methods in Germany: see Pommer and Otto, *Weissenhof 1927 and the Modern Movement*, p. 64; and Martin Wagner, *Amerikanische Bauwirtschaft*, Berlin, 1925.

25   Despite May's efforts to get rents down by designing ever smaller and more minimal plans ("minimal housing" was the subject of the first conference of CIAM, held at Frankfurt in 1929: see *Die Wohnung für das Existenzminimum*, Frankfurt, 1930) neither May's nor any other of the modernist Siedlungen were ever within the reach of any but the most affluent skilled workers. Indeed, most of these Siedlungen were inhabited by members of the educated middle classes. See von Saldern, "Die Neubausiedlung der zwanziger Jahre", 36, 53–4; and Bullock, "Housing in Frankfurt 1925 to 1931 and the New Wohnkultur", *Architectural Review* 162, 1976, 335–42.

26   All these contradictory features of the Frankfurt Siedlungen were presented with pride in successive issues of *Das Neue Frankfurt*, in Ernst May and Fritz Wichert (eds), *Frankfurt am Main, 1926–1930*, (continued under different editorial leadership, until 1934; from 1932–34, *Die neue Stadt*, Josef Gantner, ed.). On the responses of inhabitants of the Siedlungen in Frankfurt, see Lane, *Architecture and Politics*, p. 103. On reactions to the new Siedlungen in general, see von Saldern, "Die Neubausiedlung der zwanziger Jahre", 67–70.

27   At Weissenhof, Mies had "encouraged the architects to adopt the 'lightest shade of color possible,' preferably an 'off-white.'" See Pommer and Otto, *Weissenhof 1927 and the Modern Movement*, p. 79. Taut and Stam used strong exterior colors, Gropius paler colors, and Le Corbusier experimented with primary colors in the interior. In Gropius's work of the later twenties, color was reduced to accents. See Nerdinger, *Walter Gropius*, especially pp. 74–83, and Mies's Tugendhat house was of course entirely white.

28   It should be remarked, though, that this focus on the new dwelling was not as socially radical as many writers have believed, since it reaffirmed traditional family structures. Working women were accommodated, but the family and home continued to be seen as the basic social unit, as they always had been among anti-socialist thinkers. See Pommer and Otto, *Weissenhof 1927 and the Modern Movement*, p. 73, and Nicholas Bullock and James Read, *The Movement for Housing Reform in Germany and France, 1840–1914*, Cambridge, Engl. and New York: Cambridge University Press, 1985, chs. 1 and 4.

29   Taut, *Ein Wohnhaus*, Stuttgart, 1927, and *Bauen: Der neue Wohnbau*, Leipzig, 1927. See also the poster "Wie wohnen", by Willi Baumeister, Staatsgalerie Stuttgart, Graphische Sammlung, published in Vittorio Magnago Lampugnani, "Neue Sachlichkeit: A History of German Modern Architecture – Part 3", *A & U* 261, June, 1992, 50–61, fig. 11.

30 Paul Tillich, "Kult und Form", *Die Form* 5, 1930, 578–83.
31 See the summary of historiography in Nerdinger, "Walter Gropius: Beitrag zur Architektur", in Hartmut Probst and Christian Schädlich (eds) *Walter Gropius*, Berlin, 1986, vol. 1, 47. See also Pommer and Otto, *Weissenhof 1927 and the Modern Movement*, p. 80, who describe the Weissenhof Siedlung as representing "a last moment before rationalist orthodoxy eliminated the early diversity of the new architecture".
32 On rationalization, standardization, and increasing height, see for example, Gropius, "Flach-, Mittel- oder Hochbau", in *Das Neue Berlin*, 1929, 75–80, and in *Moderne Bauformen* 30, 1931, 321–8; May, "Rationalisierung des Bauwesens", *Frankfurter Zeitung*, April 14, 1926; "Die Wohnung für das Existenzminimum", *Das Neue Frankfurt* 11, 1929, 209; "Einzelreihen- oder Doppelreihenbau", *Zentralblatt der Bauverwaltung* 36, 1929, 581. Zeilenbau was also thought to provide better access for all inhabitants to light, air and sun. On Taut's and Behne's criticisms of Zeilenbau, see von Saldern, "Die Neubausiedlung der zwanziger Jahre", 41.
33 Ludwig Hilberseimer, *Entfaltung einer Planungsidee*, Berlin: Ullstein Verlag, 1963, p. 22, quoted in Richard Pommer's excellent "'More a Necropolis than a Metropolis': Ludwig Hilberseimer's Highrise City and Modern City Planning", in Pommer et al., *In the Shadow of Mies: Ludwig Hilberseimer; Architect, Educator, and Urban Planner*, New York: Rizzoli, pp. 16–53. […]
34 See note 31, above. It could be argued, perhaps, that the influence of modernism after the war, and especially in America, on high-rise skyscrapers and regimented public housing, confirms these criticisms of modernism. But Franz Schulze has argued that high-rise architecture was an indigenous American phenomenon, and that Mies and others learned it from America, rather than vice versa.
35 An emphasis on standardization, rationalization, and the search for inexpensive, machine-oriented, building methods was present among modernists from the very start of the Weimar Republic. See Pommer and Otto, *Weissenhof 1927 and the Modern Movement*, pp. 61–71 and Lane, *Architecture and Politics*, pp. 59–61, 129–30. See also Walter Gropius and Gilbert Herbert, this volume.
36 Nerdinger, "Walter Gropius: Beitrag zur Architektur", pp. 48–9, 51–3. Nerdinger is entirely persuasive in seeing strong elements of continuity in Gropius's thought between 1911 and the late twenties and early thirties.
37 See for example, Adolf Behne, *Der moderne Zweckbau*, Munich, 1926; *Neues Wohnen, neues Bauen*, Leipzig, 1927; *Eine Stunde Architektur*, Stuttgart, 1928. May and Wagner, like Gropius, both wrote a great deal about rationalized and inexpensive building methods. But as editors of *Das Neue Frankfurt* and *Das Neue Berlin*, they stressed the broad cultural and communitarian importance of Neues Bauen.

Figure 42   Walter Gropius and the Bauhaus, mass-produced houses at Siedlung Törten-Dessau, 1926–8.

Figure 43
Grete Schütte-Lihotzky and
Ernst May staff, Frankfurt
Kitchen, 1927.

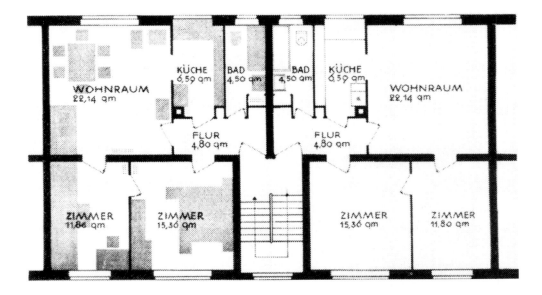

Figure 44   Plan of 3-room dwelling (65 sq.m.), Frankfurt am Main, Bruchfeldstrasse, 1926

Figure 45   Ernst May and staff, Bruchfeldstrasse Housing, interior court showing community center

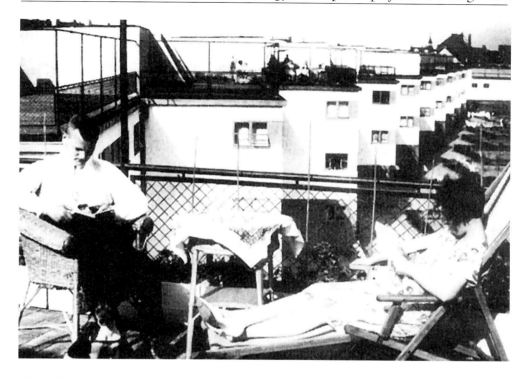

Figure 46   Couple reclining on the roof terrace, Bruchfeldstrasse Housing

Figure 47   Lyonel Feininger, frontispiece, *Bauhaus Manifesto*, April 1919.

9

Mass housing as single-family dwelling
The post-war American suburb

Here, extracts from social critic John Keats's famous and widely-read *The Crack in the Picture Window* of 1956 set the stage for the contempt for "tract houses" that has been so prevalent among American architects and social critics (Figs. 48, 49). But Levittown historian Curtis Miner, writing about the Pennsylvania Levittown, makes clear the attractions of these tiny dwellings (quickly built, inexpensive to buy, each with its own yard), and their architecturally innovative character (Figs. 50, 51). Levittown plans showed clearly a development toward the "open" living spaces of modern architecture. Notably, entrances have almost always shifted to the side to accommodate the automobile; hence the traditional front porch of rural and small town dwellings is absent. Art historian David Smiley, drawing on recent discussions of the American "culture industry", and working with plan books and magazine articles of the 1940s and 1950s, demonstrates that American consumers demanded houses that offered a mixture of traditional and modern components, and thus "participated in the reshaping of an authentic modernism" [Smiley] (Figs. 52, 53). Architect and landscape historian Georges Teyssot traces the history of American front lawns, which, in tract housing, came to be continuous, providing a new kind of shared public space while serving as a kind of substitute for a larger, more rural site (Fig. 54). Architectural historian Sandy Isenstadt analyzes the development of the "picture window" in the context of American views of nature and landscape, and suggests that the tract house reflects an American desire for "spaciousness", rather than the influence of any major modern architects (Fig. 55).

The crack in the picture window
John Keats (1956)

"If we don't like it, we can always sell it and get another one later on", [John Drone] said, completely unaware he was echoing her thought. "The way things are now, I guess we might even sell it at a profit. Where is this place?"

"Right here in Virginia", Mary [Drone] said.

Only a man of vision, a real-estate promoter, say, could have seen promise in that bleak stretch of pine barrens in Fairfax County which was to be the site of Rolling Knolls Estates. (Yes, Virginia, there is a Fairfax County, but Rolling Knolls Estates is a mythical development firmly grounded, unfortunately, on the shoals of fact.)

When the Drones arrived that next Saturday in a rented car, they found bulldozers squirming over the landscape, battering down the pines, leveling the knolls, churning the area into a level red-clay sea, out of which skeletal houses were rising. A concrete entrance-drive turned off the lane-and-a-half, high-crown, macadam county highway. It stopped abruptly beside the one completed structure – a gaily-painted little house bearing the legend "Sample Home – Office". Floodlights apparently illuminated it at night.

It was quite early in the morning, but cars were parked for half a mile along the county road, and the Drones found themselves part of a slowly-moving line of young house-hunters. In a dream they inspected the tiny building, stared at the strange, yet somehow uncomfortable-looking modernistic furniture, at the picture window which seemed to make the living room so much larger. There were two small bedrooms and a little bath, and the bath was part of a central unit which on one wall was the closet, on another the "utility closet" containing the hot-water heater and oil furnace, and on the fourth wall, the kitchen range and icebox. The living room was built in the form of a shallow L, with the short leg of the L leading off the kitchen and identified as the "dining alcove". There was an attic which could be expanded into a set of bedrooms, the salesman said, and the house was solidly based on a concrete slab.

"This unique foundation", the salesman said, "does away with the need of expensive excavation. It cuts down the building cost and is one reason why all this can be offered for the amazingly low price of $10,500".

Since the house was a simple rectangle with a steep-to roof, it was basically a Cape Cod design, the salesman said, summoning up mental pictures of sun, sand, sparkling surf and sea breezes. And, because of the picture window, borrowed from California ranch homes, and because of the one-floor plan which made it easy to add another room at a later time, the house was also something of a California rambler.

"We call it the California Cape Cod Rambler", the salesman said with quiet pride.

John Drone listened and nodded sagely, while the salesman showed Mary the Formica-topped sink, the tiny kitchen that was to make housework so simple, and the dining alcove so handy to the stove.

"Everything is easy to reach, right at hand", the salesman explained.

Truer words were never spoken, for a tall woman would have been able to stand in the dining alcove, reach into the kitchen, and prepare dinner.

John and Mary looked around at the neat, clean little house and compared it to their Jubal Early apartment. There was, of course, no comparison. For one thing, the house boasted forty-eight square feet more floor space than their apartment. It did not occur to Mary until much later that the one closet in the house was even smaller than the one closet at the Jubal Early Homes, nor did it occur to John that the expansible attic was simply an air space, and therefore could appropriately be used for summer bedrooms only by deceased, unrepentant sinners. Indeed, the only question in the Drones' minds was, How soon would the other houses be built, and when could they move into one of them?

It seemed there was a waiting list. There was also the matter of John's Veterans Administration loan guarantee, and to get a certificate of eligibility for such a guarantee took a certain amount of time, for Veterans Administration had its own waiting lists. Next, John would have to obtain a Veterans Administration appraisal on the house he was to buy, and next, to discover a bank or other lending agency willing to accept a four-percent mortgage.

"Don't worry", the salesman said. "'Bout the time you folks are ready to buy and move in, we'll have the house for you".

"And there's nothing down?" John asked, looking for some catch.

"Ab-so-lutely nothing", the salesman said. "Just the settlement charges. Of course", he said, "you'll have to pay for a credit check we'll make on you, and you'll have to pay the appraisal fee, and for the title search, guarantee and insurance, assume your share of the taxes, insurance on the house, and pay a few notary fees. But it shouldn't come to more than $275.76 – approximately, of course".

"Oh", John said.

He didn't make that much money in a month, and they were able to save nothing, but perhaps by relentless economy, by borrowing from Mary's mother, they could scrape together the settlement fee by the time a house was ready. And so, without further reflection, John entered his name. […]

Mary Drone's washing machine jittered to a stop, and as she lifted the lid to peel the wet wash from the inner walls of the contraption, year-old Kim burst into a desperate keening.

"Oh, God, what now?" Mary muttered, colliding with the opened door of an under-the-sink cabinet as she barged out of the tiny kitchen on her way to the dinette and the living room to the source of the wails.

She found Kim shrieking beside the open door of the utility closet – the space containing the hot-water heater and furnace. Kim, holding one red hand in the other, her eyes tight shut, seemed to be drawing a giant breath. Then she let it go, splitting the shattered air anew.

"She crying", Chip observed.

"Did you touch that hot-water pipe again?" Mary demanded, torn between tears and anger. She lifted the howling child to her shoulder, noticing as she did that it was time to change Kim's diaper.

The front door banged open.

"Yoo hoo! It's me!" Gladys Fecund called, hopping into the room. Then, seeing the maternal tableau, she asked with gay concern:

"Oh, dear, what's the matter now?" She patted Kim's tiny back. "Do oo hurt its 'ittle self?" she asked.

"She burned her hand on the hot-water pipe", Mary said. "I don't know why they didn't put insulation around those pipes".

"Do you want me to get some olive oil for it? Olive oil is wonderful for burns".

Mary, who as a matter of fact had been about to get a salve from the bathroom shelves, bit her lip and told Gladys never mind, it wasn't much of a burn. She just wasn't going to let another woman tell her how to care for a child. Mary put Kim down, went to the children's bedroom for a new diaper, and returned to find Gladys at the door again, ushering in her four children.

"It's not a bit nice out – for them to play", Gladys said. "It's going to rain. It's raining a little now".

"I really can't stay a minute", she said, pushing yesterday's papers off the couch to sit down. "Maybe just until the rain stops".

"Let me heat up the coffee", Mary said wearily, diaper pins in her mouth. "I'll be through in a sec".

She finished with Kim, stepped around the Fecund children squirming on the floor, and was well on her way to the kitchen when Chip's husky four-year-old cries of wounded rage beat at her ears.

"Gimmie! Mine!" her son was bellowing.

"Give it back, Jackson", Gladys was saying. "It's not yours. It's Chip's tricycle.. ".

Three hours later, 1:15 P.M., Gladys's minute was up and she packed off her brood and decamped. Mary hadn't the faintest idea what they'd discussed, since most of the conversation had necessarily been conducted in fits and starts, coming spasmodically through a thick field of children's static. Vaguely, Mary decided the morning's chat had increased her sum of knowledge to this extent: that three persons unknown to her, but known to Gladys, had their names down on waiting lists for new cars; that Mrs. Voter thought she was going to have a baby but the doctor didn't think so. Meanwhile, it was raining.

Mary moodily gathered up the coffee cups and the saucers with their ground-out cigarette butts, and piled the debris in the littered sink. She hadn't done the breakfast dishes because she'd picked up the children's room and had sorted the wash first thing after John left on his mile-long walk to the bus stop. She saw the washing machine lid open, started to close it from force of habit, and realized she hadn't taken the wash out to dry. Chip was making Kim cry in the living room, but Mary was beyond the point of caring much about it one way or another. The beds were unmade. Gladys's kids had scattered Chip's and Kim's toys all over the house. Mary sat on the high kitchen stool and, while waiting to wonder where to begin, lit a cigarette and watched the rain fall softly over Rolling Knolls. It gathered in little pools, and gullies formed, and the gullies became tiny canyons, winding through the sparse sod.

And then it was 1:30. Mary came out of her trance with a start. In three and a half hours, John would be home. She started to extract the wash from the machine, but remembered it was time for lunch. She fixed lunch for herself and the children, piled the dishes in the sink, put the children down for their naps, made the beds, put the papers back on the couch, returned to the kitchen and did all the dishes. It was still raining. It gave every promise of raining all day and all night, and Mary knew she wouldn't hang the wash outside. Once again, she'd have to string it wetly through the house.

Gloomily, she ran the first two clotheslines across the living room, fastening them to the nails John had driven in the walls for the purpose.

Adam Wild was buying his wife a dryer.

John should buy her a dryer. They could put it in – well, they couldn't put it in the kitchen. There wasn't room to turn around there, as it was. And certainly they couldn't put it in the living room; it would never fit beside the couch. Likewise, there wasn't space enough to put it in the dinette or in the bathroom, or in the children's room unless they bought the kids a two-deck bunk bed and got rid of the two sections of that old studio couch. So the dryer would have to go in what Mary called the master bedroom – just as it had in the Wilds' house. But, she thought, they wouldn't need it long – just until Kim was out of diapers, really. Then, she thought gaily, they could sell it!

The possibility of a little windfall cheered her immensely. Why money from the sale of the dryer could buy them …

A scalding, numbing pain shot through her right leg. Moving down the clothesline, intent on her work, she'd barked her shin against Chip's tricycle. It hurt like sin, and the tears came automatically. It was at this point the door shuddered open, and a wet wind blew in.

"Watch out, can't you see the wash is up? You're getting the wash all dirty", Mary very nearly screamed.

"I'm sorry dear", a familiar, monotonous voice said.

"Oh, it's you", Mary said.

And it was. John Drone, master of all he surveyed, had returned to his castle and to the bosom of his admiring family. He closed the door.

"Hi", he said brightly over the clothesline. "What's for chow?"

Now certainly it was not just John Drone's bumping into the wash that led Mary to shriek at him as he returned from his day at the office. The cumulative effect of Mary's rancid day led her to shriek, and although she never once allowed the thought conscious expression, somewhere deep inside her she knew perfectly well that the house she inhabited had helped spoil her day; that it was harming her marriage and corroding her life. In fact, the corrosive process was well under way, for the Drones had lived in their new rambler for six months. The pattern of their lives was bearing out the truth in Winston Churchill's dictum: "We shape our dwellings, and then our dwellings shape us".

The shape of Mary's dwelling was vile.[…]

Among the factors affecting Mary's emotional health were her memories of other living conditions. Like John Drone, she had spent part of her youth in one of the big, three-story family houses on Elm Street. It might have been difficult to heat and hard to clean, but it did have space. It sheltered three generations of a family; granted privacy to age, play space to youth, offered hospitality to guests and – in sum – satisfied the needs of every person dwelling therein. If the Elm Street house seemed a somewhat inefficient machine for living, nevertheless *living* is what happened within its comfortable walls. Compared to the big houses on Elm Street, the California Cape Cod Ramblers of Rolling Knolls were so many ill-made, inefficient machines for insufficient existence.

Of course, when John and Mary needed living space at war's end, they were in no position to pick and choose. They had to take what was offered within their means, and, as we've seen, a combination of ruthless circumstances had thrust them into Rolling Knolls. On the day Mary inspected the sample house, her first thoughts were that the one-floor plan and general compactness would make housework quick and simple. With the drudgery done, the rest of her day could be a lilting song.

"It only takes two hours to clean", the salesman had said.

Well, it might have, at that. Despite the foul design of the rambler that didn't ramble, Mary's day might have been considerably more bearable than it was – but only if her house had not been built in Rolling Knolls. In development life, other forces than the shape of the specific dwelling help to shape the dweller. To see these forces at work, let's visit Mary again, on a clear day. Let's visit her on a sunny Tuesday:

The dishes are dry, the beds are made, the children fresh and scrubbed, and woman's work is done until lunch and naptime. It is one minute before 11 A.M. What lilting air will Mary sing? Specifically, what is there to do with her free time in Rolling Knolls?

She can take her children out to play. Only this, and nothing more.

And where will she take them?

Why – to the front lawn, of course. There is no other place. There is no park in Rolling Knolls or near it. […]

American sociologists… have begun to make notes on development life.

"In these communities", said Harold Mendelsohn of American University's Bureau of Social Research, "there is no real privacy. The women become involved in one another's emotional problems. And, unless they take part in community activities, they are apt to be shunned and lead incredibly lonely lives, surrounded by the endless monotony of the development itself and trying to cope with the monotony of their children and house-work. Their husbands may drive off to the city each day, but for the women, there is no escape. It's often a tough life for them..."

On our clear, sunny, sample Tuesday, Mary Drone, desperately bored by toilet-training, deeply discouraged by the daily attack on the inadequacy of husbands (a matter she knew only too well), retreated into her tiny house and forced the warped door shut. Mechanically, she prepared lunch and put the children down for their naps. Moved by subconscious need, she lowered the venetian blinds across her picture window to shut out the ghastly view of the mirror of her empty life staring at her across the treeless, unpaved street. Listlessly, she picked up a woman's magazine and began to read. The story concerned a gay, bubbling young creature who, whilst engaged in her secretarial duties, fell in love with the darkly handsome stockroom clerk, not knowing he was really a director of the firm working in disguise.

Later that afternoon – after romance had culminated in marriage, a stately Long Island home and, therefore, happiness – Mary's children woke from their naps and Mary began to think of supper, John's return, and her evening. Supper would have to be something simple; she'd make it out of cans.

Mary took down a prepared spaghetti dinner from her shelves, a can of peas, and, casting around for dessert, decided on mixed fruit. She emptied the spaghetti and the peas into saucepans, put the saucepans on the stove; emptied the canned fruit into a bowl and put the bowl in the refrigerator. Then she ran a tub of water and, leaving the door ajar so that she could keep an ear out for her children, shed her shirt and bluejeans and bathed.

Then she dressed in perfume, blouse, silk stockings, tweed skirt, dark shoes and brace-lets. In three other Rolling Knolls estates, three other chatelaines underwent similar ablu-tions. Gladys, Maryann, Jane and Mary were making themselves fresh and lovely, not for their husbands, but for each other, for Tuesday evenings meant bridge at Maryann's. Indeed, when Buster, Lawrence, Henry and John returned to their manors, their ladies denied them the perfunctory, sterile, connubial kiss – "You'll smear my lipstick", each lady said.

Four husbands did the dishes and put the children to bed, while four wives that evening confused Goren with Blackwood and discussed babies and the characters of absent neighbors. And once again, Mary felt caught in a deadly trap.

The real nature of the trap was this: Mary had fallen into a world of women without men. She had moved into a house that could never be a home. She had moved into a neighborhood that could never be a community. She had moved into a strange, new way of life – a kind of life America had never seen before.

In the old Elm Street neighborhoods of this nation, both in small towns and large, the houses are each different from the other, inhabited by people of differing ages, occupa-tions, dress, manners and beliefs. The houses, sufficient to meet the needs of each of their inhabitants, are centers of family life. In Elm Street, one housewife did not necessarily meet – or even necessarily know – all other housewives on the block. For one thing, the housewives of Elm Street might well have little in common.

In Elm Street the husband still plays more or less his traditional role in the family. Thus, an Elm Street wife's social acquaintances were often those introduced by her husband. Going out of an evening most usually meant going to the home of a husband's friend. And, while the husband's friends might share a common business neighborhood, they most certainly did not share a common residential neighborhood, much less the same residential block. Therefore, an Elm Street woman's social life was apt to carry her to different parts of town, to homes different in detail from her own. Such variety lent richness and perspective to her own life.

In Rolling Knolls, however, there were no husbands. Men were overnight lodgers or casual weekend guests. They left each morning for the city, which satisfied their need for change and the society of others. When they came home at night, they were apt to want to stay there. They seldom visited their business acquaintances socially, for such acquaintances might well live miles away in some other development at the far end of the metropolitan sprawl. Husbands came to Rolling Knolls as they came to the Jubal Early Homes, to eat and sleep, and when they left in the morning, ownership of Rolling Knolls passed by default to a matriarchy.

Thus the women assumed the lead in development social life. They introduced their friends to their husbands. And, because they were all anchored close to their inadequate houses by the needs of their young children, their friends were necessarily one another. Their friendships were recruited entirely within their neighborhood block. Thus, the lawn date in the morning. Thus, the bridge date in the evening. And always with the same people – people horribly like themselves.

It is a hideous travesty to suggest the housewives of Rolling Knolls had "something in common" when the bitter truth is they had only too much in common. It is true that the dwelling shapes the dweller. When all dwellings are the same shape, all dwellers are squeezed into the same shape. Thus, Mary Drone in Rolling Knolls was living much closer in every way to 1984 than to 1934, for she dwelt in a vast, communistic, female barracks. This communism, like any other, was made possible by destruction of the individual. In this case, destruction began with obliteration of the individualistic house and self-sufficient neighborhood, and from there on, the creation of mass-produced human beings followed as the night the day. The job was done quickly enough, for Rolling Knolls dwellers mostly came that way. […]

Days dragged into weeks, and weeks into months and just when it seemed nothing could save the Mary Drones of this land from a fate worse than life, television burst upon America. It came to Mary Drone thus:

She was sitting moodily in her kitchen, listening to the racket of her jittering washer, when the phone rang.

"We've got one!" Jane Amiable's excited voice said. "Could you and John come over tonight to watch it with us?"

That evening, after the children were abed, John and Mary knocked at the Amiables' door.

"Shhh!" Jane whispered sharply. "Come in. Find a seat".

In wonder, the Drones entered the Amiables' house as though it were a cathedral. They made their way into the darkened room, bumped into the huddled forms of the Fecunds, and sat gingerly on the rug. At the end of the room, perched on a table, was a tiny box with a picture window. From time to time the picture blurred, or streaked, or skipped merrily up and down, but Henry Amiable squatted constantly below the altar, reaching up to turn the dials, and the show – such as it was – went on.

It reminded John Drone vaguely of something he'd seen once, as a child. He couldn't place it, but the memory he could not name persisted. He was seeing vaudeville once again, this time in microcosm.

During the evening, John and Mary took turns at leaving the room to return to their house to make sure the children were safe and soundly sleeping. And each time they left or entered the Amiables' house, Jane would say "Shhh".

From this point, things moved briskly. Television even penetrated the fastnesses of Colorado, appeared in the lonely mountain cabins of Tennessee's Cumberland Plateau. But chiefly it swept through the developments, and every house in every Rolling Knolls everywhere acquired a television set, and every television set developed expensive maladies, and a whole new realm of larceny unfolded before the glittering eyes of appliance dealers and repairmen. But that is another story – perhaps another book. We're concerned here with what television did to the lives of development dwellers.

For the first months, a wondrous change was wrought. From seven P.M. on, in those days, there was not a light to be seen in Rolling Knolls. Every house but one was dark, and apparently uninhabited, but within every shuttered living room there gleamed a feeble phosphorescence, a tiny picture flickering in that glow. Over the bewitched community there swelled a common sound. Sometimes it was a fanfare, introducing a commercial. Sometimes it was the thin, jubilant cry of a studio audience in New York wildly cheering a contestant who had just announced he came from Detroit, Michigan. Sometimes it was the dumb-de-dumb-dumb musical signature of a period crime piece. But whatever the sound, it was a common sound, rising above the darkened houses, for everyone watched the same shows.

There is no question that TV, as television became known, at first lifted a great burden from the rounded shoulders of Rolling Knolls housewives. To their infinite joy, they discovered the Twentieth Century's built-in baby-sitter. […]

Mary Drone, unwilling and unable to endure the chatter of her neighbors, at first took refuge in her television set. She became aware of Arthur Godfrey. For weeks she watched, fascinated by the rasping chuckles, the strange silences, the peculiar blankness of that pudgy face, the earnest pleadings to buy this and that. She laughed when the studio audience laughed, and at the end of the program she couldn't remember what in the world had seemed so funny. She had the eerie feeling Godfrey was boring, but she watched and listened anyway.

Then came the morning when she gave it up and emerged in defeat to the lawn date.

"I've been watching TV", she apologized to Jane Amiable, completely unaware this was also Jane's first morning out in weeks.

"I kept watching and watching, waiting for something good to come on, and afterwards I wondered why I'd been watching".

"My mother wrote that she'd just got a set", Jane said. "She asked me to tell her what the good programs were, but it turned out we'd been watching the same channels. Do you know what the good programs are? Everybody says there are some good programs on TV".

"I think", Mary said, "they must all come on after we're in bed".

"One thing", Gladys Fecund said, "TV is a godsend for the children. I turn it on while I'm fixing supper and the kids sit there out of the way and watch".

"No child", Mrs. Voter ruled, "should be allowed to look at the things they have on the children's programs".

This latter point was soon resolved by the children themselves. For months, little glassy eyes stared blank and vacant. Then the kids gave it up as a bad job and went back to play, but not before some special conditioning had set in. It remained for three-year-old

Jackson Fecund to sum it up. He was sitting in the living room when the venetian blinds suddenly came rattling down across the picture window.

"Mommy!" he wailed, "Mommy! The picture's lost!"

Picture window paradise

Curtis Miner (2002)

> *To the outsider, Levittown, Pennsylvania, seems like a vast mirage, a city of 4,000 spanking new ranch homes where a short year ago were acres of corn and wheat ...*
> Ladies Home Journal, March 1953

On Monday, June 23, 1952, John and Philomena Dougherty packed up their belongings, and with their two daughters in tow, drove from a government housing project in northeast Philadelphia to their new home in the suburbs. Their journey was not unusual. Between 1950 and 1960, twenty million Americans moved from cities to suburbs. It was the largest internal migration in the country's history, outstripping many times over the legendary westward migration of the nineteenth century. What made the Dougherty's journey newsworthy – and, in retrospect, historic – was their objective: to be the first official residents in the new development of Levittown in Bucks County.

If mass suburbs were postwar America's new frontier, then Levittown, Pennsylvania, was its California. By the time it was completed in 1958, its 17,311 dwellings spread out over four municipalities in lower Bucks County and housed seventy thousand people, a population which made it equivalent to Pennsylvania's tenth largest city. It was, and remains to this day, the largest self-contained planned community constructed by a single builder in the United States. The scale and scope of the project insured that it would become synonymous with suburbia itself, a prototype of residential development frequently criticized but widely imitated.

The community was the brainchild of Levitt and Sons, a New York building firm founded in 1929 by attorney Abraham Levitt (1880–1962) along with his two sons, Alfred S. (1912–1966), an architect, and William J. (1907–1994), who would become its president, principal salesman, and unofficial spokesman. During the 1930s, the firm erected custom-designed houses in suburban Long Island for upper middle class clients. But during the early forties, as the country mobilized for war, Levitt seized the opportunity to build for a new market. In 1942, the firm won a federal contract to supply twenty-two hundred defense housing units for the U.S. Navy in Norfolk, Virginia. The project would forever change the way the company did business.

The need to manufacture houses quickly and efficiently compelled Levitt to think outside the box. Under the traditional system, skilled contractors fabricated one house at a time using craft techniques and traditional building materials. The result was sturdily built and often distinctively designed homes, but the process was slow and expensive. Levitt responded by imposing a factory-like rationale. With a scientific eye for efficiency, Levitt broke down the twenty-six-step construction process into more than one hundred separate tasks. Laborers, working in teams, would then be assigned just one step in the construction process, which they would repeat at each house site. As one crew finished its assigned task, it was quickly followed by another crew, which would perform its task before moving on to the next structure.

William Levitt, known to nearly all as Bill, characterized the operation as an assembly line in reverse. Instead of the product moving down the line to workers' stations, employees and materials moved down the line to a stationary product. The system reduced Levitt's dependence on skilled labor and the amount of time normally devoted to planning out the next task, even if it may have made house building less than stimulating ...

Levitt's defense housing contract provided a trial run, but it was not until after World War II that his mass production techniques were really put to the test. Returning veterans and their new families had spiked demand for new housing, but the key ingredient was federal support for home financing. By offering long-term, low-interest mortgages and reducing or eliminating down payment requirements, the Federal Housing Authority and, later, the GI Bill of Rights, helped place homeownership within reach of millions of Americans. Buoyed by these incentives, Levitt in 1947 set about transforming four thousand acres of potato fields on Long Island into the largest mass housing development of its day.

The scale of Levittown, New York, and the speed with which it was built – less than five years – made Levitt a household name. *Time* pronounced him "the Henry Ford of Housing" and placed him on its cover. In 1950, his firm built one out of every eight houses in the United States. His product was also a huge hit with consumers, particularly the veterans who lined up to purchase (or in some cases rent) one of the seventeen thousand units, many of them identical Cape Cods, for the unheard of low price of $7,990.

Levitt and Sons was not without its critics. [...] Publicly, Levitt refused to yield ground. "What would you call the places our homeowners left to move out here? We give them something better and something they can pay for". Privately, however, Bill Levitt recognized some of the development's shortcomings, particularly its visual monotony, and vowed to improve.

Levitt got his chance in 1951. Early that year, the United States Steel Corporation announced plans to build a massive steel plant along the banks of the Delaware River in lower Bucks County. Located twenty-two miles north of Philadelphia and just over the river from Trenton, New Jersey, lower Bucks was situated between two major urban centers, making it an ideal location for residential growth. The arrival of a major new employer only sweetened the proverbial pot. Even before U.S. Steel officially broke ground for its new Fairless Works, Levitt agents began buying land for the second development. By summer, Levitt had closed deals with between one hundred and fifty and one hundred and seventy-five individual property owners, mostly farmers, for more than fifty-seven hundred contiguous acres in Falls, Bristol, and Middletown Townships and Tullytown Borough.

By buying the property "in one fell swoop", as he called it, Levitt now had the chance to create not just rows of houses but a coherent community. "I'm not here just to build and sell houses ... I want to build a town to be proud of", Levitt told the *New York Times*. He also announced his intention of offering a wider range of housing styles and types, within the limitations imposed by his factory system. "Levittown, Pa., will be the least monotonous mass housing group ever planned in America", Levitt boasted shortly after announcing plans, in July 1951, for a planned community of sixteen thousand dwellings.

At the center of Levitt's new development was the individual neighborhood. The final master plan designated forty of them, ranging in size from fifty-one to nine hundred and ninety houses, with a mean size of four hundred and thirty. Every three to five neighborhoods were massed together to form a "master block", roughly a square mile area bounded by parkways and greenways. Although the goal of Levittown was to house people, and lots of them, by arranging them around thoughtfully landscaped neighborhoods drawn to human scale, Levitt hoped to create the look and feel of a garden community. Interior streets were intentionally curved to impede traffic and break up sight lines. Access to each neighborhood was limited to three or four entrance points. Although dependent on the automobile – an estimated ninety-seven miles of roads crisscrossed the community – project architect Alfred Levitt was determined that Levittown not be tyrannized by it. Houses on perimeter streets were to face inward, away from the main thoroughfares such as the Levittown Parkway, which would be softened by intensive landscaping. For the same reason, the company also banned property owners from erecting fences, which it deemed unsightly and unnecessary.

At the same time, Levittown's maze of curvilinear streets and irregularly shaped sections demanded some sort of internal logic to help orient both visitors and residents. Each neighborhood was bounded by a single circumferential, or "collector", street, which provided access to all interior streets and carried the same name as the neighborhood. In turn, each interior street began with the same first letter as the neighborhood. Stonybrook Drive, for instance, encircled the Stonybrook section and provided access to interior streets such as Sunset Lane, Summer Lane, Shadetree Lane, and so forth. (Levitt purposely did not use the term "street" because of its urban connotations, and substituted "lanes" in the eastern sections and "roads" in the western sections.) The alliteration was especially important during the early years, when street signs were virtually the only features that distinguished one section from another. One pioneering resident joked, "even cats and dogs can't find their porch stoop".

A critical component of Levittown's master plan was its schools. Levitt and Sons allocated land for elementary schools near the center of each master block so that no child would need to walk more than a half-mile to school or cross a major intersection. Levitt also hoped that by having children attend schools in their own neighborhood, residents would be encouraged to identify with other families in their section. Little League baseball fields, swimming pools, and "parklets" were distributed according the same logic. If parents sent their children to the same school and enrolled them in the same leagues, they would be more likely themselves to socialize with one another, creating a harmonious and, therefore, attractive environment.

When it came to shopping, Levitt and Sons took a more centralized approach. Based on its experience in New York, the firm concluded that neighborhood-based commerce disrupted traffic patterns and produced unsightly commercial strips. For Pennsylvania, architect Alfred Levitt proposed a main shopping center near the development's southeastern perimeter. The center's location shielded neighborhoods from traffic and congestion while at the same time making it accessible to shoppers who did not live in Levittown. When completed in 1955, the sixty-acre Levittown Shopping Center, later renamed Shop-A-Rama, was the largest outdoor pedestrian mall east of the Mississippi, with space for ninety stores – many of them chains such as Sears, Food Fair, Kresge's, McCrory's, Grants, Woolworth's and Sun-Ray Drugs – and six thousand automobiles! During its heyday, the shopping center served as Levittown's ersatz Main Street, hosting activities such as "Miss Levitteen" beauty pageants, Easter parades, and political rallies (for John F. Kennedy and Richard M. Nixon, among others).

The heart of the Levittown plan was the single-family house [*Fig. 50*]. Between 1952 and 1958, Levitt and Sons built six different models, from the modest, two-bedroom, misleadingly named Rancher – actually a modified Cape Cod, first introduced in 1953 – to the more upscale, three-bedroom Country Clubber, introduced in 1952 but updated and expanded two years later. Borrowing from Detroit's automakers, Levitt offered each model in several different styles and model years. Differences in styles were limited almost entirely to rooflines, carport placement, foundation angles, and colors; interior floor plans were largely identical. Moreover, Bill Levitt believed that his system of mass production required he build only one house model per section. The result, particularly in the early sections, were entire neighborhoods of nearly identical Levittowners, Ranchers, or Country Clubbers.

Levitt trusted most consumers would willingly trade individuality and conventional building elements for cost-effectiveness and efficiency. By substituting radiantly heated concrete slabs for basements, Levitt estimated he saved consumers a thousand dollars per dwelling. (Like most of Levitt's initiatives, this controversial shortcut caught on; by 1952, twenty-five percent of all new houses were being constructed on slab.) He also reduced costs by introducing cheaper and more efficient materials – bamboo curtains, for instance, instead of solid closet doors, and specially designed countertop boilers – always bought in bulk. At the same time, Levittown models featured efficient, built-in, all-electric General Electric kitchens [*Fig. 51*], contemporary, open-plan interiors, and large picture windows, all in an effort to appeal to young, brand-conscious, style-savvy homebuyers. A popular – and cost saving – option in many two-floor models was an expandable attic that could be finished into a third bedroom or rumpus room for the kids. Each house also came fully landscaped, a feature of which family patriarch Abraham Levitt, an amateur horticulturist, was particularly proud.

Levitt billed it "the most house for the money". Judging from demand, consumers agreed. During the opening weekend in December 1951, more than thirty thousand people converged on the company's main sales office, conspicuously located opposite the train station at Tullytown, to inspect one of Levitt's three sample houses. During that first weekend alone, the firm sold more than three hundred units and averaged sixteen hundred sales over the next several months. By May 1952, the first year's production of single-floor Levittowners had been completely sold out. Priced at an astonishingly low $9,990 and requiring little – if any – money down, the Levittowner was a bargain.

Construction began in April with an army of laborers and subcontractors working with military precision. Cement was mixed on site to expedite the pouring of concrete slabs. Materials, such as framing lumber, were pre-cut in a main lumber yard, transported by truck to each house site, and bundled "combat loaded" with pieces needed first on top. Bill Levitt saw no advantage to prefabricating wall sections or roof trusses, since they would have been too bulky to transport. Other supplies, including aluminum-framed windows, asbestos siding, and kitchen appliances, arrived by train at the central warehouse – at the rate of forty-eight carloads a day – where they were unloaded and then re-packaged in house-sized amounts for delivery to the job site. During good weather, crews worked seven days a week. The result was a dazzling production record. At its peak, workers were turning out houses at the rate of fifty per day – or one house every sixteen minutes! By April 1953, four thousand houses had been constructed; by mid–1954, another five thousand units had been added. "We are not builders", Bill Levitt declared. "We are manufacturers".

Newly completed sections looked eerie, almost like ghost towns, but they never stayed vacant for long. After Levittown's first twenty families arrived on opening day, Monday,

June 23,1952, new families arrived at the rate of five hundred each month. Most were married couples under the age of thirty with children less than five years old. Newcomers came with "a suitcase in one hand, and a baby under the other", quipped one observer. In 1953, less than four percent of Levittown's population was over the age of forty-five.

The crush of school-age children placed a considerable burden on local school districts charged with the task of educating Levittown's youth. With new sections opening on weekends, it wasn't unusual for school administrators to encounter between one hundred and fifty to three hundred new faces waiting to register on Monday mornings. To keep pace, schools taught students in two shifts and cobbled temporary classrooms from trailers. Parochial schools also felt the crunch. St. Michael the Archangel, Levittown's first and largest Roman Catholic congregation, postponed construction of its church building for a full decade so that funds could be dedicated to the building of an elementary school and, several years later, a major addition.

Youth had its advantages. During the fifties, Levittown supported three little leagues, thanks in part to the community's ample supply of baseball fields, and probably played some of the most competitive pre-teen baseball in the country. In 1960, a team from the Levittown American League, competing in the first nationally televised championship game, won the Little League World Series in Williamsport. Levittown also attracted national publicity by becoming the first community in the United States to name a school in honor of Walt Disney (1901–1965). The popular animator and producer flew to Levittown for the dedication ceremonies and was greeted by throngs of residents. Original stills from popular Disney Studios films, among them Dumbo and Sleeping Beauty, donated by Disney himself, still decorate the school's classrooms.

With its green lawns and tidy, single-family homes, Levittown during the fifties seemed to conform to every postwar suburban stereotype, both good and bad. Following policies first established on Long Island, Levitt and Sons refused to sell directly to blacks. As a result, Levittown did not receive its first African American family until 1957, and then only after considerable local resistance. In other important ways, though, Levittown belied popular perceptions of suburbia. A 1953 survey revealed Levittown to be actually more diverse than the rest of the country, attracting Catholics and Jews in numbers disproportionate to their representation in the general population. Levittown's assortment of churches and synagogues – built on land donated by the developer – testified to this religious melting pot.

As one might have expected, about half of Levittown's residents in the fifties were drawn from metropolitan Philadelphia, but in some of the community's blue-collar sections it was estimated that as many as twenty-five percent of residents came from the anthracite region of northeastern Pennsylvania. Sections bounded by Falls Township, home to U.S. Steel's Fairless Works, attracted a number of transplanted steelworkers from western Pennsylvania, prompting one journalist to remark that Levittown might be better called "Kensington North, Trenton South, or McKeesport East". Levittown's proximity to Trenton and Philadelphia also attracted a significant number of white-collar commuters, including a small group of academics attracted to what they perceived to be a grand social experiment in mass housing.

Neighborhoods reflected the diverse ethnic, religious, and social mix in the early years. One resident recalled that it was not uncommon to find college professors living next to truck drivers, "a mix of Bronx born Jews and Nanticoke coal crackers". By the late fifties, though, Levittown was becoming increasingly stratified by income level. In the Stonybrook section, for instance, white-collar professionals began moving to more upscale neighborhoods within Levittown or out of the area entirely, while blue-collar families tended to stay put and build additions. This sort of class structure was virtually embedded in Levittown's design: since specific housing types tended to be clustered in particular sections, it stood to reason that particular sections – and by association, townships – would attract residents from similar socio-economic backgrounds. Middletown Township, home to forty-five hundred Levitt-built dwellings and all of its Country Clubber models, became regarded as the "status" township; Bristol Township, meanwhile, with nearly eighty-four hundred mostly lower cost homes, defined the other end of the continuum.

In 1954, partly in an effort to congeal [sic] these growing rifts, a group of concerned residents began calling for political incorporation. Although Levittown represented the largest single voting bloc in Bucks County, its power was dispersed over four separate municipalities, each with its own ordinances and regulations. By incorporating, Levittown residents would theoretically be able to cohere around common concerns and more effectively address issues affecting all homeowners. The effort was defeated, though, largely because residents of Falls Township were understandably reluctant to share their ample, U.S. Steel-infused tax base. [...]

Fifty years later, Levittown's borders are still the same, but much within its boundaries is not. Disparate renovations, additions, and modernizations have transformed its rows of indistinguishable houses into a patchwork of personalized dwellings, many completely unrecognizable from their original incarnation as Levittowners or Ranchers or Jubilees. Large enclosed shopping malls have rendered the once thriving Levittown Shop-A-Rama obsolete, reducing it to little more than a white elephant. While an impressive number of baby boomers have remained in Levittown to raise their own families, children no longer crowd its sidewalks. Perhaps the most impressive aspect about today's Levittown is not so much how it continues to distinguish itself from the rest of the country, but how much the rest of the country has come to resemble it. Thanks to the Levitts, and the thousands who pursued their dream of homeownership, suburbia is no longer a crabgrass frontier but a settled way of life.

Making the modified modern

David Smiley (2001)

[...] This essay explores the values and concerns among the array of people and institutions that produced and consumed the culture of the home. How were ideas of the home affected by the vast cultural apparatus through which they were represented? Conversely, what role did the single family house – the mythic heart and litmus test of "American values" – play in the reception and transformation of postwar modernism?

The domestic culture industry: 1946

A survey of New York's domestic culture events during a single year reveals the vast expansion of the industry after wartime restrictions. Images of full and small-scale model houses, plans, rendered views, surveys, and photographs of built houses and furnishings were widely circulated. Conferences, expositions, lectures, store displays, magazines, and newspapers fostered intense debates about the appropriate form and role of the modern house.

The 1946 National Modern Homes Exposition at Grand Central Palace in New York City provided one arena for a house-hungry public to examine new ways of planning, furnishing, and equipping their future homes. Five thousand visitors crowded the exhibit on its opening day in May.[1] One star of the show was a full-scale model of a plywood prefabricated house called the "Shelter Home" by the noted designer Donald Deskey.[2] *Good Housekeeping* magazine exhibited scale models from its "Homes America Wants" series, including what they called a "traditional little red house" and a colonial cottage as well as a "modern brick design" by Edward Durell Stone. The New York Savings Bank Association, a major supporter of the show, exhibited scale model houses, including a "strictly modern-oriented" home by John Funk featured in *McCall's* magazine. Scale models of the basementless "Answer Home" by Anthracite Industries were also exhibited.[3] In addition to the house models and exhibits were booths for home "gadgets", including storm window systems and electric fly screens.[4]

Department stores sponsored their own domestic exhibits. Macy's displayed the scale models of the winning house designs from *House and Garden*'s 1945 "Blueprints for Tomorrow" competition.[5] For their 75th anniversary, Bloomingdale's displayed the models from their "Suburban Houses for New Yorkers" competition and distributed a book of the winning plans. Based on the models, the store also enlisted noted designers – including Norman MacGregor, Edward J. Wormley, and George Nelson – to furnish full-scale interiors highlighting the store's fabrics, furniture, and other household items.[6] John Wanamaker opened its "Village of Vision" with seven full-sized, furnished model homes built by the prefabrication company Johnson Quality Homes.[7]

Cultural institutions also ventured into the web of the domestic culture industry. The School of Architecture at Columbia University offered a home building lecture series by architects Frederic Woodbridge and Harold Sleeper to assist middle-income builders and buyers.[8] *Builders News* announced the formation of a new national curriculum of home building courses, in 21 colleges across the country, leading to Bachelor of Science degrees in Light Construction, Engineering, and Marketing.[9] The advice-filled *If You Want to Build a House* (1946) by Museum of Modern Art curator Elizabeth Mock and a photographic exhibit of work by the architects featured in the book, added to the depth and breadth of the domestic culture industry.[10]

Unsurprisingly, there was a wide variety of terms by which different participants in housing culture described the modern home. Exhibitors like *Good Housekeeping*'s "Homes America Wants" and Bloomingdale's, for example, were careful to represent both "traditional" and "modern" designs. At the same time, a "pleasant middle course" hybrid emerged that some architectural writers optimistically anticipated as a step in the gradual transformation of public taste.[11] The houses sponsored by *Good Housekeeping* were praised by the editors of *Architectural Forum* as a "vote … against Cape Coddling the public". The approbation was conditional and revolved around a distinction that became instrumental and familiar in subsequent debates about the modern house: the *Forum* editors took exception to the full-scale "Williamsburg" *exterior* of a Westinghouse-sponsored model house while they approved of its fully modernized *interior*.[12] And the Bloomingdale's jury, advised by *Progressive Architecture* editor Kenneth Reid, praised one entry's "modern freedom of plan *despite* the conventional exteriors".[13]

Modified modern

The ambiguous relationship between architectural journals and popular magazines in representing modernity and the home is evident in a special issue of *Architectural Forum* from 1945. Called the "House Omnibus", it was comprised of excerpts of advice, articles, and reader surveys from several major mass-circulation magazines including *Ladies Home Journal* and *House Beautiful*. In their introduction the editors simultaneously embraced and distanced themselves from popular considerations of the modern house. They took pride in the fact that the *Forum* led the way in the "trend toward modern design" taking root in the popular imagination. At the same time, they grudgingly acknowledged that popular opinions were indicative of what "the customer wants". They cautioned readers that selections from the various magazines ranged from status-quo traditional designs to unrealistic "electronic-swimming-pool-in-the-library" fantasies.[14] Expressing the delicacy, if not the elitism, of their professional role, the editors concluded that the information taken from the popular magazines should prove valuable for the careful practitioner "prepared to move at least with the public, if not ahead".[15] [...]

In the *Ladies Home Journal*, perhaps the most interesting of all the magazines featured, architectural editor Richard Pratt took the position that readers might not want to look at ideas or homes with which they are already familiar. By showing "the best that progressive architects can produce", the *Journal* sought to "transcend" the debate between traditional and modern.[16] At the same time, Pratt displayed a less flattering, if honest, appraisal of his readers who "won't worry about the simplified forms of appearances and simplified methods of manufacture" once they are provided with a good home at a low price. Readers were uninterested in technical studies, Pratt said, "so what I do is feed them spoonfuls of [information] in beakers of Frank Lloyd Wright [and] Hugh Stubbins".[17]

Under Pratt, the *Ladies Home Journal* promoted modern design by commissioning proposals for "factory-built" houses by top architects and designers. Beginning in January 1944 and running through late 1946, Pratt's photographs of meticulously furnished and landscaped scale house models were published almost every month, along with occasional tie-in articles by the magazine's interior design staff.[18] The proposals displayed the variety and flexibility many commentators predicted would result from the application of the same mass-production processes that had already widened the choices in automobiles, clothing, and appliances. Pratt predicted, "you will not only be able to get the special sections which will make the kind of looking house you want but the kind of working house as well". Interchangeable and standard parts would produce modern living patterns with flexible and multi-use spaces, interior and exterior "living gardens", extensive glazing, new appliances, and complete mechanical services.

The *Ladies Home Journal* Houses were extremely popular. Panels of model photographs from the magazine were exhibited at the Boston Museum of Fine Arts and at MIT. In the summer of 1945, while the *Journal* series was still running, the Museum of Modern Art re-prepared and exhibited the original scale models in their *Tomorrow's Small House* exhibit. In her introduction to the catalogue, Elizabeth Mock encouraged the reader/viewer to consider the spatial potential of modern design in tandem with what she hoped would be its genuinely radical future: the capacity of prefabrication to bring "innumerable possible combinations" to the house-buying public. In a further recycling of images, in September 1945, *Pencil Points* published photographs of the Museum's models alongside laudatory letters by *Ladies Home Journal* readers.

Judging from these magazines, two overlapping views of domestic modernism emerge. On one side was a modernism based on an aesthetic of production. Like the well-known *Arts & Architecture* Case Study Houses, this was an architecture of repetitive forms and structure, flat roofs, standardized parts, modular construction, and centralized mechanical services, all of which were suggested by prefabrication and factory production. On the other side was … a modernism that stressed patterns of inhabitation such as flexibility, open planning, "engineered storage", convenience (including new appliances), and views through large areas of glass. Both modernisms – the modernism of production aesthetics and the modernism of "effortless inhabitation" – shared spatial flexibility, built-in furnishings, indoor-outdoor living, and, perhaps most importantly, the ideal of an infinite variety of personal patterns of living. For the former, prefabrication and mass production played a crucial symbolic role in shaping modernity while for the latter, they were merely instrumental. For a production-based, aesthetic modernism, modern living could only occur in a modern house that *looked* modern. For a socially-derived modernism of inhabitation, modern living could be enjoyed in a traditional-looking *or* in a modern-looking house or in some hybrid of the two. In other words, a modernism emerged that formalized a separation of exterior appearances from interior performance.

Moreover, by stressing a life of convenience and flexibility that could be lived in either a modern-looking or traditional-looking house, the popular journals reframed and created what *Architectural Forum* editors called a "modified modern": a new style from which bits and pieces could be selected and combined with other styles.[19] Abetting this process of re-defining modernism was the circulation of images among both popular and progressively-minded journals. The photographs of full- and small-scale models of houses and rooms that permeated the media had the effect of re-configuring the modern house as a catalogue of parts – a roof, a window, a kitchen, a piece of furniture – all of which could be brought to, or assembled at, a site. The circulation of images also re-configured the modern house as a sum of attributes or experiences – a flexible space, a view through an expanse of glass, and efficient storage. Increasingly, the domestic culture industry sponsored an elastic conception of modernity that made it the functional equivalent of a process of selection. […]

Selling prefabrication

Although these two modernisms – production aesthetics and frictionless inhabitation – assessed it differently, the ease with which the language of prefabrication moved within the domestic culture industry was grounded, in part, in wartime and postwar thinking about housing needs. Prewar houses such as Fuller's 1927 Dymaxion House, Kocher and Frey's 1931 Aluminaire House, or George Fred Keck's 1934 House of Tomorrow introduced prefabrication to the public, but the efforts to market these and similar houses were under-capitalized and too expensive for low-cost mass production. By the early 1940s, however – and this was pre-Levittown – there was little question that years of meager housing production would eventually reach crisis proportions. Expert and popular commentators alike knew that massive numbers of housing units were required; "a million units per year" became a mantra among architecture, builder, and shelter magazines. While there were as many different housing proposals (many pre-dating World War II) as there were speakers, the concept of prefabrication increasingly floated throughout the discussion and soon became a primary concern among a variety of contributors to the industry. Beyond the technical intricacies of the off-site assembly of buildings, or building sections, was the rhetorical capacity of terms such as "pre-assembly", "panelized construction", "factory produced", and "mass produced" to stand in for, or partially constitute, an image of modernity.

The September 1942 issue of *Architectural Forum* was devoted to the coming postwar housing crunch. Called the "The New House 194x" (referring to the unknown date of the war's end), the article asked: "Assuming prefabrication ... how can the house of 194x be made the most-wanted commodity in the competitive postwar marketplace?" In the *Forum*'s opinion, the technical mastery that had enabled the mass production of thousands of wartime housing units was far superior to their design quality. With such poor examples of industrially-built housing, they wondered how the house of the future would convince a hungry public to relinquish their pre-conceived domestic images and adopt an "appropriate" or "honest" modernity. The answer, unsurprisingly, lay in improving the design standards cast aside for emergency production. To achieve a truly modern postwar house, "progressive, forward-looking designers" would have to "catch-up" with factory-based methods of mass production. [...]

Other participants in the domestic culture industry also recognized that traditional-looking prefabricated houses could just as easily accommodate modern living; while the transformative potential of prefabrication remained central, they embraced the modified modern aesthetic of inhabitation. In fact, a 1947 "how-to" book called *The Prefabricated House: A Practical Guide for the Prospective Buyer* by architects Raymond K. Graff and Rudolph A. Matern and writer Henry Lionel Williams was illustrated almost entirely with traditional and Cape Cod-type designs, including some of their own.[20] In ironic contrast to the photos of Richard Pratt's house models in the *Ladies Home Journal*, the only indications of prefabrication in the model photographs in *The Prefabricated House* were in their captions. Moreover, the authors asserted that traditional or less radical modern design could "incorporate modern aids for housekeeping efficiency", better fit in a neighborhood, and more easily comply with building financing regulations. No prefabricator, they concluded, could afford to experiment with "ultra-modern or freakish" designs since, in the end, traditional design was "what most people want".[21] The authors explained prefabrication not by showing its historic inevitability nor by assuming a proper or "honest" expression for new technologies or needs, rather, they affirmed prefabrication as a consumer's dream: the variety born of new methods could satisfy any taste.

If journals and other advice books opened the way for the accommodating spirit of the modified modern and the prefabricated house, the mid-century department store opened the floodgates. Embedded in urban cultural life since the late nineteenth century, the department store offered the publicity and distribution infrastructures to turn the prefabricated house into a truly mass-produced and mass-consumed product.[22] The downtown department store served a huge sector of the public, provided highly accessible sites for house displays, and, extending their reach, acted as co-sponsors for off-site displays. Typically, a department store would team up with a prefabricator; the store could display furnishings and appliances alongside or inside the exhibited houses, and the prefabricator could use the store as a marketing device to compete against developer housing. In New York and other major cities, stores such as Gimbel's, Wanamaker's, Bloomingdale's, and Macy's used both full-scale model houses and small-scale house models to entice an avidly shopping public.[23] [...]

Department store displays were packed with crowds and widely published in the popular press. In 1946 the Homasote Company exhibited eight full-sized, mostly tradi-tional-looking model houses inside Macy's in New York City. The same year, as noted above, Johnson Quality Homes joined Wanamaker's in New York City and Philadelphia to exhibit "The Village of Vision", comprised of seven Johnson model homes.[24] In 1948, Gimbel's teamed up with Adirondack Homes and *Look* magazine to exhibit a furnished model of a "factory-produced" house designed by Walter Dorwin Teague.[25] Lord and Taylor, Sears, Roebuck, and Bamberger's also exhibited full-scale model houses (as well as small-scale house models) sponsored by prefabricators.[26]

Widening the scope of cultural connections, prefabricators went directly to their potential customers by building on vacant street corners – with department stores still furnishing and decorating them – and enlisting charity organizations to assist in the marketing, which lent the exhibits an air of good citizenship.[27] The year 1948 was espe-cially busy: in January, Pre-Fab Homes, Inc. built a prefabricated "cottage" at 5th Avenue and 48th Street in New York City; in April, Lustron Corporation built a simpli-fied Cape Cod model house on the corner of 6th Avenue and 52nd Street; and in July, Johnson Quality Homes built a "colonial-style" prefabricated house resembling Cary Grant's house in the film *Mr. Blandings Builds His Dream House*, again at 5th Avenue and 48th Street – a model house for a prefabricated house based on a movie about the building of a custom house![28] [...]

The integration of prefabrication into the domestic culture industry – through models and photographs in department stores, on street corners, popular newspapers and maga-zines, and professional magazines – mitigated the importance of the actual production of the house and contributed to the aesthetic of inhabitation, a vision of the modern as a sense of personal, frictionless interior convenience. Just as Graff and Matern's "Practical Guide" to prefabrication had dismissed any incongruity between modern appliances and traditional architectural form, most of the participants in the domestic culture industry recognized no meaningful contradiction between a modern means of production and traditional appearance. Increasingly, prefabrication figured as a means to an end, one that, the stores assured, would be as individual as every purchaser. The variety and indi-viduality promised by prefabrication reshaped modernity into a process of selection. That this individuality matched only part of the rhetoric of the architectural community fueled professional scorn for what they saw as misguided or deceitful production.

Variety within standardization

Despite the combined industry and department store programs, wide coverage in popular magazines, daily newspapers, and the architectural press, the well-known proposals of Gropius and Wachsmann, Fuller, and a host of other prefabrication researchers, prefabricated houses were never successfully mass marketed – traditional *or* modern. The technical capacities of the industry that had performed so well during the war did not help prefabricators compete with developer housing. The Lustron Corpo-ration, one of the best capitalized of the firms, produced only 2,500 houses in its ten-year life.[29] Even as *Architectural Forum* continued to advocate prefabrication, by 1950 they mourned that many "prefabbers have already worn a path to the bankruptcy courts".[30] [...]

But ... the sub-division – from its lot-by-lot nineteenth century beginnings to its Levitt-scaled apotheosis – remained the norm: the house is only one portion of a far more complex package. For the prefabricated house, the purchaser was asked to provide the plot survey, local zoning, building and fire codes, and soil information.[31] For the developer house, a signature and a deposit (no deposit for veterans) secured the buyer a house on a legal lot with utilities, sewers, streets, and, in larger cases, neighborhood schools and stores, all included in the price. In other words, the prefabricated house required the buyer to perform the duties of the contractor, surveyor, expediter, and real estate agent, while the developer house merely asked the purchaser to be a consumer.[32] [...]

The luster of factory-produced housing began to fade by the early 1950s but the promise of "individualization" and "variety within standardization" remained vital principles of middle-class housing design. One of the means by which variety was attained was the use of a standard plan with a selection of elevations (whole and partial) and orientations, a strategy with roots in the history of nineteenth century architectural pattern books and mail-order houses and reiterated in Depression-era building practices sanctioned by the Federal Housing Administration[33] [...] By the late 1940s, the choices offered by mass builders were less among styles than among specific features like overhangs or siding. Composed of a selection of features – picture windows, combined living and dining areas, outdoor spaces, sliding glass doors, new kitchen equipment, and the occasional breezeway – the infinite variety of housing choices provided a comforting if indeterminate "individuality".

Modified modernist

Rudolph Matern, writer and advocate of prefabrication, also practiced architecture on Long Island from the late 1930s until the mid-1960s and, with his partner Herman York, was responsible for almost 40,000 houses in Nassau County alone. The firm worked closely with Long Island builders and was active in many professional architectural associations in the New York area. Both Matern and York sold thousands of stock plans between 1946 and 1951 and served as planning consultants for home shows and expositions; their practice was instrumental in designing a mass market.[34] Matern in particular is notable for his mediation among different modernisms as an architect and through his role in the circulation of images of the modern house.[35]

The 1947 National Home Show in New York City featured a full-scale model of a "ranch-type" home by Matern. The "rambling one-story" home was, according to *The New York Times,* "indicative of the trend [that] made full use of glass in all rooms". For the 1948 National Home Show a full-scale ranch by Matern was praised for its use of the "latest home conveniences" and its flexible plan, multi-use rooms, private garden, and solarium.[36] The *Times* praised the "eye appeal" of Matern's 1949 model for a 300-house development on Long Island, writing that its low, broad lines gave a sense of both "California and New England architecture" – the former a euphemism for modern design, the latter for traditional. With a roof overhang, angled picture window forming a small garden inside and out, built-in bookshelves, expandable attic space, and a "multipurpose" room separated from the living room by an accordion partition, the house – with its three plan and four elevation variations – offered a "new conception of an economy home".[37] The 1949 project was praised in professional magazines exploring the potential markets opened by successful "builder and architect" relationships.[38]

An interview with Matern in *Architectural Forum* in 1951 offers a clear picture of this "modified modern" from the architect's optimistic perspective. He portrayed his work as a part of an architectural transition on the way to something "more" modern: "We feel we're gradually bringing up the level of home design, flattening out the roof little by little, introducing more and more open-planning and functional ideas. But we'd rather take one jump ahead of the people's tastes and sell houses than take two and fall flat on our faces, which can cost a builder his whole building season".[39] The *Forum* writer praised Matern's work for using modern technology to open up the interior, for improving the plan, and for providing more flexible work areas; in other words, for his innovations in the modernity of inhabitation, but not for any aesthetic innovation. [*See Figs. 52, 53.*]

Matern also proposed less "modified" and more strictly modern work during the 1950s, but these were designed in addition to the hybrid stylistic variety produced by Matern and York. A 1958 mass-market book called *Low Cost Homes* shows the scope of the practice; it included more designs by Matern than any other single architect. Unsurprisingly, the descriptions of the houses focused on good planning, flexible arrangements and movable partitions, built-in furniture, lots of glass and views to the outdoors, indoor-outdoor gardens, a sense of expansiveness, and, of course, breezeways. The houses were called "subdued modern", and "conservative modern", and the occasional references to colonial or "early American" were always followed by the assurance that the interior is "up-to-the-minute America".[40]

Matern's successful housing practice was based on the uncoupling of interior from exterior that we see at work in the mass marketing of single-family homes during this period. He used the technologies of mass production for interior comfort without requiring their expression or representation on the exterior. Without a moral or programmatic necessity to link the two, Matern was able to reconcile or mediate the aesthetics of production with the mores of convenience that drove mass-market building. In addition, the separation of interior from exterior gave Matern the leeway to slowly "improve" and "raise" appreciation of modern design; a dormer in one room could be balanced by a corner window in another. As the sub-division house was transformed, however, so were the aesthetic principles of modernism that Matern gently introduced in his designs. Flooding the market with his hybrids, Matern participated in a shift in the nature of modernist design categories that critics of the 1950s increasingly disparaged as "middlebrow". [...]

"Modern is as modern does"

Other discussions of the home also turned on the relation of satisfaction and ease to the precepts of modernity. In a 1945 *House and Garden* article "Modern is as Modern Does" that showed the work of a variety of modern architects such as John Funk, Walter Gropius, and William Wurster, historian Talbot Hamlin examined what he considered the transparent simplicity that undergirded modern homes. If sensitive to people's needs and contemporary living patterns, he wrote, the architect will necessarily design houses both modern and rooted in the American tradition and, furthermore, that are expressive of the individuality of the occupants. Houses conceived in terms of rational planning, comfort, flexibility, and indoor-outdoor living would result in a properly modern architecture.[41] But definitions based on performance could equally describe the work of Rudolph Matern. After a 1955 visit to Puerto Rico, Matern reported that the flexible and adaptable qualities of what he called the "Caribbean contemporary" style he found there would be suitable for houses in New York. "Modern in feeling", with overhang-protected glazing, low-pitched roofs, and indoor-outdoor plan features, the style could be built from pre-cast elements and could "accommodate numerous exterior variations around one basic floor plan".[42]

While Hamlin privileged the historicist idea of the necessarily modern object and Matern the service potential for mass production, these two descriptions created an image of the modern house ultimately based on its capacity to provide for variety and individuality.

Rather than assuming that only certain cultural actors were using the word correctly, a broader historical picture reveals that several different modernisms were at work in the making of the modern house in the immediate postwar period. Most broadly, there was the modernism of the mass production and circulation of images; enmeshed in a culture of magazines, department stores, and home shows, this modernity was constituted by its technical capacity to create and respond to a variety of ever-widening audiences. Then there was the "high" architectural modernism of the production aesthetic which believed that new techniques, forms, spaces, and materials appropriate to the time and used honestly would naturally and necessarily foster a new, modern life of precision and ease. And finally there was also a modernism of inhabitation, often dismissed as middlebrow, in which flexible planning assisted by improved technologies and new appliances provided comfort and convenience within an unprescribed variety of architectural expressions.

Operating sometimes in tandem and other times at cross-purposes, these modernisms propelled the single-family house to the center of postwar cultural debate even as they rendered moot any single idea of how the house should look. The iconic fruit of these debates was the middlebrow or modified modern house for an expanding middle class, because it was this group that most participated in the domestic culture industry … as *both* producers and consumers.[43] Since this group most actively participated in the dissemination of the new single-family housing, the middle-class values of comfort and convenience formed the basis of a modernism that suited and represented them. The capacity of the modified modern to create and sustain a sense of "variety within standardization" *without* implying a larger social or aesthetic program enabled it to become the suburban vernacular, disappointing a generation of newly modernist-trained architects. Despite the assessment by architectural culture that these houses were not modern enough, the postwar modified modern might have been considerably more modern than they realized.[44]

In a culture of infinite choice, the central feature of the middlebrow modern house was its formation through the process of browsing and selection of desirable features, attributes, and effects. Modified modern homes were assemblages of parts and "bundle[s] of features" selected from the array of products offered by architects, in department stores, and in images circulated in the magazines.[45] Represented by vaguely familiar exteriors and efficient, flexible interiors, the results were consumer collages that eschewed a classical idea of aesthetic unity. It is not an accident that many architects and critics considered these houses degraded and hopelessly compromised as aesthetic objects. The ideas of organic unity and wholeness that undergirded the spirit of "high" modernism were not compatible with the discontinuities, fragments, and syntheses introduced by middlebrow or "modified" domestic practices. That these practices of selection were fully integrated into the vast apparatus of shopping and marketing only amplified the pejorative rendering of the middlebrow as female. The modified modern was made of bits and pieces of recognizable purchases that could only have been made by a customer with no commitment to the organic purity of the production aesthetic. To the guardians of high culture, the middlebrow production of Matern and his ilk was nothing less than an assault on culture itself.

The formation of the modified modern shows that the cultural process by which the postwar house was configured was more complex than the passing down of a single set of forms. The domestic culture industry operated in a multi-directional manner. Not only did the various participants have competing and often conflicting values, but their engagement with, and construction of, modernity was filtered through the means by which they visualized and experienced it. Mass production of houses, like the mass circulation of their images, created a new terrain of interchangeable features whose spokesmen (and women) participated in the reshaping of an authentic modernism.

Notes

1   The exposition was sponsored by the Metropolitan Association of Real Estate Boards, the New York chapter of the National Association of Real Estate Boards (NAREB) which sponsored shows and "Home Weeks" across the country. "Modern Home Show Attracts Thousands", *New York Times*, May 6, 1946 (future references will read *NYT*).
2   Mary Roche, "Designers Exhibit New Type of House", *NYT*, May 2, 1946; Roche, "Designed to Grow Old Gracefully", *NYT*, May 3, 1946.
3   Roche, "Modern Home Show to Open Today", *NYT*, May 4, 1946.
4   "Gadgets on View for Modern Home", *NYT*, May 5, 1946.
5   "House Models on Display", *NYT* February 22, 1946.
6   Roche, "Exhibit Will Open for Home Planner", *NYT*, February 9, 1947. The free book included names and addresses of the architects, but the houses were not available through the store. On Nelson's collection, see Stanley Abercrombie, *George Nelson: The Design of Modern Design*, Cambridge, Mass.: MIT Press, 1995, pp. 83–101.
7   *NYT*, January 25, 1946. See also "Over-the-Counter Prefabs", *Architectural Forum*, February 1946, 7.
8   "Lectures to Guide the Home Builder", *NYT*, January 20, 1946. Woodbridge was a partner of Randolph Evans, who wrote on mass market homes; Sleeper (co-author of *Architectural Graphic Standards*) co-wrote, with Catherine Sleeper, *The House for You: To Build, Buy or Rent*, New York: John Wiley, 1948, based on his lectures.
9   The new program trained men to understand "packaged consumer service in construction". "21 Colleges Offering Training for Careers in Building Field", *NYT*, January 27, 1946.
10   Elizabeth Mock, *If You Want to Build a House*, New York: Museum of Modern Art, 1946, Edith Sonn, "Museum Display Features Houses", *NYT*, January 9, 1946.
11   The *New York Times* critic Mary Roche wrote that Deskey's "Shelter Home" "follows a pleasant middle course between the most advanced modern theories on the one hand and hackneyed traditional designs on the other ...". Mary Roche, "Designers Exhibit New Type of House", *NYT*, May 2, 1946.
12   "Model Houses", *Architectural Forum*, August 1945, 9; italics added.
13   "19 Architects Get Prizes for Houses", *NYT*, April 11, 1946; italics added.
14   "House Omnibus", *Architectural Forum*, April 1945, 89.
15   Ibid., 90. The role of magazines and other agents of the domestic culture industry is not new: mass production transformed the building industry over the course of the nineteenth century, and magazines and advice literature were plentiful in the nineteenth and twentieth centuries. Architects and builders have had tense, if not inimical, relations throughout. See Gwendolyn Wright, *Moralism and the Modern Home: Domestic Architecture and Cultural Conflict in Chicago, 1873–1913*, Chicago: University of Chicago Press, 1980; and Michael Doucet and John Weaver, *Housing the North American City*, McGill: McGill Queen's University Press, 1991.
16   "House Omnibus", 109.
17   *The Ladies Home Journal* excerpt shows work by Plan-Tech Associates, Vernon DeMars, Hugh Stubbins, and Gardner A. Dailey; "House Omnibus", 109–18. In November, 1946 *Journal* editor Pratt presented the last modernist-inspired houses and began a new series exploring traditional houses called "Regional Houses". The series was later published as Bruce Gould and Beatrice Blackman Gould (eds) *Regional Houses*, Philadelphia: Ladies Home Journal and Curtis Publishing Co., 1947.

18 *The Ladies Home Journal* series consisted of 24 projects by George Fred Keck, Carl Koch, Malcolm Graeme Duncan (two projects), A. Lawrence Kocher, Hugh Stubbins (two), Vernon DeMars (the only multi-family project except for the potential two-family by Duncan), Plan-Tech Associates, Mario Corbett (with landscape architect Garrett Eckbo), Frank Lloyd Wright, Philip Johnson (two), John Funk (two, with Garrett Eckbo), Wurster and Bernardi with Ernest Kump, Ferdinand Kramer and Calvert Coggeshall, Victorine and Samuel Homsey, Edward Durell Stone, Cameron Clark (the one "traditional"), H. T. Williams, Antonin Raymond, Ladislav Rado & Robert Hays Rosenberg.

19 "Model Houses", *Architectural Forum*, August 1945, 9.

20 Raymond K. Graff, Rudolph A. Matern, and Henry Lionel Williams, *The Prefabricated House: A Practical Guide for the Prospective Buyer*, Garden City, NY: Doubleday, 1947. See also Samuel Paul (of Matern, Graff and Paul Architects), "Prefabrication Pattern", *Pencil Points*, April 1943.

21 Graff, Matern and Williams, *Prefabricated House*, p. 8. Citing the Federal Housing Administration (FHA) refusal to guarantee loans for houses deemed "too modern", the authors point out that traditional houses have greater resale value. This was not an isolated problem: the Chicago FHA office rejected a development of flat-roofed houses saying that the "exterior design does not appear to be highly favorable from a market standpoint". "Still Too Modern", *House and Home*, November 1953, 52.

22 On the transformations wrought by the department store and mass marketing, see Susan Strasser, *Satisfaction Guaranteed*, Washington, D.C.: Smithsonian Institution Press, 1989, and Gunter Barth, *City People*, Oxford, Engl. and New York: Oxford University Press, 1980; see also William Leach, *Land of Desire: Merchants, Power and the Rise of a New American Culture*, New York: Pantheon, 1993, Daniel Bluestone et al., *The Retail Revolution: Market Transformation, Investment and Labor in the Modern Department Store*, Boston: Auburn, 1981, pp. 10–27, and Susan Porter Benson, "Palace of Consumption and Machine for Selling: The American Department Store 1880–1940", *Radical History Review*, Fall, 1979, 199–221.

23 Department store house displays preceded the war but were not typically aimed at low-cost housing. [...]

24 On Macy's: "Sale of New Homes Is Begun by Macy's", *NYT*, January 31, 1946; "House Offered for Sale by Department Store", *NYT*, February 3, 1946. On Wanamaker's: Mary Roche, "Housing Cost Seen at Store Display", *NYT*, January 25, 1946; Mary Roche, "Lower Prices for 1947 Prefabs", *NYT*, June 5, 1947. "Department Store Sub-division", *Architectural Forum*, February 1946, 7.

25 *The Times* notes that a "duplicate" could be seen at the Museum of Science and Industry's "Modern Living Exposition", "Gimbel's to Show a 4–1/2 Room House", *NYT*, April 9, 1948.

26 Henry Wright decorated the "modern living room" of the "1949 Pace-Setter House" at Lord & Taylor's in Orange, NJ, *NYT*, September 30, 1949. Sears exhibited the "Homart Model House" in Saddle River, NJ, *NYT*, May 22, 1949. Bamberger's displayed 26 scale-model ranch houses in "Climate Control for New Jersey", *NYT*, January 18, 1950.

27 Street corner displays were not entirely new: in 1934, the New York Committee of "Better Houses in America" displayed a Georgian house at Park Avenue and 39th Street. This was followed in 1936 by William Van Alen's "House of the Modern Age" on the same corner. On the former, see *Architectural Record*, October 1934, 217; *Architectural Forum*, February 1935, 173–6; on the latter, see *NYT*, May 30, 1936.

28 On Pre-Fab Homes: "Little House Draws 38,500 Visitors", *NYT*, January 11, 1948; on Lustron: "Model of Steel House to Be Exhibited Here", *NYT*, April 5, 1948; on Johnson Quality Homes, "An Honored Guest at the Dream House", *NYT*, July 23, 1948; advertisement, *NYT*, July 25, 1948. The beneficiary for Pre-Fab Homes was the Spence-Chapin Adoption Services; for Lustron, the American Overseas Aid and United Nations Appeal for Children; for Johnson, the New York Heart Association.

29 Douglas Glenn Nerr, *The House America Has Been Waiting For: The Lustron Experiment In Factory Made Housing, 1946–1954*, Dissertation, University Of Cincinnati, 1996. Of the 100 prefabricated houses Gimbel's stocked in 1946, only 30 sold. "Prefabrication Code Drafted", *Interiors*, June 1946, 14.

30 "The Builder and Prefabrication", *Architectural Forum*, April 1950, 160. See also Gilbert Herbert, *The Dream of the Factory Made House: Walter Gropius and Conrad Wachsmann*, Cambridge, Mass.: MIT Press, 1984 [*this volume*].

31 See, for example, "Sale of New Homes Is Begun by Macy's", *NYT*, January 31, 1946.

32 Other problems ensued for prefabricators. Neither zoning and building codes nor banking and loan regulations – especially those issued by the FHA – accounted for the needs of prefabricators, especially those experimenting with new materials. The FHA took a skeptical view of the "prospect" of prefabrication; *Principles of Planning Small Houses, Technical Bulletin #4*, rev., Washington, D.C., 1938 [1936], 1. In addition, until after the Korean War, metals needed for panel assemblies were federally regulated; "Urges 'Package Loans' for Homes", *Interiors*, May, 1946; Burnham Kelley, *The Prefabrication of Houses*, Boston: MIT and John Wiley, 1951, pp. 86–96; Herbert, *The Dream of the Factory Made House*, pp. 299–313.

33 The FHA advised: "When a developer uses only a limited number of house plans, variety and interest may be secured by sometimes having the end elevation and sometimes the side elevation toward the street, by the placement of the garages and by varying the setback line". Federal Housing Administration, *Planning Neighborhoods for Small Houses, Technical Bulletin #5*, Washington, D.C., 1936, 29. In the revised edition of *Principles of Planning Small Houses*, the FHA advised material variations as well as reversed and turned plans to ensure visual variety; *Technical Bulletin #4*, rev., Washington, D.C., 1940 [1936], 39. See also Gwendolyn Wright, *Building the Dream: A Social History of Housing in America*, New York: Pantheon, 1981, and Wright, *Moralism and the Model Home*.

34 "The Builder's Architect", *Architectural Forum*, December 1951, 118, 122–3. [...]

35 Matern (b. 1912) graduated from the University of Michigan and studied for one year with Eliel Saarinen at Cranbrook. In 1937, Matern (with architect George Nemeny) placed in the "20th Century Home Competition" sponsored by the Harnischfeger Corp. (a building material manufacturer); *Architectural Forum*, February 1937, 96–7. In 1939, Matern's flat roofed, expressed-frame entry (with a breezeway-garage) won the "Productive Home for the South" in the "Productive Home Architectural Competition", "Productive Garden Homes", *Pencil Points*, May 1939, 307–14.

36 On the 1947 Show: "To Show Model Home", *NYT*, February 9, 1947, "House Designed for Exhibit at Home Show Here", *NYT*, March 9, 1947. On the 1948 Show, "Exhibition Home and New Housing Facilities for the New York Area", *NYT*, February 22, 1948.

37 "Builders Offer a Low-priced House with 'Eye Appeal' at East Hempstead", *NYT*, April 10, 1949.

38 See, for instance, "The Small House" special issue, *Architectural Forum*, April 1950, 123.

39 "The Builder's Architect", *Architectural Forum*, December 1951, 122.

40 Larry Eisenger and Ray Gill (eds) *Low Cost Homes*, New York: Do-it-Yourself Series, Arco, 1958.

41 Talbot Hamlin, "Modern Is as Modern Does: An Introduction to the Intelligent Appraisal of Modern House Design", *House and Garden*, October 1945, 84–7, 138, 140 ...

42 "Home Planning Here Influenced by Style Popular in Puerto Rico", *NYT*, May 13, 1956. In the mid-1960s Matern retired to Puerto Rico.

43 The dual role of the new managerial class was emphasized by William H. Whyte, Jr. in his 1953 *Fortune* magazine series "The Transients" that became part of his 1956 *The Organization Man*.

44 For a similar argument about furnishings, see George H. Marcus, *Design in the Fifties*, New York: Prestel, 1998, pp. 35–86.

45 The term is from Thomas Hine, "The Search for the Postwar House", in *Blueprints for Modern Living: History and Legacy of the Case Study Houses*, Los Angeles: Museum of Contemporary Art, 1989, p. 173 ...

The American lawn
Surface of everyday life

Georges Teyssot (1999)

[…] The first half of the twentieth century was marked by a continual oscillation between the most extreme convictions for or against fences. It is possible to see in this debate essentially two opposing camps: on the one hand a pronounced taste for the opening and transparency of front lawn and the street side of the house; on the other the aspiration to reclusion that converges on the back yard and the rear of the house. These are the places, respectively, of bourgeois and familial intimacy. […]

The opening of the yard on the street side inexorably gained ground. This preference expressed itself overtly in a 1930 book by Leonidas Ramsey, *Landscaping the Home Grounds:* "A man's home may be his castle, but his front lawn belongs to the public. At least, this is the case in the great majority of American Homes. The universal practice of establishing building lines and setting the house back from the street has created the typical American front yard. Custom has prescribed the leaving of the front yard open, providing a view of the house and the grounds".[1] Ramsey justified this tradition by linking it to a sense of civic responsibility. "The home owner should always keep in mind that it is his duty to do everything in his power to make his street more attractive", he continued. "Unless each home owner plans his lot … as a part of the whole block or street, the street cannot present a harmonious aspect, no matter how well laid out or how important a part it plays in the city plan".[2] With this passage Ramsey announced what from then on would become not only the rule of architectural composition in the American suburb but also its unwritten moral law: the inhabitant must maintain his lawn as a community place. In 1937, for example, in a work called *Planning the Home Grounds*, this quasi-law governing the landscape in its smallest details appeared as a need for conformity – not only formal, but social as well. In fact, the chapter titled "Lawns and their Care" began with this assertion: "The semi-public area, no matter what your personal preference may be, will of necessity conform largely to the planting style of the homes which surround you".[3] An upkeep manual in 1950s California described the front lawn as a pair of arms opened toward the visitor, the better to welcome him: "Where zoning laws … exist, there is usually a required setback from the street to the building line. This leaves a strip of grass that … is the welcome mat to any visitor and goes far toward giving him his first impression of the place".[4] The landscape of the suburb is also the place of micro-tactics inscribed on the ground: "To divide one lawn from another (and to avoid offending a neighbor's sensibilities), some use rough-hewn stones as a 'natural' boundary".[5] In the 1950s and 1960s, the editors of *Sunset* magazine overflowed with practical advice: "a lawn has a spiteful way of exposing the lax gardener to his neighbors by turning brown, sprouting weeds, or looking generally shaggy and woebegone".[6] This array of regulations and instructions upholds what sociologist William Dobriner called the "visibility principle" in his noted thesis on "The Psychology of the Suburbs". A defining mark of suburbia, the visibility principle describes a visual openness that permits residents "to observe each other's behavior and general lifestyle far more easily than the central city dweller".[7] […]

The victory over the fence precipitated the removal of partitions and a sense of apparent democratic openness to greet the GI upon his return from the Second World

War. "All fences, whether fabricated or growing, are prohibited", declared a 1948 issue of the *Levittown Tribune*, the newspaper founded by pioneering suburban developer Abraham Levitt.[8] Even as the postwar freedom of the citizen was loudly proclaimed, J. B. Jackson recalled, "in the sales contract you [would] find a clause guaranteeing the perpetual inviolability of the lawn in front of the house".[9] [See Fig. 54.] The romanticized recollections of W. D. Wetherell, published in 1985 under the title *The Man Who Loved Levittown*, describes this total, almost panoramic openness of the front lawns through the filter of a nostalgia for a vanished past, of a paradise lost: "[W]e used to talk about … how there were no hedges … in the old days, no fences, no locked doors. Everyone's home was your home; we all walked back and forth like it was one big yard".[10]

Notes

1   Leonidas W. Ramsey, *Landscaping the Home Grounds*, New York: Macmillan Company, 1930, p. 54.
2   Ibid., pp. 55–7.
3   Cecile Hulse Matschat, *Planning the Home Grounds*, Boston: Houghton Mifflin Company, 1937, p. 60.
4   Frederick Frye Rockwell and Ester C. Grayson, *The Complete Book of Lawns: How to Determine What Kind of Lawn You Should Have, and Sure-Fire Methods for Constructing and Maintaining It, Lawn Grasses (and Grass Substitutes) for All Sections of the United States, and Their Particular Requirements*, Garden City, NY: American Garden Guild, 1956, p. 28.
5   P. J. McKenna and Anna B. McKenna, *Small Home Landscaping*, New York: Sterling Publishing Co., Inc., 1953, p. 49.
6   Sunset Editorial Staff, *How to Install and Care for Your Lawn*, Menlo Park, CA: Lane Book Co., 1955, p. 4.
7   Willian Mann Dobriner, *Class in Suburbia*, Englewood Cliffs, NJ: Prentice-Hall, 1963, p. 9; see also "the visibility principle may be the major force behind the suburban informal relationships rather than a psychological predisposition", pp. 62–3.
8   See "Restrictions Affecting Houses & Sample Contract", *Levittown Tribune*, June 24, 1948, 2.
9   John Brinckerhoff Jackson, "Green Desert", *Landscape* 3, Summer 1953, 3–4.
10 W. D. Wetherell, *The Man Who Loved Levittown*, Pittsburgh, PA: University of Pittsburgh Press, 1985, p. 14.

The rise and fall of the picture window

Sandy Isenstadt (1998)

As if to underscore architecture's cultural position – somewhere between material practice and civic discourse – every so often a particular building element comes to bear an extraordinary representational load. Sometimes the element – columns or keystones, for instance – carries a visibly structural load, and then becomes a broad metaphor for clarity and strength. Sometimes the meaning is more specific. In the 1930s, for example, flat roofs became a flashpoint for the articulation of a particular kind of German national identity. The pointed windows characteristic of the Gothic, owing to some combination of shape and historical use, seem everlastingly aspirational. In this essay I argue that the picture window – understood as a large rectangle of glass *and* as the view of the landscape through that glass – is precisely such an element; it's both a symbol and just a hole in the wall.

The time of the picture window has passed. This is evident in, for instance, the explicit prohibition against them in the design code of the New Urbanist town of Seaside, Florida. And it is evident also by their replacement, in much speculative residential construction in the United States, with the elaborately designed "signature window", as Michael Pollan recently observed. But in its heyday, the picture window was the focus of much attention, of optimism and contempt: harbinger of the good life to some, a symbol of suburban anomie to others. Usually assumed to be merely a commercial, retrograde adaptation of a modernist ideal – "mass-market descendants of the horizontal ribbon windows and glass walls of Modernism", in Pollan's words – the picture window is actually much more, with a richer and more complex history than is usually understood. Although not often counted among the icons of national self-representation, the picture window is sited precisely at that intersection of the Arcadian and the progressive which Leo Marx has described as the heart of an American ideology of space.[1] Recovering some portion of the picture window's history will illuminate architecture's unique amalgam of mind and matter: the ability of some mute building materials to inspire both rhapsody and reproach.

> Have you reckon'd that the landscape took substance and form that it might be painted in a picture?
>
> Walt Whitman, *Leaves of Grass*, 1855

Rise

The concept of *window* has been laden with symbolic content since at least early Egypt; landscapes in particular have been depicted and visualized as window-framed since Pompeii. The writings of Pliny contain the first record of a "contemplative use of the window", which historians believe recurs at moments of cultural confidence.[2] In Romantic sentiment, scenes viewed through windows gained special significance. Given that vision is a common metaphor for knowledge, the two terms, "picture" and "window", together created a productive paradox. The view provided access to knowledge of the world, while the frame, which nearly always figured prominently in the view, demarcated the limits of knowledge. Views through windows could thus symbolize the essence of the human condition: connection to the larger world tempered by separation from it; certainty turns to conjecture at the borders of the visible.

The specifically horizontal form of the picture window is equally old. "Horizontal" or "mullioned" windows were found in Knossos, and, contrasted with "classic" or "door-shaped" windows, they figure as a grand historical type. In Europe, horizontal windows were considered especially well suited for country houses, and, indeed, were elaborately developed in Elizabethan and Tudor homes. In England in the mid-eighteenth century, advances in glass manufacturing, including the ability to make larger and flatter panes, along with increased interest in landscape, led to a renewed emphasis on the prospect. In response to the limitation on window heights imposed by ceilings, and in accord with conventions of landscape painting, large glazed horizontal openings and, almost invariably, the sylvan scenery beyond, appear regularly in nineteenth-century domestic architecture. As architects Raymond McGrath and Albert C. Frost summarized: "To enjoy a prospect from a window, two things are necessary; first the leisurely appreciation of nature for its own sake and quite apart from its elemental associations, and second, either an unobstructed opening or clear, colorless glazing".[3] At root, then, the distinctly modern version of the picture window was a product both of landscape and of the leisure to contemplate it through clear, flat glass; it was an alloy of Romantic outlook and industrial technology.

In keeping with Picturesque aesthetic theory, the conceit of framing pictures through windows involved a conscious exercise of taste as well as the development of ideas about how the landscape elements beyond the window might be composed. Not surprisingly, landscape gardeners at the turn of the nineteenth century were the first to discuss how their work appeared from inside. Viewing landscape through glass required education and a learned appreciation for principles of Picturesque taste; and it certainly required an expanse of land amenable to improvement. It came to be assumed that those with modest incomes should, when siting their homes, concentrate on convenience, while the rich, in contrast, had the luxury to consider the view: "There is a pleasure that none but the man of fortune knows in commanding an extensive prospect every way from his house, and knowing that all he sees is his own".[4] Prospects – private prospects – were clearly linked with wealth and real property, with the leisure that follows both, and with the pleasure to be found in all.

Countless middle-class dwellings sought to emulate the homes of the wealthy. Stylistic imitation has been the most common evidence cited by historians to demonstrate such villa envy. But what was already being called, in the mid-nineteenth century, a "landscape window" – involving a large, horizontally oriented piece of glass, a sylvan scene, *and* a meditative frame of mind – was too good to go unnoticed. Although it has yet to receive proper historical treatment, the *vista* was as much the object of middle-class appropriation as were other features of upper-class houses; without the same expanses of land, however, house designers had to make some adjustments. More and more, in the second half of the nineteenth century, in books and popular magazines, homeowners were advised to consider their private landscape views – to enhance promising ones and to efface ugly ones where necessary, even as the average acreage of house lots was decreasing. In fact, even for modest homes, the relative size of windows was increasing, along with a concern for the view they looked upon.

Muntins, in particular, came under special scrutiny, especially after manufacturing improvements threatened to make them technologically obsolete. On the one hand, it was thought that they interfered with the view. Henry Hudson Holly, for example, spoke delightedly of an unmuntined window so transparent that a house guest tried to walk through it. Holly adored the flawless reflections that such windows offered from outside, and imagined oversized glass as Nature's own crystalline canvas: "Distant scenery is a picture which none but the Great Architect could paint". On the other hand, Edith Wharton and Ogden Codman, writing in 1897, advised caution when pursuing the fashion for larger windows: muntins traced the wall's surface across the open air of the view and thus maintained the sense of enclosure indispensable to domestic decorum. By doing away with muntins, they argued, clients unwittingly sacrificed their home's spatial and moral integrity to an immodest desire for a better view. Wharton and Codman concluded with the *coup de grâce* that the French, "always logical in such matters", had given up on large panes decades ago and had settled sensibly on small ones.[5]

Big glass was an affront to aesthetic thinking generally, since "framing" was the learned activity that aestheticized *nature* into *landscape*. As windows widened, window frames moved to the periphery, visually and cognitively. Loss of the muntin, in this context, further eroded the possibilities of visual composition; through the 1920s, muntins were often defended from an "artistic" point of view. In fact, what might well be termed "the muntin dispute" may be the longest-running debate in nineteenth- and twentieth-century architecture: it began with early nineteenth-century condemnations of "the bar" that intervened between landscape and viewer; continued through the early twentieth century with the Modernist rejection of muntins; and remains alive even today, in legal disputes about whether municipalities have the authority to require muntins, albeit for preserving historical character and not for framing prospects. Though often unfocused in polemical terms, discussions of the muntin explicitly pitted technical and material change against social convention; this suggests that far more was at stake than architectural style.

Serial production of building components made matters more complicated. By the end of the nineteenth century, a window composed of a central fixed pane flanked by casements or decorative bands, sometimes with an operable sash above or a decorative transom, was a stock item in millwork catalogues, a type of "cottage window", a term for windows with high meeting rails. Although comparable to large windows in Shingle Style houses, the landscape window was mass produced, intended for suburban and mostly unremarkable sites. It was designed less in response to a view than in anticipation of one. Further, being more elaborate than other windows, the picture window was typically placed in the main room of the house, usually at the front. This was significant: the landscape being thus framed was almost always a street. The "landscape window", then, implied confidence that there was something visually attractive about the surroundings being acquired along with the house.

The picture window idea

Though related to prior uses and images, the phrase "picture window" came into sustained use early in 1934, when glass manufacturer Libbey-Owens-Ford began an advertising campaign in *House and Garden* and *House Beautiful* centered on "The Picture Window Idea". While obviously admiring the unabashed use of glass characteristic of the International Style, Libbey-Owens-Ford regrounded the rationale for big windows, emphasizing not the evocation of an industrial aesthetic but rather the visual access to nature. In the advertisements, nature is admitted so freely as to become an animated part of the interior: "A Picture Window is made by setting into one wall of a room a single piece of fine polished plate glass, considerably larger than an ordinary window, so that the ever changing vista through it paints what is, in effect, a marching mural on your wall". This was in contrast to Libbey-Owens-Ford's earlier ads, that only months earlier had stressed the refined optical clarity of their glass. The company's literature from the 1920s had emphasized that glass had two jobs: to reflect light evenly from the outside, and, from within, to "give you a clear, sharp picture of whatever lies beyond it". "Whatever lies beyond it" varied in their ads from those years, including images of leisure activities, of attractive neighbors, and of transparent relations between client, architect, and window maker, all partners in progress. After 1934, though, "whatever lies beyond it" was nearly always a landscape. Libbey-Owens-Ford seemed to have taken seriously a question posed in *House and Garden* just before their new ad campaign began: "Why not consider the pictures which windows bring into our lives?"

Month after month, for several years, Libbey-Owens-Ford expounded on "The Picture Window Idea", and it was at this point that the "picture window" became an identifiable object in residential design (the first citation in the *Oxford English Dictionary* is from 1938), signifying a large piece of unmuntined glass *and* a view of landscape. Also at the time, the picture window was entirely synonymous with either window-walls or glass walls, all of which were enthusiastically taken up in the 1930s by the professional and popular journals. By 1937, Walter Curt Behrendt thought that the use of big windows had become a cliché, "an article of faith" used more to parade one's modernity than to refine it. In fact, large glass areas were the only stylistic feature common to both modern and traditional houses: "A really dramatic picture window in the living room is dear to the heart of the conservative as well as the modernist", *Architectural Forum* proclaimed in 1942.[6] Small windows, in contrast, were criticized as a kind of dead weight binding a building to a rapidly receding past. The picture window looked to be the start of broad popular acceptance for Modernism's highest ideals: formal expression of new materials and methods of construction, and the creation of a new kind of space.

If Modernism was being accepted, though, it was on terms quite different from those in which it was originally promulgated. Avant garde architects in the 1920s admired large glass areas as expressions of building technology: new materials and construction methods seemed then to demand such new expression. Transparent sheets of glass disclosed structure, mechanical systems, and the functional order within; by fore-grounding the stuff of architectural invention, transparent glass walls explained architecture to architects. The idea of revealing technology was much less motivating, however, for the rising class of affluent homebuyers; for them, transparency served other ends. For the domestic consumer, especially in the years following the Second World War, the wall-sized window was advocated for its ability to promote visual relations with nature.

In this sense, the picture window was hardly Modernism's bastard. It can be understood, rather, as an evolving vernacular element serving an expansion of the visual field since the 1800s. In contrast, professional rationales for glass walls have shifted, sometimes emphasizing the expression of technology, other times the pastoralized view. Put simply, the formal innovations of Modernism in the United States fulfilled a popular perceptual desire that preceded those innovations (any ambivalence toward that desire notwithstanding). Picture windows are thus more richly understood as a leg up on the view out, the consumer's-eye view of dematerialization, rather than as high design brought down by the masses.

In 1934, this combination of technical change and renewed relations with nature was exactly described by Libbey-Owens-Ford: "Picture Windows ... There is something distinctly modern about them ... yet something equally mellow and pleasantly old as the ages". In the advertisements, sylvan scenery seasoned Modernism's hard edges, while plate glass made looking at landscapes seem a very modern thing to do. Technological progress – Libbey-Owens-Ford was founded following the acquisition of a manufacturing patent – was presented as offering an animated picture of nature. In this sense, picture windows sought to resolve what seemed to be competing desires: the quest for material progress and the longing for Arcadian retreat.

The result was widely touted as a new view of nature, which varied from speaker to speaker but, as often as not, included a picture window. Edwin Bateman Morris, for instance, in the February 1953 *Journal of the A.I.A.*, described the view shared by millions of suburban and Thermopaned Americans. This view was cinematic – "we sit at our ease and the scene revolves before us" – and artificial, "pleasantly synthetic", Morris wrote, where "the soft gentle pink of dresses on [a clothes] line is as optically satisfying as that of the flowers waving below". In accordance with earlier concepts of nature as wilderness, "we are still children of the Great Without", only now "in a continuous synthetic open-air Sunday-school-picnic surrounding". In the democracy of visible light, anything might be observed or juxtaposed – "the blue vault of heaven" alongside the "embarrassment of other dwellers" and "geraniums, diaper-service vehicles" and "soft floating clouds, brush salesmen … a world spread out for our relaxed entertainment". This signaled, moreover, a new stage in social relations, where privacy, "the former stuffy top-secret idea of boudoir", evaporated. "Open are curtains at their windows, open at ours". Though windows had long provided opportunities for "stirring picture compositions", the new thresholds of viewing and the new relationship to nature that Morris described were a "triumph" for "those men who, as a result of patient research, put the thin vacuum between glass, and thus brought to our couch-side the sweet and beautiful world". "How", Morris asked, "did we exist before the creation of the all-seeing picture window?"[7]

> A picture window is only as good as the view it frames.
>
> Philip Johnson, *New York Times Magazine*, March 17, 1996

Fall

From the perspective of today, such enthusiasm is hard to recover. Even as Morris wrote, some critics – he called them "cynics" – demonized the picture window as emblematic of pretty much everything wrong with architecture, America, or both. In architectural circles, picture windows became the apotheosis of commercial vulgarization: the subordination of high ideals to crass consumerism. Ten years after *Architectural Forum* extolled the picture window's broad appeal, Robert Woods Kennedy condemned it as a superficial and misunderstood imitation of underlying principles. *Architectural Forum* itself, in 1957, described the piecemeal approach of "the real estate man": a character not exactly malevolent, but without moral restraint, focused on "appearances rather than a philosophy of building … the mass developer who scatters picture windows promiscuously throughout the country today". James Marston Fitch, who in 1950 applauded the "new view of nature" afforded by mass-produced glass, assumed by 1961 that homebuyers had a picture window simply because the neighbors did. Along with the chromium "gorp" dripping from postwar automobiles, picture windows were "manifestations of a profound inner uncertainty, of a corrosive lack of self-identification". Evoking Adolf Loos's and Thorstein Veblen's respective critiques of squandered social resources, along with contemporary sociology, Fitch derided picture windows as an affectation of status that "often verges on crime".[8] The transgression was this: from its development during the heroic age of early Modernism, the picture window had devolved to become just another object for mass consumption. Cheapened not only in cost but in character as well, the picture window was the utopian manifesto of transparency writ small.

Ubiquitous from coast to coast, the picture window became a synecdoche for middle-class consumer society, a kind of shorthand for everything wrong with American suburban culture – its equation of goodness with material acquisition, its fantasy of self-reliance amid numbing conformity, and its intolerance of difference, a racism invisible only from the picture window. In 1956, the sociologist John Keats detected a continent-wide "crack in the picture window"; for Keats, the postwar suburb was a reassuring pastoral package wrapped around an insipid form of settlement. The picture window had mutated from a mild anti-urban conceit – visual proof of a bucolic backdrop – into a farcical symbol of mindless accumulation and ritualized display. The image of picture windows opposite *other* picture windows became an ironic symbol: vision had been set free only to become entangled in the web of suburban social and architectural expectations. The picture window was a manifestation of suburbia's "visibility principle", as one sociologist described suburbia's confining openness, the sense in which it was an unwitting prison of perpetual disclosure. Daniel Boorstin went so far as to conclude his 1961 study of American culture, *The Image*, with a discussion of the picture window: the "thicket of unreality which stands between us and the facts of life". He saw the picture window as emblematic of a dense scrim of illusion: boredom disguised as leisure, living environments ruined by their owners' attempts to improve them and degraded by nothing more heroic than bad taste, a debasement of national consciousness that would be tragic were it not so banal. "How escape?" he asked. "How avoid a life of looking in and out of picture windows?"[9]

It would not be hard to extend this kind of critique to the present day, casting picture windows as a harbinger of spectacle, a little like a car's windshield and a lot like television: hidden technologies – under the hood, offscreen, or behind the hedge – allow distant objects or events to be experienced near-at-hand, without physical or even intellectual exertion, and sometimes even without actual distance. Small wonder, then, that early descriptions of television called it "the biggest window"; or that a child could exclaim as the blinds dropped over the picture window, "Mommy! The picture's lost!"; or that landscape itself might be shaped by how we become used to seeing it, as *Landscape* predicted in 1951: "The ultimate definition of landscape will probably be: the distant objects which are seen through a picture window. For it is distance, a remote and autonomous nature, that the picture window is intended to frame".[10] Whatever the formal innovations of landscape architects, seeing landscapes through picture windows must be counted as one of the ways in which the landscape became modern. A kind of inhabitable camera, the picture window filtered radiant energy to form images of the good life. It then became the work of urban planning and mass media, of earth-moving machines, lumber mills, lawn mowers, fertilizers, and nurseries, of federal loan guarantees, restrictive covenants, and banking practices, of electrification and highways, automobiles and appliances, developers and builders, clients and architects, to reconfigure that landscape to accord with our views of how it should be.

> Do I contradict myself? Very well, I contradict myself!
>
> Walt Whitman, *Leaves of Grass*, 1855

Outlook

The keenest disappointment caused by the picture window was that it promised relations with nature impossible to achieve: because of careless siting, windows were placed where there were no views and views were created into what had once been privacies. By the 1950s, streets were not considered appropriate aspects to look upon, while the overexposure of the domestic interior was being mocked in the popular press. Indeed, nothing so deformed the promise of the picture window as the prospect of looking *out* only to realize that one is being looked *at*: gazes were being returned from the otherwise sightless and volition-free landscape [*Fig. 55*]. There is, though, some irony in the unexamined notion that the sight of other suburbanites should be unwelcome. Most mid-twentieth-century critics assumed that the picture in the picture window *should* have remained the sylvan, unpopulated, and basically aristocratic prospect of a century earlier; few interpreted it in terms of the nascent sense of community discerned by Edwin Bateman Morris, or more recently, by Michael Pollan, who has suggested that, in our common experience, the picture window is an "image of promised land … The fact that the picture in the window was composed not of unspoiled nature but of a station wagon, a stamp of lawn, and the neighbor's split-level was nothing to regret".[11]

Such critiques suggest that the picture window has been judged, fairly or not, by standards that do not grasp its chief aspiration: the evocation of an appropriate setting for contemporary life, however much criticism that life may be subject to. To borrow a distinction applied to architecture by John Outram: suburbs are Arcadian at root, which is to say they are narrative, representational, focused on words and pictures, on recomposing the world into an idea. An Arcadian outlook characteristically seeks to fashion current social distinctions and cultural objects into a timeless narrative – into a story that accounts for why things are the way they are and why they should stay that way. Modernism, in contrast, is essentially utopian: abstract, syntactic, and focused on construction and number, on fabricating a world from an idea. Utopian standards are more visionary, even prophetic, and construe limits as a kind of corruption. The profile of Modernism's utopian moment remains sharp even today; distance from that epic time is measured in accumulated impurities. The picture window fails most conspicuously when measured against such utopian coordinates.[12]

Notes

1 Michael Pollan, "A Touch of Glass: Reflections in the Picture Window", *House and Garden*, September 1997, 132–6. Leo Marx, "The American Ideology of Space", in Stuart Wrede and William Howard Adams (eds) *Denatured Visions: Landscapes and Cultures in the Twentieth Century*, New York: Museum of Modern Art, 1991.

2 The phrase is used by Robert Atkinson and Hope Bagenal in *Theory and Elements of Architecture*, New York: McBride, 1926, pp. 319–23. They define cultural confidence as having no fear of either enemies or nature.

3 In Raymond McGrath, *Glass in Architecture and Decoration*, London: The Architectural Press, 1937, pp. 103–4.

4 Richard Brown, *Domestic Architecture*, London: Bernard Quaritch, 1852, p. 93.

5 Henry Hudson Holly, *Modern Dwellings in Town and Country*, New York: Harper and Bros., 1878, pp. 66, 204. Edith Wharton and Ogden Codman, *The Decoration of Houses* (1897), New York: Scribner, 1902, pp. 66–8.

6 Walter Curt Behrendt, *Modern Building*, New York: Harcourt, 1937, p. 173. "The House of 1942", *Architectural Forum*, September 1942, 69.

7 Edwin Bateman Morris, "How to View the Out-of-Doors", *Journal of the A.I.A.*, February 1953, 63–5. Here, Morris defines a picture window specifically as insulated double-glazing.

8 Robert Woods Kennedy, *The House and the Art of Its Design*, New York: Reinhold, 1953, p. 384. "The Real Estate Operator", *Architectural Forum's Building, U.S.A.*, New York: McGraw Hill, 1957, pp. 18–20. James Marston Fitch, "The New Architecture Started 70 Years Ago", *House Beautiful*, May 1950, 136, and *Architecture and the Esthetics of Plenty*, New York: Columbia University Press, 1961, p. 187.

9 John Keats, *The Crack in the Picture Window*, Boston: Houghton Mifflin, 1956. For Keats, the picture window represented excessive borrowing and illusory ownership, developer avarice, corporate bureaucracy, a nagging wife and an ineffectual husband, ennui and delusion, and consumer culture in general. His protagonists are John and Mary Drone. Daniel Boorstin, *The Image: A Guide to Pseudo-Events in America* (1961), New York: Atheneum, 1982, p. 259.

10 "Biggest window" cited in Cecelia Tichi, *Electronic Hearth: Creating an American Television Culture*, Oxford, Engl. and New York: Oxford University Press, 1991, p. 4. "Mommy" cited in Keats, *Crack in the Picture Window*, p. 81 [see above, this volume]. "The ultimate definition" cited in a book review, signed "P. K"., of Christopher Tunnard's *Gardens in the Modern*

Landscape, London: Architectural Press, 1938 and Kenneth Clark's *Landscape Into Art*, London: J. Murray, 1949.

11   Pollan, "A Touch of Glass", 134.

12   John Outram, "Uses and Abuses of Arcadia", *The Architectural Review*, June 1984, 78–80. William McClung applies this distinction specifically to English country-house literature in "The Country-House Arcadia", in Gervase Jackson-Stops (ed.) *The Fashioning and Functioning of the British Country House*, Washington, DC: National Gallery of Art, 1989, pp. 277–88.

Figure 48 "Something infinitely more serious than a new fad", cartoon by Don Kindler for John Keats, 1956.

Figure 49 "Owning property implied a certain permanence", cartoon by Don Kindler for John Keats, 1956.

Figure 50 Levittown, Pennsylvania, model houses, 1950s.

Figure 51
Levittown kitchen,
1950s.

Figure 52
Rudolph Matern, house,
1951, exterior.

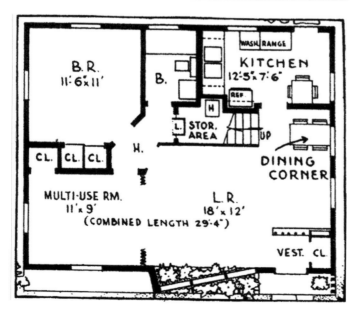

Figure 53
Rudolph Matern and
Herman York, house in
East Hempsted, Long
Island, 1949, plan

Figure 54   Continuous front lawns in 1960s housing development, Arlington Heights, Chicago, Illinois.

Figure 55   "Is there a picture in your picture window?", *House Beautiful*, January 1950.

10

Participatory planning and design
Initiatives in self-help housing, renovation, and interior decoration

A seminal writer in creating enthusiasm for "self-help" housing was architect and community activist John F. C. Turner, who studied the squatter settlements of Latin America in the 1960s, finding in them an inspiration for self-building, self-ownership, and responsive plans and street layouts (Fig. 56). Turner argued that temporary low-standard housing is often more useful to poor and marginal populations than high-standard subsidized housing; his writings gave currency to the slogan "the freedom to build", that inspired generations of squatters and socially-conscious builders and architects. Urban historian Alison Ravetz sketches the general evolution of self-help housing, including a few of the cooperative movements also discussed by Spencer-Wood, chapter 6, this volume. Architectural historian Peter Davey and architect Mats Egelius describe two of the most successful ventures of government-sponsored versions of participatory design: the work of Hardt-Waltherr Hämer and S.T.E.R.N. in Berlin-Kreuzberg, and Ralph Erskine's replanning and redesign of the Byker Wall section of Newcastle upon Tyne (Figs. 57, 58, 59, 60, 61). The important ways in which people modify their dwellings without building them from scratch are detailed by historian of vernacular architecture Alice Gray Read, historian of technology Carolyn Goldstein, and ethnographer Alison J. Clarke (Figs. 62, 63). Read shows how the inhabitants of the Mantua district of Philadelphia assert their ethnic identity by modifying the façades of their buildings; Goldstein describes the evolution of modern tools used in "do-it-yourself" work; and Clarke examines the interior decorating schemes of poor residents in London subsidized housing.

Squatter settlement
An architecture that works

John Turner (1968)

The squatter *barriada*-builder[1] who chooses to invest his life's savings in an environment that he creates, forms himself in the process. The person, as the member of a family and of a local community, finds in the responsibilities and activities of home-building and local improvement the creative dialogue essential for self-discovery and growth. The *barriada* is ground for living that the housing units, marketed or allocated by mass-consumption society, do not provide.

The *barriada* in Lima (like the *geçekondu* of Istanbul or the *villes extra-coutumiers* of

Kinshasa) is one element of a typical, rapidly growing city in a transitional economy. It is a suburb and, like the suburbs of modern cities, the *barriada* represents a step *up* from the inner city – and the vast majority of squatter home-builders are ex-city slum dwellers. Contrary to common belief, the majority of suburban or peri-urban squatter settlements in large cities are not temporary encampments of miserably poor rural migrants unable to find a job and a home in the city proper. The suburban home-builder is busy consolidating an *improved* status and, by doing so, he is further improving it and himself. Typically, he and his very young family have escaped from the depredations of the inner-city slumlord (often a renter of clandestine shacks costing half a minimum wage) thanks to a steadier and better-paid job – enabling the wage-earner to commute, the family to buy their water from lorries until it is laid on and to start building a permanent house. At least one quarter of Lima's population now live in *barriadas* and the majority of these 500,000 people are of "consolidating" blue-collar class families. They are the (very much poorer) Peruvian equivalents of the Building Society house-buyers of the suburbs of any city of the industrialized world.

The cities of the incipiently industrializing or transitional world, such as Lima, respond far more readily to the demands of the poor majority, than cities of the industrial or post-industrial world, like Chicago or New York, respond to their poor minorities. Because the poor are the majority in Lima and because the government controls neither the material nor the human resources necessary for the satisfaction of essential housing needs, the poor must act for themselves – and if the official rules and regulations get in their way these, along with any policemen who may be sent in to enforce them, are generally swept aside. Consequently, the very poor are able to find some corner for their private life, even if it's only a temporary shack in one of the interstices of the city – on an unguarded lot, in a ravine or even under a bridge. And the somewhat less poor are able to choose between renting one or two tenement rooms and squatting on the periphery. The urban poor in wealthy and highly institutionalized mass-consumption society do not have these freedoms. At best, like the Algerian and Portuguese immigrants to Paris, they are able to set up very poor *bidonvilles* on the edge of the city; more commonly, like the ghetto inhabitants of the United States cities, the poor can only rent tenements, from slumlords or from public housing authorities. There they must stay until they can make the far higher grade of suburbia in one leap – unless, of course, they are an ethnically discriminated minority in which case their environment will hold them down forever, or until they burn *it* down.

The man who would be free must build his own life. The existential value of the *barriada* is the product of three freedoms: the freedom of community self-selection; the freedom to budget one's own resources and the freedom to shape one's own environment.

The freedom of community self-selection

Barriada inhabitants, unlike institutionally or corporatively sponsored and controlled project "beneficiaries", are self-selected. The *barriada* squatters have a homogeneity of purpose but maintain the heterogeneity of social characteristics vital for cultural stimulation and growth. The project beneficiaries, as one result of the perhaps inevitable political constraints, have a far greater homogeneity of social character but are rarely unified by common purpose – except in opposition to their "benefactors". Anyone, or any household is free to join a *barriada* association as long as there is enough land to go round and as long as dues are paid – the only common rule is that the member must live on his plot.

As dues are low (and not always collected) and as a family with a very low income can afford to build a shack and live in the typical *barriada*, the lower socio-economic limit is very low indeed. On the other hand, the *barriada* offers many opportunities to the small businessman, the (lower-echelon or exceptionally unpretentious) professional or, even, to the aspiring political leader. It therefore attracts a wide range of individual interests and, naturally, the wider the range of its members the better served the community and the greater the opportunities of those who most need them.

The freedom to budget one's own resources

The outstanding difference between the *barriada* and orthodox modern housing is between the ways in which they are built: the squatter – when his tenure is secure enough to risk investment in permanent structures – builds by stages, in accordance with his priorities and budget; the modern housing development is completed to "minimum standards" at least, before it is occupied.

The traditional "progressive development" procedure is essential for those with low and uncertain incomes who are using their property and environmental improvements as socio-economic boot-straps. Those who are constantly threatened with loss of income through unemployment or because they have no health insurance and little free medical care, must depend for their security on relatives or on home-ownership. A new, largely young immigrant population will have few relatives on whom to depend for food and shelter in time of need – both necessities are too scarce to share for more than very brief periods. The young low-income family obliged to spend one-third or more of their cash income on rent for a slum tenement in constantly increasing demand is extremely vulnerable: as the landlord can get a higher rent when his tenants change he will have little patience with those in arrears. Eviction in time of domestic crisis is a sure way of destroying a poor man's hope – without which he will never seek opportunities or progress. But if the family is the owner, or *de facto* possessor of their home, even if it is no more than a shack on a plot of undeveloped land, they have an excellent anchor for their hope. In time of need their cash expenditure can be reduced to a much lower minimum as they have no rent to pay; in addition to that vital advantage, the family (or the abandoned woman with children) can get income from their property by renting part (or attracting another man), by using it as a shop or workshop or, in the last resort, by selling it in order to move on to greener pastures. "Property security" is a vital function of housing for the "consolidating" masses in cities like Lima and it is eliminated by the "instant development" procedure. The threat of foreclosure on the mortgage demanded by heavy, initial capital outlay can be an even greater one than that of eviction. The family can lose a good part of their savings as well as their home. The disadvantages so impressive from the point of view of the modern middle class – the necessity of living in provisional or incomplete structures and without all utilities for long periods – are small by comparison with the advantages. In addition to the incalculable value of securing their hope and sustaining their expectations through the steady improvement of their inalienable homes and local environment, the squatter families have far more space, light and fresh air than in the rented slum.

The freedom to shape one's own environment

Not only does the authoritarian "instant development" procedure demand the mortgage of a life's savings but it also imposes a sudden and drastic change of space-use and of personal relationships, both within the family and with neighbors. Perhaps only a minority of such families can use a modern standard dwelling effectively, even when they are in great need of a home of their own. Their highest priority is for secure tenure, but it is unlikely to be for plastered masonry walls and ceilings, let alone for modern kitchenettes and bathrooms. These are extremely costly items and, unless furnished properly, their naked dinginess is often alien and unattractive while the honestly poor shack is often personal and warm. The most important architectural advantage of the squatters' procedure is the consequent adaptability of space and structures to the changing needs and behavior patterns of the family. Over one generation of a family the changes can be immense: a young couple can have had a dozen children and the household can have expanded into an extended family with 15 or 20 members (with the arrival of grandparents and sundry relatives) and it can have shrunk again to an aging couple living alone or with an unmarried child or two. In the same period the family's life-style can have changed from that of the semi-peasant to that of the modern urban middle or lower-middle class. The typical *barriada* house starts as a shack or as a group of shacks and ends up as a two- or even three-story house – often subdivided into several separate dwellings occupied by the original squatters' children or rented in order to provide the owners with an income in their old age. The ground floor is often used as a shop or workshop (7 percent of the houses in Pampa de Cueva were used in these ways five years after its establishment). This freedom to manipulate one's own living space is extended to the community as a whole: it is the local association that generally decides on the number of schools, open spaces, markets and so on. Local community associations work hard to establish all kinds of facilities and services, from primary schools to sewer systems, but they often fail, mainly through lack of the administrative know-how and credit assistance which their governments should be providing them with instead of uneconomic and inflexible housing projects.

That the mass of the urban poor in cities like Lima are able to seek and find improvement through home-ownership (or *de facto* possession) when they are still very poor by modern standards is certainly the main reason for their optimism. If they were trapped in the inner cities, like so many of the North American poor, they too would be burning instead of building. The mass-designed, mass-produced environments for an increasingly homogenized market of mass-consumers are no more than assemblies of material goods devoid of existential meaning. They are not the product of dialogue. Decisions are made for a producer's market by those themselves bound by highly institutionalized norms and procedures. The occupant buys or rents a ready-made unit in much the same way as he gets his motor car or TV set – and if it is a flat or in a tightly controlled subdivision, he can do little more with his house than he can with the other manufactured "goods" essential for his way of life. The intense dialogue that takes place between squatters planning an invasion, and the continuing dialogue of its development and administration are, with rare exceptions, totally lacking in the modern housing process.

Notes

1 A *barriada* is the Peruvian term for squatter settlement.

Self-help housing

Alison Ravetz with Richard Turkington (1995)

Squatting

[...] Squatting embraced a number of dichotomies: it could be either an individual or a group effort; it could be pragmatically or ideologically motivated; and it could use new or rehabilitated buildings, in either conventional or unconventional ways. Its one invariable principle was that it was for housing the homeless: oneself or others. Beyond that, there might be secondary purposes, which could include taking a political stand or living an alternative lifestyle. These dichotomies largely account for the complex factional history of squatting movements, as well as official reactions to them. If anything, Labor administrations were the most hostile to squatters, for challenging orderly programs of housing provision and allocation. Conservatives were more willing, at least from time to time, to do "deals" with squatters, whose self-help and initiative they might use to break through impasses in housing policy.

Contrary to popular assumptions, squatters seldom if ever invaded inhabited property, even when its owners were absent. They were concerned with empty, and so predominantly pre–1914 property, whether houses or institutional buildings. "Skippering" – individual squatting by down-and-outs – had little general impact: for since it was furtive, those practicing it did not try to restore services or make other changes, but simply moved on when squats became too fouled. Collective squatting campaigns, in contrast, sought both to draw attention to the scandal of homelessness and to exploit the legal status of squatting in order to get access to homes as rent-paying tenants. As Colin Ward pointed out, this was of necessity a post-1945 phenomenon, for it depended on buildings left empty for reasons of speculation, or in expectation of slum clearance.[1]

A squatting campaign after the First World War left little lasting record.[2] That following the Second World War began with mass invasions of disused service camps in 1946. Eventually over a thousand camps were affected, involving some forty thousand people. Life in the camps was organized democratically with a weekly levy, communal kitchens, nurseries, and rotas for building work. Whitehall was not at first ill disposed towards the squatters and leant on local authorities in the areas concerned to take over the camps. Many did so and some of the camps that were squatted eventually evolved into permanent council estates [*state-owned and subsidized housing, Ed.*].

The next stage of the campaign, which took place mainly in London, was more confrontational, involving takeover of a number of empty hotels, luxury flats and other buildings. The Duchess of Bedford Mansions, a block of empty luxury flats in Kensington, were occupied by several hundred families, the fathers of many of them ex-servicemen. The Communist Party claimed to play the leading role, and although this was disputed by other participants, the police and press so far believed it that, in the event, five Communist borough councilors were brought to trial for conspiracy. The eventual outcome of the occupation was a negotiated settlement and peaceful evacuation. Some of the families concerned were resettled, first in residential Homes or Part III accommodation,[3] and later in normal council housing.[4] Solidarity, self help and inspired improvisation remained high in the memories of those who took part, evoking memories of wartime cameraderie. There was however no sign that the squatters' ambition was to achieve anything other than conventional family housing.

Twenty years later there were hopes of a new family squatting campaign imitating the successes of the 1940s.[5] It owed one of its origins to a protest of homeless families in a Part III hostel in Kent, where fourteen excluded husbands illegally moved in with their families. Two of the men were jailed, but the outcome was improved conditions, both there and in other hostels. The other origin lay in growing awareness of the scandal of empty houses. In the London borough of Redbridge, a Conservative controlled council had boarded up a street of substantial houses, in anticipation of town center redevelopment (the plan for which was eventually abandoned). Squatters broke into some of the houses and as far as possible made them fit for people to live as normal families.[6] Countering action by the council led to sieges, violent evictions by bailiffs, deliberate wrecking of interiors and services, and demolitions. In retaliation, some of the squatters carried out a campaign of personal harassment against individual councilors. Support for the squatters came from the surprisingly wide alliance of ratepayers, political and religious groups, and eventually some of the houses were patched and handed over to short-life housing associations, with Ministry approval.[7]

Similar campaigns took place in many parts of London and a number of towns and cities, where office blocks and other empty buildings were occupied. The internal history of the movement shows a complicated array of organizations and alliances throughout the 1970s. Their achievements included two London-wide unions, a "squatters' charter", the establishment of advisory services, a squatters' "estate agency", handbooks, and an organized campaign against the proposal in 1974 to convert squatting from a civil to a legal offence. Squatters even invaded the 1979 Ideal Homes Exhibition where they briefly set up an "Ideal Squat".[8] [...] Altogether, considerable numbers of people were squatters: a conservative estimate was some 25,000 in London and 30,000 in total, but other estimates were much higher.[9]

The entirely new aspect of this later squatting movement was the involvement of single homeless people. This was apparent at Redbridge, where single would-be squatters were resented for spoiling family squatters' chances of re-housing.[10] The unmet housing needs of single people were the motive for a notorious squat of 144 Piccadilly in 1969. This large empty mansion was taken over by a hippy commune who at one stage invited in the Hell's Angels, whereupon the Skinheads came to fight them, with much ensuing violence and a police raid. This helped to color public perceptions of all squatters as hippies, but for the most part young single squatters were more influenced by pacifist direct action and the painstaking local community action of campaigns against slum clearance. Many found inspiration in the "free city" of Christiania in the heart of Copenhagen,[11] seeing themselves, therefore, as urban pioneers who followed different objectives from the family squatters. "As well as raising questions about the *amount* of housing available, squatters increasingly challenged the *nature* of housing and the quality of community life".[12] Their sense of community led them to develop street art, theatre, festivals, carnivals and communal street parties of a kind not seen since the demise of working-class neighborhood culture some twenty or more years before. Their global as well as local consciousness led them to become involved in wholefood shops, bookshops, recycling, community gardens, wind and solar power, and geodesic domes. In pursuit of its ideals one small West London squat (later converted to a housing co-op) declared itself the "free and independent republic of Frestonia".[13] [...]

The campaigns of single squatters appeared to die away in the right-wing policies of the 1980s, but there still remained uncounted numbers of squatters particularly in inner London, and the main reason for squatting was, as ever, people's need of homes when no other affordable property was available. In 1994, the Criminal Justice and Public Order Act threatened squatters as much as [New Age] travelers, and some local councils were already taking independent action to clear them out of their boroughs.

The longer-term achievements of single-person squatting were less obvious than those of the family squatting campaigns, although in some respects more pervasive. While some of the squatters must have joined the New Age travelers, they also contributed a generation of veterans to community and environmental politics, finding channels in various forms of advocacy planning such as Community Technical Aid Centers, the Tenant Participation Advisory Service, legal aid centers, and a host of local initiatives. More generally, they merged into the loose movement known as "community architecture" which embraced both individual architects and consultancies, including those involved in the rehabilitation of hard-to-let council estates and multi-story flats. Squatters also brought new populations and cultures to the areas they colonized, such as Hebden Bridge in West Yorkshire, where they attempted and partially succeeded in saving condemned houses, in some cases converting them to alternative domestic patterns to those of the conventional nuclear family.[14]

Housing co-operatives and alternative communities

Housing co-operatives shared the now familiar dichotomies of others kinds of self-help housing. They had, of necessity, to pertain to groups rather than individuals, but they could be pragmatic (as a route to normal housing) or ideological, to allow their members to practice a chosen lifestyle, whether in new or old houses. In operation, they were likely always to bear some traces of the ideological, if only because of the unfamiliarity of the tenure within the mainstream British housing system. [...]

For ethnic or other minority groups the co-op became the vehicle of special kinds of dwelling and layout, to meet needs and provide a sense of security and identity. It could also be an expression of group philosophy and community ideals. Thus many groups purposely included dwellings for the elderly and wheelchair-bound. Funds permitting, some opted to include an old people's lounge or clubroom, and some were still more ambitious than this. Two of the most innovative were those of the Weller Streets and Eldonian Community, both in Liverpool and initiated by local residents, and both seeking to use their own experience to proselytize and train further groups. The Eldonians, in particular, set out to create a "village" which would include not only members' homes but shops, new local industries, training opportunities, a community "health villa" and projects for leisure and tourism.[15] At this scale of activity they resembled the Coin Street Community Builders on the South Bank of the Thames who, with ownership of extensive and valuable metropolitan land, developed a series of housing co-operatives through "shell groups" of local people (who would not themselves be the occupants), together with a building and exhibition center, an extensive street market with shops and restaurants, public riverside gardens and a museum and arts center.[16]

At such a scale, the housing co-operative shared something of the scope of the larger alternative community. The difference was that it operated, when it could, with official funding and for the most part provided conventional housing for people who could be considered "ordinary" members of the public. By definition, alternative communities set themselves apart from the normal world and among other things this meant that they were usually, though not invariably, rurally based. Typically they started from small beginnings with insecure finance, and consequent effects on the type of property they were able to occupy. A favorite choice was the large country house or redundant farm, which were adaptable for use as educational and craft centers. The main objective of urban groups was more likely to be simply to work out forms for living together, but they also took on crafts and various forms of social service. As well as large villas, the row of small houses that could be knocked through was suitable for their purposes.[17]

The active period for the foundation of alternative communities was the 1970s. Most were very small and broke up after a short life in which sharing domestic space raised many problems of decision-making, privacy, child and house care.[18] The most durable examples were those with a strongly religious basis. Monastic orders, of course, had endured for hundreds of years, with a way of life actively followed throughout the twentieth century. A new initiative of this century was the Camphill community, begun according to the teachings of Rudolph Steiner as educational and curative centers for children with mental disabilities, and continued in the form of new "villages" for adults with such disabilities. In the dozen or so Camphill villages throughout the country a new pattern was established where "families" of house-parents, children, "villagers" and volunteers lived in large purpose-built or adapted houses of a dozen or more workers and clients who shared meals, outings and cultural activities, as a family. The Camphill villages were also partly self-supporting, with workshops, gardens and farms. By the 1990s, some of their houses were being registered as residential Homes under "care in the community" policies; but the care that was given was within the already established framework of an alternative way of life.[19] [...]

It was ... mainly squatters, communards and alternative communities who experimented with new patterns. Some tried co-operative living only to revert to conventional privacy and self-containment, as did the free and independent Frestonians when they re-formed themselves as a housing co-op.[20] Exciting and innovative ideas put forward by others remained in the realm of fantasy, as did the Hebden Bridge proposal for a unified terrace incorporating children's houses, workshops, music room, organic garden and wind generator.[21] Though less ambitious, the unknown numbers of houses shared by young people who chose to share expenses, catering and other chores were probably influenced by these examples. As for conventional housing, although the postwar women's liberation movement continued to rail against the self-contained home, it appears that it was driven by strong cultural imperatives, both for families and single people. Indeed, as a contributor to *The Freewoman* had pointed out in 1912, had there been any widespread desire for co-operative housekeeping, people could well have developed their own schemes within the homes they already had.[22]

The significance of self-help housing

While for obvious reasons the exact amount of self-help in housing is unknown, it is clear that, even discounting "conventional" self build, upwards of a million people may have been involved throughout the century – more, that is, than all the subjects of institutional housing. But since so many different groups with different purposes were involved, this provides little guide to the real significance of these housing alternatives, for which a more discriminating approach is needed.

In the main, self-help in housing was an opportunistic response to housing need among the poor or marginalized, whose aim was usually to get access to a normal, self-contained home within the usual range of tenures. For the most part it was for the young and energetic, as well as the skilled, or those who were able to acquire skills quickly. But in desperate need, people of all kinds created homes out of anything that was at hand – including vehicles, sheds, boats – and then self-help demonstrated not only people's ingenuity but their ability to be satisfied with self-chosen standards which could diverge very significantly from official standards or what was generally thought to be a proper home ...

Technically innovatory self-help was only socially innovatory when it expressed a different culture (as the gypsies) or new forms of social organization. Innovations with tenure were potentially more socially alternative, and in this respect co-operative tenure is interesting. It was often adopted for the duration of a self-building scheme, only to be relinquished when the individual builders became owner occupiers, and it could also be treated as a slightly unusual form of renting. But the tenure had more radical potential than this, whether to create wider environments, or to bring about a new relationship to their homes among the members, through being collective rather than individual owners. In the early 1990s it was still too soon to see how far such potential might be realized, and little was yet known of the operation of housing co-ops following their pioneering phase, when the enthusiasm of the founder generation might have waned.

By far the largest number of social innovators were the squatter communards – not those who sought conventional ends, but the self-styled "urban pioneers", who did report a different and "unique" connection to their homes,[23] although in the long run they could find themselves involved in a role not unlike that of landlord.[24] Older houses that were squatted lent themselves well to social experiments, especially when whole terraces could be adapted to a group. Thus twenty elegant terraced houses of the Villa Road housing co-op, saved in defiance of Lambeth Borough Council, made it possible for 160 people "to remain together as a community ... retaining many of the collective arrangements and physical adaptations ... over the years".[25] The dilapidated condition of such houses was regarded as an asset, allowing as it did a repudiation of conventional housekeeping and a stimulus to creativity.

Self-help in housing, therefore, has different functions: in one case it can be a means to an end and in another the end itself, and it is misleading to lump these together. The first case demonstrates the power of groups in getting homes for people whom the system does not serve; the second is part of a quest for alternative social forms.

Notes

1 Colin Ward, "The Early Squatters: Squatting from the Middle Ages to the Second World War", in Nick Wates and Christian Wolmar (eds), *Squatting: The Real Story*, London: Bayleaf Books, 1980.
2 Ibid.
3 Alison Ravetz with Richard Turkington, *The Place of Home: English Domestic Environments 1914–2000*, London: Spon, 1995, p. 84.
4 Noreen Branson, "London Squatters 1946", Proceedings of a conference held by the Communist Party History Group, May 1984, *Our History*, Pamphlet 80, 1989.
5 Ron Bailey, *The Squatters*, Harmondsworth: Penguin, 1973.
6 Ibid.
7 Ibid.; Steve Platt, "A Decade of Squatting: The Story of Squatting in Britain since 1968", in Wates and Wolmar, *Squatting: The Real Story*.

8   Wates and Wolmar, *Squatting: The Real Story*.
9   Frederick Shaw, *The Homes and Homeless of Postwar Britain*, London: Parthenon, 1985.
10 Bailey, *The Squatters*.
11 Mark Gimson, "Everybody's Doing It", in Wates and Wolmar, *Squatting: The Real Story*.
12 Platt, "A Decade of Squatting", p. 38.
13 Ibid., p. 93.
14 Andrew Ingham, "Using the Space", in Wates and Wolmar, *Squatting: The Real Story*.
15 Ruth Owens, "Parker Morris in the Pub", *Architects' Journal*, June 29, 1984, 52–61; Robert Cowan, Patrick Hannay, and Ruth Owens, "Community-Led Regeneration by the Eldonians", *Architects' Journal*, March 23, 1988, 37–63.
16 *Community Action*, "Coin Street Community Plan in Action", no. 83, Spring, 1990, 15–9; *Architects' Journal*, "Studies in Practice: Coin Street Design Team", June 7, 1989, 93–6.
17 Michèle and Kevin (of The Teachers), *Directory of Alternative Communities in the British Isles*, 4th edn, Bangor: The Teachers, 1983.
18 Andrew Rigby, *Communes in Britain*, London: Routledge and Kegan Paul, 1974.
19 Anke Weihs and Joan Tallo (eds), *Camphill Villages*, 2nd edn Gloucester: Camphill Press, 1988.
20 Ruth Owens, "Bramley Housing Co-Op, Freston Road, London W.11: Appraisal", *Architects' Journal*, April 29, 1987, 37–46.
21 Ingham, "Using the Space".
22 Lynn F. Pearson, *The Architectural and Social History of Co-Operative Living*, London: Macmillan, p. 122.
23 Ingham, "Using the Space", p. 173.
24 Tom Osborn, "Outpost of a New Culture: Squatting Communities as an Alternative Way of Life", in Wates and Wolmar, *Squatting: The Real Story*.
25 Nick Anning and Jill Simpson, "Victory Villa: Challenging the Planners in South London, Villa Road", in Wates and Wolmar, *Squatting: The Real Story*, p. 149.

S.T.E.R.N. work

Peter Davey (1987)

It is a commonplace that on August 13, 1961 the Wall cut Berlin in half along class boundaries. To the west are the prosperous, leafy middle-class districts; to the east are the old city center and the working-class areas. In London terms, it is like dividing the parks, Kensington and the rich outer western suburbs from Westminster, the City and the East End. In fact, Berlin's division was not nearly so neat. Among many anomalies on the western side, old inner working-class districts like Wedding and Kreuzberg have been cut off from their *raison d'être*, the city center.

While West Berlin struggled to found a new commercial center in Schöneberg round the Kurfürstendamm, these western working-class areas seemed peripheral. During the '60s and '70s, Kreuzberg in particular was laid waste by grand plans for motorway connections leading to East Berlin. They were evolved under [Hans] Scharoun's period as planner for the whole city … and had little hope of ever being implemented, but property in their tracks was either knocked down or allowed to become vacant. Even the War had been less destructive; after 1945, the fabric was much battered but the fundamental urban structure of street and block remained. The process was accelerated by large-scale demolitions to make way for comprehensive redevelopment funded by central government grants. Yet at the same time, Kreuzberg was under intense pressure because the Wall had prevented nearly 50,000 workers traveling daily from East Berlin to the west;

new workers were urgently needed and many of them came from Turkey. These *Gastarbeiter*, workers but not citizens, found that virtually the only places in which they could find accommodation were the old working-class areas where they had to live in squalor. The population of Kreuzberg is now 50 percent Turkish; in some nursery schools 80 percent of pupils are immigrants.

When the IBA [*Internationale Bau-Ausstellung*, International Building Exposition] was set up in 1979, the Altbau (rehabilitation) section was given the task of "saving this urban wreck" and made responsible for the urban regeneration of two chunks of Kreuzberg: Luisenstadt and SO 36 (the remaining parts of the old south-east 36 postal district).

The two are rather different in nature. Luisenstadt was originally developed according to a plan by [Karl Friedrich] Schinkel's contemporary Peter Joseph Lenné. From 1841, a picturesque series of streets and squares emerged. They were defined by low blocks of housing enclosing large semi-private interior open spaces ... Under the pressure of imperial industrialization, extra stories were added to the perimeter housing and the interiors of the blocks were developed as a mixture of flats and factories.

The development of SO 36 was much more directly a result of Berlin's industrial revolution. From the mid-1860s, workers streaming into the city from Silesia were housed in the large deep blocks (so designed to reduce the cost of perimeter roads) which surrounded Görlitzer Bahnhof. In the virtually gridiron plan, there were no squares or parks. The blocks are high (four or five stories of flats over shops on the ground floor) and within their perimeters was an intricate pattern of small dark courts defined by a mixture of more flats, flatted workshops and small factories. From the first, SO 36 was squalid and overcrowded. Even today, it is easy to understand the reaction of the politicians and planners of the 1920s down to the '60s to the fetid Kreuzberg mixture – pull most of it down and start again. But by the late '70s, it was clear that this solution was making the human problems worse. The remaining buildings were even more overcrowded, or else empty; businesses were rapidly leaving the area, causing local unemployment. The squalor remained.

For Hardt-Waltherr Hämer, director of Altbau, there was only one solution: conserve as much as possible of what remained of Kreuzberg and enhance it to make tolerable living conditions and stabilize business confidence. This was to be done by "careful urban renewal" (*behutsame Stadterneuerung*) – a gradual program, completely opposite to the policy in force when Hämer took over. That had envisaged rebuilding 1,600 dwellings and totally modernizing 4–5,000 more. Hämer pointed out that this would mean that 12 to 15,000 residents would have to leave the area within three years and several hundred businesses would have to go too.

By March 1983, the Senate of Berlin had agreed to a 12 point careful urban-renewal program.[1] This laid down that the work in Kreuzberg should be carried out with the participation of the residents, be gradual and should respect the character of the area. This character is not only virtually unique in Europe as one of the last and densest enclaves of the first industrial revolution but it has positive aspects as well. Strong local communities exist (German as well as Turkish); the mix of functions is fundamentally vital; the dense urban structure is inherently energy conservationist and it is cheaper to repair and improve the fabric rather than pulling it down and rebuilding [*Fig. 57*].

Step by step

The step-by-step approach adopted by IBA Altbau first of all involved reusing the empty buildings – particularly in Luisenstadt which had been more affected by the consequences of '60s planning and where Altbau had powers to act as development authority. The rehabilitated buildings later became a reserve to accommodate people who were displaced when their blocks were improved. By moving people to the previously empty blocks (and the few new blocks built under IBA aegis, for instance Block 88 by [William] Holzbauer),[2] it has been possible for 95 percent of inhabitants affected by rehabilitation to remain in Kreuzberg – 61 percent in their original flats.

To be able to keep many people in their original surroundings, Altbau had to evolve a special way of working. Block architects are appointed to be responsible for the overall program of repair of each block and to ensure that the inhabitants are fully consulted and involved. The first priority is to stabilize the rundown fabric – make the buildings watertight, better insulated and structurally sound. Then, after discussion with tenants (modernization financed by public funds cannot be enforced against the will of the tenants concerned) decisions about individual flats can be implemented. Proper kitchens and bathrooms are installed; very small flats are merged to make less cramped living conditions. Both these measures lead to an overall reduction in the number of flats in each block – hence the need for the reserve of accommodation in new buildings and renovated abandoned blocks. While improvements are done to a decent level, as far as they can be they are done by tenants on a self-help basis [*Figs. 58, 59*]. Standards are not as high as they were under the previous regime where blocks were in effect gutted and completely new flats built inside the shells. For instance, heat is wherever possible provided by an IBA-developed gas fired core system (living room and kitchen) rather than full central heating which would be beyond the reach of most tenants' budgets. Keeping as much as possible of the very tight rectangular jigsaw planning of [the] Kreuzberg mix ensures that geometry assists fuel economy by allowing waste heat to be absorbed by neighboring flats.

But keeping the geometry certainly poses problems. Occasionally parts of the meanest courtyards have been knocked down to let in more light but, in general, the yards remain dark and grim (to a non-Berliner's eyes). When two flats are knocked together, improvements can often be made by giving the resulting plan prospect to the street or at least another court, but for many the only amelioration can be in painting and greening the yards.

Much work of this kind continues (250 courts are in the program) – it is the micro end of a large-scale program for improvement of public facilities in Kreuzberg. Russian tanks demolished a good many of the tactically important block corners in the last days of the War. Some of the resulting gap sites have been turned into neighborhood gardens – an idea that would be anathema in the Neubau area of IBA where turning the corner is one of the chief formal problems of block design. But the lost corners let light and air into the inner units and paradoxically, by losing part of their outward form, the blocks gain potential for inner life.

Pavements in some of the relatively broad streets have been widened, relaid and planted with trees. Three existing schools will be converted to cater for over 2,000 pupils[3] and there is a large program of children's day centers (particularly needed to cater for large Turkish families). These are usually built within the courts and grow out of converted ground floors of the perimeter …

Other social injections organized by IBA include [Otto] Steidle's old people's home on Köpenickerstrasse …, a women's center, gymnasia, youth centers and a children's farm. As Hämer says, more important than the figures "is the fact that from a situation which had become hopeless, from resignation and resistance, some hope, a first sign of self-confidence and a growing identity with the quarter were able to emerge". In fact, success is becoming a problem in itself. Though squalor is far from abolished and Turkish children still play in noisome puddles, the quality of Kreuzberg has improved so much that the yuppies are beginning to move in; Kreuzberg is becoming the Fulham or Greenwich Village of Berlin. So one of the main battles now faced by Hämer's organization is to hold down rents charged by the private landlords enough to allow poorer tenants to afford improvements to their flats.

The battles will go on. Altbau has been reconstituted as S.T.E.R.N., *Gesellschaft der behutsamen Stadterneuerung Berlin*. It will continue its work in Kreuzberg – and elsewhere – after IBA ends this year.

Notes

1   The 12-point careful urban-renewal program: 1. The residents and the local business community must be involved in planning rehabilitation measures, and these must be carried out in a manner conducive to conserving the existing building stock. 2. Planners, the residents and the local business community must agree on the objectives and implementation of rehabilitation measures; technical planning and social planning must be operations pursued in parallel. 3. Kreuzberg's characteristic features must be preserved, and trust and confidence must be reestablished in the endangered neighborhoods; defects which threaten the substance of buildings must be remedied immediately. 4. Minor modifications of layouts should permit the development of new forms of living. 5. The rehabilitation of apartments and houses should be undertaken on a step-by-step basis and gradually expanded. 6. The context should be upgraded by minimizing demolition work, laying out green spaces inside the block structures and restoring façades. 7. Public amenities, streets, squares and green spaces must be rehabilitated and supplemented to meet local needs. 8. The participatory and material rights of the parties concerned must be specified in the social planning. 9. Decisions concerning urban rehabilitation measures must be taken in an open process and discussed to the extent possible in the locality; efforts must be made to strengthen the involvement of those affected. 10. Irrevocable financial pledges are required to strengthen confidence in urban rehabilitation; the funds must be disbursed without delay in order to be available for the scheduled expenditures. 11. New forms of trusteeship are to be developed; fiduciary renewal functions (services) must be kept distinct from construction measures. 12. This concept of urban rehabilitation must be safeguarded beyond the year 1984.

2   Other new buildings in the Altbau area include Alvaro Siza's corner block on Ickensteinstrasse and Schlesische Strasse (*Architectural Review*, September 1984, 40–1) and Hinrich & Inken Baller's reconstruction of the Fraenkelufer block (*Architectural Review*, September 1984, 30–5). The austere Rationalism of the first was widely acclaimed by architects; the flamboyant expressionism of the Baller work made it the most popular of all IBA buildings in a poll carried out by a city newspaper.

3   These heavy red *klinker-brick* Prussian barrack-like buildings are being reorganized to let in more light, provide smaller spaces for small groups and specialist subjects, and allow for team teaching (see *Architectural Review*, September 1984, 39).

The Byker Wall
Mats Egelius (1990)

On approaching Byker (1969–81) in Newcastle-on-Tyne, one sees a high, curving wall of brick and it is hard not to be impressed by this enormous mural. Patterns formed by bricks in five different colors are an excellent means of reducing the scale of this massive wall, besides showing the visitor how to find the entrances in this one-and-a-half kilometer long building.

The residents will readily explain the protective function of the wall – that it shuts out traffic noise and cold driving north winds – and how the cheerfully colored cowls outside the kitchens act as sound traps. The residents have certainly learned much from official sources and extensive media coverage. The dailies, Sunday supplements and TV have analyzed this successful rebuilding of a part of the town, and how its people got a chance to exercise influence during construction.

Once through the wall, the other side is found to be full of life, the access galleries are full of activity and a small-scale colorful community extends within the curve of the wall [*Fig. 60*]. Any initially critical attitude dissolves on seeing the apparently contented inhabitants; Byker attracts tourists, and its people are ready to show their visitors the sights.

Old Byker, an area of mineworkers' dwellings, is now only a grim memory of appalling housing. During the 1880s, small two-up-and-two-down brick houses were built here for shipyard workers and others in rapidly expanding heavy industry, and 18,000 people were crammed into an area that now houses 7,850. Sanitary standards were abysmal. There was, however, a strong sense of community, not just within the traditional extended families, and social control was strong. Local businesses flourished, and in 1959 there were 115 shops and most goods and services were available locally.

The political slogan for rebuilding was "Byker for Byker people". Renovation and improvement were unsuitable remedies for houses on the point of collapse and a deficient urban structure. This was confirmed in 1968, in an independent public-opinion poll that found 80 percent of respondents in favor of total rebuilding. The local-government planners and architects had worked out a proposal for a wholly new area protected by a solid wall to the north and east that would shut out the noise of a planned motorway and urban railway. The decision to build something new was in line with the Newcastle development plan.

During a period of expansion in the 1960s, Newcastle was to be transformed from a gray city of heavy industry to a modern administrative center for north-eastern England. The planning committee, on which the Conservative party had the majority, wanted to allocate resources from the local-government authority to private enterprise. The Conservatives chose [Ralph] Erskine, who was working on the Killingworth housing estate just outside Newcastle, and who was known to have the social commitment that would be needed to solve the sensitive issue of renewing Byker.

On being offered the commission in September 1968, he asked for a month to think it over and gain some idea of the social problems in Byker. Two of his employees – his elder daughter Jane, and Arne Nilsson – moved to the area to live there. Then Erskine reached agreement with the authorities over how the work should be done. His priorities were that he should take account firstly of what the residents of Byker wanted, secondly of what people in the immediate area wanted, and thirdly what the client wanted. Some other important goals were set out in a memorandum dated November 1968.

At the lowest possible cost for the residents, and in intimate contact and collaboration with them particularly, and with relevant authorities generally, to prepare a project for planning and building a complete and integrated environment for living in its widest possible sense. This would involve us in endeavoring to create positive conditions for dwelling, shopping, recreation, studying and – as far as possible – working in near contact with the home. It would involve us in considering the wishes of people of all ages and many tastes.

We would endeavor to maintain as far as possible valued traditions and characteristics of the neighborhood itself and its relations with the surrounding areas and the center of Newcastle.

The main concern will be with those who are already resident in Byker, and the need to re-house them without breaking family ties and other valued associations or patterns of life. We would endeavor to exploit the physical character of the site, more especially the slope to the south, its views and sunny aspect.

Once he had accepted the commission, Erskine opened a small office in a disused undertaker's in Byker and began a tenants' influence policy by simply leaving its door open. Vernon Gracie, who ran the comprehensive activities of the office, lived upstairs, and Byker people, who soon found their way to their architect, began to talk about vandalism, leaky pipes, even the apartments they were to move into.

The first tangible result of these contacts was a pilot project, Janet Square, built in 1971–72 on a site that had been cleared earlier [*Fig. 61*]. Forty-seven families agreed to take part in tenants' planning activity before moving in. At the start, they were highly suspicious of what the authorities were up to, but when the project was complete everyone knew it had been worthwhile; for example, countless meetings and questionnaires revealed the residents' liking for open-plan layouts and primary colors.

Once lived in, the pilot area proved disappointing, but the local authority showed its support for Erskine. The trouble was that, just like what it replaced, the area was felt to be dark and cramped; its back street idea and unbroken dark brickwork was not used later. The idea of making a square a pleasant meeting place was much liked, but people living on the square were disturbed by kids at play. The pilot project revealed a Byker hierarchy that the Erskine team had not perceived earlier: those who moved in from a high-status area up the hill had trouble mixing with folk from down the hill, near the Tyne.

Contact with the reference group made it clear that people did not just want refurbished streets and houses – they had clear ideas of a wholly new Byker. They wanted to preserve Byker's small corner shops, pubs and laundries, the bathhouse and other meeting points. They agreed that the proposed number of apartments should be reduced, and actively discussed traffic solutions, green areas and playground equipment. But what they wanted first were results, instead of more of the promises and discussions that had gone on since the 1950s. [...]

After the pilot project but before making any further enquiries of the Byker people, work began on building the Wall. It was to shut out the noise of a planned motorway, although the idea of a building containing dwellings in the form of a continuous, curving wall has fascinated architects since Le Corbusier drew his plans for the Bay of Algiers in the 1930s. In the 1950s, when Team Ten's work extended the idea of the function of a linear wall as a symbol of the creation of identity, Erskine advanced his idea of a wall as a protection in cold climates against chilly north winds.

In the opinion of the residents of Byker, the Wall is less successful than the low-level housing it surrounds, but many of them who live in the Wall are pleased, praising its wonderful views and the form of its access galleries. Its colossal format is toned down by its wave-like form and its variations in height, color and materials. From the Wall itself, one sees never more than a part of it. Its galleries are narrow and often their visual perspectives are shortened, for example by pergolas. Where the internal stairways open onto the galleries, there are often small projecting meeting places, formed as greenhouses. The light and airy galleries, roofed in corrugated plastic, have lots of sitting places and flower boxes. [...]

The low-level dwellings, which comprise 80 percent of the project, are less remarkable. Erskine and his fellow architects succeeded in creating attractive, traffic-free surroundings, with a great many open spaces, all of varying quality, ground texture and scale. Lampposts, bollards and cobblestones make the surroundings interesting. Among the decorative elements, one notices classical embellishments, which came from the demolished town hall; the Byker office was instrumental in saving them. In summer, the narrow alleys of Byker are tunnels of flowers and climbing plants. An additional measure of economic support for the care of plants was a precondition for this green town: a lot of good soil was acquired, and the office provided free advice, having started by planting a reserve of a number of trees, so that the new area could be leafy right from the start.

Over the years, the greenery has become rather jungly, and an architect might think that administrators could well take out their machetes and clear a view of some houses. The residents use and look after their gardens in different ways: some cultivate roses, herbs and climbing plants, but few seem to have the use of a lawn mower. Along the pathways, the mixture of asphalt, plants and stone is very successful. Animals do well in Byker: Erskine provided nesting boxes that top off roofs and crown rainwater pipes in a light-hearted way, and birds have nested elsewhere too. Some residents try to keep pigeons off their balconies with wires and nets, while down below dogs run about, and bark at visitors, and plainly ignore notices stating that "It Is Forbidden By Order, on Penalty of a Fine of Fifty Pounds to soil the pavements".

Byker is an exciting labyrinth of a place, but difficult to see as a whole and without a palpably main street. The central pathway, flanked with trees, has the name and position of former Raby Street, but as an urban artery it cannot compare with the busy commerce of the old main street. The new shopping square is a disappointment, and its few shops are carefully enclosed within steel gratings and heavy doors after closing time. Vandalism is not particularly common in Byker.

While Byker was building, Erskine made regular visits and the architects in the local office traveled often to Stockholm, where all important decisions on design and form were taken. The Byker office decided most questions of administration of the new buildings, which allowed it to be more influenced by the residents.

Byker has much in common with Erskine's earlier projects. The novelty concerned foremost building administration. Many improvements were initiated by Vernon Gracie, who learned at first hand how dreadful it was to live in Byker with vandalism, thefts and other unpleasantness of the demolition and building period. As a result, he proposed new guidelines for demolition: to pull down only small areas of about 250 houses at one time, so that new areas could be occupied as soon as possible. The tenancy service began to give very early notice of new apartments to make it easier for people to move in. This gave them time to get used to their novel situation and, for example, to save money for new furniture while their apartment was building. A couple of months before an area was ready, the future tenants were invited to a meeting at which an architect described the new area and provided detailed plans of each apartment, showing exact dimensions for floors, windows, cupboards and so on; tenants were also offered an opportunity to swap apartments. [...]

The Byker model for residents' influence has been praised, discussed and criticized. Its ideas for reference groups, and its novel methods of administration, have become models that have inspired many others to improve the processes of planning in Newcastle and other places in Europe. In 1978, the Department of the Environment commissioned an investigation by Peter Malpass that established that the slogan of "Byker for Byker people" had been only partly realized. Of the new dwellings, only 50 percent were occupied by former residents of Byker, while over 5,000 households had left Byker. The investigation suggested that the authorities had seen the process of residents' influence as just a question of information; they took for granted that the architects would try to achieve a consensus, the process being seen in fact as a means of concealing conflicts.

The idea of the architects having a local office made for simpler communications between them and the builders, which saved money during construction. For the architects, it was inspiring and informative so directly to see the results of their work. The office existed for more than ten years and the number of its employees rose to twenty. [But] when work in Byker began to tail off, ... [it] soon became necessary to wind up the office.

Making a home in a Philadelphia neighborhood
Alice Gray Read (1986)

In most parts of the United States, a new house built to order is an uncommon luxury. The vast majority of the population, particularly in the urban Northeast, lives in second-hand houses or "off the shelf" models designed and built by profiteering developers for an anonymous public. In large industrialized cities, domestic architecture has been taken out of the hands of residents so completely that developers and architects rarely know the people for whom they design and rarely concern themselves with residents' opinions when a project is complete. The gulf between designer and occupant is compounded in cities such as Philadelphia and Boston, for a large percentage of the current housing stock is old. Most urban residential neighborhoods were built in the nineteenth and early twentieth centuries according to the tastes of the period. These houses stand twice removed from their present owners: they were built by strangers and they were built nearly a century ago.

In these cities, this great displacement of architectural authorship to designers outside the community has modified the meaning of *house* and *home*. The significance of a house has been reduced to the brick and wood of which it is made. There is no longer a singular identification of building and resident as in communities where houses have the same name as their owners. As physical shells, the existing houses that fill large urban neighborhoods are relics of turn-of-the-century design principles that have now been discarded. An unoccupied house exists in the same strange void of meaning as an empty theater. The actors that defined the space with drama are gone and a new company has not yet possessed the stage. The house is anonymous and mute. Only when it is touched by an owner, lived in, and made over inside and out does it begin to bear the identity of its occupants. It is they who see "character" in its empty rooms and transform an existing house into their home. In a sense, the city is an enormous and complex ruin of anachronistic forms occupied by residents who constantly must modify and reinterpret their found spaces to accommodate new needs and changing priorities. Renovation is the decorating, furnishing, painting, and planting that homeowners do to claim a house as their own and to make it a part of their community.

Remodeling is usually done by a homeowner for his or her own use in response to some specific need or perceived inadequacy in the existing design. A homeowner may find suggestions for renovation from popular magazines or retail stores' advertisements, but, within a coherent community, design ideas are often passed through local networks of neighbors and friends. The actual work of renovation may be done by the homeowners themselves or by builders and handymen from the immediate area. This local economy is so consistent that remodeling styles often characterize neighborhoods within the city and distinguish one area from the next.

Materials available to a homeowner or handyman are plentiful, flexible, and inexpensive, allowing a broad range of choice for even the simplest details. With a repertoire enriched by whole catalogs of decorative options, renovation must be addressed as a self-conscious and articulate form of architectural expression. By considering renovations this way, it becomes possible to approach the spatial aesthetic of a community that has never had the opportunity to build new. This essay explores the architectural aesthetic of one urban community – the Mantua section of west Philadelphia.[1]

Bounded by railroad yards on the north and east and by a deteriorated commercial strip on the south, Mantua is a dense urban neighborhood of two-story brick row houses set on long, uniform blocks. Developed in the mid-nineteenth century as high-density housing for workers, Mantua has been a stopping place for a succession of railroad and factory workers of differing ethnic backgrounds who remained only until they could become established more comfortably elsewhere. The area was notorious for unrest during late nineteenth-century labor struggles against the railroads and was the scene of periodic street violence that did not encourage the munificence of Philadelphia City Hall. The area has thus suffered from poverty, abuse, and governmental neglect. Since World War II, it has become a relatively stable black community consisting largely of families from rural areas of the South. Homeownership in Mantua, rare in the past, has risen recently in some neighborhoods, for the housing, while deteriorated, is sound, inexpensive, and pleasant.

In Mantua today, the almost ancient masonry establishes a background rhythm against which current householders must set their new variations, adding their own strains to the work that has gone before. Brightly painted porches, awnings, flower gardens, and outdoor carpeting are the more recent flourishes played out in elaborate variation down each neighborhood block. Layer upon layer, new construction is added to old. Little is removed. Over the years, a neighborhood street becomes dense with detail. Awnings, railings, furniture, and gardens each take their place as families grow and become part of the life of the community.

The buildings of Mantua acquire a visual density, and social ties among neighbors fill the space between them. In a sense, "remodeling" is almost a metaphor for the whole of neighborhood life. The expressed intent of homeowners and elected block captains is to "beautify" their area and to distinguish it as a community – in their words, to make their houses their homes. An additive, outward-looking approach to building is a consistent style of architecture in Mantua that exists independently of ideas on house renovation that prevail in the rapidly expanding areas of white "urban renaissance".

In Mantua, improving a house or beautifying a neighborhood invariably means adding to it either in actual construction or in decoration. Brick is painted, cornices are sheathed and redecorated, siding is added. Astroturf covers porch decks and steps; stone facing conceals façades; and bright paint sets off railings and trim. Porches and gardens receive special attention as outside living spaces with a view of the street. Dependencies such as awnings and cornices extend the surface of the wall out toward the sidewalk so that the façade itself acquires depth. The façade literally becomes three-dimensional, enclosing space of its own. In effect, the house is a structural frame from which layer upon layer of construction extends out into space (Fig. 62). In the language of aesthetician Robert Plant Armstrong, it is an architecture that may be described as "extensive" as it reaches out from a central core, extending to engage a larger space than it actually encloses.[2]

The elaboration of porch and garden strengthens the area between street and house and blurs the border between inside and outside. The ubiquitous porch is an extension of interior living space, profusely decorated, furnished, and commonly used as a summer living room. Railings and posts are often articulated with two or three different colors of paint. The porch deck is covered with outdoor carpeting, and another textured surface such as form-stone, stucco, or paint is added to the first-floor façade, thus distinguishing the entire porch area as a finished room. To complement this extension of living area toward the street, a walkway from the sidewalk to the door is generally kept visually open and physically direct. The property line dividing public space from private front walk is rarely marked by a gate or fence. The walk itself is identified by a railing, strip of carpeting, or painted concrete that offers a broad passage up the porch steps to the front door.

A suburban curving stepping-stone path across a sea of green lawn would be foreign in this part of Philadelphia, as would the pedimented and paneled entrance doors common in other parts of the city. In Mantua, the entrance door does not receive the same attention that is lavished on the porch and garden. Doors are plain, painted the same color as window trim, and are rarely adorned with doorknockers or wreaths. The absence of specific marking at the doorway – the inside/outside boundary – or at the property line – public/private boundary – further softens any spatial division between the individual house and the neighborhood as a whole. The porch and the garden negotiate these transitions as "in-between" spaces where public and private, inside and outside may coexist.[3]

This in-between space is essential to the social life of Mantua. Neighborhood life is street life, and it requires participation. The covered porch offers a place to sit outside during the summer in a shaded spot open to the breeze. Here, residents are separated from the public way yet close enough to be both audience and actors, maintaining both the possibility of distance and the possibility of involvement. Neighborhood life is built around talk from sidewalk to porch, words passed without interruption or excuse.

This place for sitting out in front of the house is so essential to neighborhood life that there can be no compromise. The backyard will not serve as a substitute. It is a service area, used only as a storage space, a laundry yard, or a pen for dogs. Residents of houses that were built with no front yard or porch will not furnish a back lot. Rather, a sitting area in front of the house is made out of a piece of the sidewalk, always within the lot lines of the house and always adjacent to the front door. Acting with the consent of the community, individuals literally stake out a part of the street to serve as a part of the house. A covering on the ground is enough to identify an area of the sidewalk as a spot claimed by a particular homeowner or to distinguish a part of the public way that is set aside and maintained by a shopkeeper.

Whether this front space is given or made, homeowners plant it and furnish it with grass-green carpets, hanging baskets, and other details, creating a pastoral setting for summer afternoons. Decorative elements for the front garden are frequently drawn from the vocabulary of the country – roses, picket fences, and box hedges – and a lush Astroturf lawn may be set down across the sidewalk to the curb of the street. Vegetables are not considered appropriate for front gardens. Those who plant them draw local criticism. Ambitious flower gardens, by contrast, are the subject of pride and encouragement. Enthusiastic gardeners may extend their attention to planting boxes placed across the sidewalk on the concrete curb or hanging baskets suspended from street-side trees. Into these city gardens passersby become fleeting visitors or trespassers on a sidewalk that is no longer neutral ground.

The sidewalk is common ground held by a neighborhood that has the same stolid existence as the houses themselves. The street is the arena for community interaction and cooperative physical design, just as the individual house is the arena for a householder's interior design. Within such a cohesive neighborhood, the design of a single house is meaningless if divorced from the whole block. The exteriors of houses have become the interior of a neighborhood.

The block of houses presents a visual pattern of three-dimensional form and color stretching out horizontally and parallel to the street. Most of the emphasis is on the ground story – even on the ground plane. A line of awnings cuts low across the visual horizon, and railings and fences, flower gardens and furniture reinforce the horizontality of the picture. Often the first story is distinguished from the others by a change in color or façade sheathing. A wall surface underneath a porch roof often is more strongly identified with its neighbor than with the façade above, reinforcing the horizontal theme. A section cutting through the street makes this low and horizontal emphasis even more apparent. It directly addresses pedestrians on the sidewalk, for decorative elements seem within reach. In linear perspective, the vanishing points of all horizontal lines are at eye level. This is a very human horizon to which the space between ground and sky is concentrated in distance. The low architecture of Mantua gathers detail and color within a narrow band close to this horizon.

As horizontality is emphasized, the vertical plane of the façade wall is weakened. In graphic design, an artist may use color tonality to create depth in a composition. Darker colors and cooler colors – blues and greens – will appear to be farther away than light warm colors – reds and yellows. In juxtaposition, these contrastive colors create a visual modulation that contradicts the planar surface of the actual work. Painted façades along a block of houses in Mantua often work on the same principle. A pattern of color exists independently of the masonry structure, apparently lifting off the surface of the front wall and unfolding in its own rhythm, dissolving the vertical plane in favor of a variable pattern not unlike those of Afro-American quilts.[4] As with quilt designs, the colors are chosen from within a close range of hue density so that they complement each other in much the same way as pastel colors. Along this "quilted" block, each house is picked out individually in bright colors. Unlike the cacophony of individualism on the American strip, however, these singular houses converge in a pattern that contains all while allowing each to stand alone.

Within the design of a single façade, a similar compositional logic applies. The house front is a congeries of separate pieces clearly delineated by changes in color or by a contrasting band that traces the extent of that color and separates the shape from other areas. Parts of the façade are picked out with color: the triangle of the gable end, the rectangles of windows and doors, the triangular form of projecting awnings, the terminal stripe of a cornice. Each part is crisply isolated from every other part as if called out by name.[5] White-painted mortar joints on stone walls emphasize the irregular stones as abstract shapes that exist independently of the wall itself. Visually dissolving any sense of solidity, the patterning of brick relies on principles of formal isolation and emphasis in order to create an animate surface from static building materials. It becomes a wall that will not stand still.

Making a house a home in the Mantua section of Philadelphia means more than a new coat of paint. It implies an affective transformation of an anonymous masonry shell into a personal architecture that not only accommodates domestic life but also participates in a broader visual aesthetic shared by the neighborhood. These houses are singular statements not of an isolate individualism but of an individualism strengthened by its communal base. Houses do not retreat from one another behind their façades but reach out to contribute to a larger sense of place and, in doing so, establish an arena for personal expression. Together these houses create an identity that allows neighbors to belong to their neighborhood as villagers belong to their country towns. In Mantua, renovation is a part of the necessary making of a home, at once individual and communal, arbitrary and ordered.

Notes

1   This study began while the author was working on the design of a church building for a congregation in Mantua. It was initially an attempt to understand local spatial preferences so that the new building might respond more effectively to its users. The church was never built, but this study may suggest one way in which architects might begin to learn from their clients.

2   The notion of "extensive" as opposed to "intensive" design is taken from Robert Plant Armstrong's *The Affecting Presence: An Essay in Humanistic Anthropology*, Chicago: University of Chicago Press, 1971.

3   The idea of an architectural space partaking of two worlds – an "in-between" – was suggested by Dutch architect Aldo van Eyck, in his lectures at the University of Pennsylvania in 1979. See also his observations published in *Via I*, Philadelphia: University of Pennsylvania Graduate School of Fine Arts, 1966.

4   Sally Price and Richard Price, *Afro-American Arts of the Suriname Rain Forest*, Los Angeles: University of California, 1980. A marked similarity between [a] Mantua house … and an Afro-American quilt was pointed out to the author by Henry Glassie and John Vlach at the Vernacular Architecture Forum meeting in Newark, Delaware, May 4, 1984.

5   Many of the characteristics of Mantua houses are parallel to qualities of African art and dance emphasized by Robert Farris Thompson in *African Art in Motion*, Los Angeles: University of California Press, 1980. Thompson describes dance of the Niger River area as characterized by low horizontal movements with specific attention to the ground plane. He also sees in African art the accomplished arrangement of discrete elements into a decorative composition.

Do it yourself
Home improvement in 20th century America

Carolyn M. Goldstein (1998)

The suburban ideal, and the postwar building boom that made it accessible to growing numbers of Americans, provided a context for do-it-yourself to become a mass cultural phenomenon in the early 1950s. Popular magazines proclaimed the trend's arrival. "This is the age of do-it-yourself", *Business Week* announced.[1] While the possibilities for do-it-yourself home improvement had been emerging for several decades, it now became an acceptable, desirable, and even expected activity for large numbers of American families.

On the most basic level, do-it-yourself was a response to economic and labor-market conditions of the immediate postwar era. A shortage of skilled labor encouraged home-owners – especially veterans and industrial workers who had acquired technical skills during the war – to improve their homes with their own two hands. Doing their own repairs also saved homeowners the cost of hiring professionals, and regular maintenance eliminated the need to pay for large jobs later on. *Business Week* identified the high cost of labor as the "overwhelming, immediate reason" that homeowners took on remodeling projects in their spare time.[2]

But the appeal of do-it-yourself transcended cost–benefit analysis. For many American families, home-improvement activities provided a way of obtaining the house and life-style to which they aspired – a way of participating in the American dream. Do-it-your-self resonated as a quintessential expression of that dream, especially as it was defined by the dominant values of the 1950s: domesticity, leisure, and independence.

The do-it-yourself ethos was well-suited to the era's emphasis on domesticity. Contemporary surveys showed a dramatic rise in the proportion of the nation's wealth being spent on home pursuits in the Cold War period. Historian Elaine Tyler May has characterized this era as one of "virtuous consumerism", in which spending reinforced a family-centered way of life. She writes, "Americans responded [to the Cold War] with guarded optimism by making purchases that would strengthen their sense of security. In the postwar years, investing in one's own home, along with the trappings that would presumably enhance family life, was seen as the best way to plan for the future".[3] For many families, do-it-yourself home improvement was an economical way to upgrade their dwellings according to the middle-class standards of the day.

An emerging culture of leisure defined the home as a place of relaxation. After the war, the forty-hour work week became the norm, leaving time for two-day weekends. Union contracts included paid vacations and set a standard in the workplace for others to follow. Middle-class Americans expected to spend free time at home doing things that were plea-surable and relaxing. The quest for fun led many American families to embrace outdoor living and to pursue projects, such as building outdoor barbecues, that contributed to a culture of backyard togetherness and entertaining.[4]

Do-it-yourself also seemed to represent independence from the corporate world. Popular writers grounded the do-it-yourself idea in the American past by linking it to Yankee ingenuity and an imagined agrarian, democratic past. They invoked Henry David Thoreau as the "patron saint of the theoretical do-it-yourself-man".[5] [...]

The popularity of magazine articles promoting do-it-yourself provided an incentive for the publication of a new wave of books and instruction manuals aimed at the absolute novice. Through easy-to-use formats and extensive photographic illustrations, these how-to publications addressed non-specialists more deliberately than their early-20th-century predecessors had. The *Better Homes and Gardens Handyman's Book*, first published in 1951, aimed "to provide basic know-how, as clearly and simply as possible, for the average man who putters around, just keeping his house in comfortable working order".[6] An introductory section listed basic hand tools all homeowners should own and gave instruction on how to use them. More than 1,500 step-by-step pictures showed such tasks as "how to use a hammer" and "how to build a workbench". The book emphasized home repairs and improvements that required little or no skill. It told how to make minor plumbing and electrical repairs, but stopped short of providing instructions on how to install such systems in their entirety. Paneling with plywood, building storage units, and laying flooring were among the most complicated projects included. [...]

The do-it-yourself marketplace

The popular interest in do-it-yourself – and the enthusiasm for home remodeling it generated – revolutionized the design and retailing of building materials, tools, and other supplies. Although many manufacturers and dealers had begun to develop and market tools and materials for do-it-yourselfers in the early decades of the century, they responded most seriously to these potential customers only after 1945. During the postwar period, as part of an overall effort to convert wartime manufacturing facilities to peacetime uses, many industrial leaders redesigned and repackaged their products to meet the needs of amateur builders interested in changing or upgrading their homes. The transformed marketplace expanded the possibilities for do-it-yourself amateurs and raised expectations for the types of projects homeowners could take on. Many new products had professional skills designed and built into them. Widely available in self-service hardware stores and home centers, these products placed large and small repair and remodeling tasks within the grasp of nonspecialists. As products such as power tools, paint rollers, and drywall became everyday household supplies, do-it-yourselfers began to master increasingly ambitious and sophisticated home-improvement projects.

Tools and supplies for amateurs

To ride the wave of postwar prosperity and attract the business of American home-owners, manufacturers began redesigning building tools and supplies soon after 1945. Traditionally, the hardware industry had addressed the needs of professionals and specialists in the building trades. In seeking a mass market for their goods, producers of repair and construction supplies marketed directly to the do-it-yourselfer by providing products and kits that greatly simplified projects and repairs. Amateur-friendly tools, often packaged with accessories and manuals offering detailed instructions and project suggestions, substituted for the hired specialist and made it possible for amateurs to tackle tasks that had once been out of reach. To make these products more accessible and inviting to novices, manufacturers packaged them in bright colors and gave them special names to associate them with domesticity and infuse them with the do-it-yourself spirit.

The demands of war had led many manufacturing firms to develop new tools, techniques, and synthetic materials. Now they applied this knowledge to adapting industrial-purpose tools and machinery for home use. At trade shows and in industry publications, producers conferred about how to redirect the hardware industry to attract the attention of the nation's growing number of homeowners. The National Hardware Show, established in 1946, provided a forum for manufacturers and retailers to work together to develop new ways of designing for and marketing to amateur builders. Within a few short years, the hardware industry's new orientation had caught the attention of the business and popular press, which heralded the arrival of a do-it-yourself market. The dramatic rise in sales of a variety of hand-held electric tools for amateurs was an early indicator. Before the war, the power-tool industry had total sales of $25 million; by 1954 sales climbed to $200 million. Whereas less than two dozen different types of power tools were available for home use in 1940, *Business Week* counted about a hundred in 1952.[7]

The electric drill was one of the first industrial-purpose tools to become a staple of home workshops [*Fig. 63*]. Several companies had attempted to sell power drills to farmers and amateurs before the war, but only after 1945 did they find a sizable market for this product. Black & Decker's quarter-inch power drill was one of the earliest successes. According to company lore, Black & Decker managers discovered the potential market when they noticed that many of their employees took industrial-purpose drills home with them to make repairs and alterations to their houses. To reach the consumer market, Black & Decker packaged these tools in brightly colored boxes, advertised in national magazines, and began distribution through department stores, appliance dealers, and hardware stores. In 1949, the company launched a new series of drills and other power tools under the name "Home-Utility Electric Tools".[8] Other manufacturers soon introduced similar products and marketing strategies. Within a few years, Skil introduced a "Skil Home Shop Tool" line of hand-held power drills and saws, and Porter-Cable launched a campaign for its competing products under the brand name "Homemaster".[9] [...]

New materials also widened the possibilities for do-it-yourselfers in the immediate postwar years. The building boom and materials shortage during and after World War II had led builders to adopt plywood as a standard construction material.[10] Made of layers of wood laminated tightly together, plywood was cheap, workable, and versatile. Usually sold in standardized four-by-eight-foot panels, the material was suitable for house construction but was difficult to cut with a handsaw for smaller projects. By the early 1950s, the Douglas Fir Plywood Association began marketing smaller pieces of plywood for the home carpenter under the brand name "Handy Panels", as well as pre-finished panels for a variety of decorative effects.[11] With these innovations, plywood became a mainstay of do-it-yourself home improvement. [...]

By the 1970s, undertaking repair and remodeling work on one's own had become so commonplace that even some of the most technically challenging home-improvement projects could be accomplished by amateurs.

Painting and decorating

The manufacturing and marketing of paint, wallpaper, and floor coverings similarly transformed painting and interior decorating from professional remodeling tasks into projects suitable for the amateur. New types of equipment aimed at nonspecialists moved the jobs of refinishing walls, floors, and ceilings from the exclusive province of contractors to the domain of homeowners in the decade between 1945 and 1955. [...]

Shortages of lead and oil during World War II, coupled with a desire to circumvent the influence of professional painters and create new markets, led manufacturers in the 1940s to focus development and marketing energies on water-based resin emulsion paints that could be easily used by homeowners. The National Chemical and Manufacturing Company's Ultra Luminall and Sherwin-Williams's Kem-Tone were among the first such brands on the market.[12] Emulsion paints – which after 1949 used latex as their main binder – covered plaster, old paint, and wallpaper in one coat, without primers. They could be thinned and cleaned up with water, dried into washable yet colorfast films, and had little odor. Using them involved, as every Kem-Tone ad pointed out, "No muss, no fuss, no bother".[13]

[…] By the early 1950s, surveys by home-improvement magazines indicated that between seventy and ninety percent of readers did their own painting.[14] […]

The development of new synthetic materials further increased the design possibilities for would-be remodelers and provided them with easier ways to decorate on their own. Companies used plastics to manufacture a broad spectrum of decorative laminates, wall paneling, and floor coverings.[15] In the 1950s, vinyl overtook linoleum as the most popular floor covering. Originally available in large rolls requiring special cutting tools and installation skills, both materials were soon sold in standard-sized tiles or small squares. Within two decades, vinyl tile was available with a self-adhesive back for easy installation. Amateurs needed only ordinary hand tools to cover old walls with light-weight panels such as Marlite, a masonite product with a melamine plastic finish introduced by Marsh Wall Products, Inc. Plastic decorative paneling was available in different colors and sizes, as were prefinished hardwood panels, introduced by the U.S. Plywood Corporation in the mid-1940s under the names Plankweld and Weldtex.[16] […]

Equally important to the amateur builder or handyman was the transformation of the way home-improvement products were bought and sold after World War II. Because most repairs and remodeling projects had been executed by professional contractors in the years before 1940, hardware stores and lumberyards had catered primarily to these skilled men. Average consumers or would-be do-it-yourselfers found few retail outlets readily accessible to them …

[But] beginning in the 1920s and 1930s, hardware-store owners and managers gradually began catering to homeowners interested in making basic repairs and taking on remodeling projects.[17] The rising popularity of do-it-yourself in the 1950s encouraged many building-supply retailers to redesign their stores to specifically target amateur handymen and women as their primary customers. To bring themselves up to date with other contemporary shopping environments, they incorporated self-service merchandising techniques pioneered in supermarkets. […]

By 1970, independent hardware stores and old-line chains such as Sears and Montgomery Ward's began to face competition from a new kind of retailer: the home center. The managers of these stores explicitly designed their displays and marketing campaigns for the do-it-yourselfer rather than the professional builder.[18] Home centers were bigger than hardware stores and had a much wider selection of merchandise. Whereas most hardware stores stocked less than twelve thousand items in the early 1980s, home centers such as Lowe's, Payless Cashways, and Hechinger's kept forty thousand or more items on the shelves.[19] By offering many different types of products under one roof, these stores provided one-stop shopping, eliminating the need for separate visits to the paint store, nursery, and lumberyard. Home centers attempted to provide shoppers with the security of knowing what was available and aimed to ensure that products would be in stock.

Notes

1 "The New Do-It-Yourself Market", *Business Week*, June 14, 1952, 60.
2 Ibid., 61.
3 Elaine Tyler May, *Homeward Bound: American Families in the Cold War Era*, New York: Basic Books, 1988, pp. 165–6.
4 On the culture of leisure in the 1950s, see Karal Ann Marling, *As Seen on TV: The Visual Culture of Everyday Life in the 1950s*, Cambridge, Mass.: Harvard University Press, 1994, pp. 51–3.
5 Darrell Huff, "We've Found a Substitute for Income", *Harper's*, October 1953, 27.
6 *Better Homes and Gardens Handyman's Book*, Des Moines: Meredith Publishing Company, 1951.
7 "The New Do-It-Yourself Market", 69; and "The Shoulder Trade", *Time*, August 2, 1954, 62–8.
8 "The New Do-It-Yourself Market", 72, 74; and *Home-Utility Electric Tools*, Towson, Md.: The Black & Decker Manufacturing Company, 1949.
9 See, for example, "A $245.00 Workshop Complete For Only $96.75 – Built with My Skil Home Shop Tools", *Popular Mechanics*, October 1951, 293; and "New Porter-Cable Home-master 1/4" Drill", *Popular Science*, October 1954, 259.
10 Robert Friedel, "Scarcity and Promise: Materials and American Domestic Culture during World War II", in Donald Albrecht (ed.) *World War II and the American Dream*, pp. 42–89; and Thomas C. Jester (ed.) *Twentieth-Century Building Materials: History and Conservation*, New York: McGraw-Hill, 1995, pp. 132–5.
11 "The New Do-It-Yourself Market", 62.
12 "War Paint Stays", *Business Week*, May 4, 1946, 73–4; and "Mix Paints Go To Town", *Business Week*, February 14, 1948, 58, 63.
13 "Paint for Brush-loving Amateurs", *Modern Packaging* 16, October 1942, 64–5.
14 "The New Do-It-Yourself Market", 62.
15 Jeffrey L. Meikle, *American Plastic: A Cultural History*, New Brunswick: Rutgers University Press, 1995, pp. 184, 256–7.
16 Jester, *Twentieth-Century Building Materials*, p. 135.
17 "The Building of America", *Do-it-Yourself Retailing*, June 1986, 86–95.
18 Burt Murphy, "The Home Improvement Market", *Mechanix Illustrated* 78, March 1982, 8.
19 Jay Gissen, "Nice Number, 40,000", *Forbes*, November 21, 1983, 292. On Lowe's, see Dan McIntyre, *No Place Like Lowe's: 50 Years of Retailing for the American Home*, North Wilkesboro, NC: Lowe's Companies, Inc., 1996.

The aesthetics of social aspiration

Alison J. Clarke (2001)

The modern household ... defined as a site of provisioning, social relations and economic management, holds a vital historical position in relation to the modern State and class politics.[1] This chapter uses ethnographic examples to explore how the increasing emphasis on home decoration as a practice, its intersection with class, gender and ethnicity, is related to the construction of ideal and actual contemporary social worlds. It does not simplistically suggest that the external abstract forces such as "class" and "the State" are countered through the appropriation of domestic environments. Rather, it considers "home" as a process, as opposed to an act of individual expressivity, in which past and future trajectories (inseparable from external abstractions such as "class") are negotiated through fantasy and action, projection and interiorization. The householders in this study are representative of the broader section of informants in that their homemaking marks a particular stage in the life cycle of the family (and the individual women concerned). Whether physically or mentally transforming or transposing their homes, the process in which they are engaged is socially aspirant, not merely in terms of accumulating and articulating cultural capital,[2] but in terms of the ambitions and projections of ideal social relations.

The study is based on ethnographic research concerning the provisioning of households in north London ... The ethnographic site in north London consisted of a street referred to as Jay Road, with a cross-section of housing: 1960s blocks of council (State owned) flats and maisonettes; semi-detached 1930s homes; Edwardian rented and small owner-occupied maisonettes as well as larger Victorian family houses occupied predominantly by middle-class families on adjoining streets. The ethnic groups found in the area and included in the study range from those of Greek Cypriot [to] West African, Jewish, Asian, South American, West Indian and Irish descent. The main street in the study was selected because it lacked any outstanding features although it does have an array of particularly mixed housing types. In short, the street is typical of north London in being cosmopolitan but manifestly ordinary.

Day-dreaming ideal homes: the process of envisaging

[...] Home decoration, though tied to key life cycles and events, is the principal means by which members of households attempt to invert, reinvent or perpetuate their material worlds. The physical act of "decorating" requires the household to draw on (or negate) both traditional and contemporary cultural, social, aesthetic and technical knowledge to varying degrees. But crucially, it also requires a process of envisaging or imagining even at its most basic level.

Walking along Jay Road, in the shadows of blocks of council flats, maisonettes and Victorian terraced houses, there are Devonshire fisherman's cabins, baronial mansions and rose-covered country cottages that thrive in the imaginations of the street's householders. These imaginings are not merely "dream homes", plucked from the pages of lifestyle magazines and used as a blueprint for home decorating choices, rather they act as conceptual and value-laden configurations informing or undermining everyday household decisions. While the single occupant of a spacious three-bedroom 1930s semi-detached house on Jay Road conjures up a fantasy seaside residence to explain her taste in fabrics, the occupant of a cramped one-bedroom maisonette on the other side of the street talks of the garden she would have at "her" rambling imaginary home in southern Ireland. [...]

The following section focuses on the decoration of State-designated homes, namely a council housing estate in north London, named Sparrow Court, in order to place the home-making activities of its occupants in the context of a local and class-specific housing culture. Do the inhabitants of State housing use home decorating any less than their middle-class counterparts as an activity of creativity, daydreaming and expressivity? In a strictly delineated, State-designed environment, where the interior and exterior world of the households is standardized and regulated by an external entity (the council/State) the ethnography goes on to reveal the ways in which the occupants appropriate, interpret and generate agency through their standardized spaces. In so doing, it challenges the understanding of home decoration and consumption as a merely expressive or normative activity. Rather, the interior worlds of these households, although they may remain to all intents and purposes physically private, are used as projections of very real relations with the larger external world.

Sparrow Court: behind lace curtained windows

Sparrow Court council estate was built in the mid-1960s and is situated along one side of Jay Road opposite a row of late Victorian terraced maisonettes and 1930s semi-detached houses …Organized in three-story blocks of approximately thirty units as it is, access to the upper stories of the estate is made by ascending a central stairwell leading to an open balcony, running to the right and left, overlooked by the kitchen windows of each unit. This relatively narrow balcony with open railings is the only thoroughfare, and it allows little room for external storage, decoration or individual exterior customization of flats.

The block of housing is easily identifiable as State housing. It has uniform green/blue PVC doors and standardized external fittings, but it is a relatively low-density, well-maintained and neighborly housing arrangement with an ethnically diverse range of households ranging from five-children families to single elderly-person households. It is common for neighbors in Sparrow Court to recognize and greet each other, but this is usually the limit of their intimacy. Despite this semblance of community and the comparatively small scale and green setting of the housing block, inhabitants view the estate as an ostensibly urban dwelling with the associated problems of theft and the protection of privacy.

Only in exceptional circumstances do neighbors actually see the contents of each other's homes. The ability to contain "domestic dramas" within the walls of individual households is considered paramount for the smooth running of everyday life on the estate. […]

Estates such as Sparrow Court are suspended between a constant tension of privacy and sociality that impacts on the broader moral economy of households.[3] Suzy, a mother in her late thirties, consciously maintains an aloofness from her neighbors. Her husband Jim, who is out working most of the day, views the boundaries of his home more protectively than Suzy who spends a considerable amount of her time alone in Sparrow Court:

> Jim is one of those people who likes to keep himself to himself and he doesn't like to interfere in anybody's life or them interfere in his but I'm more like, I'm not saying gossipy but I have a chat and I like talking to people. I invite people round for *a* coffee sometimes and he'll say, "what did you invite her in for? You have her in every week". But I say, "I'm here half the time on my own!"

The negotiation of living inside and outside, for retaining autonomy and maintaining sociality, is a tentative and on-going process particularly for women raising children on the estate. While it is unusual for adult neighbors to speak to one another, let alone be welcomed into each other's flats, it *is* deemed acceptable for children to congregate on the estate and occasionally enter each other's homes in the summer months. […]

Although households are separated by thin walls, and literally built one on top of the other, the layout of the flats and the positioning of the windows make it impossible for passers-by to casually glance inside a tenant's flat. Despite this and the studied distancing from each other's affairs (with the exception of overtly public incidents) informants frequently try to envisage the interiors of one another's homes. The flats in Sparrow Court do not vary from a standardized layout of rooms, but this seems to add to, rather than detract from, neighborly interest in specific individuals' interpretation of household space, as revealed in the informants' following conversational extracts:

> Yeah the girl next door, have you seen it? She's done her loft and she sews up there and everything. She's boarded it all out. Her boyfriend did it before he went to Africa … but mine is twice as big as hers, it covers the whole flat.

> Well, she's got two kids 'cos I think the little one's room is there [pointing to neighbor's flat above] and they moved their living room to the big bedroom as far as I can tell.

> Well she had a big sofa and chairs moved in from the catalogue [mail-order purchase], and her washing machine was out on the landing so I think they're having a clear out.

Despite this interest in neighbors' private domains there is very little in the way of formal or informal sociality conducted in each other's homes. Mail-order catalogues might be passed from door to door for shared perusal but it is rarely anticipated that neighbors will step beyond each other's thresholds.

Getting your house in order: strategies for sociality and aspiration

[…] The following case studies focus on the distinctiveness of the home decorating activities of three women bringing up families on low incomes in Sparrow Court. They highlight the ways in which home decorating and interior decoration are used to establish relations with an outside and ideal social world. Rather than construct their homes as "havens" these households use "home", and its provisioning, to project themselves beyond their immediate surroundings. The informants share identical spatial layout. Their flats comprise an entrance hall leading to a central living room, kitchen, bathroom and two or three bedrooms.

All three households have a steady but minimal income supplemented by sporadic cash injections from entrepreneurial activity or members of family outside the immediate household. But, as Sandra Wallman's pioneering study of urban households in south London revealed, economic measures of capital, land and labor do not alone explain the diversity of households in industrial societies and the range of resources they deploy:

> The livelihood of a London household involves all kinds of work. It depends on the achievement of a sense of identity and belonging; on its ability to differentiate between us and them in apparently transient and impersonal urban settings; and on its capacity to manage social relationships and information, as much as it depends on informal economic organization and on some member of the household having a job in the formal economy.[4]

While Wallman treats consumption as a by-product of employment and services rather than as an integral or productive aspect of household resourcing, in the following case studies, consumption, in the form of home decorating is seen as a focal point, rather than a "reflection", of the construction and negotiation of "household philosophies".

Historical narratives and future trajectories, revealed through the ethnographic detail of home-decoration practice, highlight the home as process.

1. Kelly: "a man about the house"

The first case study considers the role of home decoration in the life of a woman running a household as a single mother. Aged around forty years old, Kelly relies on social welfare and sporadic cash supplements from her ex-partner, casual work and occasional entrepreneurial activity. She has rented her three-bedroom flat on the Sparrow Court council estate for over ten years and lives there with her two children aged seven and fifteen years. Kelly has no savings and would only ever be able to move house by taking part in the council-housing exchange scheme, which would be unlikely to benefit her because her flat is extremely large and well situated in comparison to other council properties in the borough. Her ex-partner, the father of her children, makes very occasional visits to the family's home (he now lives abroad) but he generally acts as an absent but much-loved father figure. Towards the end of the three-year span of the ethnography his visits had decreased dramatically and after several years' work as the sole child-carer Kelly has begun to reconsider the direction and future of her own life, as well as her children's. As both children are settled at local schools Kelly has become determined to pursue a new social life. As a first-generation black British woman she has relatives in the West Midlands and Jamaica. Her older sister, whom she stays in contact with by telephone, is a solicitor. She does not regularly meet any members of her extended family, and she moved to London more than fifteen years ago when she met her ex-partner. Kelly openly seeks to detach herself from what she describes as her "traditional Jamaican working-class roots" and considers herself middle class even though, unlike her sister, she has no formal college education or qualifications. In this context, several years ago Kelly changed her Christian name from what she considered to be an "old-fashioned" form to a more suitable and trendy version more indicative of her own self-image.

For Kelly, then, a woman all too aware of the constraints of externally imposed definitions, aspiration is an empowering concept. Despite her comparatively friendly relations with neighbors, her reliance on State housing, and the stigma associated with council estates is a constant source of unease for Kelly, which she counters through her interior-design schemes. Kelly last fully decorated her flat in 1989 and describes it as an "oasis of tranquility". Situated on the upper story of Sparrow Court at the point furthest from Jay Road it is protected from the noise of passing traffic. Although Kelly is conscious of her flat as a council property she consistently counterbalances her antipathy towards Sparrow Court with the "specialness" of her specific flat and its interior design. In order to feel confident about the prospect and ambition of leaving behind her home of over ten years by meeting a new partner, she goes through a process of re-amelioration regarding her flat and prepares to spring clean and refurbish the living room:

> Honestly I mean even when it's hot outside it's cool in here. It's just so nice in the winter I mean it's not that cold I can economize on bills heating and that, but if I can find myself someone … I'm going out now because I'm going to find myself a partner. Yeah this is what it's all about!

Kelly stands apart from other informants in the street due to the overwhelming enthusiasm she expresses for formal principles of interior decoration. Her living room has a white fitted carpet, white walls, a white leather three-piece suite and a mirrored rear wall which, she says, is used to accentuate a "monochrome feeling". She made the ruched curtains herself, "before everyone else had them", in shiny pale pink using exclusive cut-price designer fabric from a friend working in a prestigious fabric shop in the West End. [...]

Although the living room is the largest single space in the flat, which she shares with her two children, it is very much designated and decorated as an adult space. A large coffee table, a gift from Kelly's ex-partner, with a beveled glass top, chinoiserie engraving and Egyptianesque legs stands in the center of the room. In the corner an ornate flower stand features a climbing plant. A bookcase hidden around the corner from the doorway in a recess holds a pile *of Hello!* photo-gossip magazines, the stereo system, paperbacks and a selection of school and family photographs. The room has a palatial feel of relaxed and modern luxury. There are no toys or children's items present.

Kelly sees the room as an expression of her talents as a designer, the one room she has managed to completely redecorate in her "own taste" according to sound decorative principles since she moved to Sparrow Court. While expressing dismay at the state of her unfinished kitchen (she paid the next-door neighbor to install shelves last winter but still has not finished decorating) Kelly views her living room as a testament to her "know-how" and individual artistic flair. She also couches the significance of the room in spiritual terms:

> Most people wouldn't think of doing a room like this because it could be clinical. When it was just done it just looked so therapeutic. Colors are really important we take it for granted but it really is important about how we feel about things, you know, and so most of these colors together could look clinical but it's funny it just opens it up and makes it look airy.

[...] The white, spatial living room of Kelly's flat stands in stark contrast to the clutter of the rest of the house. The other rooms have been left unaltered since moving to the flat over ten years earlier. The children have attached posters to their bedroom walls but Kelly points out that they are still waiting to decorate these rooms. The bathroom also remains unchanged since the beginning of the tenancy and Kelly is concerned about a rising-damp patch in the corner. Rather than rely on the council to deal with such problems Kelly waits until her ex-partner makes one of his sporadic visits and hopes that he will take on some home-improvement tasks. She has occasionally "borrowed" her next-door neighbor's husband, to move heavy household items, but is wary of over-stretching this relationship. Without "having a man about the house" Kelly has confined her efforts to the living room, and her effort to spring clean and refurbish the living room coincides with a determined decision on Kelly's part to find a new partner:

> I've just got myself together I've started going out again and if I go out I'd like to entertain, right? So if I start [decorating] then I feel comfortable when I go out. It's no good projecting this image and then you invite people back and "oh!" [feigns shocked disappointment] because I hate pretending. When I decorated three years ago I didn't even finish the kitchen so I've got that to do, the bathroom and every-thing and then I'll feel comfortable about myself. I've got to take them down [looking at the curtain pelmets] and clean everything.

Kelly is detached from her extended family but has a large network of friends across London. Several years ago she began a dress-designing company with a best friend. They turned their own experience making clothes in the home into a made-to-measure "couture clothes" business. Specializing in glamorous party dresses the two women rented a small shop and used contacts at fabric shops to support their enterprise. Despite a certain amount of success the enterprise folded when her business partner "found herself a nice rich man friend" and left the shop. Since then Kelly has intermittently used her home dressmaking skills to make one-off party dresses for paying friends and contacts. [...]

2. Lola: assimilation and aspiration in "bring a bottle" culture

Lola, her husband and three children share exactly the same layout of rooms as their neighbor Kelly in their three-bedroom flat in Sparrow Court. They are comparatively new residents and after living in the property as council tenants for a year took the option of purchasing the flat by taking on a large mortgage. This home marks, for Lola and her husband, a major life transition. Prior to living in Sparrow Court they shared a multiple-occupancy house with several other immigrant families in Camden, London. When the couple first arrived in the UK they had few possessions with which to construct a home; "When I came from Chile I didn't bring any special things just my clothes and bed linen as I didn't know where I was going to sleep and I decide [sic] to bring those".

Over a ten-year span Lola and her husband have moved from sleeping on friends' floors, to bringing up their new babies in communal homes, to sharing a co-op house, to renting a council flat that has finally become "their own home". This process has involved decisions, conscious and otherwise, over the extent of their Anglicization. By moving to Sparrow Court they have severed many of their ties with their ethnic community which initially facilitated their lives in a new host country. Although they regularly attend Chilean party events their decision to make Sparrow Court their permanent home has had direct consequences for their everyday social lives, as Lola points out: "None of my friends live around here – *none* of them. I don't know any Chileans living around here. I say hello to the neighbors and that but we are not really friends – my friends live south of London or at Camden".

Lola is a full-time house parent and, except for occasional visits to friends' homes at weekends, spends each day at Sparrow Court alone while her children attend local Catholic schools. Since moving to the area her husband, Philipe, who works in south London, has had to work longer hours to increase his training as an electrician and earn more money to cover new living costs. Initially he spent most weekends studying but more recently spends an increasing amount of time involved in home-improvement projects. It is principally Lola, then, who has become the member of the family responsible for acquiring information about local amenities and for making friends on the estate. Lola is not at all confident in this position. She is reluctant to leave the house alone and limits her provisioning to one weekly shopping trip to the supermarket. Although Lola's children are becoming increasingly involved in school and social activities (such as attending friends' birthday parties) Lola herself remains relatively isolated.

While the children gain confidence in their new social groups, their parents work on transforming their home, and through the negotiation of objects and styles struggle to make an appropriate home for their first generation Chilean/British children. The children instruct their parents in the mores and nuances of British taste and culture, which they bring home daily from their peers and apply when flicking through the pages of furnishing catalogues together. Lola and her husband mediate their children's new values and tastes and try to combine, through the provisioning and decoration of the home, some version of Anglo-Chilean identity.

In this sense, the children become the driving force behind Lola's and her husband's most recent spate of home decoration. Unlike their neighbor Kelly, the couple cares little for their living room or its potential for home entertainment. While their Chilean friends frequently host extravagant house parties, the Santoses, aware of the importance of "not upsetting the neighbors" or drawing undue attention to themselves in Sparrow Court, feel that such festivities are an aspect of culture they left behind in their ethnic community in Camden along with the associated social relations. Now "out of the circuit" Lola explains that in her own culture the home would be decorated and furnished almost exclusively through gifts from friends and family rather than through private consumption. Similarly, the English "bring a bottle" culture (whereby a guest is expected to make a contribution to their host's hospitality) is anathema to Chilean sociality and hospitality:

> If I had house parties I would receive lots of gifts but I can't. The Chileans are always having house parties to early in the morning – but now they are learning they must hire a hall or a place because of the noise. They play the music very loud and until 5 o'clock in the morning and they have trouble with the neighbors so now they hire a place. Chileans like parties and they spend a lot of money and they invite you and give you food and you don't have to buy anything like an English party where you bring a bottle – not Chileans they spend hundreds.

The living room, the most public room, has changed little since the Santoses arrival at the flat three years earlier, even though they are buying the property through the "right to buy" scheme. There are dust patches on the walls where the previous occupants hung their pictures. It contains only an ageing television, a makeshift table and two pieces of flimsy garden furniture. There are no comfortable seats and few ornaments. Lola disassociates herself from many of the objects in this room, as they are "hand-me downs" from a series of other Chilean families setting up home in Britain. In a complete inversion of Kelly's home it is the private rooms, in particular the children's bedrooms, which have received maximum decorative attention.

While the living room has an air of neglect and aesthetic indifference, on entering the children's bedrooms one is struck by the immaculate, "show-home" finish of newly decorated and refurbished rooms. The wall-to-wall fitted carpets have been replaced by shining wood-effect laminate. The bedroom doors have been removed and re-hinged to allow room for hand-made customized louvred cupboards. The bed linen matches a set of stenciled toy boxes and the walls are covered with bright wallpaper coordinated with pretty swagged curtains in modern plaid fabric.

In the bathroom the entire bath suite has been replaced by a large walk-in shower. Like the bedrooms, the bathroom features hand-made cabinets crafted by Philipe. The windows have been fitted with double-glazing and ceramic tiles have replaced the linoleum flooring. Gradually, then, beginning with the children's rooms and bathroom, the flat is being overhauled and modernized in a style most appropriately described as modern European.

The Santoses want their children to have opportunities equivalent to or better than their English peers and are very aware of their own children's perception of deprivation (the older child, for example, complains that English families all own cars). This move towards a more materially comfortable lifestyle has to be weighed tentatively against a loss of core "Chilean values" as perceived by the parents. Since they embarked on the refurbishment of their home the girls have become, Lola believes, unappreciative of the "value of things": "We just bought a new bedroom suite and Susannah [the eldest child] started saying she wanted this she wanted that. I told her, I said 'this is the first piece of new furniture I've had in fifteen years of marriage, things just don't come to you like that.'"

Their newly decorated house is defiantly non-traditional British, with its non-carpeted floors, walk-in shower room and café-style kitchen. But it also defies the lavishness or "Dynasty style" Lola associates with her Chilean friends in Camden. Rather they have created a metropolitan style that brings together home crafts (cabinetry, home sewing, hand painting) and modern design styles. Although much of the furniture is brand new, Philipe customizes the items, including especially designed cupboards and lamps for the children's rooms, and Lola makes the bed linen and curtains herself from Ikea fabric. While Philipe is solely responsible for home improvement, Lola spends much of her time at home adapting patterns from women's magazines to make linen items for the home and the children. This home is indeed a labor of love. [...]

3. Sharon: "the creative home and the ideal of mothering"

Sharon and her partner David have two younger children and a teenager who has left home to live with his grandmother (following a family argument). They are both in their early forties. They have an identical space to that of Kelly and Lola with a large living room, medium-size kitchen and three bedrooms. They are situated on the upper story of the block. The family is very settled in their home, and Sparrow Court in general, having lived in the flat for over fifteen years. Unlike many of the families on the estate they use their garden plot (situated some distance for the dwelling) regularly as a place to keep the pet rabbit and hang a hammock in the summer. Their children are well known on the estate as they frequently play outside. The couple rent their flat and live largely on Dave's casual income as a part-time painter and decorator.

As in their neighbor Kelly's flat, the kitchen is the least decorated room, serving as a place of functional tasks rather than aesthetic interest or coherence. The living room is the center of the home. It contains a deep, green velveteen three-piece suite, a worn shag-pile carpet, a large television/home entertainment center, wall display units and cupboards, a dining table and four chairs, and an enormous American jukebox. On the living room wall, as well as pictures acquired from car-boot sales, are old sepia photographs of Dave's great-grandparents and elderly West Indian relatives displayed in a prominent, symmetrical composition. As Sharon has become estranged from her own mother, Dave's family has become the closest extended kin. She frequently expresses love and admiration for her mother-in-law who has been teaching her traditional feminine skills that she did not acquire herself as a child, such as home dressmaking.

Since buying her first sewing machine three years ago Sharon has dreamed of having her own space, a sewing room up in the loft, where she could embark on a home-craft pursuit that she could return to without clearing from the dinner table when the kids get home from school. In the drawers of the living-room cabinets Sharon keeps all of her home-making magazines and books that she buys at the local newsagent or as offers from the cable daytime television "home-craft" shows she loves to watch. She also has an extensive collection of unused home-craft materials such as ribbons, threads and hooks that she picks up at car-boot sales and "50p shops".

Over the last decade Sharon has consistently tried to implement a series of home-improvement schemes. She has, for example, been stripping the paint from the doors and banister. This process has taken so long she worries that by the time she finishes bare wood "will be out of fashion again!" This home-improvement scheme is at the focus of a running joke and playful antagonism between Sharon and her husband, Dave. Sharon does not work outside the home and the family relies on Dave's part-time employment in the building trade for most of their income. Sharon's paint-removal task falls within the realms of Dave's paid expertise but he never gets around to doing their own home improvement. Sharon complains that she is full of ideas and schemes for home decoration but because of the kids she never has time to carry any of them through: "you've got to stop to go shopping and stop to get the kids' dinner ready. And I couldn't just stop and leave it I had to stop and clean up all the dust and everything, so it was taking me forever".

As well as using a converted loft as a creative space for making clothes and home-crafts for the children and their bedrooms, Sharon envisages it as a useful storage area. If she could move extraneous furniture into the loft she could complete her bedroom design (another project in progress for over ten years). If her husband had not mismeasured the cabinet units he finally got around to making for the bedroom, it would not be necessary for the radiator to be moved and extra furniture to be stored in the loft that he has been promising to convert for ten years. Similarly Sharon would like a dishwasher in the kitchen, but her husband argues that until he moves the kitchen doorway to another position there will not be enough room for the plumbing. Until he moves the doorway Sharon cannot redecorate the kitchen and introduce her ambitious wall-of-glass-bricks idea inspired by the television home-decorating program *Changing Rooms*.

Within the household a "circular logic" operates preventing the successful completion of the home as a coherent project of redecoration. Encompassing all rooms in the house, Sharon's role as would-be homemaker and Dave's role as provider and facilitator, this "circular logic" revolves around a pivotal character – a rogue squirrel. Dave will not rearrange the kitchen until he has completed the loft idea they have been discussing for years. But he refuses to do this as a rogue squirrel has made a nest in the roof and "it gives him the creeps". While Sharon uses this in defense of her husband's inactivity (along with the fact that he does home improvement as a job outside the home), she is quick to guard against any sense of emasculation she may be conferring on him: "He's not really scared of it [the squirrel]. It's just that it might jump out at him and you know [mock scream]! I rang the council but they want twenty-five quid to come out and I thought 'bugger that'".

Over the three-year period of the ethnography Sharon repeatedly mentions the "bloomin' squirrel" in relation to her thwarted ambitions for the home: "cos when I get around to converting my loft I'll have somewhere – the only thing that's stopping me is the squirrel up there". Sharon and David's home could not be described as a haven of coherent home decoration or aesthetic normativity. Despite Sharon's consistent desire and efforts to transform the home through her own labor, time and creativity, the home seems to have reached a happy but static situation. The "would-be" loft has become the most important, if conceptual, space in the home. It is the focus of much hope for change in terms of Sharon's own personal fulfillment, her commitment to the kids as a "better" mother and the family's overall improvement. Here we see vividly the home as process: how its decorative schemes (implemented and failed through a light-hearted playoff of gender relations) are the interiorizations of external concepts such as "proper" mothering.

Conclusion

The home-improvement aspirations of the above informants clearly challenge the homogeneous and normative models of working-class homemaking. While it would be easy to assume that the rise of the "home" as a privatized arena of consumption exists in inverse relation to a State of declining sociality experienced by the occupants of the housing estate, such an assumption fails to explain the extent or nature of the investment made by the households in their interior worlds. In these particular examples, there is an extraordinary disparity between the amount of attention paid to how a place should look, as if it is firmly within the public domain, as against all evidence which indicates to the contrary that they are very rarely exposed to the view of an outsider. Kelly, Lola and Sharon conjure up their "ideals" (as manifest in a man, class aspiration, the kids, immigration or home creativity), and it is as though instead of being inspected by actual visitors they are being viewed and judged by these same ideals.

This is not to suggest that people have become more materialistic and, having abandoned sociality, merely turn to an "interiorized" social world. [...] Rather, this ethnographic example shows how the ideal home, as used to influence the construction of the actual home, becomes an internalized vision of what other people might think of one. Far from being a site of crude emulation, the house itself *actually* becomes the "others". The house objectifies the vision the occupants have of themselves in the eyes of others and as such it becomes an entity and process to live up to, give time to, show off to. As against actual observers it is an interiorized image of the other that can actually be worked on and fed into the aspirations and labor of the occupants. So the proliferation of home decoration and the popularization of design has become a key, contemporary component of a relationship that was never simply between an internal private sphere and an external public sphere, but a more complex process of projection and interiorization that continues to evolve.

Notes

1 Victoria de Grazia with Ellen Furlough, *The Sex of Things: Gender and Consumption in Historical Perspectives*, Berkeley: University of California Press, 1996, p. 153.
2 Pierre Bourdieu, *Distinction: A Social Critique on the Judgment of Taste*, London: Routledge, 1979.
3 For contrast see Marianne Gullestad, *Kitchen Table Society: A Case Study of the Family Life and Friendships of Young Working-Class Mothers in Urban Norway*, Oslo: Universitetsforlaget, 1986, for the actual sociability of Norwegian housewives where the home is constantly "primed" for potential neighborly visits.
4 Sandra Wallman, *Eight London Households*, London: Tavistock, 1984, p. 23.

Figure 56   La Paz, Bolivia, squatter settlement: tin-roofed adobe housing built on irregular street pattern, 1974.

Figure 57   Berlin, street in Kreuzberg district restored by S.T.E.R.N., with shops and apartments, 1980s.

Figure 58
Berlin, tenant wall
decorations under
aegis of S.T.E.R.N.
(façade and frieze by
Hanefi Yeter), 1980s.

Figure 59
S.T.E.R.N. and Stefan
Koppelmann,
do-it-yourself cooper-
ative building at 16
Admiralstrasse, Berlin,
1980s.

Figure 60   Ralph Erskine, Byker Wall development, Newcastle-upon-Tyne, 1969–81, view of inner face of wall.

Figure 61   Byker Wall development, Janet Square, 1971–2.

Figure 62
Mantua district, Philadelphia, "A typical Mantua house before and after renovation", drawn by
Alice Gray Read.

Figure 63
Ads for electric drill and electric sander,
1949–61

11

Twentieth-century apartment dwelling
Ideals and realities

No type of modern domestic architecture has been more widely debated than the high-rise towers so often constructed by public authorities in the 1960s and 1970s. Inspired by the early writings of Le Corbusier about the need for apartment towers in wide green spaces, and by the later writings of Team Ten and the Smithsons about the possibilities for creating "streets in the air" (Figs. 64, 65), postwar builders and government agencies turned to high-rise structures (see also Fig. 4) as a solution to housing shortages and the need for minimal dwellings – as a solution to the need for mass housing, especially for the poor. The rapid evolution of steel and concrete construction and the perfection of the electric-powered elevator now made such buildings cheaper to build than they had been in the earlier twentieth century. Alison Ravetz sketches the outlines of this development and shows the great disillusionment of the public and of government agencies with high-rise housing, which came to be seen as a breeding ground for crime and social alienation. Anthony Burgess's *A Clockwork Orange* (1963), a corrosive novel of teenage crime and violence in urban apartment towers, highlighted and probably contributed to this public disaffection, as did Stanley Kubrik's 1971 movie based on the novel (Figs. 66, 67). There soon followed a series of highly-publicized demolitions of housing towers in both Britain and the United States; the best-known of these was the demolition of Pruitt-Igoe housing (1955) in St Louis in 1972 (Figs. 68, 69). Yet social welfare specialist James S. Fuerst, writing in 1985, found widespread satisfaction among high-rise apartment dwellers in New York public housing, and sociologist David Popenoe, studying the Swedish new town of Vällingby, where tiny apartments were constructed in both high-rise and low-rise versions (Figs. 70, 71), observed extremely positive reactions, together with a comfortable sense of being "at home", among all the residents there.

The center of Paris
Le Corbusier (1924)

The center of Paris

The "Voisin Plan"[1] for Paris is the result of combining two new essential elements: *a commercial city* and *a residential city* [*Fig. 64*] …

The *residential city* would extend from the Rue des Pyramides to the circus on the

Champs Élysées and from the Gare Saint-Lazare to the Rue de Rivoli, and would involve the destruction of areas which for the most part are overcrowded, and covered with middle-class houses now used as offices. [...]

This plan makes a frontal attack on the most diseased quarters of the city, and the narrowest streets: it is not "opportunist" or designed to gain a yard or two at odd points in over-congested roads. Its aim is rather to open up in the strategic heart of Paris a splendid system of communication. As against streets ranging from 20 to 35 feet in width with cross roads every 20, 30, or 50 yards, its aim is to establish a plan on the "gridiron" system with roads 150, 250 to 400 feet in width, with cross roads every 350 or 400 yards; and on the vast island sites thus formed to build immense cruciform sky-scrapers, so creating a *vertical* city, a city which will pile up the cells which have for so long been crushed on the ground, and set them high above the earth, bathed in light and air.

Thenceforward, instead of a flattened-out and jumbled city such as *the airplane reveals to us for the first time*, terrifying in its confusion ..., our city rises vertical to the sky, open to light and air, clear and radiant and sparkling. The soil, of whose surface 70 to 80 percent has till now been encumbered by closely packed houses, is now built over to the extent of a mere five percent. The remaining 95 percent is devoted to the main speed-ways, car parks and open spaces. The avenues of trees are doubled and quadrupled, and the parks at the foot of the sky-scrapers do, in fact, make the city itself one vast garden.

The density, which is too great as things are at present, of the districts affected by the "Voisin" plan would not be reduced. It would be *quadrupled*. [...]

I wish it were possible for the reader, by an effort of imagination, to conceive what such a vertical city would be like; imagine all this junk, which till now has lain spread out over the soil like a dry crust, cleaned off and carted away and replaced by immense clear crystals of glass, rising to a height of over 600 feet; each at a good distance from the next and all standing with their bases set among trees. Our city, which has crawled on the ground till now, suddenly rises to its feet in the most natural way, even for the moment going beyond the powers of our imaginations, which have been constrained by age-long habits of thought. [...]

From one sky-scraper to another a relationship of voids and solids is established. At their feet the great open spaces are seen. The city is once more based on axes, as is every true architectural creation. Town planning enters into architecture and architecture into town planning. If the "Voisin" plan is studied there can be seen to west and southwest the great openings made by Louis XIV, Louis XV and Napoleon: the Invalides, the Tuileries, the Place de la Concorde, the Champ de Mars and the Étoile. These works are a signal example of *creation*, of that spirit which is able to dominate and compel the mob. Set in juxtaposition the new *business city* does not seem an anomaly, but rather gives the impression of being in the same tradition and following the normal laws of progress. [...]

The great artery running *east to west*, which is today totally lacking, would act as a channel into which would pour the traffic which is bottled up in the shapeless network of streets of today. This great artery would deliver us from the present street system, so shut in upon itself, and would open up a way into the country at its two extremities. [...]

The "Voisin" scheme and the past

In this scheme the historical past, our common inheritance, is respected. More than that, it is *rescued*. The persistence of the present state of crisis must otherwise lead rapidly to the destruction of that past.

First of all I must make a distinction, of a sentimental nature, but one of great importance; in these days the past has lost something of its fragrance, for its enforced mingling with the life of today has set it in a false environment. My dream is to see the Place de la Concorde empty once more, silent and lonely, and the Champs Élysées a quiet place to walk in. The "Voisin" scheme would isolate the whole of the ancient city and bring back peace and calm from Saint-Gervais to the Étoile.

The districts of the *Marais*, the *Archives*, the *Temple*, etc., would be demolished. But the ancient churches would be preserved.[2] They would stand surrounded by verdure; what could more charming! And even if we must admit that their original environment has thus been transformed, we must agree that their present setting is not only an unreal one, but is also dreary and ugly.

Similarly the "Voisin" plan shows, still standing among the masses of foliage of the new parks, certain historical monuments, arcades, doorways, carefully preserved because they are pages out of history or works of art.

Thus one might find, surrounded by green grass, an exciting and delightful relic such as, say, some fine Renaissance house, now to be used as a library, lecture hall or what not.

The "Voisin" scheme covers five percent only of the ground with buildings, it safeguards the relics of the past and enshrines them harmoniously in a framework of trees and woods. For material things too must die, and these green parks with their relics are in some sort cemeteries, carefully tended, in which people may breathe, dream and learn. In this way the past becomes no longer dangerous to life, but finds instead its true place within it.

The "Voisin" scheme does not claim to have found a final solution to the problem of the center of Paris; but it may serve to raise the discussion to a level in keeping with the spirit of our age, and to provide us with reasonable standards by which to judge the problem. It sets up *principles* as against the medley of silly little reforms with which we are constantly deceiving ourselves.

Notes

1   As it is the motor-car which has completely overturned all our old ideas of town planning, I thought of interesting the manufacturers of cars in the construction of the *Esprit Nouveau* Pavilion at the Paris International Exhibition of Decorative Art, since this Pavilion was planned as a dwelling and as a unit of modern town planning. I saw the heads of the Peugeot, Citroën and Voisin Companies and said to them:

"The motor has killed the great city. The motor must save the great city. Will you endow Paris with a Peugeot, Citroën or Voisin scheme of rebuilding; a scheme whose sole object would be to concentrate public notice on the true architectural problem of this era, a problem not of decoration but of architecture and town planning; a sane reconstruction of the dwelling unit and the creation of urban organs which would answer to our conditions of living which have been so profoundly affected by machinery?"

Messrs. Peugeot would not risk themselves on our venturesome scheme. M. Citroën very amiably replied that he did not know what I was talking about, and did not see what the motor-car had to do with the problem of the center of Paris. M. Mongermon, of the Voisin Company, without any hesitation agreed to finance my researches into the question of the center of Paris, and so the resulting scheme is called the "Voisin" scheme for Paris.

2   This was not one of the objects of the plan, but was merely the result of their falling into the architectural composition of the scheme.

Urban structuring

Alison and Peter Smithson (1967)

Identity

This study is concerned with the problem of identity in a mobile society. It proposes that a community should be built up from a hierarchy of associational elements and tries to express the various levels of association – the house, the street, the district, the city. It is important to realize that the terms used, street, district, etc., are not to be taken as the reality but as the idea, and that it is our task to find new equivalents for these forms of association for our non-demonstrative society.

There should be a basic program for the dwelling in terms of the activities of the family, considering them individually and in association with each other. (THE HOUSE)

The dwelling thought of in terms of human association should take account not only of the family but also those additional responsibilities which vary in all countries and with all families – this additional activity gives identity to the dwelling and its inhabitants.

Traditional Street considered as active environment is now being changed by increased mobility.

Re-identifying man with his environment cannot be achieved by using historical forms of house-groupings: streets, squares, greens, etc., as the social reality they represent no longer exists.

The principle of identity we propose is the basis of the Golden Lane Project – a multi-level city with residential streets-in-the-air [*Fig. 65*]. Outside the house is the first point of contact where children learn for the first time of the world outside. Here are carried on those adult activities which are essential to everyday life – shopping, car cleaning, scooter repairs, letter posting. (THE STREET)

Off the street "deck", accessed from it and the house, is the extension to the dwelling – the "yard-garden". The ever changing vignette patterns of sky and city seen through the yard-gardens from the ground and from the street deck itself enhance the passing stranger's view.

The street decks are intended as ample spaces, wide enough for two mothers with prams to stop to talk and still to leave room to pass. A more complex geometry that "rational lot division" answers to the need for an environment active and creative socially. Outside the street people are in direct contact with the larger range of activities which give identity to the community. (THE DISTRICT)

Even in a small town compactness is essential. With loosely organized quarters, each associated with a certain sort of work – banking, docks, shipping concerns, furs – and varying in height and density to suit their needs, the complex would rise finite in the fields, with the uneven skyline and defined boundaries of an Italian or Greek hill town.

Streets-in-the-air are linked together in a multi-level continuous complex, connected where necessary to work and to those ground elements that are necessary at each level of association. Our "hierarchy of association" is woven into a modulated continuum representing the true complexity of human associations.

Districts in association generate the need for a richer scale of activities which in their turn give identity to the ultimate community. (THE CITY)

Any new combinations of dwellings with their immediate access that would make for a new way of living in the city must nearly always expect to have to lace-in between existing buildings and mesh over existing road and service networks. Their function is renewal; of the dying centers and derelict areas among railway viaducts and old industrial sites. The "elements" can expect little help from their surroundings in terms of environment but must by their unblemishable newness carry the whole load of responsibility for renewal in themselves.

The horizontal street mesh would slot into the vertical circulation of other buildings in an attempt to fuse many different kinds of multi-level buildings already in existence (offices, department stores, parking garages); to make a city conceived as a cluster of population pressure points, not an abstract pyramid of density figures. Such an idea offers, "a germ of a city convincingly urban, many valued, growing – not one valued, fixed, and closed in a single hierarchy of forms".

The high-rise estate

Alison Ravetz with Richard Turkington (1995)

… After a delay of one or two generations, the multi-level city heralded at the turn of the century began to take shape. For the most part its translation into conventional British council housing [*state owned and subsidized, Ed.*] was a travesty of what the architectural visionaries had had in mind and only a very few examples stood out from the general debasement. Such classic cases included Ernö Goldfinger's Trellick Tower in west London, proposed for listing by English Heritage in the 1990s and fiercely defended by some of its occupants; and the renowned Alton West estate at Roehampton, which owed much of its quality to the parkland in which it was set.[1] In mundane practice, the simple and sometimes elegant freestanding tower was elaborated into the cruciform, T or Y-shaped "point" block, while the slab could become a building raised above ground on legs or *pilotis*, as Le Corbusier had advocated; but instead of being used for flowing green space as he had envisaged, the ground level had to be allotted to stores and carparks. The slab placed on a podium could be developed into a deck access complex. No use was made of flat roofs, and entrances to buildings that might house hundreds or thousands were small and mean.

More importantly than their lack of architectural quality, most high-rise estates made little if any physical link with their surroundings, but they stood in isolation, neither containing urban amenities within themselves (as was the case with Le Corbusier's "Unités") nor having around them anything more than council estates normally provided. On urban sites they mostly occupied tight plots where any surrounding space was appropriated by road access and car parking. But in the interests of mixed development and what was often described as "architectural emphasis", they were also sometimes placed in suburbs or on the edges of towns, where there was no apparent reason to save land and where tightly crammed dwellings contrasted oddly with liberal amounts of "public open space" within the estate. Large deck-access estates became, in effect, labyrinths impenetrable to outsiders, the invariable telltale being a profusion of direction signs with arrows pointing to block names or flat numbers divided into "odds" and "evens" …

The alien nature of estate architecture increased with their scale. Before 1939, most flatted estates contained a few hundred dwellings or less. In its Quarry Hill Flats, with around 900 dwellings, Leeds had boasted the largest such estate in Europe; but after the war, the Aylesbury estate in Southwark housed 8,000 people in over 2,400 units, in blocks up to a third of a mile long. Some of the large central London estates were, it is true, endowed with shops, cinemas and other amenities which could be used by a wider public. The outstanding but untypical example of this was The Barbican in the City of London, built for over 2,000 high-income council tenants and incorporating the London Museum, a public day school, church and theater. [*See Fig. 4.*] The far commoner case, however, was the estate that looked spuriously self-sufficient and repelling to outsiders. Broadwater Farm, made notorious in the 1980s by a youth riot and murder, provided an example: its gleaming white, deck-access complex placed without any relation to the surrounding north London streets, where it appeared to have landed like a capsule from outer space. Indeed, it was often the designers' purpose to make such estates look as different as possible from normal environments, as in the notorious Southgate estate at Runcorn new town, endowed by Sir James Stirling with colored plastic ("legoland") cladding and large, round, "porthole" windows.[2]

Living in flats

In the second half of the century flats became an established form of housing for the single and the elderly, though still not entirely without some taint of welfare origins. If not as terminal, they were still likely to be treated as only temporary homes. But outside a small luxury market, family flats were almost exclusively council owned, and held in low esteem. Like some of the peripheral council estates, they easily developed into reservoirs of people living on welfare payments and with larger than average amounts of unemployment, of large families, and perhaps drug traffickers. It was hard to remember that in their opening years many such estates operated well, with tenants who were appreciative of them.[3] In prewar walk-up flats, the ideal situation found in Kensal House might be thought overdrawn, were it not for many similar accounts from other estates: "each balcony has its tenants leaning elbows on the rail, smoking, gossiping, happy, like a group of cottagers perched above each other on a steep cliff".[4] It was evidently possible for something like this to occur even on a large, postwar London estate of maisonettes [*an apartment on two levels, Ed*.] and high flats: "If it's someone's birthday on your landing, we always have a bit of a sing song along the balcony. If it's a wedding or a funeral, everyone turns up and cleans the landings and the stairs because there'll be visitors coming … and that's why I say I wouldn't want to live nowhere else".[5]

But increasingly the legacy of the high-rise boom was the estate that failed to stabilize socially and seemed to be a disaster from the beginning. This applied to the architecturally pretentious, deck-access estates of Southgate, just mentioned, to the system-built, deck-access estates of the 'YDG' type in Leeds, Hull and Sheffield, and to Hulme in central Manchester – this last the product of a long planning history which dated back to the 1930s, when local people had fought off slum clearance and redevelopment.[6]

Yet in terms of dwelling interiors, the technical standards of flats were often high, and to a large degree successful. Even councils' early walk-up flats, although cramped and sometimes lacking bathrooms, improved on the earlier tenements by being self-contained. In the 1930s a number of authorities used the "improved" flat with superior internal standards, notably staircase access and individual balconies.[7] The Quarry Hill Flats, in particular, with their first use of a waterborne system of refuse disposal and other features, represented the most advanced living standards of their time.[8] High internal standards continued to be applied after 1945, making it possible for the Parker Morris Report to refer to "standards which before the war were scarcely dreamt of for anything but the luxury market".[9] This no doubt accounts for the high levels of satisfaction that residents of flats commonly reported, even on estates that were otherwise regarded as failures.[10] Maisonettes shared such standards and at first were felt to have particular advantages in being cheaper to build than houses, making rents lower, while it was possible for them to have individual gardens, at front or back. Their popularity did not last, however, and they soon became "possibly the most unpopular type of council dwelling of all".[11] The reasons for this are not entirely clear, but an important factor was doubtless the alternate layering of living rooms and bedrooms, which made maisonettes even noisier than flats.

While both flats and maisonettes benefited from Parker Morris space standards and fittings – which could even include such things as refrigerators and wallpaper – there was no effective attempt to address the practical problems of vertical living. Postwar high-rise dwellings were built with an apparently total absence of inquiry into the operation of existing walk-up flats. The introduction of lifts, while seeming a self-evident improvement, enabled architects and managers to imagine that they were replacing conventional with "vertical" streets or "streets in the air" without any serious consideration as to the practicalities involved. Normal practice was to provide pairs of lifts which stopped on alternate floors. Economies and minimal technical standards resulted in slow speeds with frequent breakdowns, which were not only frustrating but provided maximal opportunities for vandalism, graffiti and use of lifts as urinals. The confined space of the lift had to be shared with people from different floors who were not neighbors in any meaningful sense. When lifts broke down, dingy and menacing staircases had to be used. It is not surprising therefore, that flats on the first floor were most in demand. The top floor was the favorite of people who felt able to trade problems with lifts for peace and long distance views; but those on the ground floor moved away whenever they could, because of noise and general disturbance.[12]

Deck access design tried to address some of these problems. Sited at strategic deck and bridge crossings, their lifts could be fewer in number but larger and more efficient, while the decks themselves were intended to provide opportunities for socializing, thus restoring the friendly, busy atmosphere of the neighborhood street, without its traffic noise and danger.[13] In reality, decks involved a superfluity of hard-to-maintain stairs, passages, landings and illumination; far from being convivial, they were cold, draughty and menacing places where the prudent did not linger.[14]

The main victims of living off the ground were children, with their mothers. The high-level playgrounds provided on some of the larger estates were soon closed for safety reasons; but nationwide there were in most years one or two fatalities of children falling from windows and balconies. Once let outside to play it was impossible for parents to control, or indeed even to see their children, many of whom got up to ingenious games which easily developed into vandalism.[15] One consequence was that children old enough to play outside were kept inside the home, where parents desperately tried to keep them quiet for fear of annoying the neighbors.[16]

A home in a high flat thus brought a special kind of "encapsulation", where "to reach one's own floor, to step out onto a long, empty corridor or a small, empty landing, to be faced with closed doors and to have this happen *time after time* can give an impression of being alone in an unfriendly world. To look out of a twentieth-story window at a miniature world peopled by midgets is to look on a planet of which one has no 'natural' experience… even to hear noises from other flats, while seeing no one, can contribute to an eerie sense of loneliness".[17] Inward-looking people who mainly saw the home as a refuge may not have minded, indeed may even have enjoyed, such detachment; but it could not be maintained in families with children without giving rise to health and stress problems.

Daily problems of domestic living were intensified as the scale and height of flats increased. They included the disposal of refuse… and an inexplicable habit among some tenants of discarding unwanted appliances by lobbing them over balconies.[18] But the most serious problem of all was universally agreed to be noise. Flats had more contiguous neighbors than houses with in addition all the noises generated by the block: lifts, plumbing, people tramping along access balconies, and in the case of deck-access blocks decks that ran above the ceilings of inhabited rooms, often bedrooms. Bare concrete stairwells and open courtyards compounded the problem, particularly of noisy play.

Problems of security also affected flats more than houses. In the early years of high-rise building, no security devices were provided on block entrances, so that anyone could enter and wander round unchallenged. Intercom systems began to be fitted in the 1970s but these could not be used on deck-access estates where decks had the function of through streets. Yet these were not streets in any ordinary sense: in particular they were not overlooked by windows, as streets of houses would be, and the rows of front doors along them could belong to dwellings on three different levels. This exemplified a special phenomenon of high-rise estates: unfamiliar kinds of space which were neither public nor private, and which lacked any defined function. At the same time, the important buffer space between the home and the public street, traditionally provided by the front garden, was absent.

The new high-rise environments, therefore, lacked cultural roots or social consensus as to their proper use. Successful usage would have required much cooperation and control, particularly over children. This had in fact often been achieved in the interwar walk-up flats which had resident caretakers whose authority was not questioned; but on postwar high-rise estates, which in any case had more complex layouts, problems were critically increased when for reasons of economy one council after another took the step of replacing resident caretakers by mobile teams of cleaners. The problem of children was addressed by a policy decision to remove them from high blocks, or at least from higher floors; but at best this was only partially successful[19] and it was a policy that could not always be maintained under pressures of family growth and housing demand.

All the inherent problems of high-rise living were intensified by the adoption of indus-trialized system building in the 1960s.[20] The amount of heating needed in high blocks, which were quickly chilled by high winds, had always been underestimated; but poorly designed and hastily erected blocks using patent, prefabricated systems had their own inherent heating problems, as well as dampness, condensation, fire risk and noise. All gas heating systems installed in them were banned after the collapse of Ronan Point in a gas explosion in 1968 and the electrical systems that replaced them were often ineffective, expensive to use, often not allowing the user to control use from within the home. It was not uncommon for the cost of heating to rise to as much or even more than the rent itself, and in consequence many tenants were disconnected from the supply, or cut themselves off. They then resorted to portable paraffin heaters which created further problems of condensation and mold growth. For many years, the response of housing managers was to deny the existence of the problems or else to blame them on the tenants, who were given spurious advice which included leaving windows open in all seasons, avoidance of vapor-producing activities such as boiling kettles or even "deep breathing". The problems were in reality so serious that they eventually led to a tenants' "dampness campaign" which later developed into a national movement, the National Tower Blocks Network.[21]

In due course the problems of high flats, and of system building in particular, became too obvious to be officially ignored and, some years after the Ronan Point disaster, blocks here and there began to be deliberately demolished. Less desperate measures included the "lopping" of upper storys, a device particularly useful for converting blocks of maisonettes into conventional houses, and the reroofing and recladding of blocks, to provide both better insulation and a more attractive appearance. Blocks were also divided into separate layers allotted to different populations.[22] Such initiatives showed that under certain circumstances high-rise housing could operate successfully: it served well as sheltered housing, for instance, and when sold off and converted, as up-market, owner-occupied homes. But radical transformations were also possible without turning out the original population, as the experience of the Priority Estates Projects and numerous other cases of estates improved through tenant consultation showed.[23] Nor was it always necessary to carry out major structural work: estates could be changed from "hard-to-let" to much-in-demand through intensive management,[24] through the introduction of such apparently simple things as carpeted and well-lit entrance halls, or the use of "concierges", who more than covered their wages by the consequent reduction of vandalism and unlet flats.[25]

The essence of the problem of council flats was that, unlike the English house, their use by families was not rooted in a long, evolutionary process. In addition, they were the products of monolithic and large-scale design which gave little scope for the users to modify through their ordinary domestic behavior. Besides fatally underestimating repairs and maintenance, such design was inflexible, cowing even its housing managers. On the deck-access estate of Hunslet Grange in Leeds, for example, the local managers found that small children who ran along decks got lost and could not find their way home, because the long rows of white-painted front doors were all identical. The estate's architect, however, refused to agree to a variation of colors on the grounds that this would destroy the "visual unity" of his architectural design. The result was that this most expensive and difficult to live in of all housing was assigned to some of the poorest and the largest families in society. This was partially mitigated in the early stages by the fact that the first residents were likely to be local people who appreciated having up-to-date housing standards in their own neighborhoods. But on outlying high-rise estates, and increasingly on all of them over time, tenant populations became both more heterogeneous and more deprived. Thus [a] fatal combination of environmental with adverse social factors accelerated obsolescence, to the extent that many estates, both pre- and postwar flats, had a shorter life than houses – much shorter in fact, than many of the postwar prefabs whose planned life was only ten years... In the case of the Quarry Hill Flats the life was only around thirty-five years, but Southgate and Hunslet Grange lasted for little over fifteen. In effect the estates of council flats degenerated into new and in a sense purpose-built slums, a situation without precedent since some of the worst workers' housing of the industrial revolution.

While equally serious problems could be found on peripheral council estates, high flats were less amenable to physical change and more visible to the general public, with whom their over-ambitious and failed utopianism brought the whole idea of public housing into disrepute. As we have seen, their contribution to the housing stock as a whole was only small, but nevertheless flats and maisonettes made up over a third of all council housing in 1991. About a fifth of the 170,000 high-rise (12-story and above) and over 30 percent of the walk-up flats fell into the worst 10 percent of the English housing stock.[26]

It was an open question how far into the future flats could continue to serve as family homes. The Priority Estates and other initiatives demonstrated that those schemes of improvement which worked best were the product of joint physical and managerial change, with partial demolition, separation of different household types, perhaps some diversification of tenure, and tenant management. The reallocation of neglected and vandalized spaces could give residents more control over and pride in their environments, as well as protecting these from abuse by outsiders, notably commuters using them as carparks. But ultimately the degree to which estates could be converted into "normal" residential environments was probably limited, not least because any scheme of improvement demanded high levels of commitment to collective action. Many residents gave this gladly at times of crisis or when there was a real prospect of change; but it was unclear how far such a level of commitment would be sustained, or need to be sustained, into the future.

Notes

1   E. R. Scoffham, *The Shape of British Housing*, London: George Goodwin, 1984.
2   Jane Morton, *From Southgate to Hallwood Park – 25 Years in the Life of a Runcorn Community*, Liverpool: Merseyside Improved Houses, 1994.
3   Ibid.
4   Ascot, *Flats: Municipal and Private Enterprise*, London: Ascot Gas Water Heaters Ltd., 1938.
5   Morris Parker, *Home for Today and Tomorrow* (Ministry of Housing and Local Government), London: HMSO, 1961, p. 70. [*The Parker-Morris report of 1961 established new standards for public housing; these were made mandatory in 1967 for new towns, in all council housing in 1969, and for all public housing in 1980. Ed.*]
6   Alison Ravetz, "Factors Contributing to Estate Write-Offs and Their Relevance to Current Theory and Practice: Quarry Hill Flats and Hunslet Grange Leeds", in Alan Ferguson and Duncan Sim (eds) *System Building: Making It Work*, Stirling: Housing Policy and Practice Unit, University of Stirling, 1992; Hulme Study, "Stage One: Initial Action Plan Commissioned by the Department of Environment and Prepared by Capita *et al*"., 1990; Martin Spring, "Hulme Brew", *Building* 28, January 1994, 41–6.
7   Ravetz, "From Working-Class Tenement to Modern Flat: Local Authorities and Multi-Story Housing between the Wars", in Anthony Sutcliffe (ed.) *Multi-Story Living: The British Working-Class Experience*, London: Croom Helm, 1974.
8   Ravetz, *Model Estate: Planned Housing at Quarry Hill, Leeds*, London: Croom Helm, 1974.
9   Parker, *Home for Today and Tomorrow*, para. 117.
10 Ministry of Housing and Local Government [MHLG], "Living in a Slum: A Study of St. Mary's, Oldham", *Design Bulletin* 20, London: HMSO, 1970.
11 Anne Power, *Property Before People: The Management of Twentieth-Century Council Housing*, London: Allen and Unwin, 1987, p. 54.
12 Ravetz, "Tenancy Patterns and Turnover at Quarry Hill Flats, Leeds, *Urban Studies* 8, no. 2, 1971, 181–205.
13 Alison and Peter Smithson, *Urban Structuring: Studies of Alison and Peter Smithson*, London: Studio Vista, 1967.
14 Morton, *From Southgate to Hallwood Park*.
15 Parker, *Home for Today and Tomorrow*.
16 W. F. R. Stewart, *Children in Flats: A Family Study*, London: NSPCC, 1970.
17 Ibid., p. 8.
18 Anthea Holme, *Housing and Young Families in East London*, London: Routledge and Kegan Paul, 1985.

19 GHS (General Household Survey) nos. 1–., Office of Population Censuses and Surveys, Social Survey Division, London: HMSO, 1971–.

20 Patrick Dunleavy, *The Politics of Mass Housing in Britain, 1945–75: A Study of Corporate Power and Professional Influence in the Welfare State*, Oxford: Clarendon Press, 1981.

21 Community Links, *The View: The National Tower Blocks Bulletin*, 1988–, London: Community Links, 1988–.

22 Institute of Housing, *Trends in High Places*, London: IoH, 1983.

23 Anne Power, *The PEP Guide to Local Housing Management and Estate Action. 1. The PEP Model. 2. The PEP Experience*, London: Department of Environment and Welsh Office, 1987; John Thompson, *Community Architecture: The Story of Lea View House, Hackney*, London: RIBA Community Architecture Group, 1985; Ruth Owens, "Born Again", *Architects' Journal*, March 18, 1987, 48–57; NHTCP (National Housing and Town Planning Council), "High-Rise Living", *A Housing and Planning Review* 42, no. 1, 1987.

24 Morton, *From Southgate to Hallwood Park*.

25 Brent Community Law Center, *Making an Entrance* (Gloucester House, Brent), London: Brent Community Law Center, n.d.

26 Department of Environment, *English House Condition Survey 1991*, London: HMSO, 1993.

A Clockwork Orange

Anthony Burgess (1962)

[*The dialect spoken by Alex and his droogs is "nadsat", a language invented by Burgess, who has one of his characters describe it thus (114): "'Odd bits of old rhyming slang,' said Dr Branom ... 'A bit of gipsy talk, too. But most of the roots are Slav.'" Misspellings are in the original. Stanley Kubrick's 1971 motion picture, based on the novel (Figs. 66, 67), has come to be as well or better-known than the original. Ed.*]

"What's it going to be then, eh?"

There was me, that is Alex, and my three droogs, that is Pete, Georgie, and Dim, Dim being really dim, and we sat in the Korova Milkbar making up our rassoodocks what to do with the evening, a flip dark chill winter bastard though dry. The Korova Milkbar was a milk-plus mesto, and you may, O my brothers, have forgotten what these mestos were like, things changing so skorry these days and everybody very quick to forget, newspapers not being read much neither. Well, what they sold there was milk plus something else. They had no licence for selling liquor, but there was no law yet against prodding some of the new veshches which they used to put into the old moloko, so you could peet it with vellocet or synthemesc or drencrom or one or two other veshches which would give you a nice quiet horrorshow fifteen minutes admiring Bog And All His Holy Angels And Saints in your left shoe with lights bursting all over your mozg. Or you could peet milk with knives in it, as we used to say, and this would sharpen you up and make you ready for a bit of dirty twenty-to-one, and that was what we were peeting this evening I'm starting off the story with.

Our pockets were full of deng, so there was no real need from the point of view of crasting any more pretty polly to tolchock some old veck in an alley and viddy him swim in his blood while we counted the takings and divided by four, nor to do the ultra-violent on some shivering starry gray-haired ptitsa in a shop and go smecking off with the till's guts. But, as they say, money isn't everything.

The four of us were dressed in the heighth of fashion, which in those days was a pair of black very tight tights with the old jelly mould, as we called it, fitting on the crutch underneath the tights, this being to protect and also a sort of a design you could viddy clear enough in a certain light, so that I had one in the shape of a spider, Pete had a rooker (a hand, that is), Georgie had a very fancy one of a flower, and poor old Dim had a very hound-and-horny one of a clown's litso (face, that is), Dim not ever having much of an idea of things and being, beyond all shadow of a doubting thomas, the dimmest of we four. Then we wore waisty jackets without lapels but with these very big built-up shoulders ("pletchoes" we called them) which were a kind of a mockery of having real shoulders like that. Then, my brothers, we had these off-white cravats which looked like whipped-up kartoffel or spud with a sort of a design made on it with a fork. We wore our hair not too long and we had flip horrorshow boots for kicking.

"What's it going to be then, eh?"

There were three devotchkas sitting at the counter all together, but there were four of us malchicks and it was usually like one for all and all for one. These sharps were dressed in the heighth of fashion too, with purple and green and orange wigs on their gullivers. Each one not costing less than three or four weeks of those sharps' wages, I should reckon, and make-up to match (rainbows round the glazzies, that is, and the rot painted very wide). Then they had long black very straight dresses. [...]

... But poor old Dim kept looking up at the stars and planets and the Luna with his rot wide open like a kid who'd never viddied any such thing before, and he said:

"What's on them, I wonder. What would be up there on things like that?"

I nudged him hard, saying: "Come, gloopy bastard as thou art. Think thou not on them. There'll be life like down here most likely, with some getting knifed and others doing the knifing. And now, with the nochy still molodoy, let us be on our way, O my brothers". The others smecked at this, but poor old Dim looked at me serious, then up again at the stars and the Luna. So we went on our way down the alley, with the worldcast blueing on on either side. What we needed now was an auto, so we turned left coming out of the alley, knowing right away we were in Priestley Place as soon as we viddied the big bronze statue of some starry poet with an apey upper lip and a pipe stuck in a droopy old rot. Going north we came to the filthy old Filmdrome, peeling and dropping to bits through nobody going there much except malchicks like me and my droogs, and then only for a yell or a razrez or a bit of in-out-in-out in the dark. We could viddy from the poster on the Filmdrome's face, a couple of fly-dirted spots trained on it, that there was the usual cowboy riot, with the archangels on the side of the US marshal six-shooting at the rustlers out of hell's fighting legions, the kind of hound-and-horny veshch put out by Statefilm in those days. The autos parked by the sinny weren't all that horrorshow, crappy starry veshches most of them, but there was a newish Durango 95 that I thought might do. Georgie had one of these polyclefs, as they called them, on his keyring, so we were soon aboard – Dim and Pete at the back, puffing away lordly at their cancers – and I turned on the ignition and started her up and she grumbled away real horrorshow, a nice warm vibraty feeling grumbling all through your guttiwuts. Then I made with the noga, and we backed out lovely, and nobody viddied us take off.

We fillied round what was called the backtown for a bit, scaring old vecks and cheenas that were crossing the roads and zigzagging after cats and that. Then we took the road west. There wasn't much traffic about, so I kept pushing the old noga through the floorboards near, and the Durango 95 ate up the road like spaghetti. Soon it was winter trees and dark, my brothers, with a country dark, and at one place I ran over something big with a snarling toothy rot in the headlamps, then it screamed and squelched under and old Dim at the back near laughed his gulliver off – "Ho ho ho" – at that. Then we saw one young malchick with his sharp, lubbilubbing under a tree, so we stopped and cheered at them, then we bashed into them both with a couple of half-hearted tolchocks, making them cry, and on we went. What we were after now was the old surprise visit. That was a real kick and good for smecks and lashings of the ultra-violent. We came at last to a sort of a village, and just outside this village was a small sort of a cottage on its own with a bit of a garden. The Luna was well up now, and we could viddy this cottage fine and clear as I eased up and put the brake on, the other three giggling like bezoomny, and we could viddy the name on the gate of this cottage veshch was HOME, a gloopy sort of a name. I got out of the auto, ordering my droogs to shush their giggles and act like serious, and I opened this malenky gate and walked up to the front door. I knocked nice and gentle and nobody came, so I knocked a bit more and this time I could slooshy somebody coming, then a bolt drawn, then the door inched open an inch or so, then I could viddy this one glaz looking out at me and the door was on a chain. "Yes? Who is it?" It was a sharp's goloss, a youngish devotchka by her sound, so I said in a very refined manner of speech, a real gentleman's goloss:

"Pardon, madam, most sorry to disturb you, but my friend and me were out for a walk, and my friend has taken bad all of a sudden with a very troublesome turn, and he is out there on the road dead out and groaning. Would you have the goodness to let me use your telephone to telephone for an ambulance?"

"We haven't a telephone", said this devotchka. "I'm sorry, but we haven't. You'll have to go somewhere else". From inside this malenky cottage I could slooshy the clack clack clacky clack clack clackity clackclack of some veck typing away, and then the typing stopped and there was this chelloveck's goloss calling: "What is it, dear?"

"Well", I said, "could you of your goodness please let him have a cup of water? It's like a faint, you see. It seems as though he's passed out in a sort of a fainting fit".

The devotchka sort of hesitated and then said: "Wait". Then she went off, and my three droogs had got out of the auto quiet and crept up horrorshow stealthy, putting their maskies on now, then I put mine on, then it was only a matter of me putting in the old rooker and undoing the chain, me having softened up this devotchka with my gent's goloss, so that she hadn't shut the door like she should have done, us being strangers of the night. The four of us then went roaring in, old Dim playing the shoot as usual with his jumping up and down and singing out dirty slovos, and it was a nice malenky cottage, I'll say that. We all went smecking into the room with a light on, and there was this devotchka sort of cowering, a young pretty bit of sharp with real horrorshow groodies on her, and with her was this chelloveck who was her moodge, youngish too with horn-rimmed otchkies on him, and on a table was a typewriter and all papers scattered everywhere, but there was one little pile of paper like that must have been what he'd already typed, so here was another intelligent type bookman type like that we'd fillied with some hours back, but this one was a writer not a reader. Anyway, he said:

"What is this? Who are you? How dare you enter my house without permission". And all the time his goloss was trembling and his rookers too. So I said:

"Never fear. If fear thou hast in thy heart, O brother, pray banish it forthwith". Then Georgie and Pete went out to find the kitchen, while old Dim waited for orders, standing next to me with his rot wide open. "What is this, then?" I said, picking up the pile like of typing from off of the table, and the horn-rimmed moodge said, dithering:

"That's just what I want to know. What *is* this? What do you want? Get out at once before I throw you out". So poor old Dim, masked like Peebee Shelley, had a good loud smeck at that, roaring like some animal.

"It's a book", I said. "It's a book what you are writing". I made the old goloss very coarse. "I have always had the strongest admiration for them as can write books". Then I looked at its top sheet, and there was the name – A CLOCKWORK ORANGE – and I said: "That's a fair gloopy title. Who ever heard of a clockwork orange?" Then I read a malenky bit out loud in a sort of very high type preaching goloss: "– The attempt to impose upon man, a creature of growth and capable of sweetness, to ooze juicily at the last round the bearded lips of God, to attempt to impose, I say, laws and conditions appropriate to a mechanical creation, against this I raise my sword-pen –" Dim made the old lip-music at that and I had to smeck myself. Then I started to tear up the sheets and scatter the bits over the floor, and this writer moodge went sort of bezoomny and made for me with his zoobies clenched and showing yellow and his nails ready for me like claws. So that was old Dim's cue and he went grinning and going er er and a a a for this veck's dithering rot, crack crack, first left fistie then right, so that our dear old droog the red-red vino on tap and the same in all places, like it's put out by the same big firm – started to pour and spot the nice clean carpet and the bits of his book that I was still ripping away at, razrez razrez. All this time this devotchka, his loving and faithful wife, just stood like froze by the fire-place, and then she started letting out little malenky creeches, like in time to the like music of old Dim's fisty work. Then Georgie and Pete came in from the kitchen, both munching away, though with their maskies on, you could do that with them on and no trouble, Georgie with like a cold leg of something in one rooker and half a loaf of kleb with a big dollop of maslo on it in the other, and Pete with a bottle of beer frothing its gulliver off and a horrorshow rookerful of like plum cake. They went haw haw haw, viddying old Dim dancing round and fisting the writer veck so that the writer veck started to platch like his life's work was ruined, going boo hoo hoo with a very square bloody rot, but it was haw haw haw in a muffled eater's way and you could see bits of what they were eating. I didn't like that, it being dirty and slobbery, so I said:

"Drop that mounch. I gave no permission. Grab hold of this veck here so he can viddy all and not get away". So they put down their fatty pishcha on the table among all the flying paper and they clopped over to the writer veck whose horn-rimmed otchkies were cracked but still hanging on, with old Dim still dancing round and making ornaments shake on the mantelpiece (I swept them all off then and they couldn't shake no more, little brothers) while he fillied with the author of *A Clockwork Orange*, making his litso all purple and dripping away like some very special sort of a juicy fruit. "All right, Dim", I said. "Now for the other veshch, Bog help us all". So he did the strong-man on the devotchka, who was still creech creech creeching away in very horrorshow four-in-a-bar, locking her rookers from the back, while I ripped away at this and that and the other, the others going haw haw haw still, and real good horrorshow groodies they were that then exhibited their pink glazzies, O my brothers, while I untrussed and got ready for the plunge. Plunging, I could slooshy cries of agony and this writer bleeding veck that Georgie and Pete held on to nearly got loose howling bezoomny with the filthiest of slovos that I already knew and others he was making up. Then after me it was right old Dim should have his turn, which he did in a beasty snorty howly sort of a way with his Peebee Shelley maskie taking no notice, while I held on to her. Then there was a change-over, Dim and me grabbing the slobbering writer veck who was past struggling really, only just coming out with slack sort of slovos like he was in the land in a milk-plus bar, and Pete and Georgie had theirs. Then there was like quiet and we were full of like hate, so smashed what was left to be smashed – typewriter, lamp, chairs – and Dim, it was typical of old Dim, watered the fire out and was going to dung on the carpet, there being plenty of paper, but I said no. "Out out out out", I howled. The writer veck and and his zheena were not really there, bloody and torn and making noises. But they'd live.

So we got into the waiting auto and I left it to Georgie to take the wheel, me feeling that malenky bit shagged, and we went back to town, running over odd squealing things on the way. […]

So off we went our several ways, me belching arrrrgh on the cold coke I'd peeted. I had my cut-throat britva handy in case any of Billyboy's droogs should be around near the flatblock waiting, or for that matter any of the other bandas or gruppas or shaikas that from time to time were at war with one. Where I lived was with my dadda and mum in the flats of Municipal Flatblock 18A, between Kingsley Avenue and Wilsonsway. I got to the big main door with no trouble, though I did pass one young malchick sprawling and creeching and moaning in the gutter, all cut about lovely, and saw in the lamplight also streaks of blood here and there like signatures, my brothers, of the night's fillying. And too I saw just by 18A a pair of devotchka's neezhnies doubtless rudely wrenched off in the heat of the moment, O my brothers. And so in. In the hallway was the good old municipal painting on the walls – vecks and ptitsas very well developed, stern in the dignity of labor, at workbench and machine with not one stitch of platties on their well-developed plotts. But of course some of the malchicks living in 18A had, as was to be expected, embellished and decorated the said big painting with handy pencil and ballpoint, adding hair and stiff rods and dirty ballooning slovos out of the dignified rots of these nagoy (bare, that is) cheenas and vecks. I went to the lift, but there was no need to press the electric knopka to see if it was working or not, because it had been tolchocked real horrorshow this night, the metal doors all buckled, some feat of rare strength indeed, so I had to walk the ten floors up. I cursed and panted climbing, being tired in plott if not so much in brain. I wanted music very bad this evening, that singing devotchka in the Korova having perhaps started me off. I wanted like a big feast of it before getting my passport stamped, my brothers, at sleep's frontier and the stripy shest lifted to let me through.

I opened the door of 10-8 with my own little klootch, and inside our malenky quarters all was quiet, the pee and em both being in sleepland, and mum had laid out on the table my malenky bit of supper – a couple of lomticks of tinned spongemeat with a shive or so of kleb and butter, a glass of the old cold moloko. Hohoho, the old moloko, with no knives or synthemesc or drencrom in it. How wicked, my brothers, innocent milk must always seem to me now. Still, I drank and ate growling, being more hungry than I thought at first, and I got fruit-pie from the larder and tore chunks off it to stuff into my greedy rot. Then I tooth-cleaned and clicked, cleaning out the old rot with my yahzick or tongue, then I went into my own little room or den, easing off my platties as I did so. Here was my bed and my stereo, pride of my jeezny, and my discs in their cupboard, and banners and flags on the wall, these being like remembrances of my corrective school life since I was eleven, O my brothers, each one shining and blazoned with name or number: SOUTH 4; METRO CORSKOL BLUE DIVISION; THE BOYS OF ALPHA.

The little speakers of my stereo were all arranged round the room, on ceiling, walls, floor, so, lying on my bed slooshying the music, I was like netted and meshed in the orchestra. Now what I fancied first tonight was this new violin concerto by the American

Geoffrey Plautus, played by Odysseus Choerilos with the Macon (Georgia) Philharmonic, so I slid it from where it was neatly filed and switched on and waited.

Then, brothers, it came. Oh, bliss, bliss and heaven. I lay all nagoy to the ceiling, my gulliver on my rookers on the pillow, glazzies closed, rot open in bliss, slooshying the sluice of lovely sounds. Oh, it was gorgeousness and gorgeosity made flesh. The trombones crunched redgold under my bed, and behind my gulliver the trumpets three-wise silverflamed, and there by the door the timps rolling through my guts and out again crunched like candy thunder. Oh, it was wonder of wonders. And then, a bird of like rarest spun heavenmetal, or like silvery wine flowing in a spaceship, gravity all nonsense now, came the violin solo above all the other strings, and those strings were like a cage of silk round my bed. Then flute and oboe bored, like worms of like platinum, into the thick thick toffee gold and silver. I was in such bliss, my brothers. Pee and em in their bedroom next door had learnt now not to knock on the wall with complaints of what they called noise. I had taught them. Now they would take sleep-pills. Perhaps, knowing the joy I had in my night music, they had already taken them. As I slooshied, my glazzies tight shut to shut in the bliss that was better than any synthemesc Bog or God, I knew such lovely pictures. There were vecks and ptitsas, both young and starry, lying on the ground screaming for mercy, and I was smecking all over my rot and grinding my boot in their litsos. [...]

After that I had lovely Mozart, the Jupiter, and there were new pictures of different litsos to be ground and splashed, and it was after this that I thought I would have just one last disc only before crossing the border, and I wanted something starry and strong and very firm, so it was J. S. Bach I had, the Brandenburg Concerto just for middle and lower strings. And, slooshying with different bliss than before, I viddied again this name on the paper I'd razzrezzed that night, a long time ago it seemed, in that cottage called HOME. The name was about a clockwork orange. Listening to the J. S. Bach, I began to pony better what that meant now, and I thought, slooshying away to the brown gorgeousness of the starry German master, that I would like to have tolchocked them both harder and ripped them to ribbons on their own floor.

High-rise living
What tenants say

J. S. Fuerst (1985)

High-rises for low- and moderate-income families have been denounced by critics ever since government began to build them. But apparently residents have a different opinion.

During the 1950s and 1960s most conventional public housing built in large cities was high-rise. Administrators jammed as many units on each site as the federal agencies would allow. Since planners clamored for green space, housing authorities – working with limited space and limited budgets – seemed to have no choice but to build high-rises.

The greatest need for public housing was among large families; consequently multi-bedroom units abounded. Robert Taylor Homes, for example, a multi-story project in Chicago, was typical with an average of three bedrooms and five children per unit. A considerable number of these projects were built for the most underpriviledged. The miseries of stacking masses of large, broken, and bruised families next to and on top of one another were not well recognized by the housing authorities. In time, though, the terrible social conditions wrought by this poor judgment brought general denunciations of public housing high-rises from architects and sociologists all over Europe and the United States. Soon, conventional wisdom declared that elevators and families don't mix.

In 1968, U.S. District Court Judge Richard Austin, in the *Gautreaux v. Chicago Housing Authority* case, went so far as to forbid the building of any new high-rise public housing for families with children. Generally this decision seems to have been extended to privately owned, publicly subsidized housing projects. Later, federal court ruled that Cedar Riverside – one of the more successful "new town-in-town" projects in Minneapolis – could not build any more high-rise additions because they had an adverse environmental impact upon the area.

Most critics have relegated high-rise public housing (if not public housing in any form) to the dust heap. Yet there have been successful high-rises built as part of public housing programs in the last 25 years which refute these prophecies of failure. In 1950, a state and city financed high-rise program was developed by the Chicago Housing Authority which won praise from *Progressive Architecture Magazine* "for startlingly new designs of outside balconies and use of color in its high-rises". *Architectural Forum* editorialized that "public housing, since the war, has done more in Chicago to improve design and planning of high-rise apartments at lower rents than all private building in the U.S. during the same period". Other high-rises, such as Ping Yuan, an eight-story project in San Francisco's Chinatown, have been just as successful. Ping Yuan is a high-density project, filled with large, low-income Chinese families. Though such conditions have spelled difficulties elsewhere, the great need for housing in the Chinese community, a good design, great *esprit de corps* among the tenants made turnover low and waiting lists long for many years.

Successful high-rises are also found in Boston, Pittsburgh, and New York City. Even Oscar Newman, author of *Defensible Space* – a sharp critique of high-rise public housing – cites a number of high-rises such as Riverbend and Brownsville as more than acceptable. A most successful one is the New York City Housing Authority project in Forest Hills, New York.

Likewise *Housing* by John Macsai (1976) detailed 65 multifamily units all over the U.S., 12 of which were high-rises for families of low- and moderate-income. Judging by low turnover, virtually no vacancies, and willingness to replicate these developments, managers of 10 of these 12 indicated great successes.

The same study showed that in a comparison of 135 low- and moderate-income families living in high-rises felt more secure than those in low-rise buildings. The authors point out that high rises in this study were all built in New York City and were of recent design; "In other words the high-rises were designed, located, and tenanted with far greater care… This situation may easily account for the lack of significant difference in satisfaction levels".

By all odds, these projects should have been towering infernos of social problems. In fact, many have been quite successful. In [some] cases, residents have expressed considerable satisfaction. Real estate firms operating these projects indicate success as measured by the usual criteria: moveouts were low, vacancy losses were minimal, waiting lists were long, payments to HUD were adequate, and the financial returns were satisfactory.

The clearest confirmation of the success of high-rise projects, however, comes from tenant surveys. Tenants were surveyed in a Chicago subsidized development, 820 Belle

Plaines. This high-rise is a 24-story, 265-unit project built in 1969 and managed and developed by M. Myers and Associates.

The "Uptown" community, where Belle Plaines is located, is a "neighborhood of entry" for immigrants and a home for refugees from poverty-stricken areas. It contains many halfway houses for alcoholics, former mental patients, ex-convicts, and many unemployables.

It also contains a good many middle-income families and is adjacent to the higher rent neighborhoods of Lakeview, and Lincoln Park, and Edgebrook. Although there is some social disorganization and a crime problem, Uptown's diversity of race, nationality, and income keeps it from being a racial or economic ghetto.

A preeminent fact about 820 Belle Plaines has been its consistent low vacancy rate. One hundred of the 200 tenants were questioned as they came into the building during a three-day period. This provided the bulk of the information for the survey. The managers of Belle Plaines and a neighboring high-rise, 833 Buena, provided a random list of names of families with children in the two high-rises who were also interviewed for their comments.

Aesthetics

Some of the harshest criticisms of high-rises relate to their antihuman character and their lack of spiritual quality. Critics such as Lewis Mumford, Jane Jacobs, and Wolf von Eckhardt revolt against the high-rises' architectural barrenness.

For example, von Eckhardt says:

> High-rises work against nature, against man, and against society by eliminating all spiritual values which existed in the past. Human symbols such as churches, which towered above the city are below the skyscraper.

The tenants in 820 Bell Plaines feel somewhat differently. One rather articulate resident, on hearing Eckhardt's comments, asked: "Does von Eckhardt expect us to believe that our country is shrinking from its values because we live a few bricks higher than the churches?"

Another replied:

> From my twentieth floor apartment I can see sailboats on Lake Michigan, a green stretch of Lincoln Park, and lights twinkling from the top of Sears Tower. My high-rise experience has extended my environment and given me perspective.

Planning critics attribute "anomie" and human isolation to high-rises. Tenants provide a refreshing rejoinder to these allegations. "When they talk about isolation in a high-rise, I don't know what they are talking about. We have many friends in the building. In fact, we came to the building because of our friends, and are staying because of them. True, we make adjustments in routine. We take the kids to the park rather than letting them out to play in the garden. But our life style doesn't change".

"People, regardless of where they live, isolate themselves everyday. Buildings, houses, town houses do not cause isolation. There is a far deeper cause and it occurs in suburbs as well as in cities, in low-rises as well as in high-rises".

Architectural critics point to the lack of amenities in high-rises – particularly outdoor space.

The tenants' comments indicate a realism not shared by the critics. They answer:

> In an ideal world everyone should have private outdoor space, and perhaps in years to come we will develop a lifestyle where most jobs are not concentrated in a few square miles, so that people must flock there and live without elbow room. Until then, what is a viable alternative? I can't afford the time or money to live further from the downtown area. A clean, well maintained high-rise is certainly preferable to anything else available to me.

Much tenant satisfaction was attributable to the low rents relative to the unsubsidized housing market. Some of the tenants were students remaining until the completion of studies. Others were renting only until they could save enough money to buy a home. Many tenants remained because of the cheap rent.

In fact, one-third gave "cheap rent" as their prime motivation in moving to the building. Eight percent did not think the rent was too high and the same proportion believed they could not do better in the open market.

Income levels at Belle Plaines varied from under $1,500 to well over $15,000 a year. Management does adjust rents to income, but does not evict tenants as quickly as conventional housing does when their incomes climb past the federally determined ceilings for participation in such projects.

Tenants

Fifty percent of the tenants are Black, 25 percent Asian and 25 percent white including Spanish American. Our interviews indicated that tenants felt no discomfort with the racial mix, though most believed that some limits would be necessary.

Twenty percent of the families in Belle Plaines receive either Old Age Assistance or Aid to Dependent Children. Yet these are prompt rent-payers and none have had to be evicted for delinquencies in rent. Virtually all of the tenants queried said that the present income distribution of the families was satisfactory to them. No one objected to the presence of families receiving public assistance. Indeed, few families seemed aware of the income mix of the project except that there was some mention of "elderly families who probably receive old age benefits".

Children in multi-story buildings has been a persistent dilemma. A common complaint for years among families with children is that they can find few management firms willing to rent to them. Landlords have been reluctant to permit large numbers of children in a building because of potential damages. To meet this need, public housing was built almost exclusively for such families. Some concluded that high-rises for low-income families with children did not work. Oscar Newman added to the allegations by drawing on a few crime studies of New York City public housing high-rises:

> [One of] the alarming aspects of high-rise development is the danger of raising children in them. For low-income families with children, high-rise apartment buildings are strictly to be avoided. These families should be housed in walk ups no higher than three stories.

[…] Belle Plaines contains about 130 children, and Buena houses 190 children. Managers of both buildings said they control the number of children in the apartments. Nine out of ten tenants believed their building could handle children with no difficulty – and saw no reason against some increases.

A 1973–74 study prepared by the Chicago Council for Community Services, for the U.S. Office of Child Development, quotes a mother living in South Commons, a Chicago high-rise, low-rise complex, "I find that living in a high-rise actually brings my family closer together". Similarly, a tenant in Cedar Riverside, a successful Minneapolis subsidized high-rise, said, "This is a good place to bring up kids. The pediatrician is right on the Plaza. […] I can let the children play without worrying about cars. […] My kids sit on the 20th floor balcony drawing all the roof angles and the sight lines. That's the way to learn to draw".

A study on children in high-rises by A. M. Pollowy of the University of Montreal indicated that generally for families with children, high-rise height seemed to have little effect on personal attitudes. Those living very high up are no less satisfied than those living near the ground.

Height is a vital question in an elevator building. The residents of these projects preferred differing heights. There were only a few who stated that height made much difference. Several similar studies by others have indicated that "the height of the buildings seemed to have little effect on attitudes".

Architect Ezra Gordon has argued that seven stories is a desirable height because it kept the tenants in touch with the ground and trees. John Black, another architect, believes that 22 stories is an acceptable height, though once the buildings are tall enough to require elevators, the exact height is of negligible importance.

There is nothing in the height of a building to stop a family from functioning well if the basics are there. Certainly to live in a well-run high-rise is preferable to living in a poorly kept slum walkup.

Density

Connected with neighborhood and crime is the question of density of population. Crime has nothing to do with height. It depends upon the neighborhood. Crime did not result from height but from the packing of too many problem families into one project. Many architects believe that restrictions on density are overemphasized. John Black has said that "density per se is irrelevant; the only criterion is market acceptance". Ezra Gordon has said acceptable density depends on neighborhood patterns. In a highly built-up area like Uptown, it is possible to have 250 units per acre whereas in other areas this would be completely unacceptable. The important question is the number of persons, particularly children, per unit rather than the number of units per acre. For example, a building could have 100 units per acre but if there are five persons to each unit, this would be 500 persons, including perhaps 300 children to the acre, which would crowd the area with teenagers and youngsters. In contrast, a high-rise might have 250 units with 600 people, yet only 130 children to the acre, and tenants would feel less crowded.

The question of density was central to the discussion of the consulting team chosen by the Department of Housing and Urban Development to study the fate of Pruitt-Igoe, the St. Louis public housing project that received national publicity when it was dynamited ten years ago [*Figs. 68, 69*]. The prestigious study team, headed by architect Walter Netsch, never recommended the complete destruction of that project. Recognizing that the density had been far too great – the project was empty when the team studied it – the team recommended that the density be reduced by destroying one out of every three buildings. The team recommended converting and rehabilitating the remaining buildings, providing fewer, larger apartments and space for community services, libraries, and recreation space. Finally, the team suggested the adoption of a more restrictive tenant selection procedure, based on models used by the private sector. Thus, even the oft-cited example of Pruitt-Igoe as proof of the undesirability of high-rise buildings is less than valid.

Conclusion

Whether the tenants who spoke highly of their situation were all telling the truth may be open to question. People are wary of disparaging their own homes. However, low turnover and low vacancy rate are undeniable evidence of the degree of tenant satisfaction.

Thus, contrary to popular notions currently in vogue in planning circles, tenants can and do live happily in high-rises with diverse ethnic groups, with different income groups, and with children. Moreover, such buildings can, with subsidies, pay off for the investors, the developers, and the mortgage holders. Most important, they can provide good housing for a large number of low- and moderate-income families without the need for extensive community facilities or cash subsidies to tenants.

At least from the point of view of the dwellers, it provides satisfying, inexpensive housing without isolating people, depriving them of spiritual comfort, or violating their rights as citizens. As Ralph Rapson, architect of Cedar Riverside, said, "I don't advocate high-rises for everybody. But to house so many people, what is the alternative?"

Vällingby

David Popenoe (1977)

Vällingby after twenty years: first impressions

The typical approach to Vällingby is by subway. Shortly after leaving the downtown area of Stockholm, the train emerges from its tunnel, providing the traveler with some spectacular views of the city as it glides over several high bridges which bind together Stockholm's islands. The cityscape, dominated by six-, eight-, and ten-story apartment blocks, has a sense of order; everything seems to be in its place. There is also a feeling of openness which is uncharacteristic of most cities, a feeling created by waterways, interconnecting fingers of parkland, jagged hills, and outcroppings left in their natural state. Yet very little open space seems transitional or unused.

One passes from the inner city through the prewar suburbs of small, single-family houses (looking much like California bungalows) only to abruptly encounter further high-density expressions of city life. One does not meet the expected uniform decline in building densities with distance from the central business district that the real estate market generates in most Western cities. Stockholm's densities are very uneven; the high-density developments may be followed by green parkland or, in one instance, what looks like a working farm with grazing sheep. The dark green of the wooded areas, the shimmering blue of the waterways, and the lovely pastels of the built-environment, make the trip to Vällingby, especially on a sunny day, a memorable one. It is hard to believe that this is all part of a major city.

Just as one has begun to feel that the city may at last be ending, the Vällingby development area emerges in the distance. Each subway stop soon becomes encased by a sizable urban center, or centrum,[1] surrounded by apartment buildings – some as high as ten stories. The apartment buildings, in turn, are encompassed by heavily wooded parkland. Finally, the main Vällingby centrum comes into view, built on a hill which commands the surrounding area.

The subway tunnels through the hill under Vällingby centrum, the visitor disembarks from the train in partial darkness and heads up the escalator toward the light. A step outside and one is back in the city, which was supposed to have been left behind. Vällingby centrum is a large, pedestrian shopping mall [*Fig. 70*]. The scene is dominated in spring, summer, and fall by open-air stalls selling fruits, vegetables, and flowers; sparkling fountains; people walking to and fro and sitting on benches as they watch the urban milieu. The feeling is calm and peaceful, yet with a touch of gaiety, especially on a bright, sunny day. The environment is colorful, alive, and ever-changing, as new people continually enter the field of view.

One immediately recognizes that the centrum is not just a retail sales venture. Prominently in view are the modernistic church, the community and youth centers, and office buildings. Attached to the centrum on the periphery are high apartment buildings that overlook the urban scene like giant sentinels. The centrum is a place to walk through on the way home from work, also to linger for a while. It is more like a downtown district than a U.S. shopping center; that, of course, was the planner's intention.

The centrum, with its high buildings and urban ambience, is surrounded by a green belt, which sets it apart from the garden apartments and town houses which make up the bulk of the Vällingby area [*Fig. 71*]. Pedestrian walkways underpass the traffic arteries around the centrum and lead across the green belt to the housing beyond. The Vällingby residential areas are heavily wooded and quite hilly; one can follow the paths for hours, through parklike settings, seldom having to cross even a minor roadway. Lateral paths veer off from the main walkways, leading to the garden and high-rise apartment complexes. There is scant feeling of being in either a city or a traditional suburb; the overall impression is of being in a large park, within which apartment houses have been placed.

Much of the parklike area between the residential buildings is given over to children's activities. Conspicuous visual features are the day-care centers: long, colorful, interconnecting buildings with attached playgrounds and play facilities. Tot-lots, children's parks, wading pools, and sports grounds also are frequently in evidence. The apartments look out on these facilities the way houses overlook streets and back yards in the American suburb. [...]

In the following pages, the residential environment of Vällingby is described and analyzed in terms of three major components... The first is the environment itself, the tangible and perceived world of things which surround the resident. In urban areas, of course, a large part of this environment is built, or man-made. The second component of the residential environment is its demographic structure, the kinds of people who live there. The major units of demographic structure have become well standardized in sociology, including age, sex, class, race, ethnicity, and stage of the life cycle. Third, is what I have labeled community system characteristics: those aspects of the community which give it structure as a social system, apart from the nature and behavior of particular residents who happen to live there.

The elements of the Vällingby environment

The major environmental elements in Vällingby are the apartment building, the individual dwelling unit, the pedestrian path, the street, the parking lot, play and sitting areas, service facilities (schools, day-care centers), neighborhood and town shopping centers, the automobile, other people in the process of utilizing the environment, vegetation and landscape (especially hills and rocks). These are the tangible things one sees, uses, or comes into contact with in the close vicinity of the dwelling unit, on a regular, usually daily, basis.

The most conspicuous element of the environment is the apartment building – typically three-story, often faced with stucco, and painted with the muted and earthy pastel colors which one associates with Europe. The buildings can be quite long, often as much as a block without a break in the denser areas of Vällingby. But clusters of such buildings, sometimes forming superblocks, are separated from one another by seas of grass, bushes, and trees. This quickly distinguishes them from their counterparts in more urban settings. In the more recently built sections of Vällingby, and in the areas adjacent to the centrums, the low-rise buildings are interspersed with ten-story tower blocks.

The six-to-eight-story "slab" buildings which are characteristic of more recent Swedish suburbs can also be found in Vällingby. They are not as high as the tower blocks but are far more massive and obtrusive in appearance. [...]

The architecture of Vällingby is actually quite diverse. Many different architects were used, and different styles sometimes vie for one's attention in a limited area. Some architects have denounced this as "eclecticism"; but it was instrumental in saving Vällingby from the often monolithic uniformity of the later suburbs.

The individual dwelling unit, unlike in the U.S. suburb, is probably the least prominent element of the Vällingby environment to the outside observer, although it may be the most important for the resident. The outsider encounters only two aspects of the dwelling: the balcony (almost all Vällingby apartments have balconies) and the entrance door. The small balconies tend to look alike, though the residents often dress them up with flowers. Many Swedes take the same care in dressing up their balconies as they do in their dwelling interiors; in spring, summer, and fall these efforts make a delightful addition to the outdoor visual scene. The balconies are also used to a limited extent for drying and airing clothes and rugs, and sometimes for the storage of household accessories such as toys.

Entrances to the dwelling units are clustered typically in groups of six, two to each floor, opening off an interior stairwell with one large door to the outside. One must go into the building and up at least half a flight of stairs to encounter the individual entrance, which invariably has a mail slot and a name on the door. Beyond the door is what seems a totally private world.

Adjacent to almost every apartment building, but usually on one side only, is an open parking lot which empties onto the area's traffic circulation system. Because of the sharp physical separation between pedestrian and automobile, together with the abundance of mature vegetation, the traffic system is not always very obvious to the observer on foot. Yet the car is never more than a stone's throw from the apartment unit. Almost no Vällingby households have two cars, and a significant percentage (35–40)[2] have no car at all, so the small parking lots and narrow streets (by U.S. standards) seem adequate. Driving a car through Vällingby is a very different experience from walking. One sees a contrary face of the same environment, a face which is more typical of the U.S.

Most streets have sidewalks, and it is sometimes necessary for the pedestrian to use these sidewalks to get where he is going. Planners frequently comment on how inadequate the separation of vehicular from pedestrian traffic is in Vällingby compared to the separation in later Stockholm suburbs. Yet to an American this distinction is lost. One can walk virtually the length of the Vällingby area (except for one major gap in the middle) and never cross a street. The pedestrian paths are for the most part paved, wide, and well lighted; they often lead through heavily wooded areas where one is but dimly aware of the presence of buildings. Sometimes the buildings themselves, jutting up in a sudden and unexpected way from the crest of a hill, add to the beauty of the scene. It is no wonder that many Vällingby residents ... take walks for pleasure; indeed this is their major form of exercise and regular recreation.

Many persons, young and old, also ride bicycles. Cyclists share the paths with pedestrians but are not allowed inside the centrums. Motorized bicycles (Mopeds) are restricted to the street system, although they sometimes stray on to the pedestrian paths. Cycling is mainly a recreational pursuit, yet the bicycle is also a not unimportant vehicle for shopping, work trips, and visits to friends. While bicycle riding is not uncommon in U.S. suburbs, it is mainly limited to the young. In Sweden, it is an activity of all stages of the life cycle except for the very young and the very old.

The pedestrian circulation system in Vällingby, together with the pedestrian-only character of the shopping centers and the diminution of the need for and visual presence of the automobile, gives Vällingby an environmental character that is relatively unknown in the U.S. There is an atmosphere of peace and quiet, fostered also by the tall trees and mature shrubbery, which normally is difficult to obtain in a residential environment of this density. The human scale that comes with an area designed mainly for pedestrians can be found in the U.S. only in those special environments, typically nonresidential, from which the car has been excluded: boardwalks at resorts, pedestrian malls in downtown areas and shopping centers, historical districts like Williamsburg, amusement parks like Disneyland. These environments give a unique kind of contentment and even exhilaration in the United States; they are much sought after. But one drives to get to them, and they are invariably surrounded by a sea of parked cars – the "real world" in an almost extreme form. In Vällingby the human scale is natural and spontaneous, built into daily living. It is not the destination for a special trip but the basic dimension of a way of life... Vällingby residents are well aware of, and greatly appreciate, this environmental quality. It is uppermost in the minds of a majority of Vällingby dwellers in their positive evaluation of the area.

The other elements that Vällingby residents rate very highly are the vegetation and landscape, and the proximity of the suburb to "the country". Vällingby lies on a very attractive site: hilly, heavily wooded terrain bordered on two sides by an arm of Lake Mälaren which marks the outer boundary of the city. The Vällingby area was originally the site of farms which supplied produce for the city of Stockholm. It is easy to forget that when Vällingby was first built it had the same raw look which is characteristic of new developments everywhere, and it came in for the share of criticism faced by all new developments because of this fact. Now, as is also true in Levittown, the vegetation has matured and become a focus of great pride and positive feeling.

It is significant that the residents often combine, in their positive assessment of

Vällingby, the pedestrian orientation with the assets of nature. Thus Vällingby is often described as quiet and peaceful, with lovely walkways, and close to nature and beauty. The natural world would seem to be the world par excellence at the human scale. The pedestrian facilities provide access to Vällingby's natural assets, allowing these assets to be more than a mere backdrop.

Plantings and even woodland in a heavily populated area require a high level of maintenance. In the American suburb, most maintenance rests in the hands of the individual property owner, a situation that leads to a network of social pressures and often sporadic deterioration in quality. In Vällingby, "gardening" is done by trained employees – except in the cases of the balcony flower boxes and indoor plantings, and the small gardens connected with single-family homes.[3] This gives an even level of maintenance throughout the area, a level that in Vällingby seems quite high. The public spaces, the equivalent of the private yards in the United States, appear well cared for and indeed are often planted with masses of flowers and shrubbery which are well beyond the means of the average citizen.

… The Vällingby multifamily dwelling is oriented to public open spaces. These open spaces far exceed their U.S. counterparts in variety and quality. The facilities range from small tot-lots with a sandbox, through larger playground areas with play apparatus of some kind, to large, supervised play parks which throughout the year (except during summer vacation months) have planned programs of activities for children up to the age of about twelve. Finally, clusters of low, colorful buildings surrounded by fenced-in play areas signal the Swedish day-care centers with facilities for the care of babies (over seven months old) and infants, toddlers, kindergartners [sic], and schoolchildren during after-school hours. There are also wading pools (used for skating in the winter) and sports fields.

These facilities give the Vällingby environment a domestic quality which is not characteristic of most public park areas; and the children generate in the environment a liveliness which one does not always associate with apartment living. Facilities for children and youth are generally within view of the dwelling units; the squeals of the children can sometimes be heard through the open windows. These facilities and spaces represent an extension of the living environment of the apartment dwelling, just as a private yard is an extension of the house in the United States. The Vällingby apartment dwellers have no private yard space – all yard space is publicly owned. As in the American suburban yard, however, the activities of children in the "public yard" tend to prevail. […]

The American suburb seldom has a true focal point; it typically consists of street after parallel street of detached houses. While one often encounters a school, a church, or a shopping center, it is rarely the case that the adjacent residential areas *focus* on these facilities. Rather, the facilities are distributed on pieces of land which happen to be available. The church seldom draws exclusively from its local area, and the automobile provides a freedom of movement which may well lead away from the nearest shopping center to a preferred one at greater distance. In Levittown, only the elementary school is designed to be a neighborhood focal point, but it is quite distant from the average home and is not perceived as a focal point by most residents.

In Vällingby, all paths lead to the town centers, or centrums. These hubs of activity represent concerted attempts by the planners to bring physical and functional focus to clusters of about 10,000 persons, and the planners have achieved a degree of success in their attempts, certainly in physical terms. The high-rise apartments around the centrums can be seen from great distances and provide a strong sense of orientation to persons walking the paths through the outlying residential districts. During the day, at least, the centrums, which are bustling with activity, provide a social counterpoint to the calm and quiet of these districts. In a sense, one can go from country to city in the distance of a few hundred yards. No apartment unit lies more than five or six hundred yards from a centrum, so residents are always within easy walking distance; the great majority of Vällingby residents do their regular shopping entirely on foot.

An additional element of the environment should be mentioned, though it is not commonly classified as environmental – the presence of strangers. The people who are visually encountered on the pedestrian path system are typically strangers, as on a city street. For the most part, however, these strangers are limited to fellow residents of the 4,000–10,000-person clusters of which Vällingby is composed. Over time, therefore, some of these strangers become familiar faces, as in a socially enclosed residential district of a city or in a small town of similar size. This element is seldom found in American suburbs, where streets are usually not throughways for pedestrians. When residents leave their homes in the United States, they typically are enclosed in an automobile. It is the automobile, therefore, which takes on the quality of being unknown or partially known.

A final word about the Vällingby environment. One has there a pervasive sense of being linked to the city. The subway runs above ground the length of Vällingby, and a subway stop is never far away. The constant shuttling back and forth of trains, by day and well into the night, is a continuing reminder that Vällingby is a part of something else. There is an easily accessible world beyond, a world which is much larger and more interesting for those whose mood or necessity would carry them in that direction. […]

Households illustrating a high degree of congruence with the environment

The characteristic Vällingby household

Despite growing demographic diversity in Vällingby, one household and family type emerged from the demographic analysis as most characteristic of the community today, in the sense of occurring more frequently than any other single type: the family of middle-aged adults whose teenagers are leaving home. This is the type into which the original Vällingby settlers, who came as young families with children, now fall. Within this category, nine of the twenty-five households in the interview sample were remarkably similar in life-style and attitudes toward Vällingby, as well as in age, family size, and class level. The common elements shared by most of these nine cases have been put together into the following composite case, a descriptive sketch of the characteristic Vällingby household. In many respects, such as age, income level, family size, and residential accommodation, this composite household is similar to the typical or statistically average household in Sweden as a whole.

The characteristic Vällingby household consists of two working or lower-middle-class adults in their forties or fifties, with one teenager still living at home. Both adults work, the man going into downtown Stockholm on the subway and the woman working locally. They have lived in their present one- or two-bedroom apartment seven or eight years and own one car, which is used mainly on weekends and for summer vacations.

Almost every day, on the way home from work, food shopping is done by the wife at a small grocery store which is no more than a few hundred yards away; other purchases, such as household supplies, are made several times a week at the neighborhood centrum. Aside from work trips, she and her husband go into downtown Stockholm no more than once or twice a month, often on Saturdays, for shopping or occasionally for entertainment.

In the evening, after supper, the adults take care of household chores, read the Stockholm newspaper, take a walk around the Vällingby area in nice weather, watch about one hour of television, and go to bed by eleven o'clock. On weekends, they visit friends or relatives in the Stockholm area by car, take a long walk, or in spring, summer, and fall, drive to their summer "stuga", or cottage.

The family's summer cottage typically is located by a lake or the sea, several hours' drive from Stockholm. It is grouped with perhaps five or six others, forming a small neighborhood; sometimes the parents' cottage is nearby. Trips to the cottage are made as often as possible. The husband may drive to the cottage every nice weekend in the spring, for a change of scene and to do maintenance and repair work on either the cottage or the boat that the couple also owns, and the family spends most of its summer vacation there, about three or four weeks. One week of the vacation is spent visiting one set of parents in their home county. Often the teenager past the age of thirteen or fourteen stays in Stockholm for the summer or takes a vacation apart from his family; usually he or she holds a summer job. Every few years the family will take a trip to southern Europe or North Africa, commonly for a week during the colder months.

At least one of the spouses was raised in the Stockholm area and has parents who still live there. Visiting with relatives is common; major holidays such as Christmas and Easter are almost always spent with close relatives. Apart from relatives, the couple has only a few friends, usually met through work, and the entertaining of friends at home is not common, taking place about once a month or less. [...]

Neither spouse is a member of any community organization apart from work, neither reads more than a daily newspaper and sometimes a magazine, and regular exercise is limited to occasional walking, bicycle riding (they own several bicycles), and activities having to do with the summer house and boat. Regular participation in cultural or educational activities is rare, and they seldom eat out in restaurants.

The characteristic family likes Vällingby very much, pointing out that it is quiet and near woods and lake, has all the services that are needed, is "settled", and is close to the city. They can think of few problems in Vällingby, except perhaps for some rowdy youths or the growing visibility of alcoholics in the centrums; these phenomena are regarded as problems in the abstract, not as serious social problems which directly affect their lives.

Though they have no plans to move, they would like to have a larger apartment. There is nowhere else they realistically would rather live than in the Stockholm area: "Of course, it would be nice to live in a small town or farm, but we wouldn't be able to find work there". It might also be desirable to live in a single-family detached house, they feel, but it would be much more work, and they might have to give up their summer cottage. They talk of living during their retirement years at the summer cottage, keeping a small apartment in town so they can be near their children.

In summary, the characteristic Vällingby household is quite home- and family-centered. Outside activities for the adults revolve mainly around work and summer cottage. Their life is not culturally or intellectually rich by upper-middle-class standards, and their social life is focused on extended-family members and a few friends from work and perhaps childhood. [...]

The teenager in Vällingby

The teenagers in the household sample expressed a higher level of contentment than their parents. Only one of the teenagers whom I interviewed stated that he was bored in Vällingby, and the great majority indicated that they would be happy to live in Vällingby as adults, although they felt that at their age it was rather unrealistic of them to state a preference of this kind. A few preferred to live "in the city", others on a farm or in a small town; in these cases, however, negative reaction against Vällingby was surprisingly weak.

What did they like about Vällingby? It is near nature, quiet and peaceful, yet also near the city – these were common answers. They also liked the services and facilities which Vällingby provides, such as public transportation and recreation; very few could think of any services or facilities for young people which might usefully be added to the community. Similarly, few could think of any "problems" in Vällingby.

In marked contrast to the American suburban situation, teenagers in Vällingby have almost no transportation problems; there is no dependence on parents to drive them places within the community or even within the metropolitan area. Public transportation is well suited to their needs, and its cost is low. As an indication of their geographic mobility, many youth from the age of about ten or eleven are allowed to make trips by themselves into downtown Stockholm for specific purposes. In addition, teenagers in Vällingby can walk to school, bike riding is common, and many boys get motor bikes at age fifteen. Because the minimum legal age for driving a car in Sweden is eighteen, the automobile plays a relatively insignificant role in their lives. Some teenagers are even anti-automobile; they plan never to own a car or to get a driver's license when they become of age. [...]

Patterns of environmental fit in Vällingby: some conclusions

No single residential environment can work well for all types of people; the range of human needs and interests is far too great. Yet Vällingby provides a close environmental fit for a surprisingly wide range of individuals and families. In this respect it must be ranked at the top of urban settlement types. It works well for the young family, especially if the family is not too large or too desirous of personal, private space. It works even better for older families, because it is especially well suited to the needs of teenagers and working women. For parents whose children have left home, it provides a maintenance-free dwelling close to desired services and facilities and often close to the children themselves. It seems to work just as well for singles and young couples with no children, and for many pensioners.

Neither urban nor suburban in the U.S. sense, Vällingby combines some of the advantages as well as the disadvantages of both settings. In the process of attracting persons with such diverse needs and interests, it has become a very heterogeneous settlement, quite unlike most in the United States. This demographic balance gives it an urban flavor which most suburbs lack. Yet with its natural environment and its air of peace and contentment, Vällingby is very un-urban; indeed, it is almost rural in character.

Which households are not congruent with Vällingby? The large family finds apartment living of any kind difficult; the need for a sizable amount of living space becomes paramount. Since they can afford it, the middle- and upper-middle-class families often find the lure of the single-family house irresistible. They are willing to give up the benefits of a Vällingby for the space, the status, and the privacy of a separate dwelling unit. Those whose roots or preferences lie in rural or small-town living find any form of urban settlement an uncomfortable place to be, and Vällingby is no exception in this regard. At the opposite extreme, every society has a small handful of people whose tastes and interests run to urbanity and cosmopolitanism – Vällingby can be a dull place to them. Finally, the lonely of the world find an urban way of living difficult, whether in city or suburb. Vällingby does not offer much help for their problem, although the best environmental alternatives are by no means clear.

Yet the range of persons Vällingby serves, and serves well, remains perhaps its most unique and positive characteristic. In the United States, new residential environments are becoming more highly specialized: for families, rich or poor; for singles; for senior citizens; and so on. The specialized environments have many social drawbacks, such as the loss of diversity and the fostering of needless residential mobility. Moreover, these environments become fragile commodities in the buffeting of the urban real-estate market. As neighborhoods change, what works today may not work tomorrow; the environment can quickly head down the path of premature obsolescence.

If anything, Vällingby has improved over the years as a stable, desirable, and efficient residential environment. One can reasonably conclude that it works even better for its present population than it did for its original settlers.

Notes

1 The term used by the Swedes to designate the combined commercial, social, and cultural centers that form the core of Vällingby districts.
2 Based on data from the Grimsta district…
3 Some Vällingby apartment residents do tend garden plots; these lie on the edge of Vällingby or outside the area in adjacent districts.

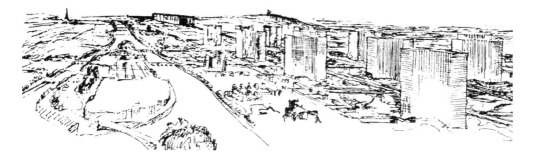

Figure 64 Le Corbusier, "Plan Voisin", sketch for the "Center of Paris", 1925.

Figure 65 Alison and Peter Smithson, "Streets in the Air", GLC Robin Hood Lane, Tower Hamlets, London, begun 1968.

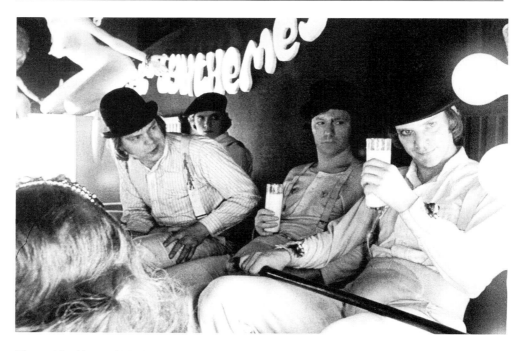

Figure 66   Alex and his droogs at the Korova Milkbar, from *A Clockwork Orange* (1971, directed by Stanley Kubrick).

Figure 67   Dim vandalizing a building, from *A Clockwork Orange* (1971, Stanley Kubrick).

Figure 68   Minoru Yamasaki, Pruitt-Igoe housing, St Louis, Missouri, 1955.

Figure 69   Pruitt-Igoe housing being demolished in 1972

Figure 70
Vällingby,
Sweden, general
view (high-rise
apartments in
background).

Figure 71
Vällingby,
Omega housing
area, 1958.

12

Some possible futures

This section raises questions about the relevance of the past to the future, and suggests possible models for further development. With housing density necessarily increasing, along with mobility, the pressure for relatively smaller dwellings in new relationships to one another will also increase. The "cohousing" movement, which began in Denmark in the 1970s, and now is widespread in Europe and America, offers one possible model. Cohousing, which draws upon the cooperative traditions already reviewed by Spencer-Wood and Ravetz, seeks to create relatively dense new communities in which residents give up some privacy and join in a number of collaborative activities. Usually, there is an effort to include a variety of residents – single and married, young and old, well-to-do and not so well-to-do. The important Danish example of Trudeslund (Figs. 72, 73) is surveyed by Kathryn McCamant. The desire to replicate older kinds of community with modern means is also apparent in the prefabricated housing groups being mass produced by Ikea (Fig. 74), reported on here in a *New York Times* article by John Leland. In apparent contrast to these kinds of community-oriented housing is the American trailer or mobile home, one of the most successful products of prefabrication, analyzed by political scientist Allan D. Wallis, and John Brinckerhoff Jackson (a principal founder of modern landscape history). The mobile home offers single-family dwellings at low cost (and with easy financing) to more than twenty million Americans. These buyers sacrifice interior space in exchange for modern household technologies; they also, sometimes, value the possibility of movement – movement to lightly settled areas, or even to wilderness areas (Fig. 75). In this aspect, the "trailer" or mobile home reminds us of the kind of "home" described by Reyner Banham in Chapter 3. And it also has some affinities with the Walden hut documented by Maynard in Chapter 7.

On the other hand, as both Wallis and Jackson make clear, the "trailer" or mobile home is frequently not mobile at all: often it travels directly from the factory to an isolated site and stays there, or it sits in a trailer park in perpetuity (Fig. 76), or, as Jackson shows, it is employed by long-established ethnic communities for new housing. It is also quite commonly remodeled and extended by its inhabitants (Fig. 77).

The more affluent housing purchasers of the future may have other opportunities as well. In the United States, at least, there is a new tendency among young professional people to invest in large and elaborate "McMansions" (on small lots), often part of a builder's housing development, and sometimes gated off from the rest of public space. The advertisement for "Harriton Farm" in Villanova, PA makes clear the appeal to tradition and stability that such housing developments offer (Fig. 78). And for those who still (or again) want to "live downtown", there is the remodeled loft, described here by architect and housing historian Norbert Schoenauer (Figs. 79, 80).

How cohousing works
The Trudeslund community

Kathryn McCamant and Charles Durrett, with Ellen Hertzman (1988)

> I know I live in a community because on a Friday night it takes me 45 minutes and two beers to get from the parking lot to my front door.
>
> Trudeslund resident

People drift into the common house. The few minutes before dinner are a time to relax and catch up on each other's lives. At one of the tables, a little girl tells her parents about her day at preschool. Shrieks of laughter come from the playroom down the hall. The cooks put the last touches on the salad. By six o'clock the dining hall is bustling with life as people find their seats. It's dinnertime at Trudeslund.

For the 33 families who live in the cohousing community of Trudeslund, this was a typical evening. For us, it was the first of many such evenings we would spend in the Trudeslund common house. We were not certain that first night how we would adjust to eating regularly with 50 or more people, but our wariness was soon dispelled. After experiencing the convenience and pleasantness of common dinners and community life as a whole, we wondered why we had ever considered living any other way.

Dinner is served in the common house every night (except for two Saturdays a month when the room is used for private parties). Each of the private houses also has a full kitchen, so that residents may participate in common dinners as often as they like. Many residents eat in the common house three or four times a week, and have more intimate family dinners at home the other evenings. Some eat almost every night in the common house, using the time they save from shopping, cooking, and cleaning up to spend with their children. We quickly came to appreciate having several extra hours each day. Community dinners are not only convenient, but also pleasant social gatherings filled with interesting conversation. On any given evening, 50 percent of the residents, and often more, take part.

The one responsibility required of every adult resident is to cook dinner. Two adults, assisted by one child, plan, shop, prepare, serve, and wash up after dinner. Cooking for 60 may seem like an enormous job for two people, but with a well-equipped community kitchen, it's not much more complicated than cooking for six in a normal kitchen – you just learn to use ten times as much of everything. Residents sign up for dinners at least two days in advance and pay for the meal after dinner, when the cooks have divided the cost by the number eating – typically about $1 to $1.50 for adults, half price for children under thirteen, and free for toddlers under three.

The first time we prepared a common dinner – enchiladas for 80 – was an intimidating experience. But the satisfaction we felt at the end of the evening made up for all our anxieties. Our next efforts were considerably easier as we learned the ropes of cooking for large groups. One resident, a doctor, told us he had been very apprehensive about cooking for the community; he had never really cooked for himself, let alone for 50 people. To his surprise, he had not only succeeded, but discovered he actually enjoyed cooking and began to cook more at home as well. With more than 60 adults in the community, each has to cook only once a month. Cooking one day a month is well worth the time and trouble when you can just show up for dinner the other 29 days. Trudeslund residents are convinced that they have the best dinner system of all – it's dependable, yet flexible enough to accommodate the changing needs of each family. We have to agree.

The place

As our primary base and home for six months, Trudeslund is the cohousing community we know best. Situated in the town of Birkerød, just north of Copenhagen, its 33 residences and large common house were completed in the spring of 1981. Utilizing the natural features of the sloping, wooded site, the residences line two pedestrian streets [*Fig. 72*], with the common house located at the highest point where the streets meet. With cars kept at the edge of the site and the houses clustered together, much of the lower end is left wooded, making it a favorite place for children to play. Architecturally, socially, and practically, this community has succeeded in creating a very "livable" environment.

Shared resources

Common dinners are only one of the practical advantages of living in Trudeslund. A cooperative store, located in the common house, is stocked with household goods, from toothpaste to cornflakes. Each household has a key, so that residents can pick up goods at any hour. They write down what they take in the account book and receive a bill at the end of the month. We wondered if goods ever disappeared without being noted in the account book. Indeed, there are occasional discrepancies (probably because people forget to write items down, rather than purposely steal) which must be made up from the community budget. Residents know that serious problems with the accounts would cause the store to be closed.

The store is run by one of nine "interest groups". Every adult is a member of one such group. Other interest groups are responsible for the outdoor areas, special children's activities, the monthly paper and minutes of meetings, the heating system, the laundry room, general maintenance, social events, and overall coordination of community activities.

Two washing machines and one dryer accommodate the laundry needs of the more than 100 residents. If both machines are full, clothes baskets are left in line with washing instructions. When one resident takes his laundry out, he puts in the next load in line, so no one has to wait around for an empty machine. Detergent is bought in bulk as part of the common budget. While all the houses were designed to accommodate a washer and dryer, only one family has chosen to install its own.

Also located in the common house are a workshop, a darkroom for photography, a television room, a walk-in freezer used by the community store and individual families, a guest room, and a music room where teenagers can "jam" on drums and electric guitars without bothering anyone. A more recent addition is the computer. A study the government conducted of different possibilities for working at home provided every household in Trudeslund with a personal computer connected to a central computer in the common house and outside computer lines. The computers have not, however, facilitated better communication among neighbors. For most, it is easier and more social to go to the common house and put a notice on the bulletin board than to network by computer.

These facilities are only a small part of Trudeslund's practical advantages. In such a community it's easy to borrow occasional necessities or share ownership. For instance, two families share a car, while five others own a sailboat together. There is only one lawn mower. Items needed only occasionally, such as tools, typewriters, and camping equipment, can generally be borrowed or shared, instead of each family owning one of everything. Twenty-nine of the households have also pooled their resources to buy a 17-room vacation house in Sweden. The sharing of resources gives all residents access to a wider variety of conveniences at a lower cost per family than is possible in traditional single-family houses.

Advantages for children

With nearly 50 children living in Trudeslund, there is no lack of playmates. The pedestrian-oriented site gives them lots of room to run without worrying about cars. The community serves as a large, extended family – children have many people besides their parents to look after them, to whom they can turn for assistance, or just to talk to. It becomes second nature for the older kids to keep an eye on the smaller ones, and the adults know every child by name.

Child-care is still needed during the daytime, when most of the parents are at work. After considering many possibilities, including local public facilities, the community decided to start its own after-school program and to send preschoolers to existing child-care centers in the neighborhood.

Initially, a "child-care corps" of five to seven adults rotated responsibility for 12 to 15 youngsters from noon to early evening when their parents came home. Other adults were also expected to help out at least five days a year. During the first two years, this system was adjusted several times, becoming more and more loosely structured until it dissolved almost completely. Because the children had grown older and were more familiar with the community and each other, they no longer required such structured care. Many adults also found that a forty-hour-a-week job simply did not permit them the extra time to run a child-care program.

After school, older children may hang out in the common house, play outside, or go home. The evening's cooks are usually working in the community kitchen and other adults are around if a child needs assistance.

Afternoon tea, a vestige of the after-school program, provides a meeting place for both children and adults every afternoon at three o'clock in the common house. Although officially an activity for the kids, adults also enjoy afternoon tea. On the days we were working at home, we always looked forward to tea time, the cohousing equivalent of the office coffee break.

Baby sitters are never lacking in the community. One couple, needing some time alone, went away for several days, leaving their sons, ages two and seven, with neighbors. The boys were quite comfortable staying with their neighbors and the parents knew they need not worry. As we watched the Trudeslund kids playing after dinner – their interaction with each other and with the adults, their self-confidence, and their ability to articulate their thoughts – we could truly appreciate the benefits that children derive from a sense of community.

A social atmosphere

The obvious practical advantages – child care, common dinners, shared resources – are not the main reasons why people choose to live in Trudeslund. One resident, John Nielsen, wrote:

Our primary motive for wanting to live in a community was the desire for a richer social atmosphere – for both children and adults. The many practical advantages which we later discovered, we hadn't even thought of in the beginning.[1]

One of the objectives stated by Trudeslund's initiators in the development program was to create a social network that would provide more support for the nuclear family:

> We want to open the family up toward the community, but still have it [the family] as a base. We want to have the necessary daily functions in the private dwellings, but transfer as many as possible of the other functions to the community, thereby encouraging social interaction.

The rich social atmosphere at Trudeslund is most evident on a warm day along the walkways between houses. Here children play, people relax with a beer after work, and families enjoy leisurely Saturday morning breakfasts. All the dwellings have private patios in back, but people seem to prefer sitting in front along the main circulation paths, where they can visit with neighbors or just watch the activity [*Figs. 72, 73*].

The community's design encourages social interaction by providing small courtyards along the walkways, complete with sandboxes and picnic tables, and patios and garden areas directly outside each house, with visual access from the houses themselves. Neighbors tend to congregate around the picnic tables and sandboxes where they can watch the children play. People sit on their front patios whenever weather permits, enjoying the comfortable vantage point just outside their front door.

In the houses, the kitchen-dining area – the room most families "live" in – looks onto the street, allowing parents to watch children playing outside, or to ask a passing neighbor about a recipe. As John Nielsen describes it:

> In Trudeslund we don't draw the curtains, so one can look in and glimpse life in the different houses. But from the front room [the kitchen-dining area] one also feels part of what happens on the street. Perhaps some would call it nosiness. I call it openness and sharing life.[2]

Each house also has a living area away from the street, which affords complete privacy. The sensitive relationship between the community area and private dwelling allows for many kinds of socializing. In fact, contrary to many outsiders' apprehensions, we never heard a resident complain about lack of privacy. Living in a close community, people learn to respect each other's occasional need to be unsociable.

Building a dream

Looking at Trudeslund today, it is easy to forget the difficult process necessary to transform the initial ideas into reality. In December, 1978, 20 families formed a group to build a cohousing development on a site available for sale, but zoned for single-family houses. At that time, only eight cohousing communities had been built in Denmark, though many were in the planning process. Under pressure to submit a project proposal quickly to secure the site, the members of the group did not have sufficient time to clarify their objectives. Only after a dramatic division that caused half of the original members to drop out, followed by a cautious restructuring of goals, was the group able to formulate a development plan.

With their goals and objectives agreed upon and the development plan formulated, the group held a limited architectural competition, inviting four firms to submit design proposals. After much debate, Vandkunsten Architects, a young, innovative firm, was selected to design and supervise construction of the development.

The two and a half years from the first planning meetings to the completion of construction were hectic and often frustrating. The group's commitment to making all decisions democratically meant numerous long meetings. Two of the participants later wrote:

> We had a flood of work groups going – many meetings in small groups where problems were discussed, and community decision meetings with two-foot-long agendas. Everyone was involved in the work. In the most active period there was at least one meeting a week for the least involved, and three or four for the most involved, after which came "homework" to prepare for the next meetings.[3]

Economic pressures, especially climbing interest rates, disciplined the group's ambitions and kept them to a tight time schedule.

To this day, the architects remember the process of working with the Trudeslund group as very exasperating. According to project architect Michael Sten Johnsen:

> Here we have a group of people who are used to being treated individually by virtue of their education, income, and influence; that they wished to act as a community was a dilemma throughout the project.[4]

Many of the participants were well-educated professionals who had strong opinions on the planning and development of the project, but few had previous experience with group decision making. Although the project is regarded as a success by the residents and has been widely publicized, the architects feel they failed to realize their architectural ideals because of the compromises made during the design process. The architects wanted to push cooperative concepts further than the residents were willing to go. They advocated even smaller houses to reduce costs and promote the use of community areas. Residents, most of whom had growing families, were already taking financial risks and did not want homes so unconventional that they would have difficulty selling them later. Conflicts between client and architect are common, but the participatory nature of this project, where strong-willed architects confronted equally strong-willed residents, made for a fiery design process.

Still, most residents involved in the planning process agree that their participation was vital to the project's success. Not only did their involvement result in a design that fit their specific needs and desires, but it helped to define the group's ideals and to strengthen community spirit: "We learned each other's strong and weak sides, and to be open with each other".[5]

In retrospect, residents acknowledge that they would have done some things differently. Many feel they overemphasized the design of the individual houses in relation to the common areas. One participant explained:

> It's difficult to imagine what you want in a common house because you've never had anything like it before. But everyone knows what they want in their own kitchen.

Although the group attempted to restrict the floor plans to four basic designs, individual preferences – particularly with regard to the kitchens – resulted in 33 different variations. Today, most residents agree that standardized kitchens would have been fine, since they eat dinner so often in the common house. Standardization would have reduced construction costs – a lesson from which more recent communities have benefited.

The houses, although not luxurious, are quite comfortable. Ranging in size from 970 to 1,500 square feet (90 to 140 square meters; m²),[6] they feature vaulted ceilings and wood floors [*Fig. 73*]. The one-story houses on the lower, southern side of the pedestrian street allow the two-story houses on the north side to enjoy sun and views of the trees. Unfortunately, the attractive interior design does not make up for the lack of sound insulation between rooms; from any room, a person can easily hear what's going on in the rest of the house.

The houses are privately owned, using a financial structure similar to that of American condominiums, where each resident owns a house and a portion of the common areas. Cohousing is generally more affordable than single-family houses, but Trudeslund's location and the time it was built make it one of the more expensive developments. Situated on valuable property near the train station with a direct line into central Copenhagen, Trudeslund is also close to a forested recreation area, lakes, and the pleasant town of Birkerød. The cost was further increased by 1980–81 interest rates, which had reached an all-time high of 21 percent. Upon completion, the price of a house and a share of the common facilities ranged from 777,000 to 1,000,000 Danish Kroner (DKr) (approximately $91,400 to $117,600).[7] These prices were comparable to single-family residences in the surrounding area that had no common facilities.

Houses in Trudeslund have sold quickly and their resale value has steadily climbed. While a developer might consider this a measure of success, the residents find it disconcerting that their community is moving further out of the economic grasp of many people. Because the houses are privately owned and no limitations on profits were written into the initial contracts, there is little the group can do to control resale prices. The ability to make monthly house payments is the only formal determinant for who lives at Trudeslund. For most households, this means two incomes are necessary. Whereas other communities have built smaller units to accommodate single-income households, at Trudeslund single-income households often rent out a room in order to make ends meet.

Residents contend that other living expenses are less for families at Trudeslund than for households living alone. A resident explained:

> Although our monthly house payment increased, our total lifestyle costs decreased because of the common facilities and shared resources available here. Common dinners in particular have cut down the amount we spend on food and the frequency with which we eat out.

Despite the issue of affordability, the residents are quite a diverse group. Adults range in age from 28 to 67. There are four households with no children, nine single parents (seven of whom are fathers), and several singles. Professionally, they include 13 engineers and computer programmers, 11 elementary and secondary school teachers, four doctors, three economists, two dentists, two nurses, a journalist, and a manager of a chain of radio equipment stores. Fluctuating from year to year, there may be a few full-time parents, someone going back to school or temporarily unemployed, and soon, a few retirees.

At first we feared that with such an interesting group of residents and so many community activities, residents might feel little need to participate in the surrounding neighborhood. Quite the contrary, Trudeslund residents are active in the local theater, politics, schools, and sports teams. The common house is often used for meetings, including practice for the local samba band. Through Trudeslund's social network, residents become aware of neighborhood activities they may have never known about before.

The residents of Trudeslund readily admit they have not built a utopia; that was not their intention. Old problems remain unresolved and new ones have appeared. There are long, frustrating meetings, compromises and disagreements over what needs to be done and how to do it. Some residents, dissatisfied with the level of community participation, point out how many hours the common house sits empty. Yet the residents of Trudeslund have built a special place, whose unique qualities can be observed every night in the common house when the children are playing and the adults sip their coffee, talking long after dinner is finished.

Notes

1 John Nielsen wrote a postscript ("Efterskrift") for *Veje til Bofællesskab* in November 1982, a year and a half after moving into Trudeslund (Byggeriets Udviklingsrød, 1983), 136.
2 Ibid., 138.
3 H. S. Andersen and John Nielsen, "Økonomisk risiko og hardt arbejde ved bofaellesskabsprojekt", *Blød By* 13, 1981, 22–3.
4 Michael Sten Johnsen, "Apropos Trudeslund", *Arkitektur* 6, 1982, 248.
5 Nielsen, *Veje til Bofællesskab*, 137.
6 All measurements have been converted from meters and rounded off to the nearest five for readability. Therefore the meter measurements are the more precise of the two.
7 We have converted Danish Kroner (DKr) to United States dollars at an exchange ratio of 8.5:1. Exchange rates have experienced radical fluctuations over the last decade ranging from 4.8 DKr to the dollar to 12.6 DKr to the dollar.

A prefab utopia
What happens when a furniture company builds a community

John Leland (2002)

On a rainy afternoon in Helsingborg, a coastal town in southern Sweden, a young couple were moving into a BoKlok development so new the grass hadn't grown in around it yet [*Fig. 74*]. You could tell something about their world by the capitalized names on their boxes: the BONDE entertainment unit, the EKTORP sofa, the LEKSVIK hat-and-coat rack, the PAX wardrobe. Sophia Stringer, 28, an athletic-looking woman who manages a local soccer team, brought up the back end of one box. She and her partner had won a lottery, competing with 400 people for the 30 apartments in the development. Priced about 25 percent below comparable apartments in the area, the apartment features polished oak floors, high ceilings and a loft-style layout, with a small living room pushed against an open kitchen. The closets are deep, the rooms small. Bright new Ikea fixtures – natural beech cabinets in the kitchen, closet organizers in the bedroom – added just a dollop of conspicuous design, a modernist Scandinavian take on the generic and ready-made.

BoKlok represents the new frontier of Ikea's design ambition. Instead of just selling furnishings, the company is trying something much bolder: actually building homes. Groups of homes, in fact – housing developments built according to the same principles that guide the design of Ikea furniture. The homes are small modernist units, prefabricated and mass-produced to minimize the price and organized to maximize interaction among residents. "I don't think we're creating communities", said Joakim Blomquist, one of the five members of the BoKlok team, measuring his words. "It's up to people to create their own. But this is not only housing".

"This is very consequent", said Alexander von Vegesack, director of the Vitra Design Museum in Weil am Rhein, Germany. "If you do the entire living environment, then of course you should end up thinking of cheap, well-designed houses as well. I don't know if it really will happen on the same scale that they are developing furniture. But what I saw in the south of Sweden was very positive. It was a new way of housing that looked interesting and was functional. And it was very light, with natural materials – very appealing for human use".

The scale of the houses and the way they are arranged are largely a response to the high Scandinavian divorce rate. The big houses of the 20th century didn't fit the micro-families of the 21st. Madeleine Nobs, one of the architects, saw the project in an overtly missionary cast. "So many architects are making houses for their own way of how they want to live", she said. "We started with research, not just making beautiful drawings".

Like a typical BoKlok resident, Nobs is a single mother with two children. To her, one of the big problems for such singles is isolation. With an Ikea faith in design solutions, the architects tried to fix this problem. They constructed the buildings in an L shape, Nobs said, to force greater contact among building residents, and dug a small, communal garden in front, so neighbors would be joined in a small project: better living through geometry. "The BoKlok idea is that you have to be close to your neighbors and have dialogue. That means so much".

To cut costs, the company expects the residents to manage the development cooperatively, taking two-year turns on a governing board. The boards can be instruments in what the writer Roland Huntford calls benign Swedish totalitarianism. When one woman in Helsingborg wanted to build a wall behind her apartment to keep the wind off her patio, the board turned her down, saying that the units had to be uniform. Other neighbors who wanted to put up satellite dishes to watch foreign television were similarly rejected. In some developments, everybody gathers twice a year for a huge cleanup and repair of the grounds. Neighbors in each unit take turns tending the grass and hedges – the equivalent of the do-it-yourself assembly at Ikea. "We meet all six together and have coffee and discuss lawn work", said Therese Henriksson, 32, who shares a ground-floor apartment with her 2-year-old daughter, Maja. "So you know you get that piece of paper in your mailbox every six weeks. Yippee! It's my turn to cut the lawn".

Ikea is not the only design company trying to extend its reach to cover the whole domicile. Michael Graves is developing a prefab house for Target. In 1999, Philippe Starck and a partner, John Hitchcox, started a company called Yoo to build high-end homes that reflect Starck's design, from the layout to the lemon squeezer in the kitchen. Customers choose one of four design palettes – Classic, Minimal, Nature and Culture – each corresponding to a lexicon of portentous and expensive attributes. The first American venture, with condos selling from $330,000 to more than $1 million, is in motion for South Beach in Miami.

Blomquist says that there are no plans to build BoKlok housing in the United States, where higher land prices might dilute the cost-cutting measures. But the project has expanded into Norway and Finland; the company is "close to a decision to start in Denmark" and is researching the feasibility of BoKlok England. And in Sweden, there are currently more than 1,000 BoKlok units.

The problem with trying to conceive ideal housing, even on a small scale, is one of overweening ambition, said Ruth Eaton, an architectural historian and the author of "Ideal Cities: Utopianism and the (Un)Built Environment". "You build little pockets of them, and a lot of them work quite well", she said. "The idea of building an ideal little street is quite laudable. But you can't put the same thing everywhere. That's where utopias go wrong. They say, 'I've worked out the perfect solution – this is applicable anywhere.' You can't take over the world, because conditions are too different, calling for different solutions. Yes for Stockholm, no for Timbuktu".

Mobile homes
Form, meaning, and function
Allan D. Wallis (1997)

The question of form

The distinction between the mobile home and the house trailer involved a shift in attitude, as well as use. Manufacturers no longer made trailers that could also serve as dwellings, but dwellings that happened to be mobile [*Figs. 75, 76, 77*]. […]

On being house-like vs. vehicle-like

[…] Details of the mobile home which distinguished it from the house trailer and reflected the buyers' changing preferences were more house-like doors and windows. The trailer door was, at most, 6 feet high, and swung outward, like vehicle doors. House doors are around 7 feet high and swing inward, allowing a storm or screen door to be attached. With increased ceiling height in the mobile home living room, it became possible to use taller doors. They still had to swing out, but screen doors could be attached inside. Many manufacturers introduced doors with jalousie windows, and Trailorama's 1955 pull-out double-wide unit featured a sliding glass patio door.

Along with house-like doors, many manufacturers were featuring more house-like windows. […] The changing treatment of windows and doors reflected the fact that these features were meant to be seen from the interior, as part of a home rather than as part of a vehicle. This shift was also evident in other aspects of interior decor. The café curtains common in railroad passenger cars and yachts were replaced with venetian blinds by the mid–1940s and, a decade later, by floor-to-ceiling drapes tucked neatly behind valances. Interiors of this period were often finished in a light colored plywood such as birch veneer. The same material often covered the ceiling, and all surfaces were lacquered. Built-in furniture was usually made of plywood, often from left over scraps of wall paneling sheets. Floors were covered with linoleum. The result was an interior as shiny and hard as the metal sheathed exterior. In such spaces, the use of draperies must have had a visually softening, as well as a sound-deadening effect. [...]

In the mobile home, larger, better-appointed kitchens and bathrooms were expected. Many ads focused on kitchens finished with attractive cabinets, double sinks, built-in stoves, clocks, and knickknack shelves. Even small details, like a set of canisters displayed on a counter, suggested more space and greater conventionality. In bathrooms, tubs became more common, along with vanity sinks and mirrored walls. [...]

As house-like interior details became more popular, vehicle details faded out. The clever placement of storage areas above cabinets or below beds, and the use of collapsible or transformable furniture, such as Pullman berths, had become associated with the spartan nature of the travel trailer and the house trailer. Mobile home owners wanted to identify with a different image and way of life. Often this meant giving up features that remained eminently practical in the enlarged but still restrictive confines of the mobile home.

The split imagery of interior and exterior

Even though house trailer and early mobile home interiors were becoming more house-like in plan and decor, exterior design remained tied to a vehicle-based imagery. [...]

Experimentation with the external appearance of mobile homes concentrated primarily on two images: one derived from the trailer aesthetic, which treated the unit as part of a car/trailer ensemble, the other based on a house aesthetic, which promoted the image of a permanent dwelling in a park setting. [...]

Modifications by owners

Among those deciding what the mobile home should look like are the owners themselves.[1] They often have been responsible for determining how their units would be placed on a site, expanded, modified to accommodate local weather, and decorated. Many of their changes and additions were to make their homes more comfortable, particularly by providing more space for activities and storage; others were to make their homes more attractive and socially acceptable.

Just as the mobile home manufacturers were guided by different images of their product as they tried to style it to meet market needs and avoid local resistance, the modifications users made suggest similar images and strategies. On the one hand, there were owners who saw the mobile home as part of a park/trailer ensemble. They did not mind if their homes looked like trailers, with hitch and lights attached, while surrounded by house-like, site-built additions. On the other hand, there were those who seemed to have had a house/subdivision image in mind. Their modifications were clearly intended to make their dwelling indistinguishable from a site-built house. [...]

In their attempt to find more room, owners frequently built additions. The most common of these was a shed, attached to the entry, that served as a mudroom and utility porch. [...]

If a family expected to stay in a park for a long time, or if it owned its lot, it usually added some kind of shed. Several manufacturers, such as Alum-O-Room and Add-A-Room, began marketing prefabricated sheds. Along with their recommendations for landscaping mobile homes, the Borgesons suggested adding a shed-type porch or cabana. "Mobile home dwellers" they wrote, "are not Gypsies. They put down roots, build picket fences, plant".[2] By the early 1960s, shed additions were popular enough for *Trailer Topics* to feature articles like "Immobile Mobile Homes", without intended irony. Details were offered, for example, on how H. B. Ellis added a 14′ × 20′ living room with a fireplace onto his mobile home. "At first glance", the article observed, "the casual passerby wouldn't notice that this pleasant home is really a mobile home".[3] Farris and Lorraine Bynum's "House With a Trailer Inside" consisted of a 41′ × 8′ trailer with a 12′ × 48′ site-built addition on one side. Since Farris, an itinerant electrician, had retired, he and Lorraine could enjoy "the conveniences of a mobile home and a conventional home as well. That is kind of like having their cake and eating it too".[4]

Often a shed addition started as an awning-covered, concrete pad carport. Later, part or all of the area would be enclosed, forming a long, narrow, unpartitioned space. In warm climates this space might be left screened, while in colder regions, it would be insulated and warmed with a stove or some other source of heat. The floor level of the slab and the main unit were usually two feet apart, and when the shed was enclosed, the difference in levels was rarely rectified. The metal siding of the unit was usually left exposed as one of the walls of the new interior space, and exterior details such as attached shutters, skirting, and lights, become part of an interior space with little if any modification. While in most respects the shed additions on mobile homes were not unlike ones tacked onto site-built houses, the final ensemble often looked as if the mobile home was the addition rather than the shed.

A variation of the shed addition has spaces on both sides of the home, with one side an activity room and the other a carport and utility area [*Fig. 77*]. A common Southwestern version of this double shed consisted of one large roof covering the entire unit and additions. Open space between the roof and the mobile home allowed air to circulate in the summer. The resulting ensemble often looks something like a box car tucked in a hay barn.

More elaborate than the double shed was an arrangement in which two or more mobile homes or trailers were connected with site-built sheds and breezeways into what might be called a compound unit. In some cases the compound consisted of two units joined longitudinally, with new doors cut for circulation, effectively forming a double-wide. Other units were arranged in an L- or H-shaped configuration. In the L-shaped arrangement, a new entry was usually constructed at the crux of the two units. In the H-shaped arrangement, the connecting piece might be a site-built room or a separate trailer which served as an entry.

The compound unit took advantage of the low cost of used trailers. They provided instant space complete with wiring, plumbing, and a waterproof exterior all at a low cost and without too much labor. Owners often attempted to make all floor heights the same, with entry porches and shed additions elevated as well. And they might put a new roof over the ensemble, preventing leaks and giving the whole more visual unity. Compound developments were more common in rural areas where occupants owned their lots, neighbors were more tolerant, and building regulations were not enforced. [...]

The way in which people modify their units, working within site and budget constraints, produces a rich and varied form of housing. The contrast between site-built additions and the factory-made core can be provocative and at times humorous. Often it is the site-built shed that looks like the original core and the mobile home like the addition. Sometimes there appears to have been a literal collision, in which a trailer has smashed into a site-built house and stayed there. Ironically, these kinds of modifications, which demonstrate better than anything else the capacity of the mobile home to evolve into a genuine dwelling,[5] are often disparaged by manufacturers, who fear they will provoke images of trailer camp slums.

Complexity in the experience of living in houses

It might seem easy to dismiss the changes which both users and manufacturers made to the form of the mobile home as superficial mimicking of features on traditional, site-built housing. Borrow a window detail here, a roofline there, and before you know it, Mr. Potato Head is starting to look like a house. Certainly some of the models designed upon such casual borrowing were silly if not ugly; yet, there was something else carried over in this process. Changes in the layout of the mobile home, particularly of public and private spaces, suggest a response to the experience of living in houses. Two important dimensions of this experience identified by psychologists are complexity and adaptability.

Complexity[6] is experienced, in part, in the differentiation of interior from exterior. One aspect of the complexity found in the ordinary house is that its floor plan cannot be read from the outside. Ask people who live in a site-built house to describe it, and they will often begin by telling you the number of bedrooms it has; but ask people in a mobile home and they will tell you its exterior dimensions.

In the single-wide mobile home with a shotgun corridor, the interior organization can be read from the external elevation, and the shape of the exterior is apparent from inside. There is a transparency, or thinness, which is more than physical. The double-wide and single-wide with extensive shed additions, by contrast, restore the complexity of the typical site-built house. The desired independence of interior from exterior may have to do with the public and private faces of the house, what occupants show to their neighbors, and the image they give themselves.[7]

In modern housing in general, much of the complexity of dwellings has been lost. The "free plan", advocated since the 1920s by architects of the modern movement and adopted by builders because it reduced costs makes tighter living areas seem more spacious by eliminating partitions between rooms. But the free plan also requires combining functions and accepting an informality which may not always be desired. Another change dictated by construction economics and technology has been the disappearance of attics and basements. The basement, which was once needed for the furnace and its bulky fuel, can now be eliminated because furnaces can be placed in closets and fed by gas. Similarly, the attic, which provided dusty storage and extra play space, has been replaced by the garage, which is often too stuffed with items to leave room for the car. These spaces not only had specific purposes, they also invited unintended activities and meanings (the attic as a children's clubhouse, the basement as the dark and mysterious place where children often fear to go).[8] Both the owners of sparse modern homes and of mobile homes seem to prefer house forms with greater complexity and hence modify their dwellings to achieve it.

The transformation of house trailer into mobile home also suggests the importance of adaptability in the experience of dwelling. By adding to and changing the form of their housing mobile home users were not only attempting to make their homes look more acceptable, they were also personalizing them. […]

Thinness

The changes in mobile homes – whether through conventionalization or syncretism – resulted in objects of unmistakable thinness. This quality is most apparent in the physical structure of the mobile home: in its lightness, shallow cross-section, and the tactile experiences of living in it – the way walls bellow in the wind, floors deflect under foot, and roofs resonate with the sound of falling rain drops. Its thinness is evident in the shallow recesses and the characteristic appliqué look of details, whether structural or ornamental. "Thinness" is also apparent in something more subtle and figurative: in the imitative borrowing of elements, such as the photographed grain of an expensive wood laminated to the surface of cheap paneling, or details borrowed from different styles collaged on a single object. The figurative thinness of the mobile home consists of the way it casually borrows characteristics from other often unrelated objects. Both the literal and figurative aspects of thinness are indicative of how meaning, form, and use are associated with one another in the mobile home, and in American vernacular design in general. [...]

Twentieth-century advocates of industrialized building have frequently cited disposability as an important characteristic of modern house construction because it allows technological improvements to be easily introduced. Yet nineteenth-century stick-built construction already provided an economical form of disposable building. The framing members of a 2″ × 4″ structure could be easily shipped throughout the Midwest, especially to areas where timber was scarce. Before long, prefabricated houses were available through mail-order and catalogues and were widely distributed. The mobile home clearly falls within this tradition of building, its thin cross-section a strong confirmation of vernacular standards.

The need to build quickly and cheaply, which propelled the diffusion of stick-built construction, promoted an architecture that was not only physically thin, but figuratively thin. Figurative thinness, as suggested earlier, refers to the relationship between the physical features of a building, their meaning, and the way they are used. The figurative thinness of stick-built architecture is well illustrated in what architects Robert Venturi, Denise Scott Brown, and Steven Izenour call the "decorated shed", which occurs "where systems of space and structure are directly at the service of program, and ornamentation is applied independently of them".[9] These ornaments may be expensive materials or they may be painted on. [...]

The predisposition to accept such an aesthetic is itself a manifestation of modern society's search for a way to manage change and, in America, to cope with constant migration and expansion. It was a way of taking an architectural kit of parts and by applying the pieces to new forms and a new landscape, to achieve a sense of familiarity and, hence, bring the environment under control. The result is an environment of borrowed, standard elements in a familiar yet individual collage.

The mobile home is composed almost entirely of materials that make allusions to other materials: metal siding with a wood grain pattern printed on it, interior paneling laminated with the photographic image of decorative wood, ceilings made of a material that looks like stucco but is actually foam padding, plastic hardware finished as if it were antique brass. [...]

As transparent as these imitations are, they are necessary for the acceptance of the object as a whole. [Bringing together] imitative ready-mades to form an essentially new object is characteristic of many of the most original artifacts of the American environment: the fast-food franchise, the gas station, and the speculatively built suburban house. On a larger scale, it is the method underlying the merchant builder's subdivision, the enclosed shopping mall, and the mobile home park.

Notes

1 Portions of this section appeared originally in "The Mobile Home: Lessons in Industrial Vernacular Design", *Open House International* 9, no. 3, 1984.
2 Lillian and Griffith Borgeson, *Mobile Homes and Travel Trailers*, New York: Fawcett Publications, 1959, p. 28.
3 H. B. Ellis, "Our Immobile Mobile Home", *Trailer Topics*, January 1961, 36.
4 Dick Poplin, "The House with a Trailer Inside", *Trailer Topics*, January 1962, 39–40.
5 I am using the term *dwelling* here in the phenomenological sense as developed by Heidegger in "Building Dwelling Thinking", in *Martin Heidegger: Basic Writings*, New York: Harper and Row, 1977, pp. 323–39, and by Christian Norberg-Schulz in *The Concept of Dwelling*, New York: Electa/Rizzoli, 1985. (See also Heidegger, Chapter 3, this volume.)
6 For an analysis of the psychological and cultural significance of the quality of complexity, see Amos Rapoport and Robert E. Kantor, "Complexity & Ambiguity in Environmental Design", *AIP Journal* 33, no. 4, July 1967, 210–21; and Rapoport, *Human Aspects of Urban Form*, New York: Pergamon, 1977, pp. 207–20.
7 On the analysis of social and personal images of housing, see Franklin Becker, *Housing Messages*, Stroudsburg, Penn.: Dowden, Hutchinson, and Ross, 1977.
8 A discussion of some of the intended and unintended functions and meanings of attic and cellar are found in Perla Korosec-Serfaty, "The Home, from Attic to Cellar", *Journal of Environmental Psychology* 4, no. 4, 1984, 172–9.
9 Robert Venturi, Denise Scott Brown, and Steven Izenour, *Learning From Las Vegas*, Cambridge, Mass.: MIT Press, 1977, p. 85.

The mobile home on the range

John Brinckerhoff Jackson (1994)

New Mexico contains an extraordinary variety of dwellings; I doubt if any other state has as many. We have Pueblo Indian, Spanish-American, Anglo-American, and Navajo houses. Some ancient house-types are eight or nine hundred years old, and how they were used is still not entirely understood. Chaco Canyon, the largest archaeological site in the United States, is from that point of view the greatest of mysteries. But we have house-types like the trailer (or mobile home) that are new and evolving, and the brief counterculture of the 1960s also made its contribution.

What is unusual about many of these house-types is that they can be found side by side in the same small community; and that in many cases they are lived in by the families who originally built them. This means that it is easy to find out how they were built and how they are used. [...]

When I first came to New Mexico in the 1920s, I was attracted by the Spanish-American villages scattered throughout the ranch country where I was staying. They seemed very foreign, very un-American. In those times most families supported themselves by farming and raising cattle or sheep. It was a hard life; many men worked as sheepherders or cowhands on ranches in Wyoming or Colorado and were away from home for months at a time.

The villages were half-hidden in the immense open rangeland, near a stream that watered the small fields of corn and chili and beans. The surrounding landscape was organized in an almost medieval manner. Easterners are not always aware that communal control of the land and its use, with a large common for the livestock, existed in the Spanish Southwest before New England had been heard of. In some places the system still survives. [...]

Architecturally speaking, the houses were far from remarkable: one-story structures with two or three rooms, usually of adobe. Often they had a pitched roof of corrugated tin that shone in the sun, and a long front porch. They were all very much alike, for there is a limit to the variety that can be introduced into the plan of a house with two or three rooms. None had running water or electricity, and almost all had dirt floors. They were painted different colors, however; bright green or pink or brown, with white window and door trim, and entirely without ornamentation. The manner in which they were sometimes connected in rows to form three sides of a common courtyard or plaza gave the village an almost urban aspect. Throughout the day the houses were quiet. They were scantily furnished, yet their interiors gave the impression less of poverty than of an austere formality. When I visited such a house I went not to the front door (painted white and locked) but to the kitchen door, and (as was the custom among neighbors) I entered without knocking. The mother-in-law, babysitting, said nothing by way of greeting. I asked where Manuel was. She answered that he was out, getting a load of firewood. And Joe? "Joe is out seeing about a job", she said, adding that Linda was also out, having gone to the store.

This was almost always the case: at every house everybody was out; being "out" meant taking some part in the life of the village. [...] We who live in town think of the countryside as where people farm or enjoy the beauties of nature. Actually, it can be a stimulating place, and politically speaking even the most somnolent village has much to offer, for that is where we see custom in action, regulating movement and ways of work and relationships between neighbors. It is where we eventually recognize that an established order is not easily changed. Remaining at home would not only be lonely, it would mean that you were deprived of the excitement of community existence and its opportunities. [...]

When I set out in 1990 to refresh my memory of the past, I found many changes in the New Mexico landscape, the most striking being what had happened to some of the villages I had once known. They had degenerated into rural slums of a very abject kind. [...]

Yet, some of the villages *have* survived. The men now work for wages in the service sector or do odd jobs in town. Thanks to the automobile, the environment they depend on has expanded well beyond the village and ranch, and they think nothing of commuting thirty or forty miles to work. The roads are paved and buses take the children to a consolidated school. When they come home in the afternoon and run down the street, their bright clothes and loud voices bring life to the village and mark the time of day. Every household seems to have at least three cars, one of them a pickup. Cars in varying stages of mobility are parked outside the bar, the convenience store, in front yards, in deserted corrals, and in vacant lots. With hoods raised, they seem about to devour the young men adjusting the carburetor, and Spanish music comes from their radios. Though the villages are probably just as poor, comparatively speaking, as they were in the past, some now have more movement and more vitality. [...]

A great deal of this new housing throughout New Mexico – and for that matter throughout the whole country – consists of trailers. They are everywhere: tucked in between houses, attached to houses, even on top of houses; in alleys and gardens and out in the fields. In fact, there are New Mexico villages where trailers outnumber conventional dwellings and where the newly arrived tourist cries out in delight at the glimpse of an adobe house. I was sorry to see that the old close relationship between houses, suggesting as it did a relationship between members of the same extended family, had been replaced by a more scattered arrangement, like that among friendly but self-sufficient neighbors. The newer, freestanding houses seem to prefer the margins of the road leading out of the village to the traditional compact pattern of plazas. [...]

Now, two generations later, America has more trailers than ever before. Called mobile homes in the trade, they are larger, more comfortable, and more expensive. More than thirteen million Americans [*now more than twenty million, Ed.*], most of them from young blue-collar families, live in trailers and (for the time being, at least) call them home. There is, however, strong public prejudice against them. [...]

Over the years the educated public, led by architects and urban planners, has drawn up the indictment of the trailer. It is part aesthetic judgment, part structural critique, with a touch of compassion for those who are unfortunate enough to have to live in one. To begin with, the trailer is an industrial product, mass-produced, low-cost, and disposable. It comes out of a midwestern factory and is shipped by truck, quickly unloaded, and soon ready for occupancy. It has bypassed the craftsman and the architect and the landscape architect, and the owner (or consumer) has no opportunity for self-expression, or even a say in the ordering of the interior or in the outside decorations. Some trailers come completely furnished – the ultimate in standardization. And then, coming as it does off an assembly line, the trailer ignores local architectural traditions and local environmental constraints. Its uncompromising shape and boxlike appearance make any real composition of a group of trailers impossible. No matter how we site them in relation to one another, we never achieve anything like a traditional village. [...]

Most would agree that these are valid criticisms; we could probably add to them. But from the point of view of those who live in trailers I think they miss their mark. From what I have learned, the villagers who have moved into trailers are in general satisfied. They wish their trailer were larger and had better insulation. They object to the floor plan. Nevertheless, to them the advantages of the trailer far outweigh its faults. What they especially appreciate is how little the trailer costs, compared to even the smallest house, and how easy it is to finance. They regretted leaving the old adobe house with its associations, but it was a joy to move into a brand-new home, clean and never used.

Newness is something we do not always appreciate, but I am convinced that a large minority of Americans have never owned a new car, though they would like very much to. That is why there are spray cans to produce the smell – whatever it may be – of a new car interior. A new trailer has the same exciting appeal: stickers on the windows, books of instructions, and that indefinable smell of newness. It takes only a few days to realize how convenient and comfortable the trailer is, and how easy to maintain. The fact that it resembles all the other trailers in the vicinity is if anything a source of reassurance, for it means that the choice was a popular one, endorsed by other families. The most welcome feature of trailer living for the villager is that it brings with it no new responsibilities, no change or expansion in the traditional domestic routine. Nor does it alter the old relationship with the outside world: the man or woman of the family can as usual leave home in the morning, only with the trailer there is no chopping of wood, no feeding of livestock. Life is simplified and begins, as it always has, when we join others in work and conversation. Moreover, with fewer domestic chores the wife is at last free to move into the community. Trailers, as we all know, are rarely mobile in the literal sense of the word, but because of their impersonality, their fungibility, they are like automobiles: easy to trade and sell. When a better job becomes available somewhere else, the family can at least consider the wisdom of selling, and of finding similar accommodations wherever they go.

I need not belabor the point: for a great many families the trailer is a sensible way of living. Indeed, it almost seems as if those shortcomings which critics never tire of mentioning – the lack of individuality, the functional incompleteness, the dependence on outside services and amenities, and even the lack of such traditional architectural qualities as firmness, commodity, and delight – all are what make the trailer useful and attractive to many of its occupants.

I am no blind admirer of the trailer or mobile home. I have seen at first hand what is wrong about its plan and construction. But I still think it is the most practical low-cost dwelling we have, and that it is well adapted to a way of life that is becoming increasingly common in both urban and rural America. That way of life is identified with the blue-collar worker: the man or woman without capital, without any marketable skill, and with only a limited formal education. The man or woman of the family (in many cases both) has to work by the hour or the day at an unskilled or semiskilled job away from home, with little assurance that it will last. These factors obviously have their effect on the kind of house they can afford, and how they use it. [...]

This was the kind of dwelling I saw in the cities and towns of New Mexico, and in the industrial communities. I naturally associated it with urban working-class areas, so it came as something of a surprise to see those prefabricated houses and trailers in remote villages. What reconciled me to their presence, whatever their style or lack of style, was that they were being used, being lived in, in much the same manner as were the older houses, and when I went into a few of them I was entirely reassured. The resemblance between the lifestyle of the younger villagers and that of their families or grandfathers whom I had known a half-century earlier was striking. The houses were much more comfortable, much healthier than the old ones ever were, and they were better furnished. No wonder the families were proud of them and glad to show them off. I sensed that certain traditional relationships – between the house and the family, the house and the community, the house and the place of work – had changed little or not at all. They were much the same as they had been for generations in the old adobe houses. I was satisfied in that these brand-new houses or trailers were bona fide vernacular. [...]

The working-class house has been largely immune to the appeal of the monofunctional space. The house may well contain many rooms, but most of them serve several uses, uses which can change from hour to hour or from day to day. The garage serves as a storage room, then becomes a workshop. The kitchen is where we watch television and cook and eat; the dining room – if there is one – is for homework. The out-of-work brother-in-law sleeps on the living-room couch, and the men in the family tune up the second-hand car on the patch of lawn. These are strictly temporary expedients. All, or almost all, spaces in the house can be shared and used in a variety of ways. This reflects what I would call a vernacular concept of a space: a space has no inherent identity, it is simply defined by the way it is used. [...]

Hospitality [in the working-class dwelling] ... is informal and unpremeditated: no special rooms, no special days or hours, no special china or special cooking area called for, and the guests who appear, often uninvited, are not there for negotiating alliances or soliciting favors: they come to be included in the daily routine of the family.

I find nothing to criticize in this. It seems entirely consistent with the vernacular concept of the dwelling as a refuge from the workaday world, a place for the rituals of privacy, not for the pursuit of influence and power. As I have tried to indicate, the wage-earner dwelling delegates as many functions as it can to the public realm, reserving for itself the role of providing shelter and perpetuating family awareness. Unlike the middle-class house, the vernacular house is not a jealously guarded territory, and the outsider undergoes no entrance examination. As a member of the extended family or of the neighborhood, he or she is automatically included in the domestic order.

Hospitality, in short, is less an initiation into the house as an autonomous territory than it is a celebration of the super-family, and the best kind of celebration, the most generous kind of hospitality is that which is staged *outside* the home. The graduation party, the wedding reception, the grandparents' anniversary, the family reunion take over the school gymnasium, the parish hall, the hall of the local protective fraternal order, and for the time being the super-family uses it as if it belonged to them and no one else. From behind the closed doors come sounds of revelry: of flash photos, of laughter and long, emotional toasts. Benny Vigil and his Rock Caballeros play from eight in the evening until dawn. Outside in the darkness a shiny car, decorated with crepe paper flowers and streamers, waits for the bride and groom, and off they go for a weekend in Las Vegas.

This is the kind of event and the kind of space the vernacular dwelling *has* to have to survive. Its dependence on its immediate environment is not a servitude, it is something that can always be counted on, something morally dependable. For that is what distinguishes vernacular space from territorial space: it belongs to *us*. We have no legal title to it, but custom, unwritten law tells us we can use it in meeting our daily needs. Vernacular space is to be shared, not exploited or monopolized. It is never a source of wealth or power, it is in the literal sense of the term a common ground, a common place, a common denominator which makes each vernacular neighborhood a miniature common-wealth. Thus the contemporary way to study the vernacular dwelling is to see it not as an autonomous realm but as a structure which achieves completeness by relating to its environment.

Harriton Farm, Villanova, PA, advertising brochure

Pohlig Builders (2001)

Harriton Farm [*Fig. 78*] is a unique opportunity to own a personally crafted residence in one of the most coveted locations in the country. This community will be a rare combination of history, craftsmanship and demeanor that far transcends the ordinary. The land on which we are building has been in the same family since the early 1700s. It was once part of a larger farm, the history of which goes back nearly a hundred years before the American Revolution, and which later became the home of a leader in the Continental Congress who signed the Declaration of Independence. This long heritage is important to the family whose generations have lived here and preserved the land – and it is important to us.

The community we're creating here is a reflection of our own pride and heritage as well. The land plan we have created is environmentally sensitive. It preserves over twenty acres of open space as well as the existing historic buildings and natural features that give

Harriton Farm its character and beauty. We did not take our task lightly, and our plan was years in the making. We approached the project with a sense of respect – and an eye on the past. Each home will be individually designed to meet the owner's needs and to reflect the area's architectural heritage. The homes will be an example of our dedication to excellence in design and craftsmanship. No two will be alike, but all will share a stylistic character reminiscent of the elegant northside neighborhoods of the past. Each home will be a work of art.

The aura that accompanies a Main Line address has taken many years to create. The Main Line has become more than a location. It is a state of mind. Its character is a reflection of those who brought their families, their pride and their priorities to this special place, infusing it with an air of refinement and quiet dignity. Each generation has contributed its own personality, while retaining the most important elements of the past. This tasteful blending of old and new has made the Main Line what it is today … a place whose reputation for gracious living is known throughout the world. We are honored to build here and excited to create a new chapter in the history of Harriton Farm. We are dedicated to making it a fitting addition to the Philadelphia story.

Residential conversions

Norbert Schoenauer (2000)

The conversion of factories and warehouses into loft apartment buildings is a phenomenon of the second half of the twentieth century. After World War II, the vacancy rate in loft buildings was high because of the gradual departure of manufacturing industries and warehouses from inner-city locations. The economic base in North American cities shifted from manufacturing to service industries, and the dispersal of factories was aided by the new interstate highways. The first loft conversion was probably made clandestinely by an artist in search of a studio and, although it was illegal, a place to live for a reasonable rent.

A well-documented loft conversion area in New York City is SoHo (named for its location south of Houston Street). Before the mid-nineteenth century, SoHo was a fashionable residential neighborhood, but when residents moved to uptown Manhattan, garment industries and wholesalers moved into newly erected five- to six-story loft buildings, many with cast-iron façades, in SoHo. Just before World War I, garment factories and wholesalers moved to the upper Thirties along Seventh Avenue (the present garment district) and left their vacated loft buildings for low-profile commercial enterprises.

In the early fifties artists began to move into SoHo loft buildings. They were drawn not only by cheap rent, but also because they required space for their artwork, which had a tendency to be on a large scale. For sculptors, industrial buildings were ideal for studios since they were designed for heavy live loads and were serviced by freight elevators. Apart from painters and sculptors, other artists, for example, dancers, graphic designers, architects, and musicians, also found the typical deep lofts exciting spaces to live and work in [*Figs. 79, 80*].

By the early sixties, SoHo was an important residential neighborhood for artists and soon thereafter, when smart shops and restaurants moved in, the area also became attractive to the modish middle-class. "Loft spaces were sought after not only because they were part of a new chic scene in New York, but also because they were reasonably priced living spaces – in fact, comparative bargains – in the expensive and tight housing market of New York".[1]

In Lowell, Massachusetts, textile mills built next to sources of water power and later abandoned were converted into subsidized housing for the elderly and low-income residents. But it was not only New England textile mills that were converted into housing, but also heavy industrial buildings, as exemplified by the industrial structures (decommissioned in 1974) of Boston's Charlestown Navy Yard. The spine of the foundry and the machine-shop building were converted into six-story-high atriums, the main circulation space of the 367 apartment units of this project, called Constitution Quarters; ground-floor apartment units are entered from the spine, like town houses from a small stoop. Although the interiors of the dwelling units are up-to-date, the historic integrity of the buildings' exteriors from the 1850s remained essentially intact.

In Boston Harbor's Lewis Wharf is the 400-ft (122-m) long and 80-ft (24-m) wide Granite Building, which was built during the 1830s but after World War I gradually lapsed into disuse. In 1972, Carl Koch and Associates converted this old six-story warehouse into a mixed-use building. The ground floor was transformed into shops and restaurants, the floor above into offices, and the top four floors into dwellings. Built for the well-to-do, the dwellings are generally roomy with high ceilings. In contrast to the crowded housing built in the inner city, the Lewis Wharf rehabilitation project offers the advantage of a distant view over the harbor, and the luxury not only of mooring a yacht and parking a car close to home, but also of living within walking distance of downtown.

New York City high-rise office buildings, too, have been transformed into apartment buildings. Turtle Bay Towers, a twenty-four-story typical stepped-back office building with 12-ft (3.6-m) ceilings and 8-ft (2.4-m) high windows, erected in 1929 on Manhattan's East Side, was converted by Bernard Rothzeid & Partners into a luxurious residential building with 341 apartment units. The addition of greenhouses, the full width of several apartments, located adjacent to set-back ledges, as well as the provision of bedroom lofts to the linear dwelling units, created an interesting spatial zoning. This project was carried out under a New York City tax abatement program to encourage the conversion of commercial properties into residential use to give a boost to inner-city housing.

Abandoned schools in old residential neighborhoods have also been successfully converted into housing, often the only adaptive reuse acceptable to a neighboring community. Churches, too, have been converted into dwellings, but their transformation into private homes is much more difficult in comparison to an institutional conversion, for example, a library. Most nonresidential building types, however, do lend themselves to conversion into dwellings, and the limits of the existing physical envelope seldom hampers the ingenuity of architects, as many projects illustrate.

Notes

1 James R. Hudson, *The Unanticipated City: Loft Conversions in Lower Manhattan*, Amherst, Mass.: University of Massachusetts Press, 1987, p. 95.

Figure 72   Trudeslund, Denmark, 1980s, village-like street.

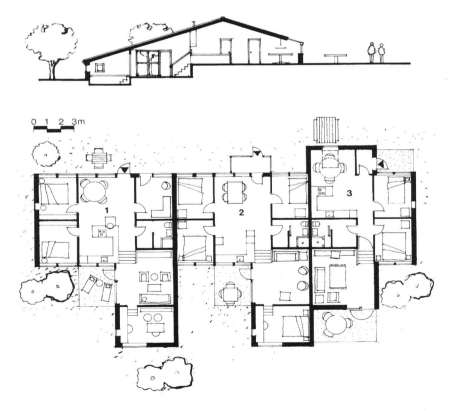

Figure 73   Trudeslund, Denmark, 1980s, typical house plans and section through
House Two.

Figure 74
Ikea, BoKlok prefab community, 2002.

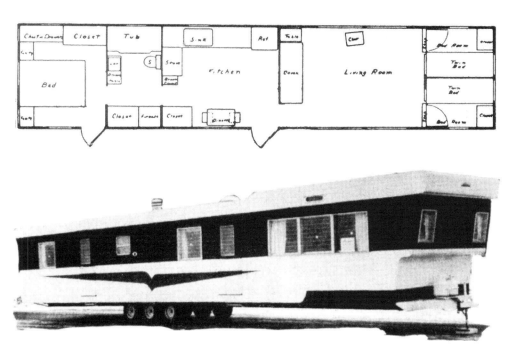

Figure 75   Mobile home, exterior and plan, 1950s.

Figure 76
Trailer park,
"Freedom
Acres", Muncie,
Indiana, begun
1947.

Figure 77
Double-shed
additions to
trailer outside
Phoenix,
Arizona.

Figure 78
Pohlig Builders,
Harriton Farm
model house,
Villanova,
Pennsylvania.

Figure 79
New York City loft building:
commercial building at 462
Broadway, 1879.

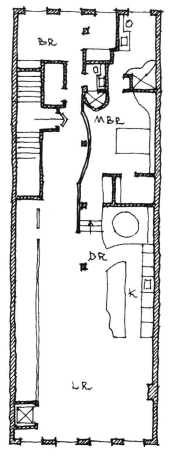

Figure 80
New York City loft dwelling, plan.

13

Where is home?

For most writers in this anthology, the notion of home or dwelling is deeply affected by one's relationship to a conception of homeland or home place. Yi-Fu Tuan contends that all people everywhere and in all periods have had a vital attachment to a home place, an attachment which cannot be dissolved except by a thoroughgoing destruction of that place. The experiences of inhabitants of the communal apartments created in St. Petersburg out of the luxury apartments of Imperial Russia as a Stalinist response to acute housing shortage seem to bear out Tuan's argument (Figs. 81, 82). As described by Ilya Utekhin, ethnologist and long-term resident in one of these dwellings, these were cramped and difficult places, where inhabitants had to resort to complicated sharing and queuing regulations in order to make daily life tolerable. Yet as these communal apartments have been dismantled in the post-Stalinist era, many inhabitants have elected to remain in the older communal types of dwellings, viewing them as "home".

Can older ideas of home and place survive in the twenty-first century? Using the example of the Czech village of Lidice, completely obliterated by the Nazis in 1942, poet and essayist Deborah Tall argues that the violence of twentieth-century war, the phenomena of mass dispossessions and displacements, and the patterns of modern mobility have led to an almost universal experience of "irretrievably lost places". The Mad Housers of Atlanta, GA (Figs. 83, 84), described by journalist Bo Emerson, are part of a larger movement among socially-conscious people today (younger architects and ordinary citizens) to create "housing for the dispossessed". It remains to be seen whether such initially temporary shelters can produce the kind of attachment that Tuan describes, although Monira Al-Haroun's photograph of Walter Turner (Fig. 84) suggests that they may. Yet in the controversial 1984 television series *Heimat* (shown here in a series of stills introduced by the editor – Fig. 85) director Edgar Reitz tried to show that the most fundamental of twentieth-century experiences – world wars, new technologies, mass communications – make it impossible to recapture older ideas of home and place.

Attachment to homeland

Yi-Fu Tuan (1977)

Place exists at different scales. At one extreme a favorite armchair is a place, at the other extreme the whole earth. Homeland is an important type of place at the medium scale. It is a region (city or countryside) large enough to support a people's livelihood. Attachment to the homeland can be intense. What is the character of this sentiment? What experiences and conditions promote it?

Human groups nearly everywhere tend to regard their own homeland as the center of the world. A people who believe they are at the center claim, implicitly, the ineluctable worth of their location. In diverse parts of the world this sense of centrality is made explicit by a geometrical conception of space oriented to the cardinal points. Home is at the center of an astronomically determined spatial system. A vertical axis, linking heaven to the underworld, passes through it. The stars are perceived to move around one's abode; home is the focal point of a cosmic structure. Such a conception of place ought to give it supreme value; to abandon it would be hard to imagine. Should destruction occur we may reasonably conclude that the people would be thoroughly demoralized, since the ruin of their settlement implies the ruin of their cosmos. Yet this does not necessarily happen. Human beings have strong recuperative powers. Cosmic views can be adjusted to suit new circumstances. With the destruction of one "center of the world", another can be built next to it, or in another location altogether, and it in turn becomes the "center of the world". "Center" is not a particular point on the earth's surface; it is a concept in mythic thought rather than a deeply felt value bound to unique events and locality. In mythic thought several world centers may coexist in the same general area without contradiction. It is possible to believe that the axis of the world passes through the settlement as a whole as well as through the separate dwellings within it. Space that is stretched over a grid of cardinal points makes the idea of place vivid, but it does not make any particular geographical locality *the* place. A spatial frame determined by the stars is anthropocentric rather than place-centric, and it can be moved as human beings themselves move.

If a cosmic world view does not guarantee uniqueness to locality, what beliefs do? Evidence from different cultures suggests that place is specific – tied to a particular cluster of buildings at one location – wherever the people believe it to be not only their home but also the home of their guarding spirits and gods. Ancient cities in the Near East and in the Mediterranean Basin enjoyed this kind of particularity. The original inspiration for building a city was to consort with the gods. Early Mesopotamian towns were essentially temple communities. Ritual centers and the more important settlements in the Nile Valley also had religious foundations, since they were thought to occupy sites on which primordial creation had taken place. It is difficult for the modern mind to appreciate the extent to which religion intermeshed with human activities and values in ancient times. When life seemed uncertain and nature hostile, the divinities not only promoted life and protected it, they were also guarantors of order in nature and in society. The legitimacy of laws and institutions depended on them. The withdrawal of the presiding presences meant chaos and death. Conquerors did not raze a city to the ground simply out of wanton fury; in such destruction they appropriated a people's gods by rendering them homeless, and in appropriating the gods the conquerors acquired a civilization. This belief throws light on the paradox that, although the city is the embodiment of civilization, the Sumerians listed "the destruction of cities" as one of the divine institutions upon which civilization is founded.[1] […]

Rootedness was an ideal of the ancient Greeks and Romans. The French scholar Fustel de Coulanges explored this theme in detail more than a century ago. He stressed the importance of piety and of ancestor worship. A son was obliged to make sacrifices to the souls of the dead, those of his dead father and other ancestors. To fail in this duty was to commit the greatest act of impiety. An ancestor became a protecting god if provisions were carried to his tomb on the appointed days. He was good and provident to his own family but hostile to those who had not descended from him, driving them from his tomb, inflicting diseases upon them if they approached. Love for one's own kin and hostility, rather than mere indifference, to strangers was a common trait of place-bound religions. Each family had its sacred fire which represented the ancestors. A sacred fire "was the providence of a family, and had nothing in common with the fire of a neighboring family, which was another providence".[2] The altar or family hearth symbolized sedentary life. It must be placed on the ground, and once established it could not be moved except as the consequence of unforeseen necessity. Duty and religion required that the family remain grouped around its altar; the family was as much fixed to the soil as the altar itself. The city was a confederation of families. Just as each family had its fixed hearth, so the city had its hearth in the council house, where the officials and a few especially honored citizens took their meals.[3]

The people of ancient Greece and Italy believed in exclusiveness. Space had its inviolable bounds. Every domain was under the eyes of household divinities, and an uncultivated band of soil marked its limit. On certain days of each month and year the father of the family walked around his field. "He drove victims before him, sang hymns, and offered sacrifices. By this ceremony he believed he had awakened the benevolence of his gods towards his field and his house … The path which the victims and prayers had followed were the inviolable limit of the domain".[4]

In antiquity land and religion were so closely associated that a family could not renounce one without yielding the other. Exile was the worst of fates, since it deprived a man not only of his physical means of support but also of his religion and the protection of laws guaranteed by the local gods. In Euripides's play, *Hippolytus*, Theseus would not impose the death penalty on Hippolytus because swift death was regarded as too light a punishment for his heinous crime. Hippolytus had to drain the bitter dregs of his life as an exile on strange soil, this being the proper fate for the impious.[5]

The Greeks valued autochthony. Athenians took great pride in being natives, in the fact that they could trace their long and noble lineage in one locality. Pericles proclaimed, "Our ancestors deserve praise, for they dwelt in the country without break in the succession from generation to generation, and handed it down free to the present time by their valor".[6] Isocrates argued that Athens was great for many reasons but that her strongest title to distinction lay in the people's autochthony and racial purity. He declaimed:

> We did not become dwellers in this land by driving others out of it, nor by finding it uninhabited, nor by coming together here a motley horde composed of many races; but we are of a lineage so noble and so pure that throughout our history we have continued in possession of the very land which gave us birth, since we are sprung from its very soil and are able to address our city by the very names which we apply to our nearest kin; for we alone of all the Hellenes have the right to call our city at once nurse and fatherland and mother.[7]

This profound attachment to the homeland appears to be a worldwide phenomenon. It is not limited to any particular culture and economy. It is known to literate and nonliterate peoples, hunter-gatherers, and sedentary farmers, as well as city dwellers. The city or land is viewed as mother, and it nourishes; place is an archive of fond memories and splendid achievements that inspire the present; place is permanent and hence reassuring to man, who sees frailty in himself and chance and flux everywhere.

"The Maori [in New Zealand]", Raymond Firth wrote, "had a great respect for land *per se*, and an exceedingly strong affection for his ancestral soil, a sentiment by no means to be correlated only with its fertility and immediate value to him as a source of food. The lands whereon his forefathers lived, fought, and were buried were ever to him an object of the deepest feeling … 'Mine is the land, the land of my ancestors' was his cry".[8] The Maori revealed their deep-rooted affection in a number of ways. For example, a prisoner, when about to be slain, might ask to be conducted first to the border of his tribal territory so that he could look upon it once again before death. "Or he might ask that he should be allowed to drink of the waters of some stream which flowed through the borders of his home".[9] Tales of heroic deeds added respect to affection for land. Among the most important of these tales were accounts of the arrival of ancestral canoes in New Zealand more than twenty generations ago.[10]

European students are acquainted with the speeches of Pericles and Isocrates in which these patriots proclaimed their piety for Athens and the Athenians. In the United States, where knowledge of classical antiquity is less emphasized, students may nonetheless acquire a feeling for what profound attachment to ancestral land can mean in the eloquent address of an Indian chief. On the sad occasion when native Americans had to cede land to Governor Stevens of Washington Territory, an Indian chief is reported to have said:

> There was a time when our people covered the whole land as the waves of a wind-ruffled sea covers its shell-paved floor, but that time has long since passed away with the greatness of tribes now almost forgotten. I will not dwell on nor mourn over our untimely decay, nor reproach my pale-face brothers with hastening it. We are two distinct races. There is little in common between us. To us the ashes of our ancestors are sacred and their final resting place is hallowed ground, while you wander far from the graves of your ancestors, and, seemingly, without regret … Every part of this country is sacred to my people. Every hillside, every valley, every plain and grove has been hallowed by some fond memory or some sad experience of my tribe. Even the rocks, which seem to lie dumb as they swelter in the sun along the silent seashore in solemn grandeur, thrill with memories of past events connected with the lives of my people. The very dust under your feet responds more lovingly to our footsteps than to yours, because it is the ashes of our ancestors, and our bare feet are conscious of the sympathetic touch, for the soil is rich with the life of our kindred.[11]

Profound sentiment for land has not disappeared; it persists in places isolated from the traffic of civilization. The rhetoric of sentiment barely alters through the ages and differs little from one culture to another. Consider the meaning of the German word *Heimat* as given in a South Tyrolean almanac for the year 1953. Leonard Doob, who discovered this superb specimen of Heimat sentimentality in our time, provides the following translation:

> Heimat is first of all the mother earth who has given birth to our folk and race, who is the holy soil, and who gulps down God's clouds, sun, and storms so that together with their own mysterious strength they prepare the bread and wine which rest on our table and give us strength to lead a good life … Heimat is landscape. Heimat is the landscape we have experienced. That means one that has been fought over,

menaced, filled with the history of families, towns, and villages. Our Heimat is the Heimat of knights and heroes, of battles and victories, of legends and fairy tales. But more than all this, our Heimat is the land which has become fruitful through the sweat of our ancestors. For this Heimat our ancestors have fought and suffered, for this Heimat our fathers have died.[12]

Rootedness in the soil and the growth of pious feeling toward it seem natural to sedentary agricultural peoples. What of nomadic hunters and gatherers? Because they do not stay in one place and because their sense of land ownership is ill-defined, we might expect less attachment; but in fact the strongest sentiment for the nurturing earth can exist among such people. American Plains Indians have migratory habits. The Comanches, for example, change the location of their principal encampment from year to year, yet they worship the earth as mother. It is for them the receptacle and producer of all that sustains life; in honor it is second only to the sun. Mother earth is implored to make things grow so that they may eat and live, to make the water flow so that they may drink, and to keep the ground firm so that they can walk on it.[13] The Lakota of the Northern Plains have the warmest feeling for their country, particularly the Black Hills. A tribal legend describes these hills as a reclining female from whose breasts issue life-giving forces, and to them the Lakota go like children to their mother's arms. The old people, even more than the young, love the soil; they sit or recline on the ground so as to be close to a nurturing power.[14]

The attitude of American Plains Indians may be influenced by their own agricultural past or by contact with agriculturalists. Australian aborigines, who cannot have been affected by the values of soil tillers, provide a clear example of how hunters and gatherers can be intensely attached to place. Aborigines have no rules of land ownership and no strict ideas of territorial boundary. They do, however, distinguish two types of territory – "estate" and "range". Estate is the traditionally recognized home or dreaming place of a patrilineal descent group and its adherents. Range is the tract or orbit over which the group ordinarily hunts and forages. Range is more important than estate for survival; estate is more important than range for social and ceremonial life. As the aborigines put it, range is where they could walk about or run; estate is where they could sit. Strong emotional ties are established with the estate. It is the home of ancestors, the dreaming place where every incident in legend and myth is firmly fixed in some unchanging aspect of nature – rocks, hills and mountains, even trees, for trees can outlive human generations. In times of scarcity, which are frequent along the margins of the desert, the people will leave their own range to forage in other groups' ranges, but seldom for long.[15] As a member of the Ilbalintja tribe explained to the anthropologist Strehlow, "Our fathers taught us to love our own country, and not to lust after the lands belonging to other men. They told us that Ilbalintja was the greatest bandicoot totemic center amongst the Aranda people, and that, in the beginning, bandicoot ancestors had come from every part of the tribe to Ilbalintja alone and had stayed there for ever: so pleasing was our home to them".[16]

Landscape is personal and tribal history made visible. The native's identity – his place in the total scheme of things – is not in doubt, because the myths that support it are as real as the rocks and waterholes he can see and touch. He finds recorded in his land the ancient story of the lives and deeds of the immortal beings from whom he himself is descended, and whom he reveres. The whole countryside is his family tree.[17]

Modern society has its nomads – hoboes, migrant workers, and merchant seamen, among others. What are the consequences of rootlessness? Do they long for a permanent place, and if so, how is this longing expressed? Migrant workers with their families adapt to the nomadic life out of necessity, not choice. Merchant seamen, in contrast, opt for the sea and rootless wayfaring. They may join the merchant marine in their teens or in early manhood. The ship is their home, the mates are their family, yet there appears to be a craving for a permanent locality as an anchor for their imagination when out at sea. Robert Davis, in an unpublished M.A. thesis, wrote of the seamen he knew personally thus:

> They had a craving for a headquarters somewhere along the shore, a place where they could leave their trunk, if they had one; a place to which they could project their minds, wherever they might wander, and visualize the position of the furniture, and imagine just what the inmates of the place were doing at the different hours of the day; a place to which they could send a picture postcard or bring back a curio; a place to which they could always return and be sure of a welcome.[18]

Attachment to the homeland is a common human emotion. Its strength varies among different cultures and historical periods. The more ties there are, the stronger is the emotional bond. In antiquity both the city and the countryside may be sacred, the city because of its shrines, which house local gods and heroes, the countryside because of its nature spirits. But people live in the city and form emotional ties of other kinds, whereas they do not live in the sacred mountains, springs, or groves. Sentiment for nature, inhabited only by spirits, is therefore weaker. A people may, however, become strongly attached to a natural feature because more than one tie yoke[s] them to it. As an example, consider the peak of Reani, the crowning point of the island of Tikopia in the South Pacific. This peak is a landmark of singular importance to the seafaring islanders for at least three reasons. First, it enables the ocean rover to estimate how far he is from land and whether he is on course; this is the practical reason. Second, it is an object of sentiment: the wanderer, when he departs, loses sight of the peak below the ocean waves in sorrow, and, when he returns, greets its first appearance above the waves with joy. Third, it is a sacred place: "it is there that the gods first stand when they come down".[19]

A homeland has its landmarks, which may be features of high visibility and public significance, such as monuments, shrines, a hallowed battlefield or cemetery. These visible signs serve to enhance a people's sense of identity; they encourage awareness of and loyalty to place. But a strong attachment to the homeland can emerge quite apart from any explicit concept of sacredness; it can form without the memory of heroic battles won and lost, and without the bond of fear or of superiority vis-à-vis other people. Attachment of a deep though subconscious sort may come simply with familiarity and ease, with the assurance of nurture and security, with the memory of sounds and smells, of communal activities and homely pleasures accumulated over time. It is difficult to articulate quiet attachments of this type. Neither the rhetoric of an Isocrates nor the effusive prose of a German *Volkskalender* seems appropriate. Contentment is a warm positive feeling, but it is most easily described as incuriosity toward the outside world and as absence of desire for a change of scene. To illustrate this deep undramatic tie to locality, consider three human groups of widely divergent geographical and cultural milieus: the primitive Tasaday of the Mindanao rain forest in the Philippines; the ancient Chinese (their attitude revealed in a Taoist classic); and a modern American farm family in northwestern Illinois.

The outside world discovered the Tasaday in 1971. As yet very little is known about them. They appear to have lived for generations in complete isolation, even from tribes that share the Mindanao rain forest with them. Their material as well as mental culture is perhaps among the simplest in the world. They are food gatherers; their hunting skills are elementary. They seem to lack rituals, ceremonials, or any kind of systematic world view. They are not curious to know about the world beyond the small confines of their home-land. Their language contains no word for sea or lake, although the Celebes Sea and Lake Sebu are less than forty miles away.[20]

> "Why didn't you leave the forest?"
> "We can't go out of our place".
> "Why?"
> "We love to stay in our forest. We like it here. It is a quiet place to sleep. It is warm. Not loud".[21]

In China the ideal of the simple and sedentary life is stated in the Taoist classic, the *Tao Te Ching*. One passage in it reads: "Let us have a small country with few inhabitants … Let the people return to the use of knotted cords [for keeping records]. Let their food be sweet, their clothing beautiful, their homes comfortable, their rustic tasks pleasurable. The neighboring state might be so near at hand that one could hear the cocks crowing and dogs barking in it. But the people would grow old and die without ever having been there".[22]

The last example is from the American heartland. Six generations of a farm family – the Hammers – have lived and died in Daviess County, northwestern Illinois. Here is a people for whom the riches and wonders of the outside world do not beckon. One middle-aged Hammer explained: "My dad never traveled far and I don't have to. We have so many kinds of recreation right on our own farm. We have a nice stream for fishing, we have hunting. I can hunt deer, squirrels, rabbits – anything you want to hunt. I got them here, right on the farm. I don't have to travel".[23] Young Bill Hammer and Dorothy, married in 1961, went to California for their honeymoon but quickly returned because, as Dorothy put it, "It's so unreal to be gone".[24] Loyalty to the homeland is taught in childhood. In 1972, nine-year-old Jim Hammer was asked what his mother had taught him. He replied:

> "What did Mom teach me? For one thing, she taught me how to mow the lawn. She showed me how to tie my shoes … And she tries to teach me to live decent. Like some people don't have a very good life because they don't settle down in one place and don't stay very long. They could live in Illinois for a while and then move to Cali-fornia. I like Illinois; it's just my home state".[25]

Notes

1   John S. Dunne, *The City of Gods: A Study of Myth and Mortality*, London, Sheldon Press, 1974, p. 29; J. B. Pritchard, *Ancient Near Eastern Texts*, Princeton: Prince-University Press, 1955.
2   M. D. Fustel de Coulanges, *The Ancient City*, Garden City, New York: Doubleday Anchor Books, n.d., pp. 36–7. (First published as *La Cité antique* in 1864.)
3   Martin P. Nilsson, *Greek Popular Religion*, New York: Columbia University Press, 1940, p. 75.
4   De Coulanges, *The Ancient City*, p. 68.
5   Euripides, *Hippolytus*, 1047–50. See Ernest L. Hettich, *A Study in Ancient Nationalism*, Williamsport, Penn.: The Bayard Press, 1933.
6   Pericles's funeral oration in Thucydides, *The History of the Peloponnesian War*, book 2: 36, trans. Richard Crawley, Chicago: The University of Chicago Press, Great Books, vol. 6, 1952, p. 396.

7 Isocrates, *Panegyricus*, 23–6, trans. George Norlin, Cambridge: Harvard University Press, vol. 1, 1928, p. 133.

8 Raymond Firth, *Economics of the New Zealand Maori*, Wellington, New Zealand: Government Printers, 1959, p. 368.

9 Ibid., p. 370.

10 Ibid., p. 373.

11 Clarence R. Bagley, "Chief Seattle and Angeline", *The Washington Historical Quarterly* 22, no. 4, 253–5. The speech is reported by Dr. Henry A. Smith in *Seattle Sunday Star*, October 29, 1877. Although the sentiment is Chief Seattle's, the words in English are those of Dr. Smith, whose feeling for rhetoric may have been influenced by classical learning.

12 Leonard W. Doob, *Patriotism and Nationalism: Their Psychological Foundations*, New Haven, Conn.: Yale University Press, 1952, p. 196.

13 Ernest Wallace and E. Adamson Hoebel, *The Comanches: Land of the South Plains*, Norman, Okla.: University of Oklahoma Press, 1952, p. 196.

14 Chief Standing Bear, *Land of the Spotted Eagle*, Boston: Houghton Mifflin, 1933, pp. 43, 192–3.

15 W. E. H. Stanner, "Aboriginal Territorial Organization: Estate, Range, Domain and Regime", *Oceania* 36, no. 1, 1965, 1–26.

16 T. G. H. Strehlow, *Aranda Traditions*, Melbourne: Melbourne University Press, 1947, p. 51.

17 Ibid., pp. 30–1; see also Amos Rapoport, "Australian Aborigines and the Definition of Place", in W. J. Mitchell (ed.), *Environmental Design and Research Association*, Proceedings of the 3rd Conference at Los Angeles, 1972, 3–3–1 to 3–3–14.

18 Robert Davis, *Some Men of the Merchant Marine*, unpublished Master's thesis, Faculty of Political Science, Columbia University Press, 1907; quoted in Margaret M. Wood, *Paths of Loneliness*, New York: Columbia University Press, 1953, p. 156.

19 Raymond Firth, *We, the Tikopia*, London: George Allen & Unwin, 1957, pp. 27–8.

20 John Nance, *The Gentle Tasaday*, New York: Harcourt, Brace, Jovanovich, 1975, pp. 21–2.

21 Ibid., p. 57.

22 *Tao Te Ching*, chapter 80; quoted in Fung Yu-Lan, *A Short History of Chinese Philosophy*, New York: Macmillan, 1948, p. 20.

23 Archie Lieberman, *Farm Boy*, New York: Harry N. Abrams, 1974, p. 36.

24 Ibid., p. 130.

25 Ibid., p. 293.

Filling dwelling place with history
Communal apartments in St Petersburg

Ilya Utekhin (2003)

… To great extent, local history remains unwritten, existing but in oral form, with no way to check the stories told against a document other than other people's narratives. The facts simply do not exist apart from this or that interpretation. Correspondingly, the researcher is bound to take for the truth what is thought to be true by the community members: their interpretations may vary, but some basic lines remain the same in all narratives.

This chapter focuses on the so-called communal apartment (CA), a special type of dwelling characteristic to Leningrad (St. Petersburg) and other big Soviet cities, where several families share all the facilities; today, up to 20 percent of the population of St. Petersburg lives in this way. During most of the Soviet period, the CA was the predominant type of dwelling in Leningrad. As far as we can judge, the communal apartment has never been studied by either ethnographer or anthropologist. [...]

The communal apartment as a phenomenon of Soviet housing was the outcome of both practical and ideological circumstances. Housing problems in Moscow after the revolution and in St. Petersburg in the 1930s became acute due to migration to the cities. The Bolshevist government had neither resources nor intention to launch a large-scale construction program, but tried instead to resolve housing shortages through the redistribution of living space: "Palaces to working people!" was a popular slogan when private property on real estate was abolished by a governmental decree in August 1918 and it became possible for authorities to use the dwelling spaces confiscated from former proprietors [*Fig. 81*]. The distribution of space was regulated by a "sanitary norm", which gave a person the right to a specific amount of living space, but there was no guarantee. As a result, in many "former rich people's" apartments in the center of the city, tenants belonging to different social strata began living together – sometimes among them were the former proprietors of the building or of the apartment.[1] Such situations provoked frequent disputes between the new dwellers and their class-antagonist former owners, which is reflected in the Soviet press of the late 1920s, where the letters of workers called for banning former owners from living in their former places, even in cases when they have been successfully incorporated into the new political and social realities of the Soviet state, having become trade union members or employees of Soviet enterprises. Second, for some time before a separate flat for each family became the goal of Soviet housing policy in the 1930s,[2] an illusion existed as a part of official ideology that living together would bring about a sense of camaraderie between people, leading to the formation of a true collectivist personality, including liberating women from the domestic slavery typical of the old way of everyday life. The socialist reform of everyday life supposed a collectivization of all the aspects of everyday life, such as eating, sleeping, and child rearing – all to be separated from family life, which had to be utterly transformed ... The community was regarded as a potential source of order and educational [and] moral influence. This trend propelled not only [the] creation of house-communes in already constructed buildings, but an abundance of utopian social and architectural projects [for] new communist cities and buildings. [...]

The official discourse since the 1930s stressed that a separate apartment for each worker's family was the goal of Soviet housing policy from the beginning. However, many facts contradict this claim. The reality for the vast majority of the population in the big cities was the CA. The very term "CA" meant initially "an apartment without a householder" where order was maintained by the tenants themselves. In fact, the self-organization turned out to reveal the worst qualities of people involved in a struggle for survival in a time and place of over-population; order usually came from an outside authority, such as the housing administration, *militsia*, or the People's Court. Numerous instructions and rules intended to regulate the interior order in the apartments were elaborated, with detailed prescriptions concerning potentially controversial issues in CA everyday life; such instructions themselves were a sort of canonization of spontaneously established practices that had proved to be the most efficient.

Living in CAs brought about the specific communal mentality. First was the organization of privacy: several people – usually belonging to the same family but not necessarily so – lived in the same room. There was among neighbors an almost complete transparency of life: all everyday practices, concerns, and events were perceived by other tenants who could see, hear, feel [and] smell ... what all other tenants were doing. Such neglected privacy led to an oversensitivity to violations of privacy and its substitutes. And there were concerns related to hygiene since CA residents shared toilet, bathroom, and kitchen facilities. The maintenance of the common spaces followed the principle of minimal suffi-cient effort (no one tried to achieve the cleanest possible state), and the responsibility was distributed between the members of the community, who performed the duties of cleaning by turn.

Any kind of collective living has two crucial aspects: to distribute existing – however limited – resources among the members of the group and to share the overall effort and costs needed to maintain the living space [*Fig. 81*]. This means always sharing some-thing – be it the shelf in the kitchen, the right to use the bathroom, or the obligation to clean the floors. Queuing was an important dimension of everyday contact among neighbors; it was often institutionalized through written schedules. Sharing was emotionally charged with envy, and people were extremely sensitive to overall fairness. Although close relationships did develop among neighbors, endless conflicts were typical in the CAs. People regularly addressed written complaints to authorities, denouncing their neighbors and getting rid of the competition, so to speak. [...]

Local history in CA communities exists in the form of oral narratives and so belongs to folklore. It is important to determine the place of the information about local history in the whole body of folklore knowledge transmitted from older tenants to the younger genera-tion. CA folklore comprises a range of genres, from gossip to etiological statements.

Let us take a newcomer at a CA as an example. Even if he speaks the same language and belongs to the same culture as his new neighbors, in the beginning he does not share a special kind of cultural competence of the dweller, he is not yet "our folk". [...] To get a full-scale membership in the community, the newcomer should acquire the local stan-dards of action and interpretation, to master the specific cultural competence necessary to be incorporated in the community through getting his own status and the right to modify the existing order by his very participation.

What does this local competence consist of? Imagine a visitor who has come to a CA for the first time. He is not acquainted with the neighbors, so he enters the kitchen and his greeting is general, not personally addressed. He [has] to ask where the toilet is located. He does not know where to find soap and a towel, on which cooker he is allowed to put the teapot, where he might get the matches, etc. His ignorance is logical, as he knows that he has the right to use [only] the things – and the places – of the person whose guest he is. A mistake would lead to a conflict, directed against the person responsible for the situation, that is, the dweller who invited the guest but failed to explain to him the minimal necessary amount of information.[3]

It would hardly be possible to formulate the whole amount of this information through a set of rules and norms, because they are too many, comprise too many excep-tions, and are modified in the course of their application. Thus, new residents know, in principle, that to set a bag down on a neighbor's table is risky; you can expect to find your bag lying on the floor ... The cultural competence of a participant of the community enables him to use these special terms of the rules' application, whereas a stranger does not possess but a very general idea about relevant behavior, having no idea of the rules' application: he is not aware of the status of the things and places [that represent] the rela-tions between the neighbors.

Accepted norms exist in a more or less stereotypic verbal form and ascend to the local rationality or to a precedent. The first case is illustrated with the following example. The laundering is usually performed in the bathroom or in the kitchen. Although both ways are possible (and explicitly mentioned in the official regulations), they are never combined in one apartment. The motivation of the choice may be purely functional, but often it is not. Really this choice is more often determined by custom only and makes part of the habits that are never thought about nor expressed openly, except for the cases of a violation of the custom by a newcomer. "Don't you know that the bathroom is to be used to take a bath? No one will wait until you finish if he wants to wash his hands. So go and launder in the kitchen as all the people do!" Or "You should know that people cook here. What a silly idea to do laundry in the kitchen when the bathroom is made for it!" Both explanations have [a] rational appearance.

[Appealing] to a precedent is evident when people say "We've always done it this way" or "as early as in time of my grandfather we already had a hook here". It is a kind of knowledge of what is not evident, but necessary for mastering the "normal way". Besides this knowledge, knowledge about neighbors' personal stories, characters, and inclinations is needed for complete incorporation into the everyday life of the community. One can gain reliable information about a neighbor from one's own observations and from personal communication with the neighbor; at the same time, some information comes from what other people say about the neighbor. The curious nature of gossip consists in the fact that it would be meaningless to attempt to retell the gossip to a stranger in a comprehensible form. The whole meaning of gossip can be understood only by those who belong to the same community and share – partly, at least – its interests. Generally, gossip is that which differs from the normal way of things – and so incites special attention, explanation, and commentary able to excite envy or interest aimed at disclosing one's privacy. [...]

Seemingly less important to everyday behavior is another type of data: information about former dwellers and their relations to those who actually live in the apartment as well as about the circumstances that motivate features of the environment. To some extent this has to do with the motivation of why the space is organized and distributed in a particular way, and where the "survivals" (e.g., old geyser, or someone's skis on a shelf in a public place) come from. This kind of information should not be underestimated, as it forms a substantial part of conceptual mapping of the territory. A newcomer lacking this knowledge needs explanations about what belongs to this or that neighbor, and to what extent the community in general recognizes the rights of the neighbor (say, to use a shelf or a corner in the corridor) ... This sort of information has direct implications for one's behavior. [...]

A part of the body of local history knowledge that we may consider separately consists of the ideas the actual dwellers have about the origin and past of their building and their apartment. Being located in the center of the city and mainly constructed before the 1917 revolution, practically each building has its own particular face, sometimes its name (after the name of the former owner), and often historical and architectural value. Few residents remember the distant past from their own experience; what people know about the history of the building was told to them in oral narratives. This information being a sort of past perfect, it is not relevant to everyday behavior but is important for people's self-identification.[4] It is unwrapped before strangers and newcomers in order to show what is special about the place (and, so, about its actual dwellers) and is important to the community. After the revolution, big apartments were granted to more or less significant communist functionaries and high-ranking military officers. This fact is remembered, even though there is no one left in the apartment of the descendants of those initial dwellers. In our material concerning different apartments of the same building, a strikingly similar story was told by various speakers about how the apartment became communal. More than once our informers explained the initial sharing of the apartment by the wish of the dwellers to find ... good company: "he [an army general] was bored alone with his family, and so he invited some people, all of them well-educated intelligentsia, to live together". Another version: "He [a party functionary] invited some people from the ground floor to take temporary shelter in his apartment after the 1924 flood, because ground-floor premises suffered severe damage. Those people remained in his apartment long after that and, moreover, brought their relatives to live together, and thus the apartment became densely populated". Practically the same explanation is given in another apartment where the engineer lived who directed the last decoration [work] in the building (this fact is confirmed by his daughter still living in the apartment). The presumably voluntary character of his decision to share the apartment is remarkable: people believed that it is uncomfortable for a family to live alone in an apartment. So, the tenants themselves looked for suitable company. This idea can have some real foundations: the new élite was not accustomed to living in luxurious conditions with the number of rooms greater than the number of dwellers.

It is plausible, however, that another real, though far from voluntary, prototype of this idea existed: the so-called right to self-compression (*samouplotnenie*), that is, the right to choose people with whom to live together in order to reduce per capita dwelling space in the apartment. This idea existed in the 1920s and meant that if some tenants had more space than was prescribed by the sanitary norm (4.5 square meters per person), they were obliged to share their living space; after the official notice, they had a definite term during which they were allowed to choose those with whom to share the dwelling. After this term expired, ZHEK (housing administration) did not take into account the [wishes] of the "compressed" tenants while [allotting] the living space to other people.

To avoid the company of strangers, tenants formalized their cohabitation with their household servants or invited relatives from the countryside. Traces of this situation can still be found in some apartments where former masters and servants, or their descendants, live together. In other cases, the masters left the apartment, while the servants remained. "He was a banker ... I don't remember the name ... We have a neighbor woman who should recall – not the banker himself, of course, but ... this neighbor's mother worked as chambermaid at the banker's family. She doesn't like mentioning this fact, that the mother was a chambermaid. Perhaps, it seems humiliating to her".[5]

Samouplotnenie (self-compression) and simply *uplotnenie* (compression) might have affected both the dwellers who lived in the apartment from pre-revolutionary times and the post-revolutionary dwellers, members of the new élite, for some reason fallen into disgrace. Those legendary personages who occupied the whole apartment, be it before or right after the revolution, are usually conceived as outstanding personalities. The few data that remain about their habits and way of life are linked with the historical topography of the place. [In practically] every big CA there are some tenants – not necessarily elderly people – who can explain the initial purpose of each room. Living for a long time in the former dining room or in a small room intended for domestic servants, one can nevertheless keep in mind the whole of the apartment and be able to restore mentally the initial plan. The remaining original decoration is the main guideline; the story of the apartment is the story of rebuilding and partitioning, the story of communal living unfolding in an unfavorable environment. Leaving no traces of a past, some cases of rebuilding delete the supports to memory; however, the rebuilding works and partitions were usually made in the cheapest way, and so traces remained. [...]

The garret and other peripheral places are thought to shelter the secrets of the founders. When the former dwellers had fled after the revolution, it was supposed that they left their treasures in a secret place in the building. Looking for a hidden treasure, the dwellers checked the walls and the floors, the garret and the cellar. Interior rebuilding involving divisions of big apartments added mysteries and riddles to the place: doors that are never opened appeared – in the staircases and inside the apartments. They were left because it was too expensive to make walls instead. Few inhabitants have an exact idea of the complicated planning of the building, and sometimes most curious things are said about where these doors lead to. Sometimes the curiosity is instigated by the sounds coming from behind the doors.

CA people feel that they live in a special place – this feeling is totally alien to people living in the new buildings built on the same projects outside the center of the city. There hardly can be a memorial plate on a [new apartment] building – this construction is not intended to be a memory, but is just a sleeping place of doubtful individuality. On the contrary, the center of the city being rich in literary and historical connotations, the memory affects even those people who are not interested in history or literature, though only through the names of the streets and buildings. Living in a CA from birth, people feel themselves deep-rooted in the history of the place.

The period after the revolution is usually remembered as the time of a well-organized CA life, in spite of the high density of CA population. The most remarkable object of nostalgia is the clean state of the staircases and the care by the *dvornik* about the common use places outside the apartment. "Dvornik" is the term to denote workers responsible for cleaning the staircases and the courtyard.[6] The significance of dvorniks for CA everyday life became much lesser after the introduction, mainly in early 1950s, of central heating (before that, *dvorniks* were responsible for wood supply). With the night guard of the *dvorniks* suspended, the first graffiti appeared on the walls of the staircases. [...]

Two ... historical periods (the years after Stalin before perestroika and perestroika itself) are manifest in the current structure of community: some participants of early events are still living at the same place, others moved elsewhere recently. Their conflicts, thefts, births, deaths, and marriages are parts of the actual landscape. Although changes as late as the 1980s have led to far less overcrowding, the deterioration of housing generally is the usual subject of comments. Significant in the chain of the signs of decay was the [abolition], in late 1950s, of night-watch duties of the dvorniks. Residents remarked that perestroika brought widespread deviant behaviors and worse than ever technical state of the premises. [...]

The common motives of people's opinions about the past reveal their reflections on the general changes over time both in their living environment and in society in general. In the past, life in CAs was more intense and the tenants were more numerous, but there was also more order, people say. There were no deviant drunkards and drug addicts; the apartments were cleaned more often, and people were more honest, and theft inside the apartments was unlikely. Such Golden Age nostalgia is typical of classic CA mentality, whereas the new generation appreciates increasing privatization of life and tolerance to various lifestyles.[...]

The privatization of life in the CAs today makes people think less about rules and norms. At the same time, there is an absence of leadership within the CA. In the Soviet times, in the cases when the tenants could not come to an agreement, the order usually came from an outside authority such as the housing administration. Today the order comes from the *uchastkovyi militsioner* (local police officer responsible for the area) or the *domovoi komitet* (house committee elected by the tenants). Before World War II, each CA elected a leader responsible for the order in the particular apartment (*kvartupolnomochennyi*). The leader was obliged to enforce the orders of the housing administration and to represent the CA before it in any hearings. In the post-Stalinist era people in many CAs refused to accept the leadership role and thus had no formal leadership. To be a nonformal authority was different: "Here people do not like to express their claims. But they always have millions of claims, they are always discontent. So *kvartupolnomochennyi* is the person who is entitled to express the claims to a transgressor. When he does so officially, he speaks not as a private person, but on behalf of the collective. And this is a quite different role, it is easier [than to do it privately]".[7] Nevertheless, no one wanted to be kvartupolnomochennyi or to undertake formal responsibility for resolving problems in the CA.

Instead, some energetic people actually did perform the duties of the kvartupolnomochennyi but without any formal authority. Their active position originated from the wish to live in better conditions, not from the desire to achieve power. "His opinion was always taken into consideration. He even edited the rules on a piece of cardboard posted in the corridor. Now somebody must have discarded these rules. I remember them in the lumber-room, perhaps, someone took the sheet to cover something".[8]

The rules written by the informal leader, as far as we can judge, were more detailed than any official rules control of everyday practices. With all the pedantry possible, he wrote that while sweeping the corridor, one should have the dustpan at hand, [in order] to take up the dust by parts and not to bring it in a heap through all the corridor; that telephone conversation should be brief; that smoking was not allowed in public places, because it damaged people's health; that the rooms' doors should be closed; that no noise is allowed after eleven o'clock, etc. In the bathroom he posted up notices such as "Please, do not turn the tap too strong". [...]

Individual initiative led some people to modify their environment with their own effort. Here is a typical story: "Pal Sergeich, navy officer, a remarkable person, very businesslike. There was [in the kitchen] a big tiled stove, and they [ZHEK, that is, housing administration] gave an order to remove it. He took all the tiles and held them somewhere, and then called the workers and they covered the walls in the kitchen with the tiles. These are the walls we have now. It was his initiative. He always paid attention to problems and conflicts". We know a case when a tenant installed a bath in the kitchen (in an apartment without a bathroom), despite the neighbors' opposition. He did it with his own money. Then all the neighbors gradually became accustomed to using the bathroom; from the beginning this bath was intended for common use. Today, we would not find such leadership within the CAs. [...]

It should be noted that the mastery of a community memory by an individual is one of the most important factors in a person's self-identity as a community member. Here I touch on the uses of local history. Old dwellers' status and their claims to special rights in Soviet times were supported not only by customary law but also reflected in the active legislation. Thus, they had privileged rights to get an additional living space; even today some old people are sure one day the state will provide them with separate apartments just because they are old dwellers, living here since blockade times. This status and implied references to historical motivation of this or that claim are tools in conflicts and controversies inside the apartments. References can be made not to one's personal involvement [in] the history of a particular community but to the history of the place (building, district, or city). The Russian term for the old dweller of Leningrad is *korennoy leningradets,* which means literally "Leningrad-er according to his roots". It is an extremely interesting phenomenon for a city whose population during all its history suffered the impact of active migrations and fell drastically and then increased at least two times during the Soviet period.

The special feeling of identity to some extent may be related to the place with all its historical connotations, not only to the given community that is a natural environment of CA inhabitants. In recent years, real estate agencies made a profitable business out of what is called rasselenie, that is, moving CA dwellers to separate flats out of the city center and selling the former CAs to rich private owners. However attractive may seem the perspective of receiving a separate and private flat instead of a CA room, many CA residents vehemently opposed making such a change in their lives. Sometimes neighbors from the same apartment are so used to living together that they agree to move to newly constructed buildings provided that they get flats in a same building, together with their former CA neighbors. Sometimes, they refuse to change their lives, though such a change is [needed] to better one's living conditions. Of course, to some extent such a change is warranted by workplace location or nearby colleges as well as favorite and familiar shops, convenient municipal transport, etc.: The person is caught in the social nets that are partly related to the apartment. [...]

Together with those people who are deeply related to their place or their CA collective there is another ever growing group of inhabitants in today's CAs. These are temporary residents whose attitude to the place is sharply different. For them, the given CA is a temporary residence, and so has no special value. Local history is less relevant to such people, whose attitude to the place is evident even in their lack of responsibility for order and cleanliness in the apartment. Here is an interview with a resident about the temporary residents.

> If someone moves to a room of the apartment, is he aware about the past of this room?
>
> *If the former dweller of this room was interested in such things and told them to the new resident, yes. But the question is that those who come here to live these days, they are, probably too young, in their mind. They take it for a residence, and they don't care a damn about who built this house and who lived here. They are temporary, themselves.*

> How many are there such dwellers compared to those who live here permanently?
>
> *Half. As for me, I consider myself a permanent resident, because it matters much to me ... not the square meters of "zhilploshchad" [living space], but the notion of home. And they, if they have 25 meters' room and hear that 26 meters are proposed instead somewhere, they will move immediately. And to me, if somebody proposes a place three times bigger someplace else, I will stay here anyway.*

> Did you have had real offers of this kind?
>
> *Yes, some private companies dealing with "rasselenie" went here more than once and made offers. They wanted to build offices here. They offered a three room apartment for this one room where we live, because we have [a] high ceiling, a fireplace, a view. Naturally, we refused ... Some neighbors were furious. They live here until they can save up enough money to move somewhere else.*

Home as something more than a temporary place for rest and sleeping, where one's things are held, should also include, as the resident above believes, an element of relation to the given district and building – especially when one has grown up in the CA and his personal story is unthinkable outside the context of the history of the apartment and, broader, of the place. The business workers and the temporary neighbors are ready for any kind of mobility, while at least some of the old CA dwellers are not: They hardly can agree to substitute their communal home with something else.

Notes

1 For a concise outline of the Soviet housing policy that led to the creation of the CA, see Timothy Sosnovy, *The Housing Problem in the Soviet Union*, New York, 1954. On housing policy in the early Soviet period, see A. Chernykh, "Zhilishchnyi peredel: politika 20-h godov v sfere zhilya", *Sotsiologicheskie Issledovaniya*, no. 10, 1995, 71–8. For the newest research on the social history of the CA in St. Petersburg, see E. Guerasimova, "Sovetskaya Kommunal'naya Kvartira", *Sotsiologicheskiy Zhurnal*, no. 1/2, 1998, 222–44. See also Svetlana Boym, *Common Places: Mythologies of Everyday Life in Russia*, Cambridge, 1994 to catch the ambience of communal culture, as well as our recent book with a detailed study of the practices of CA everyday life (Ilya Utekhin, *Ocherki Kommunal'nogo Byta*, Moscow: O.G.I., 2001).

2 This question is complicated; an array of opinions on this topic are found in official discourse and in discussions in the press in the 1920s. It became clear in the 1930s, however, that CAs represented a temporary difficulty in construction of Socialist society that later turned out to be permanent. It is worth mentioning that the failure of the communal living in reshaping people's mentality in a truly communist way was sometimes explained by the fact that these communal dwellings used old buildings not fit for new everyday life. The space itself was resistant to new ways of living. One may also recall the fact that in the first years after the Bolshevist revolution the workers who had recently moved into the so-called palaces had many reasons for feeling uncomfortable; particularly, they experienced difficulties in heating and in getting to their workplaces located on the periphery of the city.

3 From "Rules for Using the Toilet". The use of the toilet by nonresidents of the apartment (relatives, guests of residents) was carefully monitored and violations of hygiene by them were taken care of in the common toilet (Ilia I. Kabakov, *In the Communal Kitchen: New Documents and Materials*, Paris: Galerie Dina Vierny, 1993, p. 177).

4 In some cases, however, even past-perfect information is used to explain actual features of environment. Thus, a resident explained why there were yearly problems with leakage in the apartment where she lived. She said that during World War I in that building a military hospital was located, and a special open gallery for walking was constructed along the façade of the building. Its floor was, at the same time, the roof of a part of the apartment, and it was made of copper tiles. The tiles were removed in the 1920s, during one of the Bolshevist campaigns for collecting scrap metal. Leakage problems have occurred since then.

5 [Interview with] Galina R., 39, 1997.

6 *Dvor*; on cultural significance of the courtyard see B. A. Ruble, "St. Petersburg's Courtyards and Washington's Alleys: Officialdom's Neglected Neighbors", in *Cuitat real, ciutat ideal: Significat i funcio a l'espai urba modern* (ed.), Pep Subirós, Barcelona, 1998, pp. 12–27.

7 [Interview with] Rosalia Y. 72, 1998.

8 [Interview with] Susanna P., 63, 1998.

Dwelling
Making peace with space and place

Deborah Tall (1996)

To say we dwell somewhere implies permanence, or at least continuity. But at root "dwell" means to pause, to linger or delay. We dwell on a subject, but eventually give it up. So what does it mean to dwell somewhere? How long do we have to stay? J. B. Jackson takes on the question, but speaks of habits rather than years, of a place becoming customary. Habits are acquired, they form over time. With disuse they are forgotten. To dwell in a place rather than simply exist in it seems to hinge on allowing such adaptive habits to form, an act of accommodation.[1]

It used to be easier. A home and its land were once widely understood as belonging to a family forever. Even today, most people in the world are born and die within a radius of a few miles. But 20 to 30 percent of Americans move each year, and the average American moves fourteen times over a lifetime. Permanent residence is at odds with our notion of property – property as commodity, as route to profit, rather than something attained to keep. The American dream requires that you own your home, but Americans rarely stay in a house longer than five years. To change not just your home or town, but the region of the country you live in, is understood as a way to change your life, and we aim to do that often. Numerous milestones – college, marriage, birth of children, a new job, divorce, retirement – almost require a change of location.[2] In fact, to stay in one place for life is often interpreted as being unambitious, unadventurous – a negation of American values. Moving up in the world means moving on.

The easy replacement of home ignores its emotional charge for us, ignores how important familiarity is in the constitution of home. Frequent dislocation, or the sudden destruction of a known environment, can be fundamentally deranging. It means the loss of personal landmarks – which embody the past – and the disintegration of a communal pattern of identity. People relocated from condemned slums, for instance, often suffer terribly no matter how much more "attractive" the new housing provided. Home is where we know – and are known – through accumulated experience.

When an entire place or landscape is destroyed, the sense of betrayal and disorientation is acute. Harvey Cox's shattering story of a Holocaust survivor from the Czech village of Lidice illustrates such loss in the extreme:

> The Germans had arbitrarily picked this hamlet to be the example of what would happen to other villages … They came into the town, shot all the men over twelve, then shipped the wives to one concentration camp and the children to another. They burned the village completely, destroyed all the trees and foliage and plowed up the ground. Significantly they demanded that on all maps of Czechoslovakia the town of Lidice must be erased. The woman survivor confessed to me that despite the loss of her husband and the extended separation from her children, the most shocking blow of all was to return to the crest of the hill overlooking Lidice at the end of the war – and to find nothing there, not even ruins.[3]

The poetry of John Clare evokes a similar sense of violation, in his case as a result of the Enclosure Act, which in the late eighteenth and early nineteenth centuries vigorously transformed the common open-field system of rural England into private holdings in the name of efficiency. Instead of the long strips and winding trails of the old communal arrangement, small square fields and straight connecting roads were rapidly imposed on the land, virtually erasing its prior boundaries and landmarks. Even streams were diverted to fit the plan. The landscape was reconfigured on a blank map; what people had lived in for generations became unrecognizable. […]

John Clare and others like him who had rarely been outside their own parishes were caught in a moment of violent physical and social transformation. Removed from Helpston, where his family had farmed for generations, Clare suffered catastrophically from the loss of familiars and the location of his memories; he left an eloquent record of his pain.

> I've left mine own old home of homes
> Green fields and every pleasant place
> The summer like a stranger comes
> I pause and hardly know her face

The disorientation of removal for Clare was such that even the dependable sun "seems to lose its way / Nor knows the quarter it is in". Outside Helpston "the very wild flowers seemed to forget me" – as if it had been the known landscape that confirmed his existence.

Unable to write about his love of nature in general terms, Clare lost, with his displacement, the crucial particulars that gave his voice a body. Over the next few years, his connection to the external world increasingly slipped. He spent the last twenty-seven years of his life in an asylum writing such lines as "I am – yet what I am, none cares or knows".[…]

All over Europe, from the Renaissance on, the landscape was increasingly divided as in England. A side effect was the prizing of "shapeliness" in the land, regarding the landscape as a work of art. Landschaft had become *landschap* in the hands of Dutch and Italian painters. Landscape painting reflected the growing visual preference for a landscape composed of balanced parts, while at the same time it helped to disseminate that as an ideal. Some claim people only learned to "see" landscapes by learning to appreciate landscape painting. At its most extreme, says Samuel Monk, "Nature was scarcely seen at all, for the lover of the picturesque was bent upon discovering not the world as it is, but the world as it might have been had the Creator been an Italian artist of the seventeenth century".[4] Our view is still controlled to some extent by that aesthetic norm – highway planners provide us with scenic overlooks that command us to admire the land from a carefully contrived viewpoint.

Though enclosure was largely economic and agricultural in motive, it had aesthetic implications, and it made social distinctions more visible too – between rich and poor, between places for work and places for leisure. It was in this landscape that the great English gardens were created – by, as Raymond Williams puts it, "a self-conscious observer [who] was very specifically the self-conscious owner" of a pleasing stretch of land.[5] Private property now provided both topographic and social place; one's place was no longer communally defined. The notion of place in which one owns and cares for a plot of land still exerts enormous influence on contemporary Americans. The extent and condition of our property, and our choice of style in dwelling, create a powerful emblem of our identity and status.

At the same time, though, we are awash in a landscape of mobility that eschews connections to particular plots, has no need or desire for great distinction between places, and is essentially utilitarian about the land, often lacking environmental conscience. Place has come to mean proximity to highways, shopping, and year-round recreation, rather than natural situation or indigenous character. In some ways, that has been liberating. In the hierarchy of landowners, admission to place is hard won and restricted; in the landscape of mobility, new communities – be they townhouse tracts or trailer parks – can crop up on the spot and rapidly assimilate new members.[6] Yet we remain caught between nostalgia for place in its traditional sense and cool detachment, between a sense of responsibility for the land and the freedom of indifference. We've been told we live in a global village, which sounds a little like a Landschaft; but in truth, the technologically shrunken world has left us without much of a foothold.

Numerous modern writers have applauded the condition of "perpetual exile" as ethically healthy, a necessary severance from the sentimentalities of nationalism, for example.[7] Others, though, prominently Simone Weil, have argued strongly for attachment: "To be rooted is perhaps the most important and least recognized need of the human soul … A human being has roots by virtue of his real, active, and natural participation in the life of a community, which preserves in living shape certain particular treasures of the past and certain particular expectations for the future".[8]

Given how often I have moved, my community is widely scattered. I have close friends all over the world; none of them know each other. We have only our own brief intensities of common experience to bind us, our telephone calls and letters. Friendship is tethered to loss, dependent on mental reconstruction instead of daily enactment. Sometimes I feel stranded at the center of a fragmented orb, my life divided into a series of experiences and places that can never be brought together – except in the solitude of memory. My family too is deposited all over the continent. Crucial junctures in our lives take place in hospital hallways or over bad coffee in airports.

In many ways, though, our upbringings prepare us for this essential solitude. The privacy of the typical American home molds us in an image of separateness, turns us of necessity inward. Nowhere else in the world has isolation been such a common pattern of settlement as in America, especially historically in rural America. As settlers moved out onto the rectangular grids the country was carved into, their farmhouses were almost invariably set toward the middle of the plot, very rarely clustered at the corners near adjoining blocks of land so as to provide proximity to other families. In Quebec, by contrast, farm plots were made long and narrow so that houses could be set side by side along a road. Congress, debating the Land Ordinance Act, briefly worried about the lack of any central focus in the grids. Congressmen from New England believed the lack of a central meetinghouse would lead the settlers into sin. But no gathering of towns or villages was conceived of in the grand design; each family went it alone. The itinerant merchant materialized, and the mobile library; social life atrophied. These settlers were people who had come primarily from urban centers in Europe. Their survival in such extreme solitude became an anti-communal American ideal.[9]

Individualism and mobility are at the core of American identity. I am admittedly the observer and writer I am in part because of the freedom I have had to wander. Mobility is, for many of us, essential to personal and economic development. "Mobility is always the weapon of the underdog", says Cox.[10] "… Space symbolizes hope; place, achievement and stability".[11] A fixed place can obviously be seen as a trap, home to drudgery and hopelessness. "Roots are ruts", complains a rising young executive.[12] "To be rooted is the property of vegetables", scoffs the geographer David Sopher.[13] To Sopher's mind, the prevailing "domicentric" bias in our thinking has turned "rootless" into the stigmatizing image of the shifty vagabond and made all wandering peoples suspicious – Gypsies, tinkers, the Wandering Jew. When people are seen as lacking loyalty to a place, lacking perhaps even the ability to be loyal to places, it is easy to persecute them, to view them as threatening to communal stability. The privileged and unadventurous may rightly fear that mobility threatens established traditions, and so they exaggerate the healthy attachment to place into rigid exclusivity and sentimentality. For the underprivileged or disaffected, though, mobility may represent a lifesaving escape, the eluding of oppressive inherited values and the stranglehold of tradition. For a phase of one's life, at the very least, it is a great relief to be free of the influences and expectations that a home place holds, just as one often needs to escape the clutches of one's family in order to mature. Place requires "encounters and obligations", points out James Houston; it means accepting certain limitations. Space, on the other hand, is "the arena of freedom".[14]

As a national ideal carried to an extreme, though, mobility has created the circumstances for widespread fragmentation and damage – to people, communities, and the land. The avoidance of ties to a place, which take years to build, removes constraints, allows us to be indifferent to our towns and cities, to ignore their human and environmental plights, to say *but this isn't mine*. To cling to the right of mobility with all the freedoms it bestows is ultimately to contribute to destruction.

In other traditions, a balance between wandering and staying is aspired to, the understanding that a full life involves both venturing out and returning. In the allegorical world of mythical and religious journeys, the greatest challenge of the journey is to return home, to share the lessons of one's experience, to incorporate the journey into its place of origin. While remaining in a single place can indeed be imprisoning, wandering compulsively makes one a non-citizen. There is a delicate dialectic to play out. "Before any choice", says the French geographer Eric Dardel, "there is this place which we have not chosen, where the very foundation of our earthly existence and human condition establishes itself. We can change places, move, but this is still to look for a place, for this we need as a base to set down Being and to realize our possibilities – a *here* from which the world discloses itself, a *there* to which we can go".[15] Or, as the poet Richard Hugo jokes: "If you are in Chicago you can go to Rome. If you ain't no place you can't go nowhere".[16]

I come from a people in diaspora who only lightly touch the place on earth they happen to be living. My grandparents fled the pogroms of Russia and the poverty of Eastern Europe, lost the coherence of their villages, but reestablished it, to some extent, in the immigrant streets of New York. Then their children, my parents, fled the city for an American-dream suburban life, severed from the intimate communities of their childhood. None of the many homes my parents made for me and my sister resembled what they had come from. Their goal was to get as far as possible from that life, with its poverty and ghetto narrowness. Suburbia may have offered a new form of community to them, but it was more truthfully a series of stepping-stones to status. To me, the streets outside our increasingly pricey homes looked exactly the same – mass produced and bare, something for us to buy into, move on from.

Housing developments still grieve me. Ubiquitous and interchangeable, they are also such an ominously forced form of neighborhood: house colors legislated to a single shade, or choice of similar three, landscaping controlled by the neighborhood association. Even the street names have in recent years been reduced, strangled into intimacy. Moving beyond earlier schemes based on a theme (trees, racetracks), newer developments often choose a single name and cram together, say, a Windsor Court with a Windsor Mews, a Windsor Drive, Road, Avenue, Lane, and Place. A friend tells me how, visiting his mother, having forgotten which Windsor she was living on and all the houses an identical rosy beige, he drove around desperately in her car, pressing the garage-door opener, waiting to see which door would open in welcome.

No wonder we return from these visits "home" dispirited. The developments many of our parents retire into have no connection to childhood for us. Even if our families remain in our hometown, the place is often so drastically altered that our landmarks are as completely obliterated as John Clare's. We are left disoriented, unable to find our way to old haunts. Most of the fields and woods are probably gone anyway, and to see a building or a business in American suburbia that has survived intact a twenty-year or thirty-year lapse is a rarity. It's a tissue-paper world, ripping before our eyes, even more temporary than we are.

Because we've been left so little to rely on, we're forced into self-protective amnesia. If our places change so radically, so quickly, what do the lives we lived in them mean? The rhythm of change and persistence, the balance of past and present, has been warped. We ourselves have been thrown out.

Maybe my persistent yearning for a full-fledged home derives more from my Jewish background than I have allowed. Most American Jews come from irretrievably lost places. We remain half-at-home here, alert enough to pack in a hurry if need be, the ghost of the Holocaust too close for comfort. To not belong, to imagine constantly an elsewhere, becomes a chronic unease. It does not compel, or perhaps even allow, loyalty to one's present place, the making of a solid home. That is the resistance I am trying to overcome. When the landscapes in which we find ourselves are not diffused with *our* meanings, *our* history or community, it is not easy to attach ourselves to them. It cannot be a natural connection, but must be a forged one. It is easier to turn inward from a strange land than to attempt to bridge the gap.

Historically, the physical life of Jews in diaspora, in ghettos, was cramped and oppressive, often literally cut off from the cultures that surrounded and ruled them. In compensation, think some, the temporal dimension of Jews' lives – their history – gained disproportionate importance. "Their spatial existence was always a tenuous and painful reminder of their isolation from the surrounding world", says the critic Stephen Kern, "and was far less important to them than their existence in time. Thus the Wandering Jew is at home only in time".[17] Cultural identity had to be internalized, kept abstract, free of attachment to its physical setting. Yiddish is said to be the only folk language in the world that has no base in nature; its vocabulary is bereft of plants and animals, almost the entire natural world.[18]

Jews have perhaps had a complicated, ambivalent relation to nature from the start. Though natural symbols survive in ritual, Judaism is the religion that by and large defused the tradition of sacred place. It is the religion that imaginatively placed divinity *outside* nature, the religion in which God, instead of existing *as* nature, used the forces of nature as punishment (plagues of locusts, floods). Cox finds it revealing that the Hebrew concept of God "arose in the social context of a nomadic, essentially homeless people".[19] The pagan gods the early Jews set out to overthrow were the numerous place-defined, local nature deities. For Jews, holy places were not crucial because their single God was a spirit who could be worshiped anywhere. "Anywhere" meant that the where of one's life faded in significance. Identity depended on human community and common belief, not on shared location.

That tendency toward placelessness helped define the thinking and writing of numerous twentieth-century artists and intellectuals who remain highly influential. Proust is an interesting literary example, a writer for whom the meaning of places depends entirely on their personal associations. "The places that we have known belong now only to the little world of space on which we map them for our own convenience. None of them was ever more than a thin slice held between the contiguous impressions that composed our life at that time; remembrance for a particular form is but regret for a particular moment, and houses, roads, avenues, are as fugitive, alas, as the years".[20]

His plaint is close to my own on occasion, close to the fact of quickly vanishing landscapes. But for Proust, the implications are more extreme. Says Kern:

> If there is a single illusion that Proust most wanted to dispel it is that life takes place primarily in space. The spaces in which we live close about us and disappear like the waters of the sea after a ship passes through. To look for the essence of life in space is like trying to look for the path of a ship in the water: it only exists as a memory of the flow of its uninterrupted movement in time. The places where we happen to be are ephemeral and fortuitous settings for our life in time, and to try to recapture them is impossible.[21]

Places are ephemeral when they are treated as dispensable, when we are not embraced by their traditions or when the traditions have drained away. Even for the exiled modernist James Joyce, Dublin is what solidly persists when chronological time breaks down in his work and fantasy takes over. Place is the concrete, time the fluid. For most of us in this century, it is the reverse. "Most individuals feel almost naked without their wrist-watches", notes Wilbur Zelinsky, "but how many carry compasses, maps, or field glasses …?"[22] We continuously, unconsciously, transform space into time, say a city is four hours away rather than two hundred miles.

E. V. Walter, a sociologist specializing in the study of place, points to Freud as another figure whose temperamental affiliation with time rather than space has had a crucial influence on our thinking. "Freud moved theory of the mind away from grounded experience and helped to build the couch as a vehicle abstracting patient from place. Despite his own existential recognition of the inner need that yearns for place, Freud's psychology never integrated personal identity with the sense of belonging, and the real power of places".[23] […]

This is our inherited thinking, an essential severance from place true for many of us, not just those historically in diaspora. We have been taught to live consciously in time rather than in place, with our lives divided into well-defined passages. Without the continuity of place, our sense of time is exaggerated, becomes all omnipresent drama. Wendell Berry, too, wishes psychotherapy were more attentive to restoring our connection to places. "The lost identity would find itself by recognizing physical landmarks, by connecting itself responsibly to practical circumstances; it would learn to stay put in the body to which it belongs and in the place to which preference or history or accident has brought it".[24] But that is not, typically, how nowadays we "find" ourselves.

We almost cannot, when the stage sets on which we play out our lives are struck with each act. We are left with only the plot. The where of our immediate past is often unrecognizable, our further past unlocatable. Many of us are unable to trace back our ancestry beyond a generation or two. Even if we can, we have little idea, often, of *what* we've come from, what places and experiences have, unbeknown to us, filtered into our personalities, helped shape our values and temperaments.

A weak sense of the past encourages a weak sense of place. When people are attached to their forebears, they want to remain close to where they lived, continue their traditions, tend their graves, embody their hopes. Many may remain where they were born out of habit or spiritual duty, but the staying itself is conducive to life because the lived-in land then becomes an extension of the self, the family, the group; to endanger the land is to wound one's collective body.

Lacking that connection, as most of us do, how do we come to feel loyal to a place and choose to dwell there? What makes a location *feel* like a place at all? In my own life, transplanted to upstate New York, I have been hunting down stories, discovering what is legible and instructive in my landscape. In thirteen years here, I have found festering wounds beneath fine scenery, but I have found as well a palimpsest of lives by which I might patch together a sense of connection, a poultice for my own placelessness. My place's traditions are not my own; I have had to adopt them. But having a sense of place may, by now, require a continual act of imagination.

Notes

1 John Brinckerhoff Jackson, *Discovering the Vernacular Landscape*, New Haven, Conn.: Yale University Press, 1984, p. 91.
2 Wilbur Zelinsky, *The Cultural Geography of the United States*, Englewood Cliffs, New Jersey: Prentice-Hall, 1973, p. 56.
3 Harvey Cox, "The Restoration of a Sense of Place: A Theological Reflection on the Visual Environment", *Ekistics* 25, 422–3.
4 Samuel Monk, Quoted by David Lowenthal and Hugh C. Prince in "English Landscape Tastes", *Geographical Review* 55, no. 2, 1965, 195.
5 Raymond Williams, *The Country and the City*, Oxford, Engl. and New York: Oxford University Press, 1973, p. 124.
6 Jackson, *Discovering the Vernacular Landscape*, pp. 152–6.
7 Lee Quinby, *Freedom, Foucault, and the Subject of America*, Boston, Mass.: Northeastern University Press, 1991, pp. 147–8.
8 Simone Weil, *The Need for Roots: Prelude to a Declaration of Duties toward Mankind* (1952), trans. Arthur Wills, New York: Harper Colophon Books, 1971, p. 43.
9 John Stilgoe, *Common Landscape of America, 1580–1845*, New Haven, Conn.: Yale University Press, 1982, p. 104; Zelinsky, *The Cultural Geography of the United States*, pp. 47–9.
10 Harvey Cox, *The Secular City*, New York: Macmillan, 1966.
11 Yi-Fu Tuan, "American Space, Chinese Place", *Harper's Magazine*, July 1974, 8.
12 Vance Packard, *A Nation of Strangers*, New York: David McKay, 1972, p. 1.
13 David E. Sopher, "The Landscape of Home: Myth, Experience, Social Meaning", in D. W. Meinig (ed.), *The Interpretation of Ordinary Landscapes*, Oxford: Oxford University Press, 1979, p. 137.
14 James M. Houston, "The Concepts of 'Place' and 'Land' in the Judaeo-Christian Tradition", in David Ley and Marwyn S. Samuels (eds), *Humanistic Geography: Prospects and Problems*, Chicago: Marroufa Press, 1978, p. 226.
15 Eric Dardel, quoted by E. Relph in *Place and Placelessness*, London: Pion, 1976, p. 41.
16 Richard Hugo, *The Triggering Town: Lectures and Essays on Poetry and Writing*, New York: W. W. Norton, 1979, p. 7.
17 Stephen Kern, *The Culture of Time and Space, 1880–1918*, Cambridge, Mass.: Harvard University Press, 1983, p. 51.
18 Maurice Samuel, quoted in Houston, "The Concepts of 'Place' and 'Land'", 228.
19 Cox, *The Secular City*, p. 47.
20 Marcel Proust, quoted by E. Relph in *Place and Placelessness*, London: Pion, p. 144.

21 Kern, *The Culture of Time and Space, 1880–1918*, p. 50.
22 Zelinsky, *The Cultural Geography of the United States*, p. 55.
23 E. V. Walter, *Placeways: A Theory of the Human Environment*, Chapel Hill, N.C.: University of North Carolina Press, 1988, p. 97.
24 Wendell Berry, *The Unsettling of America: Culture and Agriculture*, New York: Avon Books, 1977, p. 11.

The shelter people

In hidden corners of Atlanta and environs, huts for the homeless just seem to spring up. Call it … stealth housing

Bo Emerson (2002)

Nick Hess, the smooth-domed leader of one of the oddest construction crews in Georgia, gathered buckets of nails, bundles of hammers and his battery-powered circular saw last Sunday and hiked under dripping skies to a small grove of hardwoods in a concrete wilderness within view of Midtown's skyscrapers.

Once at the site, Hess, 32, and a half-dozen colleagues went to work, laying a simple concrete block foundation and raising modular walls. These builders, most of them computer geeks, are not skilled with the Skilsaw, but within two hours they were putting the roof on the finished structure. A homeless man who'd been sleeping under plastic tarps was waiting to take possession.

"We do the most affordable housing in the metro area", said Jim Devlin, a 41-year-old Little Five Points resident in an Aussie hat, as he pounded nails. "We build it and give it away".

These are the Mad Housers, a band of volunteers who deal with the problem of homelessness by cutting to the chase: Every Sunday they build houses [*Figs. 83, 84*].

Very small houses.

The base model is only 6 feet wide by 8 feet long, with a ceiling that's 10 feet high at the peak. Cost to the Mad Housers: about $350. Cost to the client: zero.

For someone who's been burrowing in kudzu, sleeping in Hefty bags or hunkering under a highway bridge, 48 square feet of floor space makes a world of difference.

It's a weather tight, insulated miniature home, with roll roofing, a locking front door and a cheery wood stove piping in the corner.

One of their clients is Walt Turner, a 52-year-old auto mechanic and tree service worker, who has added a room to his hut plus space for the portable toilet. "This is the way I came up", says the former farm boy, surveying his cluttered domain a few miles away from Sunday's construction site. "I know about cooking on a wood stove 'cause my mama had to get up every morning and make breakfast on one".

Granted, what the Mad Housers do is at the margins of the law. Their huts, which they give away, are generally sited on property that they don't own. But for Mad Houser Vice President Hess, the choice between doing the right thing and doing the legal thing is a no-brainer. "We've been yelled at before and we'll probably get yelled at again".

Beth McCracken, who is studying to be a social worker at Kennesaw State University, wrote a paper on the Mad Housers for a class on grass-roots movements, and was so impressed she launched a fund-raiser to pay for a new hut. "Technically they try to fly under the radar", says McCracken, 34. "I think they're awesome. They're taking on a cause that's overwhelming – the city can't handle it – and they're helping out, one person at a time".

According to longtime member Frank Jeffers, 59, the original Mad Housers, who first cohered in 1987, were politically provocative. They built huts in "ostentatious places" to raise awareness of the homeless problem.

But quality control was low. The plywood was thin, the huts uninsulated, the windows too big. "They leaked heat like a sieve and they were totally unsecure", says Hess. "It was a good first pass".

Like many of their huts, that group fell apart in the mid-1990s. The Mad Housers regrouped about two years ago, focusing on shelter, not politics.

Today the Mad Housers succeed by thinking inside the box. For example, consider their unique wood stove design, created by Jeffers: It is built of four nested galvanized shop buckets, with a lid and a 2-inch-diameter vent pipe to carry smoke up through the roof. Perforations at the base control air flow. Cost: about $30. (Clients receive instruction in using the cheap stove, and its safety record is good, says volunteer Kurt Haas.)

The low-budget group, composed of activists, software writers and the formerly homeless, works the same way. The Mad Housers operate on a minimum of fuel, efficiently turning income into shelter. Their huts are exactly the length of two sheets of plywood and the width of one and a half, meaning a minimum of cuts per sheet. Classed as "emergency shelter", the huts are intended to finesse housing codes that apply to permanent dwellings.

Sometimes their overhead is so low they bump their noggins. At a recent "build" they used a plastic bottle filled with water for a level, and they were forced to flatten the hut site by digging in the dirt with pointy pieces of wood and their bare hands.

"We need a shovel", says Devlin during a Mad Houser meeting at a Midtown coffee shop. At the meeting they discuss the upcoming Sunday's construction activities and ways to capitalize on National Hunger and Homelessness Awareness Week, which starts Sunday.

They also talk about a van. Hess, a computer programmer at Weather.com, reports that insurance on a "company" van will cost $1,500, the entire Mad Houser bank account. No van, man.

Their profile is low and their donations are low too. Yet support comes from a wide range of folks (including an anonymous donor who communicates only through a Washington lawyer).

Middle school students from Atlanta and Boy Scouts from Lilburn have helped on Mad Houser projects, with funds donated by the Georgia Vietnam Veterans Alliance. A Powder Springs church joined them on a build, and this summer the Furniture Bank of Metro Atlanta donated warehouse space so they could do some of their carpentry inside.

But they've yet to be embraced by the mainstream. Folks in Habitat for Humanity (where starter houses cost $46,000) prefer not to comment on the guerrilla builders. Hess doesn't even want to approach the "big box" retailers such as Home Depot for free plywood. He figures few corporations want to claim charitable deductions to habitual trespassers.

In the meantime, the slumping economy and promises of a cold winter keep business brisk. All two dozen of their huts are full, and there's a waiting list six deep, with requests for huts in places far from downtown Atlanta. (There are potential clients camping in woods around Marietta.)

Some supporters are troubled by the group's underground tactics, but sympathetic to their goals. Phil Greeves of Lilburn says he'd prefer it if the Mad Housers got permission instead of hiding their huts, but he acknowledges that in most cases they'd be denied.

Adam, Greeves' son, built a hut two years ago to fulfill the community service requirement for his Eagle Scout badge. The project changed their opinions about the homeless. "These were not unproductive people", says the father. "They were working Monday to Friday, and on the weekends they'd come out and help with the house".

On the ethics of madhousing, Bill Bolling, founder of the Atlanta Community Food Bank, comments, "I would say you ask forgiveness instead of permission in this case. This is a small legal question vs. a big social issue".

Mad Houser Peter Richards, a teacher at Paideia School, sums up the question this way: "In America", he says, "you have two choices if you're homeless: charity or trespass".

The city hasn't prosecuted any Mad Housers in recent memory, says Sandra Walker, spokeswoman for Atlanta Mayor Shirley Franklin, though the city has asked that some structures be removed. "It's an unfortunate situation", says Walker. "It's what [the Mad Housers] feel they have to do, but certainly we have to respect the right of the property owners, and follow the laws".

The Mad Housers will always remove huts if asked by the property owner, says Haas. The group tracks ownership by checking plats, and on at least one occasion disassembled a village when the property changed hands. It will also take down a hut if a resident causes a problem for the neighborhood.

Haas says he doesn't know whether the huts pose a liability risk for landowners, but adds, "In general the sites where there is a clear property owner, the property owner is tacitly aware they [the huts] are there".

Many "hutters" stay a short while, saving enough money to get an apartment or subsidized housing, at which point they turn their huts over to the next in line. Others stay longer. "This reminds me of Boy Scouts", says Joe, a Ghanaian expatriate who has been in his rustic shelter for five years.

If constructing stealth housing is a trend, it's a quiet one. Jim Reid, a perennial candidate for public office in San Francisco, has designed a 10-by-10 house to be mass-produced for that city's homeless, but none is currently in use, perhaps because of the $12,000 price tag.

A similar movement rose and fell in Chicago, and a group in Canada called the Peterborough Collective is trying to raise interest in similar shelters. "It can snowball, even if it's not a big ball", says Richard Van Slyke, an independent videographer who has been taping a documentary about the Mad Housers for four months.

One thing that Van Slyke and others notice about the group is that it is motivated by a desire to do the right thing, even though few of the Housers seem to connect that desire with a religious affiliation.

Salma Abdulrahman, a telecommunications software programmer, says her urge to volunteer with the group doesn't grow out of her Muslim faith as much as from her basic character.

"We're all human beings, we're all people, when you come down to it", says the 24-year-old. "I'd be doing this if I were any religion. It's just part of my personality".

On a drizzly, mackerel-clouded Sunday at another hut site, Abdulrahman is demonstrating her philosophy by hauling wheelbarrows full of firewood from hut to hut, while Jeffers wields a chain saw.

This small village of huts is located on the bones of a ruined amusement park called Funtown. Turman once visited Funtown as a child, when school buses brought a pack of teenagers up from his Heard County high school. Now he lives next to the defunct merry-go-round, which is reduced to a weed-cracked concrete pad.

Here residents carry their water and heat with wood. They grow vegetables and make their own charcoal under Joe's guidance. Turman powers his portable TV with a 12-volt car battery.

"We're just trying to get society back into some kind of balance", says Jeffers, pausing for some cowboy coffee perking on a galvanized drum fire. "Some people have got so much more and other people don't have any heat".

What they provide, says Hess, is hope and dignity, along with a dry place to sleep. "Once you give people a certain amount of hope", he says, "civilization begins there".

Funtown: a third world village in the middle of the city

The Ferris wheel was hauled off long ago. The bumper cars are gone. Algae grows in the empty swimming pool and the concession stands tilt in slow-motion collapse.

Funtown, an amusement park that once drew revelers from around the metro area, is a ruin. But there is new life on Funtown's grave.

In this wild, secluded corner of Southwest Atlanta, hidden among the scrub mimosa that push up through Funtown's asphalt walkways and parking lots, is a village of about 12 tiny huts, built by the Mad Housers over the last 10 years.

While some residents of the village have gone on to less primitive housing, others find themselves happy with this simple life: carrying water, cutting wood for their durable homemade woodstoves, and growing vegetables.

Walking on the nearby streets was scary for Barbara Ann Triplett, who lived here for a few months, but once inside the village she felt safe. "Every one of them [the other residents] was there to protect me", she said.

Another resident from the early days of the village said the mosquitoes and ants were a problem, not to mention the scary isolation and the cold weather (this was before the huts were insulated), "but other than that it was fine", she adds with a smile.

This resident left before the gen-car arrived. The gen-car changed everything.

Always looking for ways to humanize the environment for the residents of their huts, the Mad Housers, led by president Frank Jeffers, figured out a way to turn a junked 1985 Mercury Capri into light and hot water.

Jeffers, whose group builds emergency shelters for the homeless, calls it the "co-generation car" – gen-car for short. Mad Houser Bill Callison bought it for $200 (it already had 250,000 miles on it), then the transmission burned out. He had it towed to the site. Callison and Jeffers began upgrading the Capri, and eventually had it outfitted with two 90-amp alternators and an array of six golf-cart batteries in the trunk. Nearby "hutters" connected themselves to a home-made electrical grid, and, voilà, there was 12-volt light.

By running the car for a few hours three times a week, the residents could recharge the battery array enough to run lights and portable television sets for the seven hutters who were interested.

Jeffers also retro-fitted the car's cooling system, running hot water from the water pump to a coil of copper tubing in a nearby 50-gallon drum. Water inside the drum was heated through this primitive heat exchange, while water from the coil was returned to the car's radiator. Residents had hot water for dishes and bathing.

"For less than $10 a week in gasoline we had power and hot water for about seven people", says Callison.

Unfortunately the gen-car is no more. After five years supplying the needs of the village, it died last spring. Still, says Callison, "that was the best $200 I ever spent".

Edgar Reitz's *Heimat*

Barbara Miller Lane (2006)

The television series called *Heimat: a German Chronicle* was directed by Edgar Reitz and screened on German television over a period of eleven weeks in September and October of 1984. It was also shown in movie theaters. Ultimately regarded as a classic of modern film, *Heimat* initially encountered widespread adverse criticism because of its apparently value-free representation of everyday life in Nazi Germany. The scope and significance of the series is, however, much broader than this.

Reitz's *Heimat* (home, homeland) chronicles the life of two German families in the Rhineland from 1919 to 1982 (in the imaginary farming village of Schabbach, in the real province of Hunsrück – the latter the site of Reitz's own youth). The film series portrays the life of three generations of "little people". For many of his actors, Reitz employed local people from the Hunsrück area and directed them brilliantly.

Heimat has many themes. One is regionalism versus nationalism: how do the people who live in a small town in a relatively remote village identify with the national population, if they do? And how do they view the world outside the nation? Another is memory: how do people remember? Through personal memory, stories, photographs, films? Each seems to have its role. Glassisch Karl, the frequent narrator and village "idiot", collects family and village photographs and uses them to introduce each new sequence. Eduard, the brother of Paul Simon, is an early photographer, who records each family and village event with his big camera. Several sequences underline the propaganda uses of photography and film under the Nazis. The photography switches back and forth between black and white and color, and the rationale is not always clear. The viewer is led, through all this, constantly to question the veracity of the photograph or film, and thus of memory itself. The series is also about leaving home and coming back.

Heimat focuses on the lives of the Simon and Wiegand families, especially on Paul Simon, son of the village blacksmith, and Maria Wiegand, daughter of the town's wealthiest farmer. Maria and Paul marry and have two children (Anton and Ernst). Paul proves to be a *Weggeher*, a "departer"– he leaves the town and his family suddenly in 1927. We see him walking away along the country road with fields on both sides, the only road to the remote country town. Maria remains in Schabbach throughout the entire period. But Paul and Maria, their families and the villagers themselves are transformed by their experiences of the twentieth century [*Fig. 85*].

The first episode begins with Paul Simon's return from the Western Front in 1919. He has been a French prisoner of war. Paul returns to the village eagerly, ready to take up a role in his father's smithy. But already his encounters during the war with foreign places and peoples, and with modern technology, have filled him with *Fernweh*, "The Call of Far-Away Places". He becomes obsessed with trying to build a radio, and when he succeeds, he gathers the villagers together for a picnic at a nearby ruined castle. Here he is able to broadcast for them a Viennese concert by world-famous tenor Leo Slezak, performing on radio for the first time. Later, a chance airplane ride with an American flyer reinforces his longing for the outside world. He leaves the town and his family without explanation and goes to America, where he eventually founds a nationally successful electric company. He attempts to return to Schabbach in 1939 but is turned away by Nazi officials. He succeeds in returning only in 1947.

In the interim, the Simons, Wiegands and other villagers go to other parts of Germany and return, marry, take lovers (Maria's is part Jewish, and they have a child, Hermann). The children grow up. Some of the villagers remain aloof from the Nazi Party (especially Paul's mother, Katharina); others join; a few become powerful within it. Some are implicated in the Holocaust, but the film does not emphasize this. The men fight in the war – as pilots, propaganda officers, infantry soldiers – and experience the rapidity and immediacy of modern communications. Many also witness the terrible destruction of bombing and bombardment. But after the end of the war, the occupying Americans are greatly liked and admired; they represent "the big world" to some of the Schabbach people.

When Paul returns in 1947, he is a rich and portly American with a Stetson hat, a big car, a Negro chauffeur. The road to Schabbach is now lined with telephone and electric lines. Paul wants to help the villagers and offers chocolate bars, powdered milk, baby food, groceries of all kinds. He admits to having been terribly homesick. He attempts a reconciliation with Maria, but she rejects him. He shows that he has almost no understanding of the war, or of what local people have experienced. ("I never thought my boys would be in the war", he says, and "I don't understand Germany any more".) He leaves, dejected, before his mother's funeral.

Paul is able to help his son Anton establish an optics factory, and to help Maria's illegitimate son Hermann (another *Weggeher*) become a composer of avant garde electronic music. But he cannot return "home": he can never revisit the Schabbach of his youth. He establishes foundations in Germany and the United States to create "homes for the homeless of all the world". One of these is his family house in Schabbach.

Reitz has directed sequels to the first film series: *Zweite Heimat*, 1992, which chronicles the life of Hermann in the 1960s, and *Heimat 3*, 2004, which traces Hermann's life from 1989 to 2000. These sequels have received great critical acclaim.

Figure 81
St Petersburg communal
apartment, plan.

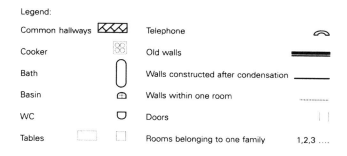

Legend:

Common hallways		Telephone	
Cooker		Old walls	
Bath		Walls constructed after condensation	
Basin		Walls within one room	
WC		Doors	
Tables		Rooms belonging to one family	1,2,3 ....

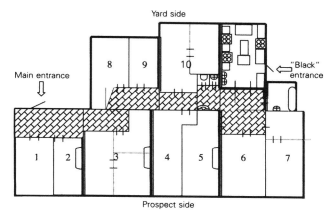

Figure 82
St Petersburg communal
apartment, view of
communal kitchen.

Figure 83 Construction of Mad Houser hut, Atlanta, Georgia, *c*. 2002.

Figure 84 Atlanta, Georgia: Walter Turner sits in front of his dwelling, one of several huts in a Mad Houser community, 3 November 2003.

Figure 85
Scenes in the life of Paul Simon, from
Heimat, a German Chronicle, 1984 television
series directed by Edgar Reitz.

Text source credits

Bachelard, Gaston, "The Oneiric House", in Joan Ockman (ed.), *Architecture Culture 1943–1968: A Documentary Anthology,* New York: Rizzoli, 1993, pp. 110–3, from a chapter titled "The Childhood House and the Oneiric House", in Bachelard, *La Terre et les reveries du repos* (*The Earth and the Reveries of Rest*), Paris: J. Corti, 1948, pp. 106–12, trans. Joan Ockman.

Banham, Reyner, "A Home is Not a House", in Joan Ockman (ed.), *Architecture Culture 1943–1968, A Documentary Anthology*, New York: Rizzoli, 1993, pp. 370–8. Originally published in *Art in America*, April 1965, Brant Publications, Inc.

Beckham, Sue Bridwell, "The American Front Porch: Women's Liminal Space", in Marilyn Ferris Motz and Pat Browne (eds), *Making the American Home: Middle-Class Women and Domestic Material Culture, 1840–1940*, Bowling Green, Ohio: Bowling Green State University Popular Press, 1988, pp. 69–89. ©The University of Wisconsin Press. Reprinted by permission.

Blackmar, Elizabeth, "The Social Meanings of Housing, 1800–1840", in *Manhattan for Rent, 1785–1850*, Ithaca, N.Y., and London: Cornell University Press, 1989, pp. 126–38, 313–6. Copyright ©1989 Cornell University Press. Reprinted by permission.

Burgess, Anthony, *A Clockwork Orange*, New York: W. W. Norton, (1962) 1983, pp. 1–2, 17–24, 31–4. Copyright ©1962, 1989, renewed 1990 by Anthony Burgess. Used by permission of W. W. Norton and Company, Inc. Reprinted by permission of the Random House Group Ltd.

Clarke, Alison J., "The Aesthetics of Social Aspiration", in Daniel Miller (ed.), *Home Possessions: Material Culture Behind Closed Doors*, Oxford and New York: Berg, 2001, pp. 25–43.

Colomina, Beatriz, "The Split Wall: Domestic Voyeurism", in Colomina (ed.), *Sexuality and Space*, New York: Princeton Architectural Press, 1992, pp. 73–128, 74–86. Used by permission of the author and publisher.

Cromley, Elizabeth Collins, *Alone Together: A History of New York's Early Apartments*, Ithaca, N.Y., and London: Cornell University Press, 1990, pp. 38–50, 62–76, 104–10, 217–27. Copyright ©1990 Cornell University Press. Used by permission of Cornell University Press.

Daunton, M. J., "Public Place and Private Space: The Victorian City and the Working-Class Household", in Derek Fraser and Anthony Sutcliffe (eds), *The Pursuit of Urban History*, London: Edward Arnold, 1983, pp. 212–33. Copyright ©1983 by Edward Arnold. Reproduced by permission of the author and Edward Arnold.

Davey, Peter, "S.T.E.R.N. Work", *Architectural Review* 181, April 1987, 87–9.

Douglas, Mary, "The Idea of a Home: A Kind of Space", in Arien Mack (ed.), *Home: A Place in the World*, New York: New York University Press, 1993, pp. 261–81.

Downing, Andrew Jackson, "What a Farm-house Should Be", in *The Architecture of Country Houses: Designs for Cottages, Farm Houses, and Villas*, New York: D. Appleton, 1850, pp. 135–141.

Earley, Tony, "The Hallway", in *Somehow Form a Family*, Chapel Hill, N.C.: Algonquin Books of Chapel Hill, 2001, pp. 19–49. Reprinted by permission of Algonquin Books of Chapel Hill.

Egelius, Mats, "The Byker Wall", in *Ralph Erskine, Architect*, Stockholm: Byggförlaget, 1990, pp. 148–60.

Emerson, Bo, "The Shelter People: In Hidden Corners of Atlanta and Environs, Huts for the Homeless Just Seem to Spring Up. Call It … Stealth Housing", *Atlanta Journal-Constitution*, 16 October 2002.

Freeman, Dawni, "Home and Work: The Use of Space in a Nebraska Farmhouse", unpublished paper, Bryn Mawr College, May 2003.

Fuerst, J. S., "High-rise Living: What Tenants Say", *Journal of Housing* 42, 3, May–June 1985, 88–90.

Goldstein, Carolyn M., *Do It Yourself: Home Improvement in 20th Century America*, New York: Princeton Architectural Press, 1998.

Gropius, Walter, "Program for the Founding of a General Housing-Construction Company Following Artistically Uniform Principles", 1910, in Hans Maria Wingler (ed.) *The Bauhaus: Weimar – Dessau – Berlin – Chicago*, Cambridge, Mass.: MIT Press, 1969, pp. 20–1.

Groth, Paul, *Living Downtown: The History of Residential Hotels in the United States*, Berkeley and Los Angeles: University of California Press, 1994, pp. 101–9. Copyright © 1994.

Heidegger, Martin, "Building, Dwelling, Thinking", in *Poetry, Language, Thought*, trans. Albert Hofstadter, New York: Harper and Row, pp. 143–61 ("Bauen Wohnen Denken", from Heidegger, *Vorträge und Aufsätze*, Pfullingen: G. Neske, [1954] 1959). Reprinted by permission of HarperCollins Publishers.

Henderson, Susan R., "A Revolution in the Woman's Sphere: Grete Lihotzky and the Frankfurt Kitchen", in Debra Coleman *et al.* (eds), *Architecture and Feminism*, New York: Princeton Architectural Press, 1996, pp. 221–53.

Hepworth, Mike, "Privacy, Security and Respectability: The Ideal Victorian Home", part 1, in Tony Chapman and Jenny Hockey (eds), *Ideal Homes? Social Change and Domestic Life*, New York: Routledge, 1999.

—— "Homes and Gardens: the Rural Idyll", part 2 of "Privacy, Security and Respectability: The Ideal Victorian Home: Homes and Gardens", in Tony Chapman and Jenny Hockey (eds), *Ideal Homes? Social Change and Domestic Life*, New York: Routledge, 1999.

Herbert, Gilbert, *The Dream of the Factory Made House: Walter Gropius and Konrad Wachsmann*, Cambridge, Mass.: MIT, 1984, pp. 3–11, 39–57.

hooks, bell, "homeplace: a site of resistance", in *yearning: race, gender and cultural politics*, Boston: South End Press, 1990, pp. 41–9, 232–3.

Hubka, Thomas C., "Pattern in Building and Farming", in *Big House, Little House, Back House, Barn: The Connected Farm Buildings of New England*, Hanover and London: University Press of New England, 2004 (1984), pp. 113–9, 209. © 1984 by Trustees of Dartmouth College. Reprinted by permission of University Press of New England, Hanover, NH.

Isenstadt, Sandy, "The Rise and Fall of the Picture Window", *Harvard Design Magazine*, Fall 1998, 27–33.

Jackson, John Brinckerhoff, "The Mobile Home on the Range", in *A Sense of Place, a Sense of Time*, New Haven, Conn.: Yale University Press, 1994, pp. 53–67. Copyright © by Yale University Press.

Kaiser, Harvey, *Great Camps of the Adirondacks*, Boston: David R. Godine, 1982. Reprinted by permission of David R. Godine, Publisher, Inc. Copyright © 1982 by Harvey Kaiser.

Keats, John, *The Crack in the Picture Window*, Boston, Mass.: Houghton Mifflin Company; Cambridge, Mass.: The Riverside Press, 1956, selections from third printing of 1957, pp. 7–10, 39–43, 49–50, 58–61, 78–81. Copyright © 1956, and renewed 1984 by John C. Keats. Reprinted by permission of Houghton Mifflin Company. All rights reserved.

Kerr, Robert, *The Gentleman's House (or, How to Plan English Residences)*, London: J. Murray, 1864, 1871 (Johnson Reprint, 1972) pp. 63–141.

Lane, Barbara Miller, "Modern Architecture and Politics in Germany, 1918–1945", English original of "Die Moderne und die Politik in Deutschland zwischen 1918 und 1945", in Vittorio Magnago Lampugnani and Romana Schneider (eds), *Expressionismus und neue Sachlichkeit*, Deutsches Architekturmuseum, 1994, pp. 224–49.

—— "The Home as a Work of Art", selections on Finland and Sweden, in Lane, *National Romanticism and Modern Architecture in Germany and the Scandinavian Countries*, Cambridge and New York: Cambridge University Press, 2000, pp. 79–162. Reproduced with permission of the author and publisher.

—— "Edgar Reitz's *Heimat*", commentary on *Heimat, eine deutsche Chronik*, television series 1984, fifteen and a half hours. With English subtitles: Facets Multimedia, Chicago, Illinois: video 1987, 1996; DVD 2005.

Le Corbusier, "The Center of Paris", in *The City of Tomorrow*, Cambridge, Mass.: MIT Press, 1971, from *Urbanisme*, Paris, Editions Crés, 1924, trans. Frederick Etchells, 1929, republished in facsimile in 1947, pp. 275–88. Copyright © FLC/ADAGP. Paris, and DACS, London, 2005, trans. © MIT Press.

Leland, John, "A Prefab Utopia – What Happens When a Furniture Company Builds a Community", *New York Times Magazine*, 1 December 2002, 92–6.

Loeb, Adina, "Excavation and Reconstruction: An Oral Archaeology of the deLemos Home", unpublished paper, Bryn Mawr College, May 2003.

Marcus, Sharon, "Seeing through Paris", in *Apartment Stories: City and Home in Nineteenth Century Paris and London*, Berkeley: University of California Press, 1999, pp. 17–29, 32–8, 42–3, 205–18. Copyright © 1999.

Maynard, William Barksdale, "Thoreau's House at Walden", *Art Bulletin* 81, 2, June 1999, 303–25. Used by permission of the author and publisher.

McCamant, Kathryn and Charles Durrett, with Ellen Hertzman, "How Cohousing Works: The Trudeslund Community", in *Cohousing: A Contemporary Approach to Housing Ourselves*, Berkeley: Ten Speed Press, (1988) 1994, pp. 21–35.

Miner, Curtis, "Picture Window Paradise", *Pennsylvania Heritage* 28, 2, Spring 2002, 12–21.

Olsen, Donald J., *The City as a Work of Art: London, Paris, Vienna*, New Haven, Conn., and London: Yale University Press, 1986, pp. 125–31. Copyright © 1986 by Yale University Press.

Pevsner, Nikolaus, *An Outline of European Architecture*, Middlesex: Penguin Books, Ltd, 1943, 7th edn 1968, "Introduction", pp. 15–17. Reproduced by permission of Penguin Books Ltd.

Pohlig Builders, Harriton Farm, Villanova, 2001, advertising brochure.

Popenoe, David, "Vällingby", in *The Suburban Environment: Sweden and the United States*, Chicago: University of Chicago Press, 1977, pp. 52–62, 85–8, 107–11.

Rapoport, Amos, *House Form and Culture*, Englewood Cliffs, N.J.: Prentice Hall, 1969, pp. 1–9, 130–4. Copyright © 1969. Adapted by permission of Pearson Education, Inc., Upper Saddle River, N.J.

Ravetz, Alison with Richard Turkington, "The High-Rise Estate", in *The Place of Home: English Domestic Environments 1914–2000*, London: Spon, 1995, pp. 51–60.

—— "Self-Help Housing", in *The Place of Home: English Domestic Environments 1914–2000*, London: Spon, 1995, pp. 109–18, 225–36.

Read, Alice Gray, "Making a Home in a Philadelphia Neighborhood", in Camille Wells (ed.), *Perspectives in Vernacular Architecture*, vol. 2, Columbia: University of Missouri Press, 1986, pp. 192–9. Reprinted by permission of The University of Missouri Press. Copyright © 1986 by the Curators of the University of Missouri.

Schoenauer, Norbert, "Residential Conversions", in *6,000 Years of Housing*, revised and expanded edition, New York: W. W. Norton and Company, 2000, pp. 466–8. Copyright © 2000, 1992, 1981 by Norbert Schoenauer. Used by permission of W. W. Norton and Company, Inc.

Sidlauskas, Susan, "Degas and the Sexuality of the *Interior*", in *Body, Place, and Self in Nineteenth-Century Painting*, Cambridge and New York: Cambridge University Press, 2000, pp. 20–60, 161–72. Copyright © 2000, Cambridge University Press. Reproduced by permission of the author and publisher.

Smiley, David, "Making the Modified Modern", *Perspecta* 32, 2001, 40–54.

Smithson, Alison and Peter, *Urban Structuring*, London: Studio Vista, and New York: Reinhold, 1967, pp. 21–8.

Spencer-Wood, Suzanne M., "The World Their Household: Changing Meanings of the Domestic Sphere in the Nineteenth Century", Chapter 10 in Penelope Allison (ed.), *The Archaeology of Household Activities: Dwelling in the Past*, London and New York: Routledge, 1999, pp. 162–89. Used by permission of the author and publisher.

Tall, Deborah, "Dwelling: making peace with space and place", in Wes Jackson and William Vitek (eds), *Rooted in the Land: Essays on Community and Place*, Yale University Press, 1996, pp. 104–12.

Teyssot, Georges, "The American Lawn: Surface of Everyday Life", in Teyssot (ed.), *The American Lawn*, New York: Princeton Architectural Press, 1999, pp. 21–2, 24–6, 37–8.

Tuan, Yi-Fu, "Architectural Space and Awareness", in Tuan, *Space and Place: The Perspective of Experience*, Minneapolis: University of Minnesota Press, (1977) 2001, pp. 101–17, 218–20.

—— "Attachment to Homeland", in Tuan, *Space and Place: The Perspective of Experience*, Minneapolis: University of Minnesota Press, 1977, pp. 149–60, 222–3.

Turner, John, "Squatter Settlement: an Architecture that Works", *Architectural Design*, August 1968, 355–61. Reproduced by permission of John Wiley & Sons Limited.

Utekhin, Ilya, "Filling Dwelling Place with History: Communal Apartments in St. Petersburg", in John J. Czaplicka and Blair A. Ruble (eds) *Composing Urban History and the Constitution of Civic Identities*, Washington, D.C.: The Johns Hopkins

University Press, 2003, pp. 86–109. © 2003 by the Woodrow Wilson International Center for Scholars. Reprinted with permission of The Johns Hopkins University Press.

Wallis, Allan D., "Mobile Homes: Form, Meaning, and Function", in Wallis, *Wheel Estate: The Rise and Decline of Mobile Homes*, Washington, D.C.: The Johns Hopkins University Press, 1997, pp. 125–65: 133, 136, 139–43, 149, 156–65. © 1991 Oxford University Press, Inc. Used by permission.

Wright, Frank Lloyd, "Building the New House", in *The Natural House*, New York: Horizon Press, 1954, pp. 37–47. Copyright © 1954 The Frank Lloyd Wright Foundation, Taliesin West, Scottsdale, Ariz.

Zola, Émile, *L'Assommoir (The Dram Shop)* (Paris, 1876), tr. and ed. by Robin Buss, London: Penguin Books, 2000, selections from chapters 1, 2, 4, 5, 10. Reproduced by permission of Penguin Books Ltd.

Illustration source credits

Albertina, Graphische Sammlung, Vienna: 10, 11
Arcaid, Kingston upon Thames: 4
Architectural Forum: 52
Architectural Record, 11 (July 1901): 15
Artists Rights Society (ARS) New York/ADAGP, Paris/FLC, copyright: 64
Black & Decker Corporation: 63
Calzarette, Rita: 51
Cameron, Robert: 6
Carpentry and Building Magazine, New York, 1897: 28, 29
Chamberlin, Powell and Bon: 4
Christopher Wood Gallery, London: 23
Cohen, Jeffrey A.: 79
Country Life, 1968, and IPC Media: 25
Downing, Andrew Jackson, *The Architecture of Country Houses*, New York: D. Appleton, 1850: 32
English Heritage, National Monuments Record: 24
Ernst May und das neue Frankfurt, 1925-1930, Frankfurt am Main, 1986-7: 44, 45, 46
Erskine Tovatt, Architects and Planners: 60, 61
Farm Security Administration Collection, Library of Congress: 16
Gerasimova, Katerina, "Public Privacy in the Soviet Communal Apartment," in David Crowley and Susan E. Reid (eds), *Socialist Spaces*, New York: Berg: 81
Hall, Peter, *Cities of Tomorrow*, Oxford: Blackwell, 2002: 68, 69
Henderson, Susan R.: 43
Homes of American Authors, New York: Putnam, 1853: 33
House Beautiful, reprinted by permission of *House Beautiful*, copyright January 1950, and Hearst Communications: all rights reserved: 55
Journal of the Society of Architectural Historians, 34, 1 (March 1975): 2
Kaiser, Harvey: 37, 38, 39
Keats, John, *The Crack in the Picture Window*, Boston, MA: Houghton Mifflin Co., and Cambridge, MA: The Riverside Press, 1956: 48, 49
Kerr, Robert, *The Gentleman's House*, London: Murray, 1864: 26
Koppelmann, Stefan: 59
Lane, Barbara Miller, 3, 27, 34, 35, 42, 47, 54, 56, 57, 70, 71, 78
Larsson, Carl, *Ett hem*, Stockholm: Bonnier, 1899: 36
Loeb, Adina: 12, 13
Lutyens, E. L., *Houses and Gardens by E. L. Lutyens*, London, 1912: 41

McCamant, Kathryn, and Charles Durrett: 72, 73

McDougal, Stuart Y.: 66, 67

Musées de la Ville de Paris: 19

Museum of the City of New York: 14

Muthesius, Stefan: 65

New York Times, 1949: 53

The New Yorker: 7

Philadelphia Museum of Art, The Henry McIlhenny Collection: 31

Photofest, Inc., New York: 21, 22

Read, Alice Gray: 62

Reitz, Edgar, Filmproduktionen: 85

Rotkin, Charles E., *Europe: An Aerial Close-up*, Philadelphia: Lippencott, 1962: 1

S.T.E.R.N., Berlin: 58, 59

Schoenauer, Norbert, *6000 Years of Housing*, rev. and expanded ed., copyright 2000, used by permission of W. W. Norton & Co., Inc.: 80

Sears Roebuck Modern Homes, New York, 1908: 30

Silk, Monira Al-Haroun: 83, 84

SKIL Power Tools: 63

State Museum of Pennsylvania, the Pennsylvania Historical Museum, and Levittown, PA Public Library: 50

Texier, Edmund, *Tableau de Paris*, Paris, 1852: 20

Thiede, Klaus, *Deutsche Bauernhäuser*, Königstein im Taunus: Langewiesche, 1937: 8

Tunbjörk, Lars: 74

University Press of New England, Thomas C. Hubka, *Big House, Little House, Back House, Barn*, copyright 2004, used with permission: 40

Utekhin, Ilya: 82

Von Eckardt, Wolf, *The Challenge of Megalopolis*, New York: Macmillan, 1964: 5

Wagner-Rieger, Renate (ed.), *Die Wiener Ringstrasse*, Wiesbaden, Franz Steiner, 1976: 17, 18

Wallis, Allan: 75, 76, 77

Bibliography

Ábalos, Iñaki. *The Good Life: A Guided Visit to the Houses of Modernity*. Barcelona: Editorial Gustavo Gili, 2001.

Albrecht, Donald (ed.), *World War II and the American Dream*, Washington, D.C.: National Building Museum and Cambridge, Mass.: MIT Press, 1995.

Alexander, Christopher, *Notes on the Synthesis of Form*, Cambridge, Mass.: Harvard University Press, 1964.

Allan, Graham and Graham Crow (eds), *Home and Family: Creating the Domestic Sphere*, Basingstoke: Macmillan, 1989.

Allison, Penelope (ed.), *The Archaeology of Household Activities: Dwelling in the Past*, London and New York: Routledge, 1999.

Appadurai, A. (ed.), *The Social Life of Things: Commodities in Cultural Perspective*, Cambridge and New York: Cambridge University Press, 1986.

Applegate, Celia, *A Nation of Provincials: The German Idea of Heimat,* Berkeley, Calif.: University of California Press, 1990.

Archigram: ouvrage publié à l'occasion de l'exposition « Archigram » présentée du 29 juin au 29 août 1994 dans la Galerie Nord, Centre national d'art et de culture, Georges Pompidou, Paris: Editions du Centre Georges Pompidou: Diffusion, Seuil, 1994.

Arias, Ernesto G. (ed.), *The Meaning and Use of Housing: International Perspectives, Approaches and their Applications*, Aldershot: Avebury, 1993.

Ariès, Philippe, *Centuries of Childhood: A Social History of Family Life*, New York: Knopf, 1962.

Ariès, Philippe and Georges Duby (eds), *A History of Private Life*, 5 vols., Cambridge, Mass.: Belknap Press of Harvard University Press, 1987–1991.

Arnold, Dana and Andrew Ballantyne (eds), *Architecture as Experience: Radical Change in Spatial Practice*, London: Routledge, 2003.

Bachelard, Gaston, *The Poetics of Space*, trans. Maria Jolas, Boston: Beacon Press, 1958.

Bailin, Miriam, *The Sickroom in Victorian Fiction: The Art of Being Ill*, Cambridge, Engl. and New York: Cambridge University Press, 1994.

Barbey, G., "Spatial Analyisis and the Experience of Time: Identifying the Dimensions of Home", in Ernesto G. Arias (ed.), *The Meaning and Use of Housing: International Perspectives, Approaches and their Applications*, Aldershot: Avebury, 1993.

Barkin, Kenneth, "Heimat: Eine deutsche Chronik", *American Historical Review* 96, no. 4, October 1991, 1123–6.

Barley, M. W., *The English Farmhouse and Cottage*, London: Routledge and Kegan Paul, 1961.

Bartram, Michael, *The Pre-Raphelite Camera*, London: Weidenfeld, 1985.

Baumgartner, M. P., *The Moral Order of a Suburb*, Oxford and New York: Oxford University Press, 1988.

Baxandall, Rosalyn and Elizabeth Ewen, *Picture Windows: How the Suburbs Happened*, New York: Basic Books, 2000.

Beecher, Catherine E., *Treatise on Domestic Economy*, New York: J. B. Ford, 1869.

Beecher, Catherine E. and Harriet Beecher Stowe, *The American Woman's Home, or Principles of Domestic Science*, New York: J. B. Ford, 1869.

Benjamin, Walter, "Paris, Capital of the Nineteenth Century", in *Reflections*, trans. Edmund Jephcott, New York: Schocken Books, 1986.

Berry, Wendell, *The Unsettling of America: Culture and Agriculture*, New York: Avon Books, 1977.

Bingaman, Amy, Lise Sanders and Rebecca Zorach (eds), *Embodied Utopias: Gender, Social Change, and the Modern Metropolis*, London and New York: Routledge, 2002.

Birdwell-Pheasant, Donna and Denise Lawrence-Zúñiga (eds), *House Life: Space, Place, and Family in Europe*, Oxford and New York: Berg, 1999.

Blackmar, Elizabeth, *Manhattan for Rent, 1785–1850*, Ithaca: Cornell University Press, 1989.

Blau, Eve, *The Architecture of Red Vienna, 1919–1934*, Cambridge, Mass.: MIT Press, 1999.

Bloom, Nicholas D., *Suburban Alchemy: 1960s New Towns and the Transformation of the American Dream*, Columbus: Ohio State University Press, 2001.

Bloomer, Kent C. and Charles W. Moore, *Body, Memory, and Architecture*. New Haven, Conn.: Yale University Press, 1977.

Blueprints for Modern Living: History and Legacy of the Case Study Houses, Los Angeles: Museum of Contemporary Art, 1989.

Booth, Chris, Jane Darke and Susan Yeandle (eds), *Changing Places: Women's Lives in the City*, London: P. Chapman, 1996.

Bormann, F. Herbert, et al. (eds), *Redesigning the American Lawn: A Search for Environmental Harmony*, New Haven, Conn.: Yale University Press, 1993.

Boudon, Philippe, *Lived-in Architecture: Le Corbusier's Pessac Revisited*, Cambridge, Mass.: MIT Press, 1972.

Bourdieu, Pierre, "The Kabyle House: or, the world reversed", first published in 1970 ("La Maison Kabyle ou le monde renversé"), in Jean Pouillon and Pierre Maranda (eds), *Échanges et communications. Mélanges offerts à Claude Lévi Strauss à l'occasion de son 60e anniversaire*, The Hague: Mouton, 1970, pp. 739–58.

—— *Distinction: A Social Critique on the Judgment of Taste*, London: Routledge, 1979.

Boym, Svetlana, *Common Places: Mythologies of Everyday Life in Russia*, Cambridge, Mass.: Harvard University Press, 1994.

—— "The Archeology of Banality: The Soviet Home", in Henry Schwarz and Richard Dienst (eds), *Reading the Shape of the World: Toward an International Cultural Studies*, Boulder, Colo.: Westview Press, 1996, pp. 111–34.

Bratt, Rachel G., Chester Hartman and Ann Meyerson (eds), *Critical Perspectives on Housing*, Philadelphia: Temple University Press, 1986.

Briggs, Asa, *Victorian Things*, Harmondsworth: Penguin, 1990.

Bullock, Nicholas, "Housing in Frankfurt 1925 to 1931 and the New Wohnkultur", *Architectural Review* 162, 1976, 335–42.

—— "First the Kitchen – then the Façade", *AA Files* 6, 1984, 59–67.

—— *Building the Post-war World: Modern Architecture and Reconstruction in Britain*, London and New York: Routledge, 2002.

Bullock, Nicholas and James Read, *The Movement for Housing Reform in Germany and France, 1840–1914*, Cambridge and New York: Cambridge University Press, 1985.

Burgess, Anthony, *A Clockwork Orange*, New York: W. W. Norton, (1963) 1987.

Burnett, John, *A Social History of Housing 1815–1970*, London: Eyre Methuen, 1980.

Cairns, Stephen, *Drift: Migrancy and Architecture*, London and New York: Routledge, 2004.

Calhoun, Craig (ed.), *Habermas and the Public Sphere*, Cambridge, Mass.: MIT Press, 1992.

Camesasca, Ettore, *History of the House,* London: Collins, 1971 (originally Milan, 1968).

Caminos, Horacio, John F. C. Turner and John A. Steffian, *Urban Dwelling Environments: An Elementary Survey of Settlements for the Study of Design Determinants*, Cambridge, Mass.: MIT Press, 1969.

Cammarota, Anne Marie, *Pavements in the Garden: The Suburbanization of Southern New Jersey,*

Adjacent to the City of Philadelphia, 1769 to the Present, Madison, Wisc.: Fairleigh Dickinson University Press, 2001.

Carter, Thomas, "Living the Principle: Mormon Polygamous Housing in Nineteenth-Century Utah", *Winterthur Portfolio* 35, 4, winter 2000, 223–54.

Casey, Edward, "Retrieving the Difference Between Place and Space", in Andrew E. Benjamin (ed.), *Architecture, Space, Painting*, London: Academy Editions, New York: St Martin's Press, 1992.

Casteras, Susan, *Images of Victorian Womanhood in English Art*, Rutherford, N.J.: Fairleigh Dickinson University Press, 1987.

Chandler, Marilyn R., *Dwelling in the Text: Houses in American Fiction*, Berkeley, Calif.: University of California Press, 1991.

Chapman, Tony and Jenny Hockey (eds), *Ideal Homes? Social Change and Domestic Life*, New York: Routledge, 1999.

Cieraad, Irene, *At Home: An Anthropology of Domestic Space*, Syracuse, N.Y.: Syracuse University Press, 1999.

Clark, Clifford Edward, *The American Family Home, 1800–1960*, Chapel Hill: University of North Carolina Press, 1986.

Clark, Peter and M. J. Daunton (eds), *The Cambridge Urban History of Britain*, Cambridge and New York: Cambridge University Press, 2000–.

Clayton-Payne, Andrew, *Victorian Flower Gardens*, London: Weidenfeld and Nicolson, 1988.

Cogan, Frances B., *All-American Girl: The Ideal of Real Womanhood in Mid-Nineteenth-Century America*, Athens: University of Georgia Press, 1989.

Cohen, L., "Embellishing a Life of Labor: An Interpretation of the Material Culture of American Working-class Homes, 1885–1915", *Journal of American Culture* 4, 1980, 752–5.

Coleman, Debra, *et al.* (eds), *Architecture and Feminism*, New York: Princeton Architectural Press, 1996, pp. 221–53.

Collymore, Peter, *The Architecture of Ralph Erskine*, rev. edn, London: Academy Editions, 1994.

Colomina, Beatriz (ed.), *Sexuality and Space*, New York: Princeton Architectural Press, 1992.

—— "The Exhibitionist House", in Richard Koshalek and Elizabeth A. T. Smith (eds), *At the End of the Century: One Hundred Years of Architecture*, Los Angeles: Museum of Contemporary Art and Harry N. Abrams, 1998.

Contosta, David R., *Suburb in the City: Chestnut Hill, Philadelphia, 1850–1990*, Columbus: Ohio State University Press, 1992.

Cowan, Ruth Schwartz, *More Work for Mother: The Ironies of Household Technology from the Open Hearth to the Microwave*, New York: Basic Books, 1983.

Cowling, Mary, *The Artist as Anthropologist: The Representation of Type and Character in Victorian Art*, Cambridge and New York: Cambridge University Press, 1989.

Cromley, Elizabeth Collins, *Alone Together: A History of New York's Early Apartments*, Ithaca, New York and London: Cornell University Press, 1990.

—— "A History of American Beds and Bedrooms", in Thomas Carter and Bernard L. Herman (eds), *Perspectives in Vernacular Architecture, IV*, Columbia and London: University of Missouri Press, 1991, pp. 177–86.

Crowley, David and Susan E. Reid (eds), *Socialist Spaces: Sites of Everyday Life in the Eastern Bloc*, New York: Berg, 2002.

Crowley, John E., *The Invention of Comfort: Sensibilities and Design in Early Modern Britain and Early America*, Baltimore, Md.: Johns Hopkins University Press, 2001.

Csikszentmihalyi, Mihaly and Eugene Rochberg-Halton, *The Meaning of Things: Domestic Symbols and the Self*, Cambridge and New York: Cambridge University Press, 1981.

Czaplicka, John J. and Blair A. Ruble (eds), *Composing Urban History and the Constitution of Civic Identities*, Washington, D.C.: Johns Hopkins University Press, 2003.

Darley, Gillian, *Villages of Vision*, London and New York: Granada, 1978.

Daunton, M. J., *House and Home in the Victorian City: Working Class Housing 1850–1914*, London: Edward Arnold, 1983.

Davey, Peter, "S.T.E.R.N. Work", *Architectural Review* 181, April 1987, 87–9.

Davis, Sam, *The Architecture of Affordable Housing*, Berkeley: University of California Press, 1995.

—— *Designing for the Homeless: Architecture that Works*, Berkeley: University of California Press, 2004.

De Certeau, Michel, *The Practice of Everyday Life*, trans. Steven Rendall, Berkeley: University of California Press, 1988 (originally Paris, 1980).

De Grazia, Victoria, with E. Furlough, *The Sex of Things: Gender and Consumption in Historical Perspectives*, Berkeley: University of California Press, 1996.

Dean, Andrea Oppenheimer and Timothy Hursley, *Rural Studio: Samuel Mockbee and an Architecture of Decency*, New York: Princeton Architectural Press, 2002.

D'Emilio, John and Estelle B. Freedman, *Intimate Matters: A History of Sexuality in America*, New York: Harper and Row, 1988.

Deutsche, Rosalyn, *Evictions: Art and Spatial Politics*, Cambridge, Mass.: MIT Press, 1996.

Dickerson, Vanessa D. (ed.), *Keeping the Victorian House: a Collection of Essays*, New York: Garland, 1995.

Douglas, Mary, *How Institutions Think*, Syracuse, N.Y.: Syracuse University Press, 1986.

Douglas, Mary and Baron Isherwood, *The World of Goods*, New York: Basic Books, 1979.

Downing, Andrew Jackson, *The Architecture of Country Houses: Including Designs for Cottages, Farm Houses, and Villas, with Remarks on Interiors, Furniture, and the Best Modes of Warming and Ventilating, with Three Hundred and Twenty Illustrations*, New York: D. Appleton, 1850.

Duncan, James S. and Nancy Duncan, *Landscapes of Privilege: Aesthetics and Affluence in an American Suburb*, New York and London: Routledge, 2004.

Earley, Tony, *Somehow Form a Family: Stories that Are Mostly True*, Chapel Hill, N.C.: Algonquin Books, 2001.

Egelius, Mats, *Ralph Erskine, Architect*, Stockholm: Byggförlaget, 1990.

Ellis, Russell and Dana Cuff (eds), *Architects' People*, Oxford and New York: Oxford University Press, 1989.

Elsaesser, Thomas, "Tales of Sound and Fury: Observations on the Family Melodrama", in Bill Nichols (ed.), *Movies and Methods: An Anthology*, New York: Columbia University Press, (1976) 1985.

Ezell, Marianne, "My Grandmother's Houses in the Ozarks", Cities Senior Thesis, Bryn Mawr College, 1993–94.

Falke, Jacob von, *Art in the House. Historical, Critical, and Aesthetical Studies on the Decoration and Furnishing of the Dwelling*, trans. from 3rd German edn by Charles C. Perkins, Boston: L. Prang and Company, 1879.

Fausch, Deborah, "Ugly and Ordinary: The Representation of the Everyday", in Steven Harris and Deborah Berke (eds), *Architecture of the Everyday*, New York: Princeton Architectural Press, 1997, pp. 75–106.

Fishman, Robert, *Urban Utopias of the Twentieth Century: Ebenezer Howard, Frank Lloyd Wright, and Le Corbusier*, New York: Basic Books, 1977.

—— *Bourgeois Utopias: The Rise and Fall of Suburbia*, New York: Basic Books, 1987.

Flagge, Ingeborg, et al. (eds), *Geschichte des Wohnens*, 5 vols, Stuttgart: Deutsche Verlags-Anstalt, 1996–99.

Forty, Adrian, *Objects of Desire: Design and Society 1750–1980*, New York: Pantheon Books, 1986.

Foy, Jessica H. and Thomas J. Schlereth (eds), *American Home Life, 1880–1930: A Social History of Spaces and Services*, Knoxville: University of Tennessee Press, 1992.

Franklin, Jill, *The Gentleman's Country House and Its Plan, 1835–1914*, London and Boston: Routledge and Kegan Paul, 1981.

Fraser, Derek and Anthony Sutcliffe (eds), *The Pursuit of Urban History*, London: Edward Arnold, 1983.

Frederick, Christine, *Household Engineering: Scientific Management in the Home*, 5th edn, Chicago: American School of Home Economics, 1923.

Friedman, Alice T., *Women and the Making of the Modern House: A Social and Architectural History*, New York: Harry N. Abrams, 1998.

Frisch, Karl von, *Animal Architecture*, New York: Harcourt Brace Jovanovich, 1974.

Futagawa, Yukio (ed.), *Ralph Erskine: Byker Redevelopment: Byker Area of Newcastle upon Tyne, England, 1969–82*, text by Mats Egelius, Tokyo: A.D.A. Edita, 1980.

Gans, Herbert J., *The Levittowners: Ways of Life and Politics in a New Suburban Community*, New York: Pantheon Books, 1967.

Gay, Peter, *The Bourgeois Experience: Victoria to Freud*, 5 vols., Oxford and New York: Oxford University Press, 1984–98.

Gerard, Jessica, *Country House Life: Family and Servants, 1815–1914*, Oxford and Cambridge, Mass.: Blackwell, 1994.

Ghirardo, Diane (ed.), *Out of Site: A Social Criticism of Architecture*, Seattle: Bay Press, 1991.

Gilborn, Craig A., *Adirondack Camps: Homes away from Home, 1850–1950*, Syracuse, N.Y.: Adirondack Museum and Syracuse University Press, 2000.

Girouard, Mark, *Life in the English Country House: A Social and Agricultural History*, New Haven, Conn.: Yale University Press, 1978.

—— *The Victorian Country House*, rev. and enl. edn, New Haven, Conn.: Yale University Press, 1979.

Glassie, Henry H., *Folk Housing in Middle Virginia*, Knoxville: University of Tennessee Press, 1975.

—— *Vernacular Architecture,* Bloomington: Indiana University Press, 2000.

Gledhill, Christine (ed.), *Home Is Where the Heart Is: Studies in Melodrama and the Woman's Film*, London: BFI Pub., 1987.

Glendinning, Miles and Stefan Muthesius, *Tower Block: Modern Public Housing in England, Scotland, Wales, and Northern Ireland*, New Haven, Conn.: Yale University Press, 1994.

Goffman, Erving, *The Presentation of Self in Everyday Life*, Garden City, N.Y.: Doubleday Anchor Books, 1959.

Goldstein, Carolyn M., *Do It Yourself: Home Improvement in 20th-century America*, Washington, D.C.: National Building Museum and New York: Princeton Architectural Press, 1998.

Gottmann, Jean, *Megalopolis: the Urbanized Northeastern Seaboard of the United States*, New York: Twentieth Century Fund, 1961.

Gowans, Alan, *The Comfortable House: North American Suburban Architecture, 1890–1930*, Cambridge, Mass.: MIT Press, 1986.

Grier, Katherine, *Culture and Comfort: People, Parlors and Upholstery: 1850–1930*, Rochester, N.Y.: The Strong Museum, 1988.

Groth, Paul, *Living Downtown: The History of Residential Hotels in the United States*, Berkeley: University of California Press, 1994.

Gullestad, Marianne, *Kitchen Table Society: A Case Study of the Family Life and Friendships of Young Working-Class Mothers in Urban Norway*, Oslo: Universitetsforlaget, 1986.

Habermas, Jürgen, "The Public Sphere", in Robert E. Goodin and Philip Pettit (eds), *Contemporary Political Philosophy: An Anthology*, Oxford and Cambridge, Mass.: Blackwell, 1997, pp. 105–9.

Haine, W. Scott, *The World of the Paris Café: Sociability Among the French Working Class, 1759–1914*, Baltimore, Md.: Johns Hopkins University Press, 1996.

Hall, E. T., *The Hidden Dimension*, Garden City, NY: Doubleday and Co., 1966.

Halttunen, Karen, *Confidence Men and Painted Ladies: A Study of Middle-Class Culture in America, 1830–1870*, New Haven, Conn.: Yale University Press, 1982.

Hammer-Tugendhat, Daniela and Wolf Tegethoff (eds), *Ludwig Mies van der Rohe: the Tugendhat House*, Vienna and New York: Springer, 2000.

Handlin, David P., *The American Home: Architecture and Society, 1815–1915*, Boston: Little, Brown and Co., 1979

Hanson, Julienne, *Decoding Homes and Houses*, Cambridge and New York: Cambridge University Press, 1998.

Hardy, Dennis, *Alternative Communities in Nineteenth-century England*, London and New York: Longman, 1979.

Harris, Steven and Deborah Berke (eds), *Architecture of the Everyday*, New York: Princeton Architectural Press, 1997.

Hayden, Dolores, *Seven American Utopias: The Architecture of Communitarian Socialism, 1790–1975*, Cambridge, Mass.: MIT Press, 1976.

—— *The Grand Domestic Revolution: A History of Feminist Designs for American Homes, Neighborhoods, and Cities*, Cambridge, Mass.: MIT Press, 1981.

—— *The Power of Place: Urban Landscapes as Public History*, Cambridge, Mass.: MIT Press, 1995.

—— *Redesigning the American Dream: The Future of Housing, Work, and Family Life*, New York: W. W. Norton, (1984) 2002.

—— *Building Suburbia: Green Fields and Urban Growth, 1820–2000*, New York: Pantheon, 2003.

Hayward, Mary Ellen and Charles Belfoure, *The Baltimore Rowhouse*, New York: Princeton Architectural Press, 1999.

Heidegger, Martin, *Vorträge und Aufsätze*, Pfullingen: G. Neske, (1954) 1959.

Heimat, eine deutsche Chronik, television series 1984, fifteen and a half hours. With English subtitles: Facets Multimedia, Chicago: video 1987, 1996; DVD 2005.

Henderson, Susan R., "The Work of Ernst May, 1919–1930", dissertation, Columbia University, 1990.

—— "A Setting for Mass Culture: Life and Leisure in the Nidda Valley", *Planning Perspectives* 10, 1995, 199–222.

Herbert, Gilbert, *Pioneers of Prefabrication: The British Contribution in the Nineteenth Century*, Baltimore, Md.: Johns Hopkins University Press, 1978.

—— *The Dream of the Factory-Made House: Walter Gropius and Konrad Wachsmann*, Cambridge, Mass.: MIT Press, 1984.

Herf, Jeffrey, *Reactionary Modernism: Technology, Culture, and Politics in Weimar and the Third Reich*, Cambridge and New York: Cambridge University Press, 1984.

Heynen, Hilde, *Architecture and Modernity: A Critique*, Cambridge, Mass.: MIT Press, 1999.

Heynen, Hilde and Gülsüm Baydar (eds), *Negotiating Domesticity: Spatial Productions of Gender in Modern Architecture*, London and New York: Routledge, 2005.

Hill, Jonathan (ed.), *Occupying Architecture: Between the Architect and the User*, London and New York: Routledge, 1998.

—— *Actions of Architecture: Architects and Creative Users*, London and New York: Routledge, 2003.

Hillier, Bill and Julienne Hanson, *The Social Logic of Space*, Cambridge and New York: Cambridge University Press, 1984.

Hine, Thomas, "The Search for the Postwar House", in *Blueprints for Modern Living: History and Legacy of the Case Study Houses*, Los Angeles: Museum of Contemporary Art, 1989.

Hoch, Charles and Robert A. Slayton, *New Homeless and Old: Community and the Skid Row Hotel*, Philadelphia: Temple University Press, 1989.

Hodder, Ian (ed.), *The Archaeology of Contextual Meanings*, Cambridge and New York: Cambridge University Press, 1987.

Hoganson, Kristin, "Cosmopolitan Domesticity: Importing the American Dream, 1865–1920", *American Historical Review* 107 (2002), 55–83.

Hollows, Joanna, "The Bachelor Dinner: Masculinity, Class and Cooking in *Playboy*, 1953–1961", *Continuum: Journal of Media and Cultural Studies* 16, no. 2, 2002, 144–155.

hooks, bell, *yearning: race, gender and cultural politics*, Boston: South End Press, 1990.

Hubka, Thomas C., *Big House, Little House, Back House, Barn: The Connected Farm Buildings of New England*, Hanover and London: University Press of New England, (1984) 2004.

Hudson, James R., *The Unanticipated City: Loft Conversions in Lower Manhattan*, Amherst: University of Massachusetts Press, 1987.

Hughes, Thomas P., *Networks of Power: Electrification in Western Society, 1880–1930*, Baltimore, Md.: Johns Hopkins University Press, 1983.

—— *Human-built World: How to Think about Technology and Culture*, Chicago: University of Chicago Press, 2004.

Hunter, Christine, *Ranches, Rowhouses, and Railroad Flats: American Homes: How They Shape Our Landscapes and Neighborhoods*, New York: W. W. Norton, 1999.

Isenstadt, Sandy, "The Rise and Fall of the Picture Window", *Harvard Design Magazine*, Fall 1998, 27–33.

—— "Visions of Plenty: Refrigerators in America around 1950", *Journal of Design History* 11, 4, 1998, 311–21.

—— *The Modern American House: Spaciousness and Middle-Class Identity, 1850–1950*, Cambridge, Engl. and New York: Cambridge University Press, 2006.

Jackson, John Brinckerhoff, "The Westward Moving House", *Landscape* 2, 3, 1953, 8–21.

—— *Discovering the Vernacular Landscape*, New Haven, Conn.: Yale University Press, 1984.

—— *A Sense of Place, a Sense of Time*, New Haven, Conn.: Yale University Press, 1994.

Jackson, Kenneth T., *The Crabgrass Frontier: The Suburbanization of the United States*, Oxford and New York: Oxford University Press, 1985.

Jacobs, Jane, *The Death and Life of Great American Cities*, New York: Random House, 1961.

Jester, Thomas C. (ed.), *Twentieth-Century Building Materials: History and Conservation*, New York: McGraw-Hill, 1995.

Kaiser, Harvey, *Great Camps of the Adirondacks*, Boston: David R. Godine, 1982.

Keats, John, *The Crack in the Picture Window*, Boston: Houghton Mifflin Company; Cambridge, Mass.: The Riverside Press, 1956.

Kelly, Barbara M., *Expanding the American Dream: Building and Rebuilding Levittown*, Albany, N.Y.: State University of New York Press, 1993.

Kent, Susan (ed.), *Domestic Architecture and the Use of Space: an Inter-disciplinary Study*, Cambridge and New York: Cambridge University Press, 1990.

Kerber, Linda K., *Toward an Intellectual History of Women: Essays*, Chapel Hill, N.C.: University of North Carolina Press, 1997.

Kern, Stephen, *The Culture of Time and Space, 1880–1918*, Cambridge, Mass.: Harvard University Press, 1983.

Kerr, Robert, *The Gentleman's House; or, How to Plan English Residences, from the Parsonage to the Palace; with Tables of Accommodation and Cost, and a Series of Selected Plans*, London: Murray, 1864.

Kertzer, David I. and Marzio Barbagli (eds), *The History of the European Family*, 3 vols., New Haven, Conn.: Yale University Press, 2001–4.

Kilborn, Richard, "Retrieving and Remembering the Past: Edgar Reitz's *Heimat* (1984)", *Forum for Modern Language Studies* 31, 1, January 1995, 84–98.

King, Anthony D., *Buildings and Society: Essays on the Social Development of the Built Environment*, London and Boston: Routledge and Kegan Paul, 1980.

—— *The Bungalow: The Production of a Global Culture*, London and Boston: Routledge and Kegan Paul, 1984.

Korosec-Serfaty, Perla, "The Home, from Attic to Cellar", *Journal of Environmental Psychology* 4, 4, 1984, 172–9.

Kronenburg, Robert, *Portable Architecture*, 2nd edn, Oxford and Boston: Architectural Press, 2000.

Laermans, R., "Learning to Consume: Early Department Stores and the Shaping of the Modern Consumer Culture", *Theory, Culture and Society* 10, 4, 1993, 79–102.

Lampugnani, Vittorio Magnago and Romana Schneider (eds), *Expressionismus und neue Sachlichkeit*, Frankfurt am Main: Deutsches Architekturmuseum, 1994.

Lane, Barbara Miller, *Architecture and Politics in Germany, 1918–1945*, Cambridge, Mass.: Harvard University Press, (1968) 1985.

—— *National Romanticism and Modern Architecture in Germany and the Scandinavian Countries*, Cambridge and New York: Cambridge University Press, 2000.

Lane, Jonathan, "The Period House in the Nineteen-Twenties", *Journal of the Society of Architectural Historians* 20, December 1961, 169–76.

Lawrence, Denise and Setha Low, "The Built Environment and Spatial Form", *Annual Review of Anthropology* 19, 1990, 453–505.

Lawrence, Roderick J., "Public Collective and Private Space: a Study of Urban Housing in Switzerland", in Susan Kent (ed.), *Domestic Architecture and the Use of Space: an Interdisciplinary Study*, Cambridge and New York: Cambridge University Press, 1990, pp. 73–91.

Le Corbusier, *The City of Tomorrow*, Cambridge, Mass.: MIT Press, 1971 (*Urbanisme*, Paris, Editions Crés, 1924), trans. Frederick Etchells, 1929, republished in facsimile in 1947.

Lefebvre, Henri, *Everyday Life in the Modern World*, trans. Sacha Rabinovitch, New Brunswick, N.J.: Transaction Books, 1984 (originally Paris, 1968).

—— *The Production of Space*, trans. Donald Nicholson-Smith, Oxford and Cambridge, Mass.: Blackwell, 1991 (originally Paris 1974).

Levittown, PA: Building the Suburban Dream, Harrisburg: The State Museum of Pennsylvania, 2003.

Lifshey, Earl, *The Housewares Story: A History of the American Housewares Industry*, Chicago: National Housewares Manufacturers, 1973.

Lilley, Ed, "The Name of the Boudoir", *Journal of the Society of Architectural Historians* 53, June 1994, 193–8.

Loeb, Adina, "Excavation and Reconstruction: An Oral Archaeology of the deLemos Home", unpublished paper, Bryn Mawr College, May 2003.

Logan, Thad, *The Victorian Parlour: a Cultural Study*, Cambridge and New York, Cambridge University Press, 2001.

Loyer, François, *Paris: Nineteenth-Century Architecture and Urbanism*, trans. Charles Lynn Clark, New York: Abbeville Press, 1988.

Lupton, Ellen and J. Abbott Miller, *The Bathroom, the Kitchen, and the Aesthetics of Waste: a Process of Elimination*, Cambridge, Mass.: MIT Press, 1992.

McCamant, Kathryn and Charles Durrett, with Ellen Hertzman, *Cohousing: A Contemporary Approach to Housing Ourselves*, Berkeley, Calif.: Ten Speed Press, (1988) 1994.

McCracken, Grant, *Culture and Consumption. New Approaches to the Symbolic Character of Consumer Goods and Activities*, Bloomington: Indiana University Press, 1988.

Mack, Arien (ed.), *Home: A Place in the World*, New York: New York University Press, 1993.

McLeod, Mary, "Everyday and 'Other' Spaces", in Debra Coleman, Elizabeth Danze and Carol Henderson (eds), *Architecture and Feminism*, New York: Princeton Architectural Press, 1996, 1–37.

Marcus, Sharon, *Apartment Stories: City and Home in Nineteenth Century Paris and London*, Berkeley: University of California Press, 1999.

Marling, Karal Ann, *As Seen on TV: The Visual Culture of Everyday Life in the 1950s*, Cambridge, Mass.: Harvard University Press, 1994.

Marshall, John and Ian Willox, *The Victorian House*, London: Sidgwick and Jackson, 1986.

Martin, Brenda and Penny Sparke (eds), *Women's Places: Architecture and Design 1860–1960*, London and New York: Routledge, 2003.

Martinson, Tom, *American Dreamscape: The Pursuit of Happiness in Postwar Suburbia*, New York: Carroll and Graf, 2000.

Masotti, Louis (ed.), *Suburbia in Transition*, New York: New Viewpoints, 1974.

Massey, Doreen, *Space, Place and Gender*, Cambridge: Polity, 1994.

May, Elaine Tyler, *Homeward Bound: American Families in the Cold War Era*, New York: Basic Books, 1988.

Meinig, D. W. (ed.), *The Interpretation of Ordinary Landscapes*, Oxford: Oxford University Press, 1979.

Miller, Daniel (ed.), *Home Possessions: Material Culture Behind Closed Doors*, Oxford and New York: Berg, 2001.

Mintz, Steven and Susan Kellogg, *Domestic Revolutions: A Social History of American Family Life*, New York: Free Press; London: Collier Macmillan, 1988.

Mockbee, Samuel, "The Rural Studio", *Architectural Design* 68, 7/8, 1998 (special issue, *The Everyday and Architecture*, guest-edited by Jeremy Till and Sarah Wigglesworth), 73–9.

Moore, Barrington, *Privacy: Studies in Social and Cultural History*, Armonk, N.Y.: M. E. Sharpe and New York: Distributed by Pantheon Books, 1984.

Moore, Charles, Katheryn Smith and Peter Becker (eds), *Home Sweet Home: American Domestic Vernacular Architecture*, New York: Rizzoli, 1983.

Motz, Marilyn Ferris and Pat Browne (eds), *Making the American Home: Middle-Class Women and Domestic Material Culture, 1840–1940*, Bowling Green, OH: Bowling Green State University Popular Press, 1988.

Mulvey, Laura, *Visual and Other Pleasures*, Bloomington: Indiana University Press, 1989.

Mumford, Eric, *The CIAM Discourse on Urbanism, 1928–1960*, Cambridge, Mass.: MIT Press, 2000.

Münz, Ludwig and Gustav Künstler, *Der Architekt Adolf Loos*, Vienna and Munich, 1964. English translation: *Adolf Loos, Pioneer of Modern Architecture*, London, 1966.

Nash, Suzanne (ed.), *Home and Its Dislocations in Nineteenth-Century France*, Albany: State University of New York Press, 1993.

Nerdinger, Winfried, *Walter Gropius*, Berlin and Cambridge, Mass.: A. Koch and Harvard University Art Museums, 1985.

—— "Walter Gropius: Beitrag zur Architektur", in Hartmut Probst and Christian Schädlich (eds), *Walter Gropius*, Berlin, 1986.

Newman, Oscar, *Defensible Space: Crime Prevention through Urban Design*, New York: Macmillan, 1972.

Nichols, Bill (ed.), *Movies and Methods*, Berkeley: University of California Press, 1976.

Norberg-Schulz, Christian, *The Concept of Dwelling*, New York: Electa/Rizzoli, 1985.

Oliver, Paul (ed.), *Encyclopedia of the Vernacular Architecture of the World,* 3 vols., Cambridge and New York: Cambridge University Press, 1997.

Oliver, Paul, *Dwellings: the House Across the World*, Austin: University of Texas Press, 1987.

Olsen, Donald J., *Town Planning in London: the Eighteenth and Nineteenth Centuries*, New Haven, Conn.: Yale University Press, 1964.

—— *The Growth of Victorian London,* New Haven, Conn.: Yale University Press, 1976.

—— *The City as a Work of Art: London, Paris, Vienna*, New Haven, Conn.: Yale University Press, 1986.

Ozment, Steven, *Flesh and Spirit: Private Life in Early Modern Germany*, New York: Viking, 1999.

—— *Ancestors: The Loving Family in Old Europe*, Cambridge, Mass.: Harvard University Press, 2001.

Pardailhé-Galabrun, Annik, *The Birth of Intimacy: Privacy and Domestic Life in Early Modern France*, trans. Jocelyn Phelps, Cambridge: Polity Press, 1991.

Pearson, Lynn F., *The Architectural and Social History of Cooperative Living*, New York: St Martin's Press, 1988.

Pevsner, Nikolaus, *The Buildings of England* series, Harmondsworth: Penguin, 1952–83.

—— *An Outline of European Architecture*, Middlesex, England: Penguin Books, Ltd., (1943) 7th edn 1968.

—— *A History of Building Types*, Princeton: Princeton University Press, 1976.

—— *Pioneers of Modern Design from William Morris to Walter Gropius*, New Haven, Conn.: Yale University Press, (1936) 2005.

Pollock, Griselda, "Modernity and the Spaces of Femininity", in *Vision and Difference: Femininity, Feminism and Histories of Art*, New York: Routledge, 1988, pp. 50–90.

Pommer, Richard, "'More a Necropolis than a Metropolis': Ludwig Hilberseimer's Highrise City and Modern City Planning", in Pommer *et al.*, *In the Shadow of Mies: Ludwig Hilberseimer; Architect, Educator, and Urban Planner*, New York: Rizzoli, pp. 16–53.

Pommer, Richard and Christian F. Otto, *Weissenhof 1927 and the Modern Movement in Architecture*, Chicago: University of Chicago Press, 1991.

Popenoe, David, *The Suburban Environment: Sweden and the United States*, Chicago: University of Chicago Press, 1977.

Rapoport, Amos, *House Form and Culture*. Englewood Cliffs, N.J.: Prentice-Hall, 1969.

—— *Human Aspects of Urban Form*, New York: Pergamon, 1977.

Ravetz, Alison, with Richard Turkington, *The Place of Home: English Domestic Environments 1914–2000*, London: Spon, 1995.

Rawlings, Irene, *Portable Houses*, Salt Lake City, Utah: Gibbs Smith, 2004.

Read, Alan (ed.), *Architecturally Speaking: Practices of Art, Architecture, and the Everyday*, London and New York: Routledge, 2000.

Reed, Christopher (ed.), *Not at Home: The Suppression of Domesticity in Modern Art and Architecture*, New York: Thames and Hudson, 1996.

Rendell, Jane, Barbara Penner and Iain Borden (eds), *Gender Space Architecture: An Interdisciplinary Introduction*, London and New York: Routledge, 2000.

Rigby, Andrew, *Alternative Realities: A Study of Communes and their Members*, London and Boston: Routledge and Kegan Paul, 1974.

Riley, Terence, *The Un-Private House*, New York: Museum of Modern Art, distributed by Harry N. Abrams, 1999.

Roberts, Marion, *Living in a Man-Made World: Gender Assumptions in Modern Housing Design*, London and New York: Routledge, 1991.

Rosaldo, Michelle and Louise Lamphere (eds), *Woman, Culture, and Society*, Stanford: Stanford University Press, 1974.

Rowe, Peter G., *Modernity and Housing*, Cambridge, Mass: MIT Press, 1993.

Rudofsky, Bernard, *Architecture without Architects: An Introduction to Non-pedigreed Architecture*, Garden City, N.Y.: Doubleday, 1964.

Rybczynski, Witold, *Home: A Short History of an Idea*, New York: Penguin, 1986.

Rykwert, Joseph, *On Adam's House in Paradise: The Idea of the Primitive Hut in Architectural History*, New York: Museum of Modern Art; distributed by New York Graphic Society, Greenwich, Conn., 1972.

Saegert, Susan, "Masculine Cities and Feminine Suburbs", in Catharine R. Stimpson *et al.* (eds), *Women and the American City*, Chicago: University of Chicago Press, 1981.

Sanders, Joel (ed.), *Stud: Architectures of Masculinity*, New York: Princeton Architectural Press, 1996.

Schama, Simon, *The Embarrassment of Riches: An Interpretation of Dutch Culture in the Golden Age*, New York: Knopf, 1987.

Schoenauer, Norbert, *6,000 Years of Housing*, New York: W. W. Norton, 2000.

Schroeder, Fred E. H., *Front Yard America: The Evolution and Meanings of a Vernacular Domestic Landscape*, Bowling Green, Ohio: Bowling Green State University Popular Press, 1993.

Scully, Vincent J., Jr., *The Shingle Style and the Stick Style: Architectural Theory and Design from Downing to the Origins of Wright*, rev. ed., New Haven, Conn.: Yale University Press, 1971.

Shafer, Jay, www.tumbleweedhouses.com

Shaw, Frederick, *The Homes and Homeless of Postwar Britain*, London: Parthenon, 1985.

Sidlauskas, Susan, *Body, Place, and Self in Nineteenth-Century Painting*, Cambridge and New York: Cambridge University Press, 2000.

Siegal, Jennifer (ed.), *Mobile: The Art of Portable Architecture*, New York: Princeton Architectural Press, 2002.

Sies, Mary Corbin, "Toward a Performance Theory of the Suburban Ideal, 1877–1917", *Perspectives in Vernacular Architecture* 2, 1986, 197–207.

Silverstone, Roger (ed.), *Visions of Suburbia*, London and New York: Routledge, 1997.

Sinclair, Cameron, Kate Stohr and Architecture for Humanity (eds), *Design Like You Give a Damn: Architectural Responses to Humanitarian Crises*, London: Thames & Hudson, 2006

Smith, Terry, *Making the Modern: Industry, Art, and Design in America*, Chicago: University of Chicago Press, 1993.

Smith-Rosenberg, Carroll, *Disorderly Conduct: Visions of Gender in Victorian America*, Oxford and New York: Oxford University Press, 1985.

Smithson, Alison and Peter Smithson, *Urban Structuring*, London: Studio Vista and New York: Reinhold, 1967.

Snodin, Michael and Elisabet Stavenow-Hidemark (eds), *Carl and Karin Larsson: Creators of the Swedish Style*, exhibition catalog, London: Victoria and Albert Publications, 1997.

Sørensen, Knut H. and Merete Lie, *Making Technology our Own: Domesticating Technology into Everyday Life*, Oslo and Boston: Scandinavian University Press, 1996.

Sosnovy, Timothy, *The Housing Problem in the Soviet Union*, New York: Research Program on the USSR, 1954.

Souden, David, *The Victorian Village*, London: Collins and Brown, 1991.

Spain, Daphne, *Gendered Spaces*, Chapel Hill: University of North Carolina Press, 1992.

Spencer-Wood, Suzanne M., "Toward the Further Development of Feminist Historical Archaeology", *World Archaeological Bulletin* 7, 1993, 118–36.

Spigel, Lynn, "From Theatre to Space Ship: Metaphors of Suburban Domesticity in Postwar America", in Roger Silverstone (ed.), *Visions of Suburbia*, London and New York: Routledge, 1997, pp. 217–39.

—— *Welcome to the Dreamhouse: Popular Media and Postwar Suburbs*, Durham, N.C.: Duke University Press, 2001.

Springer, Kathryn, *Frank Lloyd Wright, Hollyhock House and Olive Hill: Buildings and Projects for Aline Barnsdall*, New York: Rizzoli, 1992.

Stilgoe, John, *Common Landscape of America, 1580–1845*, New Haven, Conn.: Yale University Press, 1982.

Strasser, Susan, *Never Done: A History of American Housework*, New York: Pantheon Books, 1982.

Sutcliffe, Anthony (ed.), *Multi–story Living: The British Working Class Experience*, London: Croom Helm, 1974.

Taut, Bruno, *Die Neue Wohnung: Die Frau als Schöpferin*, Leipzig: Klinkhardt and Biermann, 1925.

Taylor, Lisa (ed.), *Housing: Structure, Symbol, Site*, New York: Cooper-Hewitt Museum, 1990.

Teyssot, Georges, "The Disease of the Domicile", *Assemblage* 6, June 1988, 73–97.

—— (ed.), *The American Lawn*, New York: Princeton Architectural Press, 1999.

Thornton, Peter, *Authentic Decor: The Domestic Interior, 1620–1920*, New York: Viking, 1984.

Till, Jeremy and Sarah Wigglesworth (eds), *The Everyday and Architecture*, *Architectural Design* 68, 7–8, 1998.

Toker, Franklin, *Fallingwater Rising: Frank Lloyd Wright, E. J. Kaufmann, and America's Most Extraordinary House*, New York: Knopf, 2004.

Topham, Sean, *Move House*, London: Prestel, 2004.

Tosh, John, "'New Men'? The Bourgeois Cult of Home", *History Today* 46, 12, 1996.

Tuan, Yi-Fu, *Space and Place: The Perspective of Experience*, Minneapolis: University of Minnesota Press, 1977.

Turner, John F. C., *Housing by People: Towards Autonomy in Building Environments*, New York: Pantheon Books, 1976.

Turner, John F. C. and Robert Fichter (eds), *Freedom to Build: Dweller Control of the Housing Process*, New York: Macmillan, 1972.

Turner, Victor Witter, *Dramas, Fields and Metaphors: Symbolic Action in Human Society*, Ithaca: Cornell University Press, 1974.

Upton, Dell, *Architecture in the United States*, Oxford and New York: Oxford University Press, 1998.

Upton, Dell and John Michael Vlach (eds), *Common Places: Readings in American Vernacular Architecture*, Athens: University of Georgia Press, 1986.

Van Zanten, David, *Developing Paris: The Architecture of Duban, Labrouste, Due, and Vaudoyer*, Cambridge, Mass.: MIT Press, 1987.

Venturi, Robert, *Complexity and Contradiction in Architecture*, New York: MOMA, 1966.

Venturi, Robert and John Rauch, *Signs of Life: Symbols in the American City*, Exhibition at the Renwick Gallery of the National Collections of Fine Arts, Smithsonian Institution, from February 26 through September 30, 1976, Washington, D.C.: Aperture, 1976.

Venturi, Robert, Denise Scott Brown and Steven Izenour, *Learning from Las Vegas*, Cambridge, Mass.: MIT Press, 1972.

Vidler, Anthony, "The Scenes of the Street: Transformations in Ideal and Reality, 1750–1871", in Stanford Anderson (ed.), *On Streets*, Cambridge, Mass.: MIT Press, 1978.

—— *The Architectural Uncanny: Essays on the Modern Unhomely*, Cambridge, Mass.: MIT Press, 1992.

Vitek, William and Wes Jackson (eds), *Rooted in the Land: Essays on Community and Place*, New Haven, Conn.: Yale University Press, 1996.

Von Eckhardt, Wolf, *The Challenge of Megalopolis: a Graphic Presentation of the Urbanized Northeastern Seaboard of the United States*, New York: Macmillan, 1964.

Wagner-Rieger, Renate (ed.), *Die Wiener Ringstrasse: Bild einer Epoche*, Wiesbaden: Franz Steiner, 1976.

Wallis, Allan D., *Wheel Estate: The Rise and Decline of Mobile Homes*, Oxford and New York: Oxford University Press, 1991; Washington, D.C.: Johns Hopkins University Press, 1997.

Wallis, Brian (ed.), *If You Lived Here: The City in Art, Theory, and Social Activism*, Seattle: Bay Press, 1991.

Warner, Sam Bass, "The Public Invasion of Private Space and the Private Engrossment of Public Space", in *Growth and Transformation of the Modern City*, Stockholm: Swedish Council for Building Research, 1979, pp. 171–7.

Wates, Nick and Christian Wolmar (eds), *Squatting: The Real Story*, London: Bayleaf Books, 1980.

Weintraub, Jeff and Krishnan Kumar (eds), *Public and Private in Thought and Practice: Perspectives on a Grand Dichotomy*, Chicago: University of Chicago Press, 1997.

Wertheimer, Barbara, *We Were There: The Story of Working Women in America*, New York: Pantheon Books, 1977.

Wetherell, W. D., *The Man Who Loved Levittown*, Pittsburgh, Pa.: University of Pittsburgh Press, 1985.

White, Roger B., *Home on the Road: The Motor Home in America*, Washington, D.C.: Smithsonian Institution Press, 2000.

Whitehand, J. W. R. and C. M. H. Carr, *Twentieth-century Suburbs: A Morphological Approach*, New York and London: Routledge, 2001.

Wickham, Christopher J., "Representation and Mediation in Edgar Reitz's *Heimat*", *German Quarterly* 64, 1, Winter 1991, 35–45.

Williams, Raymond, *The Country and the City*, Oxford and New York: Oxford University Press, 1973.

Wilson, Kristina, *Livable Modernism: Interior Decorating and Design during the Great Depression*, New Haven, Conn.: Yale University Press, 2004.

Wingler, Hans Maria (ed.), *The Bauhaus: Weimar – Dessau – Berlin – Chicago*, Cambridge, Mass.: MIT Press, 1969.

Wright, Frank Lloyd, *The Natural House*, New York: Horizon Press, 1954.

Wright, Gwendolyn, *Building the Dream: A Social History of Housing in America*, New York: Pantheon, 1981.

—— *Moralism and the Model Home: Domestic Architecture and Cultural Conflict in Chicago 1873–1913*, Chicago: University of Chicago Press, 1985.

Wright, L., *Home Fires Burning: The History of Domestic Heating and Cooking*, London: Routledge and Kegan Paul, 1964.

Zola, Émile, *L'Assommoir (The Dram Shop)*, trans. and ed. by Robin Buss, London: Penguin Books, 2000 (originally Paris, 1876).

Additional web sites

www.architectureforhumanity.org
www.habitat.org/disaster
www.housingprototypes.org
www.madhousers.org
www.thedwellhome.com

Index

Page numbers in bold refer to illustrations.